we lucky few

we lucky few

Portraits of courage *&* sacrifice from SE Iowa

Stories of World War II

Compiled by Larry Cuddeback
and Cheyenne Cuddeback Miller

Camp Pope
2012

Copyright © 2012 by Larry Cuddeback & Cheyenne Cuddeback Miller

ISBN 978-1-929919-46-8

Library of Congress Control Number: 2012948508

Camp Pope Publishing
PO Box 2232
Iowa City, Iowa 52244
www.camppope.com

Printed and bound in the United States of America

Unless otherwise noted, all photographs (including cover photos) taken by Cheyenne C. Miller.

*This book is dedicated to
Kenneth R. Cuddeback, father and
grandfather, who volunteered to
"Stand Up and Hook Up" for our
beloved nation.*

*Proud member of the 508th
Parachute Infantry Regiment,
82nd Airborne, WWII.*

*Thank you for your service and
for being the wind at our back
throughout this project.*

ACKNOWLEDGEMENTS

We would like to thank all those people who made this book possible. Our task would have been nearly insurmountable without community help, verbal and otherwise. We were both honored and humbled by the groundswell of interest and support. Our gratitude is beyond measure.

Our special thanks to Paula Brinning of the United Presbyterian Home, Pam Green of the McCreedy Home, and Penny Stout of the Halcyon House and the staffs of all the retirement homes for their kind and courteous assistance in locating veterans. Our thanks to Peg Harris, Kathy Cuddeback, and Terry Phillips for their many hours volunteered to proof read the manuscript. A special thanks goes out to Clark Kenyon of Camp Pope Publishing, who paitently held our hands through the final stages of this project. We did our best to acknowledge those individuals who transcribed our audial recordings into print as well as those who offered names of veterans and assistance in locating them. Poor memory and misplaced notes regrettably resulted in omissions which we apologize for.

Without our families' commitment and sacrifice, this project would not have born fruition. We would like to extend a special thank-you to two little girls. To Carys Miller, who's endless enthusiasm, inquiring mind, and gentle soul made friends with many veterans. And to Isla Miller, who was content to sleep in her mother's arms for hours as each page of this book was created.

AUTHORS' NOTE

While much has been written about World War II and the Greatest Generation, this book records the stories of those veterans still living in the rural communities of southeastern Iowa as they were told to us. We hope the reader finds the individual stories inspiring and revealing. Taken collectively, however, they go a long way in telling the story of World War II. These accounts also represent the embodiment of the heart and soul of the citizen soldier from heartland America. These individuals participated in the high water mark of world history, winning the one war we absolutely had to win as a nation to survive as a free people. World War II was the pivotal, defining moment in the 20th Century. These individuals were not only a part of this history; they made history. The war experience was also the defining moment in the lives of many of these vets. Nothing else in life had a greater measure of impact.

We were once asked if the book had a theme. We weren't sure how to answer that question. We had no agenda other than recording what we were told to the best of our abilities. Upon reflection, if there is a theme, it comes from the mouths of our vets. The theme would be, simply; they did their duty, they did what had to done, they came home and carried on with their lives. For this, they deserve our nation's greatest thanks and gratitude.

We have arranged the chapters in the order in which the interviews were conducted. We explained to each veteran that we did not expect them to tell us anything that made them uncomfortable. The questions we asked the veterans were incorporated into the text to form a free-flowing narrative whenever possible. Some questions and comments were noted when we felt it was necessary for clarification or distinction. Interviews were transcribed to the best of our ability, and only edited for length and content as necessary.

These are their words.

As interviewers, we felt honored to be in their presence and blessed by their trust in confiding to us their personal accounts. When their memories journeyed back to the war era, their eyes again became those of 18 or 20 year olds. We realized that we were witnessing, and were perhaps a small part of something special, even sacred. So as you experience these stories, pause and ponder the people you thought you knew.

Larry Cuddeback and Cheyenne Cuddeback Miller

CONTENTS

FOREWORD

From the ages of four to eighteen, I frequently attended my grandfather's annual army reunion. Like clockwork, former members of the 113th Cavalry—the "Redhorsers"—converged on Washington the last weekend of July to reminisce, share food and drink, and enjoy each other's company. It was a consistent highlight of my every summer—even more so than playing baseball, riding my bike, or swimming at the pool. The guys (Grandpa—Harold Wolf, Ted, Keith, Clifford, Bill, and many others)—silver-haired versions of their younger selves (and some with an extra pound or five)—always went out of their way to make sure a pesky little kid felt included in their weekend. I felt proud to have a front row seat every year when they hoisted the distinctive Redhorser coat of arms outside my grandparents' house. The proud red horse reared up against its eternal mustard yellow background, atop bold words that read: "we maintain." I cherished being part of the group. I was mesmerized by their colorful personalities and enchanted with their abilities to recall moments, decades past, as if those moments had just occurred the week before. Despite having independent lives the rest of the year, some more successful than others, they seemed to bring out the best in each other during that magical weekend in Washington. They were like ageless brothers. While from the beginning, I understood that they had been in the Army together during "the war," it was not until I was nine (1984) that I began to process the depth and reason for their unbreakable bond. As many know, 1984 was the fortieth anniversary of the Allied invasion of Normandy, France—arguably the boldest and the most successful amphibious invasion ever—and one that turned the tide of the war in Europe. What I discovered in 1984 was that the Redhorsers had been a part of it. In subsequent years, I realized the depth of their involvement in the war—after Normandy, significant action in Northern France, Belgium, Holland and finally, victory in Germany.

The experiences of the Redhorsers are threads in a rich tapestry that touches nearly everyone with ties to Washington County. Almost all of us have immediate or extended family or family friends who served in some manner during World War II. Washington County provided nearly an entire generation of young men for this just and necessary cause. Their lives were postponed; graduating high school or attending college was delayed; weddings were accelerated or pushed off; loved ones were left behind; plans and dreams were put on hold— and sometimes never resumed. Young men who had spent their entire lives in places such as Washington, Brighton, West Chester, Wellman, Kalona, Riverside, Ainsworth, or on the farm, found themselves serving at important posts stateside, or fighting in surreal places named Anzio, Bastogne, Arnhem, Guadalcanal, Leyte Gulf, Iwo Jima, and Saipan or on ships and submarines, literally on the other side of the world. The humble sons of small town shop owners, doctors, grocers, and farmers became noble gladiators in the greatest conflict the world has ever known. The women of Washington County put their lives on hold, too. They played essential roles in holding up the home front—through formal service such as Women Accepted for Voluntary Emergency Service (WAVES), or by taking over traditional "men's jobs," and filling critical community service roles. In many ways, large and small, almost everyone "did their bit." In many ways, large and small, almost everyone sacrificed for the greater good. Tragically, some of our boys made the ultimate, and most sacred sacrifice, and never came home again. Their families were left to imagine what could have been, what should have been. Thankfully though, at the end of it all, most did come home and life picked up again, even if it was not necessarily where it had left off.

We know most of the stories of what followed their return—resuming old relationships and starting new ones; reconnecting with loved ones; marriages and divorces; baby booms and grandchildren; careers and business ventures; hobbies and other equally less threatening adventures; all with various levels of success and failure—essentially, the ups and downs of everyday life. We know that they were not perfect, but almost all gave it their best in the phases of their life that followed. We know (or knew) them as our fathers or grandfathers, uncles, cousins, teachers, coaches, mailmen, salesmen, farmers, and neighbors. When the war ended, they dusted themselves off and quickly moved on to help build a post-war America that, despite its faults, still remains the most exceptional country on Earth. What many of us have never known, though, is what they did during the war. Some of the defining characteristics of what television journalist and author Tom Brokaw aptly labeled the "Greatest Generation" have been their enduring humility and reticence to volunteer particulars of their experiences. Theirs was a generation that did not have an impulsive desire to relay the detailed adventures and horrors of war. It was not until the autumn and winters of their lives that some members of this special generation finally opened up, to the extent that they could, to share what they had witnessed and what they had endured. Some of us were blessed to hear their stories directly. Unfortunately, not all of us had this special opportunity before our loved ones passed on. Some of us may have only discovered details after reading letters, long lost in a dusty box in the basement. Others only know a possible fact or two from second or third-hand accounts. But now all of us are honored to share in the stories that follow in this book.

At the time of this writing, we find ourselves in difficult times, marked by economic uncertainty and anxiety, polarizing politics and a lack of civil discourse, and terrifying existential threats by entities that no longer see our borders as walls that cannot be penetrated. And while the world has been made immeasurably smaller by rapid advances in technology and communications, it seems to be more complicated than ever. I ask that you take a pause from that reality when you read this book. I ask that you approach the stories that follow, not merely as personal history lessons, but as insights into who we were and who we can be when we are at our best—as Iowans, Americans, and global citizens. Despite our divisions, differences, and disagreements, when we unite in a singular effort, there is simply no achievement beyond our grasp. Keep in mind the stories you will read are not of fictional superheroes, but rather, are from real people with heroic experiences—real men and women who, not so long ago, were united in a single effort and helped save the world. We are made of their fabric.

While I will always be a Washingtonian in heart and soul, I currently serve as a Naval officer overseas. Four years ago, as have many of my fellow Washingtonians, I was deployed to Iraq. It was an experience that was simultaneously invigorating and scary, and likely one of the most rewarding things I will ever do. One particular day in Baghdad, I was stopped in my tracks by something I could not have possibly imagined I would ever see in the middle of foreign desert, over six thousand miles away from home—the Redhorser coat of arms emblazoned with the words, "we maintain." While I logically concluded the symbol reflected the presence of the current generation of the Iowa National Guard's 113th Cavalry in Iraq, I genuinely felt as if my Redhorsers (Grandpa, Ted, Keith, Clifford, and Bill) were right beside me. I still think they were (and are).

We maintain.

Ian Preston Wolf
Naples, Italy
August 2012

I Think I Was Lucky

Bob Swift
Washington, IA

Navy
Pacific

Interview Date:
15 March 2010

Referral:
Craig Swift

It was a long time ago. I went into the Navy when I was 17. Two older boys from Washington and I always talked about joining the Navy together so we all went up to Des Moines. I passed my physical and they didn't. So there I was, a seventeen year old farm boy alone without any friends. I wondered, "What the hell am I doing here?" I only got homesick once.

I did boot camp in Great Lakes and then was sent to San Diego. They lined forty of us up in a row by alphabetical order and this many went to the submarines and this many went to Naval Aviation. I was fortunate to be sent to a squadron in Naval Aviation. The guy standing next to me went to the submarines. I was paid $21 a month and 25% more for flying. I was rich! When I left for the Navy, my dad gave me two bucks and that was probably all the money he had in the world.

The first thing I got to do was work on the beach crew. Then the war started. By that time I knew how to start the engines and everything inside the plane. I was a 2nd Class Machinist Mate. Our plane was a big four engine seaplane, a PB2Y235. It was called a Coronado and was twice the size of the Catalina. It was 72 feet long and had a one hundred and ten foot wing span. It was twenty-two feet high on the inside. It was a big airplane.

I was assigned to a crew in Squadron BP-13 when the war started. We were sent first to Hawaii and flew out of there. It took eighteen and a half hours of flying time to get there. It was a lot different than flying today. The navigator about died on those long trips. We didn't have the big radar and the navigator had to shoot the stars (to determine our position) and drop flares for drift.

We reached Hawaii around the end of December in 1941. I got to see the damage done at Pearl Harbor because it was still smoking. We flew out of Kane'ohe Bay which sits across the island from Pearl Harbor. There was good water there for landing. The Coronado didn't have landing wheels so we always landed in water. We flew patrols out of Hawaii quite often. Everybody was still scared and worried the Japanese were close by.

We bombed Wake Island and Admiral Chester Nimitz rode with us (as an observer). I think he was trying to make a name for himself but he was a nice guy. The Japanese were shooting back at us some but you think that they'll never hurt you. Some of the other pilots were wounded. Five of our squadron planes were involved in the raid. That was our first combat.

Question: What did it feel like to be 17 and being shot at?

Scared to hell. You don't know anything when you're 17. You just go along with what they say.

Our airplane had a crew of 12 or 13. Usually it was 13. My job was to mainly run the engines. My battle station was to man the front turret. It was a twin fifty. I shot it quite often but I don't know if I hit anything. For practice they would tow a target behind another airplane. It usually wasn't a big deal. You were just kind of along for the ride.

Our next deployment was to Midway and it was just a place to gas up so we could go further. We flew a lot at night, usually at three to four thousand feet. We had oxygen but I can only remember using it once. Usually we'd be out of gas if we climbed high enough to need it. From Midway, we went down to Perry Island (off Queensland, Australia). We flew out of there for quite some time.

We were a patrol bomber. We were looking for the Japanese more than anything, trying to keep track of where they were. We'd look for Japanese convoys and we found a couple of them. We were to report them and keep track of them as long we could and not get too close. Then the submarines would take care of them if there were any in the area. One time we had an eager beaver pilot that wanted to make a run at a convoy. The Japs were shooting at us five miles away with their big guns. You could see those black puffs of smoke from the explosions and the plane would move around. It would make you feel kind of funny. When you're doing this kind of stuff you always think it'll be someone else that gets hurt rather than yourself. I always said that I was one hundred percent lucky not to have been hurt.

The deck of the ship in the convoy that was shooting at us was crowded with people. I don't know why we weren't ordered to shoot but I am glad now that we didn't. We would have just slaughtered those people.

We didn't really have that many people shooting at us. If we ran into a twin engine Japanese bomber called a Betty, they'd run from us. They didn't fool around at all. We were a lot bigger airplane and

"Every time he'd moan, we'd stick him again with morphine. The doctor said we about killed him."

they were scared of us. Hell, we couldn't have hit them if we had tried.

We carried these survival packets on us when we flew. There were flags and messages in different languages saying we were Americans and that there would be a reward for helping us. There was also money and morphine in the packet. We had one of our crew members get injured during a flight. We didn't know what to do for him except to give him a shot of morphine in his leg. Every time he'd moan, we'd stick him again with morphine. The doctor said we about killed him.

We also acted as weather spotters. There were terrible storms in the South Pacific (that affected air and naval operations) and one of our jobs was to report and track the storms. We'd also circle the islands looking for a Japanese presence. If we saw a radio antenna, we'd try to blow it up. If we spotted a boat with anything that looked like an antenna, we sank it if we could. We could carry twelve 100 pound bombs. We could also carry a torpedo and sea mines we could drop.

We didn't run into too much activity flying out of Perry Island. We were there six to seven months. We lived in tents and had movies every night. They'd give us a case of beer every time we flew a mission. That was a big deal. We'd fly four or five missions a week. After flying eighteen missions, they fly us to Hawaii (for R&R) if we wanted to go. I never did. On the weekends, we'd hit that beer pretty hard, even though it was warm beer. You could buy cold beer, two a day, for ten cents apiece. A pack of cigarettes was a nickel. I brought a box of cigars from the states. One night on Perry, I handed them out to everyone while we were watching a movie. I'd kept the damn things too long and the cigars had worms in them. We smoked them anyway.

We had a food shortage for a while. We subsisted on beer and what they called C ration soup. You could eat that and go throw up and then drink the beer. I lost forty pounds of the weight I had gained on Hawaii on Perry Island. Usually they fed us pretty good. I can't complain about that. From boot camp on, the Navy food tasted good to me. I can't complain about anything, really.

One day on Perry Island there was a scare that the Japanese were coming. So we loaded everybody up in our airplane. We crowded 72 people in that plane and we couldn't get off the water because of the weight. We threw all our machine guns and interior armor plating overboard to lighten the load. We had trouble getting the soldiers on board to part with their guns. They didn't want to give them up. I would imagine we ran that plane across 50 miles of ocean before we got off the water.

It wasn't until we got up to Saipan that it got tougher. There were too many dead people, that was the biggest thing. I remember flying over the landing beach when we arrived and seeing all the dead bodies of Marines floating in the water. There was a ship attempting to beach and trying to avoid hitting the bodies as it went in. They had to send people out in a small craft to move the bodies out of the way.

They had one big ship there at Saipan that could pick our plane up out of the water and work on it if needed. Most of the time, we slept on our plane off shore as we had everything we needed on board. Sometimes we spent the night aboard that big ship. We did have one good beer party on the beach.

We'd sleep on the airplane's wing. One night when everybody got a little careless, some Japanese swam out and took over another plane. The crew jumped into the water, so in the morning the Japs controlled the plane. It was kind of exciting and it wasn't too far away from us. It ended up that a ship just blew that airplane all to hell. That took care of that. Afterwards, we watched ourselves. We shut the doors on the plane so nobody could get in.

We always had good food to eat. We had fresh eggs. Some of them were green but they tried. They always tried to give us some meat. We ate as good as the pilot did because we fixed the food for him most of the time. The soldiers would come out to the airplane and any food we gave them was like gold as they had very little to eat. These soldiers had been living in a hole on that damn island and a can of peaches we'd give them meant a great deal.

We spent quite a bit of time walking and just looking around the island of Saipan. There was a sugar cane factory there and it was all blown to hell. They had native people (interned) in a barb wire enclosure. They were a terrible, sorry looking

people. There were probably three or four hundred in the camp. I found a carbine and another American rifle on Saipan. I carried those damn guns all the way through service until getting back to San Diego after the war. I couldn't figure out how to disassemble the rifle but did manage to take the carbine apart and store in my sea bag. It made the trip home with me and I had it quite a while until the cops stopped me for speeding in California. They confiscated the gun and forgot all about the speeding ticket. They seemed quite tickled to get my carbine.

When the campaign to take Okinawa was going on, we operated out of a nice bay on a nearby smaller island. It was close enough then, that most of our patrols were around Formosa along the Chinese line. I can still remember the Yellow River so good it is pathetic. There were lots of little boats in the ocean. The Chinese people made their living in these boats. They lived on them as well. We'd try to sink any boat with an antenna on it by strafing it. We flew around Formosa and the Yellow Sea quite a bit. It was full of small islands. We didn't drop many bombs, it was mostly strafing.

One time we took a run on a boat that looked like it had an antenna sticking out of it. Its deck appeared to be loaded with bamboo sticks. When we got close the deck opened up and they shot the hell out of us. We got out of there with a few holes in our airplane. We lucked out there. They had all the opportunity to blow us clear away. A lot of times it was just eight or ten hours of flying around and not seeing anything. There would be these small islands down below with Japanese on them but we didn't get very close unless we could see a target.

We lost a lot of people, that's why I keep saying that I was lucky. I didn't realize it until we had a reunion and people started talking. We had 15 planes in our squadron and 270 people. We lost 135 of them. Some of planes got caught in typhoons, terrible storms. No one knew what happened to them except that they didn't come back.

The longest time I flew in an airplane was when we got a report of a plane going down near Marcus Island along the coast of China. The Japanese held that island. It took twenty-eight hours to fly there and back. It was a long flight. They added auxiliary gas tanks inside the fuselage for the trip. We landed on the water and picked them up. Normally we would not have attempted to land in the open ocean because the waves could tear apart a plane of our size. Usually we'd remain in the air, doing what we could until the smaller Catalina arrived for the actual rescue. Landing in the ocean was tough. We landed in the ocean a few times but tried to avoid it. You had to land on top of the waves and not in the valleys. Our bases were always in protected bays with quieter water.

Late in the war we would fly all night over the ocean between Korea and Japan to contact our submarines. We'd tell them where the Japanese convoys were heading. Japanese Zeroes would come out and fly right with us. You could see the Zero pilot sitting in the airplane, they were that close. They never shot at us and we never shot at them. The Zeroes were more interested in the location of our subs than us. I always figured those Jap pilots were young kids and just as scared as we were. I always kind of sat back and hoped I didn't have to kill anybody.

We flew the west coast of Japan. We dropped bombs there on factories and strafed their airports and little trains. By that time in the war, they had nothing for air defense, no fighters, no anti-aircraft batteries. When our support ship got closer to Japan, it was hit by a kamikaze. Luckily, the bomb it was carrying didn't explode but there was a hole in the side of the ship and a few people killed. The kamikaze attacked in the morning. All of a sudden the ship started shooting at it. I just missed being on board. I was getting out of our plane ready to meet the small boat they would send out to ferry us to the ship to eat. It was scary to think what would have happened if the bomb had exploded. I think I was lucky.

Ninety-nine percent of the time we were in the dark about what was going on in the rest of the war. About the only thing we were aware of is that we were slowly getting closer to Japan.

Question: What were your thoughts when you learned of the two atomic bombs being dropped?
I was tickled. We saw the first one. We were flying all that day, 300 miles from Hiroshima. It was a hell of an explosion. Of course, we didn't know what had caused it but we could see the mushroom cloud. We were told what had caused it later.

After the war we were based at Sasebo, Japan. There was a large Japanese ship anchored next to us. All the crew was on deck waving at us. I think they were just as tickled the war was over too as far as I could see. We flew over where the bomb was dropped. It was in a big valley and just wiped out everything in there. You just couldn't believe what that bomb did. The sides of the valley were scorched half way up to the top. We never went on land except for a few guys that swam ashore without permission. We could see Japanese through binoculars and they looked terrible, like they had been burnt and we were 30 or 40 miles away from where the bomb was dropped.

I spent almost five years in the Navy and then I got married was ready to get out. They flew me to the Philippines and put me on several weeks of Shore Patrol. It was pretty tough duty as there were people in that area of the Philippines that wanted to kill you. I spent 28 days on a ship getting back to San Francisco. We had some pretty tough weather and that boat was under water about half the time. I think it was made out of concrete. They were pretty safe, really.

I had two duties overseas during the war. After the first year, we were flown back to San Diego and given a 30-day furlough. I had no money to do anything. A stranger bought me a train ticket back to Iowa. If you were hungry, all you had to do was go to church and someone would invite you home for a meal. That's how it was back then.

Bob was a long time deputy sheriff and jailer back when Washington County had a two-man sheriff's department. He has also been a mechanic, farmer and the owner/operator of the popular Willows Restaurant.

MEAT HOOKS

Ezra "Easy" Jones
Washington, IA

87th Infantry Division
Europe

Interview Date:
20 March 2010

Referral:
Donald Libe

I got my draft notice in November of '42. I was originally from Missouri but living in Anamosa at that time. I went to Camp Dodge for my physical examination. They told me I would be called the last week in December for induction. I received a letter at home telling me to report February 3rd. They sent my group to Camp McCain in Mississippi for basic. I was married with a six month old baby daughter. I trained in the 335th Field Artillery Battalion. I feared that being in Mississippi during the summer heat was designed to prepare us for the Pacific. I thanked God when we were sent to New York to ship out because I knew we were heading for England. But I swear that the Germans were more tedious and brutal than the Japanese.

My unit shot the 155mm howitzer. My job was a driver and my rank was a T5 corporal. I carried a carbine. I towed a howitzer and a trailer with a caterpillar tractor. The trailer carried twelve men and 40 artillery rounds which weighed two tons. The fuses were carried separately. Some fuses were designed to penetrate concrete pillboxes. We had

four howitzers in my outfit. Our battery fired 1311 tons of ammo in six and one half months.

We landed at LaHarve, France. We made it to the front lines at Metz on December 6th. We had stopped and did some firing on the Seine River on the way up. I'm not sure what that was for. Metz was our first real combat where the Germans fired back at us. We were in Patton's 3rd Army until near the end of the war.

We were shelled one night in France. The artillery barrage lasted 20-30 minutes. I counted 32 shrapnel holes in my shelter half. It was set up about four feet from my foxhole.

I spent a month sharing the same foxhole with another driver next to the Siegfried Line. The captain told us to dig in good as we were going to be there a long time. We had straw for bedding and an oil burner for heat. I brought my cat (tractor) around and ran a drop cord from it so we had electric light. All our supplies including ammunition, food, and fuel was dropped by color coded parachutes.

I went up one time in a jeep to help set up the aiming stakes. I drove the jeep up over a hill toward the Siegfried Line to place the stakes. Lining up the barrel with the stakes would point the gun at the pillbox we were trying to knock out. The Siegfried Line was about a half mile away. We fired off ten rounds and got out of there. The next day we went up again and fired another ten rounds and pulled out. The third day I didn't even get my head over the hill before the Germans opened up on us with 88s from pillboxes all along the Siegfried Line. We still fired our ten rounds but we lost two men. The Germans had us zeroed in. Our mistake was going back to the same place three days in a row.

I spent two weeks in the hospital suffering concussion from the shelling the Germans gave us on the Siegfried Line. That happened in Belgium. We had captured a German artillery piece and the captain sent me and another guy to search for the German ammo dump. We discovered it about a half mile away. The Germans started shelling us on our way back. One round hit close enough to blow me 30 feet in the air. I didn't get hit by any shrapnel. I didn't know anything was wrong with me until I started urinating straight blood. I was sent to a hospital in Luxembourg. A lieutenant came around doing the paperwork to get me a Purple Heart. I declined, telling him to give mine to the poor guy in the bed beside mine that was in a full body cast. The guy on my other side had a leg blown off. Anyway, my outfit fired 50 German rounds through that captured gun back at the Germans. It took me a week to catch up with my outfit after I was released from the hospital.

There were three batteries of four guns each in our battalion. I was in B Battery. Our gun was the only one going forward to fire at the Siegfried Line in our division. We also had Piper Cub spotter planes. They'd radio back telling us how to adjust our fire. *(Note: The 87th was the first division to use small planes as artillery observers in WWII.)*

During the Battle of the Bulge, we took St. Vith and St. Hubert. I walked down the main street of Bastogne but it was secure by then. The worst things I saw were in Belgium, where the Germans

> *"A lieutenant came around doing the paperwork to get me a Purple Heart. I declined, telling him to give mine to poor guy in the bed beside mine that was in a full body cast."*

overran the Americans. Our division was one of 10 or 15 divisions involved in retaking the towns in Belgium. There was a lot of snow on the ground when we moved up. It was colder than the dickens. There was artillery pieces and other equipment just like ours sitting abandoned. The Germans had shot every man in that outfit and left them sitting in their fox holes. We used ropes and chains to pull the frozen bodies out of the foxholes. We lined the bodies up in rows. Then we slept in their foxholes.

Question: What was your opinion of General Patton?

My opinion of Patton was good. He was a fighting general. I saw General Patton twice. The first time was right after we crossed the Rhine. We were part of a task force that included a regiment of infantry, tank destroyers, and combat engineers that broke through the German lines and made a run. We got behind the German lines and we were surrounded for seven days. We were near Buchholz. The Germans blew a bridge in front of us which held us up. Patton made a speech to our task force before we started. He told us, "I'm not telling you to shoot at women and kids. But if you are going through a town and somebody is looking out a window, throw at shot at them. Because if you don't, somebody will be shot in the back before you go very far." The next time I saw him, he was standing there wearing his two big pistols directing traffic. This was towards the end of the war. There were times, because of all the vehicles, that we almost ran over one another.

The bridge we crossed over the Rhine River had smoke pots on each end to hide it from the German planes. One small German plane came in low over the river toward the bridge. You could see he carried two bombs. Our P-47 fighters were so high up that we didn't even know they were there. We could see tracer bullets raining down on this German plane. They shot him down and continued firing even after he disappeared under the water.

One time our whole road convoy was sprayed by a machine gun. We dismounted and took cover. Nobody had been hit. This was towards the end of the war. One guy could see where the machine gun was hidden. We had an interpreter and a PA system mounted on a truck. The interpreter told the German to surrender and come out or we'd blow him out. He was answered with more machine gun fire. So they pulled a howitzer out and made a little circle and blew him out of there. When we got up there, the German was still alive. He looked like he was about 14 years old. He was chained to that machine gun. This happened somewhere in Germany.

I saw something similar in Luxembourg. We were set up along an old railroad track. When the guns were firing, we had to pull our cats back at least 100 yards because they didn't want them blown up by German counter battery fire. I noticed a platform up in a tree. The next day I stopped in the same place and noticed the platform was still there and it looked like a body was hanging from it. I walked over there. From the ground it looked like a 15 year old German kid. He had been chained to the platform. Someone had shot him, but it wasn't me.

I only witnessed one occasion when our artillery shot at enemy armor. A German tank came out and started shooting at our guns. We fired two or three times before hitting it. That 155mm round blew its turret 20 feet in the air. There were five dead Germans in the tank.

I visited Buchenwald concentration camp after the war was over. Patton had sent a message out. "A lot of the boys over here have wondered what we have been fighting for. I want them to see what we were fighting for." Any man that wanted to go to Buchenwald was provided free transportation and given a tour. One building was 50 feet wide and a city block long. There were wooden beams every two feet across the ceiling. There were meat hooks hanging from the beams every two feet. They did not allow cameras inside this building. We were told that the Germans hung the Jews upside down by running the meat hook through the Achilles' tendon. The tour guide had us kneel down and examine the concrete floor below the hooks. You could see that the concrete had been cupped out ¼ to ½ inch deep. They said the concrete had been scratched out by the fingernails of the prisoners hanging from the hooks. That's when I said that I was glad we killed all the Germans that we did.

> *"They said the concrete had been scratched out by the fingernails of the prisoners hanging from the hooks."*

The Germans had urns at Buchenwald that looked like they would hold about 2 ½ gallons. We were told the Germans would burn 200 bodies at a time in a pit. The ashes would be shoveled into the urns. Two hundred bodies would fill ten urns.

Mary Jones: When Easy came home after the war he wouldn't talk about any of this. Then we started going to the reunions in 1973. The guys would all get together and the wives would start to hear all these stories. I wish we had tape recorders. A lot of stories were pretty horrid but there were funny ones, too. All those guys were like brothers.

Easy: I was pretty much scared all the time we were in combat. Most of the guys that got hurt or wounded were the replacements. But we had quiet times too, when there wasn't any shelling going on. There was joking and humor. It would have been terrible to endure if there hadn't been.

I would have rather fought a man with a rifle than an artillery shell exploding in the air. I give the Air Force a lot of the credit for winning the war in Europe. Our planes would literally fill the sky when the weather was good. Germany's shortage of fuel affected their ability to wage war. Our bombers get the credit for causing that.

When I came home, I hated the Germans.

Mary: My brother was killed in Italy in the battle for the Monte Casino Monastery. His body was never recovered. He was listed as missing in action for a year and then declared dead.

Easy: Of the 109 guys in my outfit, there are seven of us left alive. I'm 89 years old. Bob Lowe and Tom Tanner were in the 87th with me. Tom froze his feet so bad the first week in December that he was sent home and given a discharge. It got down to 30-35 below zero for 16 mornings in a row.

We'll celebrate our 70th wedding anniversary this year.

TROTTER

Bill Trotter
Ainsworth, IA

3rd & 70th Infantry Divisions
Europe

Interview Date:
30 March 2010

Referral:
Sheila Hildebrand, Gary Hill,
Gary Murphy, Mike Roberts
& many others

This is something that's pretty hard for me to swallow. We paid a high price.

I enlisted in 1944 because I knew my draft number was coming up. I was 24 years old and married. In fact, we had our son already and our daughter came when I was home on leave. I took my basic training in Little Rock, Arkansas. When we left Little Rock en route for Chicago, we came right through Ainsworth. That was one of the hardest things I had to do. My rank was a private first class, the bottom of the chain.

There were 14,000 of us on the ship going over. We were packed in so tight the guys couldn't even play cards.

I remember going up to the front line for the first time and seeing all those dead soldiers in the road ditches. It ties your belly in a knot. I was scared, there's no question about that.

I know you've heard of shrapnel. Most people would say it's a little piece of metal. They're right, most of the time. This is what took me out of combat. *(At this point, Bill slowly pulled an old pill container out of his pocket that housed a piece of*

shrapnel. It was a very large, very heavy piece of metal that would no doubt be lethal to whomever it hit.) I'd guess this piece of shrapnel was from an 88mm. It hit me in the shoulder. I've had people ask me if it hurt. I can't tell you how much it hurt. It took out 3 ribs, part of my lung and a kidney. This happened the 22nd day of March, 1945 in Saarbrucken, Germany. At the time, lying there badly wounded, I was certain this was it for me. I was going to die right where I lay bleeding.

Question: You were in the 3rd Infantry Division at first and then the 70th Infantry Division. Were you reassigned?
I can well remember….

When I first arrived in France, I went to the Repo-Depot, the replacement depot, and a major picked me up. I was eating my dinner, sitting on the edge of the street. This jeep stopped and he asked, "What outfit are you with?" I said, "I don't have an outfit. I'm just coming up." "Get in." I got in that jeep and we took off. It was cold then. We traveled a lot of miles and I was in the back of the jeep, freezing to death. One of the majors said to the other one, "Where are we going to drop this poor bastard off?" They dropped me off at what they thought was the 3rd Division, but it was really the 70th. I was in the 70th for a couple of weeks before I realize that I was in the 70th, not the 3rd. I was a BAR (Browning Automatic Rifle) man.

We marched, more like hiked, through France. We came to the village of Philippsbourg and went right on through and up a mountain. It was awful. I was in B Company and the Germans had us completely surrounded. Our company commander was badly wounded along with several others. I was tagged to go out on a patrol to see if I could get word back to Battalion HQ. We were out of ammunition, no communication, no food, no nothing. So after dark, the four of us in this patrol tried to get through the German lines. We were fortunate enough to get through and only lose one man. We met a patrol from C Company and the Lieutenant wouldn't let us go any further. So we stayed there one night and dug in near an intersection in the road. The next morning a 2nd lieutenant acknowledged that we had to do something, so he tagged me to make it on to Philippsbourg to get word that we were in trouble.

When I got to Phillippsbourg that evening, I saw that D Company had motorized recon units in town. Just as I came into town a jeep pulled in pulling a trailer. When he threw the tarp back I saw he had a load of ammunition, so I filled my ammo bag, my belt, and picked up a few hand grenades. For some reason I walked on up the street. It was really cold—zero degrees. I came to this one house, and I have no idea why I walked over to it and tried the door, but it opened. I walked into the house and it was dark inside. I had a short stub of a candle and lit it so I could see my way around. I climbed the stairs and went into a bedroom. There was no furniture at all in the house but there was a large rug rolled up lying against the wall. I laid it down and used it for a blanket to cover myself and went to sleep.

Early the next morning when I awakened, it sounded like there was machine gun fire right at my feet. I crawled over to the window and could see helmets and people running back and forth. I couldn't tell if they were GIs, German, or who they

"Now that's something you could write a book about: the thoughts that go through your head when you have your gun sight on a human being and pull the trigger. You don't forget it."

were. So I waited until daylight came and I realized they were the SS 6th Infantry Division. They were good soldiers. I knew I was in trouble. These Germans would charge the house if they knew where I was.

Anyway, I decided I wasn't over there to be hiding so I knocked the window out. From the second floor of the house, I could look across the street. There were two Germans on a machine gun and a rifleman on either side. I eliminated the four of them. By that time the Germans farther down the street behind a wall could tell where my fire was coming from. They threw a lot of fire at me through that window. We fought it out for about an hour, I suppose. That window came down to within ten inches of the floor. The only way I could get from one side of the room to the other was crawling on my belly. The house would have burned except it was built out of stone.

To make a long story short, I knew the Germans would charge the house. They had tried that before but I picked them off coming across the street. I had just put a fresh ammunition clip in my BAR when I saw the latch on the stairway door come down. I turned and emptied the whole 20 round clip through the door. I could hear screams and hollering so I knew I had hit people. I walked over and went through what was left of the door. There were two or three Germans lying on the stairway that had been hit. I took my boot and kicked them on down the stairs. That morning I killed 13 Germans. Now that's something you could write a book about: the thoughts that go through your head when you have your gun sight on a human being and pull the trigger. You don't forget it. I don't take any pride in the fact that I killed 13 Germans that morning.

Anyhow, I got out of that house and here is the story part. In 1995, we went back over to France and Germany, something I said I would never do. So 50 years later, we were standing in the middle of Phillippsbourg looking at this same house. It was all pockmarked from where the bullets had struck it. As we stood there, an elderly man came out of a house to our left. He asked in broken English if

I had been here during the war. When I told him yes, he invited us in to his home for wine. I'd say there were three generations living in the house. When the missus of the house noticed me glancing around while we drank our wine, she asked me if I wanted to see the rest of the house. We walked up the stairs to the landing. I turned to her saying, "You have a new door". She gave me a funny look. I walked over to the window I had been at 50 years before. For some reason I got the shakes. My wife Edie and another fellow in our tour group sat me down in a chair. *(As he sat down, the chair leg caught on a rug laid in front of the window pulling it back.)* I noticed a black stain on the floor under the window. The lady said she had tried everything to get the stain removed. I told her the Germans had shot me through the neck during the fight and the stain was from my blood. I had taken an old towel I carried under my helmet and ripped it up and had wrapped it around my neck to soak up the blood. I was real happy when an anti-tank outfit pulled into Phillippsbourg and I could get out of there. Then I made my way to an aid station.

When we were back in Phillippsbourg on the second floor of that house and looking out the window by the black stain on the floor, an older man came up the stairs. He starts saying, "machine gun, machine gun!" I relied, "No, it was a BAR." He still insisted I had been firing a machine gun because he had picked up over 300 empty shell casing fired from my BAR. I had a lot of ammunition with me and had thrown all my grenades. A BAR could be fired single shot but I didn't do that too often.

Comment: I find it remarkable that you chose to single handedly take on all those Germans in Phillippsbourg. Most people would have hunkered down to wait them out or try to slip away but you took them on.

Well, yes I did. I never thought I'd get out alive.

The BAR is a good weapon but the magazine doesn't hold enough bullets. I could slap a new clip in pretty fast. I'd go through 20 clips in most fights. It weighed 20 pounds so it was heavy to carry but it was well balanced. It didn't climb on you too bad on full automatic. It could reach out 500 yards.

> "I told her the Germans had shot me through the neck during the fight and the stain was from my blood."

I remember being in this one village and a German courier came roaring in on a motorcycle. Evidently he thought the Germans held the town. He saw us and wheeled that motorcycle around and gave it the gas to get out of town. Everybody was taking shots at him. I don't know that anybody ever touched him.

Bill asked us to accompany him to another room. He showed us a framed display case that his granddaughters Amy and Kate helped him fill with his campaign ribbons and medals. (He kept his medals in a basement storage closet until the late 1990s.) He pointed out his Purple Heart with four clusters at the top, meaning he was wounded five times. There was a Bronze Star and two Silver Stars for heroism. Bill said he was most proud of his Combat Infantry Badge, however, because only infantrymen were awarded those.

Question: Can you tell us what happened that you were awarded a Silver Star for?

Well, yes. We were advancing through a larger wooded area and we got pinned down by German tanks. I was behind a big rock. The German infantry swept around behind another big boulder. I could see that they were going to wipe out half our line. So I jumped up and ran out and emptied my magazine. I probably got to within 15 yards of the Germans. I killed quite a few of them. That gave us a chance to regroup and strengthen the front line.

One thing you may have never thought of was that during WWII there were twelve million men and women in uniform during the course of the war. Only 14% of those were in the infantry and they suffered 88% of the casualties. I was scared the whole time in combat. We had so many patrols…and most of our patrols never came back. I remember this one night a patrol was going out and we knew who made up the patrol because they had a contest. Everyone was given a chew of tobacco. A target was set up 15 feet away. Whoever fell short spitting at the target went on patrol.

This one time I had to go out on patrol because three patrols had already been sent out and none of them had come back. We walked to the edge of a village. I came in through the back door of a house. It was just getting daylight. As I was walking up the cellar stairs to the kitchen, I heard a man talking. I looked up and there was a German soldier standing on a balcony with a burp gun in his hand. I shot him and then got the hell out of there.

We were in the Hurtgen Forest. You'd be down in your foxhole and the German 88s would come in and hit the tree tops and the shrapnel would rain down on us. So being in the hole didn't make any difference. We got to where instead of jumping in a hole we'd stand up and wrap our arms around a tree, hugging it. We had better protection doing that than being in a foxhole. We were in the Hurtgen a couple of weeks. The visibility in the forest was bad. It was foggy, wet, and cold. It was bad. Our commanding officer there was a dunce. He was more concerned about making a name for himself than about the men.

I was in the Battle of the Bulge with the 70th Infantry Division. So many times, like during the Bulge, the German infantry came at us in waves. You'd mow down a bunch and there'd be another bunch right behind them. I've never been as cold as I was during the Battle of the Bulge. We didn't have the clothing for it. I picked up an old blanket somewhere. The wind would be so strong that I'd have one end over my shoulders and the other end of the blanket would be blowing straight out horizontally. I was miserable. I've been cold ever since the winter of '44-45. I had foot problems from the frostbite I suffered that winter. My feet still bother me. The weather over in Europe was bad enough without any combat.

We spent so much of our time in heavy forest during the Bulge. Mountains and slopes with rocks and tree roots made getting a foxhole dug with your entrenching tool quite a chore. Those Krauts were mighty good with their mortars. I remember going 87 days during the Bulge without changing my clothes. I got pretty ripe.

One thing people don't realize is that when our tanks go through a village they shoot it all up and keep going. But the Germans are still there and the

infantry coming behind the tanks had to deal with them. You can hide just as well behind a pile of rubble as you can in a standing building.

Question: Was there a specific action for being awarded the Bronze Star?

Oh, yes. We were crossing the Saar River one evening just as it was getting dark. Our boat upset midway. Oh Lord, the water was cold. The strong current carried the boat downstream for a half mile. We reached shore right in front of an old castle. As usual, the Germans had their machine guns up in the castle. Trying to be quiet landing a capsized boat in a strong current can't be done. I'd say a third of the fellows that were in the boat were hit. Well, we finally charged the castle. When we got close enough, I ran towards the door. But when you've been in cold water up to your shoulders, you don't run very fast. I never tried the lock on the door. I just emptied my magazine through the door and started kicking it in. As I stood on the outside of the door, blood came running out from under the door. I can remember how the blood looked in the snow…we always had blood in the snow.

Another time we had this three man patrol out. We came into a town and the Germans were in it. We wormed our way in and got down in a basement of a house. It was raining and we were soaked to the skin. Then it started to rain harder. I told the other fellows that in about five minutes the Krauts are going to be pouring down these steps to get in out of the rain. I positioned myself at the bottom of the stairs with my BAR and the other two were on either side of me. I was right. It wasn't but a few minutes and here comes five or six of them down the stairs. They were in front of me, within ten feet. That's where they died. I don't believe the other two guys with me fired a round.

At night we were in the woods so much of the time. I always carried my knife in my boot when I slept. That way, when you were crawling up to a German position you didn't have to rise up to get to it. You'd lay your hand down and the knife was there. It's not a nice thing to see. *(Bill lifted up his shirt sleeve and showed us a scar.)* That's from a German knife. We clashed you might say. We went down in the snow and rolled around. I got

> *"I can remember how the blood looked in the snow…we always had blood in the snow."*

up and he didn't. I still have that knife. I should break it into pieces and get rid of it. I recently came across the knife in a storage box in our basement in Ainsworth. I ran my hand down the blade. It is still very sharp.

Another time we were dug in inside this German village. A buddy with me named D.C. Knott and I dug in beside a house. It was bitterly cold. We had word that no one was to go into the house. We were to stay in the foxhole. It was quiet during the night and colder than the devil. Even though there wasn't any heat in the house, D.C. decided one of us should sleep in the house while the other one stayed out on the hole. I don't think it ever happened before, but that night the commanding officer came through to check on us and Knott wasn't there. So he was written up.

The next day we were to push on into Saarbrucken, Germany. We were to jump off at daylight. A heavy weapons company with .50 caliber machine guns and mortars was supposed to come and back us up. My platoon jumped off at eight o'clock but the heavy weapons company hadn't showed up. There was an open 150-yard wide field that we had to cross and a wooded hill on the far side. I was scared to death to go across it because I knew what would happen.

We got about 3/4 of the way across and the Germans opened up with their artillery. The lieutenant beside me was hit with the first round. He was in bad shape. I pulled him over behind a grassed hummock for a little protection. German machine guns were firing over us. I crawled forward trying to find some protection. I raised my head enough to see a ditch coming down off the high ground ahead of me. I headed for that ditch, crawling on my belly. I was sure the Germans would have somebody covering the ditch but it was the only protection there was so I crawled to the base of it.

I laid there a while listening to the machine guns firing. Then I crawled about a third of the way up the ditch. I tipped my head up enough to look forward and I saw this German grenade, potato mashers we called them, go sailing over my head.

> *"'Private Trotter rushed forward, alone….'"*

It exploded but didn't hit me. But I had seen the direction it had come from.

I lay there for several minutes before looking up to the high ground. I could see a German helmet. I lay there a little longer. I aimed my BAR where I saw him last and raised my head again. I could see two helmets but they disappeared. Then I could see where they were. I sighted my rifle down to that area. It was not long before both heads popped up. I shot both of them.

I lay there a little longer and then crawled on up the ditch to a grassy area. I lay there for another minute and I got to my feet and ran toward the German trench. The Germans had picked up a machine gun and were turning it around. I shot them and ran to the German trench. The German infantrymen were in a ditch covering the hill. How I got up behind them, I don't know, but I did. I shot another machine gunner and went into the head of the ditch firing my BAR. I think I captured 12 Germans. I don't know how many were killed.

I well remember the sergeant when the GIs came up the hill where I was. The Germans who were able had run off. The platoon leader came up and stood a while and looked around. He turned to me and said, "Trotter, you son of a bitch!" That was my commendation. I knew enough of the German language by then to get the prisoners to do what I wanted. They understood "Rausmit Ihn!" and the muzzle end of my BAR jabbed in their back.

They gave me a Silver Star for that.

Note: Bill's (second) Silver Star Citation for this act of bravery reads:

"On 21 March 1945, at 1600 hours, in the vicinity of Saarbrucken, Germany, when a counterattacking enemy force threatened to overrun his Company's positions, Private Trotter rushed forward, alone, in the face of intense machine gun and small arms fire to halt the German drive. Firing short bursts from his automatic rifle, Private Trotter advanced to within fifteen yards of the enemy group, killed four Germans and captured eight. This action enabled his Company to regroup and throw back the attack and subsequently establish adequate defensive positions."

Question: I think the Medal of Honor would have been more appropriate. What do you think would have happened if Bill Trotter hadn't taken the initiative and got around behind the Germans?

There would have been more of the platoon killed, that's for sure. On our flank was the 100th or Century Division. Excuse my language, but we were attacking a German town named Bitche. That was its name. The 100th Division took the town and got credit for it. From then on, they referred to themselves as sons of bitches.

My best buddy over there was an Indian from North Carolina right off the reservation. His real name was Sampson. I called him "Sammy". When our artillery would go over us he'd always say, "Hitler, count your children." One time we were pinned down near Niederbronn, France. I was on one side of a boulder and Sammy was on the other. I told him, "Sammy, for God's sake, keep your head down." It wasn't too long and I don't know why, but Sammy peaked around the corner of the rock. They got him right through the head. His head just exploded. To show you how tough I was…I cried.

> "The fear of the Lord is with the infantryman…."

The fear of the Lord is with the infantryman when he is in his foxhole and the tanks are coming and all you have is a rifle. And maybe there'd be 50 or 100 German foot soldiers behind the tanks. You were scared. All you could do was try to get a little deeper in your hole. There was one instance when a German Panzer tank turned over our foxholes, trying to push the dirt in on us. Fortunately, the tank turned off right before it got to me. But there were still the storm troopers to take care of.

Question: Did your bazooka teams hunker down or was it pointless to shoot at the Panzers?

Both. It happened many times. Sometimes the German tanks would straddle a foxhole and asphyxiate our guys with their exhaust. Our bullets would just bounce off a tank.

We never had much support from our own tanks when we advanced. The French 10th Armored was attached to us. I received a Bronze Star from the French for liberating a German village. I can't really recall the circumstances. It's been too many years and too long ago. I remember the French officer kissed me on both cheeks. I don't know whatever became of that medal.

Question: What was your opinion of the French soldiers?

I was never around enough of them to form an opinion. The Germans were very good soldiers.

I think the one thing the Germans learned from WWI was the value of a machine gun. That MG 42 they had was a great weapon. It was a wicked weapon. Close in they were mighty deadly. If you heard it once, you knew what it was. Our machine gun would fire 600 rounds a minute and that was a lot of bullets. But the German one would fire 1200 rounds a minute. The Germans would time their firing in short bursts.

I was at Dachau at the end of the war. Dachau was close to Munich. I got a ride into Munich after the war ended. There was a large country estate on the edge of town surrounded by a brick wall and cast iron fence. The gate was open so I walked in and sat down on a concrete bench to rest. I hadn't been there long when two Rangers came in with three German prisoners. The Rangers lined the three Germans up against the brick wall and walked back nearly to where I was sitting. They turned to face the prisoners. They both raised their tommy guns. One of them said, "Now!" and that was it. The war was over, but those things happened. I don't know why that happened nor will ever know. It may have had something to do with Dachau.

Don't get me started on Dachau. I want to be able to sleep tonight.

Question (asked at a later date): I know you don't want to talk about Dachau, but what would be your response to those people that claim the Holocaust was all a hoax?

If they had kicked the gates of Dachau open like I did, they wouldn't think that. There were sights and smells you'd never forget. As soldiers, we had no knowledge of the camps until seeing them in person. There were hundreds and hundreds of bodies there. Some were still alive. They were very weak and filthy. I have no idea if they survived or not. They were hungry and we gave them food. But they couldn't eat.

Question: Did you have a difficulty adjusting to civilian life when you came home?

When I got home, I had lost a lot of weight and was limping badly. I'd had a rough time but my wife had it just as rough. She had received five different telegrams from the government that I was listed as missing in action.

They say it takes eight or nine people to support one infantryman, providing food, supplies, and postal service right on up the line. Many times I asked myself, "Why me?" Our platoon went in with 87 guys. Four of us came home. Charlie Pence, our executive officer, had his leg shot off. He's gone now. I had another friend visiting here a few weeks ago from Vancouver. He had a leg shot off. I was close to Charlie when he stepped on the mine.

I was pretty much a loner during my time in the service. I didn't know very many people. We went to one reunion. I told Edie there was no reason to go as I would not know anybody there. For some reason we went anyway. I saw this fellow walking toward me in the hotel where the reunion was being held. He looked up at me and said, "Hello, Trotter, you long-legged son of a bitch." I knew right then who it was…D. C. Knott.

There was a box of things I sent home during the war stored in the basement of our house in Ainsworth. I don't believe it had ever been opened. One time when my granddaughter Amy was home we opened it. She is very interested in military history. There was a Nazi flag inside that must have been 20 feet long and 8 feet wide. I gave the flag to her. She lives in Washington, D.C. and plans to donate it to some historical society that would want to display or preserve it.

I tore that flag off the city hall in Saarbrucken. The German towns had a lot of Nazi flags flying. A good burst of a BAR through a window and those Nazi flags turned to white flags pretty fast.

> *"When Bill held out his hands to him, Tom asked, 'Daddy, do you remember me?'"*

Question: Did you come across German towns or villages with nothing but white sheets hanging from the windows announcing their surrender?

No, not too much. A lot of German houses and businesses got shot up, especially when the tanks rolled through.

Question: Do you have any regrets?

Yes I do. But probably not in the way you asked the question. I still have quite a bit of pain in my back and shoulders. When I was shot in the neck, another fraction of an inch would have hit a major vein and I would have bled to death. The cold weather and the towel I wrapped around my neck helped stem the blood flow.

Incidentally, we have made three trips back to France. Our granddaughter Amy accompanied us. Note: The house in Phillippsbourg is still there and the bullet pockmarks on the sides are still there. The 70th Division veterans association's tour guide has it marked as "The Bill Trotter house".

Edie Trotter: You go over to France and see all the white crosses in the cemeteries. You are very grateful. It was a thrill for me to see those fellows march down the street where they had fought, carrying the American flag. It was a very special moment, very gratifying. Bill got home April 14, 1946. We drove up to Iowa City to pick him up. Our son Tom was four years old. When Bill held out his hands to him, Tom asked, "Daddy, do you remember me?"

Bill: I have often been asked to speak to school kids. You get up in front of a bunch of third or fourth graders and they all ask the same question, "Did you shoot anybody?" I have lied to kids many times. I take no pride in it.

I have no lingering animosity towards the Germans today. They have completely changed. The Germans today don't talk about the war. I waited 60 years before I would talk about it.

I operated a feed and grain business and ran the elevator at Ainsworth after the war. One of my biggest worries when I came home was that they wouldn't let me into church if they knew how many Germans I had killed. I'm 92 years old and still carry that burden. It's not something you are proud of.

One thing that disappoints me today is that most of the kids here and half the adults know nothing about WWII. You can't say that about the French people.

Edie: It was a different time and a different generation. Those fellows grew up during the Great Depression. They knew what it was like to do without because that was the only way you could live. That made a difference. They came home and got on with their lives.

Bill: I went on the one day Honor Flight in September 2010 to see the WWII Memorial. In one sense, war really never settles anything. The old men make the plans and the young men die. I wish people here, today could see Dachau. It would make them realize what the war was all about.

Bill with his BAR, Germany 1945. Photo courtesy of Edie Trotter.

I Wished I Was Back on the Farm

David Brinning
Washington, IA

113th Cavalry Group
Europe

Interview Date:
13 April 2010

Referral:
Personal Contact

I was in the local National Guard, the Troop. We were in Texas for a year of training and Pearl Harbor happened before we came back. So we didn't get to come back. We went overseas in February of '43. The North Atlantic was rough and we got our first taste of seasickness. I was in B Troop, 125th Cavalry Squadron, part of the 113th Cavalry Group. There were about 125 of us in our troop. We were the old F troop at one time but they changed us to B Troop. Three troops made up a squadron. My rank was a T4, the same pay as a sergeant.

We landed in England and did a lot of training up by the Scottish border. Anti-aircraft gunnery and stuff like that. We knew the invasion of France was coming. We were all young guys and a little leery about how well the Germans were trained.

We went in D-Day plus 4. The Rangers and paratroopers went in first. I drove an M8 Armored Car right in on Omaha beach. The Navy was still shelling inland when we landed and the Germans were trying to shell Omaha beach.

There were dead bodies all over when we landed at the beach. The worst I'd ever seen. There were

German dead as well. They all had turned black. I wonder if that wasn't from their diet they were on.

The 113th was the outer security attachment for General Bradley's headquarters. Bradley was "a soldier's general." He was a nice guy from Kirksville, Missouri. We faced outward to protect his headquarters. My main job was that of a radio operator in an armored car. We had a long distance radio and a walkie-talkie. We mainly talked to other armored cars.

We always slept under our armored cars at night. I looked out one morning and saw some shiny boots pacing back and forth. We rolled out from under the armored car and there was General Patton wearing his pearl handled revolvers. We got to our feet and saluted him. This happened two or three nights after we had landed. Patton spent some time talking to us asking where we were from and how we were doing.

Not long after we crossed the channel a German ME 109 fighter plane flew over us. He cut his engines and circled us a few times. No one knew what he was until he got right over us. Then everyone started shooting at him. We didn't get him. We had a 50 caliber machine gun in the turret of our armored car. We shot at some other planes but I don't know if we got them or not. One guy claimed we shot one down.

The most combat we had was during the Battle of the Bulge when the Germans broke through. We were guarding First Army Headquarters. The Germans were trying to surround us but ran out of fuel and supplies. They even put wood burners on the tanks to move them. They'd just creep along. It was mostly infantry we faced. The First Army headquarters was at Spa, Belgium. There were mineral water springs at the resort and some of the guys tried bathing in them but I never did.

We'd set up outposts in our half-tracks or armored cars about ten miles behind the front lines to guard the First Army Headquarters which would be ten or more miles to our rear. We slept in the half-tracks but oh boy did it ever get cold during the Bulge. There weren't any heaters in our half-tracks but we were issued insulated winter clothing. They made us quit using our radios and strung telephone lines for communication. Usually it was just our one vehicle with a crew of five or six. We'd be out for several days at time, although it varied. I never dug a foxhole during the war.

"She had a lamp shade made out of human skin in her office."

We were up on a hill in Belgium one day and the Germans were down in the town. We tried to keep quiet so as to not draw attention to ourselves but the Germans starting firing at us. We shot back with our 50 cal. They didn't come up the hill after us. We had a 37mm cannon on the half-track but didn't use it much. You had to turn the turret to use the 37mm and the fifty was much more maneuverable so we used it most of the time. There was also a stationary 30 caliber machine gun inside the turret next to the 37mm. Every fourth round was a tracer and we'd use them to mark a target so we wouldn't even need to aim the 37mm. The 37mm wasn't much good. It couldn't penetrate much.

Question: Did you ever see any of the V-1 buzz bombs or V-2 rockets?

Oh, yeah! But you couldn't see the V-2s coming. The rockets were what really scared us because you had no warning. The buzz bombs flew lower and slower. You could hear them coming. When they ran out of fuel you'd better be ducking. We had buzz bomb attacks in England as well as in Europe. The buzz bombs weren't very accurate but the Germans launched them at the general area where First Army Headquarters was located. They were a great psychological weapon.

We crossed the Rhine at the bridgehead at Remagen. The 8th Armored Division had gotten there before the Germans were able to blow the bridge. The Siegfried Line didn't amount to anything where we crossed it. The Germans were already on the run but I remember seeing some of the pillboxes and barriers.

Question: Did you ever wonder, in the thick of combat, what in the world you were doing there?

Oh yeah! I wished I was back on the farm. I was ready to go home and settle down. I lost a brother over in the Pacific. He was in the Philippines when Pearl Harbor was bombed. He was part of the ground crew in the 17th Air Corps and was captured by the Japanese when the Philippines fell. He died in a prison camp. His name was William and he was two years older than me.

We were near the Buchenwald prison camp when the war ended. There were still prisoners there. They walked around like zombies. Big hay racks were stacked full of bodies of dead prisoners. There was a woman that ran that place. She had a lamp shade made out of human skin in her office. We saw it before someone stole it. It's probably back here in the United States somewhere.

Question: Did you bring any souvenirs home?

I had a P38 pistol with me when I was ready to get on the boat to come back home. I think I had taken it off a dead German officer. We were told to turn stuff like that in before boarding and I was honest enough that I did. That was the last I saw of it.

The only time I saw General Eisenhower at our headquarters was right after we landed in France. They didn't really want him that far forward because it wasn't safe. The reporter Ernie Pyle was with us a while near the end of the war. Then he headed over to the Pacific and got killed (by Japanese machine gun fire during the Okinawa campaign).

Married men with kids got to come first. Guys like me that were in the longest had more points and were among the first to leave our outfit for home.

Question: Who are some of the other locals that served in the Red Horse?

Bob Stirling was in. I might be the only one left from my original troop except for Bob Stirling. There were some boys from Pleasant Plain. Kenny Hahn was a good friend of mine. He's gone. Bob Porter left us for OSC training so he really wasn't with us much. Of course there was Wilbur Wright and Harold Wolf. There was Bob Carson from Conesville. They kept sending out our guys as cadres to form other outfits. They'd get a higher rating that way. Raymond Edwards died just a year or so ago.

My memory isn't as good as it used to be. You know, I'm getting old.

Dave came home and farmed his entire life near Wellston in Dutch Creek Township until retirement.

TRIBUTE

I had six uncles and several friends that were in WWII. They never talked about the war. They just came home and went about their lives. They went to church and raised their families. I think that most of them felt lucky to have made it home alive. It wasn't a time to sit around and talk about what they had done. The majority of the other men their age went through the same thing or worse. They certainly didn't think of themselves as heroes.

In the 1980s I was very fortunate to get to know Wilbur Wright, Dave Brinning, and Don Bealer. They were proud members of the Red Horse Outfit. They were the Iowa National Guard Cavalry Unit right here in Washington before the war. They trained on horses. The unit was converted to Mechanized Cavalry and went into Normandy after D-Day. Oh, the stories I pried from them! If I would have only had the sense to turn on a tape recorder back then, I'd be able to write a book myself. Sadly to say, the Red Horse Outfit has dwindled to only a couple of living members. They had their final reunion last July.

I am greatly honored to call some of "The Greatest Generation" my friends, and THANK YOU ALL!

Respectfully,
Steve Sheetz
Keota, IA

THE GOOD LORD HAD HIS ARMS WRAPPED AROUND ME

Don "Coon" Rath
Riverside, IA

1st Marine Division
Pacific

Interview Date:
20 April 2010

Referral:
John 'Lefty' Wilson

I enlisted November 9th in '42. I did boot camp in San Diego at the Marine Corps base. I worked for a farmer after graduating from high school. One day I was out plowing corn and met the neighbor named Foster on the fence line. He was president of the local draft board. He asked me how old I was. When I told him I was 20, he said that he would be calling me up pretty soon. I informed him that would not happen, as I would enlist first and join the Marines. He advised against that, saying he would have to call someone else who was probably married in my place to fill his quota. I replied, "Tough, I'm going to enlist." I had always admired the looks of the Marines and hearing their tales and always wanted to be one. So I enlisted with the Marines in Cedar Rapids. My younger brother Harold went to the Army.

When I was in Camp Pendleton, we were told about a new First Armored Amphibious Tank Battalion that was being formed. The tanks had not even been made yet. Major Metzger, our commander, said he would go over our records

and individually picked those that qualified. I was one of those selected. There were a bunch of disappointed fellows out there that didn't get selected as we all wanted to stay together if we could.

While we were waiting at Pendleton for our tanks to arrive, the Hollywood movie folks used our Marine outfit in the production of *Guadalcanal Diaries*. I've seen myself in that movie. I'm the one made up with a white bandage on his arm with blood running down it. I became friends with Lloyd Nolan, the star of the movie. He spent a lot of time socializing with us Marines. We both smoked Camels and we would exchange cigarettes. He was a swell guy.

Our tanks were amphibious landing craft with turrets placed on them. I was the machine gunner and the radio operator. I sat next to the driver. Our first tank had a 37mm gun and our later had a 75mm that packed a lot of punch. The 37mm was a wicked little gun, great for direct fire. We were the first to hit the beach. Our mission was to establish a beach head. We were trained to support the infantry that came in behind us with our big guns, to use it like artillery.

We shipped out of San Diego on January 9th of '44 and refueled in Hawaii. We walked around the island and were given tubs of pineapple to eat. From there we went straight to our first landing on the Kwajalein Island in the Marshalls.

Question: How did you feel going in on your first landing?

I was scared. Anyone that tells you they weren't had something wrong with them. We were also the first on Guam. We were sitting down on the flat and the Japanese were up in caves on the mountain. They were raining down artillery on us something terrible. It was amazing how many shells were flying around and exploding and that many people don't get hit. If you could get in a foxhole, a shell could explode pretty close to you and not get you if you weren't exposed.

One time we were all sitting outside our tanks aboard an LST waiting to go in on a landing. Everyone was talking, chattering away. Johnny Green from Sigourney piped up, saying, "You know, in about fifteen minutes we'll be going in. Some of us won't be coming back." Everybody shut up. It got so quiet you could have heard a pin drop.

"We got shot up so bad that we didn't have enough tanks left to hit Iwo Jima next."

Our amphibious tanks were loaded on LSTs. They'd drop the ramp to unload us and we'd swim them to shore. I thought we were goners going in to land on Guam. Three of us were sitting up on the bow of the ship. We looked up and saw five Japanese torpedo planes coming directly at our LSTs. You could see the white streak of the torpedo in the water coming closer and closer. You'd just freeze, waiting for the blow. It was "good bye cruel world" time. At the last instant, the ship made a hard left and the torpedo passed right in front of us and struck an LCM that was a smaller craft and only had a crew of eight. That torpedo practically cut that LCM in half. A destroyer escort swung around and put its five inch guns on it and finished sinking it. They never even looked for survivors. I thought that was strange, but there probably

weren't any survivors. I think the good Lord had His arms wrapped around me.

We were told that Guam had been all shelled out by the Navy and we'd only be there a few days. They promised there would be very little resistance but that was the biggest mistake they ever made. We got shot up so bad that we didn't have enough tanks left to hit Iwo Jima next. We lost a third of our battalion's tanks on Guam. The pillboxes on Guam were back a little ways from the beach but close enough to see them. I remember the lieutenant coming over the radio when we landed, saying, "There they are. Go get them." We had a good gunner on our tank. He knocked out a lot of them.

That first night on Guam we were down on the flat next to the beach. Every time I go down on the Iowa River bottom and look up to the bluffs, it reminds me of Guam. You could hear the Jap machine guns firing all night from the hills. About the middle of the night, Tokyo Rose started broadcasting on our frequency. She asked, "How are you mosquito bitten Marines doing on Guam? I am going to play you a song by Bing Crosby and I want you to really enjoy it because we're going to push you right back into the ocean." There for a while, I kind of wondered if maybe she was right, that they might get the job done.

Over in front of our tanks there were hospital tents set up full of wounded guys. There were guys moving about one night and I didn't know if they were Japs or our own people so I was afraid to shoot. The next morning we learned that some Japs had slipped through and bayoneted all the wounded laying in the tents. It was awful. Guam was really tough. It was the worst of the three invasions for our outfit.

I was in C Company. We had a lot of men wounded but only one killed on Guam. That guy was on my tank. He got a piece of shrapnel in the middle of his forehead. A mortar round hit our tank turret. Two more of the crew was wounded. We had three guys in our company that had gone in at Guadalcanal and had lots of experience. One of them told me that he was just as scared as I was but as a leader, he wasn't supposed to show it. Sitting in those foxholes at night with all the shells coming in, you had to wonder if one had your name on it. The old veterans would joke around when it got really tense to try to ease our tension.

There had been an American base on Guam when the Japanese took it. A number of the native women had been married to sailors and could speak English as good as you and me. The Japanese used them to service their soldiers. I saw them kiss the ground at our feet. They said, "We knew you would come back!"

Question: There were a lot of native Okinawans there. What happened to them?

I don't know, but I think they got shot down just like the Japs. One morning there came this lady carrying a little baby. She was wearing a great big full skirt that hung clear down to the ground. She was walking right up to a bunch of our people. Who did it I don't know, but all at once, "kerbang", somebody shot her. Anyway, a lot of the guys were mad, asking, "Why in the hell did they shoot that woman?" Then someone checked under the skirt and discovered it was full of explosives. She was trying to get amongst a bunch of troops and blow herself up. It was a good thing somebody did shoot her. One of the guys scooped the baby up and took it somewhere where it could be cared for.

During the last big push on Okinawa, the Japs brought out their big battleship, the *Yamamoto*, with its eighteen inch guns. The Japs claimed this ship was unsinkable. The Japanese sailors were told to fire up all their ammunition and then ram our ships. Our subs and torpedo bombers kept pounding it only on one side. It started listing and finally capsized and that's how we got it.

The biggest Kamikaze attacks of the war were directed at the fleet anchored off Okinawa. Me and another guy named Neely were on top of our tank firing the 50 caliber at the kamikazes when the lieutenant yelled at us and told us to crawl under the tank as there was so much flak falling to the ground that we'd get hurt. There was so much flak falling that people did get hurt. That was the biggest fireworks I'll ever see. All the navy ships as well as those of us on land were shooting everything we had at them. We were later told that 144 Jap planes had been shot down.

Toward the end of the Okinawa campaign there were some Japanese holed up in a cave by the harbor. A Japanese interpreter spent two days on a loud speaker urging them to surrender. Told them the exact time we'd open up on the cave entrance with everything we had if they didn't come out. They refused. We had our tank gun trained on the entrance and there was a God awful explosion when the time ran out. There were 72 big guns in our outfit alone firing all at once. I didn't see how anyone could have survived but pretty soon a Japanese officer wearing a sword stuck his head out waving this little white flag. He was mowed down. The interesting thing to me is that I have watched this scene on the History Channel and know that I was there in person.

They used flame throwers to burn the Japs out of the caves. In reality, they don't so much get burnt but die from all the oxygen being burned up. One cave had 47 Japanese nurses in it and only three or four survived the flame thrower. There was another cave by a big rock that had a big Japanese artillery gun in it. They tried about everything to knock it out. Dive bombers spent two days dropping bombs at the entrance without success. Finally our major said he would knock it out with our amphibious tanks. He took eight or ten of them and they kept firing as they rolled forward. Finally they got right up to the cave entrance and fired directly down into the cave. They were able to destroy everything in that cave.

After finishing Okinawa we went back to our base at Guadalcanal. One Sunday we were sitting around doing nothing and five of us decided to go shoot some pigeons. So we went out in the brush and started shooting away at these pigeons roosting up in the trees. Pretty soon we looked around and we were completely surrounded by Navy Shore Patrol. We didn't know what we were doing wrong. They told us to line up and unload our weapons. They took us back to main camp in 6x6 trucks. We still didn't know what all the fuss was about. We finally were told that Admiral William F. "Bull "Halsey's ship was anchored out in the bay and he had a day camp set up on shore and we had been shooting into the tree tops above him. They questioned us while we were riding on the trucks, wanting to know our names and outfit. One of our group was a platoon sergeant named Green that was up for a promotion to the rank of lieutenant. This little incident would have sunk his prospects for a promotion so we all gave them fictitious names and told them we were with the 4th Tractor Battalion which had come ashore the preceding day. The officer questioning us said that he was going to call our CO. When he returned, he said that there was no radio communication established with our outfit yet because it had only come in yesterday. So that's how we got out of that. They gave us some regulations for the island and told us that we'd better read them before doing any more shooting. We killed some pigeons but they wouldn't let us take them with us. But Johnny Green made lieutenant.

My wife and I were married in Las Vegas. She came out to visit me in California while I was undergoing training. This house we are sitting in was purchased by my wife during the war for a thousand dollars. I got real lucky gambling one night on Guadalcanal and won almost $1200. That's where the money came from as we were both pretty much broke before that.

I was on Guadalcanal when the war ended. Everyone was celebrating, firing their guns into the air. One of my good buddies came by and asked me for some money to go buy beer at the Negro camp. I gave him $120 and he took off in a stolen jeep. He never returned that night. I found out later that the shore patrol had chased him because of the stolen jeep and my buddy drove off a cliff on a curve in the road and was killed. I went to see my Captain and told him about the missing money and he was able to get all but $12 returned to me.

The actor William Shatner of Star Trek fame and I became good friends during his visits to

Riverside. He told me that when he was struggling to get into acting that he'd have to sleep in his old pickup truck because he was so broke.

To be honest about it, I have had a pretty exciting life.

I WAS LUCKY

John Capper
Wellman, IA

3rd Marine Division
Pacific

Interview Date:
27 April 2010

Referral:
Personal Contact

I was in the 638th Platoon, 12th Marine Regiment, 3rd Marine Division. I was in the Mortar Section and with the artillery. I was lucky in that my primary job was to drive the radio jeep. I also drove trucks or prime movers as we called them. I did my first training in San Diego. I enlisted in 1942. There were five of us from Wellman that decided that we all wanted to join the Marines. Bill Ulin, Gus Martin, Bernie Goodwin, myself, and another guy, Irwin 'Red' Moothart, that didn't pass the physical, all went in together. We served in the 3rd Marines and survived the war.

Guadalcanal was pretty well secured by the time our Division landed. There was both jungle with coconut trees and open prairie where we were at. We had to do some police work, that's about all. The natives kept out of our way.

The Japanese navy came in close and shelled the Marines on Guadalcanal. I heard the story about a Marine mortar man dropping a (very lucky) round down a destroyer's stack, blowing it out of the water. I thought that was really something. Those mortars were quite a good weapon for the kind of war we had over there, as most of the fighting was close in.

Most of the 3rd Division landed on Bougainville (also in the Solomon Islands) to clear part of the

island so the CBs (Navy Construction Battalion, also nicknamed the Seabees) could build an airstrip. The Japs mostly stayed up in the hills on Bougainville until the end of the war. I had to stay back on Guadalcanal to take care of some things so I lucked out again. After Bougainville our Division was rebuilt with replacements and we trained for the invasion of Guam.

We sat aboard ship waiting until other Marine Divisions secured Saipan and then we landed on Guam. I remember everyone got tired of waiting on those ships. Both islands are in the Marianas. I think the British might have had control of Guam. The natives were mostly black but there were some whites among them. They were all real friendly and glad to see us.

The infantry always went in first after the Navy got done shelling the island. In the one main town on Guam, Agama, only the church and the bank were still standing. The navy had made a shambles out of everything else. A lot of coconut trees were destroyed. The Japs were up in the hills and we set up the artillery down on the flats. The Japs had pillboxes up in the hills and were firing down on the infantry. Our motor section tried to keep them pinned down.

The 12th Marines had 75mm field howitzers which were good out to seven or eight miles.

Another Marine unit had the big 155s. There were also Marine tanks involved. We had a forward observer who was really good. He'd call in for a spotter round and adjust the fire. He could put the next round right in the bucket. Those forward observers were in some bad stuff. We had one guy who went forward to help a forward observer and when he came back his hair had all turned white as snow. He had got that scared. You just can't imagine. I never had to go with any of the forward observers but I had to take hot food up to them on Guam with my jeep once.

I got scared a few times, when it got in close. You tried not to think about it. You just did your job. That's what most of the guys did.

We had a tent city set up on Guadalcanal. A single engine Jap plane would come on moonlit nights and do his bombing. We called him Washing Machine Charlie. We'd just crawl into our fox holes. I had mine fixed up pretty good with coconut logs and dirt over the middle of the top. You didn't want to close it clear up on either end or the concussion would get you. There was an anti-aircraft battery set up on a neighboring island called Christmas Island and they'd shoot some of the bombers down, catching them coming in. The Japs didn't get away with too much.

The mosquitoes were the worst thing on Guam and we had several cases of malaria there. We'd sleep under mosquito netting on fold up cots with a frame over the top for the netting. There were these little lizards on Guam that ate mosquitoes. We'd catch them and put them under the netting next to us while we slept. I had what we called ding fever for about three days but that was the only sickness I ever had.

I shouldn't tell this story. We had a crew of blacks assigned to our mortar section on Iwo. They were supposed to carry ammunition to us. They were scared to death. One time we got down to seven rounds for each of our guns. That wasn't good. The blacks would get so scared they'd stop and crawl under their ammunition truck. If somebody dropped a firecracker on that truck, where would they be? The dummies. That's the reason we got so low on ammunition.

> *"You tried not to think about it. You just did your job."*

We had some American Indians in the 3rd Marines and a few Mexican Americans. They were good people. I don't remember any Indian code talkers, however.

I would help here and there, handling ammunition, whatever or where ever I was needed when we were engaged. Very little enemy artillery was shot back at us but some mortars were. There were four guns in each battery and four batteries in the 12th Marine Regiment. I don't think we lost any guns during the war. We didn't suffer many casualties. Some, but we didn't get hurt too bad. It was the infantry and people like that which got hurt the worst. The Japs had all these caves they hid their artillery in. They would swing their guns out and fire a few rounds and go back inside. That way we didn't have a chance to get at them. But the Japs never had time to get a good aim and couldn't hit much of anything. They were a lot more accurate with their mortar fire.

Question: What was your opinion of the fighting ability of the Japanese soldier?
Dumb. They were dumb. Whenever they attacked, they'd yell, "Die Marine" or "Banzai!" On Guam, several days after we landed there, one night they came down out of the hills with sticks to beat us up. They didn't even carry guns. They were all drunk on sake. Sake is pure alcohol and strong stuff. About a dozen made it through the front lines back to us. Well, you know what happened to them. Another night a bunch attacked our field kitchen with sticks because they were hungry. The mess crew fought them off with some fire logs and one of the cooks had a tommy machine gun. He laid them out good. We were never sure where that group of Japs came from. They must have been dug in some place and we had bypassed them.

Question: What was a cook doing with a Thompson sub machine gun?
I reckon he had it sent from home or picked it up someplace. It wasn't a military issued Thompson. It had the magazine drum rather than an ammo clip. A lot of the Marines carried personal sidearms sent from home.

At night we'd be in our fox holes and we knew where everyone else was supposed to be. You didn't get out of your foxhole at night for any reason, including going to the bathroom. We did a lot of shooting at nothing. One night there was clearly something making noise in the brush which drew a lot of fire. We found a dead horse there the next morning. That poor horse picked the wrong time to be wandering about. Our policy was to think about yourself and shoot first; worry about what you hit in the morning. We didn't have too much trouble with the Japs trying to infiltrate us at night. One time on Guam we had two Japs carrying white flags somehow sneak through the front lines and come in back where we were. I'll never know how they managed to do that. One of them was nicely dressed and just as clean as could be.

Question: Were these two taken prisoner?

We took some, not very many. I think there were only around a hundred prisoners taken in all of Guam. The Japanese soldiers on Guam were all veterans. Guam was one of the places the Japanese Army sent their soldiers for rest and recuperation. These guys knew what they were doing. That's what made it a little rough. It was quite a deal.

Army infantry came in on Guam after the Marines landed. They were not as well trained as us. I know that they lost men from friendly fire when they'd get out of their foxholes at night. We used passwords at night to prevent that. There were also super trained Marines called Raiders. They were special and were usually guys like orphans without families. We had some attached to our outfit. They'd move around at night like cats to infiltrate enemy positions to locate strong points and gun emplacements.

About a quarter mile from where we had our artillery set up on Guam the Japs had a radio station set up. It took a while before any one realized it was there. They had constructed a concrete wall around a cave that was tucked into the side of a bluff. There was no way we could get at it. Finally we put together a half ton of TNT and dropped it down from the top of the bluff into the cave entrance. That took care of it.

I brought home a Japanese prayer belt I took off a dead Jap on Guam. It supposedly has a thousand stitches and each stitch represents a prayer from

> *"There were also super trained Marines called Raiders. They were special and were usually guys like orphans without families."*

a different woman. It wasn't safe to try to get too many souvenirs because the Japs would booby trap them with a bomb. The dead Jap I took the prayer belt off of was pretty fresh, let's leave it at that.

I carried a 30 caliber carbine until they issued all the truck drivers rising guns (also called the grease gun). They shot a 45 caliber bullet but weren't that great of a weapon.

I dug in soon after I got on Iwo Jima. I came in a Higgins boat. I drove my jeep clear across the island and got separated from my outfit. I spent the first night in a fox hole beside my jeep near the airstrip. The Japanese left me alone. I was lucky. They had higher value targets than a radio man. They especially targeted the guys carrying the flame throwers. I rejoined my outfit in the morning. We didn't have to move our guns after landing as we could reach every corner of the island. Bazookas worked pretty good on the caves if you could get close enough. But the flame thrower was the weapon of choice.

The Japs were really dug in on Iwo. They even had tanks buried. It was hard to get at them in those caves. TNT worked about as good as anything.

We had the island pretty well secure when the first crippled B-29 landed there. The Japanese airstrip wasn't near long enough but we saved the crew and plane. There were sulfur mines on Iwo. There wasn't much for vegetation except a few broken down trees. Everyone was pretty happy when the American flag went up on Mount Suribachi. Those guys that took that mountain had special training. The one big mistake made was bringing them down and having them help the rest of us Marines fight in the lowlands because they didn't know what they were doing. It wasn't good, because we lost a bunch of those fellows because they weren't trained for that type of fighting.

We could dig down with our hands through the sand on Iwo and the ground was hot enough to warm up our C rations. We got one canteen full of water per day. You didn't take any baths or shave with it. I didn't know at the time that Iwo was considered part of Japan. I just knew we were there to take the island. A lot of times I wondered why we had to take the dumb thing. Bernie Goodwin got blown out of his fox hole on Iwo and got banged up pretty good but he came out of it okay.

I was on Iwo until it was over and then we were sent to Guam. It took over five weeks to take the island. From there I was sent home, back to New Jersey aboard an old LST with eighteen broken (ship) ribs. The trip took thirty days. We played a lot of pinochle. I was in the Brooklyn hospital with appendicitis when the war ended in Europe and I didn't get to celebrate. From my hospital room I could hear car horns honking, ships blowing their horns, people hollering, and loud music. And there I laid.

Question: What's your opinion of the Japanese people today?

Not too good. I just can't get over it. They did some really bad things during the war. Take Guam for example. The Japanese worked those nice people like slaves from dawn to dusk and if they didn't bow to the Rising Sun every morning, it was curtains for them. That wasn't human, to treat people like that.

I was a lucky, lucky man all the way along. I was proud of myself for joining the Marines. We had really good training. Once a Marine, always a Marine.

Semper fi, John.

John, with his jeep, on Guam. Photo courtesy of John Capper.

LIKE GETTING RID OF A BUNCH OF DEAD HOGS ON THE FARM

Bob Huber
Washington, IA

Navy Construction Battalion
Pacific

Interview Date:
30 April 2010

Referral:
Paula Brinning

I volunteered for the CBs (Navy Construction Battalion, also nicknamed the Seabees). My dad was an engineer and I wanted to be one as well. I was only 17 when I graduated from high school in Toledo, Ohio in 1944, and knew I would be drafted. I would have turned 18 in August so I volunteered in July and was sent to Sampson, New York, for basic training. I had my CB training in Providence, Rhode Island. After that, I went by train to San Francisco, where we shipped out for the South Pacific.

The CBs did all the construction work in the South Pacific and the U. S. Army Corps of Engineers did the comparable in Europe and elsewhere. But we really had no idea what that would involve until we got there. We went in with the Marines. The first island we stopped at was Guam, where there was already a U.S. military base. Then we sailed for Saipan and then on to Okinawa. We used Saipan as a staging area. We spent our time there loading LSTs with construction equipment and supplies for the

invasion of Okinawa. I was a Machinist Mate, 2nd class in rank.

The heavy bombers flying out of Guam could carry enough fuel to hit the Japanese home islands and return to base. The short ranged Corsair fighter aircraft escorting them couldn't. Our mission on Okinawa (located much closer to Japan) was to construct a runway and base for the fighters to operate from.

By this time in the war, the heavy fighting was in the Philippines under MacArthur and on Okinawa. At Okinawa, the Marines and the CBs came in on the west side of the island and the Army attacked from the east side. That way we were able to cut the island in two. The Marines attacked northward and the Army went south. We went with the Marines. The Japanese had all these big guns fortified in the mountains but they all pointed south toward where the best beaches for an invasion force to land were located. Our aerial reconnaissance planes had spotted this so that is why we invaded where we did. The highest concentration of Japanese was in the south where the Army went.

In the north where we went, there wasn't much opposition other than Okinawan natives with knives tied on to bamboo sticks, and that wasn't much competition for machine guns. They would just keep coming (attacking). They'd be wearing these headbands and yelling. We'd just mow them down and there would be a whole pile of them. They'd keep coming and we'd shoot them and they would pile up, shoot them and they'd pile up. Finally, when there was a lull in the fighting, I was a bulldozer operator and they told me to dig a great big trench and push all the bodies in it and cover it up. It was like getting rid of a bunch of dead hogs on the farm. Dig a hole and cover it up. *(Note: While the large island of Okinawa was part of Japan, the native people living there were ethnically dissimilar to those on Japanese home islands and were treated by them as an inferior race.)*

Question: How did you feel doing that, did it bother you at all?

No, not a bit. You did what had to be done. If there was any consolation, it was knowing they would have done the same to us, given the opportunity. When the Japanese Army saw what we had done, most of them went and hid up in the hills. The Japanese would venture out at night to harass us. We had been told that the water on Okinawa was no good so we had brought a whole bunch of barrels ashore filled with drinking water. The Japanese would mortar our stockpile of water barrels at night probably thinking they were filled with gasoline. I imagine they wondered why they didn't catch fire and blow up when they made a direct hit. We weren't even using the barreled water as there were freshwater springs on the island providing us with good drinking water.

When we first landed on Okinawa, all the CBs carried a carbine and we had our own machine gun crews but we didn't get in on too much actual combat. We weren't dressed in regular soldier uniforms. Not all the CBs were even military. There were contractors, carpenters, electricians, plumbers, the whole works. There were 65 year old civilian volunteers working along beside us.

The construction of the airstrip for the Corsairs

went on 24 hours a day, seven days a week. We had air raids all the time. It was too noisy to sleep at night so I volunteered for the night shift. Big spot lights were set up so we could see. I'd stop and crawl under my dozer for cover when there was an air raid. That was mainly to avoid being hit by falling shrapnel from our own anti-aircraft batteries shooting at the Jap planes. You would have been a goner if any of that big shrapnel hit you. It hit my dozer.

The Japanese soldiers hiding out in the neighboring hills would also sneak down in the darkness and snipe at us. Because we were working under the spot lights, there was no way we could see what was going on beyond the dome of bright light. And because of the volume of noise, you couldn't hear anything either. You'd notice an equipment operator slump over like he had fallen asleep and realize he'd been shot.

> *"You'd notice an equipment operator slump over like he had fallen asleep and realize he'd been shot."*

There were a lot of big family burial mounds on Okinawa. These mounds had a small doorway and concrete crypt where the bodies would be laid out. After the body decayed, the remains were collected and put in a funeral urn.

Question: Were there any of these burial mounds in the area where you were constructing the airfield?

Yes. We dozed them out. The family relatives would come and pick through the debris to salvage what urns they could. They'd haul them away. Of course, it didn't mean anything to us at the time.

It took us six weeks to build the airstrip. We used crushed coral. We had brought a rock crusher in with us. We'd pack the crushed coral with a roller and then sprinkle salt water on it. It would get as hard as concrete.

The safest place to be in Okinawa during an air raid was the air strip we built. The Japanese must have had terrible bomb sights as the closest they ever came to hitting us was five miles away. They would also send in kamikazes. Our base was sitting up on a mound, like a plateau. The Japanese must not have realized this. One kamikaze came in too low and slammed into the mound rather than us. The bomb failed to detonate. I wouldn't have gone out there for anything, but a bunch of the guys went out and practically stripped that plane apart for collecting souvenirs.

After the initial invasion, the natives got real friendly. They'd tell us where the Japanese soldiers were hiding up in the hills in exchange for money or K rations. After the war was over, I did not have enough points to go home for a while. I was put in charge of a work force of native Okinawans that we employed to repair roads and culverts, things like that. They would work for rations. I was told to carry a gun but didn't need it.

We were all loaded up and ready for the invasion of the Japanese home islands when the war ended. I have had no desire to ever own a Japanese car. I can understand why they have written WWII out of their history books. They got trimmed good.

I was discharged in May 1946, and enrolled in civil engineering at Iowa State that September. I met my wife Elsie there. Upon graduation, I worked in both Red Oak and Corning, Iowa, then relocated to Washington in 1960 and served 35 years as the Washington County Engineer.

I Felt Really Blessed

Marion Turnipseed
Washington, IA

8th Air Force
Europe

Interview Date:
4 May 2010

Referral:
Bob Huber & Marion Cuddeback

I was always interested in airplanes and used to hang around the airport out here. Four of us enlisted at the same time in December of '42. Besides me going, there were the Hamill twins and their cousin, Doug Dowell. The four of us went to Des Moines and enlisted. President Roosevelt was going to close enlistments pretty soon because they weren't getting enough men in some of the service branches. I would have been drafted in January but I would have spent Christmas at home if I had waited. As it was, I spent Christmas in St. Petersburg, Florida doing basic training. I was there for five months. During that time, we could select where or what we wanted to do after basic.

I decided to go to gunnery school, because after six weeks of training you became a buck sergeant. Gunnery school was in Harlingen, Texas. On the train trip some more guys boarded at a stop in Clearwater, Florida. Bob Bauer and Carl Adams from my high school graduating class at West Chester were among those boarding. We stayed together for the entire training period until shipping overseas. They were both killed doing the same thing I was doing on a B-24. Bob was killed flying out of Italy and Carl flew with the 8th Air Force based in England.

Part of our gunnery training was shooting skeet. We shot a box of shotgun ammo every day.

We got pretty good toward the end, hitting 23 out of 25 clay pigeons. We'd ride in the back of a pickup truck traveling 30 miles per hour down a set track and the clay pigeons would fly out at in all directions. This is how they taught us angle shooting and target leading.

A week before we graduated from gunnery school they changed the completion rank from sergeant to private. So we only got one strip instead of the three promised. That really got to us. If we had been buck sergeants when we went to aircraft mechanics school in Biloxi, Mississippi, we would have slept in the NCO quarters and had a pay increase.

We flew our brand new B-24 bomber from Florida to Brazil, across to Africa and around Spain to England. We landed in England on May 10, 1944. Our air base was 80 miles north of London. This whole area of northern England was just saturated with B-24 and B-17 bomber bases. The lighter bombers (B-25s and 26s) that flew shorter missions were based in southern England. They didn't even have oxygen in their planes as they flew lower altitudes. The B-24 was officially named the Liberator.

Where we were based in England, the guys working in the mess hall were on permanent KP duty. They were former gunners with the 15th Air Force that had refused to fly any more so were court martialed to serve on permanent KP duty as punishment. Early on in the war it was almost suicide to fly bombing missions. The losses were just horrific. The 8th Air Force lost so many bombers from fighters and anti-aircraft guns that they almost gave up. I think one plane out of three in our original group was shot down. Today, there would be different thoughts if something like that happened again. Back then, the total effort of the country was put in to what we were doing, of course.

I was the flight engineer because I had been to mechanic's school. If anything mechanical went wrong during a mission, it was my job to fix it. I did things like adjusting voltage regulators, transferring fuel from the auxiliary tanks to the main tanks, starting and shutting off the auxiliary generator at takeoffs and landings. I was also the top turret gunner. We could strip our 50 caliber machine guns apart blindfolded and reassemble them.

Planes would take off from all these bases and would circle around until all of them were up and at the proper altitude to get in formation. We'd take off with anything better than ground zero visibility, which meant you couldn't see your wing tips. The clouds would be so thick that you couldn't see anything until you were four miles high and above them. Then you'd break out on top and there would be the sun shining. A lot of times, especially in the winter, you hadn't seen the sun since your last mission. With all those hundreds of planes in the air with no visibility, it was pretty dangerous. It scared the heck out of me.

Each bomber group had an old war weary plane sent up to form up on. Ours was an old B-24 painted yellow with red polka dots. Every group had a plane like this and that's how we located our group. We'd get into formation and the old painted plane would peel off and fly back to the base. Our lead plane would have streamers hanging down so we could spot it easier. The lead plane was called the pathfinder and was equipped with a radar dome so he could bomb through cloud cover. When we couldn't see the target, all the planes would drop when the pathfinder did.

"With all those hundreds of planes in the air with no visibility, it was pretty dangerous. It scared the heck out of me."

Our planes were heavily loaded at takeoff. We carried 2,700 gallons of fuel and up to 8,000 pounds of bombs. At takeoff, everything was supercharged and the engines turned wide open and you'd still barely get off the ground. I've seen the landing gear drag pine tree tops at the end of the runway. A B-24 would burn 75 gallons of fuel in the first five minutes of takeoff.

One time in the winter, we were taking off and the temperature was just right for icing. We had icing boots on the props and wings as well as the vertical and horizontal stabilizers. There was also a heavy fog. The first three planes that took off iced up and crashed before they got it shut down. A couple of my friends were on one of those planes. It landed in a plowed field that was quite soft. They crawled out and were not seriously injured but the plane was destroyed of course.

I kept a daily diary of our missions. Our first mission was bombing an airfield south of Paris. The plane flying upper echelon above us got hit, blew a motor right off the plane and down he came. I looked up and that plane was going to smack right into us. The co-pilot saw it too and lunged at the controls, ripping them out of the pilot's hands and dived our plane clear. It just missed us. We had a number of flak holes in our plane by the time we landed. This was our first mission and I thought, "Wow!"

Another time we took off carrying four blockbusters. They each weigh 2,000 pounds and there was one bomb in each of the bomb bays. The clouds were solid. We were to form at 22,500 ft. When we got our new plane, it was one that had been painted. Most hadn't been painted to save on cost. The paint alone weighed 200 pounds. The other unpainted planes with that heavy of a load could make it to 22,500 ft. But we couldn't. We could only make it so high in that light air. We tried twice and the plane felt like it was going to shake apart. We had to turn back to base but we had to land at a higher speed to support all that weight.

We were in the mess hall eating when there was this tremendous explosion. Another plane that had turned back because it had lost an engine had crashed while attempting to land. They said the pilot tried to bank into the dead engine and didn't have enough speed up. Several other parked planes were destroyed in the crash.

Our bombs were brought by train and then hauled to the base by truck. One Friday evening a load came in and the guys unloading were in a hurry and decided to roll them off the truck rather than lift them out. The bombs were supposed to be unarmed but one detonated. The concussion from explosion of the bomb dump blew the big hangar doors off and hot metal shrapnel landed around us. The bodies of the workers and their truck could not be found. There was so much destruction that we were relocated to a different air base. There were also poison gas bombs stored at our base but they were in a different bomb dump a little ways off from the one that blew up. They had to move out the civilian population living downwind as a precautionary measure.

After my sixth mission my ear started hurting. My eardrum ended up rupturing and I spent three weeks in the hospital. So I got behind on my missions. When my crew had their 30 missions completed, I still had nine to go. At that time, 30 missions were all you had to do. I was relegated to a fill in status for crews needed a temporary flight engineer. I sat around for two or three months with nothing to do. We couldn't have a fire in our Nissan huts until 9 p.m. because of fuel rationing so I sat around all bundled up trying to stay warm and playing solitaire. I didn't know many people other than my old crew. You didn't try to get acquainted with anybody because they were probably going to die the next day.

Finally in December, I got assigned permanently to Lieutenant Robert's crew. They were a replacement crew, not part of the original crews. By then the number of missions required had been raised to 35. I finished my 35 missions with that crew on February 15th, 1945. Sometime later, they got shot down and all were lost.

You see planes going down all around you and you'd get holes in your airplane but I was never injured, other than my eardrum. I felt really blessed. Someone was looking out for me.

> "You didn't try to get acquainted with anybody because they were probably going to die the next day."

Comment: I read where the 8th Air Force lost 50,000 men.

It was especially terrible early on in the war. The *Luftwaffe* fighters would just flock over the bombers. Our fighters had to turn back so we'd be on our own until the P-51s came along. The P-47s were also modified to give them great escort range. What a blessing it was to look up and see those little silver spots around in the sky above you.

Question: What was a typical mission like?

They'd get us up at one or two o'clock in the morning. Sometimes we wouldn't have gotten to bed until eleven the previous night. Around D-Day, they gave us pills to keep us going. When they wore off, you ought to have seen the people melt. The first thing after getting up in the morning was breakfast at the mess hall and then to the briefing room. They'd feed us real eggs on mornings of a mission. Otherwise, we ate powdered eggs. There'd be a big map of the continent of Europe with red yarn showing our flight path. Towns with heavy flak guns to avoid would be marked as well as areas relatively safe to take evasion action. We'd fly a route to the IP (Initial Point) where would we make our turn to the target. When we approached the target, the bombardier took over the control of the airplane. From then on, you flew straight and narrow regardless what happened. You flew right into the flak. You didn't take evasive action for any reason. That was when it got kind of hairy. You'd look up in the sky where a plane had previously been and it was just black with smoke. I have trouble talking about it yet.

The Germans shot some 105s at us but it was mostly the 88s. They'd just go *bang, bang, bang!* We got too close to Hanover one time and it was full of flak guns. Our plane was rocking from all the concussion and one piece of shrapnel came through the glass canopy of the top turret where I was sitting. That was the closest I came to being hit. Everything loose around me got sucked out into the air stream.

It was thirty to forty below zero at the high altitudes we were flying. We wore long underwear under our uniforms and an electrically heated sheep skin suit over them. We wore a tight fitting nylon glove under our bulkier heated gloves in case a gun jammed and we needed to work on it. That saved our fingers from freezing to the metal.

On one mission while I was sitting in my top turret gun scanning the skies for enemy fighters, the BX cable that supplied both my oxygen and the electricity for my heated suit got kinked. I had my hand on a dead man toggle switch that rotated my turret and gun. The radio operator sitting below me noticed that my feet continued to move in only one direction so he looked up and could see that I had passed out. They said I was blue in the face from lack of oxygen and had the shakes from being cold. I don't know how long I had been out but they estimated it was for 15 minutes. Of course, I was getting partial air during that time. I had a headache that night but otherwise I was okay.

Question: Do you remember your mission on D-Day?

I was over the coast of France at 8:00 AM but it was too cloudy to drop our bombs. We had very definite targets but because of the poor visibility it was too risky. It was our fourth mission.

Question: Did your twin fifties ever jam on you?

No, because I never shot at any enemy planes. I only saw the *Luftwaffe* on one mission. We were flying 160 mph in one direction and he was going 300 mph from the other and he closed on us so fast I probably couldn't have got a shot off if I had seen him coming. In November, our bombing group lost 16 planes on one mission from enemy fighters. Towards the end of the war, the Germans were down to young pilots and lacked fuel because we had bombed their refineries. So our bombing did some good.

The Germans had a manned rocket before the ME 262 jet. It took off vertically and could make about two passes at our bombers before running out of fuel. It landed on skids. It was really fast.

We had bombing missions to knock out the V-1 buzz bomb launching installations on the coast of northern France, especially around D-Day or when the fighting was in that area of France. The V-1s were fired off a ramp and they were real crude and

flew at about 300 ft. It was a pulse jet engine and the fuselage was the bomb. South of London, the British had big balloons anchored by long cables. If the buzz bombs hit a cable, it would upset their gyro (causing them to veer off course). The British Spitfire fighter pilots would ease in and use their wings to tip the buzz bomb's wing which upset the gyro. Then they had to get the heck out of the way because the there was no way of knowing which direction it would go.

I remember this one day a B-24 off to our side had one engine all ablaze. The crew must have exhausted all their fire extinguishers and everything they had available to them. We counted the chutes as the crew bailed out. We always did that and reported the number of chutes at the debriefing. They all got out.

That plane just kept on flying at our speed, still maintaining formation. We watched and watched it. Flames were just streaming off it. Pretty soon the wing got so hot that the fuel blew and down she went.

My last four missions were to Magdeburg, Germany. I can't remember for sure what we were bombing. It was probably railroad marshaling yards or factories. The first day the flak was pretty bad. The next day, we went to the damn place but there was more flak. The Germans had anti-aircraft guns mounted on railroad cars and they could run them around the country. The third day there was more flak. By the fourth day, there was flak everywhere.

My original plane was named the Renegade. My original crew finished up the first week in August. The replacement crew flying the Renegade was shot down in September. That worked on me, too. I thought my nine lives were running out. After each mission's debriefing, we were given a double shot of whiskey in our canteen cup. You tried to find a guy who didn't drink and get his whiskey allotment. We hadn't eaten in eight to ten hours so you can imagine what four shots of whiskey would do to you on an empty stomach but it was a blessing. Then we'd go to the mess hall.

The Army Air Corps took photos of us dressed in civilian clothes and we carried them with us on our missions. The idea behind this was to provide

> *"I was over the coast of France at 8:00 AM but it was too cloudy to drop our bombs. We had very definite targets but because of the poor visibility it was too risky."*

photos so the underground could make fake identification papers for us if we got shot down and avoided capture. The German prison of war camps were mainly full of airmen that had been shot down.

Sometimes bombers with engine trouble would seek a neutral country such as Sweden or Switzerland to land in. There was the thought among us that some of the engine trouble was faked by guys wanting to get out of the war.

Question: Did you ever bomb Berlin?
No, I never had a mission to Berlin. The first Liberators were used in submarine patrol in the Atlantic because no other bomber had its range. The B-24s could fly a little faster and could carry a heavier bomb load than the B-17s. That's why they were built. We bombed the Ruhr River valley where all the industry was located, cities like Cologne, Coblenz and Frankfurt.

We dropped supplies during a break in the weather during the Battle of the Bulge. We flew in at tree top level and climbed to 300 feet to drop the parachutes. There'd be Germans on the ground shooting at us with everything from pistols on up.

I came back to the states on a hospital ship that was part of a big convoy. There were over 400 airmen aboard but it wasn't because we were injured, we just needed a ride. I'll never forget seeing the padded cells on one deck where they put the guys suffering from shell shock. Those guys were banging their heads on the walls and hanging on the cell bar doors. They acted like animals. It was pathetic.

We sailed into New York City. It was quite a sensation to see the Statue of Liberty. We were all given a 30-day furlough. I was home in April when President Roosevelt died. I was sent to a redistribution center at an air base in California. Oh, the food they put out there! I bet the salad bar was as long as this room with every kind of green you could imagine. There was even fresh milk and entertainment.

I spent the summer of '45 in Wichita Falls, Texas, in helicopter mechanics school. I started getting nightmares, waking up wet with sweat. I kept dreaming that I was on the catwalk beside the open bomb bay doors on a B-24 in flight and was about to fall out. This went on for two or three weeks and I was starting to get concerned. I was about ready to go see the Army head shrinker, but we were going to the NCO club every night drinking that cheap 3.2 beer, and that got me over it.

You Lived With Fear

George Grove
Washington, IA

45th Infantry Division
N. Africa, Europe

Interview Date:
14 May 2010

Referral:
Paula Brinning

I turned 21 in May and they were drafting us for a year's training. In September I was to go in for a year's training and then come back home. This is in 1941. So I was sent down to Ft. Leonard Wood, Missouri, where I got my basic training. I was a spoiled brat. I was the only child in the family and I just got away with murder, so to speak, because my parents were fairly old and they didn't think they were going to have any more children. When I showed up on the scene my parents were so excited they couldn't do enough for me, and in the process they ruined me pretty bad. And I mean I was a stinking child.

So I got into the Army and we were taking Basic Training, and man, all of a sudden I had to obey! You know, "You'll do this, Grove! You'll do that!" Well, one day, to show you how fast they brought me around, we would have roll call at 5 AM and then we would walk across the parade field and pick up anything that didn't belong to Mother Earth. This is in the early part of my training. We were walking along policing the grounds and all of a sudden, "Hey, Grove!" "Yeah, what is it, Sarge?" And he pointed to a gum wrapper lying on the ground. I said, "Oh?" and went like that. That's a

no-no. You don't do that in the Army. That was my beginning of my realizing I had to shape up or ship out. He didn't say a word. He motioned to one of his men to come over and get me. I was told to take the gum wrapper and go out there in those hills of Missouri. I was ordered to dig a hole 6x6, six feet down, and bury the gum wrapper in it. I didn't get done till eleven o'clock that night and my hands, of course, were blistered. All I could think of is, "I want my mommy!" But, Mommy wasn't available! So there was a lesson.

Well, after eleven o'clock that night I went back to the barracks and just passed out. At four o'clock in the morning they came in and woke me up and said, "You're on KP." That's kitchen police. So I went on KP. After that I went back to the barracks and the sergeant said, "Well, I hope you learned your lesson." I said, "Well, I'm sure it helped." When I got through with my training the sergeant comes around and says, "Grove, I wish everybody had learned a lesson as well as you did." Because from that point on I was a totally different soldier. I said, "Yes, Sergeant, but all the boys weren't as bad as I was." So that was the beginning of my service.

I was trained in the 120th Combat Engineers attached to the 45th Infantry Division in Texas, which had been an old National Guard unit. Texas has lots of sand. So we had to learn how to keep our rifles from not getting jammed with sand or dust. We learned a lot of lessons, but I was in the right frame of mind now. I've been thankful for it every day because I've seen a lot of boys that didn't get turned around, and it's sad. After that training we moved up to Ft. Chesapeake Bay, and they trained us as an amphibious division. We'd get on the ships out in the bay and practice climbing down the nets to get into a landing ship and hit the beach. From there we went to the mountains of Virginia to learn how to handle ourselves in mountain conditions. All of this was fantastic training but, man, it was driving us bananas! We were just getting sick and tired of it. Then we went up to northern New York and learned how to handle our equipment and ourselves in 50 below zero. Finally we asked, "Why, stars, when was this training going to quit?" We were just getting sick and tired of it. They said, "Well, we're going to shoot you down now to Virginia and get you ready to get on a ship." And we all shouted, "Hooray!"

So we went down and got all issued out and boarded a ship. Of course, back then you couldn't sail in a straight line because of the submarines so we zigzagged. We could've crossed the Atlantic in seven days if we'd gone in a straight line. I remember standing on the stern of the ship looking at a mounted five inch gun. It was for shooting submarines. All of a sudden a signal went off…like a horn, and it meant for us to go down to our quarters. Well, I said, "Man, I'm not going down there! If a torpedo hits this ship, we'll be the first ones to get it!" Well, the guy behind the gun says, "If you don't, Curly, you're going to get in a lot of trouble." Well, I said, "I've been in trouble before, and I'd rather be in trouble than be dead!" He said, "You'd better be careful." I said, "Well, I'm going to stay here by you." He says, "Well, if the officer comes by he's going to make it hard on you." I say, "I'll take my chances." Well, while we were talking we noticed a little string of water, and it was a torpedo that missed us by about a hundred yards. That's just how dangerous it was. The German subs usually tried to pick off the last

ships in a convoy. We were the last ship, and there was another ship on the other side of the convoy that they hit. That was my first contact with what we were into.

We landed on the northern coast of North Africa. Did you ever hear of Patton? General Patton, I think he's a pretty popular man. He was working in North Africa, had a campaign going and trying to clean things up there so that we could get ready to go to Europe. So we went and joined him. We didn't see much combat. Engineers weren't in the front with the infantry. Only when we had to sweep a mine field did we get up in front and then the infantry went through. Anyway, while we were there we got to know Patton, and oh brother! Big black boots and oh, he was a big shot! Everybody hated him! We always said, "Patton's in our guts." He made a name for himself but he sacrificed a lot of boys to do it.

After the Germans were driven out of North Africa, we got back on our ship and we hit the shores of Sicily. That's a little island off of Italy, down at the toe of Italy. We landed, and I don't know how to say it any better way, all hell broke loose. We looked at each other and said, "Boy, I wish we were back in training!" They were bombing us, they were shelling us. We went into the shore. I started to crawl down the net and water was bringing the boats up, the landing boats. And if you didn't jump in when they said "jump" the boat went back down. We had boys that ended up between the ship and the landing craft wearing a 46 lb pack. They were gone. That's where I saw my first sight of death with our boys.

> "I saw one of my buddies get killed. I can't explain it, but it's quite a psychological experience."

We hit the shore and we started moving inland as fast as we could. German planes were strafing and their artillery shelling us. I saw one of my buddies get killed. I can't explain it, but it's quite a psychological experience. To show you how inexperienced we are, they were bringing artillery in and piling it up for the artillery to back up the infantry. There's a whole bunch of artillery shells sitting on the beach for the artillery which would be coming in later. When we were getting strafed I ran over and hid beside one of those boxes. If that box had gotten hit, I couldn't have told you this story. It would have just wiped me out. So after you get through a few experiences like that, you become a veteran real fast.

If you could survive the first five days, you learned what to do and what not to do. If you can get onto that point your chances are much, much better. To begin with, you make a lot of mistakes that could cost you your life or get you injured.

We went from that point, advancing up through Sicily to the city of Palermo. There was a big Italian hospital that the Army took over to treat our injured boys. Patton came up there one day. My unit was just outside the hospital, about a few hundred feet. We were rubbing our feet and getting ready to make the landing on Italy from Sicily. Patton comes along and he walked through the hospital. I don't know if you've ever heard this, but what he said was heard around the world. He walked up to a young man on the bed and he said, "What the hell is wrong with you, soldier?" The soldier, not realizing it was Patton, replied, "Well, who the hell cares?" Patton slapped him, just like that, and knocked him down. The doctor of the hospital came over and said, "You are not supposed to do that." Patton said, "Who do you think you are talking to?" "I'll find out." The doctor called FDR and told him what Patton did, and the President took his command away. Best thing to ever happen. Patton was pretty bad. But he was brilliant, he was a tactician. Patton really knew how to fight, but he used a lot of boys foolishly. The command was turned over to General Patch. So that slap was "heard around the world" and I was just a few hundred feet from it. I didn't hear the slap but I heard it go around the world.

Question: What was your job in Sicily?

I was in charge of mine detecting and working on the mines. I was a technical sergeant. I was responsible for keeping the mine sweepers operational and to learn how to effectively use them. We were losing boys all the time. We'd go ahead of the infantry and sweep for land mines and remove them. We would be right out there in the front getting clobbered. So it was a very difficult, rough outfit to be in.

> *"If you could survive the first five days, you learned what to do and what not to do. If you can get onto that point your chances are much, much better."*

Question: It sounds very dangerous. Did you have Germans shooting at you a lot?

It's worse than that. I'm very fortunate to be here. I got wounded pretty badly up in Italy. We had the mine detectors and then my job was to make sure that they're okay and show the boys how to use them. Before I became a tech sergeant I was out sweeping mines. We learned one of the tricks that the Germans pulled. You know the Italians gave up, so the Germans came into the picture immediately to take over because the Italians were saying, "To heck with this war." The German mine had a little on/off switch. We learned what it was. But they reversed it, so when you turned it to safety position, it exploded. We lost a lot of boys turning those things to what they thought was off. Well, we had to lose quite a few boys until somebody lived long enough to say, "Don't touch those switches!" That was the way the Germans fought the war. They just used every technique that they could think of. So from then on, we just picked up the mines and put them in a truck and they were hauled out.

After Sicily, we got on our boats and headed for Salerno, Italy, which is just below Naples. We hit the shores of Salerno, and now we were combat engineers, combat active. We had learned so many things through experience we began to realize that we needed to do so as not get into a situation where you got killed. So, about in ten days you were a real veteran because you learned so much, and we learned most of that in Sicily.

When we hit the shores of Salerno, we moved right in. We started working our way up, past Naples, and on up, headed for Rome. I got hit by a shell on our way up to Rome. It came in within about three feet of me and exploded. But it was an anti-aircraft shell. If it had been anything else and had exploded on contact, I couldn't have told you this story. But it buried itself and then the timing device exploded. But the shrapnel came up and caught me right in this leg and really just chewed it up. Of course, I reached down… and had a handful of blood. I thought, "Whoa!" and passed out. So the next thing I knew I was in a station hospital at Naples. I was there for three or four months.

We had what was called a medical unit that was right behind us that took care of emergencies. When you get shot up, they get you fixed up and then push you on down the line. It's a process. So they got me patched up and had a tag on my big toe that said, "Amputation." Well, when I got down to the regular hospital at Naples the doctor looked at it and he said, "Well, let's have another x-ray." So they brought an x-ray machine in. I was out of it. I mean, they knock me out. I couldn't stand the pain. He said, "You know, we might just save that leg for that man. Let's try." They went in there and took that shrapnel off and he said, "That nerve's still okay. I believe we can save it." That's why I have a leg today. I'm very fortunate and very thankful. But at the same time, they said, "This is going to give you trouble when you get to be old. You'll find out that." And boy, when I'm walking sometimes I say, "Lift. Lift." Because if I don't I stumble.

Question: What were you doing when you were wounded?

When that shell came down we were just below the Anzio beachhead. There was a town there and I was working on some mine detectors and the shell hit beside me. And that's all I can remember at that point.

Question: Did you land at Anzio?

I didn't land in Anzio because I spent four months in the hospital and then came to Anzio later. So when they got me fixed up they said, "Well, Grove, you'll never have to see action anymore. You got wounded and we'll put you in as quartermaster or someplace where you won't be active." I said, "I want to go back." "You dummy. If you do, sign here." So I signed there and where do you think I ended up? Anzio. Got on a ship and went up and hit Anzio and it was the worst part of the whole war for me. We were on a beachhead eleven miles long and three miles deep. There were three divisions there. We had the 34th on one side of us and a British division on the other. We couldn't get a foxhole because of the sand. So they sent up a shipload of sandbags. And you'd fill a sandbag and build a bunker because we were stuck there.

"I saw a part of war I never want to see again. But that's war. It was something that we had to go through."

The Germans were shelling us. Before I got back with the 45th they had gone inland quite a few miles but the Germans were just too much for them. So they were pushed back to the Anzio beachhead and spent four months there. So I had quite an experience on the Anzio beachhead and it was one that I could've gotten along without very well. We lost a lot of boys and I had to keep the minesweepers and everything fixed up but we couldn't use them because we couldn't move. We were stuck there, just existing. I was very fortunate that I didn't get hit again.

The Germans had a big railroad gun just outside of Rome. In fact, it was big enough that when we got there I could crawl into the breach. We called it "Anzio Auntie". You knew they were going to shoot that gun at seven, ten o'clock, and twelve o'clock. They just had it timed. That was one of the things the Germans didn't learn. They were so precise. Someone would say, "Uh-oh, Anzio Auntie will be coming!" And of course the projectile travels faster than sound. So it would hit the dirt and you couldn't wait for the sound. So we hit our bunkers and then all of a sudden whewwww! Boom! And the noise would come afterwards. We were getting so many of our boys killed and the wounded had to be evacuated by ship. I was very fortunate to have lived through that experience. I saw a part of war I never want to see again. But that's war. It was something that we had to go through.

We finally got off at the Anzio beachhead. We were supposed to be in southern France by that time to cut the Germans off when we hit the beaches on D-Day. So when D-Day hit that took the Germans away. They left us right away because they needed to be in France. We were just trying to figure out what was going on because the shelling had stopped. The news came down that the D-Day boys had struck and that was why the Germans were gone. So we advanced inland and went up to Rome. On the way we saw this big railroad gun and looked it all over and said, "That's the Anzio Auntie!" It had killed so many of our boys.

I captured an Italian motorcycle. It was a tricycle, a three wheeler, and I carried a lot of reels of wire on it. I captured that thing in Italy, and so when we got ready to go on over into Germany the old man says, "Well, if you can rig that up, Grove, and use it haul those reels of wire on, it'll give us another jeep!" So he gave me permission. I took the muffler off of it because I love to hear it cackle, which was a no-no.

Well, we weren't going to join the troops in France because we had to be reorganized; we lost so many boys. Our unit was a mess, disorganized and everything. So we spent some time in Rome and that was a wonderful experience. Declared an open city, we didn't have to worry about anything. I had a chance to go through the Vatican and see so many of the sights in Rome. It was quite an education. I got one of the most wonderful educations in what this world is like." I was all across Italy, all across France, all across Germany.

I enjoyed those few days spent in Rome. Then we came back and got ready to get on a ship and go over to southern France. We were supposed to have been there sooner but Anzio killed that. So we landed and we hit very little resistance and started working our way north and eastward. The Germans withdrew. They were pulling back to the Fatherland to defend it. The British and our boys were pushing them for all they were worth. France was a pretty country, but not as pretty as Germany. Germany was the most beautiful country of all of them. It was just marvelous.

So we worked our way across France, but I was not in combat anymore. They put me in as a sergeant of communications. We strung telephone lines. We didn't have the modern equipment of today. We had to string a line from headquarters up to each one of the lines. We strung a lot of lines. That was my job all the way over into Germany; to be in communication and set up the lines and telephones, which I fairly enjoyed doing.

When we got over to the Rhine River, just above Worms, the Germans were waiting for us. I don't know why I'm here. We lost so many boys trying to get across the Rhine. We had rubber rafts and the German artillery shells would blow them out of the water. They finally got enough infantry across to establish a foothold in Germany. After we crossed on the rubber rafts, we were supposed to return,

but I didn't want to do that because the shelling was so bad. So I climbed up a tree and here come some Germans. They were coming over to the riverbank to stop our invasion. I didn't say a word; I was quiet. You talk about being quiet! All they needed to do was look up and see me, and they could pick me off like that. I was sweating blood there almost, just sitting there. But they didn't see me; they finally left and I came down. I ran over to one of the rafts and got back across the river as fast as I could. That was a very close call.

After crossing the Rhine we're on our way to Munich. We're down on the southern part of Germany, down close to Worms. We arrived in Munich, and of course by this time the resistance was getting less and less. We were winning the war and the fighting was finally stopped.

When we started moving across Germany I was so amazed to realize that people are the same no matter where you're from or where you're at. The French people were the same and the German people were the same as us. It's the cotton-picking politicians that got us into that mess! The people in France were wonderful! The people in Germany were wonderful! I talked to people in Germany that were just sick about what happened. They had a son that was drafted and they didn't have anything to say about it. He had to go and he was only fifteen years old. They were bringing in all those inexperienced young men to fight and they were just getting slaughtered. And the German people were about as sick of that as all of us were. But that's what you learn, that people are people, whether you're French or German or English or whatever. We are all created in the image of God. We learned to accept each other and help each other, no matter what we were. I helped a lot of German people and families.

After the war ended in Europe, we were slated to go to the Pacific. But they called it off. Guys with enough points were to be sent back to the states and placed in a training outfit to train new recruits for Japan. Well, I was one of the few that had enough points. And I would not have enough points had I not gone back and rejoined my old outfit. Most of our guys had to go on to Japan. So, I felt pretty fortunate. So there I stayed until the

> "All they needed to do was look up and see me, and they could pick me off like that."

A-bomb was dropped and we got ready then to come home. I had to wait around six weeks before I could get on a ship. They were going to fly me home for training but they said, "War's over. We don't need you guys anymore." I landed in Boston. On the way home, I got the infectious hepatitis. Your blood turns yellow. Infectious hepatitis causes yellow jaundice. I was as yellow as a Chinaman. I spent most of the trip in the sick bay. It was about eight days or so. When I got to the states they put me in a hospital and I was there for two months. And I thought I was coming home to be discharged, but they had to get me back up into shape before they'd give me a discharge. My folks about went nuts. We lived near Shenandoah, over on the other end of Highway 92, in the town of College Springs. They were trying to make contact but the Army wouldn't tell them anything until I was ready to come home. After about four weeks I was fit to be tied, but I finally got my blood up to where they would let me go. I came home and I can't begin to tell you what a thrill that was. My folks met the train in Villisca. It was a reunion you can't explain. It was so wonderful. So many friends and my parents really went through a lot. They didn't know I got wounded until later, and I wrote and told them I was okay. And they said, "Well, what happened?" So I wrote and described what it was. That pretty much gives you my story until I got back home.

Question: As a combat engineer, were you involved in any building of bridges?

There are two types of engineers. The engineers built the bridges. Combat engineers blew up bridges. We blew up bridges. And the regular engineers rebuilt them. Sometimes we blew up a bridge and then went on ahead and they would come on up and build a temporary bridge over a river. So I was a combat engineer, and we were always up where the action was.

Question: If our troops were advancing, why would you blow a bridge?

We blew the bridge because the Germans were coming across it. And they were going to get over there and we thought, "We can blow that up and stop those guys from getting over here." That's the thing to do, and we blew up bridges on little rivers. Around Epinal we blew up a bridge. Lots of times we didn't know why we did it. The orders would

come in: blow up such-and-such a bridge. We were trained on how to put the C4 on the bridge and blow a place out from under it. I didn't do much of that because I was more in with the minesweepers. Most people think the infantry were in a dangerous area. But we were ahead of the infantry a lot of times just to sweep for mines and blow bridges; do those things. And we got clobbered pretty good." So I'm very fortunate to be able to tell you about it. I saw a lot of action.

Question: When you got clobbered, as you put it, was it usually artillery or small arms fire?

It was artillery.

Question: At Anzio, you mentioned that they had to take the wounded out to ships. Were the ships hospital ships with red crosses on them or were they just regular ships, and did they get shelled by the Germans when all that happened?

They were regular landing ships. The hospital ships had a great big cross and the Germans didn't bomb those. There were some rules in war and the Germans followed them, too. So they didn't bomb the hospital ships but they would go after the landing crafts going out to the ships.

Question: Did you carry a carbine?

No, just the sidearm, because my hands needed to be free for what I was doing. I also had a German Luger. It was a beautiful pistol. I took it off a captured German major. He wasn't going to need it anymore. It was much better than our Colt .45. The Germans had quality; they had the best quality. We had quantity. Our quantity won the war. Their quality was very good.

Their German tanks were so much better than our Sherman tanks there was no comparison. When we got into a fight with the Panzers we'd backed off and let our tanks go at them. The German tanks would come up and just pushed our boys back. They knocked out a lot of our tanks.

I sent 54 boxes of German flags, Lugers, ammunition, and German helmets home after the war. That's not something you could do today but it was okay back then.

The German officers were outstanding. But we learned that they would shoot their own people if they refused an order. If we didn't like an order, we would argue or at least discuss it with a sergeant. They didn't. For them it was simply, "You do what

I tell you to!" or Bang! I couldn't understand that. We realized that that's what we would run into when we got into Germany. I heard the stories. I talked to German families, and they told me things I could hardly believe. But I also experienced it. They gave an order and they did it, or they shot them. We may have argued a lot of times, but we won the war. The American was a much freer-thinking man. I noticed that when I was talking to some of the German prisoners. The Germans tried to get all of their men to learn English and French. They took France and then they were going to take Britain. From Britain they were going to come over and clean us up. Hitler was going to run the world.

Hitler was going to run it from the Eagle's Nest, which we captured. Have you ever heard of the Eagle's Nest? It's way up in the Alps. We walked in to the Eagle's Nest, and it was a beautiful building up in the mountains. There was no resistance because all the Germans had run away. We rode on an elevator up through solid rock and crawled out into an open area where his SS men trained and were entertained. They had a big kitchen filled with American appliances purchased before the war. There was a big meeting room.

"I don't know how to explain it, but walking into the Eagle's Nest…we couldn't believe what we saw. We just stood there. Wow!"

Question: How did it feel being in the same room that Adolf Hitler had been in?

It's a strange feeling and I don't know how to explain it. We're in a different frame of mind. When you've been in combat, you learn to protect yourself, always being alert. I don't know how to explain it, but walking into the Eagle's Nest…we couldn't believe what we saw. We just stood there. Wow! We walked into the kitchen and saw that American stuff and we wanted to take a hammer and knock it to pieces.

Then when we left the Eagle's Nest and by this time things were looking pretty good in our favor. I've talked with many GIs and I have found very few that have been through what I have. I saw a lot.

Question: Were there any other U.S. troops at the Eagle's Nest when you got there?

Not at the Eagle's Nest. The 3rd Army was down at the bottom and they sent a bunch of boys up with us. The 45th Infantry captured the Eagle's Nest. We drove up the switchbacks in jeeps. You didn't take your heavy equipment up. We went around in jeeps with our machine guns with the idea that we were going to run into resistance but we didn't run into any. We got onto this elevator and went up to the top. There wasn't anybody there. We were the first ones to put our foot in there.

One of the things about being a combat engineer was that we were so much ahead, even ahead of the infantry, because we had to get those mines so that they could get through there. When I came home, it took about five years before I could even talk about it. People would ask me things and I would say, "Yeah, it's pretty rough over there." I couldn't sleep at night, or at night I'd wake up. After I got married, we were sleeping in our bedroom, and I got up and started to pull the blinds down and tear them to pieces. My wife Virginia asked me what was wrong. I had a flashback of where I was and I was trying to get out. It took about five years to work through that. Then, where I finally got to where I could talk about it, a teacher at one of our schools wanted me to come and talk about WWII. At first I said, "No way." But the teacher said, "Just come one time." So I relented. I didn't tell them all of that stuff. I told them things that were of interest. The teacher said, "You've got to come back. Did you see those young people? They just soaked that up!" I said, "Yes, I did." So I went back for three years and talked to them. I'm glad I did now. Stubbornness sometimes can get you in trouble. Those kids were all sitting there glued to their seats because I was bringing World War II to them on a first person basis. So it was quite an experience.

Question: You said you entered the draft in 1941. Was that after Pearl Harbor?

No. I'll give you the Pearl Harbor story. I was walking guard duty in Ft. Leonard Wood and the sergeant came out and handed me an old WWI Enfield and three rounds of ammunition. Until then I was carrying a wooden rifle, just to have something to carry. We didn't have anything! Our nation was so non-military it was pathetic. So they gave us these wooden rifles to walk our guard duty, and he came out and said, "Japan just bombed Pearl Harbor, and we're in war." From that point on I was in for the duration. Can you imagine walking around looking for Jap planes in the middle of Missouri? Now it seems foolish because we were just so inexperienced.

When they said Jap planes hit Pearl Harbor everyone wondered, where's Pearl Harbor? I never heard of it. Our sergeants and officers were just as ignorant as we were. So it took us quite a while to get ourselves going from there. From there I went through almost a year's training before I got back on a combat ship and went over there, which was in '42. So they trained us, got us ready.

Question: Did you ever get used to being scared?

Never. I never got used to it. You got used to making the right decisions. But you always knew you could be killed at any minute. It's a strange thing, when I went into North Africa we didn't run into any resistance. When we went into Sicily we were just scared to death. We hit the shores and got in there, and we didn't know what to do. We became very disorganized. We were trying to get in and set up a CP, and we saw our buddies getting shot. We saw the boys falling down in the water, and I can't explain it, but it's very difficult for you to accept it. You live with fear. You finally learn to handle it. There's a difference between living with it and handling it. After a while you get to say, "Well, when my time comes, that's it." I hoped that I would get killed because I saw so many boys with their legs blown off.

I remember one time there was a weapons carrier that went around us. A weapons carrier is a vehicle that carried weapons a lot for the infantry. This weapons carrier went around, and there were a couple of guys in the back. They got up ahead of us, and all of a sudden boom! What happened was they had picked up a bomb and it detonated itself. It just blew them all to pieces. You have to steel yourself. You get to the point where you just don't think about it, and move on. We all took care of each other. We were all in the same boat. I don't have friends today anything like the friends I had in the service. I don't have anybody who'd die for me today.

> *"Can you imagine walking around looking for Jap planes in the middle of Missouri?"*

Anzio was the worst part; that was really terrible. When I think of Anzio, I think I'm very fortunate to be here. Just think of sitting on a beachhead being bombed and digging out sand to fill the sandbags. The minute you hear the artillery come in, it's too late because the projectile travels faster than the sound. But you might hear a sound and, boy, you hit the ground. Maybe that artillery round hit ten or fifteen feet away from you and you'd be okay because you were on the ground. If you were standing up it might just whack you right in two. A concussion will kill you as much as shrapnel. We learned very quickly that if there's any question, you hit the ground and waited to see what would happen. You learned how to keep yourself alive that way; you learned so many things on what not to do but it took time to do it, and if you lived through it your chances became better all the time because you were learning what to do and what not to do. You'd see boys that did things they shouldn't have done and they got shot up. It's quite an experience.

I'd be in a battle where I'd witness so many of our Sherman tanks getting knocked out and then read in the *Stars and Stripes* about how we knocked off so many of the German tanks. It was just a reversal. I said to one of the boys when I was back at headquarters, "Why in the world did they print in the Stars and Stripes that we won that one? We got pushed back and we had to back up until we could get reorganized." He said, "They do that to make people think we're winning the war." And there were a lot of times we weren't winning the war. It was the quantity that won us that war. We had the British, we had the Americans, Canadians; we had a lot of fellows and a lot of people. We had a British outfit at Anzio on one flank. Every morning and every afternoon the British had to have tea. We couldn't believe it! They had their little pots to make their tea. I don't care what was happening; they would make tea while they were being shelled. That tea was more important than their lives! That was just one of the things that intrigued us. They were very good; the British were very wonderful. You could depend on them. They told you what they were going to do and they did it. Even more so than our own boys because they were trained that way. The Canadians were good, too. I never could quite understand the French people; they were a whole different breed. I thought the Germans were good and they were. But the French were so…how would you define it? All they cared about was dancing and we couldn't trust the French soldiers. They didn't seem like they were dedicated to their country like Germany and like we were. The French just seemed different, I don't know how else to explain it.

Question: What did you do with all those souvenirs you shipped home?

I kept them and showed them off for years. I took some of it to show all the classes where I spoke. I sold all that stuff when we sold our house. I made around five thousand dollars off of all of those antiques. Some of the stuff I wished I hadn't sold, but I let it all go. So I don't have any of it anymore. And I didn't want it; it reminded me too much of what I'd been through.

My wife and I moved to a cottage here at the UP Home. If you come in from the west side of this deal, the first cottage on the right hand side is where I spent three years with my wife, and then she passed away. Then I moved into this assisted park. It was one of the best decisions we ever made. It was wonderful to help raise our children's children.

I found out that I'd been blessed with 90 years of a wonderful life and wonderful family so I have a lot to be thankful for.

Question: Did you know your wife before you went overseas?

Oh, no. She was from Albia and when I got home I didn't want to talk to anybody; I didn't want to do anything. I was stubborn. I don't know what it was, I can't give any explanation. I probably needed to go to a psychiatrist. I was just within myself. I came back and finally the minister of our church said, "We've got some young people that would sure like to have you come over and be their youth leader." I said, "Oh, I don't want to do that." He said, "Come over and talk to them." So I went over one evening with the minister and talked to them. I realized that I had something for them to appreciate. So I said I would be the sponsor for the young people. Well, we had a Presbyterian YPCU convention in Lake Geneva, Wisconsin. So I took half a dozen of my young people and took them up there for the YPCU convention. They had a big telescope and you could see things that you couldn't believe, it was fantastic. I was sitting there waiting for my turn and I had my foot back. And all of a sudden this gal tripped over it. I said, "Oh, I'm sorry!" "Oh, that's all right." Then she got up and left. She didn't look like a kid; she looked more like a sponsor. She was, but I didn't know it. And this is the last day, so I went down to the last supper and tried to find her and couldn't. I went around and went to the last meeting and stood in the doorway and waited. I wanted to see her and I wanted to know where she was from. Cupid hit because I wasn't having that problem at all until I saw this gal. So I stood in the doorway and everybody came in and she never came in. I walked in and noticed her sitting about four rows down with her young people! She was a sponsor. She had a blanket right beside her. I went over there and said, "What's that blanket doing there?" "That's reserved for somebody." I said, "It sure is." I took the blanket and I threw it over the chair and sat down, and we got married in June. It was fabulous; she was a great girl. We had four children. We really had a wonderful life.

Interview transcribed by Laura Felton, Iowa State University.

A LONG RIDE HOME

Kermit Hotopp
Washington, IA

94th Infantry Division
POW, Europe

Interview Date:
18 May 2010

Referral:
Dwight Sutton

I am originally from a little town named Bangor, located northwest of Marshalltown, Iowa. Uncle Sam wanted me. I got drafted in 1944. The war started when I was a senior in high school. My dad had obtained a farm deferment for me so I was a couple of years late getting into the war after graduating from high school.

I took my basic training in Arkansas and was later sent to Ft. Benning in Georgia for more training. Then I was sent to a post on the east coast. I can't remember its name. I thought I'd never forget any of that. Perhaps you should have come to talk to me a couple of years earlier. Anyway, we were housed and fed there briefly on our way overseas. Troops were being retrained to serve as infantrymen at this base. They had been pulled from noncombat outfits. The Army was in need of infantrymen real bad and these guys weren't too happy to have been included.

I knew a guy in the Headquarters Company that was responsible for assigning replacements and he told me we could volunteer to go to a specific war theatre. That's how you found things out, by talking to people, as the Army didn't ever tell

you much. Four or five of us talked it over in the barracks one night and decided we wanted to go to Europe. Everything we heard about the South Pacific was not good. Of course, what we heard about Europe wasn't much good either. It was kind of like having the choice was between bad and worse. They didn't waste any time. In three or four days we were shipped out.

Every service man being sent overseas was entitled to a 30 day furlough before leaving the states. They gave our little group only nine days. Unlike the troop trains we were used to riding, we found out that we would have to pay our own way. We only had money for a train to Atlanta. One of the guys borrowed enough money from an elderly lady he knew in Atlanta to get us most of the rest of the way home. I thought if I could make it to Burlington, my uncle in Oskaloosa could drive me on home. People were good about helping servicemen in those days. A gentleman asked to sit next to me on the train. He asked where I was headed to and I told him, "Union, Iowa, but I was running out of money" He said, "I work for the railroad and I am going to see that you get home." He talked to the train conductor and got everything arranged. I had to switch trains several times and rode the rest of the way for free. I was offered a car ride home to my parent's house. I only had a short stay, but that's the way I got home.

My Port of Disembarkation was Ft. Meade, Maryland. My arrival time was scheduled for midnight. I was a little late but no one said anything. I was sent to the mess hall for a late supper. The cook wasn't real busy that time of night so he came over and sat with me to visit. The next morning we started boarding the fifth largest transport ship in the world. It took about a day for them to get us all loaded. The first day out it looked like we would be sailing in a convoy. It was just like I imagined it would look, with ships everywhere. But the next morning we were all alone. Our ship was so much faster than the others that we got way ahead during the night. We had some bad weather and the sea got rough. You could hardly stand up. It was not a pleasant experience. Then a German submarine got on our tail. Our ship changed course every seven minutes (to elude the U-boat). It took us an extra day to cross the Atlantic. We made it in eight which was pretty fast in those days. We landed in Glasgow, Scotland, and immediately boarded a train bound for the southern tip of England. Once there, we were put in these small ships. The English Channel was too rough to cross so we were stuck in those cramped, little boats for a week before finally landing in France. We had to wade ashore as the harbor, I think it was Cherbourg, had been blown up by the Germans. This was in January of 1945 so the sea water was cold.

We were taken to a big warehouse with a little heat. In the morning we took a train across northern France. They'd feed us twice a day. The train would stop and we'd get out and eat right beside the tracks. One morning we were supposed to have pancakes. Container after container was opened in search of syrup. Finally, they gave up and served the pancakes with peanut butter on top.

We were sent (as replacements) to Patton's Third Army in Luxemburg. I was assigned to Company G, 302nd Infantry Regiment, 94th Infantry Division. There were only about a dozen of us going to the 302nd. We were dropped off at an aid station and told to catch a ride on a truck hauling supplies or people on up to the front.

I remember this one ambulance in particular. It carried a wounded soldier who had a crease across the top of his head. He was holding his helmet on his chest. It had a bullet hole through the top of it. This wounded soldier had come *that* close to being killed. He wouldn't let go of his helmet. Someone said, "Give me that helmet, soldier." "No sir, that helmet is going home with me." They finally let him keep it. This was at a winery. They were using the wine cellar as an aid station. The road we were trying to get to the front on was supposed to be reserved for medical traffic only, but we had to use it as there were so few roads open.

Question: Were you getting a little apprehensive about then as to what you were getting yourself into?

I was apprehensive all the time. But *(laughing)*, it was starting to get a little worse.

We finally made it over into Germany and to our division. Company G had a forward platoon occupying an outpost a little over a mile in front of our lines. A guy hauled me up there on a captured German motorcycle. The outpost was in a little farming village. There were five houses and a church built into the side of a hill. The farmers lived in the village and farmed the surrounding countryside. Our people had put the civilians in the church and we had the five houses.

I was there six days and didn't see hardly any action. It was kind of dull, actually. Sometimes you could hear things off in the distance and that was about it. The sixth night we were to place over one hundred anti-tank mines on the blacktop road leading into the village. We never got the mines laid out. We were supposed to do it after midnight and that's about the time the Germans hit us. And they hit hard. I was assigned to a machine gun but we had hardly any ammunition for it. That's how hard Patton was crowding things. He didn't wait for nothing. It was always move, move, and move.

We were set up the farthest house to the east. We'd take turns manning the machine gun and I had just gone inside the house after ending my watch. I heard some commotion and then rifle fire. The Germans hit our house first as we were on that edge of town. They about completely blew up that house we were in. We suffered powder burns from the explosion. I think they had hit us with artillery. So we had to leave that house. We ran over to the middle house. All the anti-tank mines were stacked in the driveway between that house and the adjoining barn. My face had been burnt so bad that my eyes swelled shut. I could only get the one eye opened a slit to see. Because of that, I wasn't much good to the rest of the platoon so they had me guard the door. Pretty soon the Germans set that house on fire as well. No one wants to be in a house on fire with anti-tank mines piled next to it so several of us ran to the last house on the western edge of the village. It was just starting to break daylight.

We had radio communication with the fifth house and the soldiers there were trying to tell us how to route to them. Several of our guys took off for the front door of the fifth house but got shot. They radioed us and told us to come around the back of the house and climb through an open window. I was picked to be the first one to attempt this. I had one hand holding my eye open and the other grasping my rifle and I was running as fast as I could go. I could see the bullets digging in the dirt around me as I ran. When I got to that window, I didn't waste any time. I just dived through it and a couple guys inside caught me. There wasn't very many of the others that made it.

> *"Pretty soon the Germans set that house on fire as well. No one wants to be in a house on fire with anti-tank mines piled next to it...."*

The Germans brought a tank up and started shooting at the walls of the house to get us to come out. The Germans knew how to pour concrete. They were good at it. None of the tank rounds penetrated those concrete house walls. In the afternoon, a German approached carrying a rifle with a white flag tied on to the bayonet. He spoke perfect English. He said we had five minutes to come out or they would bring that tank around and put the muzzle through the back window and fire one round. That would have been the end of us. That's all there was to it. So we surrendered.

Question: The time you spent in that last house, you were in no shape to fire your M-1?

I did, though. We just kept fighting. What else can you do?

We figured that after killing so many Germans, they would just shoot us when we came out. But they didn't. There were forty-eight of us in that little town and only eight were alive when we were captured. At the time, we didn't realize our little outpost was fighting an entire German division. It was the SS Mountain Division and they were good troops. They were tough.

The Germans took us to a nearby castle and put us all in a large meeting room. It was full of other prisoners from our regiment. I recognized a couple of replacements that had come over with our group. Interrogations went on all night. I was in pretty bad shape, probably half way in shock. I laid down under one of the benches that lined the walls and passed out. The next thing I knew, it was morning and a guard was poking me in the butt with a bayonet. I was the only prisoner left in the room. It was my turn to be questioned. This is when I got an idea as to how good their military intelligence was. I was only rattling off my name, rank, and serial number as I had been taught. The German officer said, "You don't have to tell me anything. I already know everywhere you were stationed after entering the military. You went in the military on June 6, 1944, and were sent to Little Rock, Arkansas," and he named the camp I was at. He proceeded to go right down the list and only missed one place I'd been, and I had moved around a lot. I couldn't believe they knew that much about an Iowa farm boy!

Henderson Wilson was my machine gunner. He got covered up with a pile of bricks in the first house we were in. He had an ear about torn off. I had a leg wound besides the powder burns and the Germans took us both to a military hospital. There were a few other Allied troops there, probably twenty to thirty, but it was mostly German wounded. We were there one week.

I've got to tell you about Henderson Wilson. Henderson Wilson was a genuine hillbilly from the mountains of Tennessee or Kentucky. He got drafted like the rest of us. He trained with the 94th Division from the beginning down in Louisiana. One day he went over the hill (AWOL). His occupation was running a moonshine still in a cave up in the mountains and that's where he was. He had the camp daily newspaper sent to his parent's home so he could keep track of the 94th's deployment. Upon learning that his outfit was being sent to Europe, he travelled to the port of disembarkation and quietly boarded with the rest of the troops. He wasn't discovered until the next day after the ship was well out to sea. He spent the voyage in the brig and was released to rejoin his unit upon reaching France. Henderson told me that he skipped out of training because all they were teaching was how to shoot and fight and he could already do that better than any of them, so it was a waste of his time. He wasn't lying, either. He was a heck of a good guy to have with you, I'll tell you that. We were together the entire time we were prisoners of war.

When we were walking to the castle right after being captured, Henderson was providing me a visual account of what was going on because I couldn't see much with my bad eyes. I had lost my helmet when the artillery round hit the first house we were in. Henderson offered me an Army issue knit cap. He thought my burnt head looked cold and it was. It sure hurt going on. He asked me if I knew where the knit cap came from. I told him that I didn't have any idea. He asked, "Remember Johnson, one of the new replacements that came in two or three days ago? It was his. He won't be needing it. He had his head blown clear off."

All the Allied POW's were together on the second or third floor of this big hospital. The only guards were stationed at the stairwells at the end of the hallways. So we could come and go freely as long as we stayed on our floor. I got sick one night and sat on a bathroom bench. This German officer came in and took a look at me and asked, "Are you all right?" I know I must have looked like a mess. He spoke perfect King's English. He sat down beside me and started talking to me like we were buddies. He said, "I think this war is about over, don't you?" I replied, "I sure hope so." "Me, too," he said. "I've got a lot of good friends over in England and I can't wait to see if they are all right." This is the type of people we were fighting. But they had a vicious nature as well.

Near as I could tell, we received the same medical treatment that the German soldiers did. Every morning a young nurse came and took me down to the operating room where they were performing surgery on the German wounded. I think she was probably fresh out of nurse's training school. Before I could see again, she'd lead me by the hand. She was ordinary people. The doctors put some ointment in my eyes and on my face. I don't know what it was but it sure felt good. You can see that they did a good job on me as there is no scarring. The burns on my hands and other places were pretty much left to heal on their own. The Germans also provided entertainment for the patients, bringing in musical bands to perform in the hallways. We were allowed to go out and to watch. The music was different than we were accustomed to, of course, but it was good. For a week, we had it as good as one could ever hope for as a POW. Then we were transported to Stalag 12 prison camp.

The prison camp was already overcrowded. All the sleeping bunks were full. Henderson found a large table and we slept on it during the short time we were there. It was not good there. We were supposed to be fed twice a day but usually it was only once a day. What food we were given was not good. There were no eating utensils. You had to scrounge up a tin can to eat out of. My first meal was a potato with a big maggot crawling around inside of it. I couldn't eat it. Another POW gladly took it off my hands. He ate it like it was candy. The prison camp wasn't anything like that program they had on TV (*Hogan's Heroes*). The officers were segregated from the enlisted men and lived in separate barracks. The guards were tough men.

We were there a little over one week. The guards came in one night told everyone that could to get to their feet to stand and line up outside. A lot of the guys were in too bad of shape to do that simple task. We were lined up in columns and marched to the railroad tracks and loaded in box cars. The German box car was smaller than ours at home. They crowded fifty of us to a box car and there wasn't room for everyone to sit down. It was a long trip. The train would only travel during daylight and our planes would take turns strafing it. The

> "My first meal was a potato with a big maggot crawling around inside of it. I couldn't eat it. Another POW gladly took it off my hands. He ate it like it was candy."

train would stop every morning and we'd form burial details. We were fortunate in that only one bullet struck the very front of our car and missed people. After several days of this, our officers convinced the Germans to paint the letters POW on top of the train. That stopped the strafing attacks.

We were not fed anything while on the train. Everyday they'd put two garbage cans in each box car. One was used for a latrine and the other had drinking water. Every morning they'd empty one can and fill the other. The guards made a group of prisoners perform this task. I'm not sure they didn't get the garbage cans mixed up some days as the water sure wasn't very palatable.

I was raised around enough German Americans to understand the language even though I couldn't speak it very well. We rode this train for a little over a week without being issued any food. I was wearing an expensive Swiss made wristwatch. I was pretty proud of that watch. At a stop in a town, the German guard that had been eyeing my watch agreed to swap two loaves of bread for it. I told him he'd need to produce the bread first before he got the watch. Soon he came running back with a loaf and a half. As near as I could make out from my limited understanding of the German language, the guard had stolen the bread and that's all I was getting. So we made the swap through this little ventilation hole in the front of the box car. I hid the bread inside my field jacket. Henderson warned me not to let anyone else see the bread as I'd probably be killed for it. I suspect he was right. We rationed the bread between the two of us during the remainder of the train ride.

The last morning we were on the train a P-51 came swooping in and started firing on us. He evidently spotted the POW painted on the top of the train because he quit firing almost as soon as he started. But the fighter plane had hit the locomotive engine and a big cloud of steam poured out from it. So there we sat, for a day and a half. Finally they unloaded and we started marching in column. There was a lot of GI's there. That column stretched for a mile. We were all in pretty bad shape and were just shuffling along. Everyone had diarrhea. You wouldn't think one would need to go

to the bathroom without eating for a week, but that wasn't the case. A guy that had to go would step off to the side of the road to the grader ditch, squat, and hurry, pulling his pants back up in order to return before the rear of the column passed. Then they would try to work their way to the front of the column before the next bout of diarrhea hit, to buy themselves more time. Anyone unfortunate enough not to complete his task or too weak to get up before the rear of the column passed by him, was shot by the guards. I saw them shoot two or three guys that afternoon. The process of leaving the column to find relief and rejoining it and moving to the front repeated itself all day, every day we marched. It was just a continuous thing we had to endure.

They'd march us into villages at nightfall and have us sleep in the barns. They would have to divide us up as the barns weren't that big. Every morning they'd roust us out and march us again. Nothing to eat, of course. This went on for over a week. The same thing, day after day. We marched.

> *"The same thing, day after day. We marched. Guys were getting shot. Diarrhea."*

Guys were getting shot. Diarrhea. Get to the front and drop off again to use the road ditch. We were so weak, we weren't moving very fast. The Germans must have had their routes carefully picked out as invariably, at dusk, we come to a town to sleep. The last day, that evening, I looked at the town and turned to Henderson, saying, "This town looks familiar. We've been here before." They had been marching us in a circle all day. Evidently there was no place else to go (to avoid the rapidly advancing Allied armies). We slept in the same barn we had the night before.

The next morning Henderson woke me up. He asked, "Do you hear something? Those are tanks, our tanks because they sound different than the German tanks." It was a dismal, drizzly March morning. The ground was muddy. You could hear those tanks and halftracks growling in that mud, all day long. There was a single guard posted at the gate. He had a wooden peg stuck in the end of his rifle barrel so we knew he wasn't going to be shooting anyone. A whole mob of prisoners gathered at the gate. The guard ignored us. Someone unhooked the gate latch and it was like a herd of cattle breaking out. So there we were, out in the middle of the street. This old German guard set his rifle against the fence and walked off.

This town reminded me of What Cheer (Iowa), built on two hills with the main part built in the valley in between. It kind of made me homesick. When we got down to the bottom of the hill, there were several German women. One fairly heavy set woman came up to me, and said in pretty good English, "We're going to fix all of you something to eat. Don't leave town. It will take quite a while. Don't leave town." We weren't all that anxious to leave regardless, not knowing what was going on outside of town. There weren't many German soldiers to be seen but we did discover a large pile of discarded German weapons. The firing pins had been mostly removed and there wasn't any ammunition so they were not much good to us.

The women brought out this big tub like my granddad used when butchering. They had that full of something that looked like a brownish colored Cream of Wheat. They had enough to feed all of us. It was the first real food we'd had since being captured. We remained in the town all day. We could hear our armor grinding through the mud all day. Our tanks arrived finally after night fall. A Lieutenant sought me out and informed me that trucks would be arriving in about an hour. Any of us who wanted to leave could ride in the back of the trucks and be transported to the rear. I don't know why he didn't talk to one of the officers. People always seemed to come to me like I was the spokesman or leader. I never could figure that out. *(Note: Anyone knowing Kermit would see no great mystery here as he has a gentle, commanding leadership presence.)* Henderson says to me, "What are we going to do?" I replied, "I'm getting on the first truck out and getting as far behind the front line as I can." After a while, these 6x6 trucks came in full of gasoline jerry cans, which are not the easiest thing to ride on but we did. Those trucks were in a hurry. Being in Patton's army, everybody was in a hurry. It seemed like we rode forever. Finally the trucks stopped in the middle of road. It was pitch dark. The driver said we were at an abandoned German supply depot and we were to get off here. Luckily,

> *"One fairly heavy set woman came up to me, and said in pretty good English, 'We're going to fix all of you something to eat. Don't leave town. It will take quite a while. Don't leave town.'"*

we wandered into a supply building that stored a number of the German long, heavy overcoats (Greatcoats), the kind that ran clear to the ankles. They were very good coats, better than anything we were issued. We wrapped ourselves in a couple of these and slept our first real sleep in weeks. It was a peaceful sleep.

Ambulances arrived in the morning and took us to hospitals. They took all our clothes away from us and burned them. Then we had a shower. Oh, that was Heaven! They gave us pajamas to wear and sent us to this big room. This little gal of a nurse came in carrying a medical tray and asked, "Who has diarrhea? I have something that will take care of it." She repeated the question two or three more times and no one would say anything. Finally she stomps her feet and said, "All right, I know that every one of you has the GI shits so get up here and get some medicine for it." I was the first one up there and Henderson was right behind me. The medicine worked, cleaned us right up.

A little after this I got really sick and was sent to another hospital where a number of doctors ran tests on me. I was told that I had diphtheria. I had figured as much as I had the same symptoms that my sister had when diphtheria almost killed her. I was placed in a private room because I was contagious.

One morning after the war was over, I heard the darnedest commotion out in the hallway. It was Henderson Wilson trying to pay me a visit. The nurse was arguing with him, insisting he couldn't see me because I was contagious. I could hear him telling her that we'd been together from the start and he was shipping out for home and that she couldn't keep him out. Henderson was a big, burly guy who could normally do about anything he pleased and in through the door he came. He blurted out, "I just wanted to say good bye, Kermit," and turned around and left. I never saw him again.

Several days later, a doctor came in and said that this hospital had to relocate. He said that I was too sick to move so they'd leave me for the next hospital that was moving in the next day. He told me not to worry. They'd leave plenty of notes for the new medical staff to find me. I was too sick to worry about anything. The only electricity to the building was provided by portable army generators and they were moved along with everything else. It was a long, dark night alone.

The new medical staff was just as good and dedicated as the previous one. I had good care and treatment. I was stretcher bound for a long time and in a number of other hospitals. I recall being flown in a C-47 from a hospital in Verdun to the big one in Paris. You can't eat when you have diphtheria so I had another thirty days without food added to the starvation diet of a POW. I had lost a little over sixty pounds. Regaining that weight proved difficult. My wife was a heck of a good cook but I was skinny for a long time.

I was sent home to the states on a hospital ship painted white. We slept in hammocks down in the hold of the ship. I got to noticing all the German writing stamped in the metal on the ship and asked a sailor about it. He informed me that the ship had been captured from Germans during WWI and refitted. On the Fourth of July, the crew pulled canvas tarps that were hiding the guns off and fired off a 21 gun salute. Hospital ships were not supposed to be armed but you wouldn't believe the number of guns they had hidden. After the celebration, the tarps went back on.

My next stop was at an Army hospital on Staten Island. My health had improved somewhat. I was gaining a little every day. I had the strength to walk around. Several days later I was put on a troop train bound for a big hospital in Oklahoma. Mid-mornings, I would always walk down to the PX to eat a big bowl of ice cream. It was a far enough walk that I would tire and need to sit down on a bench each way to rest.

One Friday morning the colonel in charge of the hospital was making an inspection. He stopped at the foot of my bed and read my chart. He said, "I see that you were a prisoner of war." I said, "Yes sir, I was." Next he asked me how I found things when I got home. I said, "Sir, I haven't yet been home, Sir." He turned to a first lieutenant accompanying him, saying, "Take care of that, will you?" After they left, I headed down to the PX for my dish of ice cream. When I returned, that same first lieutenant was waiting, pacing back and forth and he wasn't very happy, demanding to know where

the hell I'd been. So I told him. He said, "Well, get your duffel bag. I've got orders to have you on a bus out of here by noon."

There was a long bus layover in Kansas City. My mother's oldest sister lived there so I visited her. It was a welcome taste of home. The bus trip finally ended for me when it stopped in Zearing, Iowa. When I called home my mom answered. I told her I was in Zearing and asked if they could come get me. She responded, "You bet we can!"

It was a long ride home.

Kermit was still too sick to hold a job after getting discharged so he started farming. His family helped him get started. He also married his sweetheart. Much later in life Kermit moved to Washington, Iowa, and was employed as a foreman at Crane, Inc. Kermit and Henderson Wilson did not keep in touch. One day after hearing Kermit reminiscing and wondering what had become of Henderson, his daughter used the Internet to locate Henderson's family. Interestingly, they had the same phone number that Henderson had while in the service. It was then that Kermit learned that his friend, Henderson Wilson, had passed away some years previous.

TALKING TO GOD

Don Rich
Wayland, IA

101st Airborne Division
Europe

Interview Date:
28 May 2010

Referral:
John 'Lefty' Wilson

I was a senior in high school when Pearl Harbor was bombed. I was going to enlist when I graduated so I'd get a little choice on where I served but my dad talked me out of it. He said they'd take me soon enough so I might as well wait. Three of us guys that graduated together worked down at the Ordinance Plant for a while. I got my draft notice in February of 1943. In March I went to Des Moines and took one step forward and pledged allegiance to the flag of United States of America. I was in the U.S. Army.

I was sent to infantry camp in California. I had thirteen weeks of basic training. While I was out there, I read about the Airborne. So I went into the office there and asked if I could volunteer for the glider Airborne. They told me I could volunteer for the Airborne but not the gliders. I informed them that I had bad ankles which would probably break if I jumped out of an airplane. It turned out that I got what I wanted.

I convinced some of my buddies to join the Airborne with me. I basically volunteered them. We traveled to Ft. Bragg. I thought that I was in pretty good physical shape after basic training. The first morning in the Airborne we fell out and the captain asked why we had all volunteered for the Airborne? Everybody groaned but me. Then he ordered us to do 50 push-ups. He said from now on, we had to do everything on the run. You didn't

walk anywhere in the Airborne. The training was rough.

The 101st was on maneuvers when we got there. We came as replacements to fill out squads. They'd split up the 401st from the 82nd Airborne Division. Each division would get one battalion of the 401st. I was assigned to the 2nd Battalion of the 327th Glider Regiment. They made me a bazooka man in G Company. Then we shipped out to Camp Shanks in New York. We were there about a week. We had to lay everything out for inspection to make sure we had all our supplies and equipment. We were told that if we worked hard and had everything ready to go, that we'd get passes for New York City. Then the captain came out saying, "Sorry boys, they've restricted us to camp." We were pretty upset. And then he says, "If there's anyone in this outfit that can't get out of camp, then I don't want him." So you can guess what happened. Most of us tried and a good many of us made it out. Some of our guys dug under fences and got dirty and all scratched up. I decided that was no way to go out on the town. I was watching the front gate. I could see soldiers marching through with MPs accompanying them. So I slipped in with the next group going out and wandered around New York City gaping up at the tall buildings. Getting back through the front gate was more challenging. There was a guard posted and he refused me entrance. After I explained the circumstances of our captain's challenge and the fact that we were shipping overseas, he told me to slip past him when no one was around.

We took an English cruise ship overseas. It was originally designed for 360 passengers and 4000 of us were onboard. They gave us hammocks to sleep in. I couldn't sleep in one of those. I'd fall out. So I slept on a table or the floor. We only had two meals a day. We ate stewed tomatoes and fish for breakfast. I couldn't eat stewed tomatoes and the fish wasn't that good. In the evening there was boiled potatoes and fresh bread. We only received water to drink three times a day. The showers were salt water and the soap wouldn't work. You were dirtier after you took a shower than before. It took eleven days to cross the Atlantic. We were told it was the biggest convoy of the war. There were destroyers escorting us.

When we arrived in England, we had to walk to the train. We could hear Radio Berlin being broadcast on loudspeakers. About the first thing we heard was the Germans welcoming the 101st Airborne to England. It made you realize the value of secrecy.

We spent nine months in England living and training together. That was a big advantage our outfit had over some of the others. We became a cohesive unit.

While in England, I met a British family that became my second home. They were quite poor. We'd be issued fresh fruit once a month and I'd give it to the two kids. I didn't smoke so I gave the man and wife my cigarette ration. When we went out on maneuvers we'd be fed K rations. Three of us would save the biscuits for them. They had some chickens but couldn't get any feed for them. The biscuits were hard as a rock and tasted lousy. A person couldn't eat them so the man and wife crumbled the biscuits into chicken feed. Occasionally we'd get a fresh egg in return. Their kids started eating with us at the mess hall. It got to be that there were more neighborhood kids eating there than GI's so they put a stop to it. This couple invited the three of us to Christmas dinner. The wife had butchered a chicken to eat. She also served pork chops and Yorkshire pudding. The pork chops constituted their entire meat ration for

the next six months. She served pineapple she had saved since 1939. We had already eaten before we left camp but did not wish to hurt their feelings. So we ate until we were miserable and thanked them graciously. I found out after I came home from the war that my parents later sent food packages to them.

Those two other guys, Al and Proppe, became my best friends. Proppe was killed on D-Day. I did not go in on a glider because they didn't have enough of them to carry all of us. They said some of us would have to go in by ship. They waited until the last minute to tell us this. We had trained hard and were really upset we couldn't go in on those gliders. We hadn't trained for a beach landing. We sailed on an LCI ship. We were supposed to go in June 5th but a storm delayed us a full day. We spent two nights and a day aboard ship before going ashore. We landed at Utah Beach around 3 PM. The 4th Infantry Division went in there at dawn and had cleared the beach. I waded in carrying 80 pounds of equipment. If you tripped and fell, you'd drown because there was no way you could get upright again with that much weight.

> "I waded in carrying 80 pounds of equipment. If you tripped and fell, you'd drown because there was no way you could get upright again with that much weight."

We had just walked up on the beach when a Messerschmitt came over and strafed us. There was a British Spitfire right on his tail and he shot the German down. The pilot came floating down in his parachute. Some of our guys were shooting at him but couldn't hit him. I started questioning how good our training had been. The pilot had been burnt to a crisp on his exposed skin. Some of the guys wanted to kill him because the German had strafed a hospital tent set up on the beach. The pilot claimed he hadn't seen it. He was only flying 1000 feet high and with a Spitfire on his tail, I figured he was probably telling the truth. He was our first prisoner of war.

We spent the first night on the beach. Because we'd been on the ship an extra day, everybody had run out of drinking water by that evening. We dug foxholes and seep water filled the bottom of them. I dipped my empty canteen in, filled it, and dropped in a purification pill. I can't say it was the best water I ever tasted, but when you are desperate you'll drink it even if it's pretty foul tasting.

The next two or three days we moved off the beach advancing towards Carentan. The first day of combat was a little funny. We set up like a wagon train would along this hedgerow next to a road. They put me up front as lookout with a BAR so I could be the suicide guy to warn everybody if the Germans came up the road. I couldn't understand why they chose me as I was not a BAR man. All at once I heard this "clop, clop" coming up the road. I thought, oh boy, there's soldiers coming up this road. I whispered to the guys that someone was coming. I was right out in the bare open with no place to get under cover. There was a curve in the road I couldn't see around. There was another "clop, clop" and then it stopped. I figured the Germans were taking their time, looking around. Then the clopping picked up and I pulled on the trigger and it wouldn't fire. I had forgotten to take the safety off. And then their horses come around the corner.

After two days, we had run out of water again. Water was always the first thing we ran short of during the entire war. We hadn't experienced any real combat yet. There'd be a sniper once in a while. Three of us took off to hunt for water. We jumped over a fence and there were a bunch of GI's wearing gas masks. We took off running but I stopped the other two after a short distance, realizing it was futile to try to outrun a gas attack. I didn't feel anything odd so I told them I didn't think there'd been a gas attack. We continued looking for water but could not find any. So we spent another day thirsty.

We'd taken one more prisoner as we were walking towards Carentan. I found a discarded Luger on the ground among some rubbish near where the prisoner was taken. My one goal in going to Europe was acquiring a Luger so I stuck it inside my field jacket. We were warned that if we had any German weapons on us when captured, the Germans would shoot us on the spot.

There was a canal we had to cross as we approached Carentan. The bridge had been blown but my squad was able to climb the remaining girders across. We scouted ahead another 300 yards along the canal toward a small hill covered with trees. We didn't receive any fire so we returned to the bridge. Some bridge planking was brought up and the whole company crossed. Our squad was to take the point and lead the assault into Carentan.

We didn't get as far as our squad had before the Germans opened up on us with rifle, machine gun, and mortar fire. They had us zeroed in, really mowing our guys down. I heard a lieutenant in intelligence from battalion yell, "Rich, let's get that machine gun." This lieutenant was a good friend of mine. We used to play basketball together in camp. He'd always pick me to go out on patrols with him.

> *"There were so many bullets whizzing by in it sounded like I was in a bumble bee's nest."*

I didn't question the order. The lieutenant was on the opposite dike and he was going to be my loader. I jumped up over the dike, running down the best I could while carrying my bazooka. I got down to the bottom, about an eight to ten feet drop. There were so many bullets whizzing by in it sounded like I was in a bumble bee's nest. I heard the lieutenant yell, "Get the hell out of there!" I gave the bazooka a toss because I couldn't run with it and climbed back up the bank. Just as I got to the top of the bank, a bullet came in and took a chunk out of my left leg. At first it just felt like a sharp pain. I tried to get back up on my feet to keep running but my left leg wouldn't carry my weight. As I crawled out, I could hear the bullets whacking right over my head.

I crawled back through a garden to a house. I could have picked peas as I went through. A French family came to the door of the house. The lady tried to bandage my leg. Then I tried to make my way on back. I ran into another soldier wounded in the right leg. He was from the mortar squad. There was a German sniper in the marsh behind this house. He'd rise up every once in a while and shoot someone and duck back down. They finally spotted him and knocked him out. After the two of us got past the line of fire, we stood up and helped each other hobble back to the Douve River where a medic bandaged us up. There was a row boat on the river bank. The medic said we'd have to row ourselves across and there'd be somebody there to pick us up. We were carried down to the beach to an LCI ship and given another shot of morphine. That put me to sleep as the ship was departing for England. That happened on June 11th, the fifth day after we landed. I had yet to fire my bazooka or rifle.

I remember when Eisenhower and Churchill visited us right before D-Day. They told us that only half of us would be coming back. You always think that you'll be the one that makes it back. I looked to the guy standing on my right and on my left and thought, "You poor devils are going to get killed." I wasn't really all that scared when I got wounded. My thought was to get patched up as quickly as possible. You didn't get all that scared in combat if you had a weapon where you could fight back. The feeling was different when you'd get caught in an artillery barrage or a fire fight when you couldn't shoot back, and you just had to lay there and take it.

They had placed me on the second deck of the LCI with all the other wounded. The rough sea woke me up. A sailor came down the steps and he look white as a sheet. I asked him what was wrong. He said, "A torpedo just went across our bow. It wasn't six feet from us." We came that close to being blown up.

I can pick time after time when I didn't get killed and other guys did. That always bothered me. I'd survive, and this other guy who was just as good a soldier, didn't. I accepted Christ into my life and became a Christian while in England. A lot of the guys would talk about their faith. I don't remember doing much praying early on. That came later. I do remember having the feeling that everything would be okay.

I was six weeks in the hospital. They operated on my leg and sewed me up. It was a bad wound but not life threatening. I had a set of crutches to get down to the mess hall. They'd send food up if you couldn't make it but the amount was always kind of skimpy. That's how they encouraged the wounded to get exercise.

One day there was quite a commotion in the hospital. Someone was saying, "Germans, Germans!" So I got my crutches and off I went to investigate. Wounded German prisoners were being moved out of the hospital to a POW camp. The MPs were trying to keep us back,

"I remember when Eisenhower and Churchill visited us right before D-Day. They told us that only half of us would be coming back...I looked to the guy standing on my right and on my left and thought, 'You poor devils are going to get killed.'"

shouting, "There will be no killing here." I think the Germans were lucky none of them had a gun because I think they would have used it. I wasn't that gun happy by then. I think the longer you were in combat, the meaner you got.

I still had my Luger and a trench knife with me when I got to the hospital. They said that I couldn't have them in the hospital but I refused to give them up. A nurse told me that the trench knife was GI issue and I couldn't keep it anyway. She said she'd keep the Luger for me and when I awoke from surgery, it would be laying on my bed. And it was. Another paratrooper who was being discharged offered me $300 for the Luger so I sold it to him. I figured it only took me five days of combat to get one and I'd surely find another. He paid me in French currency which they had captured from a German paymaster.

Four or five guys from my squad visited me in the hospital. They told me that I'd better get out soon because they were going back into combat. I had volunteered to do some office work and typing while convalescing. The next day I asked the doctor, "How about me typing up my dismissal papers?" He said, "No, your leg is still draining." I told him my outfit was fixing to go back in and I wanted to join them. He hem-hawed a while and finally agreed to let me go. So another guy and I took off for Scotland to visit my uncle who was in an engineering unit stationed there. By the time we arrived, his unit had already shipped out for France. We spent some time there and wandered around the town at night looking for girls. An MP stopped us and told us we couldn't be out that night. Our thought was because we'd been in combat we could be out any night we chose. He explained that is was Black Night. There was a Black Night and White Night segregation to reduce the racial fighting. So we got out of there and spent our time on the edge of town with a couple of nice girls we met.

The moment I arrived back at our camp I was told to grab my helmet and weapon as we were going in. I didn't have either but knew I could pick both up after the first casualty. We were at the airport getting ready to go when the mission was cancelled. We were supposed to drop ahead of Patton's breakout but he had already over run the drop zone.

We returned to camp and remained there quite some time. A bunch of replacements arrived. Company G had lost 80 men during the invasion. Our company was increased from 160 men to 200. That gave us more fire power for Operation Market Garden in Holland. I didn't make any new buddies until near the end of the war because I didn't want to lose any more friends. Five of my squad were killed in the first 30 days after the invasion. Two of the killed were older guys in their 30s. They had orders to withdraw because the Germans had them pinched off but they refused. The Germans overran their position. It took my outfit three or four days of hard fighting to take Carentan. Even though we didn't suffer the high casualties like the paratroopers did on D-Day, we ended up losing about the same percentage of men.

The paratroopers landed in Holland the first day and the gliders followed them the second day. The gliders carried 13 men counting the pilot. The weather was decent but we caught some flack going in. We were told the Air Force had knocked out all the anti-aircraft guns but they'd missed a few. A few of the guys were already air sick and I was starting to get that way. But when that ack-ack started, I got over being sick. I knew our glider's plywood bottom and canvas sides wouldn't stop anything. Some of the guys sat on their rifles trying to protect their private areas. I do not believe we received any holes in our glider, however. Everyone else aboard the glider was a replacements Our glider landed with its nose stuck out over the edge of a canal. Just as the pilot announced that we made it down there was a heck of a jolt. Another glider had clipped one of our wings off as it landed. I don't know why that collision didn't push us off into the canal. We left the glider and headed to the assembly area.

Each group of soldiers were assigned a bridge to guard so the British tank column could go north to Arnhem. The bridge we were to guard had already been blown but we set up there anyway. One problem with the road was that it was only single lane. Two tanks couldn't pass each other. Another problem was the British stopped for tea too often.

They'd stop a battle for tea. The British had good soldiers but I thought their leadership was terrible.

We were told the enemy we would encounter in Holland would be older men and very poor quality troops. Nor would there be much German artillery. The artillery there was probably worse than it was in the Battle of the Bulge. We were shelled time after time. One night the Germans attacked us trying to drive us back. We had foxholes dug. They claimed there hadn't been an artillery attack like that since El Alamein in North Africa when Montgomery broke out. It was just a continuous roar. You couldn't hear anything because of the noise. The guy in the foxhole with me got hit real bad. The blast knocked me down on top of him. I thought I'd killed him. I couldn't get any medics up until daylight. I pert near shot one of my own guys that night. We were running out of ammunition and a guy named Simpson came crawling up behind our line, throwing bandoliers of ammunition to us. I was dug in at the end of our line. He reached up and tapped me on the shoulder. I swung my rifle around and had it on him. When I realized it was one of our guys I said, "My God, Simpson, I almost killed you!" He just laughed and went on.

The next morning the medics came and started treating my foxhole buddy. I noticed they were treating him rough. They said he wasn't hurt. I told them he was hurt and that he'd been unconscious part of the time. Finally they turned him over and discovered a piece of shrapnel in his back lodged next to his heart. He survived the wound and came to see me in Wayland after the war. One of his arms didn't work and he had to drag one leg to walk.

Comment: You must have been in quite a fire fight that night to be running out of ammo.
German infantry was attacking us. When they couldn't break through our line they would back off, regroup, and attack again. That went on all night. I was shooting a Garand by then. I never could hit much in training with the carbine so I tossed it and grabbed an M-1. I carried it along with my bazooka which was a lot of weight to pack around. I could hit more with the .45 caliber pistol than the carbine. That night the Garand barrels were so hot you could see them glowing red in the darkness. Each bandolier of ammo held 80 rounds

and I went through at least six of them. Most of our shooting was suppressive fire. Our front line curled around and we were firing across and over the other half of our own guys. They had to stay hunkered down in their foxholes to keep from being hit by friendly fire. Only half the line was actually shooting at the Germans. I could hear our BAR guy firing. He was one of the older guys. Then he stopped firing. He broke and ran back to battalion. He told the medics there, "Get out of here. The Germans broke through and are coming by the thousands." The battalion was ready to pull back. They called division. Division told them to stay there because our line was holding.

The BAR man had just lost it. This guy had always been solid. It just got to him. It was always scary to hear a BAR stop firing. They were worth about four rifles in fire power. All our machine guns were farther down the line that night.

I was sent out on a patrol the next morning to see how far the Germans withdrew. There were dead Germans with flame throwers within 20 feet of some of the foxholes. I don't know who got them, but I can tell you I killed one of them. We attacked in the day time and Germans usually attacked at night. Most of the time, you couldn't see what you were shooting at in the dark. The Germans blew a whistle when they were going to attack. When we'd hear the whistle, we knew their infantry was coming. Then we'd start firing. We were already being shelled by their artillery. I don't think we ever stopped firing that night. Every once in a while I'd toss a hand grenade for good measure. If your line of fire was heavy enough, they weren't going to get through it.

There were probably 20 of us on the reinforced patrol that next day. We went out a mile. I was carrying my bazooka. The lieutenant leading the patrol was out front. I was in the rear with my loader. The patrol was spread out about 100 yards. The lieutenant stopped and yelled back, "Are we getting fire from the right flank?" The question puzzled me. Then he yelled it again. So I answered that we were. He radioed battalion that we were receiving fire from our right flank so they ordered us back. Twenty guys out in the open wouldn't

have stood much of a chance against a company of Germans a mile from our lines.

I had a cousin named Jay in the 101st. He had flat feet and couldn't keep up on the training marches in England. So they made him a trucker. When you saw the canvas of a truck flopping in the wind because of the high speed, you knew it was him. If they had given him a tank, I think he could have won the war by himself. He'd be one of the truckers that resupplied us.

One day we had to run twelve kilometers up to the Veghel because the Germans had cut the highway the British were using. We ran in full battle gear. It was dark when we arrived. The officers decided not to attempt launching an attack in the dark. We walked around a church into an open field to dig in. The Germans caught us in a tank barrage out there in the open. Our battalion lost 80 guys in about 15 minutes. They just slaughtered us as we were trying to dig foxholes. I was lying on my back trying to dig. All you'd hear was zip bang, zip bang. That was from direct tank fire. The tanks would walk the shells up and back, across the field. I saw a medic go down a few feet away. There was a little, short captain close who never quit digging. All I could see was dirt flying after his head disappeared below ground level. I was talking to God pretty loud that night. I told Him, "If I live through this, I'll go home and try to serve You." I've tried to fulfill that promise. I was so traumatized by the shelling that I could barely function.

The next morning I was out picking up rifles. The lieutenant said we'd probably need them. Two sergeants from my barracks were among the dead. One had been blown in half. He couldn't have been cut off a cleaner if you'd used a knife. You could recognize him but his bottom half was completely missing. My buddy, Jack, told me he saw two Dutch civilians in leather jackets take off when we came in. They may have been German collaborators and that was why we got hit.

My wife Mary and I went over to Europe in 1994 and toured where the 327th had fought. When we arrived at that field and the church beside it, I broke down in tears. I could still see all those guys lying out there.

The Germans held the high ground in Holland in the area called the "Island". They were on the bluffs across the river and they could see every move you made. We moved in after dark. It wasn't safe to smoke a cigarette or talk loud in the dark or show yourself during daylight or they drop artillery in on you. Two guys went in with me carrying bazooka rounds. We occupied foxholes that had already been dug by the outfit we were replacing. Even though I was only a PFC, I was the acting commander of the bazooka section. It was my responsibility to assign the men under me their positions. I would have had sergeant stripes if the captain and I had gotten along. We no more than got in our holes when the lieutenant hollered at me, "Rich, there's a machine gun up there in front of you. Get it." I couldn't see any machine gun. Everybody got quiet. I told the guy with me to load my bazooka and then got down in the hole. I'm lying there and I still didn't know where the machine gun is. I thought, "If I shoot and miss, he'll cut me in two." Then I heard the bolt on the machine gun being worked so I fired at the sound. The bazooka rocket went right through the German and exploded when it hit the building behind him, blowing it and the machine gun up.

Question: Was that the first time you fired your bazooka in combat?

I had fired grenade launchers during the invasion at bunkers across the river. I believe that was the only time I fired my bazooka during the war.

The next morning we could see a group of Germans with a white flag across the river. They were about 300 yards away. They were carrying a stretcher into a house. We figured they were carrying a wounded person so we let them go. It wasn't too long before mortar rounds started dropping on us. One shell blew me clear out of my hole. Another guy in the foxhole with me got a piece of shrapnel in his back. I was getting ready to crawl out to a culvert to eat a K ration when the attack came. All I heard was a "swoosh" but I knew what it was. I was knocked unconscious and they thought I was dead.

The medics wouldn't come up in an ambulance. So my cousin Jay drove a three quarter ton Dodge truck up and picked me and guy with the back wound up. I was given a pill at the aid station which knocked me out for twelve hours. Then I was

sent back. I climbed back into my foxhole. There sat my K ration I was carrying with a hole through it. How that piece of shrapnel missed my hand, I'll never know.

We had a machine gunner named Gross. He and I have kept in contact over the years. He was always up on the line except for one time the captain called him back to headquarters. There were always two guys manning a machine gun. While he was gone, a shell came in killing the other guy. I can see why we lost a lot of guys. It's just hard to understand why some were taken and not others. There's a scripture that says, "God is not a respecter of persons."

Lloyd Gross spoke German. When we were in the hedgerow country during the invasion, Gross would have conversations with German soldiers. We'd be on one side of a hedgerow and they'd be on the other. They'd argue back and forth who was in the wrong army. So you can see that we were pretty close to the enemy at times.

We were 72 days in Holland. We had one shower and one change of clothes. We'd be on the line for ten days and then be pulled back off the line maybe half a mile for two days. Then you could at least wash your face. We were eating British rations. The ox tail soup was nothing but lard. I couldn't get it down. Their biscuit was worse than ours. We killed a few Dutch cows to have something eat.

When we got out of Holland, there were about 100 men left in our company. We went in with 200. At one point our captain reported that we were to down 73.

We were back in a rest area in France awaiting replacements when the Bulge hit. A lot of the guys were in Paris on a pass. Christmas was coming and we were planning a party for the local French kids. We were using the time to rest up, check our weapons, and get resupplied so we could go in again. We left on the night of December 17th for the front. They jammed us into open trucks. It was colder than heck. We were let off outside of Bastogne and walked in. We dug in south of Bastogne two or three miles at a little town called Marvie. They were trying to decide where to place me with my bazooka. The captain said, "We don't have to decide this now. There are no Germans within 40 miles." I looked up and said, "Well, they're moving fast. There are two tanks coming now!"

I grabbed a guy saying, "Let's go get that tank." We ran down to the end of the road and ran into a house. I would have got that tank if I had been thinking right. We loaded the bazooka and watched for the tank out different windows. Then WHAM! The tank blew that building in right on top of us. The German tank had fired an armor piercing round. It left a big hole through the house. I went rolling across the floor like somebody had picked me up and thrown me. I staggered into the room where the other guy was. I figured he was dead. He was buried in rubble. The bazooka was bent shut with a live rocket in it. I started digging the guy out and realized he was alive. I got him out of the building and started up the street with him, but didn't know where the medics were set up. I was half carrying him and half dragging him. I ran into a medic who took him from me. I told the medic the guy was hurt bad. I never have found out what became of him, whether he survived or not. His name was Shaw and I can't find it on any list available today. He was a replacement and sometimes the records are lacking on them.

I tried to find some of the other guys. I was wandering around still a little dazed and a guy came up holding his belly, trying to keep his entrails from coming out. That's the last thing I remember of that day until evening, when my sergeant yelled at me, "Rich, take five men and cover the right flank. We've lost contact with them." The six of us took off. I didn't have a radio, a map, or know exactly where we were to go. I don't think they knew that I didn't have a bazooka any more. We set up around a farm house. It turned out that we had crossed into enemy held territory. There was a 37mm anti-tank gun set up 200 yards behind. No food was sent up to us. We were lucky in that they brought overcoats and sleeping bags up to us. But that was only because the guys on the anti-tank gun told them there were some more men on up there a ways.

We dug foxholes on both sides of the farm house. If the Germans had attacked from that direction, we would have opened up on them. Our people would have known they were coming, but we would have been wiped out. We got into those kinds of situations a lot of times. The second or third day I got enough nerve to get out of my hole. I went into the barn and the farmer was milking his cows. He motioned for me to help myself to the milk. I filled my canteen and passed the word to the others to do the same, but to stay inside only long enough to warm up. One guy never would go in. After a tank broke through, this guy finally went into the house. He took off his boots. His frozen feet swelled up like a balloon. He ended up losing them. He was a replacement, another guy I didn't know.

The Germans came in the first day and captured our field hospital. They were wearing American uniforms and had American tanks.

Another morning I could see Germans when I climbed out of my hole. They were walking across a hill and getting behind it. The last one was pulling a sled with a radio on it. I was worried there wasn't anyone posted between the Germans and Bastogne so I told the BAR guy to fire. As soon as the BAR opened up I could hear some yelling and swearing in that direction. I think there was an engineering outfit down there and they had probably all been asleep. A patrol from G Company came up then and captured the Germans.

> "I was wandering around still a little dazed and a guy came up holding his belly, trying to keep his entrails from coming out."

I crawled out of my foxhole one night to watch the Germans bomb Bastogne. There was a small German plane we called Bed Check Charlie. He'd come every night and drop bombs. There weren't any anti-aircraft guns in Bastogne. I watched a plane fly south out of Bastogne towards me. Pretty soon the snow started kicking up all around me and I started running. He was strafing our line. I could see the pilot in the cockpit because he had the light on. I jumped back into my foxhole. It made me a little more cautious getting out of my foxhole.

I didn't have any galoshes during the Bulge. My feet got frosted and I could barely walk. So they took me off the line and made me a runner. They reasoned that I would at least be able to get in a barn or house at night and be out of the elements.

I had an overcoat, although I went three days without one. We still wore our summer uniforms.

After the 4th Armored Division arrived we were moved to the north side of Bastogne. There was a pocket of several hundred thousand Germans that we were trying to pinch off so they couldn't retreat back into Germany. We walked by a battery of the big 155mm guns. Those artillery men said that, "Three weeks ago we were in the second row of the Siegfried Line and look where we are now." At least those guys didn't abandon their guns like a lot of the others. We couldn't stop the Tiger Royal tank with our bazookas unless we got in behind it. We could stop the Panther tanks any place we hit them. Our bazooka rounds would penetrate six inches. I witnessed a shootout in a town between a Sherman and a Tiger tank. They were positioned on opposite sides of a house. The Sherman would run out, fire off a round, and scoot back in reverse to hide behind the house. The Sherman's rounds were bouncing off the Tiger. The Tiger tank was shooting through the house at the American tank. The Sherman finally aimed at the ground beside the Tiger to ricochet a round under it. That knocked the Tiger out. That Sherman was part of the 10th Armored Division that was surrounded with us at Bastogne. They were an impressive outfit.

There was also a black artillery unit at Bastogne that I can't thank enough for the job they did. If the Germans had been smart enough to attack at two different places at once, they would have overrun us. We moved all our artillery back into the center of Bastogne and placed it in a circle. We'd concentrate our artillery wherever the Germans were attacking. At one time, they were down to three shells per gun. When we'd call in for artillery support, we wouldn't say there was twelve enemy, we'd say there was fifty. Otherwise, they'd never fire. They'd tell us to take care of it ourselves. When we called for artillery from the British in Holland, we'd usually have to call back telling them to stop. They had a habit of shooting air burst rounds that exploded right over the top of us. We had a hard time getting the British to stop firing. If we ever got over two or three rounds at Bastogne we were lucky. They would have fired more had there not been a critical shortage.

> *"There was also a black artillery unit at Bastogne that I can't thank enough for the job they did."*

Guys from our company commandeered several .50 caliber machine guns that had been mounted on trucks. When we had those on the line with us, we could usually handle anything the Germans threw at us but tanks. We didn't need to call for artillery very often when the fifties were close.

When we had the Germans penned up north of Bastogne, G Company set up a line of men across a field and up a hill in case the Germans broke through the main line of defense. The captain told me to take three guys and set up an outpost between the two lines. There was no cover out there. This captain and I never got along. I said, "Give me half a chance." He was always putting me in places I didn't like. I told him I was tired of being this goat that always has to go out there. I cussed him and called him some pretty rough names. I sent two of the guys off to hide in a barn. The ground was too frozen to dig in. I told them there was no point in all four of us being killed.

The next day the company moved up to attack. I was sent back to headquarters for something. The snow was knee deep. I wasn't sure where headquarters or the Germans were at. I wore out walking up a hill and sat down in the snow. I reached for my canteen but it was empty. I was cold. I found a small stream of clear water running at the bottom of the hill. I drank my fill and refilled the canteen. I decided to follow the creek around, thinking it safer than being exposed on a hill where a sniper could pick me off. I followed the creek for 300 yards and there lay a dead horse in the creek. It was still the best water I ever drank. We were told not to drink any of the water over there. The Army set up big canvas tanks with treated water (Water Buffaloes) but I only got water once from those. We fended for ourselves the rest of the time.

One day when we were on the north side of Bastogne I was by myself for some reason. I had a foxhole there. I don't remember where G Company was. There was a group of officers up a ways from me and a platoon moving out. I heard a plane coming. We ran for these yellow flags that marked the position of friendlies so we wouldn't get bombed by our own planes. Guys were throwing flags out in every direction and then running for foxholes. This P-47 comes in dropping bombs. I swear to God I saw this platoon of men disappear right before my eyes. There were at least 20 men out there. A colonel by the name of Harper said that none of the men were hit. I saw them blown to bits. One of us is right. Several of us ran out there where we saw the platoon get hit. We could find no trace of them, not even dog tags.

After the bombing, a screaming meemie (German Nebelwerfer) came over. Those things scared the living daylights out me because you couldn't tell where they would hit. There were two officers close to me, both big guys. One had to weigh 200 pounds. They both jumped in my foxhole on top of me. I thought they had killed me.

After Bastogne, the chaplain told headquarters that the 101st was fought out and needed to be taken off the line. He said the men had given everything they've got and they didn't care anymore whether they lived or died. But General Taylor arrived back from his stateside tour and wanted to make another big show. We were pretty put out about that. General Taylor was a gung ho solider and had all kinds of guts. But I'd wish he had used his once in a while instead of mine.

Twenty replacement troops were brought into our company after the encirclement of Bastogne was broken. When we moved down to Alsace-Lorraine, the Germans had already driven the 42nd Infantry Division back across the Moder River (Operation North Wind). I was still a runner then. I met my buddy Jack on my way back from the front one night. He was leading a bunch of replacements up to G Company. He had told them to follow him and do everything he did. A German artillery shell went over. By then we knew when we needed to take cover and when not to. That round wasn't going to land close. Jack looked back and the replacements had all taken off for the timber. He had to go find them. After three days, only four of those replacements were left. One replacement had a hand grenade go off in his pocket. That took out six.

We were supposed to carry three grenades in our pockets but I generally carried six. I'd wrap tape around the handles so they wouldn't go off

> *"General Taylor was a gung ho solider and had all kinds of guts. But I'd wish he had used his once in a while instead of mine."*

in case the pin accidentally came out. I remember in Holland after I knocked out that machine gun I tossed several grenades. None of them went off. It finally dawned on me that I had forgotten to remove the tape holding the handles in.

We didn't have any problems chasing the Germans back across the Moder River. The war quieted down for us then. There'd be some artillery come across the river but that was about it. The colonel wanted us to keep sending patrols across the river. After doing this several times, our lieutenant decided all patrols across the river would be conducted on our side of the river. There wasn't any point in losing three or four guys every time we ventured across.

Half the people in the Alsace Lorraine region were French and the other half were German. We had our rations and supplies stolen one time. We were going to use an interpreter to get them back but decided the German sympathizers would understand a gun just as well. You should have seen all of the galoshes, blankets, and rations go flying out the doors.

Next we were deployed in the Ruhr Valley. It was a highly industrialized with big buildings along the river front. I remember thinking that we didn't even have electricity in our rural farm house when I left for the war. It was here when we were first told there would be a $75 fine if we were caught with a German girl. Some of them were pretty cute, too. At that time, all I was interested in was getting the war over.

We picked up a Displaced Person from Yugoslavia in the Ruhr Valley. He was a tailor. Our company adopted him. He made his own American uniform and traveled with us. We tried to smuggle him back to the United States but there was no way we could get him on the boat.

We pulled into Landsburg, Germany, after dark. Most of the company slept in the hotel but it couldn't accommodate all of us. Some of us walked down the street and took a house over. In the morning we walked back to the hotel. Everybody was laid out on the floor drunk and sick. They had helped themselves to the wine cellar. I wasn't a drinker but some of the guys drunk weren't either.

One German could have licked the whole bunch of them.

We came across the prison camp outside of Landsburg. We didn't know anything about the concentration camps. It surprised me that the Army didn't publicized them. We were all told of the Malmedy Massacre during the Bulge. The German shooting of American prisoners deterred a lot of soldiers from surrendering. Our outfit never shot any prisoners. I didn't realize until later how many were shot by others in the 101st. There was one guy they wouldn't let escort prisoners to the rear because he'd shoot every one of them.

By the time we got to Landsburg, the Germans were surrendering by the thousands. They'd walk in a hundred at a time, still carrying their weapons. One of the guys in the first jeep that drove into Landsburg was Jewish. He had a camera but was so worked up he couldn't use it. The German guards had all taken off. We captured the camp commander. General Taylor came to look at the camp. A day or two later all the local German citizens were rounded up and forced to bury the corpses. They claimed they didn't know the camp was there. I can't believe that.

I don't remember ever shooting my gun in anger during the war. I fired my gun because that was my job as a soldier. But I would not have had any problem shooting down the camp guards or their commander if given the opportunity. Landsburg Prison was where Adolph Hitler wrote *Mein Kampf* when he was a political prisoner after World War One. I saw his jail cell. Before seeing Landsburg, I was sick of war. I didn't care if I ever fired my gun again. I didn't want any more killing. My feelings about the war changed after seeing Landsburg.

When we were driving a DUKW through southern Germany, we passed some slave laborers walking along the road. We threw them all our rations and cigarettes. These were some of the healthier ones as they could still walk. They were so thin there were bones sticking out. We traveled another two miles before anyone spoke a word.

We made it to the Eagles Nest at Berchtesgaden,

"I don't remember ever shooting my gun in anger during the war. I fired my gun because that was my job as a soldier. But I would not have had any problem shooting down the camp guards or their commander if given the opportunity."

Germany. That was Hitler's hideout in the Alps. It had been bombed pretty heavily. There was a house with all of Herman Goering's stuff stored in it. We had to guard it to keep things from being stolen. We were in Austria when the war ended.

I wish I had all those foxholes I dug lined up in a row. Sometimes we had to use our helmet to dig a foxhole. Besides the limited protection it afforded, the helmet was multi-purpose. We used it to wash in and for an emergency toilet. Some days it wasn't safe to get out of your foxhole when you had to go. It was a little tough getting it clean again, especially when you didn't have any water. I did one thing during the war that most men couldn't claim. I peed in the English Channel from 2000 feet.

I've been a Methodist lay speaker and been involved in the Prison Ministry and evangelism. I try to tell people who is really in charge of this world.

Question: How long did it take you to re-adjust to civilian life after being in combat?

It probably took a year or two. For a while, every time I'd hear an explosion, I would duck behind something or jump in a hole. I attended the State Fair the next year after coming home. I about went crazy when the fireworks were going on. I was down on my knees trying to get under a seat. I'd wake up at night screaming from the nightmares. My wounded left leg still bothers me.

I farmed after the war. I quit farming before I went broke and got a job as a rural mail carrier.

I still have this little thing about being Airborne.

For further reading on Don's war experiences, see Glider Infantryman, *by Don Rich and Kevin Brooks, Texas A & M University Press, College Station, Texas, Copyright 2012.*

RAF PILOT WINGS

Rev. Everett Burham
Washington, IA

Army Air Corps
Stateside

Interview Date:
31 May 2010

Referral:
Personal Contact

I went to high school here in Washington, graduating in 1939. I went to junior college here in Washington for a year and a half. During that time, I began my flight activity at the Washington airfield. I became a pilot. A husband and wife team by the name of Snodgrass came to Washington to be flight instructors. Mrs. Snodgrass was my instructor. When I decided that I wanted to pursue my pilot activities, I transferred to the University of Iowa. I did one semester there which completed my two years of junior college.

Then I enlisted in the Army Air Corps and was sent down to Texas to train as a student pilot. Because I had already been a flyer here in Iowa, I think, in my mind, is why I was relegated to train with the British. The British already had several flight training schools they operated here in the states. I was assigned to one of their schools, BFTS No. 6, in Ponca City, Oklahoma. There was a British commander in charge of the airfield and I was trained by British pilots. It was a rather unique experience. The food was tailored to the British appetite and I was soon sick of eating mutton. I

> *"The food was tailored to the British appetite and I was soon sick of eating mutton."*

graduated as a lieutenant in the United States Air Force. I was presented with both U.S. and RAF pilot wings.

I was sent to Madison, Wisconsin, to await my appointment to be assigned overseas. I was supposed to be assigned to Billy Mitchel and fly the "hump" from India to China. Instead of getting that appointment, I was called back to San Antonio, Texas, where they made me a pilot instructor. I was really disappointed. The other two guys in my group got to go. One was killed and the other went down but was able to walk out.

I taught flight training for several years, first in Enid, Oklahoma, then Denver, Colorado, and Amarillo, Texas. I had many students. My instruction planes at Enid were called B-13 and B-15s Basic Trainers. They were single engine planes. Then I went to AT6's, also called an Advanced Trainer No. 6. I continued flight instructions for several years and never went overseas.

My last assignment as an official instructor was on the B-29 heavy bomber. I didn't necessarily instruct pilots on the B-29. I was also instructing as an engineer.

History eventually ended and I left the Air Force and came back home here to Washington. My wife and I were married in Ponca City, Oklahoma, on a Saturday. When I reported back to the base on Sunday afternoon, the guard at the main gate told me a case of spinal meningitis had been reported on the base and I was now quarantined for six weeks. So my new wife and I had only one night together, and she went home to Iowa. She did, eventually, come back to Ponca City.

I worked for the Railway Express Agency here in Washington and several other communities. I was involved in getting needed equipment to local railroads. Hubert Walker was the manager. After several years, we became re-involved with the Methodist church here. The local pastor and assistant pastor influenced me to go into the ministry. We moved to Yarmouth, Iowa, where I became the local pastor of a church and I attended Iowa Wesleyan College for two years to complete my four year degree. I then transferred to Garret Biblical Institute in Evanston, Illinois, and studied there for three years. I served as the pastor at Donnellson, Iowa, while going to school in Evanston and commuted back and forth on weekends. I've been in the ministry ever since.

Have you listened to wilder tales?

Proud to be an American

Bill McGinnis
Ainsworth, IA

Signal Corps
Europe

Interview Date:
31 May 2010

Referral:
Dave Birney & Harold Williams

I had basic training in Missouri. They had me climbing creosote treated telephone poles. That was not something I liked doing in the Missouri heat. There was a sign put up in the company's orderly room announcing a clerk/typist school. So I applied for that. I couldn't type worth a damn. The next sign that went up was for OCS prep school. So I put in for that and made it through the school. That was in New Jersey. I came out as a brand new 2nd lieutenant in charge of all the motor pools for Ford. We had 200 civilian drivers escorting vehicles around. We picked up GMC trucks and hauled radar destined for North Africa.

My dad served in France in WWI. I told my colonel that was where I wanted to serve. He told me that it wouldn't take me long to get there if I wrote a letter requesting a transfer. My wife was living with me out in New Jersey. Oh boy! Was she mad when she learned what I had done. Within a week I was back in Missouri with the 27th Signal Heavy Construction Company. My first choice was the Air Corps because I had a private pilot's license. My second choice was the field artillery

because I had studied that at Ames. But they put me in the Signal Corps.

We were shipped overseas to Scotland. I was the company executive officer. I had to do all the court martials and stuff like that. As the motor officer, I had to take all the mechanics to Liverpool to learn how to waterproof the trucks for the channel crossing. Bill Perdock was in charge of this big motor pool in Liverpool. He spent an hour driving me around the city showing me the sights.

We were in England about a month and a half before crossing the Channel. We landed at Omaha Beach about a week after D-Day. It was still an interesting place. We held up there waiting for the break out. Patton was put in charge of the 3rd Army. He was like a football player sitting on the bench, just chomping on the bit to get into the action. Our signal corps company was assigned to the 3rd Army. Our colonel told us it was our job to keep up with Patton. Well, the first day he went 50 miles! With Patton, you never went backwards, you always advanced. It'd be 40-50 miles a crack. We followed Patton across France to Paris, through

Holland, and to within 80 km of Berlin. My driver and I sold all our cigarettes and candy bars in Paris for fabulous prices when we went through. I'm a little ashamed of doing that, but that's what we did.

I had a big job. I was a supply sergeant in charge of wire and telephone supplies. I was put in with a black truck company. It was the best thing that happened to me because I didn't know a damn thing about black people. It was a good education. We had good cadre. We had a good outfit. The blacks had trained down in Ft. Hood, Texas. They performed superior to their white counterparts in every aspect. It just about killed them to hear people refer to blacks as not being fit for combat.

We had a black supply sergeant that was 45 years old. I asked him how he got in the Army at that age. He said it wasn't difficult to do in Texas. He had taken a white boy's place. He was not resentful in the least. He had gotten to visit London and Paris and soon he figured to see Berlin. He was sending more money home than his mother had ever seen before. He felt fortunate to be in the Army.

Question: Did you follow Patton when he did the pivot and head north to relieve Bastogne during the Bulge?

Before the 3rd Army headed north, I had to go into Belgium for signal supplies. On the way back we ran into a German Tiger tank. It came out of the forest on to the highway. He wasn't interested in us. We were just a jeep. The tank was looking for a convoy of food or gasoline. It crossed the road ahead of us. My driver was an uneducated kid from the south. He always said that if he saw a Kraut that he would run over him. So I turned to him saying, "There's your Kraut. Run over him!" He replied, "Don't you know what that mother is? That's a Tiger!" My driver turned around doing a wheelie. We drove back through Belgium and crossed the Meuse River. There were some British troops digging in a 57mm. One of them said, "I hear they're kicking the hell out of you Yanks down there." My driver told them they'd need something bigger than that to stop what was coming. Those Tigers had the 88mm. They were terrific guns.

We had to detour west through France to get back to my company. We met the 4th Armored Division of Patton's 3rd Army north of Nancy, France. The area was mountainous. It was cold and snowy. They were heading toward Bastogne. Not one damn jeep, 6X6 truck, or Sherman tank slid off the mountain or in a ditch. Those guys had been moving for 24 hrs straight and been in a fight the day before. In four or five hours they were in Bastogne. It was the most wonderful site I ever saw. I was just so proud to be an American on that day.

> *"We sure thanked Harry Truman when he dropped the bomb."*

After France and Holland, we didn't fight any more Germans than we had to. Patton never went back and destroyed the Germans. We'd go through them and just keep going.

We got shot at. We lost two men from land mines. The Germans would leave land mines anyplace where they thought our infantry might concentrate. Places like where railroads intersected roads were especially dangerous.

I enjoyed Europe but had no desire to go to the Pacific. We sure thanked Harry Truman we he dropped the bomb.

My rank was a 1st lieutenant when I was discharged. They would have made me a captain if I had stayed in. I wanted to come home and farm. I had been in Ames studying when I went in to the Army. I could have gone back to school and ended up being a county agent. But I had enough of standing up and trying to teach somebody something.

The real heroes don't brag that much. Do you know Art Witthoft? He was in the infantry. He was in a battle that lasted two days. They lost most of their company. What was left of the company was sitting around resting while the medics were picking up the dead. A general came up and asked to speak with the captain. Art, who was a sergeant, told him their captain got killed. The general looked around. There were only 12 guys left in the company. He gave Art a battlefield promotion to company commander. Art wouldn't tell you that story for the world. I didn't know it for a long time until his son finally told me. Art earned that promotion.

A Lieutenant Colonel

Bill Perdock
Washington, IA

872nd Ordinance Co.
Europe

Interview Date:
30 May 2010

Referral:
Dave Birney

I grew up on a farm four miles east of town. We had a dairy and delivered bottled milk to town every day. I joined after I got out of school. Actually, I enlisted the next day following graduation. It seemed like the right thing to do. That was in 1943. I went to OCS and came out a 2nd lieutenant and worked my way up to lieutenant colonel. I ran the 872nd Ordinance Company. I was a mechanic. I had experience working on cars before the war at Tucker's Chevrolet on the downtown square. I started working on cars right out of high school.

I was stationed in Omaha a while before going overseas. I was in charge of keeping vehicles repaired and running. My company was stationed in Liverpool, England, until after the invasion. Later we were in both France and Belgium. We were a technical company assigned to a headquarters and not attached to any division. We were close to the front lines. Nobody ever shot at me, but I was close enough to hear the shooting and artillery. I was involved in keeping the trucks and supplies moving. We worked on trucks, jeeps, DUKWs, and vehicles like that.

Comment: That was really important. Logistics are what win wars. Without supplies, armies surrender.

I met my wife Ellen when she was working as a waitress at Winga's Café. My mother was a Winga. I ran Perdock Motors after the war. I ended up in

the same building where I started working on cars. I had quite a career when I stop to think about it. I was also the commander of the local Army Reserve unit in Washington for several years after the war

Question; Do you remember hearing about the attack on Pearl Harbor?

Ellen Perdock: I remember my mother going outside and leaving the radio on. Usually she always turned it off when she left the house. So I was in there alone when the announcement came over the radio.

Never Saw Land

Walter Lance
Washington, IA

Navy
Pacific

Interview Date:
31 May 2010

Referral:
Dave Birney

I got drafted into the Navy in 1944. They went down the line (of the draftees) and said this many are in the Navy, the rest in the Army. I was married in 1940 and had a two year old daughter at home. I took my boots at Farragut, Idaho. It didn't amount to much. From there I went to Great Lakes and then Diesel School in Virginia for six weeks of training. Upon graduation, I had so many days to get to San Diego. Free transportation of course. I got to stop to see the family. After San Diego it was off to Hawaii.

I was in the amphibious force and a convoy was assembling ships for the invasion of Okinawa. There was a call out for a gasoline engine mechanic while we were waiting for the convoy to assemble. My CO came around and asked me if I knew anything about gas engines. I told him that I did and he suggested I volunteer for that position. I did and that's how I missed the invasion of Okinawa. I was there in Honolulu doing that for a year.

Then one day I received a notice that I had been reassigned as a diesel mechanic on a sub chaser. A sub chaser is a small boat with an ensign and 25 men and two depth charges on the back. The ship

was equipped with sonar and we spent a year at sea looking for Japanese submarines. That ship was so small that you had to be tied up on deck or it would throw you off. You couldn't stand up on deck.

We sunk two Japanese subs. I was stuck down in the engine room unless I was sleeping. When we'd locate a sub, the ship's captain would call down and tell us to shut everything down and don't even breathe hard. Then they'd drop the depth charges and get him. We must have been right over top of him.

It was kind of scary out in that big ocean. Every once in a while we'd get serviced by a big ship. We never saw land for at least eight months. That's a long time. We had no idea where we were. We nearly went crazy. All of us aboard ship thought we'd never make it home. Figured it was just a matter of time before the Japs got us so we were going to have all the fun we could. But about all you could do for fun was play cards in the sleeping quarters.

When the war ended, we went back to Pearl Harbor and I didn't have enough points to go home so they put me and another guy from Iowa on a mine sweeper headed for Japan. He didn't want to go and I didn't either. One night we were both on duty in the engine room. He says to me, "Walter, you go up on the deck and talk to the officer on duty and make sure he knows who you are." I asked him what he was going to do and he wouldn't tell me. That mine sweeper had two huge engines and the only way you could start them was by using compressed air. I was up on deck talking to the officer when the whole ship shuddered. That guy had reversed engines from full speed ahead to full reverse and ruined them. We were done. We didn't go to Japan. I think the only thing that saved the sailor that sabotaged the ship from getting into big trouble was that the officer didn't want to go to Japan either.

I received a battle star for each sub we sunk. The war was something that I wouldn't want to do again. It felt mighty good to finally get my feet on dry land. I didn't think the ensign captaining the sub chaser could even find dry land. I was discharged in January of '46. We were sent by train from San Diego to Minneapolis wearing only our tropics uniform. It was thirty below zero in Minnesota.

I can't begin to thank you enough for all you gave and sacrificed for your county. THANK YOU!! Thank you for your service, your sacrifice, your commitment to pushing back an evil the likes of which our world had never seen. You were young, you kissed your moms and sweethearts goodbye, hugged your dads and brothers, and you went half way around the world as boys and returned as men. You saw things that I'm sure you wish you hadn't, buried buddies you couldn't believe died & you may have done things you wish you hadn't been forced to do, but you did what you did to serve. So for that I say again Thank You so much for your service.

But what I found most astounding in addition to your feats of heroism and serving, those of you who returned home, went about making lives for yourselves. You taught school, you were doctors, farmers, business men & women. And you did so quietly without fanfare, and likely without complaint. If my dad, Kermit Hotopp, is any example, you did so without sharing the things you had experienced, often for many years. Thank you for blessing all of us not only by serving but by sharing your stories with Cheyenne & Larry, who are in turn able to share them with us. You deserve to have your stories heard.

Thank you again,

*LuAnn Fischer
(Daughter of Kermit Hotopp)*

Winfield, IA

How Do You Surrender?

Cecil "Cotton" Forinash
West Chester, IA & Knoxville, TN

Army, POW
Pacific

Interview Date:
5 June 2010

Referral:
Sharon Hahn

I went to the University of Iowa in 1935 and joined the Army ROTC. I joined ROTC because I needed the money. You had to take two years of ROTC back then at the University of Iowa. After two years of ROTC we got two hours of credit (for five hours of work in ROTC) and $7.00 a month. That paid my room rent. I enjoyed ROTC.

I changed my major from Liberal Arts to Business. Accordingly, I couldn't get enough hours. I took 18 or 20 hours for the next three semesters but I lacked four hours. The Thompson Act had a program in which you could go in competition for your Army commission. From there I went up to Fort Snelling, Minnesota, on that deal. But I still went on, and under the Thompson Act I didn't have to graduate. I came back from being a prisoner of war and completed my four hours and got my degree. That's where I stand on my degrees.

After the war, I went to Law School and became a lawyer. So I went back into the Army as a lawyer after having been in the infantry in the Philippines.

While in the Philippines, they asked for infantry observers. They took two people out of each regiment, and only two in my regiment could pass the physical. I was one of them, so I became an aerial observer. We were at Clark Field at that time. Before the war started we went down to Nichols Field.

I crashed up in the mountains over unexplored territory. I was just up there to fire the gun I had in the back as an observer at a towed target pulled by another plane. At about 6:00 in the morning and as we were ready to take off this tow target plane came in. Carpenter (the pilot) says, "Well, let's go on up and fool around." So we got up and fooled around, and I see a mountain on the left, a mountain on the right and a mountain straight ahead. And I was thinking I hope he's been here before, because I didn't know where we were going. He never said a word to me but all of a sudden the right wing hit something and catches fire. And we go in. Fortunately, he didn't dive in, he flew it in. The plane caught fire. I hit my head on the radio in front of me. I was bleeding like a stuck hog. I was stunned a little bit. I knew there was a fire and had better get out of this thing. I had my parachute on and I heard the pilot say, "Go out the back way. Go out the back way!" He couldn't get out. I only had a small amount of space between the top of the plane and my radio. I didn't think he could get out. I got out and he put his arms through and I put both feet against the fuselage and pulled and it didn't give. I said, "Get your parachute off and I'll get mine off because I can't pull you through the hole with the parachute on." So he took his off, I put my hands in his and put my feet back up against the fuselage. I pulled him completely out of the plane and he landed right on top of me on the ground. The pilot had burned his feet and his ears and his face from the fire.

The mountainous terrain behind us in the direction of Clark Field was straight up. He wanted to go over that and I said, "No, no, no, we can't do that. It is 100 feet high in the jungle. It's unexplored territory." I said we are going to the stream down to level ground. So we started downstream. This was early in the morning. Fortunately, the water was only around hip deep most of the time.

Well, we continued to walk until almost dusk out there in the water. My face was all bloodied. We still continued walking on down the trail way, and Carpenter said, "Oh, I've got sand in my shoes." His feet were burned, but he thought it was sand in his shoes and needed to stop. A Filipino soldier showed up and he was surprised to see that we were alive. He brought horses up with the so-called ambulance paddle to hold you in. They put us on those. We went down the trail for I don't know how far on those horses. It was quite a ways.

They had established a base camp, and they got us down to where the ambulances were, and they took us on into the hospital. We got in there about 1:00 AM. I said, "I'm going home." All I had was a cut on my forehead. And they said, "No, you're not going home. You have to stay in the hospital." I got up the next morning and I could hardly move. I was stiff and sore all over. I thought, "Boy, I'm glad I'm here." That was the only big incident that occurred while I was an aerial observer there at Fort Stotsenburg. It was an artillery post. Before that I had been at an infantry post down at Fort McKinley out of Manila.

So I continued on my duties there and we were flying a transport down to Nickles Field just out of Manila. We were supposed to fly at night and we always reported an unusual number of lights coming on down there as we were flying around looking, we could never spot where they were.

We never got them spotted. Of course we had to just assume that something was going wrong and finally we got this call in bed about 2 or 3:00 in the morning.

"Report to the squad room right away; the Japanese have attacked Pearl Harbor." I said, "Oh, no! Turn the radio on." So we turned the radio on. It was either December 6 or December 7 maybe in the Philippines. Everybody was reporting to the squad room and their planes and so forth.

About two or three days before we had a message; whether or not it was from The Department of State, Department of the Army, or the Chief of Staff, I have no idea. But the message said that the Japanese Ambassador to the U.S. had left Tokyo on two hours notice. He was sent over to make peace. He comes to the United States with no concrete proposals for peace whatsoever. His mission in the United States is to stall for time. Be on the alert.

The USS *Houston* (a cruiser) moved on out of Manila Bay, and we stayed with our airplanes. I never understood what happened. Since that time I have learned that the message was never sent to Hawaii. If that message had gone to Hawaii, I wouldn't have been a prisoner of war.

The following evening I had a call from the G-2 of the Air Force. He said, "We want you to go to the airfield and refuel and go straight to Lingayen and report what's going on. We have rumors that the Japanese are coming into the Lingayen Gulf." Lieutenant Lang was my pilot and he was supposed to get me there. But we got lost and went back to Nichols Field. I called the G-2 and told him what had happened. The pilot was lost, so I was lost too, but I wasn't in charge of that detail. So the G-2 said, "Alright. Refuel your plane, fly straight to Lingayen and when you run out of gas, jump." So I told the squadron commander that these were my instructions. I didn't know what he would say, and I had no idea whether I should do that kind of crazy thing. He said maybe try for the air field close by over by Stotsenburg. So we took off and we circled twice. I got my report and said there were about five ships there. I said there were two transports and what looked like two submarines and one destroyer. But I didn't see any activity like people unloading from ships or sea personnel.

We headed back for Clark Field. We made Clark Field and saw all of those burning B-17s that had been bombed and strafed. All we saw was four motors and a tail section. When Brady, the G-2, first briefed me, he was just so angry and so upset. He says, "When this thing happened at Pearl Harbor, I called the General (I assume MacArthur because he didn't say which one) and told him, "Have those B-17s loaded and ready to go to Taiwan right away. And he said, "No, no. no. We're going to let them hit us first." Oh, my God, how they hit us. And of course, they got the B-17s on the ground and some of the pilots got off. In any event, that was the beginning of the war.

Then I got a message to call into Clark Field. They said to wait awhile; they were going to have me do something else. So they called me at Stotsenburg, and told me they wanted me to take off over to Cabanatuan Airfield, leave them a message and fly straight back. So we delivered it and headed back to Nichols Field. We got about 40 or 50 miles, something like that, and I said to the pilot that we had a bunch of Japanese planes back there strafing us. The pilot asked what I wanted to do. He asked if I wanted to go up in the clouds and hide out or go low and straight to Manila. I said, "Let's go straight to Manila. Keep it low and go as fast as we can and get there." That old plane we were in couldn't last very long and I knew we couldn't stay in the clouds. He did that, and as we got in closer he went up in the air and got over McKinley and Nichols Field. A bullet went right between my legs. And I said, "By God, the Japanese have taken this place since I've been gone." I'd been gone since 6:00 that morning and this was now evening.

All of a sudden the motor stopped and the pilot said, "Ouch!" He told me, "I'm gone. You're out!" So I was hanging on, and they were still shooting at us. I had to turn loose because there was no way to get back in the plane. I was looking to see where the thing was on the parachute that you're supposed to pull. We started losing altitude I pulled the rip cord just as soon as I cleared the plane. Hell, they started shooting at me. They must have thought I was a paratrooper going to take the place, I guess. We were probably four or five

> *"While I was coming down I felt my back take a blow and thought, 'My God, they have shot me through the heart.'"*

(hundred) feet in altitude. While I was coming down I felt my back take a blow and thought, "My God, they have shot me through the heart." I landed near an American sergeant. He was with the 31st Infantry Regiment. I was on the ground and said, "Come and help me get out of this parachute because it is going to pull me away." He just looked at me. Pretty soon some other people came running up and said, "Call the chaplain. Call the chaplain." I said, "Call me a doctor!" And I passed out.

The next thing I remember is that I was in the hospital at Fort McKinley where they operated on me. On Christmas night of 1941, they came in this hospital and said, "Everybody who can walk, you can down to the port and we are going to take you out of here. We've got a boat a down there to take you out." I thought they meant the boat to go to Australia or something. I thought, "Oh, hell, I can walk." So I joined that group. It turned out that I was shot by an American bullet. The whole Philippine Division was down there. It was friendly fire, they thought we were Japanese.

The 57th Infantry Regiment of the Philippine Division was out at McKinley and my old regiment, the 45th Regiment was there, and I think the 1st Infantry Regiment was also out at McKinley to protect the air field. In any event, they put me on that ship, and I went over and sailed. This was after the Japs were bombing Corregidor, and they radioed us about the airplanes. "Don't worry about the airplanes, you're under our protection." We knew that wasn't true, we could see the anti-aircraft going off before it even got up to the plane. They finally got me ashore and put me in the hospital over there. I guess I was in there for a week, maybe. They released me for duty and I went back there to the 1st Air Corps and they didn't have any planes left. So I went back to see to see a Lt. Colonel and told him I wanted to go back with the Philippine Division. They were good; they were the best soldiers in the world, I think. He said, "You can't do that. I want to send you out with the Philippine Army." I said, "Colonel, I didn't come back here to go out with the Philippine Army." I was still in the Air Corps. He said they needed me with the

Philippine Army. I said I didn't want to go with them. Hell, they threw them a paper hat, and a short-sleeved shirt and a pair of shorts, and said, "Go, get 'em." I finally said, "Ok, Colonel, if you want me to go with Philippine Army I will do it." So that's how I wound up with the 31st Infantry Division, 71st Regiment of the Philippine Army.

The Japanese had already broken through the line at Abucay. As I understand, the Philippine Division was on the main road leading into Bataan, and the Philippine Division killed them and stopped them cold. The Japanese had to go back and regroup and bring in more troops.

I reported at that time to Colonel McKee, a West Pointer, I don't know why he selected me but he had me prepare a defense on Manila Beach where the Japanese came across Manila Bay and landed behind us on Bataan. Colonel McKee thought I had set up a good defense and he asked, "Have you been promoted?" The Air Corps didn't get promoted. He said, "You're going to get promoted right now. You're going to be a captain." So I became a captain.

From there we organized our defense. We had self-propelled artillery as well as regular artillery and tanks to support us because we were on the main road into Bataan. This was the Philippine Army, not the Philippine Division. The Philippine Division was made up of recruited Filipinos. That division got the best fighting people. They had doctors, lawyers, the chemists; they had the educated people. They made much more than they could make otherwise. They made the best first sergeants, best company clerks, best supply sergeants I ever had anything to do with. They would fight. They weren't going to be taken prisoner.

I thought we had the place about as ready as we could, and we had a lot of stuff going on. McKee, my colonel, said, "Forinash, you're going up to the headquarters and you're going to straighten out that damn front line. I was up there yesterday and it's a damn mess." I said, "Colonel, I can't do that, I'm just a captain." He said, "You're going up there tomorrow and straighten that up. And I'm telling Erwin that tomorrow you are coming up there to help him. So you go out there and straighten that damn line out. It's a mess." He was right it

was a mess. Your defensive weapon, primarily, is a machine gun. None of the machine guns were set up properly with fields of fire. They were supposed to have the wire down to protect that line. Hell, I knew that. None of it was there. All the soldiers were dug in and the machine guns were dug in and covered nicely, but they couldn't shoot far and they couldn't shoot right or left. So I asked the officers there, "Did you ever get down in there and sight those machine guns?" They said they didn't have any equipment. I said you go down there and look through there and see how far that gun will shoot and as high as you can get it. The top of the pit was on top of the gun; you can't shoot more than 50 yards out there. You aren't going to protect the line anyway.

I went back to see the colonel and he said, "Forinash, what did you think of it?" I said, "Colonel, you'd better get down on your knees and pray that the Japanese don't hit us on your command tonight. The Filipinos are gonna run. They are just going to go right on through." He said, "It wasn't that way two weeks ago." I said, "I don't know what it was like two weeks ago, I can just tell you what it is like now."

In the morning, an artillery officer was there at the headquarters and he was supposed to be telling us when the Japanese planes were dropping their bombs. I said, "Tommy, put your eye sights on those planes—they were headed right for our headquarters." He looked at them and said, "OK, they didn't drop anything." About five seconds later, it sounded like a freight train coming down. All five of us dove into a slit trench. They didn't kill anybody, as far as I know, but the Japs hit us. It didn't amount to anything, but that is one of the funny things that happen in war.

So the next day, the whole Philippine Division had been taken off the front line and brought back into reserve. Fortunately the Japanese didn't figure it out or they could have come right through us. At any rate, they broke through over at our left hand side and marched to Longuyanh.

I organized a defense on the beach in the town of Limay. There were these little huts standing right up to the beach. I told the engineers we can't stay there in case they set those huts on fire. I asked them to take out two rows of those huts so that at least we were protected from fire. Oh yeah, they set fire to it and the whole town burned. It was funny to me—the people were gone—but I am sure the people didn't appreciate that their houses weren't there when they came back. At any event, the Japanese broke through on our left.

We marched through Limay and headed on south. Then we went back to Limay and defended there. This all happened one night. Then we were ordered farther south to the Longuan River and arrived at first light. The Japanese were shooting and strafing us as we marched south. We didn't have any help. We tried to get each Filipino soldier to stay in his place and tell him to stay down there to defend the place but we wouldn't get more than ten yards away and they'd run off.

McKee was an interesting man. He wouldn't take cover; even when we were under artillery fire. I said, "Colonel, you know, I'll do anything I have to do when I am under artillery fire, but if I don't have anything to do, I am going to be in my fox hole." He said, "That's exactly where I want you to be." But he wouldn't do that. If an airplane was out there strafing bombs, he would be out there with his .45 shooting at those things with no chance of hitting them.

But when we got down to the river and the airplanes started strafing us, he hit the ground. I did too. He got up and brushed himself off and said, "Sorry, Son, I didn't mean to do that." That's a funny thing that happened. In any event, we worked there for a half an hour on the main line, trying to get people to stay. Nobody would stay. We were told that the general came and asked for a white flag. We saw him go by and surrender. So how do you surrender to another army? I don't know where the hell the other people were. The Filipino officers had taken off. We were all there by ourselves. A whole division, maybe nine thousand Filipino troops had taken off.

On Bataan our food situation was pretty bad. I was organizing the Filipinos along the beach. I was working them hard. We cut bamboo spears and one thing or another and tried to stop boats out in the water. They would say, "But, Sir, I am so hungry." I said, "I am hungry too but we've got to

> *"We were all there by ourselves. A whole division, maybe nine thousand Filipino troops had taken off."*

defend ourselves." We all only had two small meals a day. Everybody was getting hungry. We only had two weeks supply left when we surrendered on Bataan. MacArthur had left early on.

It didn't bother me that MacArthur left but it bothered the troops. I could understand—you aren't going to let them take your top man over there and put him in jail or prison. That made sense to me, but the soldiers —oh—"Dugout Doug" that damn coward. It was Roosevelt who ordered him to leave. The Filipino Army wasn't very good. They had a cardboard hat, shorts, a little blouse and tennis shoes and an Enfield rifle. I didn't want to join that kind of an outfit. We had American officers out there who, theoretically, were supposed to aid in the training but with no command responsibility. Of course, we took over and ran this battalion like we had on the beach, across the front line. Colonel McKee called all the shots. He had a Filipino Lt. Colonel or Major and a lot of Lieutenants but they didn't know what they were doing. But we had some American officers teaching the companies and they are the ones I held responsible. But there wasn't anything we could do.

I got malaria there at the end. How do you surrender to another army? Here I am out there at Longuan River standing on the road and nobody was there but me. I took my damn gun out and I just laid it down on the ground and decided to just stay here. So I did. I was all by myself. So I waited and up came a couple of Japanese soldiers. They wanted my pocketbook so I gave it to them. It didn't have that much money in it anyway but I had some. They took my pocketbook, took the money, gave me my pocketbook back, and took a ring off my finger and they didn't stay anything. So we went out to the road and other people were heading toward this place and off to the side they were gathering the prisoners from Bataan. They must have gotten 1,500 POWs in that area. I saw all those Japanese machine guns around there and thought if you tried to stay and fight there you'd be dead in a jiffy.

Comment: That had to be a little terrifying.

No, no, I wasn't scared. You were just relaxed and just doing whatever they told you to do and hoped for the best. I never got scared. I was never scared at any time. During combat I knew to get in the foxhole because I didn't want to be killed.

They finally gathered about 1,500 or 2,000 of us. All kinds of people were there. They started us down the road and late at night they halted us on the road. We stayed on the road that night. I think the next day we got rice three or four times as we were walking out of Bataan. Anybody could have escaped; there was no problem in getting away. But where are you going to go? What do you do? Now some people did go and got away with it. I don't know how they did it. In any event, I didn't know anybody with me.

The lack of drinking water was a big problem on the march. After the first night it was obvious the Japanese guards would shoot prisoners. The Americans had reason to be disciplined. The Filipino soldiers would get out of line to get fetid water and the guards would shoot them. I never saw them shoot an American. At least they were a little better disciplined than that. Their water discipline didn't turn out very well because they wound up with diarrhea and dysentery when they got to Camp O'Donnell.

> "They must have gotten 1,500 POWs in that area. I saw all those Japanese machine guns around there and thought if you tried to stay and fight there you'd be dead in a jiffy."

I think about the second night I ran into Colonel Erwin who had been the commander of that sub-sector. He was carrying a big ole knapsack on his back—must have weighed 30, 40 or 50 pounds. I said, "Colonel, don't try to carry that thing out of here. I don't know how far we are going to walk and you don't either. You better get rid of that thing." Nobody was carrying anything but him. "Oh no, I've got to take this out of here. I've got to have this stuff." We went into one of the towns the second night, Orion, probably. We were packed in real tight; no one could lie down or sit down. The next morning Colonel Erwin says to me, "Forinash, I don't think I can live with it." I said, "You know, Colonel, they announced over the speaker system that anybody who couldn't walk could report into a little hut just outside the gate where they brought us in." I was pleased with that and I thought they were serious about it and I went with him and took him over to that little place and left him. The prisoners left and I fell back into the march. His

story is that when I got to O'Donnell I kept looking for him to come in, I wasn't sure he could make it because he wasn't in condition anyway. The Colonel didn't come in, I knew that. I finally found somebody who claimed they saw him and said that he went out of his head and had bought it. That's all hearsay. It's not from me. It's from somebody else and that's the best I can do.

We left the 9th and got in there the 15th of April. The last night the Filipino people were still trying to help us. They had water out there that we could dip our cups into but the guards would beat the hell out of anyone who tried. The Filipinos would throw us sugar cane to eat and the guards would beat the hell out of us. You had to get whatever water any way you could. One of the miracles I had, that I know of for myself, was when I would reach into my pocket as I was walking down on Bataan in this march…I felt in my pocket and I found a bottle of iodine! I thought how in the world did I ever get that? I hadn't been wounded and was alright and there was no reason for me to have a bottle of iodine. I hadn't used it and there it was! So for me it was a miracle. I thought, well, maybe I could put it in the water and maybe it would work. So every time I got a little bit of water I put a little bit of iodine in it. I didn't have dysentery or diarrhea and like so many of them did have. You would see people in that state and they just didn't live long.

We walked to San Fernando. The last part of the trip was by train. They packed us into steel boxcars. They loaded us at night. We stayed there until the morning and the sun got hot. People on the outside were yelling move out, I'm getting burned. But there wasn't any place to move. They had us packed in there so tight that people died and were still standing up. We took about a four hour trip then, and they kept the doors closed on us the entire time. I don't know how many they carried out dead.

In any event they then took us from there over to a school yard and we spent that last night of the journey there. On the 15th we walked the five or six miles into O'Donnell. When I went in, I didn't know anybody there. We got in there and a little

Japanese captain told us, "This is the first phase of a Hundred Years War. My children will fight your children; we will fight you again until we finally defeat you." I thought, that's the message I am going to carry home. This thing is not over. I said to whoever was next to me, "Obviously if this is the first phase, they don't expect to win that one." I was serious about it.

Water was again a problem. There were several thousand people there and one faucet. People were lined up to get water and everybody carried four or five canteens down to stand in line to get water. The kitchens had the priority over the water and when they wanted the water they would come and get it. In the morning you got rice wet-cooked sort of like oatmeal (no milk of course) and not very much of it. Again at lunch you got rice again. In the evening you got a little watery soup with nothing in it. You got that three times a day for the rest of your time there.

At O'Donnell I got malaria. I think I had it on the trip in. There was no quinine, no medication. I suffered through that for a while. Then somehow some quinine appeared, and I'd get one tablet. Doctors didn't have anything. I took that pill, and it stopped my chills and fever. If you've ever had chills and fever from malaria, you'd recognize it.

So O'Donnell got 6,000—6,500 Americans in there. In six weeks 120 of them died. We calculated to see from where we stood how many days it would take before we were all gone. The Filipinos were dying 500-600 a day. They were kept separate from us. They were undisciplined. Of course you had the water problem improve but it never did get good.

I managed to survive O'Donnell with the four or five quinine pills that people gave to me. We spent six weeks at O'Donnell then moved over to Cabanatuan, and that was just as bad. I always wished I had a photo of something we saw when we were in Cabanatuan. The Japanese soldiers would have severed Filipino heads carried on a bamboo pole between them and singing their sing-song Japanese as they watched the line. Can you imagine cutting their heads off and putting them on bamboo poles and marching along the road to

> *"The Japanese soldiers would have severed Filipino heads carried on a bamboo pole between them and singing their sing-song Japanese as they watched the line."*

our camp with Filipino heads? Oh, I would have give anything for a camera so people would realize what the Japanese were like.

I started getting malaria over there just like at O'Donnell. Someone would have a pill to give me. Finally, I reached the point where they couldn't find any pills. I got malaria again. No one had pills as far as I knew. I went to the so-called hospital; I went over there to die. A captain I knew from my outfit comes by the hospital bed I was in so I said, "Where in the world have you been? I haven't seen you since we were on Bataan." I never saw him march out and knew absolutely nothing of where he was. He had two five grade tablets of quinine. He gave me two and that's a pretty big hit for a prisoner of war. I can imagine that he might also get it and need it, but he didn't. So I took a pill that killed the chills and fever for a while until they put me out in the sun. When I was well enough to leave the hospital I was on orders to catch the next Japanese ship to go to Japan.

So Colonel McKee, who was up with me on Bataan he came up to see me. He says, "Forinash, we are on the list to go to Japan. I know whoever is running this and they will take me off and you off if we want to." I said, "You leave me where I am on the list." And he does. The doctor told me I would also have to go through treatment if I ever got home to kill this malaria bug. He added, "I'm gonna sweat it out here." I said, "Colonel, they aren't going to let you sweat it out here. They're gonna take you to Japan." I said, "Just leave me on this list. I need to get out of here." And he did. He was killed on one of the ships going up later. So not that I was smart but I had a pretty good idea that was going to happen when they started moving us to Japan. The only people left behind ultimately were the people too sick to move. They took all the able-bodied, well, not able-bodied….

I was put on the Nagato Maru in the Philippines down in the hold. It must have been two hundred degrees down there. With 500 people in each hold there was no room to sleep and people couldn't sit down. It was awful and people were going crazy. As the trip went along there was yelling and screaming. They'd drop a bucket down for what you needed to do. Once in a while they would give you a rice ball down there. Finally after about three days out they finally opened the damn hold and let a hundred or so of us go up and be on deck for a little while and then put us back. Then they let another hundred up. I can't explain to you, no way, nobody could ever tell you what went on down in the hold of a boat with four or five hundred people. People were going out of their minds, screaming and carrying on. I don't know how many people died.

We sailed to Taiwan or Formosa or whatever you want to call it. As we were going along they had military pieces strapped on the front and the back of that ship for protection. I assume they had some Navy stuff too but that's all we could see as I walked on the deck. I could see 75mm artillery shells, but I didn't think it would be too bad because they couldn't calculate the roll of the ship. We would hear them shooting that thing every now and then from below deck. I think they were practicing.

I can't tell you about the trip. The slaves coming over from Africa probably had it worse than we did. They are the only people I can imagine who ever had it any worse. They held us in Taiwan for two or three days, I think, because our submarines were out there. They finally took us off and we arrived at Moji, Japan. When I got off that ship I fell flat on my face. I was about the weakest I have ever been in my life. And a couple of people helped me out and got me to the railroad train or streetcar. It was pitch dark. They packed us in those cars as tight as you could get anybody in anything. They pushed you in there. They kept pushing you until they couldn't get anybody else in. We went to Osaka.

There were 1,500 of us and they divided us into groups. I went to a factory where there were about half a dozen things they were making. I happened to be on the line that galvanized the steel metal that was coming through for barrels or whatever they were using them for—two different gauges. I was a captain and had 14 people assigned to me. Theoretically officers were not supposed to be worked. We told them that and they said alright, you don't have to work, but you don't eat either. That changed your mind whether you wanted to

work or not. So we worked on this detail. I was on the business end of taking care of a furnace, smelting the galvanizing material. One time that galvanizing material caught me right here and I still got a scar there. It burned right into my skin. First they let me go in and have some doctor pick it out. I was lucky to be in charge of that detail. Of course, I had to work. They were dying so fast that I kept telling the boss there—I would say he was a non-commissioned officer— I kept telling him how many were dying, that we're starving to death and can't work.

I lived right above right where I worked. I'd say, "Another one's gone dead. We can't do this. You have to get us something to eat." You wouldn't believe this but he brought in a 26 kilo bag of rice. I cooked it on my furnace door. I had my canteen cup and he put a little rice in the bottom of that cup and boy before long we had the best rice you ever tasted in your life.

When they got special rations he and some of the other Japanese would give us their special rations, maybe a little something. I still had 14 people when I left that detail and other people were dying but I thought I took care of them pretty good.

At Christmas we got one Red Cross box to divide between three prisoners. There was no heat. It was cold. Most of us got beriberi of some kind or another. Either you got wet beriberi which is where your legs would swell or the dry beriberi and that turned out to be worse apparently. I had the dry beriberi. Some of the guys would put their feet in cold water to get relief. Well, they'd get a break in their skin and develop gangrene. The toes or the bottoms of the feet would fall off. I was smart. We were upstairs and our kitchen was down below and it had a concrete floor. I went down and walked on that cold concrete. I don't know why, I just did it that way. And I didn't have any problems with my feet.

It was so bad they had to put us in camps. Americans were almost as bad as the Japs in Japan—taking a ration of cigarettes. I can't believe that would happen to people but it did. Americans would be issued four or five cigarettes a month and the people that didn't smoke would trade them for rice. People were starving to death already. Even

> "People were going out of their minds, screaming and carrying on. I don't know how many people died."

our so-called hospital traded these cigarettes. I told my guys, "Look we are not getting into that stuff now, don't you dare do that."

I went to his commanding officer there and told him that if he didn't put out an order to prohibit anybody from trading rice for cigarettes that I was going to have him tried by court martial when we came home. He put out the order but nobody complied with it. At Cabanatuan and O'Donnell it got so bad on the distribution of the rice that I complained about it so much that they put me in charge of the mess. I told those people in there before I left Cabanatuan that I don't want any one of you to get one more grain of rice than anybody else we are feeding here. If I catch you, you are out of here and you will no longer be on this detail. Of course after we got out of there it was beyond my control. But everybody was complaining that the kitchen was getting all the rice and that kind of stuff. You could believe that when you were hungry and nobody is around. I could understand how they would want to get more of it. But I said nobody gets more and I am going to be watching and that's the way it is. We ran an honest kitchen for once; at least everybody knew it was honest. I was only there six weeks before I got on the boat and went to Japan.

I was there from November to June at this factory. They sent most of the officers down to Zensuji where an army barracks had been. They had enclosed part of the army barracks with two other buildings behind a wire fence and then a wooden fence. The prisoners there were eating high on the hog. They had beans in their rice and received a loaf of bread for lunch. They were looking pretty good. They saw us coming in and they couldn't believe that we were so bad off. We were fed this bread and rice for about six weeks and then they stopped it. The Japanese cut us back to 380 grams of rice a day. And I had a rice can, a little ole jelly can, about that round, that high, packed three times a day plus a little watery soup with no meat. Otherwise, Zentsuji was a relatively stable camp. People were being treated better although I got my hair pulled out a couple of times, and a little Jap hit me, and of course I would just fall down. I had a man on my detail—what's his name—I thought I would ever forget it—I caught this little Japanese soldier beating him on the face

and he—Krantz was his name—he was making his face a pulp because he wouldn't go down. I said, "Boy, Boy, Boy, that's crazy. Just go down. That's all he wants." I told him, "You don't need to do that, just fall over; we aren't going to think any worse of you—just don't let him beat you to death." He said, "I wouldn't let that little S-O-B have the pleasure of knocking me down." In any event, the first time they hit me, I went down. I wasn't gonna stand there and let them beat me up. There's nothing you can do about it. That was my philosophy. Maybe it was the wrong philosophy.

The reason for striking a prisoner is that the Japanese had rules…if you breathed they had a rule that you broke! Under the Geneva Convention the Japanese were supposed to pay the officers the same pay as the Japanese received. So finally they decided they were going to pay us 50 yen a month and put the rest in the bank. We didn't have anything to buy with money. But you could only have 50 yen. All the officers ignored that rule and played bridge and poker and black jack—all kinds of stuff. And they didn't make us work. I was pretty good at cards. I had thousands and thousands of yen but they weren't worth anything. So I told Carl Walsh from Cedar Rapids, we were good friends over there, I said I'm going to run a casino game. I took all my yen and you know they cleaned me out in one night! But another night I was playing black jack. I was the dealer. I guess when it ended they were going to count us. They were supposed to tell you when the Japanese guard walked through. I didn't get a notice and I was paying off Bob Ray from Cedar Rapids, Iowa. He was a fighter pilot. He was a big fella, I don't know how he ever got into the cockpit of a P-40, but he did. While I was paying him off in walks this Japanese guard. We had much too much yen when we were only supposed to have 50 yen. So they took us over to this little wooden jail. It was November and it was colder than hell. They took our clothes off and put us in the cell. If you ever saw two people get close together—that was it. Bob was worried about it. I said, "Ah, don't worry about it. They'll let us out after they count everybody off." After muster, the Japanese officer came out and looked at us and grinned and left. So my prediction didn't work out. But 1:00 the next morning he came out and gave us our clothes back and we went back to our barracks.

There was an army bakery just beyond the two fences and you could smell it. Obviously they were getting different food than us. Finally people started going under the fences over to that bakery. They had been doing it for a long time. Carl Walsh and Bob Ray and the other Iowans got together and decided to make an attempt. On our first try, we let the guards go by. So Carl said, "I'll go." And he made it over there. That was our trip to the Japanese bakery.

One time they said they had thrown a whole batch of rice away because it had rat poison in it. So Lou Lazzarini and myself, he's a chemical man, decided we'd find it. He said, "I can identify any poison. I can tell you if there is any poison there." So we got our empty Red Cross boxes and we went down and got a whole box full of rice. Then everybody else started going down there after we did. We didn't have any trouble with the rice. There was nothing in foreign in it so we had some extra rice for a while.

In Zentsuji, an artillery captain named Smith, Dillard, a pursuit pilot, and Lazzarini, a captain in the Chemical Corps, and myself all decided that if the food got so bad that we thought we couldn't make it, we were going to escape. The only way we were going to escape was to raid the rice warehouse first. If we didn't get the rice, we'd come back in. You could get out of these places. There was no trick to getting away—but what you did after you got out was the problem of course.

So we had that agreement at Zentsuji that if one of us left we were all going. Oh I didn't tell you about the ten people that were in the Philippines. They put you in groups of ten. They had this rule that if one escapes, they would shoot the other nine. Of course you informed your other nine, "If you want to escape, fine with us. But you let us know so that we can go too."

I want to tell you another story about this. Seven prisoners had gone out of the prison camp and were coming back in when they got caught. The Japanese took these soldiers and tied their arms behind their back and tied them to a fence post. The first one was about 30 – 40 yards out. The guards put them out there in the sun and left them there. Of course, there wasn't anything that we could do about it. We were right where we could see them. So one of them broke loose from his restraints and took off running. He ran for water because he was dying from thirst, of course. After catching him, the guards took the other six down, put four of them on my side where I could see them and took three over there to the hospital where we couldn't see them. The four on my side were made to dig their own graves and then they were shot. I was told they did the same thing to the other three prisoners over on the other side.

We moved from Zentsuji in June of '45 and moved up to Rokuroshi up in the mountains north of Fukui. They had us go out in a garden and clean a spot off so they could raise vegetables. Food had gotten pretty scarce by then. Towards the very end, we four discussed making our escape. We weren't going to live through another winter. But the sky was on fire. It was American bombers. I said, "No, this war is about to end. I'm not going to take off now. " Louis Lazzarini said he wasn't going either. The other two had to made their escape without us.

They took off and I heard the dogs barking all around the warehouse. We had no idea there were dogs posted there. We had agreed that if they couldn't get any rice or supplies that they would come back. But they didn't come back and we thought they'd gone on. I saw them returned hog-tied later the next day. The Japanese wanted them to show how they had escaped. Anybody could escap,e but the problem was what to do when you got out of there. This was about two days before the end of the war.

I saw both Dillard and Smith after the war. So I asked them what had happened, and they said, "Oh we thought we could get rice at that warehouse and those damn dogs kept barking at us so we decided we were just going to go on in anyway." They walked all night and couldn't find a place to hide. A young boy saw them early in the morning and they knew then that the jig was up. On the train down to the prison camp the Japanese told them they would try them and shoot them. That was their story. Any way, they got back.

Let's see, I didn't tell you about at Rokuroshi, they decided to put the officers on the honey bucket detail. Our colonel went down to complain. He said, "You can't do that. First you are not supposed to work us and secondly you can't put us on the honey bucket detail." They said, "Your country has used a new and illegal weapon against us. We have complained to Geneva about it and you will do this."

We got back to the building and Gene Conrad said, "By God, I bet they dropped an atomic bomb on them!" And we said, "An atomic bomb? What are you talking about?" And I never did find out until l later. I said, "How did you guess that they used an atomic bomb on them?" He said, "I read an article in the newspaper and it talked about the conceivability of something like that being developed." I didn't know we had dropped an atomic bomb on them until Conrad guessed it. We could see the glow. We were up in the mountains. I could see Fukui burning. I wasn't worried about the Japanese killing us when the war ended.

So the Japanese commandant had gotten us all together and I think maybe it was the 16th of August. He said that the Emperor had brought peace to the world. We knew what he meant. All the Japs left and we took over the camp. We went downtown. We got some sake and all the food we could find. Then on September 2nd, our B-29s flew over and dropped all these 55 gallon drums of food, two of them welded together. They were bombing us with food! Of course the officers stayed there and the enlisted men went on to downtown Tokyo and that kind of thing. But we were told to stay where we are and they would come and get us. So we stayed but they didn't come until September 8th.

The relief people spent the night as I recall. An American officer died that night. He was a friend of mine. He had been ill and he died the night that they got there at the camp. They came in and took a look at us just to see who could travel and who couldn't. But most of us could travel at that point in time.

They put us on a train and we rode to Yokohama. General MacArthur was down there. He had tears in his eyes when he saw us getting off. He said he had never seen such a rag-tag outfit.

I weighed about 155 or 160 when the war started and I got down to about 110 or maybe 100 pounds. I was skin and bones. When I got back, I decided I wanted to go to Yokohama and get a shower and a clean uniform. A lot of people said they were going to wait there for an airplane. I said I am going

home, and I am sure I am getting on one of those ships. The instructions were that the kitchen is to be open at all times for the prisoners of war. So any time we wanted, we could eat. So I got on a ship.

They took us on ships in the Philippines to process us. They gave us uniforms, awarded some medals and so forth.

Question; How long did malaria give you trouble?

Sixty-three years later, about two or three weeks ago, I got these awful chills and fever. They had told me that if I ever get home I needed to take a course (of meds) to kill that malaria or they will lie dormant in you forever. I forgot all about that. This one night I got this awful temperature and it went up to 104.9 degrees. I went to the hospital and they couldn't find anything wrong. No flu, no infection, no bug, but they put me in the hospital anyway. They put me on antibiotics, two or three initially, for two days. The doctors were dosing me with antibiotics and my legs got as red as blood all the way up. I still have part of it, it hasn't gone away yet.

I finally told the doctor that I had tropical malaria. He was initially skeptical. Hopefully the antibiotics took care of the malaria. According to medical experts, the record for malaria lying dormant is 37 years. My malaria bug came back after 63 years!

I retired from the Army in 1969 as a colonel in the Judge Advocate Department. I never talked about the war unless I had to.

Interview transcribed by Kathy Tanner

CONDUCTIVE TOUR OF GERMANY

Harold Stephens
Washington, IA

30th Infantry Division
Europe

Interview Date:
11 June 2010

Referral:
Dave Birney

Well, I never quite got to the hero class, so don't expect too much.

I enlisted in 1942. I was 18 or 19 years old. I did my basic training down at Camp Robinson, Arkansas. I did my officer training at Fort Benning. I came out with a "shaved tail". The officers wore epaulets on their shirts, and they took our shirts down to the tailor and cut the tail off to make an epaulet.

I was in the 30th Infantry. I came into Italy as a replacement. Everybody was a replacement. When I checked in, I asked my company commander whose place I was taking. He said, "that good looking man lying there under that blanket." That was my first mistake.

We were part of the southern invasion of France. We landed down in the Marseille area. Originally they wanted us to invade right after (they went in at Normandy), but they found out that they didn't have enough equipment or power to invade at both locations right then. So they went ahead with D-Day and then our outfit came in there in southern France (Operation Dragoon in August 1944).

As we moved north we encountered the 19th Germany Army at Montélimar. They had a lot of horse drawn vehicles—horses that they had confiscated off the French. We attacked them, the Air Corps attacked them, the armored attacked them, everything. Well, when it was over with there was a 5 mile stretch with a thousand dead horses. It was a mess.

We went on north from there through Lyon and Bescanon, then we cut into the Vosges Mountains at Saint-Die. We got up there in the hills and were there several days, and I don't think the Germans ever knew we were there. We were getting ready to pull out and go back to reserve, but they sent me on a patrol to a little town at a road junction. They told me to go down there and secure the road junction and then get back up to the line and we would pull out at four o'clock. Well, we got down there and everything hit the fan. I was down there for two days trying to get out! And the bad part was that a whole new division was in the woods right behind us. Mag Ahmling was there. I didn't know it at the time. I always gave Mag a hard time, too…sitting up there and he wouldn't help me! But of course he didn't have anything to do with it.

We pulled out of there and went on up to the Strasbourg area and then started back down towards Colmar. We went into a little town called Kaiserberg. I think that's where Albert Schweitzer came from. We got there and went into a house. A guy came out and was more than happy to see us. He said he didn't have much but we were more than welcome to anything that he had.

That night we started hearing shells coming in. One would be short and the next one would be long. We could tell they were adjusting. I said that there has to be an observer down here some place. One of our guys went down into the basement and that dude was down there with a radio. He was calling (in our position)! Let's just say we took him out and counseled him. That was the 16th of December, and that's when the Battle of the Bulge started.

We started out the next morning around daylight. A shell came in right beside me and I got hit in the head. It hit me on the right side of the head, tore my helmet off and I started to go blind. I was carrying a Thompson submachine gun and it was in two pieces. I don't know if something hit it or if it just came apart. A little guy beside told me to grab onto his belt and took me to the aide station. That night an ambulance came and I went to the field hospital and then on to a regular hospital.

I was in the hospital for about a week before returning to regular duty. Eventually we ended up in a little town called Holtzwihr. We were issued snowsuits, and they were green on one side and white on the other. We were told that I-Company was going to come down and give us hand with the town. I went out into the street and I saw a guy down the road wearing a snowsuit. And I thought, "well, there's I-Company down there now." Trouble was, that guy took a shot at me! The Germans had been given snowsuits, too. I ducked into a little house and I could hear them (the enemy) coming. I was going to bail out a window to go back toward the street, but then I saw some guy out in the street get all shot up. That didn't look too good, so I figured I'd better find some other way out of the house. I got into a little hallway and thought I could shoot my way out because I had done that kind of thing before. I opened the door and there was a German tank pulled right up in front of me. The .88 on that tank looked as big as a tuff bottom. I dropped my weapon and went out and they took me in. I thought I was probably the only one that got caught.

I learned the next morning they had captured my

whole outfit. They had my company commander, I-Company, the whole bunch. This is when I started my conductive tour of Germany. The next night they took us across the river to Freiburg, Germany. The placed us in a building that was kind of like a stable. There was water on the floor because the heat from us humans was melting the snow.

We came down with dysentery in there, and I'll tell you what, it was something else. We had a senior officer, Colonel Huff, with us. There was also a doctor that they had captured, too. Some of the guys were taking care of their business right outside the door. The next morning Col. Huff ordered them down to the latrine about 50 yards away. He told them they had to make it to the latrines. The next day the doctor told the Colonel that he couldn't ask us to pucker up long enough to get down to the latrines. When I came down with it during the night, it was all over as far as I was concerned. I heard these guys cussing and yelling and there came the Colonel and the doctor, both with their pants down. Geez, it was terrible.

> "Our food allotment at Hammelburg was 9/10th of a quart of soup a day. ...It had little white worms in it, and we called that the protein."

Eventually, they loaded us up in 40 & 8 box cars, meaning 40 men or 8 horses. They hauled us to Hammelburg and I was there for about 6 weeks. At that camp, right across the fence from us was the Serbian POW camp. I think the Germans took the whole Serbian army prisoner.

Our food allotment at Hammelburg was 9/10th of a quart of soup a day. The soup was boiled parsley or something like that. We called it "green hornet". It had little white worms in it, and we called that the protein. We also had coffee every once in a while.

General Gunther von Goeckel (the German camp commandant), lived just outside the post. He had a cat. We assigned duties to one another, and every day we had to go out and take turns calling that cat try to get it to come over. Well, I wasn't on duty, but the next day we had a stew with little chunks of meat in it and I never saw that cat again. I didn't ask any questions.

We had a few downed pilots come through the

camp. One of them, Jesse Jumper, had a gift of gab. He went down and told Gen. von Goeckel that they couldn't hold him prisoner because he was illegally drafted. He came from the Jones-free-state-of-Mississi-black-god-ippi and it never joined the Union. So they didn't have any right to draft him to start with. Von Goeckel didn't buy that.

Every morning they would haul us out and line us up for a count. Those German guards weren't the sharpest knives in the drawer. The guard would go down the line counting "*eins, zwei, drei…,*" and a couple of us would scoot together and he wouldn't come out right. He'd have to count again.

For some reason they gave us a toothbrush and toothpaste. I don't know why, because we didn't have anything to eat. One day after he counted us a bunch of times, one of the guys put a bunch of that toothpaste powder in his mouth and swished it around and got it foaming. He got down on the ground and started gyrating and squirting that stuff out of his mouth. We all hollered "*Ein man Krank!* (He is sick!)" They carried him into the barracks and after he settled down they had to count again.

At Hammelburg, that's where Patton sent the task force in. His son-in-law was there, but he said he didn't know that. He said he was just going to let some people out of a POW camp. The task force went in and got everyone out that wanted to go. There was supposed to be an air drop that night of fuel so that we could get back to the American line, as we were about 60 miles past the front line. But the clouds rolled in and the Air Corps couldn't drop any fuel. So we all got stuck and got re-captured, along with Patton's task force. All except for Col. Waters, Patton's son-in-law. They got him out with one of those little artillery observer planes. The rest of us didn't get out.

Question: What were the German guards doing all that time?

They were heading for high ground! We had one guard that claimed he came from Jersey City and that he owned a hamburger joint there. He had come to Germany to visit some relatives and they decided to keep him and put him in the army. He

> *"We ended up going right through downtown Nuremburg. The Germans were so busy putting out fires and picking up bricks that they didn't pay any attention to us."*

had his suitcases all packed up, ready to go back to Jersey City!

From Hammelburg we were sent to a prison camp just outside of Nuremburg. My buddy Tom and I decided we'd better take off again. We bailed out one night and we were looking for a place to hide out until the next morning. We found a big mound of dirt—it looked like a levy or something. We got to the top of it and there was a bomb crater that was big enough for both of us to get in. So we stayed in it until the next morning. At daylight we decided we'd better peek out over the edge to see where we were. We were right in the middle of the rail yards in Nuremburg! Around noon the American Air Force flew over and dumped about half a dozen bombs on that rail yard. The concussion was terrible!

We didn't have a map, so the next night we started following the tracks until we came to the Autobahn, which was 8 lanes wide. We followed the Autobahn and before long we were right in the middle of Reich Stadium (Nazi party rally grounds). We were hidden up under the stage. They must have been torturing someone while we were there because there was a lot of screaming. We though, "boy, we'd better get out of here!" We ended up going right through downtown Nuremburg. The Germans were so busy putting out fires and picking up bricks that they didn't pay any attention to us.

We got out into the country and decided that we'd better hide for the day. We came into a timber and crawled under some bushes and were going to take turns watching while the other one slept. At one point while I was sleeping Tom thought he heard something. We got up and started looking around and saw some German soldiers wearing helmets and everything. We started looking around, and good land, they were all around us. The timber was just full of 'em. One guy had his squad lined up on a path, and Tom said we should go up to him and tell him that we were from the prison camp and we were lost. So we tried to communicate with him, but he didn't know what we were talking about and we couldn't understand him, either. He didn't really say anything, he just stood there and grinned. So we decided to just keep walking. We soon came to a road filled with displaced persons (D.P.s) pulling carts and riding bicycles. We got in line with them, but it wasn't long before a German officer came and recognized us. He said, "where are you boys going?" We said we were from the POW camp. He said, "ok, I'll see that you get there." He started walking us back to Nuremburg. On the way we asked him what was going on in the timber. He said it was a training school for NCOs (Non-Commissioned Officers).

He took us back to a hotel in Nuremburg and sat us down in the lobby. We sat there, smoking, and he kept asking us where our troops were. We said, "Oh, out there. They'll be along here in a little bit." Man, after we said that they had generals and colonels and everybody else in the hotel burning papers and clearing out. Pretty soon a doctor came in that spoke English. He told us that he had interned in Rochester, New York. He said, "Where are your troops really?" We said we didn't know—we hadn't seen them for three months!

They proceeded to get us out to a POW camp. Right over the fence of the compound were the Russians. Those poor guys were starving, just like a bunch of dogs. The Germans would haul out a wagon load of them every morning.

A Serbian doctor got hold of Tom and me and asked us if we had gotten our typhus shots. We told him no. He said there were all these guys dying of typhus, and he could get us a shot of the serum. Where he got it, I don't know. He had a syringe that looked like a grease gun, and he gave us the shot right between our shoulder blades.

The Germans decided they were going to move us to another location. Tom thought he should go to the nearby town and talk to the Burgermeister (mayor). He told him that he should get things straightened out, hang white sheets out the windows and such. He told him that he'd see to it that the American troops wouldn't get him when they came into town, because they were going to be there very soon. Well, he sold him on it. When the German guards found him, he was sitting in the mayor's office smoking a cigar.

I sneaked off and went down the road a ways to a hospital. I was going to tell them that I was in really bad shape. I didn't see anybody in the office

so I started wandering down the hall and found a door part way open. Some guys were lying around in there, so I looked in and said, "You guys aren't German, are ya?" One said, "Nah, we're British." They had been captured way up by Dunkirk, France. They had been there for years. There was an empty bed and they told me that the nurse, Sister Ellie, was nice. I shook the dust off and went to bed. Sister Ellie thought the doctor put me in there, of course, so I got something to eat. I was there for a day or two, and she kept taking my temperature. She finally said she was going to have the doctor come in and see me the next day. I told her that would be alright. That night I jumped out the window and took off.

A few days later I could hear our artillery coming in, so I knew they were getting close. One night there was an American patrol that came through the area. I just tagged in on the end and followed them right back to the American line. They had the password to get back there and they got me in. I couldn't join their outfit because I didn't have any identification, so they sent me back to Counter Intelligence. I had to be processed. I then was sent to a hospital in England and they fattened me up a bit.

Question: Bronze Star? Purple Heart?
Yep. And a POW medal. Boy, did I earn them.

Interview transcribed by Heather (McCall) Roth

BETTER THAN MOST

Cal Wolf
Washington, IA

Japanese Code Breaker, Navy
Pacific

Interview Date:
11 June 2010

Referral:
Personal Contact

I was in the Navy. I received a letter from the Army and realized the draft would soon get me, so I enlisted in the Navy. Luckily, I had a college degree from Iowa State and was made an ensign. I went overseas on an unescorted food supply ship. It had one cannon on its bow and that was it. I weighed 110 pounds back then. The worst part of the two week trip was the initiation when we crossed the equator. There were 140 enlisted men and 65 officers on board. We were the only outfit that did the code breaking. Think what would have happened if we had been wiped out. At the time, I wasn't scared a bit.

I spent 24 months in the Pacific. We landed at Hollandaise, New Guinea. That's on the northern end of the island. We slept on cots. Later we were sent to the Philippines. I can't remember what island we were on in the Philippines. We stayed in Quonset huts there. We had it a lot better than most. I sang in the Navy choir in my spare time.

I was assigned to the Japanese code breakers. The Japanese code had been broken before the war started. The center for code breaking was in Kansas

City, Missouri, until we went overseas. We listened in on radio transmissions.

Questions: Cal, did you have to learn the Japanese language?

No, but they taught us some words and phrases to key on in a course I took at Harvard. There were guys in each section that understood Japanese and they would review everything of interest. After listening in for a while, you picked up more of the Japanese language and could recognize more words. As the years progressed, you learned a lot of Japanese.

Question: Were you involved or made aware of when the code was broken that allowed our planes to intercept and shoot down Admiral Yamamoto?

No, I knew nothing about it. I wasn't really involved in anything that significant. It was pretty much the routine stuff that I was involved with.

The only time I was really thankful to have missed death while in the Navy was after returning stateside. A group of us were staying in a hotel in downtown Chicago. We all decided to go out drinking one evening. When we returned to the hotel, we found it consumed in fire. We would have probably been trapped on the upper floor we were staying on. It always got me to me how ironic it would have been to survive the war and die in a fire in Chicago.

John Butler and I owned the West Chester Savings Bank together for years. John married my sister Wilma. John had been a POW in Germany.

TRIBUTE

I often think about the "Greatest Generation" and think about how different the world, our country and my life would be if not for the sacrifices of these true American heroes. Not only did they leave their families, children, homes and jobs, but they were gone for 3 or 4 years at a time without ever stepping foot on American soil.

We can never imagine what it was like to jump out of a troop transport into the Atlantic at the Normandy beaches or to battle the Germans and the coldest winter in the history of Europe at the Battle of the Bulge. How can we know what it was like to fight your way across the Pacific island by island fighting an enemy that knew no bounds of cruelty?

They endured unbelievable hardships, but they never gave up and ended up saving the world from dictators and tyrants such as the world had never known.

And when it was all over they returned home, married that sweetheart left behind, remembered those who did not return with them and moved on. They went to college, started families, built successful businesses, and continued to serve their country and communities. They have continued to give back their entire lives.

I know many of these men whose stories are told in this book and they are the men that I respect the most. Not just for their service and sacrifices, but also because of who they are and what they have done in their lives.

The price this generation paid to save the world and to give us an enduring freedom can never be repaid.

Dale Torpey
Washington, IA

DIDN'T KNOW ENOUGH TO GET SCARED

"Buffalo" Bob Flynn
Keota, IA

Navy
Pacific

Interview Date:
17 June 2010

Referral:
Mandy Farrier & Terry Greiner

I graduated from high school 1940 and enlisted in January, 1941. I was sent to Great Lakes in Chicago for training. My first ship was the USS *New Orleans*, a heavy cruiser used in WWI. It was so old it was about half worthless. They didn't waste any bullets on us. I was aboard that ship at Pearl. They only paid me $21 dollars a month and took out some of that out for insurance. I thought I was worth more but that's all they'd give me.

The attack on Pearl Harbor was about as confusing as it could get. It was like being in a riot. We didn't even know what the Rising Sun was. Eventually we did, of course. The day before there was a bombing run practice. Our planes would fly over and drop sacks filled with flour, trying to score hits. We were standing out on the deck when we heard the planes approaching, thinking it was another training exercise. It was around eight o'clock in the morning. The USS *Arizona* battleship was anchored about half a city block from us. Our cruiser was old and obsolete. They weren't going to waste any bullets on us. The Japanese had better targets. They were interested in a lot bigger things than us, like the battleships and the airplane

carriers, except there weren't any carriers there at Pearl Harbor on December 7th.

The Japanese planes came in fast and low and flew right past us. You could see the white of the pilot's eyes, they were that close. Our ship was locked up. Anybody that knew anything was on the beach. All the ammunition boxes had padlocks on them. Eventually, we came to realize what was going on. We didn't even know enough to get scared, initially.

Everybody on the beach that had any type of gun was shooting at the Jap planes. We were in more danger on our ship from our own people on the beach than from the Japanese. Bullets were flying everywhere. I don't know what some of them were shooting at, maybe the moon. I didn't do nothing but stand around and look at them (the attacking planes) like everyone else.

After the *Arizona* was hit, there was so much smoke you couldn't see nothing. The air was filled with dirt and the water covered with oil.

By the time the second wave of attack planes flew over, we had the locks off the ammunition magazines and could shoot back. Smaller boats ferried the officers with the keys out from the beach. I think practically all the ships at Pearl were under lock down when the first wave came in. Anyone with any rank or had any money to spend was on the beach that Sunday morning.

It looked like there were a million people over there on the beach, so many they were stumbling over each other. Hell, the commanding general and admiral were playing golf.

Everyone was pretty rattled by the time the ships could start shooting back at the second wave of planes. The Japanese planes were flying so low that naval gunfire was hitting other ships. I don't believe ours was ever hit, however.

That night we had two of our planes come back from somewhere. They'd probably been out looking for the Japanese. Everybody that had a gun was shooting at them. They could not have survived. I never have read or heard anything about that later. There was naval gunfire all the next day as well, even though we were not under attack. The Admiral finally had to issue orders banning further shooting.

I was in charge of pots and pans when the attack came. Earlier, I had been a deck hand. The Navy spent a lot of time trying to keep the crew busy before the war. We had way more sailors aboard ship than we needed. They'd have us painting and washing the deck continually. One wave would wash over the deck and ruin everything we had done. It was a complete waste of time. I'd go hide when assigned that duty. When they finally caught me, I was detailed to mess duty as punishment. I didn't mind mess duty. At least you kept busy and felt like you were accomplishing something.

Two days after the attack, we sailed for Brisbane, Australia. When we arrived in port, the Aussies had all these American flags flying, a sight I will never forget. I guess they were glad to see us. That was the only country that made a fuss over us. I suspect there were several thousand people out there to greet us. The only people left in Australia were old men, women and children. Everybody else was fighting on the front.

I'm not sure why we went to Australia. We

weren't there very long. They never consulted me on stuff like that. We sailed back to Pearl Harbor where I was transferred to the states so they could make a Gunner's Mate out of me, which involved being in charge of a five inch gun crew. Gunnery practice involved a plane pulling a target for us to shoot at. Sometimes we'd get a little too close to the tow plane, not something we were supposed to do.

Following training, I was assigned to a battleship, the USS *Massachusetts*. We had an admiral on board and no one gets to shoot at them so it was pretty safe. We always had a ring of destroyers around us. We'd go to General Quarters when there was a sub scare but I never saw one. I think my first ship, the USS *New Orleans*, was later sunk. They'd always send the old clunker ships out front and keep the better ships farther back.

"*The Japanese planes were flying so low that naval gunfire was hitting other ships.*"

We were in the Battle of Casablanca (off French Morocco) with the French Vichy Fleet. We sank more tonnage than in any other sea battle in WWII. We were in the Atlantic for a year and a half and got far enough north that a large crust of frozen sea water circled the sides of the ship. We sailed through the Panama Canal to the Pacific. Our ship had only six inches of clearance on either side going through the locks. I never could figure out why the enemy didn't bomb the Panama Canal.

We had Marines on board every ship. They were disciplined, well trained troops. Much better trained than us sailors. We had two or three men for every job. It was wasteful. I guess they figured that if half the sailors weren't any good, the other half would be.

In the Pacific, our battleship was included in carrier task forces but never on the front line, we would be farther back. They didn't let admirals near the front. Japanese planes would fly over us and we'd pepper them. We had two different admirals. One of them was Chester Nimitz. We were in the Battle of The Coral Sea, Midway, the Philippines, I can't remember them all. *(Note: Bob was awarded nine Battle Stars for engagements in the Pacific and one for action in the Atlantic.)* There's an old boy from West Chester that was on the Death March in the Philippines. I can't think of his name.

Answer: Yes, that was Cecil Forinash. He lives down South but was recently back up here for a visit. Two weeks ago we interviewed him.

Is he still alive? God, he must be tougher than heck! I was almost on the Death March. In December of '41 they asked for volunteers to go to the Philippines. I wasn't doing anything but mess cooking but they didn't take me for some reason. Now I'm kind of glad they didn't. Most of those men didn't survive.

I couldn't tell one kind of Jap plane from the others, but we didn't have any of the Kamikazes after our ship. They were after the carriers. We had a number of the smaller Kaiser flattops (escort carriers) close to us. They finally got to the point that they'd let planes take off from them but made them land on a full size carrier because we were suffering too many casualties and losing too many planes trying to land on them. The pilots said it was like trying to land on a postage stamp. They were nicknamed, "Kaiser Coffins." It was hard enough to land on a full size carrier. I thought those pilots earned their money.

One time there was some whiskey on board and some of the crew got drunk one night and went topside and started shooting starburst shells through my five inch gun. It about scared me to death. I thought I'd get hung for that. Some of those guys had no brains when they got drunk and some not even when they were sober. You could see those starburst shells for ten to fifteen miles. There must have not been any Jap subs around or we'd been in real trouble.

In late 1945 or '46, I was transferred to troop transport ships and hauled troops back to the states. I served on both the USS *Hampton* and the USS *Winslow*.

I think Truman was right to drop the bomb, don't you? That's all there was to it. I was out in Arizona talking to a colonel who was a pilot of a B-29, and he said his plane had carried a third atomic bomb around. This guy was the right age and highly decorated and I think he was telling the truth. I used to play poker with him. *(Note: History notes that at the end of the war, one additional atomic bomb was in route to Tinian and another*

remained stateside. Two more were also being assembled stateside.)

I had a brother in the Red Horse Troop. He lasted until he got tuberculosis. He got down to 98 pounds and about died. Another brother, Taylor, served. My youngest brother also served but got in late and the war ended. He was only in six months to a year and never left the states. All four of the Flynn boys served in the military during the war. There's an outfit over at Clear Creek, name of Weber, where eight or nine brothers all served. I think the youngest may have been in Korea. The WWII vets are getting thinned out.

> *"It's still hard to talk about. Been 65 years, you'd think you'd forget."*

I left the Navy in December of '46 with the rank of Gunner's Mate First Class. After six years in the Navy, I should have been all of that. I tried to get the government to send me to school (on the GI Bill) but because I was in the Navy a year before the war started and for a year after it ended, they said I didn't qualify. I managed to get by farming, enough to survive anyway.

I went to a ship's reunion several years back, and to hear those old guys talk, we (our ship) won the war. We were in it, but I don't think we hardly won the war.

Question: Is there anything you would want future generations to know regarding WWII based on your experiences?

I want them to know that we won, but the whole thing was kind of sad. It's still hard to talk about. Been 65 years, you'd think you'd forget.

Now don't put anything in your book that you're not supposed to.

Answer: We won't.

ALL SHOT TO HELL

Dean Cooney
Rubio, IA

3rd Marine Division
Pacific

Interview Date:
23 June 2010

Referral:
David Long & John Capper

I had a permanent farm deferment, but I volunteered for the Marines when I was 19 or 20 years old. I was in the 3rd Marine Division. I don't remember what year it was but it had to be after the war had started, because when I went through Pearl Harbor it was already shot all to hell. My experiences with the enemy were on Guam and Iwo Jima. I lost a lot of friends. It was a hell of an experience. It wasn't any good at all.

We'd go out on patrols through the jungle on Guam, and it was terrible because you didn't know where the Japs were. We'd find where they had been cooking, and the smoke was still coming up from their cooking pots. The Japs would run like heck and I don't blame them. On our first patrol on Guam there were seven of us. We were walking up a trail and the Japanese were coming down it. We shot it out with them. We had two guys wounded and we hardly made it back to camp. We were camped in a little school house in Marisa which was on the far end of Guam. It was a real beautiful place, but the village closest to us was not real friendly. They were sided with the Japanese.

I was a demolition rifleman. I carried a Garand. At the end on Iwo, I carried a brand new BAR made by Winchester. I had four different rifles on Iwo because I had to carry a couple of guys out.

"I have friends now that are Japanese and I used to shoot them. During the war it was either them or me.

Question: How long did it take you to secure Guam?

Well, it was a crazy thing. They got one guy that showed up four years later. He had been hiding up in the hills and finally gave himself up. Guam was a big, rugged area. It was quite interesting. I'll tell you that the Japanese are good people. We just got all mixed up because of the war. They had bad leaders. I have friends now that are Japanese and I used to shoot them. During the war, it was either them or me.

Iwo Jima was terrible. We got all shot to hell. My group didn't land on the island the first day of the invasion. I can't remember which day we went in. I stayed at the foot of Mt. Suribachi my first night. Our executive officer got shot by a sniper. It killed him. He was the first guy in our outfit to get hit. From then on it was just terrible. The Japs were zeroed in on us. In fact, one time we got shot up by our own naval artillery because they'd called in the wrong coordinates. They killed a bunch of my friends. That's how mixed up you get in battle. I got pinned down and shot at until dark. The bullets would throw dirt over you one time and the next time it'd go over the top of you. Crossing an airfield one time I thought those bullets would never stop. They'd whistle and sound like they'd go on forever. It's the strangest sound you've ever heard.

Question: Did you take any prisoners on Guam or Iwo, or did they all fight to the death?

The ones I could have taken weren't worth taking because I blew them all up. I blew up a big gun position one time. The first guy that went in got killed. The second one got all shot up. I went in at an angle and blew it up with ten pounds of TNT with tetra booster. It makes a big, hot blast. I had to go in and place it over the ledge of the gun emplacement. Later on in the battle, they blew themselves up under ground with powder charges. So they took care of themselves.

Question: Did you ever seal up any of the cave entrances with your demolition charges?

I did a little. Flamethrowers took care of a lot of that. We had flamethrowers in our outfit, and boy, when we blasted them in the caves, there wasn't much left. Toward the end on Iwo, we had (called "Ronson" or "Zippo") tanks with flamethrowers on them, and they could burn the heck out of things quite a ways off. It was really something to see that stream of diesel fuel ignite and flare off and go into something.

In one place where I was advancing, there were three tanks knocked out. All of the crews were lying dead around the tanks. They really shot us all to pieces there. The Japs had the high ground and were looking down our necks. They were shooting down at us all the time.

One Marine outfit (the 4th Marine Division) was left aboard ship because they didn't think they'd be needed. When they finally sent those poor replacements in they got shot to hell because they didn't know what they were doing.

I've had Japs throw grenades at me and that's not good. Getting shot at is worse. I'm alive. I'm full of shrapnel, but I'm alive.

Question: Was the shrapnel from artillery? Mortars?

Mortars and stuff. You'd just get blasted. I carried two or three guys out that had been shot up on Iwo. Then you'd go back and fight at the front. My closest friend, my squad leader, took a bullet on the first day that cut his nose in two. He's still alive,

though. We'd usually carry the wounded out on stretchers. I carried one guy out over my shoulder. He bled all over me, clear down to my cartridge belt. I had to keep wearing those clothes the rest of the way. Nothing smells worse. It was nauseating.

My BAR assistant was carrying ammunition up to me from the beach because we were short of men. A mortar shell landed close to me. It blew his leg all to hell. I was hit, too. He didn't even know what outfit he was with. I had to write out the (medical) ticket for him. That's how much mismanagement there is in combat.

Question: When you were wounded by the mortar, were you evacuated?

They had to carry me out. I could see the American flag on top of Suribachi. It was beautiful. They put me on an LSM which took me to one ship and it was full. They took me to the second hospital ship and it was full. So they took me back to the first one, and the officer on deck looked down at me and said, "Take him aboard." From there I ended up in Saipan in an Army hospital. Those Army nurses were wonderful. They had the softest hands but they were the roughest girls. You could tell by the lingo they used. Later I was sent on to a hospital in Tinian and then flown back to Guam.

> "I'm alive.
> I'm full of shrapnel,
> but I'm alive."

I was walking down the street on Guam when they announced that the atomic bomb had been dropped. I couldn't hardly believe it. That sure stopped things. I didn't really know what an atomic bomb was but I knew there was a big blast.

Question: What was your opinion of the Japanese soldiers?

They fight to the end, I know that. You had to kill them or else. Some of those Japanese soldiers were way bigger than I was. Great big guys, Imperial Marines they were called. I saw of them lying there dead and I thought, "Wow!"

Our government gave Iwo Jima back to the Japanese. I think that was wrong considering the amount of American blood spilled there. I'd rather seen them bulldoze the whole island into the ocean or use it for bombing practice.

War is hell. Things can be settled without fighting a war. The leaders that choose to fight don't do the fighting. For the guy doing the fighting, you know you have to go and do it or you'll be the one that gets blasted. That's the way you had to think. And you had to be thinking all the time to survive. It was no fun to run at a fortification with someone shooting at you and dust flying up all around from the bullets hitting near you. We had ten guys in our squad on Guam and nine while we were on Iwo. Everyone in the squad was either killed or wounded.

My dad was in WWI. I had a brother that was a B-24 pilot in Europe. He bombed the Ploesti oil fields, and then he bombed the heck out of Germany. I went back to farming after coming home and did some plumbing.

It Was Quite an Honor

Richard Huber
Wellman, IA

66th Infantry Division
Europe

Interview Date:
25 June 2010

Referral:
Terri (Huber) Adam

I was drafted in '42. I was teaching school at a rural school southeast of Keota and the next year at Maple Grove. That's where I was when I was drafted. I did basic training in Colorado Springs. There were several Mexicans in the outfit. When they found out I had been a teacher, they had me write letters for the Mexicans and read them the ones they received from home. I was assigned to the motor pool. After being in for four months, I took a test to go to Officers Training School and passed it. I went to my captain and told him about passing it, and he said, "I hate to tell you this, but you haven't been in the service long enough to become an officer." He advised me to join a brand new outfit being formed at Fort Blanding in Florida, so I did and was promoted to staff sergeant.

In Florida I trained replacements during their basic training. At that time, there were ten times as many young men signing up for the Air Force as needed, and many of the extra ones were sent to us. These young men were the top of their class, and it was a privilege training them. We trained two groups to serve as overseas replacements and kept the last group to form our own outfit. From there I went to Alabama and then to Fort Benning, Georgia to train officers for three months in artillery. After that, we trained in Arkansas, learning how to shoot all our guns.

I was assigned to Battery A of the 870th Field Artillery Battalion. We were part of the 66th Infantry Division. We had four 105mm howitzers. They had an effective range of four and one half miles. My job was a forward observer. I was also in charge of communications with twenty-three men and five vehicles to work with.

In November of '44, we left New York City for Europe on a converted passenger ocean cruiser named the *Britannic*. There were thirteen thousand of us on board. We arrived in England at 3:00 AM and told to get our gear gathered up. We didn't get off the ship until 9:00 AM. They fed us scrambled eggs. They were green and my men refused to eat them. I told them to go ahead and eat their C rations instead. An officer found out what I had done and put us on hard labor for two weeks. So we piled rocks and picked up sticks the two weeks were in England. My men didn't like me much but I thought I had done the right thing.

On the morning of Christmas Eve, the men of the 262nd Infantry Regiment boarded one ship, the *Leopoldville*, and I went on another with the five vehicles I was responsible for. The English Channel had terribly rough water that day. The ship I was on was the smaller of the two and people got seasick. I had never seen so much sickness. Four or five miles out from Cherbourg, France the *Leopoldville* carrying the infantrymen got torpedoed by a German submarine. Over eight men were either killed outright or drowned. England was so short of manpower that they had been forced to bring in people from Africa to crew the ship. These people abandoned ship without showing anyone how to lower the lifeboats. They radioed Cherbourg headquarters, but everyone was at a Christmas Eve party eating supper. It was terrible.

We camped in tents four or five days near Cherbourg waiting for the higher ups to decide what to do with us. We were originally scheduled for the Bulge but without any infantry we were pretty much helpless. Our four howitzers made it across the channel.

> "There was a tall pine tree up on the hill next to the chateau. That's where I built my nest, 90 ft off the ground."

The Germans had two big submarine pens on the coast of France. Their subs would come in there for maintenance and to resupply. Both were surrounded and isolated on the land side by allied troops but protected by German infantry and artillery. We were assigned to the northern one at Lorient. Inside this five mile wide enclosure the Germans ran a POW camp full of French soldiers. By this time in the war, the threat from German subs had lessened. Their subs would mainly sneak out to Norway and bring in food to those trapped in the enclosure. Counting the French POWs, there were probably twenty-five thousand mouths to feed. The Germans had been flying in supplies with planes, but that ended shortly after our arrival. It wasn't from anything we were doing that caused them to quit.

Question: Were the Germans using the French POWs as a human shield?
Oh, absolutely.

When we went there, I was assigned to the French Army. In a way, it was quite an honor. The French unit I was with had been pulled out of the Battle of the Bulge. They had been shot up pretty badly and lost a lot of people. We were bivouacked near a beautiful chateau up on a hill. Down at the base of the hill was a barn where they kept their horses. There were also attached servant quarters. That's where the group I was with stayed. I was given a French interpreter that stayed with me all the time. He was a wonderful guy.

There was a tall pine tree up on the hill next to the chateau. That's where I built my nest, 90 ft off the ground. From that height, I could actually look out and see clear across to the submarine pit four or five miles in the distance. I had a wonderful telescope. I'd normally sit eight to ten hours a day in the tree. I was on call 24 hours a day. I built a platform out of barn wood to sit on and another one for the telescope. It was fairly comfortable. On windy days, I hung on. I sat in a seat and used a hay rope and pulleys from the barn to pull myself up and down.

There wasn't anything between the 25 French troops I was with and the Germans but four and a half miles of open countryside. The American lines were three quarters of a mile behind us.

Question: Oh my! Did the French soldiers post guards at night to watch for German patrols?
I don't recall them doing that. I don't even remember them having any guns.

One day the Germans started shooting their 88's at me while I was up in my tree. Those 88's were fast and shot like a rifle. I could hear the rounds whistle through the tree branches beside me. I kind of needed to be up there to find where the gun was located. I spotted it and put him out of business, thank goodness! I received a bronze star for that.

There was an island about a mile off shore. The Germans had a huge railroad gun located there. They didn't fire it very often but it could totally devastate anything it hit. That shell sounded like a freight train going through the sky. I think that one reason they didn't fire it much was because they didn't have identifiable targets. They really had no way of seeing what they were shooting at any great distance away.

A Piper cub airplane, nicknamed a "grasshopper," was brought in once for me to ride in and direct my fire. That was pretty interesting. The plane was from another outfit and they asked if I'd like to try it. I thought it would be better than sitting up in a tree all day. We tried to fly in straight lines over the Germans to establish artillery firing coordinates. The Germans started shooting their 88's at us and the pilot would jerk the plane to dodge the anti-aircraft fire.

One day while I was up in the tree looking through my telescope, I could see a bunch of women out hoeing in a garden (inside the German lines). This was in late March or April. I noticed one of them lifting up his skirt to relieve himself. So they weren't women! So I got to shoot at them.

Question: So you called in artillery on them?

I called in artillery on them. Somewhere it says in my box of papers how many were killed. I got a nice ribbon out of it. We had quite a funny situation. The German and Allied lines were approximately four and one miles apart. One night we'd be out on patrol and the next night the Germans would be out on patrol, coming towards us. I don't know why we did it that way, but always seemed to happen that way. One night we'd be out, the next night the Germans would be. Sometimes a guy would get separated from his squad and get lost while on patrol. If they moved around in daylight the Germans would shoot at them. Usually they'd hide out in the shadows until someone found them or wait till the next night before coming in. I'd be up in my tree at night when patrols were out. Sometimes they would signal me with flashlights when they could.

At different times the Germans would patrol during daylight. Then we'd get to have a little target practice on them. Night patrols were scary. They'd send out people to see where the Germans were the night before. I never went on patrols because I was a forward artillery observer. I was issued a .45 pistol to carry but never fired it. Patrols that got into trouble would call me for artillery support. That happened quite often. They'd radio back, and I had telephone wire strung to my guns about a mile away. The civilians coming and going with their horse drawn steel wheeled wagons were hard on our telephone cable. We had to have plenty of wire available for splicing.

The French didn't go out on patrols. It was always American troops. The French had quite a deal in that some of them fought with the Germans after they were taken over and some remained free French. They were good fighting men. They treated me royally. There were 25 or 30 French soldiers at that chateau. They gave me a pin to wear that said I belonged with their army.

Two or three times we had a prisoner exchange with the Germans. The Germans would come out about two and one half miles from their lines and meet us. Usually the prisoners exchanged were sick or wounded. I don't know how all this was arranged, but I got to go with them. When the German higher ups and our officers were meeting, the enlisted Germans and I would visit. I took a bunch of candy bars with me and traded two of them for a pair of really nice artillery field glasses with lines and numbers. My impression of the German soldiers after talking to them is that they didn't want to fight us any more than we wanted to fight them.

Two days after the war ended the Germans started coming out of the submarine pits. They'd drop their helmet one place and their gun another. They came out one at a time. It took two days steady for all of them to surrender.

We were sent to Germany after the war was over to a camp of Poles. My job each day was to go to the hospital and report the number of births and deaths and new cases of sickness. There were two young Polish nurses that spoke English that I'd go to for the information. There was one little boy seven or eight years old that followed us around like a puppy. Our main duty was to get these people relocated back to Poland. We'd arrange their departure on trains. We learned later that because they had spent so much time with the Germans, the Polish people didn't want to have anything to do with them. It about broke our hearts. I don't know what ever happened to them.

We stayed overnight in a nice house while traveling through Germany. In one room I discovered an ash tray with my name, Richard Huber, on it. I thought that to be kind of a miracle. I know I shouldn't have done it, but I stole it and brought it home with me. That's it sitting over there on the book shelf.

I had a friend that went to one of the concentration camps. He brought back photos to show me. They were terrible to look at. Why anyone would ever want to treat people like that, I'll never know.

> *"My impression of the German soldier after talking to them is that they didn't want to fight us any more than we wanted to fight them"*

We only lost one guy in my outfit and that was from artillery fire. Considering all the incoming German shelling, that in itself was a miracle.

After that we were sent down to Marseilles, France. We were given the option of sightseeing around Europe or attending the University of Ritz in France. I chose to spend my time in school. I spent six weeks studying agriculture, engineering and trigonometry. The courses were taught in English. Because I was married and had a daughter, I had enough points to go home.

One of the guys that sailed home with me had been aboard the *Leopoldville* when it went down. He was so terrified from the experience that he slept on top of the open deck the whole voyage home.

I arrived back in Iowa in November of 1945. When I was teaching school before the war, I had no desire to ever go back to the farm. After the war, I never wanted to leave the farm. My dad was getting up in years so it was a natural fit for me take over the family farm.

In October 2010, Richard received a very prestigious award from the French Government—a "Chevalier" of the Legion of Honor. On the certificate that accompanies the medal it reads:

"This award testifies to the President of the French Republic's high esteem for your merits and accomplishments. In particular, it is a sign of France's true and unforgettable gratitude and appreciation for your personal, precious contribution to the United States' decisive role in the liberation of our country during World War II.

"The Legion of Honor was created by Napoleon in 1802 to acknowledge the services rendered to France by persons of great merit. The French people will never forget your courage and your devotion to the great cause of freedom."

HELL FIRE CORNER

Tom English
Washington, IA

127th AAA Gun Battalion
Europe

Interview Date:
29 June 2010

Referral:
Linda Witthoft

Six of us were drafted in 1943 out of Villisca High School before we graduated. We were deferred until after we graduated, and then we went for our physical. We spent a long, first day at the induction center at Ft. Leavenworth, Kansas, peeling potatoes and cleaning food trays. They got us up at 4 AM and worked us to seven that night. I was really worn out and I was in good shape, having gone out for athletics all through high school.

We left Leavenworth by train for California. It took seven days and seven nights for three or four thousand homesick kids to reach California because other trains had priority. Our troop train pulled over in Kansas on a siding and sat for a day in the hot sun. We had food on the train but no baths for seven days.

Basic training was at Camp Haan near Riverside, California. Then we went to Camp Irwin where we did maneuvers. Camp Irwin was located 30 miles from Death Valley and the temperature would get to 115 degrees on the firing range. Getting caught without your fatigue jacket on was an automatic court martial. So many of the guys had taken their shirts off because of the heat and gotten so

sunburnt that they ended up in the hospital. So we had to wear our fatigue jacket no matter how hot it was.

Just our 584 radar crew was assigned to Edwards Air Force Base in California. We were restricted to base because everything was top secret. Bell Aircraft and Lockheed were testing all kinds of jet airplanes. That first night there we couldn't figure out what was going on. Those jets would take off and just roar over us. They'd fly those planes and bring them back to the hangars where the mechanics would take them apart to check everything out. Then they'd put them back together and fly them again.

Our radar crew was set up at the dry Roger's Lake clear at the north end of the base. We had cameras set up behind us to record the tracking on our radar screen. We could see a pip on our radar screen and another smaller pip coming out of it. We couldn't figure out what was going on at first. Every day we'd track another B-17 airplane at a different elevation. We started at 10,000 ft and worked up 2000 ft each day.

There'd be four star generals and admirals

behind us watching our radar screens. They made us nervous. We finally figured out later that dummy bombs were being dropped from different elevations to see how far the plane could get away before the atomic bomb hit the ground.

Question: How do you feel knowing that you were a small part in ending the war?

It felt good, it really did. We were set up on a small rise by the dry lake with our equipment and a small tent. One guy had to stay there every night on guard duty while the rest of us went back to the barracks. It was a long night out there.

I came home on my first furlough after training, and Ruthella and I decided to get married. That was on November 10th of '43. Then we were sent to Ft. Bliss at El Paso for more firing range training out in the desert. A four day train trip from El Paso took us to Camp Shanks in New York. We studied airplane identification and went on ten mile hikes.

We shipped out on July 1st of 1944 on a British ship, the HMT *Sythia*. Our battery B was assigned to the officer's mess. After fourteen days at sea, we docked in Liverpool and after a mile hike with all our heavy gear, we boarded a train for Camp Blackshawn Moor in Straffordshire, England. We received our trucks, kitchen, radar, 90mm anti-aircraft guns, and all our other equipment.

Then they moved us down to the White Cliffs of Dover to shoot down German buzz bombs coming in from Calais, France, which is 18 miles across the English Channel from Dover. It was called Hell Fire Corner. There were several other anti-aircraft units there besides my unit, the 127th AAA Gun Battalion. We were part of Operation Crossbow, the defense of Great Britain. At different times, we were alerted by British Intelligence detection teams to buzz bombs leaving their launching sites at Calais. We'd pick up the buzz bombs coming on radar and it went to a director that smoothed out all the information. By that time our shells were tipped with super secret proximity fuses which automatically steered the shell to the target. Because of our radar, we could fire accurately day or night, in rain or fog. Our battalion shot down 89 buzz bombs headed to London. When you hit one in the air, it exploded and there were pieces of

> *"Our battalion shot down 89 buzz bombs headed to London."*

metal flying all over the place. You wanted to have a place that you could duck into for protection when that happened.

My battery fired 597 anti-aircraft rounds at buzz bombs. They'd travel at 350 to 400 miles per hour and carried an 1800 lb. bomb. We didn't knock down every one we shot at.

Question: How far away could your radar detect the buzz bombs?

We could detect them about ten miles away. We'd have about a half a minute then before they were in range of our guns. We had to be ready. By the time the radar information was processed the buzz bombs would be over the White Cliffs of Dover. Then you'd hear the "commence firing" order given. We just filled the sky with 90mm anti-aircraft shells and machine gun fire.

Our radar equipment was hauled around on a semi-trailer. We had to dig that in for protection. You could only dig so far down before hitting the white cliff rock. So we had to pile up sand bags around it. One piece of shrapnel would have disabled it. Our battery had four 90mm guns and two trailers, each equipped with a quad 50 caliber machine gun. There were four gun batteries in the 127th Battalion, plus a headquarters company, but they didn't have any guns. I was in Battery B. Those big 90mm guns made quite a noisy boom when they were fired. They never issued us ear plugs, and all of us suffered high frequency hearing loss.

Back behind us there were 40mm anti-aircraft guns. Back of those were British Bofors guns. Finally, there were British Spitfire fighter planes furthest back. They wouldn't attempt to shoot the buzz bombs down because there were too many people on the ground that could be hit. They'd fly along beside the buzz bombs and tip the wing causing it to crash. From there on to London the British had large barrage balloons aloft with long cables handing down. If the buzz bombs hit a cable, they were done.

Besides the buzz bombs coming over, the Germans were shelling us with 16 inch naval guns from Calais. We lost four guys and had ten wounded from that. All they could find of one of the guys killed was some skin plastered against a concrete wall. When one of those big shells hit, it made a hole in the ground as big as this house. The British had their own long range artillery which would shoot back at the Germans when they shelled us. The British also had telescopic range finders. On a clear day, they could see the smoke rings when the Germans fired those big naval guns. It gave us some warning, but not much. Those shells made a lot of noise coming in.

Question: Did you ever see any German aircraft while at the White Cliffs?

No, never. By that time, the British controlled the skies. I do remember seeing our bombers going over heading for Germany. One morning the sky was completely filled with B-17s. It was quite a sight.

We had a monument to the 127th Anti-Aircraft Battalion up above Dover castle. Our veterans association collected money for the plaque and had it built after receiving permission to have it erected. In 1985, we went over to England on a tour and dedicated the monument to the men we lost. During the war, we slept in concrete dugout caves with a piece of corrugated metal for a roof with dirt piled on top. I found my old dugout in 1985. The metal roof had rusted out and the dirt caved in.

We left Dover on September 17th, 1944 and landed at Omaha Beach September 27th. A harbor channel had been built by sinking old ships. We camped in pup tents at St. Mere Eglise waiting on our equipment. Most of the town had been torn up in the D-Day fighting. It rained every day. We lived in the mud for two weeks.

After getting all of our equipment, we went up in Belgium and set up to protect our troops and truck convoys from strafing by German planes. We were assigned to Simpson's 9th Army. Every time the front moved on, we moved with them. Each time we had to dig in the guns and radar. We had our own generator for electrical power.

We spent much of November in Holland. After moving up to a new position, the captain came over and told us to bury six German soldiers lying dead in their fox holes. One thing we had that most outfits didn't was good shovels. The army issued folding shovels weren't adequate for the job of digging our equipment in so we begged long handled shovels from French farmers. We rearranged the bodies in the foxholes and covered them with dirt. I've often wondered if those bodies are still buried there, undiscovered.

We were shelled by 88s at this location in Holland. The Germans were only about a mile away. We were up on some railroad tracks checking out a jeep and Canadian tank that had struck land mines when they started dropping shells in on us. Everybody in both vehicles was dead. Another time one of two guys out patrolling at night along railroad tracks was shot and killed by a German. We also had noncombat casualties from things like jeep wrecks.

> *"I've often wondered if those bodies are still buried there, undiscovered."*

The weather was cold and foggy during the Battle of the Bulge. I froze my ears, hands, and toes. We were issued winter clothing but no galoshes. I wore every piece of clothing I had with me, including the summer clothing under the outer winter wear. Every night I'd take my boots off and rub my feet and put on a dry pair of socks. That seemed to help. A lot of the infantry had to have frostbitten toes amputated in a hospital. After being out in the Iowa cold scooping snow for about five minutes, my toes, fingers and ears go numb and later the skin on my face will peel off.

We were warned to check out any troops withdrawing through our position as there were Germans dressed in American uniforms during the Bulge. We were told to ask them if they knew who Babe Ruth was. Nobody in our outfit, including our captain, knew what was going on during the Bulge. Usually when we'd move and set up, we didn't even know what country we were in until talking to the local citizens.

When we sat up our equipment in this marshaling area in Belgium, a general came out and inspected us. He told us that we could not leave our equipment cable on top of the ground. We'd have to bury them. When we pulled out, the ground was frozen solid and there was no way we were getting those cables out. So we had to requisition new ones. Those cables are probably still buried there. It'd take us two or three hours to get all of our equipment ready to transport under normal conditions.

One day we were strafed by a German ME 109 but sustained no casualties. The mess tent was full of holes and pretty well wrecked. Some other equipment was damaged.

Question: Did your radar pick up the German fighter?

No, he came in too low. The 90mm guns couldn't do anything but the fifty's opened up on him. I don't think he was hit. I must tell you now, that nothing is perfect in war. We had a button we could push on our radar equipment that would identify a plane as being a friend or foe. A transponder on our planes would send back a signal identifying it as a friendly. The day after we were strafed, a plane picked up on our radar failed to send a signal back so the captain told us to commence firing. We knocked him down. It turned out to be an American P-51. I have felt bad about that for the rest of my life. There were a lot of mistakes made during the war. An official investigation of the incident did not find our unit to be at fault.

Another day we were given a march order to move up to a crossroads where the Germans were expected. We were to use our big guns as field artillery, something we had practiced while training in the desert. The fog lifted the next morning and the Air Force came in and wiped the German column out so we didn't have to move up.

After the Bulge, the American troops were advancing so fast that we couldn't keep up with them with our heavy equipment. We became a rescue unit for displaced persons, rendering first aid and providing food and clothing. We freed several slave labor camps. The Germans had brought in forced laborers from Yugoslavia, Hungary, Czechoslovakia, and Poland. The camps did farm labor and manufactured artillery shells. The slave laborers sabotaged some of the artillery rounds they assembled. We were shelled by German 88s while in Holland. A couple of those were duds, thank God.

I can still smell those camps, still see the people. They were skeletons and in very poor health. They were treated terribly. They were fed potato peeling soup. There were maybe 200 of these people in the barracks at the camps. There were dead bodies lying about the camps that we had to bury. Some had been dead so long that they were getting a little "fishy". It's a smell you never forget. We buried bodies nearly every day.

We gave these people American rations to eat. As hungry as they were, these people were hesitant to eat our American food because they'd never seen food like that. They could not comprehend how to mix the powdered milk or open the ration containers without us helping them. Then we had to send patrols out to protect the German people from retribution. We found one farmer and his whole family shot by Russian slave laborers. The Russians buried the bodies in a manure pile.

We crossed the Rhine at Wessel, Germany. The Germans had better hand grenades than we did. They were called potato mashers. We'd throw them in the water there at Wessel to fish with. The concussion and shrapnel would kill the fish and we'd cook them.

After VE Day we became part of the Army of Occupation. I was detailed to guard a wrecked radar trailer out in the middle of nowhere. I gathered up K rations and water and they dropped me off about 30 miles from our bivouac. They were worried that the locals would take the tires and strip the equipment. So I stood guard and I can tell you it was real lonesome out there. We were under orders not to fraternize with Germans. These two little kids came by one day and they spoke perfect English. They were from Los Angeles and their parents had returned to Germany. Their parents came by later and we played cards to pass the time. After being there five days, I had exhausted my supply of food, water, cigarettes and toilet paper. I think my first sergeant had forgotten about me. I flagged down a passing lieutenant in a jeep and asked him to contact Battery B. The next day I was relieved from guard duty.

During a portion of our occupation duty we were stationed at Heidelberg, Germany. I had duties of sergeant of the guard one day a month and the rest of the time I was on my own. Heidelberg is a beautiful city. We were there three months and finally accumulated enough points to go home.

> *"I can still smell those camps, still see the people… It's a smell you never forget."*

We proceeded to Marseilles, France, to ship out. It was right before Christmas, so the 12,000 troops waiting to go back to the states were fed a turkey dinner. These turkeys had been frozen and thawed out and refrozen too many times. Just about everybody that ate the turkey got the GI's (severe diarrhea). It was so bad you couldn't even get to a latrine. You went right outside your tent. It was a mess.

We waited and waited at Marseilles for ships to come in and pick us up. They kept telling us the ships were coming any day now. We finally got disgusted and went down the barracks housing the general. It was a temporary barracks. We surrounded the barracks and lifted it off the foundation and shook it like it was a ship. The general charged out on to the porch, steaming mad, and said, "All right you guys. Put me down. I promise to have you a ship in two days." In two days we sailed for New York City. It took eleven days to cross the Atlantic on a Liberty ship.

Question: What was it like seeing the Statue of Liberty?
Oh! That was so great! I cried. One bad thing almost happened. When we came into the harbor everyone ran to one side of the ship to see it. The ship almost capsized. It was scary. The first thing a lot of the guys sought when they got off the ship was fresh, American milk. The milk from France and Holland had tasted terrible. A Red Cross girl gave me my first taste of milk. I drank six pints. At the relocation center, they fed us steaks. We hadn't eaten steak for 2 ½ years. I was known as the "Chow hound of Battery B" because I could never get enough to eat.

I went by train to Camp Grant where I was discharged January 13th, 1946. I had been promoted to buck sergeant by then. There were a couple of times I didn't think I would ever make it home. I'm glad I did.

I went to Simpson College in Indianola on the GI Bill and got through in 2 ½ years. My first job teaching was at Brighton. Then I taught Industrial Arts and PE at the junior high in Washington for eight years and was the football, basketball, and track coach. Then I moved to the high school and taught a number of subjects, adding history and drafting and was the head basketball coach. I retired in 1985.

It's too bad you couldn't have talked to Hap Monroe. He passed away about a month ago. He was in the Air Force in England in a control tower. He sent all those bombers I saw going over to Germany. He saw many, many of them come back and crash while trying to land.

I'm going on the Honor Flight out of Cedar Rapids to Washington, D.C. on September 14th.

Question: As a former history teacher, do you have a message regarding World War Two you would offer to the youth of today?
If you have to serve the country, serve it faithfully. If you have to be in, do the best job you can. You know, WWI was supposed to be the "War that ended all wars" and it wasn't. The ways things are going, there will be more wars. I didn't want to serve, but I knew I had to.

You Felt Sorry for Them

Bob Stout
West Chester, IA

Army of Occupation
Japan

Interview Date:
12 July 2010

Referral:
Personal Contact

I was part of the draft. I had my physical in December and was inducted in March or April of 1946. I was 18 years old. I did my basic training at Camp Polk in Louisiana. It was very hot and extremely humid. I think that was the hottest I've ever been. It was so humid our clothes wouldn't dry unless we laid them on the barracks roof.

I was scheduled to work in an office, based on the aptitude tests I had taken. I had some Army schooling to serve in that capacity. I was sent overseas to work at 8th Army Headquarters in Yokohama, Japan. General Eichelberger was the commanding general. He was the number two under MacAuthur during the island campaigns. General Eichelberger would drive past us in the mornings as we walked to work and sometimes offer us a ride. He'd make small talk as we rode, asking us where we were from and how we were doing. Eichelberger was a good guy and very communicable. The troops during the war nicknamed Eichelberger the "Bloody Butcher" because he lost so many people. I know he was on Saipan and Okinawa.

You've see pictures of those islands. Once we landed troops, they had to stay until the islands were cleaned up. There were men from buck sergeant on up in the headquarters office that had been on those campaigns. They said the fighting was bitter.

MacAuthur was the head of CINCPAC and was in Tokyo. I never had anything to do with him. MacAuthur stayed 30 miles away in Tokyo. He always acted aloof, like he was above everyone else.

Question: How did the veterans feel about the Japanese people?
We didn't really associate with them. We were told not to eat any Japanese food. The Japanese didn't have enough food anyway. Besides that, they fertilized with human compost, and we were likely to get diseases from that.

My duties involved typing and filing letters and communications. Generally, there'd be a major or lieutenant colonel in charge of all these little offices. I Corps was based in Japan. It included the 24th and 25th Infantry Divisions. I would type up military orders to them and letters to the line companies. I started out with the rank of private 1st class and later became a corporal.

Japan was a mess. Tokyo had been fire bombed by every B-29 we had for three consecutive nights. The only buildings standing for a half dozen blocks from the sea where we stayed were made out of stone. We lived in barracks that were probably constructed by the CB's. There were MP sentries guarding our compound. Occasionally, we'd get a five day pass to tour the countryside. We could ride a Japanese train reserved exclusively for Americans. We'd ride a different electric train if we had to go to Tokyo. It would be so crammed full of Japanese that the doors wouldn't close. We found out in a hurry that you had to shove your way in if you ever hoped to ride it. The streetcars were the same way except people would be hanging on to the windows. All the cars and trucks except for the very wealthy were charcoal burners. They really smelled bad.

Question: Why do you think the military wanted to somewhat segregate you from the Japanese?

I think they were concerned about what the attitudes of the people would be that soon after the war. Fraternization was forbidden but some of it went on. The Japanese government had stirred the people up so much. They had worked them into a fevered pitch. Nine year old boys and girls had been trained with sharpened sticks to repel the Americans when we attacked the homeland. The Japanese I encountered were pretty subdued. They had lost everything. You'd see these little stalls set up on the street where they were selling their keepsakes for a few yen to buy food. It was pathetic, really. You felt sorry for them, yet it was hard to feel sorry for them, too. It had been such a bitter fight. When you thought of all the Americans that had died it was hard to feel sorry for them. Yet, you pitied them, too.

We worked five days a week, just like in an office back home. One weekend three of us explored some nearby caves we had heard about. There was a hill just honeycombed with tunnels. There were electric lights strung so you could see to walk around. It had been constructed for defense against an American invasion.

"There were always a bunch of Japanese women in the latrine, talking and giggling. It was something you just had to get used to."

I had the opportunity to visit Nagasaki on a five day pass but didn't. At the time, no one knew of the radiation danger.

Question: Did the Japanese kids beg candy bars from you?

They did a little, but there wasn't much of that. Maybe they were told to stay away from us.

Question: Were there any Japanese working for the U.S. military?

Oh my, yes! The first day I was there, I went in to use the latrine and there's these Japanese women just chattering away. So I turned around and went back to the office and asked where the men's bathroom was. Everybody grinned at me. I was informed that there would always be Japanese cleaning women in the men's latrine. They were right. There were always a bunch of Japanese women in the latrine, talking and giggling. It was something you just had to get used to. They did a good job keeping the latrines clean. They had plenty of time to do a good job as they were there all day.

Question: Did the military hire Japanese to do laundry?

No, but there were private Japanese laundries. We were not supposed to use them but nearly everybody did.

Later on in my time in Japan I was moved to another office. I spent much of my time there processing requests from officers to bring their families over to Japan to live. Enlisted men with the rank of master sergeant could also submit a request. There were still names on the waiting list when I came home.

I don't know how many occupation troops were in Japan. The 11th Airborne was north of us. They were a good outfit. The 5th Army was also in Japan. We had a military contingent in all the major Japanese cities. I saw a few Marines, but I don't know if they were occupation troops.

I never heard of any rumors or reports of Japanese guerilla warfare. Sometimes Japanese would show up at the fenced perimeter of a military installation at night and be shot by American guards. Some of the guards had an IQ so low that they should not have been in the military. I think it got bad enough that they ended up sending everyone home with an IQ of 75 or below.

The Red Cross had a presence in Japan. I had a lot of respect for them. You could go there on a pass and get a meal and sometimes overnight lodging.

Question: What was your impression of the Japanese people by the time you left?

I thought they were extremely industrious. You'd see then repairing the bombed out buildings. They'd be up three stories high on bamboo scaffolds working like mad. It looked like a bunch of ants working. Agriculture consisted mainly of rice, small grains and garden vegetables. I saw very few livestock. They ate a lot of fish. You'd see the workers eating a meager portion of rice and fish heads. I never saw any Japanese dressed in western attire. They wore either wooden shoes or ones made out of rubber tires.

I was in Japan a little over a year. I was seasick the whole way over to Japan. I decided that I'd stay in Japan rather than return to the states on a ship. Luckily, I came home on a plane.

Stan Scranton was a West Chester school mate that was on occupation duty. He married a Japanese girl and brought her back to the states. Joe Easter was stationed on the Aleutians during the war.

TRIBUTE

Wilbur D. Wright of Keota, Iowa, enlisted in the 113th Cavalry of the National Guard in Washington, Iowa, on October 13, 1940. On January 13, 1941, he entered active service. He spent one year, nine months and six days overseas serving in the European Theater of War, including D-Day on Omaha Beach and on to Germany. He was a Staff Sergeant when he separated from the Army at Camp Atterburg, Indiana, on October 27, 1945. He was glad to get home.

He wanted me to marry him, he wanted to be a farmer (he hoped I would like that idea), and he wanted a little dog. We fulfilled those dreams.

I was proud and happy to be married to Wilbur for 51 years, during which time we raised our five healthy, fun children together. When veterans were invited to visit France to observe the 50th anniversary of D-Day, Wilbur did not want to go. His remark was, "I didn't lose anything over there." He was content just as things were at home.

I am so thankful for all the veterans and those who supported them in their efforts to bring and keep peace ringing in our wonderful world.

Wilma R. Wright
Keota, IA

You Just Pray A Little Bit

Stewart Bell
Washington, IA

USS *Pennsylvania*
Pacific

Interview Date:
5 July 2010

Referral:
Paula Brinning

I left in July of 1942. It's a funny thing. I was born in Canada. I didn't have a birth certificate or citizenship. My folks had come down from Canada when I was two years old so there really wasn't a record of me. When I went up to enlist, I took a United Presbyterian Church Sunday School Certificate. I got up there and I was signing my name and filling out this thing and he said, "What's this for?" I said, "It's a Sunday School Certificate. I don't have a birth certificate." He said, "I don't want that, just sign your name. That's all I need."

The USS *Pennsylvania* was 333 ft long. We had 2,000 men on board. As the Fire Control Officer, I fired the main battery with a computer from five decks below. That included calculating the motion of the ship, the roll and the pitch, plus the range at which we were firing, which was at least 15,000 yards. If we used armored piercing shells we could shoot 20 – 25,000 yards. It was a long ways.

When we were landing troops, we used lighter, high explosives shells. We could set our nose cone and it would get so close to where we were targeting and then explode, or it would explode on contact.

I remember one story. We were in 13 different operations that landed troops. I don't know what island it was, but anyhow we got word from an

Army observer who was already on land. He said there was a pill box up there that was giving them some trouble. He gave the elevation and he gave the yards from him. We put that information into the computer, I pulled the trigger, and we laid a shell right inside that small diameter with a 14 inch gun. Taking into account the roll and pitch of the ship, that was pretty good shooting.

One time we were taking on ammunition. They would use three bags of powder with each shell. Anyhow, these bags of powder were coming in big canisters that would be five and a half or six feet tall. Everybody, including the officers, said there'd be an accident one day. One time they set a bunch of these cans down and they exploded on contact on our deck. That wiped out a bunch of men. We were told that they thought this powder had been sabotaged. That's all we knew.

But we did not have a hit on the ship and we knocked down 36 kamikazes (Japanese suicide planes). We sailed from the Bering Sea clear down into the Indian Ocean on the south. So we were all over the Pacific Ocean.

We were part of the operation that took the Aleutian Islands back from the Japanese. Attu was the first one. There were a lot of personnel on that island. When we went back for the second operation for Kiska, there wasn't a soul there but a dog. I don't know if the dog spoke Japanese but he might have! *(Laughs)*

The weather is pretty tough up there. That's the nastiest weather in the world. There's always wind and it's very rough. As I remember, it was like 33 or 30 degrees, but it felt much colder than hell. They told us not to get washed overboard because you will only last about 10 to 15 minutes in that cold water. Those soldiers got into those little landing crafts. They got soaked. I don't know how they survived, I really don't. The water was very rough. It was terrible.

I got aboard ship right after I got out of school in Great Lakes (Naval station in Chicago) in February of 1943. I enlisted in July of 1942. I went through boot camp and then had three to four months of school in Great Lakes. The USS *Pennsylvania* been slightly damaged at Pearl Harbor. I was on that ship until 1945. The main reason I enlisted in the Navy was because I didn't want to dig ditches and water didn't scare me.

Our ship was never hit (by enemy fire) during the war. We did not have any naval engagements. We had one possible naval engagement which was when we were clear down south and into the Indian Ocean. We knew that the Japanese and their ships were trying to get out of a group of islands that was south of China. We waited for them but they got past us. We were in GQ (general quarters) for the afternoon and didn't get out of GQ until the next day. That would have been a naval engagement, but we never fired a shot. Every gun was loaded for everything and then we had to unload them.

Our 14 inchers did not shoot at planes. We had four double mounts of 5 inch on the port and starboard. That's what we used to knock down the planes. We could set up a ring of steel firing from port or starboard. They could really load these guns in a hurry. They could get about a dozen men inside those mounts and the ammunition would come up an elevator into the mount. The Japanese planes never got through it.

The kamikaze planes were attacking us when we were up north in Kiska/Attu. We were surrounded by Japanese submarines. The skipper put our ship

"The way I felt when we were under attack, wondering if I would see tomorrow...I was scared the first time, I really was."

in between a salvo of torpedoes. The torpedo wake was here (gestures) and we went in between them. Thank God because I wouldn't be here today if we'd been hit with one of those.

They never unlock the doors below deck when there is something like that happening. The doors were watertight and we were stuck there five decks below. There was one way out. The two times I climbed out were just for practice.

The way I felt when we were under attack, wondering if I would see tomorrow...I was scared the first time, I really was. Everybody was scared, especially down in front. You just pray a little bit.

I'll tell you a little story. One big guy that I know of, he's dead now, he was so scared that he went behind a switchboard and shit his pants—just right there. That happened, and more than once. That's a terrible thing to say but you were that scared. I don't want to hear anyone say, "Oh, we weren't scared!" The hell they weren't! At least I was scared.

But after we had finished those two engagements up north, I forget what the next engagement was. I think it was the Solomon Islands. We went down there and we took that area within three or four days. Then we went into another group of islands very shortly after that.

You know, we got to thinking this is just another operation. We're not going to get hit. And we didn't. You get calloused I suppose, and confident. This was our life.

We had destroyers for escort ships. The destroyers sunk at least three Japanese subs up there in the Bering Sea. They depth charged them and we saw the oil slicks. We were always a flag ship with usually an admiral aboard. Skipper ran our ship, but the admiral was running the operations. We would take two or three weeks to get into an operation. Then we would go back. We always had at least 10 destroyers around us. They always took care of the admiral.

We were the 7th Fleet Flag Ship. I can't remember the admiral's name. He wasn't any of those big guys. We were always glad when the admirals left because it was spit and polish when they were aboard.

We were down in the Philippines twice. One time when we took General MacArthur back to the Philippines we ran out of ammunition below. We tied up to an ammunition ship and all of a sudden we were under air attack. Let me tell you, we cut the lines on that ammunition ship and got the hell out of there! That would have blown us all to hell if the ammunition ship had been hit.

I don't have anything against those men on the ammunition ships, but they had a different life than the rest of us. At 5:00 PM, they were through. If you wanted the ammunition unloaded, then we would have to unload it ourselves.

We were getting re-supplied from firing our main battery on the landings that were made. We were firing our main battery almost constantly. That's why we were short of ammunition. We were supporting the land troops, especially when we were up north in the Bering Sea.

When we were landing troops, we were firing over their heads all the time to keep everything (enemy response) down. The other island operations we were on were Palau, two times in the Philippines, the Solomon Islands and some others I can't remember.

One island I remember taking, after we took it, there wasn't anything left. We just more or less circled the island. Everything was quiet. There were no Japs left or anything else. We had liberty and went on this island and there wasn't a tree left on the damn thing. It was just shredded to nothing. That island belonged to England. And we (the US) had to pay England for shooting up the timber. Now this is a story that we were always told, but I don't know if it's true. *(Records indicate that this is a reference to Parry Island, which was densely populated with palm trees all the way to the water's edge. After the Pennsylvania bombarded it to support landing troops, not a single tree was left standing by the morning of February 22.)*

I can't name all 13 of the operations, but the Solomons—there were two or three different groups of islands in there that we were

> *"Let me tell you, we cut the lines on that ammunition ship and got the hell out of there! That would have blown us all to hell if the ammunition ship had been hit."*

bombarding. That's where Harry Barker was killed. That's the guy they named the VFW unit here for. Harry Barker was from here. He was about three years older than I am. Harry was a Marine killed in the landing of Tarawa. That was a tough one.

When we had liberty on an island, there'd be port and starboard watches. They'd get us a couple cans of beer and that would be our afternoon. We'd swim. We made it to Australia for liberty. We had a week down there and that was strictly our R&R (rest and recreation). I had three different liberties and that was quite a lot of fun. The policemen in Sydney were the biggest men I have ever seen. Real tall, like 6 foot 4, big men walking around like policemen do. Whenever the ship would sponsor a party we had plenty of alcohol. They made sure we had it. That's just part of life.

The guns were worn out, the riflings were gone in the 5 inch guns by the time the war ended. So, we came back to Frisco, and we were in dry dock there for about three months getting re-gunned and everything.

My wife got to be with me for 30 days out there. Otherwise, when I left, she did not know where I was for two years. My daughter was six weeks old when I left. Anyhow, my wife got to stay with me on the base. We rented a Quonset hut. When she left, we were about ready to have our first shake-down cruise after we had been in dry dock. We left very shortly after that, which was about in July or August of 1945.

We went to Pearl Harbor and got some more ammunition, got some more stores. Nobody ever told us where we were going. But we were heading north and knew we were going to Japan. This was just going to be another operation as far as we were concerned.

By that time Iwo Jima and Okinawa had been taken. We went to Buckner Bay, Okinawa. You have never seen so many naval ships in your life. The whole bay was just full of ships. But the war was over. We were told the war was over because they had dropped those (atomic) bombs on Japan.

When we got into Okinawa, we went to Condition Four. That means there is no threat, it is nothing. There is hardly a watch on a gun. There were a few men topside that were part of the watch—there had to be some there all the time even with the war over. About 6:00 that night, a goddam Jap came in and laid a torpedo into our starboard quarter. Our quarter deck was awash in a half an hour. Three sea-going tugs came along side and pumped us out. We had the screws shot off of us. We were dead in the water. They towed us from Okinawa to Guam to dry dock. This is where they were going to fix us up to make us sea-worthy.

We were 30 days getting to Guam. We ran into a 100 mph hurricane on the way and we were backing down five knots all one day. We were in dry dock for 30 days. Of course, this is after the war was over. When we left there, all we had left was two screws (propellers) that we could be repaired enough for use. We went to Pearl where we picked up 4,000 Marines. They were going home too. It filled the ship, I'll tell you. We left Pearl and were headed for Bremerton, Washington. We got maybe two days out and one screw got to vibrating. They sent a diver down to cut it off. So then we had only the one screw. It took 30 days from Pearl to Bremerton. And that was the end of it.

Question: Where did the torpedo hit your ship?
The Jap pilot couldn't have spotted it better. It was right in the quarter deck. The screws were right underneath it. We drew 33 ft and that area was awash in half an hour. A division was killed, about 50 men. They never knew what hit them. That Japanese plane had to have taken off from someplace in Buckner Bay. They were still shooting. Do you know Bob Huber? He was a Seabee. He helped construct the landing strips (for our fighter planes). The Japanese would have been up in the hills some place. This was right after Okinawa had been taken. So there were still Japs on the island.

The war had been over for two or three days when we were hit. He (the Japanese pilot) came in the next night and got a destroyer. The next night after that they were waiting for him and our airplanes shot him down.

One night, I don't know where we were, it might have been the Philippines, I'm not positive; we were getting ready to land troops in the next day or two on this one particular island. There was a Jap sub that got in that night and sunk a small (escort) carrier. I think everyone was lost. I know you never read about this in the books because no one ever said anything about it. But we knew about it. There were a lot of cover-ups.

I was married when I enlisted. I could write letters to my wife, Marge, but they were censored. Some of the officers were very decent about it, saying, "Just address it and seal it, I don't want to look at it." But a lot of the officers did read the letters, so my letters were pretty much all censored. She didn't know where I was for two years. It was very tough on her. We lived in an apartment house up on North Marion. My Dad and I owned it. When I left, that's where she was living. After I had been gone for six months or so she was running out of money. My folks had a little apartment right above them and said for her to come and live with them. So that saved my wife, really. Because you know, she had (our infant) Carmen to take care of.

I went topside at night if it wasn't too rough. A lot of times, even when it was pretty smooth, we would run into 20 ft waves—big swells. You couldn't go up topside then. We didn't lose any sailors from that, though.

We had a great sick bay. I was in it for a week one time. That's when we were in Long Beach. Our ship couldn't go clear into Long Beach because it drew so much water at 33 ft. But we were outside a breakwater and you had to get back on the last liberty boat by midnight. I missed the boat so I had to wait until the next morning to be picked up. I felt like something was crawling on me when we got back on board. We had been staying in a YMCA. I went down to sick bay to see if there was something on me. The officer said, "Pull up your shirt!" I did and he said, "You've got German Measles!"

When I was discharged from the Navy and came home I went to work after just kind of lollygagging around for a week. I had worked at *The Washington Evening Journal* before I left. The summer that I enlisted, I said to my boss in the press room, Max Marble, "You don't have very much work going on here and I can work with my Dad." He was a painter. Then December 7th came along. I wasn't actually working for *The Journal* when I enlisted. So when I came home, Elder and Shannon said, "You weren't working for us when you enlisted, so therefore we don't owe you a job." But that didn't bother me. I was living on the edge so that didn't make any difference to me.

Dick McCleary came along and he said, "Stew, I can use you. So I worked for McCleary's for five years and then I bought a newspaper. I worked there 11 years running the newspaper. Then I came back and worked for McCleary's for another 25 years running a press. So I was never out of work for very long. I knew I had to go to work; I had a daughter and a wife. I had to go to work. I always thought that a lot of those fellows that came home put on being scared and so on. A gunshot would go off and they would cringe. I heard just as many gunshots as anybody did. I didn't act like that. I knew I had to go to work. You got on with your life. You had to.

Harold Wehr and I more or less enlisted together. He was an aerial photographer and he never left the United States.

I don't know where I was in the Pacific, but I went up in the radio shack that night of D-Day on June 6. I was on watch with radar, but they also had complete radio contact with everything that was going on in Europe. I heard tanks talking back and forth. I'm not kidding. This was out in the middle of the Pacific Ocean. I could hear them talking about what they had to do. Maneuver here, maneuver there. This was short wave radio. I heard those guys talking but I don't know how. There was about a 12 hour difference between us and them.

When I was in the radio shack, I was on watch with the radar. A lot of times I was the radar operator director for the 5 inch guns.

When GQ (General Quarters) was sounded, we would turn the power on for the guns so they could be mechanized. We had a lot of steel around us. We would be in GQ from 3:00 at night until 3:00 the next day.

One Christmas we made a Christmas tree. We were also issued glasses of alcohol to take care of the guns. We were supposed to take pure alcohol and wipe them off. We spit on them and saved the alcohol for our Christmas party. No one got drunk but everybody got happy.

By the time we left our bunks, we could be fully

"I knew I had to go to work. You got on with your life. You had to."

armed and ready to fight anything within two or three minutes. That's a lot of men moving fast! Down port, up starboard…we had ladders. The top deck above our plotting room was a thick, solid steel floor. They would lock it from underneath. It was armored plate and that's where we were. All the battleships had this armored plate around the center part of the ship and the belly. The decks and also the outside walls of the ship were like that. They don't make them like that anymore. The *Iowa* and the *Missouri* were the last two battleships that were built like that.

I was talking to Dave Brinning. He left with the Cavalry Red Horse Troop in December or January of 1940. Dave and I were sitting eating dinner together and he said, "Well, it's all over isn't it, Stew?" I said, "Yup." Not many of them are left. Bob Porter died about a year ago. He was in the Red Horse.

The Navy took USS *Pennsylvania* out to the Bikini Islands atoll to see if an A-bomb could sink it. They dropped this bomb on it. Of course, nobody was aboard ship. But it didn't sink. So they sent eight men aboard to open up the sea cocks. All of them died later from being overexposed to radiation. I don't know why they didn't just torpedo it.

My rank was 2nd Class Fire Control. It is a right arm rank. There are no right arm ranks anymore. There is no fire control anymore. Right arm rank is the same as a gunnery or gun division. A quartermaster is a right arm rank. Machinist's mates and all the rest were all left arm ranks. Don't ask me why.

I went back east to Washington, D.C., on the Honor Flight. I saw some stuff that made us all cry. It was a wonderful, four day trip out there.

Question: Do you have a message to pass along to the youth of today?

If I had a message for the kids about WWII, it would be that you always hear from people that you shouldn't go to war. And I know people that stayed home and didn't go to war. But I think that as a Christian, you have to. I really believe that. I didn't feel that I was ever doing anything that was against my religion or anything like that. I never felt like that. I think that as a Christian, you have to defend where you live. You have to defend your country.

Wilma Larson was in the Navy. She is a nice woman. She is a joy, really.

A lot of the men in my division—not because I was in it—but they were pretty smart people. You had to have a certain IQ to get into school and I had that IQ. I'm not bragging or anything, but thank God I did have that IQ because that is a lot better than being a deck hand.

In terms of pay, an apprentice seaman made about $25. But as a full seaman, with three white stripes, I think I got $60. And that's pretty good money back then. My wife also got subsistence and with a child, we got a little bit more. I think Marge got $80 and that was just barely enough to keep everything going. On board ship we got 20% hazardous duty pay. I got that all during the whole war. Even though we were sitting in port, we were still a part of the crew of the ship and they didn't cut the pay.

So, it was a great life. Really it was.

Interview transcribed by Kathy Tanner.

As a young boy I grew up in the Highland area (Haskins and Ainsworth). As was customary we would visit our neighbors occasionally in the evening. World War II was the topic of their conversations and I was always listening and was horrified at the number of men that were killed. There were many injuries and fatalities from our local area. At school I drew pictures of Japanese and German soldiers with bombs dropping from US planes on to them. I was 8 years old at the time. Our class at our country school would go out and collect milkweed pods which were used for flotation life vests for the service men. Our family was very grateful to the thousands of brave men and women who served their country. Our sacrifices at home were nothing compared to the sacrifices of our young men and women. As a small boy I was very scared that the Germans and Japanese would come to the USA. Every night our family would turn on our battery operated radio to listen to newscaster Gabriel Heatter who gave quite a dismal account of the war. The kerosene lamp cast its eerie shadows as I would go to bed scared and worried. Thank you to our heroes that have allowed us to enjoy freedom. A very memorable day in my life was when our crank phones had a line ring to report that the war was over.

Gary Murphy
Washington, IA

A Mariner's Journey

Jim Schmidt
Washington, IA

SS Illinois
Merchant Marines

Interview Date:
22 July 2010

Referral:
Wendel Guy

I grew up in the sand hills of Nebraska near the town of Broken Bow. This was an isolated area at the beginning of WWII and I had been out of Custer County once. At that time I had no idea where Pearl Harbor was located.

In August of 1944 I enlisted in the Maritime Service at Denver, Colorado, and was sent to Catalina Island 27 miles off of the coast of Southern California, for eight weeks of Boot Camp. At Catalina, I was issued Maritime gear which included work clothes, shoes, a blue and a white dress uniform, and a large waterproof billfold in which to carry my identifying Z number and shipping orders. I still have the billfold and all of the shipping orders.

At this base we drilled; we were introduced to a gas chamber; we ran obstacle courses and boxed. On Saturday nights the recruits were paired up and boxing matches were held at the famous Avalon Casino. This effort was worth a good steak dinner. We also trained to jump off of a 30 ft high dock with life jacket and swim an eighth of a mile out into the Pacific and back to shore. Having never been in anything larger than the Middle Loup River in Nebraska I felt that I moved two strokes ahead and one stroke back.

Boot camp also consisted of classroom work, studying the nomenclature of ships and the sea,

how to tie a multitude of knots in a line and how to handle a line (rope). Dock side we were taught how to abandon ship in an emergency and were trained how to lower a lifeboat from a ship. Six men were placed in a typical ship's lifeboat and we practiced rowing off shore from Catalina Island. We were given minimal weapons training.

After finishing Boot, our last order was to run up and back down a small mountain back of our training base. After this run and climb, I was sure that I did not want to be a mountain climber.

After boot camp I was assigned to the SS *Illinois* a WWI Tanker owned by the Texas Company (Texaco). The *Illinois* was a very old ship docked in Seattle, Washington. It was at this time I became aware that I was a civilian, and not in a branch of the navy.

The *Illinois* sailed to the Aleutian Islands to deliver high octane aviation fuel to the islands of Adack, Attu, Kiska, Cold Bay, Dutch Harbor and several other small islands in the chain. Dutch Harbor had been bombed early in the war by the Japanese. We did not travel in a convoy for very frankly the navy preferred not to get too close to us, as we were loaded with high octane fuel and some ammunition.

Nine thousand Russian troops were stationed at

Cold Bay and it was believed that they would assist in the invasion of Japan. Cold bay was a bleak, cold and forlorn piece of rock. All that I can remember seeing was the rock and an old broken down dock and pumping station. We were cautioned not to go ashore, however at that time I did not know why. We were not told that the Russians were stationed there at that time.

The Merchant Marine ships usually carried two Navy officers and seven Navy armed guards to man the guns. There was a 20mm on the bow of the Illinois, two .50 calibers port and starboard, and a five inch gun on the stern. During general quarters drill, it was my job to pump water to the two .50 calibers. Very frankly they would only fire about one half of the time. Our ship also carried two ash cans aft, (depth charges) for submarines.

The North Pacific and the Bering Sea are very rough waters with waves up to 30 ft high. At times the sea water would flow through the open port holes where we were sleeping. One young mariner from Arkansas spent about 50% of his time hanging over the rail seasick. It also was cold most of the time and ice would form on the lines and cables just like the TV show, *Deadliest Catch*.

A tanker pitches, and at times the bow of the ship would go clear out of sight. A cargo ships rolls side to side, which is much different than a pitch. Occasionally the sun would shine and the water was very smooth and the sunshine was great.

We did not see any submarines while we were making these deliveries but they had us doing sub watch anyway. It was suggested that the Japanese released a large number of magnetic mines near the end of the war that floated with the ocean current up the Aleutian chain. You can imagine the outcome if a mine had detonated on a tanker hull filled with high octane fuel. The SS *Illinois* would have been lying at the bottom of the Pacific Ocean in 2x2 inch scrap metal.

I first worked in the Stewards department, and then transferred to the Deck department. Deck duties included standing watch at night, and a turn at the wheel, as well as chipping paint and painting the deck. I must have chipped and painted ten miles. Later I had an opportunity to become a baker; I felt that this would be a good trade later in life.

On my last trip to Attu I saw my first P-38 plane. I thought that it was unbelievably fast. On our return to the Port of Seattle I also remember that "Sparks," our radio man told us that President Roosevelt had died, I believe on April 12, 1945.

Interestingly the SS *Illinois* sank near Ketchikan, Alaska on the trip after I debarked. It was later refloated and sold to a Spanish or Portuguese company.

The second vessel that I was assigned to was a new C-I cargo ship named the *Cape Igvack*. We shipped large amounts of barbed wire to Guatemala. Barefoot natives would go down in the hold and unload the spools of barbed wire with no shoes on. The soles of their feet must have been an inch thick.

We had liberty in Guatemala, and when everyone else went to the bars, I went exploring in the seaside jungle and discovered a thatched hut with both people and pigs living under it.
I left the area immediately and definitely would not go back there today.

On this trip we also hauled heavy equipment to South America. I remember a huge truck that was lashed to the deck. I think that it was to be used to haul logs from the jungle.

My next ship was the *Cape Brenton,* another new C-I cargo ship. We delivered cargo to Buenaventura, Columbia, in South America. The Custom Officials deported three illegal Columbians and put them aboard the *Cape Brenton.* They were free to roam the ship and often would come back to the fantail where we were working and talk to us. This is how I learned my first Spanish. *Uno, Dos, Tres.* Later because of my interest in these countries, I tutored many of the Latino students at the Washington Jr. High. (1991-1997).

Near the harbor in Buenaventura there was a German ship lying keel up that the Germans had scuttled rather than having it captured by the Americans. This was a huge ship and an interesting sight. The German navy roamed the eastern and southern waters near our coasts in WWII (especially their submarines).

On the return trip, we docked on the Pacific side of the Panama Canal for a day to wait our turn to enter the locks. Some of the crew decided to go swimming in a beautiful new pool that had just been built. In our group was a young seventeen year old crew member from Washington, State. He was an excellent swimmer and also a good diver. Wanting to show off a bit he crawled up to the high board took his stance and yelled " look at me." When he opened his mouth to speak his dentures fell to the bottom of the pool. This was hilarious and he spent the next 30 minutes diving to retrieve his dentures.

Being in the Merchant Marine there were some light moments. This was one of those lighter moments that I still remember.

On the next trip we crossed a smoother Atlantic to Scotland and Wales and delivered food supplies. In Swansea, Wales, I recall that many of the roofs of the stone houses had been blown off by German buzz bombs. This was a depressing sight and there was debris everywhere. Scotland was a different story and seemed quite nice. It was here that I was introduced to fish and chips. We were also near Loch Lomond. When I was a boy in Nebraska, I never dreamed of seeing this famous lake.

We always sailed under contractual obligation. We'd sign a contract for each voyage which was regulated by the Coast Guard. When not on board ship, all pay stopped for the Mariner. We were on our own. My salary was $55.00 a month, paid by the company that owned the ship not the government. Pay doubled when we reached a danger zone.

We were an island in itself during the war, a floating depot for supplies going in and out.

I have stayed in contact with a few shipmates, however there wasn't much camaraderie aboard ship, because when we were assigned a new ship we met new shipmates.

Over 800 U.S. Merchant Ships were sunk during the war and one was sunk in the Gulf of Mexico after peace was declared with Germany. During WWII many were sunk in sight of the east coast. If a German submarine torpedoed a Merchant Ship traveling in a convoy to England, survivors many times were not rescued because of the existing submarine danger.

There were many salty old Mariners at the beginning of the war, and so many ships and crews were lost that new sailors had to be trained by the National Maritime Service to replace them. I fall into this category. Of the 250,000 Merchant Marine who went to sea one out of every twenty six who sailed lost their lives. There are approximately 10,000 who sailed in WWII still living.

Twice before his death, President Roosevelt asked Congress to include the Merchant Marine in veteran's benefits. Congress did not heed this request; however under some prodding in 1988 they did declare that those who served on ocean going ships between December 7, 1941 and December 31, 1946, be classified as veterans.

Even though the United States Merchant Marine participated in every major invasion during WWII they were denied the benefits of the G.I. bill after the war, however they do now have access to VA health care. My official discharge was issued by the U.S. Coast Guard in 1988.

After serving in the U.S. Merchant Marine, I came back to Nebraska in 1946 and farmed for five years before moving to Iowa. I graduated from the University of Iowa with a marketing degree in business. Most of my career was spent with Morton International as a regional sales representative.

As I reflect back over the past 68 years I probably would not have shipped with the Merchant Marine but would have joined either the US Navy or the US Coast Guard as the GI Bill after the war offered an opportunity for a college education. One must go back to those days and realize that money was scarce and scholarships were not so available.

I have been able to meet my goals in life, and life has been good for both Gerry my loving wife of 65 years and me. I am very thankful for a loving family, Kate and Kirk our daughter and son, our grandchildren, our great grandchildren, and our good health.

By Jim Schmidt

WE WERE AFRAID YOU WOULD JUMP OFF THE TRAIN

Thomas J. Berdo
Washington, IA

20th Armored Division
Europe

Interview Date:
2 August 2010

Referral:
Sue Stannard & Jean Potratz

I went in February of '43. My basic training was at Ft. Knox, did my armor training there as well. I was in the 20th Armored Division. I did some training to be in the Corps of Engineers, but didn't like standing in water up to my neck. Edwin Hora was in the Corps of Engineers. He had quite a record, something like three to four hundred straight days in combat. That was a long stretch. We landed in France on the 3rd of March, 1945.

I tried to transfer to the Army Air Corps before going overseas. I wanted to be a bombardier/navigator, but my left eye's vision was only 20/25 and that rejected me. Later regulations allowed for 20/25 to be acceptable so I put in for a transfer again. My CO was upset with me, saying that I had already been through tank maintenance and armorer school and I had just "wasted his time," but he finally agreed to the transfer.

The Air Corps sent me to college in Alva, Oklahoma. They made the courses fairly easy and it worked out good for me as I got a semester of college credit out of it. It was nice to live in a college dorm and be issued officer uniforms. Then another directive came down through Army channels, requiring everyone who had transferred to the Air Corps to return to units that they had

been trained for. So I was transferred to the 86th Infantry Division down in Louisiana. It was quite a shock to my system after living high on the hog to be sent back to grunt and sweat duty. The guy I was rooming with was from Pennsylvania and he didn't want to go to the infantry at all. He'd sit on his bed and tap his one knee with his trench knife hoping to disable it so he'd avoid the infantry. I don't know if he was successful or not, but he was still tapping it when I left. The losses incurred during the Battle of the Bulge were the reason behind this new transfer policy.

I had a cousin who was the Activities Director at that infantry base. It's not what you know, but rather who you know that helps you in life. He got me transferred to the quartermasters because I had been on the track team in high school. So now I was on the division track team. We even went to a couple of track meets where I found out I was out of my league.

We were the very last division sent to Europe. We went by train and one morning when I awoke, I looked out and thought, "My gosh, this looks familiar." We were going through Cotter, Iowa. I asked the guys with me why they didn't wake me up when we went through Washington? They replied, "We were afraid you would jump off the train!"

I was in the Quarter Master Company and my job kind of shifted around. I had gone to tank mechanic school but they found that my mechanical ability was somewhat suspect. I had a heck of a time with carburation. They had looked at my service record and saw that I had experience driving a tractor so that's where they put me. I worked on the L3 (light tank) and the L5 (heavy tank). The Shermans were the L4s. I had the rank of sergeant and was placed in charge of various things including rations, gasoline, and the company armorer. I worked on guns that wouldn't function properly, everything from the .45 pistol all the way up to the big 75mms. We stayed behind the front lines, taking the road of least resistance.

All the gasoline was hauled in five gallon jerry cans loaded on trucks. My job was to assign the truck drivers. Occasionally the convoys would come under artillery fire or strafing from enemy planes. I was strafed once. In 2003, a small piece of shrapnel was discovered by a doctor lodged behind one of my eyes that I didn't know was there. We were in the battle of Cologne and moving up to the Ruhr Pocket. We were on one side of the Rhine River and the German's on the other. It happened there. The whole division was moving up after dark and under artillery bombardment for a short stretch, and then two or three planes made one pass strafing us. There was quite a bit of confusion inside our truck cab with all the bullets flying around. My supply sergeant wiped a little blood off my forehead after the attack but couldn't see anything. Nothing hurt so I didn't bother reporting it. Now the fragment is apparently starting to move around a little and causing me balance problems. My daughter is attempting to get me a Purple Heart through the Veterans Administration.

I remember seeing the result of Hitler's forced labor camps and the way the Germans treated people. I saw men and women that were displaced persons. I don't remember any children. They just walked around looking like living skeletons. I saw one prison camp. The memory stays with you.

We crossed the Rhine a little below Cologne.

"In 2003, a small piece of shrapnel was discovered by a doctor lodged behind one of my eyes that I didn't know was there."

General Patton was there on the river bank as we drove by. I was close enough to have pulled his six shooters out of his holsters if I had wanted to. We were with Patton's 3rd Army at the time. Sometimes we were with the 5th Army. We moved around a lot. We went wherever they needed us. We eventually made it to Austria at the war's end. It was beautiful country. We were near Hitler's Eagle's Nest, but never got to actually see it. His beliefs were very strong about what a fighting man should be.

Question: What was your opinion of General Patton?

When you were in his army you needed to look in good condition. You needed to be shaved with your hair cut, your clothes neat, boots shined and you wore your neck tie. There was no fooling around with George. He had us all buffaloed but we respected him for what he was. His beliefs were very strong about what a fighting man should do. If you weren't holding up your end of it, then it fell on someone else. I thought he got a very raw deal there, frankly.

After Germany surrendered, we were the first division sent back to the states. We were given a thirty day leave which I spent at home and then we were to report to Camp San Luis Obispo in California. They trained me down in San Diego on how to load ships with tanks, trucks and other stuff like guns for the invasion of Japan. My wife came out to visit me in California. We had a nice situation for a while and then I had to ship out. She went back to Iowa and I went to Pittsburgh, California, a point of embarkation. We got about half way across and then that wonderful man, Harry Truman, dropped the bomb and then about a week later dropped another one and that took care of my service.

I devoted three years of my life to WWII. At the time, there seemed to be no end in sight. I figured I'd be in the service until I got knocked off. Have you talked to Jim Gallagher? He was at Iwo. He lives just across the courtyard in an apartment. How about I call him for you? He's pretty modest about what he did.

I taught at the Washington High School until retirement in 1985. I was eighteen or nineteen when I went in to military service. I didn't have any deep thoughts about joining. Everybody else was in too. There weren't any thoughts of trying to evade service. It was just something that you had to do. So you were serving your country and hoping you were fortunate enough to return home. When I was in the service, you went were you where supposed to go, one pin on the map. I'd like to say that I made a difference but I didn't, because everybody else was doing the same thing.

Comment: You were all part of the war effort that saved the country.

Yes, we were all part of the war effort. You can say what you want about dropping the atomic bomb, but I wouldn't be here if we hadn't.

DO OR DIE

Jim Gallagher
Washington, IA

5th Marine Division
Pacific

Interview Date:
6 August 2010

Referral:
T.J. Berdo

I was graduated from high school in 1941 and went to work for Montgomery Ward right away in the shoe department. I worked first in Davenport, then Marshalltown, and then was transferred to Muscatine. I just decided that with the war and such that I would join the Marine Corps. I joined in November of 1942. I enlisted in St. Louis; that's where they swore me in. They took me from St. Louis to the Marine Corps base in San Diego, and that's where I went to boot camp.

I got out of boot camp, and had the opportunity to choose where I wanted to go. At that time the Marine Corps had paratroopers and I went to parachute school at Camp Gillespie outside San Diego. Boot camp was about six weeks and then there was another six weeks of parachute training.

I wanted to be a paratrooper because I just thought I'd like it. At that time it was early on in the war and there were special outfits like the Marine Raiders and the Marine Paratroopers. They were the elite. I got jump pay of $50 a month and that had some influence on me.

The training was quick and we went overseas pretty quickly after that. It took us 21 days to go from Camp Pendleton to New Caledonia. *(New Caledonia is a series of islands in the southwest Pacific Ocean, about 750 miles east of Australia.)*

And there we trained in war and did some more training jumps from DC-3s.

When we got to New Caledonia we trained there for a while and they decided they couldn't use paratroopers in the islands in the way that we were trained because of the jungle. So we went from New Caledonia to Guadalcanal for just a bit and then on to Vella Lavella, which is a small island.

Our company guarded a PT boat station because there were Japanese still loose on the island. Then from Vella Lavella we went to Bougainville, the biggest island in the Solomon group. There a 20-mile beachhead was established. It was more of a swampy area; we did a lot of patrols.

One time we did go on a raid ten miles behind the Japanese lines and it landed us right in the Japanese company regimental command post. A day or two later, Tokyo Rose said the 1st Marine Parachute Battalion was wiped out. Well, it wasn't! We got in and we got out. We had casualties of course. The 1st Marine Parachute Battalion and 1st Marine Raider Company went with us. Our Battalion was only 750 men and that's under-strength. But the Raider Company brought the number up to around 900 or 1,000. And we were just out-numbered when we landed; we just couldn't make any headway because there were too many Japanese. Intelligence made a mistake about the area where we came in.

We disembarked from landing crafts and that's the way we went in. We landed on that raid between 4:00 a.m. and 5:00 am; it was still dark. Yeah, it was nerve-wracking. We were there the whole day and then at night, the U.S. came in and got us and took us off. They couldn't do it during the day because the Japanese had artillery. There were mainly mortars because it was fairly thick jungle. We had planes go over that reported there were a lot of trucks bringing in troops all around our area. So we don't really know how many Japanese troops were actually there.

We were on Bougainville for three or four months maybe. We did a lot of patrols. It was a swampy area so you had to go through swamps. So what you did was go on patrol until you contacted the enemy to see that they weren't building up or anything. Yeah, it was kind of scary. These were company patrols; sometimes less, but most of the time company patrols. The patrols normally lasted all day, but not overnight. We had casualties because the Japanese would let you walk through their lines and then you had to get back through them again.

At that time in the war—I think maybe we were somewhat brainwashed—but you sure didn't want to be taken prisoner. You'd fight rather than be taken prisoner. But not very many guys that I know of were taken prisoner, simply because of the torture that the Japanese put you through—at least that's what we heard of it anyway. I think some of it was true. I was not aware of anyone in my company being taken prisoner. I don't know of anyone who was missing in action, but we did have a lot of casualties, of course. But Bougainville was almost as hard on you physically as was the war because of the swamp area, jungle area, and the disease. There was a lot of malaria, hookworm, and jaundice. The U.S. finally decided to disband all Marine Paratroopers and all Marine Raiders. So we left Bougainville and went back to Guadalcanal. We waited for a ship; then we came home. It wasn't hard to go back when I came home on 30-day leave. Of course I didn't know I was going to Iwo Jima.

> *"I felt pretty good when I saw the U.S. flag flying over Iwo but then again the fighting was just getting started."*

When I went back to our outfit, the 1st Marine Parachute Regiment and the Marine Raiders then formed the nucleus of the 5th Marine Division.

I was at that time a PFC—private first class. I was a machine gunner with a 1919A4. It was a .30 caliber, of course. That's what I was when we landed on Iwo Jima. We suffered a lot of casualties there. Later on I was a machine gun section leader. It involved two guns. I was one of the few who could still operate a machine gun properly and take care of us so I did that. We got a rank raise when we got back.

We went in on Iwo on Day 1. I was in the 26th Marines. There were three regiments in our division. We were supposed to be held in reserve in case we were needed. Well, we landed about noon, because they needed us. We went up to Red Beach and took a lot of artillery and mortar fire and small arms. Of course, there were a lot of casualties. After we were there on the edge of the airport, we went around the airport, and then went down on one side of the island and then we went up on the other side of the island. We made some pretty good gains. But then again, we lost quite a few men. And when I say quite a few, I mean in your company you could have lost 15 or 20 or 30 men that day.

I felt pretty good when I saw the U.S. flag flying over Iwo but then again the fighting was just getting started. How did we do it? We just kept going.

Most of the nights we were awake. At different times there were Japanese who would get wounded out in front of where our hole was and you could hear them groaning and moaning. And pretty soon we would hear a grenade going off. They would kill themselves if they were wounded. I didn't see too many Japanese soldiers outside of their fortifications, but yes we did see some. They would try to infiltrate at night. That's when they would get shot. I know at different times out in front of our hole there would be Japanese who were shot and then you would hear them talking to us saying, "Marine, you die!"

The intricate defense that the Japanese had is just amazing. We went through an area and they had artillery on a track that they ran down into a cave then they would bring it out and fire it, and then run it back down in the hole. They had several of those, but the small arms fire is what took a lot of lives.

We would either ignore the holes if no one was around them and just keep going, or sometimes we'd blow out the holes into the caves. Of course, it was hard to close them up. We used flamethrowers because the Japanese were really afraid of them. On tanks we had these flamethrowers that looked like flames came out of the main guns.

One time we were in an area that was pretty rugged; we had some Japanese who came in behind us. We didn't know it. Somebody yelled from behind us, "grenade!" and I immediately looked out front thinking that it was coming from that direction, but the grenade came from behind. It landed right behind an M1 sitting on a rock in this big shell hole that we were in. It landed behind that M1 and it busted it out; that M1 saved my life.

Prior to that incident this one guy said, "Gallagher, you've got to be one of the luckiest guys in the world." I had been firing my machine gun for cover while our troops were moving up in an area and the Japanese kept shooting at me, too. They kept hitting below me, and below me; then above me. Finally, I moved. I just had a little indentation that I was firing from, and after I moved, that little indentation got splattered with bullets.

Yes, I was lucky but I had a lot of friends really close to me get killed. And I had one of my better friends killed right on my shoulder; we were shoulder-to-shoulder. He got hit by a sniper. I had another friend talking to me; we were in the hole. A sniper shot—probably at me—but instead hit my friend in the side. Yeah, I had a lot of close calls.

One time when a grenade went off in our hole, all I had was a machine gun. I grabbed a carbine and started up the other way to avoid where the grenade came from. I ran into a Jap. I raised up the carbine to shoot him and the carbine was on lock. So I pressed on the carbine. At that time, on one side was the clip release and the other side was the off lock. I pressed the clip release and the clip dropped out! That Japanese was evidently more

scared than I, and he jumped behind a rock. I threw a grenade and got him.

How did we know what to do? Well, we just did it, there wasn't much telling us what to do. Yeah, it was do or die.

At least 6,000 Marines were killed on Iwo Jima, and a lot were wounded there. Yeah, it was tough to get on the boat and leave all those guys that we left behind. The thing that was sad to me, too, was I had kids—replacements—that came into our section, who were 17, or 18 years-old. They didn't know anything. Some of them got killed and they hadn't even got a start in life. No, war is not good. I wondered why I didn't get hurt and so many did. But…it was hard.

On Iwo Jima, we saw one of these big B-29s land. Come to find out that Dick Paul's, brother, Don, was a navigator on that crippled plane that landed. He was one of the first planes to land. It had lots of bullet holes in it and it needed to land. I knew Dick, but I didn't personally see him at that time.

After Iwo Jima, we went back to Hawaii to Camp Tarawa on the Big Island. Then we were training to make a landing on the southern island in Japan when the war ended. Yes, I was happy I didn't have to do that. According to the information we had, we were supposed to be a diversionary force on one side while the Army landed on the other side.

We went up there as first occupation troops on the southern island in. When we got there we went to Sasebo in Kyushu, which is the Annapolis of Japan. We didn't see anybody except a few soldiers. We were there for about a week before they started coming in out of the hills.

When we got to Japan, the Japanese people were very humble. It was difficult. We had instructions to treat all of them with respect and do nothing to them. The Japanese people were surprised at the Marines. Now myself, I am not a big person. There were quite a few Marines who were 6 ft to 6'4" or 6'5". And the Japanese people were amazed at how big the Marines were. There were a lot of rumors among them about what Marines did.

My company suffered 150% casualties at Iwo

> *"I just had a little indentation that I was firing from, and after I moved, that little indentation got splattered with bullets."*

Jima. Replacements would come in as the fight went on. There weren't many of the original members left. Our company started out at 240 men at Iwo. I do know that 99 out of the original 240 men were killed. There were more than that wounded.

I was never injured the entire time I was in the service. Yes, it is amazing.

The other thing too that I have always said, is that any soldier, Marine, Sailor or Army, or whoever was in combat…anytime that you are shot at, it is just as bad for one as it is for the other.

Question: Were you sacred the entire time you were in combat?
Well, you know, not really. You were scared but you weren't. You didn't even think about it. It was probably due to my training, maybe. After I got out of the service for 40 years or maybe even longer, I didn't hardly ever even think of war. Yeah, it's probably good that I didn't.

I was awarded a Bronze Star. Well, it wasn't for anything particularly heroic. Jim's Bronze Star Recommendation reads:
Private First Class Gallagher voluntarily and with utter disregard for his own personal safety exposed himself to enemy fire, personally selecting positions for his machine guns from which he could successfully direct fire into the enemy positions. His action forced the enemy fire to slacken, thereby enabling the platoon to advance with a minimum of casualties.

I have my Parachute Wings. I was an Expert Rifleman. I got three Battle Stars. They represent Bougainville and Vella Lavella. I also have a Battle Star for Iwo Jima. Our unit also received the Presidential Unit Citation for Iwo Jima.

I don't particularly talk about it.

It's true. Once a Marine, always a Marine.
The attitude "charge hell with a bucket of water"—that was the paratrooper attitude and the Marine Corps' too. I'm an Airborne Marine that never was.

Interview transcribed by Kathy Tanner.

Japan? This Will Last A Week

Rev. Fred Bickhart
Washington, IA

Navy, Combat Intelligence
Pacific

Interview Date:
12 August 2010

Referral:
Personal Contact

I enlisted in the United States Navy in 1941 before the attack on Pearl Harbor. I graduated from high school in Corona, California, about 50 miles south of Los Angeles. It was June of 1941. I had been working at the market all through high school and I kept on working for there a while after graduating. I have a brother just older than I am. I also had three brothers and a sister. My oldest brother lived in L.A. and he was married. My brother just older than I called one day in September and said, "I'm gonna enlist in the Navy." I said, "Oh, hang on, I'll go with you." *(Laughs)*

Anyway, my brother and I headed off down to San Diego for boot camp and we went through it together. I wanted to go to quarter master school and he wanted to go to radio school so we compromised and we went to radio school.

And I was going to radio school at the Naval Reserve Armory right where Dodger Stadium is now. We were assigned to radio school during the Pearl Harbor attack December 7. On that particular date, I had gone home for the weekend to see my folks and I was hitchhiking back to L.A.

I got a ride in a car and the radio was on. That's when we learned about the attack on Pearl Harbor.

When I heard it, my first thought was, "Japan? This will last a week." I guess I was young and stupid. I wasn't too concerned but of course I was young enough that it didn't bother me. If they were going to have a fight, I wanted to be in it. That's why the service tries to get everybody as young as they can.

I finished radio school and when we finished, they sent us to Puget Sound, Bainbridge Islands, for an advanced radio school. When we got there we began learning Japanese code. It was called an orange telegraphic code, which is what the Japanese used. It was like the Morse code but it had a lot more characters to it. So we had to learn the Japanese code.

I was in an outfit called CBI which stands for Combat Intelligence. This was supposed to be Top Secret. It wasn't too big a secret, but it was supposed to be. As far as the public was concerned it was secret because they didn't know what we were doing. But we were intercepting and copying Japanese transmissions and they were breaking it down and telling the Navy what the Japs were doing. I was an interceptor; I didn't do the decoding. They had special officers who were trained in decoding and breaking down the code. The Japs never thought we could do it. My job was to record the code on paper. I would find the transmission and copy it down. Sometimes it was difficult as the transmission was going long distances. There was static. And we weren't allowed to ask the Japanese to repeat it! *(Laughs)*

Before the Battle of Midway, we sent them information that told them the Japanese were moving. We told them the exact location, the direction they were heading, the speed they were going, how many carriers, how many battleships, how many cruisers, how many destroyers, everything. The Navy says, "This is impossible. They can't know all that." So they sent scout planes out and sure enough they came back and told people that the Japanese were where we said they would be. We got a Presidential Unit Citation for our work on the Battle of Midway.

I went over to Pearl Harbor during the Battle of Midway. People can see pictures of Pearl Harbor and the attack but it is hard for them to imagine how much destruction there really was. The United States Pacific fleet was just about wiped out, except for the six ships that were out at sea.

White we were there, Tokyo Rose—whom we listened to all the time—came on. It was comical. She gave the names of the ships that had been sunk—including ours. It was pretty funny—I didn't feel very wet!

After I was out of the CBI, I went back and they knocked me around to several places. Then they sent me down to Camp Pendleton by San Diego to train for amphibious forces. We learned how to work mobile radios, generators, and all that sort of thing. Then they assigned me to a unit that had seventeen men and four officers. They were all radiomen except for a cook, a mechanic, and a seaman to do the work.

We had two big vans. One had transmitters in it and one had receivers in it. Each van pulled a

trailer with a generator for power. We had a truck for all our gear. We were preparing for the invasion of Luzon, which is by Manila. We went to Leyte for training. Our thing was to go in on the third wave and set up communications for the rest of the invasion.

I think the time I was the most scared was when we were getting ready for the invasion. We were on the ship and everybody is making jokes and we are having a big time. And then the morning of the invasion, we were up about 3 or 4 or 5:00, and had breakfast. And the place was just as quiet as a tomb. I mean nobody was joking—it was hitting us then. You are going over those nets, down into that boat and going in to shore. It was not something you read about or talked about; it was something you were going to do. You start going over those nets into the boat. We did train to scale the nets, and it is not terribly difficult, except when the ship is rolling.

Mostly the Army went in first. They went over the nets and down into the boats. We then went in at the beginning of the invasion. We were there to set up the communications for the invasion. There wasn't a whole lot of combat or resistance going on when we landed there. At that time the Japanese had designed their strategy so that they didn't resist the landing. They pulled back and hid; then they let us come in and they'd shoot you.

> "At that time the Japanese had designed their strategy so that they didn't resist the landing. They pulled back and hid; then they let us come in and they'd shoot you."

After landing, we would handle the mobile radio station until the Army got in and set up a permanent radio station. Then we would leave. But we made the landing there by Manila and then went on up to an old Navy station that the Japanese had taken over. We set up a radio station there and operated out of our vans.

There we were listening to Tokyo Rose and she said there was an ammunition ship at the dock and it was true. It was probably about 150 feet from the docks. She said, "We are going to blow it up tonight." We just laughed because it was always a big joke with Tokyo Rose. But about 2:00 or 3:00 in the morning when I was on watch, we got an air raid alert. So we automatically sent a message that we were shutting down for an air raid. There was a cement culvert about five feet deep and we used it as a bomb shelter. I thought, "If they hit that ship, it is going to level half the island. We're sunk." We heard some loud noises. The next morning we found that we had shot down three planes two or three miles away. The Japanese were coming for that ammunition ship and they were going to blow that sucker up! This was on Luzon Island near Manila.

We would hear a lot of bombardment. I remember one night there was a lot of heavy bombardment and I thought, "Well, we're really giving it to them tonight! The artillery is behind us." Then I found out that it wasn't the artillery behind us, it was the other side shooting at us! And I thought all the noise I heard was us shooting at them. If I thought otherwise, I would have been scared. *(Laughs)*

After Japan surrendered, heavy danger began. The night of VJ Day, everybody was shooting their guns up in the air. And people were shot with stray bullets and stuff. They were celebrating. I don't know if this was the most danger I faced during the war, but it was one of the most. I just stayed down.

I thought it was great when we dropped the two atomic bombs. Remember, I was in an amphibious unit. And our plans were actually being drawn up to invade Japan. And that involves amphibious units. We were slated to be part of that. The bombs saved millions of lives, and maybe one of those lives saved was mine. We were set to go in there.

The war changed me. I was a young 18. I think I was more immature than I should have been for 18. But during the war and in the Navy, if you were stationed on shore you were always applying for sea duty. We always wanted to get out there. You wanted to be out on a ship and be in the action. At least that's what kids my age wanted. The older ones, maybe, were happier to be on land. I think it is all part of both patriotic fever and warrior impulse.

Interview transcribed by Kathy Tanner.

We Blew Up the Buildings Like Mad

Howard Kiefer
Washington, IA

Army Air Corps
Europe

Interview Date:
8 August 2010

Referral:
Gary Hill

My 93 year old brain has trouble remembering. I enlisted March 31st, 1943. I figured I was going to get drafted but didn't know when. I was married in 1940. I chose the Air Force because I wanted to be a pilot. I was at Jefferson Barracks in Missouri and then spent five months in East Lansing, Michigan. I attended Michigan State University to train for being a pilot. I remember that because the air strip where we practiced landing sat in a dead zone or low air pressure pocket. The plane would drop about fifteen feet when you hit that pocket and you had to compensate for that. I had an instructor with me and we practiced on several different airplanes.

My wife accompanied me as I was sent around the country for training. We were down in Gulf Port, Mississippi. When I was getting ready to go to bomber pilot school, they found it was already full so they shipped me out to west Texas instead for bombardier training at Midland. I remember driving back to Iowa and blowing out every tire on my new Chevy coup. They were all retreads. The roads were a lot better than the tires. It was hard to get tires back then but the guys at the service stations did everything they could to help a serviceman get home. My mother sent some chicken with us to eat on our long drive back to Midland. About half way through Texas my wife and I both got food poisoning from that chicken

and ended up in a hospital. The hospital called my base to explain why I was going to be late reporting in. The hospital never charged us a dime.

From Midland we were sent to Avon Park in Florida. When we were getting ready to ship out for England, I got sick with pneumonia and my bomber crew went over without me. I may have had some help from up above that time as they were all killed on their first mission. I got sick again after being assigned to a second crew and they went over and got killed. So it happened twice. I guess that I had kind of a charmed life.

I went back to Gulf Port, Mississippi, and trained with a new crew. This time we flew our new B-17 over to England rather than going by ship. We flew above the clouds over the Atlantic and never saw water. We had a new nineteen year old navigator. He brought us down through the clouds right over our landing field in Scotland where we were supposed to be. It was pretty amazing. There were 200–300 new B-17s sitting on that airfield. They would fly them over and let them sit there. We had to fly the old beat up, shot up planes that didn't have the latest equipment. I heard that after the war all those new airplanes were sold for scrap metal. The new planes had heat in them. The old ones didn't and we had to wear all this heavy clothing to stay warm. We usually flew at 35,000 feet and it was 20 to 25 degrees below zero up that high.

My job was the bombardier. My rank was 2nd lieutenant. I sat up in front of the plane, in the glass part. Some B-17's had nose gunners but ours did not. I sat looking down over the bomb sight and a telescope or something on a little screen and you guided the plane by looking at the picture. The bombardier actually controlled the flight on the airplane with the Norden bomb sight during the bombing run.

We had one bombing mission where the plane developed electrical problems and we had to turn back. We lit on a short runway and there was about a fifteen foot drop off at the end of it. We still had our bombs aboard the plane. I was running out away from the plane along with everyone else and you could hear the bombs banging back and forth in the plane. There was leaked fuel inside the bottom of the plane and one spark and it would have been "Boom!"

My wife found a letter I wrote describing my one combat mission in the war. It was to Plzen, Czechoslovakia. The civilian population had been warned we were coming. Our target was the Skoda Armament Works. It was 22 degrees below zero at 32,000 feet. The flak was not heavy but very accurate. We lost two of our ten ship formation. We did not drop bombs on our first target run because of the clouds and had to make a 360 degree turn and come back. We really got hit on the second pass. They even had fighters up waiting for us. We were in the air twelve hours on that mission. I don't know how the civilians working in those factories were warned, but the Germans knew we were coming and they had anti-aircraft guns set up every place.

Question: So how'd you do on your one mission?

We blew up the buildings like mad. I don't think there was much left there.

Question: Did you ever see the ME 262, the German jet fighter?

Oh, yeah. We saw it. It was really fast. The Germans had a lot of planes sitting in timbers or camouflaged. We kept bombing their fuel supplies and refineries and they didn't have much fuel to put in them. If the Germans had the fuel, they would have shot a lot more of our planes down.

Question: Did you have fighter escort?

Sometimes we did, but not this time. It was too far for the P-51s.

I was lucky that I got put back all those times because of illness or I would have been over there quite a while. There's only one of my crew left and he lives Minneapolis. We go up to see him.

I farmed east of Richmond until I retired in 1996. We still own the land and my son oversees it. I spent a semester at the University of Iowa playing freshman football right out of high school. This was before the war. Back then the freshmen couldn't play varsity. I played center. I weighed 190 lb and was the second biggest player on the squad. Nile Kinnick played four or five years after I did.

REAL GLAD

Harold "Buzzy" Seitsinger
Wellman, IA

Army Air Corps
Europe

Interview Date:
26 August 2010

Referral:
Richard Huber, Jack Seward, Jr.

I grew up on farm a half mile south of Kinross. I was drafted twice. The first time was in February of '41, before the war started. I was rejected for having high blood pressure. The second time was in early June of 1942. That time they took me. I was in the Army Air Corps. Basic training was at Jefferson Barracks in St. Louis. We were right on the river and it was hot and humid. For training they had us walk two miles over and back to the mess hall for our meals. They made us take a salt pill before every meal. From there I was sent across the river to a radio school. I was there until the first of November. Then my group was put on a train. They didn't tell us where we were going or anything. We rode that train for 48 hours and had no idea where we were. We were sent to a secret plane identification school out in the swamp near Boca Raton, Florida. They really isolated us. I think we were the first class to go through the school. The first few days were spent clearing vegetation with machetes. One of the guys died from a coral snake bite while doing this.

Another guy and I put in to be tail gunners on a B-17 while stateside. We were both small in stature and they were actively recruiting guys like us. I was away on a three day pass when they came for us. So only he was taken. He later came and visited me while I was stationed in Florida. His plane was shot down on his first mission as a tail gunner in the Pacific. He was captured by the Japanese but freed by Americans when we took the island.

Next I was sent to a fighter base training camp at Baton Rouge, Louisiana. I joined a veteran outfit that had been up in the Aleutian Islands. It was kind of exciting for me. They were a close knit outfit. One day I was told to pack my stuff up, I was going back to Florida. There was reason to believe that the Germans were going to bomb the east coast of Florida. The base I was sent to had a runway and some old barracks but no control tower. I was the only farm kid there so I had the job of fixing the gasoline engines. They gave me a number of different jobs. I worked in the base telephone office. We had to use baling wire for phone line. I was there almost a year and nothing really exciting happened.

I went overseas in June 1944. I was aboard ship in the Atlantic right after D-Day and we hit the darnedest storm. We were in a convoy. The waves were so high that some of the oil tankers would go clear under water. The storm lasted more than a day and nearly everyone got seasick. Our transport was crammed full of people and I thought it would capsize. That was the most scared I was anytime while in the service.

We landed at Liverpool and were put on train. We traveled to London right after the city had been hit with buzz bombs. After staying in London a day, we continued by train to the northern most bomber air base in England. Then I was sent to radar/navigation school for three weeks to become a radar mechanic. We could pick up any plane within three miles of us. We could pick up any German planes coming over to bomb us and there were plenty of fighters in England by that time to take care of them. The instrument station I worked at had a screen just like a television.

Then I was transferred to a fighter plane base located only seven miles from the English Channel. It was pretty quiet for us until the Battle of the Bulge. They tried to get some of us to volunteer to go over to Europe to help. I told them that I couldn't stand the cold and it was getting down to 20 below over there. Verl Davisson was in the Bulge and he told me most of the men froze their feet even after wrapping their boots in wool garments. Francis Lyle from Keota was wounded before the Bulge. I learned in a letter from home that Francis was in a hospital in England. I visited him several times. Francis told me he was lucky to have been hit. He had received word that his whole outfit had been wiped out in the Bulge.

We were busy during the Bulge because we were the closest air base in England. Transport planes loaded with food, ammunition, winter clothing, and medical supplies landed at our base. It was real stormy. The transport could fly but the bombers wouldn't because they couldn't see their targets. When the sun finally came out, all the B-17s and B-24s would fly low over our base on their way to Belgium. We were told they were carrying 100 pound bombs to drop on the German army. They

were flying low so the German radar couldn't pick them up. Fighters from our base would fly escort.

I credit the Air Force with having a lot to do with winning the war in Europe. I flew over the Rhine River valley and saw all the damage done to the towns. They appeared to have been fire bombed. In the city of Cologne, there was a not a building standing without bomb damage except for the churches. I flew at least twice in a B-24 before the war was over. It wasn't a bombing mission. Occasionally they'd take up ground people like me to observe the damage. One reason that I got to go up was to work on the plane's ground radar system. It was used as a navigation tool and picked up cities, roads, and rivers when it worked properly.

Pilots traditionally were kind of crazy people. We were flying up the Rhine River. There were high line wires stretching across the river maybe 200 feet above the water. The pilot said, "I wonder if we can fly under them?" He opened that plane up and dove down and scooted under them. He said his commander would bust him for pulling a stunt like that if he ever found out.

I couldn't pick up the buzz bombs on my radar because they flew too low. By the time we'd hear them, they'd usually be past us. There for a while, the buzz bombs would come over every night about seven o'clock and then again at midnight. One landed about a city block from our barracks. Our barracks were constructed out of tin. The explosion knocked everything off our shelves, I'll tell you that!

Another time some German fighter planes followed our bombers back to their base. The Germans were flying above the bombers and high enough that our radar didn't pick them up. When the bombers approached the runway, the Germans fighters dove and strafed them. The Germans hit a few of the bombers but I only saw one completely destroyed. The Germans must have shot out the plane's hydraulic system. The plane rolled past the end of the runway and tipped over when its nose dropped in a creek. It caught on fire. No one got out. The fire trucks raced out there and started hosing it down. One guy was half way out. The

> "We were flying up the Rhine River. There were high line wires stretching across the river maybe 200 feet above the water. The pilot said, 'I wonder if we can fly under them?'"

firemen were hosing him down trying to protect him from the flames. He was hit in the chest by the powerful stream of water and knocked backwards, down into the plane. Then it exploded.

I received a letter from Arden Romine while we were both stationed in England. We wrote that there were a million and a half men in southern England. They were being trained hard and he wondered when they'd get into action. He thought combat was coming soon. He had sent that letter back to the United States because all I had was an APO address. The next day, I received a letter from home saying Arden was killed during the invasion. Arden Romine grew up south of town. He played on the Keota football team.

By the time spring came, we knew by the way our troops were advancing that the war was almost over. We had so many bombers over there that the German cities had just been riddled. England really took a beating early in the war. There weren't any young men in England any more. They had been all sent off to war.

Another interesting thing was that the black and white American soldiers didn't get along. The English girls were fascinated by the black soldiers. Some of the guys didn't like that. About all the blacks did was drive trucks. They would haul in the bombs to our base. Early in the war they had what was called "TNT bombs". Later in the war we had a different type of bomb, but I can't remember its name. Anyway, the newer bomb was highly explosive. Rather than do the work to manually unload the bombs, the blacks would back up the trucks real fast and slam on the brakes and the bombs would go scooting off. Of course, one bomb eventually detonated from the mishandling and the whole bomb dump blew. We were 15 miles from that base and the explosion was so loud it sounded only a mile or two away.

There were ten of us local boys that went in the service at the same time. I'm the only one left. Arden Romine went in when I did. Two others got shot down in an air raid but survived. I considered joining the paratroopers. It sounded like the kind of thing I'd like to do.

I had six friends killed in the war. There was a neighbor boy that lived a quarter mile down the road. We used to walk to school together. He was

raised Mennonite and his folks didn't want him to go into the service. But he got drafted and went. He was killed in the Philippines by a sniper near the end of the war. It happened while the troops were marching out to board a ship to leave. He had a wife and two kids. My older brother, Omar, was a medic and ran an ambulance. He had about the toughest job of anybody I knew. His job was to pick up the sick, dead, and wounded from the front lines. He did not carry a weapon. One time he got caught out in a bad storm with a stalled vehicle. He took refuge in a German farm house. He saw a small light in the basement and went down to investigate. A Russian soldier carrying a sword was down there. For a while in the dark, each thought the other could be a German. Omar said he was scared to death. Luckily, the Russian could understand a little English.

John Denton from Kinross was the same age as Omar. He was captured in North Africa and spent four years as a POW. He could speak the German language. He lied to the guards that his folks had moved over to the United States from Germany and they planned on going back. John received special treatment after that.

Elvin Schaefer was wounded in North Africa and again in Italy.

They flew us home as soon as the war in Europe was over. Seventy-two planes took off from our base for the flight home. The navigator on one plane got lost and they ended up over the North Pole. They couldn't find a place to land and ended up crashing. All the men aboard were killed. I was sent to Roswell, New Mexico, to start training on the B-29 to help in the fight with Japan.

I was born in 1916. I was bound and determined to get married after coming home from the service. I had lived in ten different bases while in the service. I was ready to settle down. I was married 56 years and I wish she was here with me now.

I was thankful I wasn't put in the infantry. I took a lot of tests when I went in the service. They said I had a high IQ. Maybe that's why I was sent to the Air Force and end up on radar. Still, part of me was dumb enough at the time to feel like I was missing out on all the action. I was real glad that I went in and real glad I got out.

You're Free! You're Free!

Daryl Baughman
Keota, IA

102nd Infantry Division
Europe

Interview Date:
30 August 2010

Referral:
Duane Fisher

I went in to the service the 10th of June in 1944. I had been working on the farm with my dad and for another neighbor. All my friends were already in the service so I talked to the draft board and told them to go ahead and take me. I would have had to have gone anyhow. I had one brother in the Pacific in the Medical Corps. He had malaria and came down with dysentery. My brother Bob was on an oil tanker and was almost killed two or three times by kamikazes.

I went from Camp Dodge to Fort Bliss in Texas for twenty weeks of anti-aircraft artillery training. From there I was transferred to Fort Carson in Colorado. I was there on hold for three weeks. It got bad over in Europe about that time so they sent me to Oklahoma for six weeks of infantry training. From there I was sent to Camp Kilmer and Fort Meade. Seven thousand of us shipped out on the Wakefield. We sailed unescorted to England and arrived in Liverpool in the middle of the night. Within ten minutes, we were on an old, beat up troop train to South Hampton on the southern tip of England. There we loaded on an LST and crossed the channel to Le Havre. From there it was all up hill to Camp Lucky Strike. It was raining and cold. We were beat and thought we'd get some rest there. There were tents set up with old pot belly stoves in them for heat.

At four o'clock the next morning, a sergeant

rousted everyone out and we walked back the way we had come and boarded a train that took us clear across France and Belgium. I joined my outfit, 407th Infantry Regiment of the 102nd Infantry Division, in Hurlein, Holland. We were known as the Ozark Division. This would have been January of 1945. I was a private until I got into combat. Then you automatically became a private first class.

I never got to see much of Holland. The Ruhr River was close and everything was blown up. I was lucky. The officers got together and decided not to put the replacements in combat until the Ruhr River was crossed. The Germans had all the information about us and what are plans were. When our outfit started to cross the Ruhr, they blew up a big dam upstream and flooded the valley. Our guys were crossing in small boats and a lot of men were swept away and drowned. I had a buddy from West Virginia on one of those boats that got swept away. He lost his gun and everything. Three of the guys with him were killed by direct German fire and lay dead in the boat. He took one of their guns when they made it across. He really wouldn't talk much about it.

I was a combat infantryman. We saw a lot of combat. Our division was the most northern one in the entire U.S. Army. We were awfully close to where the Battle of the Bulge was fought. I had two first cousins killed in the Bulge. I carried an M-1

Garand or a BAR. The BAR was heavy to carry. I threw my overshoes and gas mask in a ditch. Toward the end of the war, when it looked like I wouldn't need it, I'd dig a hole with my foot when no one was looking and bury ammo so I had less weight to carry.

We were up on the bank of the Rhine River in foxholes for nineteen days. Dusseldorf was across the river. Our lieutenant got killed, three or four others including my good friend, Wally Beasley, the guy from Missouri I went in with. Our guys were killed getting across the river. It was unnecessary. We weren't seeing much action. Some of the officers got together and decided that we needed to see what was going on across the river. With binoculars, we could see the Germans across the river. We already knew what they were doing. But the officers wanted some action. So they sent our lieutenant and four or five other guys across the river in the middle of the night in a boat with an electric motor. They only took guys that were strong swimmers on this recon. They got to within about a hundred feet of the eastern shoreline and the Germans opened up on them. There was no sense in it.

One of my buddies from Berkley Springs, West Virginia, was on that patrol but survived the German machine guns. His name was Wally Hill. He was an excellent swimmer and swam back clear across the Rhine River to save his life. The current swept him a mile and a quarter downstream before he made it to shore. He was so exhausted that he had to be dragged out. Later we sought out the officers that had sent the patrol out. He talked back to them. He told them what "Goddamn fools they were to have sent that patrol out."

The Germans would usually shell us with artillery at night. There'd be shrapnel flying around everywhere. We thought they were shelling us to deprive us of sleep. Every evening after it would get dark, the Germans sent up a small noisy plane for the same reason, to unnerve us. We called it, "Check point Charlie." About the scariest thing was seeing those tracers coming in from across the river at night. They'd really get your attention! You never knew if you were going to get hit or not.

> *"The Germans sent a number of their buzz bombs our way. You learned pretty quick to start running for cover when you heard one coming in or going out."*

Most combat would only scare you for a while. But for some of the men, their nerves were more or less shot.

German planes dropped bombs on us one night. Maybe I didn't know enough to be scared, but our sergeant almost went to pieces. He told us to take in a nearby factory with him. Come daylight, we discovered a big bomb that came in right close and left an eight foot hole but didn't explode.

After sitting in a foxhole for 19 days, early one morning our side lit up smoke pots. There was smoke everywhere. You couldn't see anything. Then the call came to pull back. You know, they would have done better if they had told the privates and corporals what was going on. We never knew anything during the entire war. Anyway, we pulled back and we loaded on trucks that took us to Wessel. We crossed the Rhine there.

The Germans attacked us one night after we crossed the Rhine. I was lucky that time, too. I was posted under a tree. It was raining so I had my rain poncho on. I think the Germans came in across a bridge near my position. I don't think the Germans ever saw me.

The Allied Air Force's heavy bombers hit the big cities like Hamburg and Hanover ahead of us. One day we were told 340 planes would hit cities immediately ahead of our front. We watched them fly over. It was the greatest feeling in the world to see them. Those bombers would just about level a large city.

The Germans sent a number of their buzz bombs our way. You learned pretty quick to start running for cover when you heard one coming in or going out. One veteran told me not to be afraid of jumping in the deepest ditch I could find.

We'd take a lot of ground during a day towards the end of the war. We had the Germans on the go. We'd advance on foot twenty hours a day. That wasn't marching down roads. It was walking across farm fields and open countryside on a broad front with a couple of hundred feet between soldiers. We'd be given a ten minute rest break every hour. Most of the time, I went to sleep. I'd always tell the closest guy to be sure and kick me hard enough to wake me so I didn't get left behind.

During this rapid advance, another buddy and I walked up to a slave labor camp. The Germans knew we were coming and the guards had all left. The big gate at the camp's entrance was still padlocked. We smashed our way in. There was a long building that looked like one of our turkey sheds over here. There were bunks lining both sides of a narrow alleyway stacked clear to the ceiling. I stepped in there and yelled, "You're free! You're free!" They were all standing there in a daze. It was like they didn't know what to do. The Germans would take prisoners like these out every morning and work them. I had walked up on farm fields with thirty or forty of them bent over weeding. My buddy and I received a citation for freeing those prisoners. We didn't stay there over five minutes because our outfit was on the move. They were mostly women and kids in these work camps.

We went through Harz Mountains. The evergreens were planted so thick in there that it was dark. We didn't meet much resistance there. One night we came into a large city. Someone from across the street hollered at us, saying. "If you'd been here five minutes earlier, you could have seen General Patton." Patton would hijack all kind of supplies that were supposed to go to the other units.

We went all the way through Holland, then through Hanover and Hamburg, Germany. The last few days of the war we met the Russians on the Elbe River. They were the Cossacks mounted on horses. They wore the tall, hard heeled boots and carried the long sabers.

We'd see a while pillow sheet or something a quarter mile ahead of us the last few days of the war. It would be German soldiers surrendering. A lot of times the German soldiers would bury their uniforms off to the side of the road and be dressed as civilians. They wouldn't surrender to the Russians because they feared them. I saw some German SS soldiers after the war. They were all tall, at least six feet four. They were real men. German troops on the other side of the Elbe were driven to the river by the Russian troops and had their heads cut off. The bodies were thrown into the Elbe River.

"German troops on the other side of the Elbe were driven to the river by the Russian troops and had their heads cut off."

Question: Did you actually witness this?

No, but when we got to the Elbe there were already all these bodies of German soldiers floating down it. This was near Magdeburg. I think the Cossacks did the beheading with their sabers. It happened all over. We could see the Russians across the river. We weren't supposed to cross the Elbe and neither were they.

For two weeks after we reached the Elbe, from early morning until dark, all we did was help relocate slave labor workers. The Germans had sent the slave laborers from Eastern Europe to France and slave laborers from Western Europe to Eastern Europe to work. That way they were in unfamiliar countries and had no choice but to stay and work. We used flat board barges to ferry Russian and Polish workers across to the eastern shore. On our return trip, we'd bring back slave laborers from Western Europe. Those people were loaded on Army trucks and transported west someplace. I don't know how many of these refugees (or displaced persons) we transported in two weeks, but I'll tell you one thing, it was worse than loading livestock. We were lucky because we had one guy that could speak Russian. He'd yell, "Take you time, take your time. We won't forget you." Otherwise, there'd be crowding and shoving going on. The war was over and they all wanted to get home at once. The roads would be packed with these people, five or six abreast, for as far as you could see. Most of them had everything they owned in a bag over their shoulders. In a way, those prisoners that were in the forced labor camp were the lucky ones.

One night two of the Russian came over to our side of the Elbe. They weren't supposed to do that. Anyway, these two put on a show for us. They did that Cossack dance with their hind end almost touching the ground. They had been drinking the alcohol used as fuel in the buzz bombs. They put on a heck of a show.

I went over to the Russian side of the Elbe one time. The Russians were in the river throwing Germans weapons out of the water. There were hundreds of guns lying around. It was a case of help yourself to whatever you wanted. I picked up a P38 German pistol and holster and brought them home. I also have a German dagger with the words "Blood and Honor" written on it. I picked up a German Mauser rifle in a beet field full of dead Germans outside of Krefeld, Germany. The Army postal service let me mail that gun home. I also brought home a large German flag and a uniform of sorts that the slave laborers wore.

After the war I didn't have enough points to come home, so I was transferred to 405th Regiment and was made an MP. We stayed in a big, old hotel. I had to stand guard a lot. Everything was pretty calm after the war.

I was no hero. I was just lucky. There were several times I could have gotten killed but didn't. My dad worked me hard seven days a week when I came back home to the farm. Counting 4-H, I raised cattle for 63 years. I regret not taking the time to go down to Missouri and seeing Wally Beasley's folks and telling them what happened to their son.

War Makes You Face The Truth

Mary Case
Washington, IA

Coast Guard
Stateside

Interview Date:
12 October 2010

Referral:
Paula Brinning

I enlisted Feb. 20, 1945, as an apprentice seaman. I was in Philadelphia at the time. My dad and mother were missionaries to Egypt where I was born, one of five siblings. I went all through high school over there and came back to America for college. None of my relatives except one cousin were in the service and everybody was talking about brothers who were in and going over. I felt left out. Our family didn't know what was going on. They lived over there and I'm here. I felt like a stranger not taking part in the war so I applied. I was excited. I thought "Why can't I—why not?" Some of my classmates went in from Egypt. They wrote, "Now don't go overseas."

I went down to what I thought was Shepherd's Bay in New York. Manhattan Beach was a station for Coast Guard. You could overlook the waters coming in at the end of the war and that was very moving for the girls who had lost family and for one who lost a husband so he wasn't returning.

I entered as a storekeeper, at least that's how they trained me. I had to learn to type and keep records to work out the papers for the men who were discharged. The news that President Roosevelt died came in while we were out on the pavement doing our exercises as a platoon—you know marching up and down. Everything stopped.

We were allowed to choose where we wanted to go—a destination to work. I chose to go to Detroit and a friend of mine accompanied me. She and I were friends in Detroit. There was a different group of us up there as we all split up when we left New York.

I once went up to Canada while I was there. You can just go across into Canada. In Detroit I met a Jewish girl. She was one of our office girls in the Coast Guard. This Jewish girl and her mother and father came over from Europe. They must have just escaped before the war started. She invited me to their home. It was a very simple little home with a little bit of ground with chickens. Much like they must have done in Europe. They spoke with a heavy accent. They hardly knew any English. She and I kept in touch with each other after we left for a little while. I haven't forgotten that. I thought she was special.

Question: Mary, do you recall what country in Europe they were from?

No. It wasn't Germany. I know that. At least I think it wasn't Germany. It comes to mind that it was Hungary. Would that be possible?

Comment: That would be possible. It would be close enough to Germany to get real nervous.

That's what I think of when I think of them. They were little people, you know, short. Our country is made up of people like that. It's just wonderful you know. I'm a very anti illegal—over here. I'm not a bit merciful although I am a Christian. I believe in the Bible, its admonitions, words and guidance. Now they want to come here for all our benefits. They want to change it so we won't have any benefits to offer. By the time they make the changes we won't be what they think we are.

I stayed in the Coast Guard only about 16 months until the Japanese surrendered.

Question: What was your thought when you'd heard Japan had surrendered?

Well, to tell the truth I really wasn't very knowledgeable about Japan. I was interested in MacArthur and the way he dealt with it all. I thought it was amazing that those people with their history and the emperor were willing to kill if they couldn't win. I got the impression they could not stand being defeated. I thought it was sort of a miracle that they had given in peacefully. I think we have to credit the Japanese emperor. He was a wise man.

Comment: Mary, I guess that most of the people my age and younger had no idea there were young women that served in the Coast Guard during WWII.

Well, I tried to get into the Navy because I don't think I was aware of the Coast Guard. The Navy was all filled up in Philadelphia and I was disappointed and I thought "Oh I can't get in," The lady there said, "Why don't you try the Coast Guard?" and I did and they took me right away.

Question: Did you ever get a chance to go on any Coast Guard ships?

No, I didn't. With the GI Bill I got trained as a nurse in Iowa City here because I heard it was one of the top ten hospitals in the country. After completing nurses training, I went back out to Egypt and spent three years there. On my way home I went by way of Scotland and liked the country so well I stayed there 41 years. My people came from there of course. I was curious about it.

Question: What was your opinion of the Egyptian people?

I loved them because, you know, they are a very gracious people. I got to know them better when I went back as a nurse—as an adult. Some of the aides in the hospital invited me into their humble little homes. It might just be one room with a bed in it and all neatly made up. You'd sit down and they'd bring you an orange each or a glass of water with a bit of flavoring to it or cheese. For me, the touching thing was you knew they didn't have anything. One meal I was invited to by an Egyptian missionary they served pigeon. So there were two on my plate and about that much for everybody and I never tasted such delicious meat. They were trying to get me to eat the second one and I just thought that wasn't the thing to do. I had grown up there and know my parent's attitude I thought that I shouldn't eat both pigeons. They insisted saying, "No, no, Mary. Eat it, eat it. You must eat it." Later I learned that not to eat all offered me would be an insult. I would have hurt their feelings. Like saying you can't afford this. That kind of thing. That's how I learned to love them as a people. They were so simple and so good. Of course they were Christians. Our servants honored foreigners. I felt that they would never hurt a foreigner. They would today, but they wouldn't then. There are some sad things about Egypt.

So, anyway I was sitting on the tram one day going into Cairo and the tram stopped. In the front was the driver and behind him are maybe four seats, maybe eight facing each other and the aisle. This man stumbled and caught himself on this lady's knee. I saw it. I thought well he stumbled. He had to catch himself. Everybody knew that was the end of him. He'd be chased down by that girl's family. He didn't have a chance. See what I mean? That's the culture. Now we're talking about Sharia law here.

> *"I thought it was amazing that those people with their history and the emperor were willing to kill if they couldn't win."*

135

Question: If you could give one message to the youth of today and tomorrow about WWII, what would it be?

Well, I'll never forget the look on those boys faces as they were leaving for war. I can never forget the men crossing the English Channel and arriving over there in Europe, getting off those ships dropping into the water. They had to walk through the water and the Germans had the advantage from above. How few of the men got there safely and then they had to climb cliffs or hills. That's the picture I got of that. That's what I think of when I think of the war.

Question: How soon did you know about D Day? How long did it take before you were actually aware of how bad it was or saw photos?

It was later. I guess stories came out in the news and magazines. The men didn't talk about it. You never heard about it from them. When the men came home they were different and they wanted to go to college and they wanted an education. The GI Bill was a great help. The photos of all those crosses at the military cemeteries, people still go over there and visit them you know. You don't know if that is where your son or brother is buried, but maybe there is a name on every cross.

Question: You made the comment that there were boys that came back and took advantage of the GI Bill to become something better. Why do you think that was?

I was impressed at the time they knew the way things were going before the war and they wanted to get a job and make some money. They were grown up. They'd seen the worst. I didn't know at that time about post-traumatic stress syndrome. They didn't give it a name in those days but I think the men must have suffered that, but whether they went away to college because it was a good way to get started in life or because they realized the importance of knowledge. The young kids today don't seem to get that. They get a lot of fairy tales from their studies, what they wish the world were like–not what it is or was really like.

Comment: I think maybe you've touched on something really important. Do you think some of these men coming back really wanted to amount to something because of all their dead friends they left behind? To kind of make up some for the lives that were cut short? Is part of it guilt?

I never discussed it with any of them. Nobody opened up and talked in those days that I recall. You couldn't sit calmly and talk about the war–more now that it is long over that you can do that. I think that is a very good point. Maybe it doesn't hurt quite as much now as then. And I think you're right about the guilt that they have felt, because they survived when so many around them dropped.

War makes you face the truth–your own truth and the truth of why you're living. Maybe the truth is really about God.

The war started in 1941, and that was my junior year in college in Pennsylvania. It started with Pearl Harbor. I didn't even know where Pearl Harbor was. I had an idea where Japan was but not very well. I had a friend here, Dr. Bob Gordon, who was a doctor during the war at the time of Pearl Harbor. He would not talk about it even to this day. He was later a missionary to Sudan. He worked with my brother. I couldn't get a word out of him– not anything.

Interview transcribed by Jane Cuddeback.

YOU DON'T WANT TO REMEMBER

Tom Tanner
Washington, IA

87th Infantry Division
Europe

Interview Date:
10 August 2010

Referral:
Craig Swift & Easy Jones

Three of us were drafted during the last semester of our senior year of high school. I had to finish high school after I came back from the war. We three were called up to replace three other guys from Washington who got deferments by going out to California to work in defense plants. It was hard not feeling some resentment towards them. I remember hearing about houses of those unwilling to serve being painted yellow at night.

The other two draftees were Wayne Davis, and Everett Prybil. Wayne used to run the Jones Funeral Home. Wayne and Everett went into the Navy. I traveled between Christmas and New Years of '43 to Fort McClellan in Alabama for basic training. I really wanted to be a paratrooper and tried twice to join the 101st Airborne. I got rejected both times for having bad feet. I came home on furlough the last two weeks in May and then went to Camp Shelby in Mississippi. Camp Shelby is the worst place you could go in the world in the summertime. It was hot and it rained. We slept in pup tents and the water would run into them. Lizards would be in bed with you in the morning.

We shipped out of Camp Meade, New Jersey. We were aboard the *Queen Elizabeth*. That was just like riding a Cadillac. The *Queen Elizabeth* was big enough to carry almost our entire division over.

We landed in Scotland and spent some time in Manchester, England before going to La Havre, France. We went into combat in the Alsace-Lorraine region, near Metz, France. That area of France was part German and part French. It was farm country. The houses were built back into hillsides. The livestock lived in one side of the houses.

I was in the same division as Easy Jones, the 87th. We were called the Golden Acorn Division. Easy was in the artillery. I was in the 347th Infantry Regiment, 2nd Battalion and part of the Headquarters Company. I was a wireman. I strung wire with a rifle company and operated a telephone switchboard. The German artillery would break the wire and I'd have to go back and repair it. It wasn't very nice doing that at times, especially at night. I carried a carbine when I carried a gun. It'd always get in the way when stringing wire.

Question: How long did it take green troops to become combat savvy?

It didn't take very long, maybe three days. You learned to keep your eyes open and listen. You never knew when you might get stabbed in the back. I thought the Germans were pretty combat smart. They always seemed to know where we were at.

The German 88s were vicious weapons. They'd either throw them at you in a line or in a box pattern. If you were in the trees, the Germans would aim at the tree tops rather than you. Tree splinters and shrapnel would rain down. One time I was getting shelled in a timber. A frightened calf came running through and got hit by a large tree splinter. It made quite a hole.

It was all scary. My 2nd battalion was the first of the entire division to go into combat. We came out of combat with only a handful of guys left out of three companies. One company only had twelve guys left. We were green troops and the Germans had been parked there for a month. We'd advance forward one day and the Germans would counterattack the next day and push us back. It went on like that for a long time, back and forth, without us ever gaining any ground.

It was wet and muddy. The prime movers couldn't even pick up the (damaged) tanks because they would get stuck. We didn't have much for tank support. It was too rainy for our fighter bombers to fly. Occasionally you'd see one of the old artillery spotters planes flying. They'd usually draw enemy anti-aircraft fire. Sometimes they'd get hit and go down and sometimes they wouldn't. Those fliers really had guts and did us more good than anything else tried because they could tell us where the Germans were.

One time another fellow and I were stringing wire and the Germans started shelling us. We ran into a house and tucked ourselves in under a table. An 88 hit the house. It blew that table up and it landed right down on top of us but we weren't hurt.

I was out on patrol one night with a new 2nd lieutenant and he got us lost. We hid in a creek when we saw some Germans but made it back safely. I kept telling him we were going the wrong way. You never could tell the officers anything. I didn't go out on many patrols because that was the job of the soldiers in the line companies. I went on that particular patrol because the line company was running out of men.

The Whitacres lived out north of Washington. Harry Whitacre was is our outfit. He was bayoneted in his foxhole one night while we were in the Lorraine. We had to post guards at night because the Germans would infiltrate. There'd be a password every night so we could identify ourselves. I would have liked to have had dogs over. It would have saved a lot of lives.

We were pulled out of the Alsace-Lorraine region on Christmas Eve to go up north to the Battle of the Bulge. You could see knocked out German tanks the whole drive up. Our planes had gotten most of them. The troops rode in trucks. I drove a jeep the whole way up. Oh, God it was cold! There was snow on the ground and you didn't have anything for warm clothing. All I had was a pair of mittens and overshoes for winter clothing. I was in the Bulge and that ended it for me. I was in the hospital for three months with frozen feet and hands.

They sent us in where the 28th and 106th Infantry Divisions had been overrun. We relieved the guys still alive from those two divisions. There were bodies everywhere. A lot of them had frozen to death. It was a mess. It was something you don't want to remember. Our headquarters was set up in a farm house. By the time we arrived in the Bulge, the Germans were being pushed back. One of our duties was to go out and search for the bodies of American servicemen. That's how I froze my hands and feet.

I was out on limited service duty after I was released from the hospital. I was placed in the Signal Corps and sent back to the port city of Cherbourg, France. There were six of us that rolled up copper telephone wire from France, through Holland and Belgium, all the way to Braden, Germany. I lived three months in the City University in downtown Paris while doing that. It was quite a place. The wire was shipped back to the states and sold as army surplus.

> *"One of our duties was to go out and search for the bodies of American servicemen. That's how I froze my hands and feet."*

There was a big underground telephone switchboard in Braden, Germany. I was put in charge of a group of Algerian WACS that operated it after the war. They could speak English as good as anybody. I was there about three months. That was my only opportunity to tell officers off. They would call all the time to flirt with the girls. I enjoyed telling them to get off the phone and quit tying up the switchboard.

I got to see George Patton once when we were at Metz. He was standing there running off at the head at somebody, with his pearl handled pistols and his damn dog. We were part of Patton's 3rd Army all the way.

Question: What was your opinion of Patton?

I liked him. We need more of people like Patton now. That war over there (Iraq and Afghanistan) would be over by now if Patton was running it. He wouldn't lose any more soldiers than we're losing now, the way they keep getting picked off. He'd take those places and make a war out of it. It's a political war now. We used to fight wars to win them, not to lose them. Anyway, that's my opinion.

Comment: I share those same sentiments. I see there is a bronze star in your display case hanging on the wall.

Yes, I was awarded that for stringing and splicing wire while under artillery fire. That happened while we were in the Alsace-Lorraine area. The colonel put me in for it. His name was Bowden. He was an old Army guy and a good commander. A lot of the younger officers weren't all that good.

I sailed back on a Victory ship in 1946. It was out of the water more than it was in it because of the rough seas. We were on it 14 terrible days. I was seasick 13 out of the 14 days. I was discharged out of Camp McCoy in Wisconsin.

I was in the service 28 months. I ended up with the rank of staff sergeant. Davis, Prybil, and I attended the junior college in Washington for two years after going back to high school to get our diploma. It still sticks in my craw that we had to leave school early to be replacements for those that got out of going. I would have gladly gone if they'd waited to let me finish high school. My folks owned Washington Oil and I ran that until 1979. Then I spent 23 years as the parts manager at the Chevrolet garage. I am also a volunteer fireman.

I've been doing that for 60 years. I don't fight fires any more but I man the radio when there's a fire.

Question: When you think back on the war, is there one thing or experience foremost in your mind?

It's all those guys ahead of me getting shot. Our company lost a lot of men. I saw a lot of guys get shot. It was not a pleasant experience.

John Whitacre was in the 75th Infantry Division and fought in the Bulge. He was a classmate of mine but didn't have to go until May. Bob Ross was in the Navy. Robert Martin served in Germany and married a German girl. Mary Case was in the Coast Guard. Don Nicholson was in the infantry. He came up through Italy.

I liked the German people. They just had bad leadership. I did not care for the French. They were so arrogant and egotistical it was pathetic. The English were a little different but I liked them.

I went on the Honor Flight last September. It was really something.

OH MAN, CAN I TYPE!

Arlin Nall
Washington, IA

Navy
Pacific

Interview Date:
10 December 2010

Referral:
Paula Brinning

I was drafted into the Navy either the last of November or the first part of December in '44 and got out in '46. They didn't draft too many into the Navy. I was a seaman 1st Class. I got lost in the processing center in Minneapolis. There were lots men there. They finally came over the loud speaker looking for me. They put the guy ahead of me in the Marine Corps. He was about twice my age and I was 18 ½ years old. I felt pretty lucky getting into the Navy. They expect so much out of the Marines and I thought it odd they'd take a guy that old ahead of me.

I took an APA (Attack Transport) ship to Guam. There were 20mm and 40mm guns aboard. There were 300 Marines on board heading for Okinawa and 300 civilians going to Hawaii to work. Okinawa was a slaughter house. Those Marines were heading straight into combat and were scared, telling me how lucky I was not to be going with them. We went through the Marshall Islands. There were the tops of sunken ships

> *"There were still Japanese soldiers hiding in the mountains on Guam. They'd come out at night looking for food in the warehouses."*

sticking up out of the ocean there. I was dropped off in Guam.

Guam was the Navy's distributing point for everything in the Pacific. A lot of supplies came in on different ships every day. I worked one day lining up supplies for different ships. That evening someone sought me out and asked if I could type. I replied, "Oh man, can I type!" I wanted to get out of that sun. I had a desk job from then on filing what supplies went on what ships. I worked out of a Quonset hut with a bunch of chief petty officers. We had an ensign in charge. He was young and ready to fight anybody. He was nice fellow who protected us from some of the other officers. I saw him pull a gun on some other officers interfering with us and told them, "They had better scram!"

There were still Japanese soldiers hiding in the mountains on Guam. They'd come out at night looking for food in the warehouses. We called it pilfering. Sometimes they'd do some shooting when they got close. Our sentries would shoot back. A friend of mine guarding a warehouse one night had the lantern he was carrying shot out of his hands. We slept in a food warehouse so it was a little scary. There were also Japanese POW's on Guam. There'd be a seaman guard for each group of 25 prisoners. I saw two groups but there were a lot more than that on the island.

They sent some Marines up in the mountains to look for the Japanese. The story that went around was that none of the Marine patrol came back alive. So they sent some of the natives from Guam up and they came back with Japanese prisoners.

A buddy and I were out in a restricted area one night. A place we should not have been. We got shot at. The bullets were hitting the coral around us. We got out of there in a hurry. I'm not sure who was shooting at us. It was probably our own guys. I'm still hesitant to talk about it for fear of getting in trouble. There were a couple of British soldiers killed one night by friendly fire.

We moved out of our Quonset huts into a four man tent. There were two guys from Kentucky and a big Indian from Arizona living with me. The southern boys set up a moonshiner's still and stayed drunk most of the time. They didn't get along with the Indian. They picked a fight with him and one got sent to prison. It's a wonder someone didn't get cut up. I would have hated to mess with that big Indian. The Indian's father owned a big ranch and raised horses. Bing Crosby purchased horses from him.

Guam was full of big rats. They'd come right in our tent and climb over us at night. The biggest rats in the world are found on the Marianna Islands where Guam is located. Some of the rats were shell shocked and acted crazy. They had no fear of people. We rode tame water buffalo for entertainment.

Guam had a big airbase. A neighboring island, Tinian, had an airstrip. The bombers that carried the atomic bombs were based there.

We were ready to get off that island when the war ended. Guam was only 30 miles long and seven miles wide. There weren't many places to go or much to do. It was a hot, old island. There was no place to go on leave. Their capital city had been blown to bits. Nine thousand people had lived there.

At the end of the war, unused materials were pushed over the cliff into the ocean. All kinds of stuff. I remember all the beer being dumped. They figured it would spoil.

It was a long time ago. I've forgotten a lot. If the Japanese had won it would have been terrible. They would have killed half of us off and made the rest slaves.

I worked 28 years for the railroad and then worked as the janitor at the UP church. I mowed your grandparent's lawn next to the church.

An Experience of a Lifetime

Don Nicholson
Ainsworth, IA

7th Army
N. Africa, Europe

Interview Date:
19 October 2010

Referral:
Tom Tanner

I was in partnership farming with my father when I was drafted. Our farm was on the eastern edge of the county and bordered Louisa County. I suffered pneumonia in the winter of 1942 and my doctor got me medically deferred for several months. I left for the Army in August of '42. I was 24 years old. I had my eight weeks of basic training in Camp Robinson down in Arkansas.

After basic, a large group of us was sent by train to Bloomington, Illinois, to attend an automotive trade school. We were housed in hotels and had our meals in the nearby commissary. We were taught how to make all kinds of repairs on vehicles. I was a mechanic. I started out a private and worked my way up to staff sergeant. I joined my outfit, the 31st Ordinance Company, at Fort Benning, Georgia. We were at Benning for four months to continue our training. We bivouacked in the woods during that time.

In May, 1943, we departed New Port News, Virginia aboard an old Greek ship that was dirty and smelly. We bunked in hammocks hung down in the hold. The food was bad. People got seasick and then about half of us came down with food poisoning. We had no idea where we were sailing to. They didn't tell us anything. We were part of a big convoy. We changed course a lot, zigzagging to avoid German U boats. There were several destroyers and I

think one Navy cruiser along as escort. The cruiser had a light plane launched by catapult that searched for U boats during the daylight hours. I remember one day seeing a destroyer shooting off ash cans (depth charges). We never learned whether they were targeting a submarine or just practicing.

We had no idea where we were in the Atlantic until seeing the Rock of Gibraltar and sailed into the Mediterranean Sea. We landed in Oran, Algeria. By that time, the fighting in North Africa had ended. Our forces had tried to trap the German troops in Tunisia but many escaped to Italy where we had to fight them again. We rode in trucks to our camp in the barren countryside. Africa was hot and the water they gave us had been treated with so much chlorine to make it safe for drinking that it did not quench our thirst. You'd drink and drink and still be thirsty. We saw the natives threshing grain by riding horses over it and then tossing it in the wind to separate the grain from the chaff. At night, you could hear the jackals yapping. All that briefly helped me forget myself and the thought we were fighting a war.

We were part of General Patton's 7th Army. Of course that was before he was relieved and reassigned to England. I didn't really have an opinion of Patton other than the desire of avoiding him.

We were moved back closer to Oran when our trucks and equipment arrived in port. I worked as a mechanic on any type of wheeled vehicle. Our task was to prepare for the invasions of Sicily and Italy. We remained in Algeria until Sicily had been taken and after the Allies gained a foothold in Italy. We landed at Naples, Italy after some of us were sent to Palermo, Sicily to retrieve 22 trucks that had been left behind. The trucks were ferried across the Straits of Messina on an LST to the toe of Italy where we drove them the rest of the way to Naples.

Some of my unit arrived in Naples before I did. Not long after they got on shore, two German Stuka dive bombers flew over the mountains and bombed them. Luckily, no one from my company was hurt. After I arrived in Italy, two Messerschmidt 109s strafed us at noon one day. They came in low and fast, right at tree top level. Some guy in another outfit opened up on them with a .50 caliber machine gun mounted on a halftrack. The German fighters veered off a little to target him. Nobody in our company was hit but there were some casualties.

The Allies soon had control of the air. About the only German planes flying would be at night for photo reconnaissance purposes. They'd drop flares and our anti-aircraft batteries would shoot at the planes, but I never saw any of them hit. I used to look up and watch the waves of Allied bombers heading north. It was quite a sight. First came the heavy bombers, the B-24s and the B-17s. Then the formations would be the medium bombers, the B-25s and 26s. Finally, the fighters, the P-51s, P-38s and 47s and the A-10s would go over and being so much faster, could catch up to the bombers. Some days it looked like there were a thousand planes going over.

As we advanced north I could see how ineffective some of our bombing missions had been. We'd come to an unscathed river bridge but the adjacent hills and buildings would be pockmarked with bomb craters. Normally, we'd move up to within ten miles of the front after it had advanced 50 miles or so. Then we'd set up again to repair wheeled vehicles, artillery, small arms, gun sights, and things like that. Different sections of the 31st specialized in repairing specific items. Other

than wheeled vehicles like jeeps and trucks, I had occasion to work on halftracks and one tank. We erected camouflaged netting over the work area and slept in tents. It got awfully cold in Italy during the winter months.

The Allied advance got stalled because of the mud and the fortress of Monte Cassino. We were in Florence for a long time when that was going on. We were usually pretty knowledgeable about what was going on in the front and couldn't understand why it took the command so long to decide to go ahead and bomb the monastery. It seemed like the obvious course of action to take at the time. The mud was bad enough at times that mules had to be used to get supplies to the front lines.

The Army attempted a second landing at Anzio to cut off the Germans. That was a death trap. It was a very costly invasion and nearly everything was lost. The Germans held the high ground and had a 24 inch rail gun that would fire five rounds and roll back under ground. Our planes couldn't get to it.

> "The Army attempted a second landing at Anzio to cut off the Germans. That was a death trap. It was a very costly invasion and nearly everything was lost."

Later in the war there was a manpower shortage. Most of the replacement troops were needed at the front. We were given permission to hire Italians to help us. Italy had surrendered when we invaded and some of the Italians were not too pleased to us being there. But others were glad to have a job that paid them something. Usually we didn't have too much problem getting replacement parts. When we were short a part, we'd salvage it from a wrecked vehicle. New engines took several months to arrive from the states. Our goal was to have the vehicle looking like new when we sent it back to the front.

I had two cousins and friends on the front lines so I felt like I was doing what I could to help them. I was given two four days passes for R&R in Rome. It took a full day to travel to Rome each way but I did have time to see the sights including the Vatican, the Coliseum, and the Catacombs.

We were in northern Italy near the city of Milan when the war in Europe ended. Some guys in my company were sent out to help guard all the surrendered German soldiers but I was not one of them. We returned to Naples and boarded a new

Liberty ship named the USS *General Stewart* to transport us to the Pacific to help on the invasion of Japan. There were 3000 of us aboard ship. The two atomic bombs were dropped while we were in the Mediterranean Sea. We learned of this from the ship's newspaper. We were somewhere in the Atlantic when it was announced over the PA that the Japancsc had surrendered and we would head north to New York City. Everyone was just ecstatic! Caps were thrown in the air. Officers and enlisted men were hugging each other. Shirts were being ripped off each other's back and thrown overboard. Some guys were screaming and others were crying with happiness.

I was discharged in St. Louis after 37 months of military service. All but 10 months were spent overseas. It was an experience of a lifetime, but I wouldn't want another one like it.

Question: What do you remember about learning of the attack on Pearl Harbor?

I was home and we heard it on the radio on Sunday afternoon. It came as a complete surprise. There were no thoughts of Japan attacking us. I didn't know where Pearl Harbor was for sure but it didn't take long to find out by listening to the news bulletins. I knew immediately that it meant war and that I would probably be involved in it.

Davida Nicholson: My family heard it on the radio at home as well. My brother, Earl Fisher, served in the Air Force. He was the radio operator on General Omar Bradley's plane. Bradley mentions my brother by name in his book *(A Soldier's Story)*.

So Many Dead People

Bob Stirling
Washington, IA

113th Cavalry Group
Europe

Interview Date:
26 October 2010

Referral:
David Brinning

I was in the hospital getting my tonsils out when the war broke out. That was a shame as I couldn't even say anything. I was in the Red Horse Troop which was part of the 113th Calvary Group. We were on maneuvers in Texas. My time was up and I was getting ready to be discharged. They told me to forget being discharged. I remember someone saying, "Boy, you are going to have to stay." And stay I did!

We were paid $21 a month while stateside. Six dollars were taken out every month for cleaning. By the time you purchased items like gloves and toothpaste, there wasn't much left over. When we had horses, I would take one out every Sunday to ride. When we switched over to motorcycles, I was put in charge of them. I'd take one of those every Sunday and about 15 others would join me. Mac Donaldson was a lieutenant and he'd go along just to keep everybody straight. Next we were given a little schooling and spent time on the firing range.

We had a man get shot and killed one night in the room the camp guards stayed in. Nobody could understand how it happened. I was welding a universal joint on a halftrack next to the guard building when I heard the shot. I ran in and there was a guy holding a smoking gun. They maintained it was an accident. We had a replacement sergeant come in by the name of Pete Hoskins. He was a nice fellow and was quietly asking around about the shooting. About the only thing known was that the two guards didn't get along. He turned out to be an FBI agent, but I was the only one to know that. The guard who killed the other guard was court martialed. The shooting was declared accidental and the guy fined six cents for the cost of the bullet. Pete Hoskins stayed with our unit until we got overseas. Then he was transferred out.

After war was declared, we were given a little schooling and spent time on the firing range. I was sent to Ft. Riley, Kansas, to learn welding. The rest of it was just routine, the same things day in and day out. It was 20 below the day we shipped out for England. We boarded a French merchant marine vessel. I was T-4 or buck sergeant at this point. I was in charge of lining up the men for KP duty aboard ship. I never ate what the men did. The French chef would always fix a fancy meal for me and him to share. We ate pretty good.

We weren't confined to our base in England. We could get passes. I was a married man and had no desire to do any running around. I stayed in the base and did my welding.

One of the biggest problems was young 2nd lieutenants right out of school thinking they were always right when they weren't. One time I got into an argument with one of them. We got into a shoving match. Then he took a swing at me and I decked him. He reported that to the colonel. Colonel Chase came to see me. He asked, "Bob, did he really need knocked down?" I replied, "Yes, and he needed a lot more than that." Colonel Chase added, "Well, that's all I wanted to know. He wanted me to break you but I won't."

They had Studebaker halftracks, something they had just come out with. They held three men, two in the front and a guy on the machine gun in the back. We were tasked with trying them out while in England. You could run it out on a peat bog and it wouldn't sink. But if you got out on foot, a person would sink. I couldn't hardly believe that. Those halftracks were quiet and you could slip up undetected.

We went into Normandy on the 3rd wave. I've never seen so many dead people in all my life. We were out far enough when the first wave went in that the German artillery couldn't reach us. We moved in the next morning. I had camouflaged my jeep. It was also set up to run under water. I had installed a pipe for the air intake and one for the exhaust. I had Captain Coulter ride in my jeep. I told him "to hang on, here we go" as I drove down the ramp on the LST. We went under water and the jeep hit bottom. It started sputtering and jerking but pretty soon it crawled up out of there. I was holding on to the steering wheel and had the foot feed pedal clear to the floor. The Germans had been driven back far enough by then that we were not getting shot at. When we drove up to the top of the hill, we encountered German SS Panzer Division troopers riding horses. Those horses were trained to lie down, so you had to kill the horse before you killed the man. All those guys were six foot tall or better, every one of them, and tougher than all get out too, mister. They were the best the Germans had.

Question: Was there still a lot of debris and bodies on the beach?

They were cleaning it up when we got there. There were still bodies scattered around. They were burying them with bulldozers. Have you ever wondered what the notch in the dog tags was for? That was so a dog tag could be lodged between the

> *"When we drove up to the top of the hill, we encountered German SS Panzer Division troopers riding horses. Those horses were trained to lie down, so you had to kill the horse before you killed the man."*

teeth so the dead could be identified when they were dug up later for proper burial.

Captain Coulter said we needed to scout the area with the jeep. My jeep had six bullet holes in it by the time we rejoined our outfit on the hills. We could see where the SS troops had killed cattle just to be shooting something. The French had the prettiest shorthorn cattle and the Germans were shooting them for fun.

Question: Did you actually see them do it?

Oh, yes! Here's another thing not very many people know. If the French women refused to become prostitutes for the Germans, they'd cut their wedding ring finger off. The French would show us the "V" for victory sign and say, "Viva la France!" Then they'd take a spade out to the hedgerows and dig up bottles of wine and give them to us.

The Americans would pick up all the damaged vehicles and put them in a pile. If you needed a spare part, they wouldn't let you get it from the pile. We had what we called the moonlight requisition. A couple of our guys would take a half gallon of wine and visit the guard while several others went in the back to get what was needed.

I had something I wasn't supposed to have. I had brought two, 50 round clips with me for my Thompson sub machine gun. When Captain Coulter saw them, he made me give one to him. We always had a horse hitch reign tied around the barrel of the Thompson. You'd put your foot on the reign to keep the muzzle from climbing when you shot.

The 113th's main job was to direct artillery for other units. We would scout ahead in camouflaged vehicles going across country. Some of the guys rode muffled down motorcycles. Charlie Snyder, the former sheriff, was a motorcycle rider. We also scouted in jeeps and halftracks. The halftracks had a big roller on the front of them that could knock down small trees. We'd radio in targets and coordinates.

General Patton had his headquarters right beside us one time after D-Day. We were picking up strays, soldiers that had been separated from their units. Patton would ride around standing up in his jeep, holding onto the windshield. He wore his two, pearl handled pistols and was the cockiest little devil you've ever seen. There was a reason they called him blood and guts. He cared about nobody but George Patton. I had no time for him. I didn't like him or the way he acted.

One morning the Germans stood some men up on a hill. A German shouted down in perfect English, "You Americans go home or this is what will happen to you." Then they machine gunned the prisoners. That stayed with me a long time.

Another thing that really bothered me was when I pulled out a photo of a family out of a dead German's pocket. That really worked on me. A week or ten days later we captured another German. He had the same family photo in his pocket. The Germans issued these photos to soldiers to make us feel bad for shooting somebody's daddy.

The hedgerow country was tough fighting, especially when we turned the corner to split the German forces. I was hit near the Belgium border in July. We were scouting 20 miles ahead of the front lines. A woman came down into an orchard to visit a grave. I told the captain that we'd better take her prisoner, "She is going to go back and tell them (the Germans) right where we're at." The captain disagreed with me. About an hour later a barrage of 88's came in. There was about 40 of us. If my count is right, all but four of us were killed. A German soldier came up and looked at me. I was bleeding pretty good. Then he walked on. I should have shot him but I figured there would be too many others around. I laid there nine hours. It took that long for our forces to push the Germans back. I had shrapnel in one arm and a leg. My thumb was hanging down the back of my hand. I put some gauze in the holes to stop the bleeding the best I could. I had seven operations on my leg. Every time I'd go see a doctor, he'd smile and start sharpening his knife.

About five years ago I walked into a coffee shop in Wapello. I saw a guy sitting there that looked familiar but I couldn't place him. I walked over and asked him if he was ever with the 113th Calvary. He said he had been a medic in the 113th. I told him, "Then you are the medic that picked me up." Isn't that something? Two weeks later he was driving a tractor pulling a wagon down a road. A woman came up over a hill and slammed into the wagon, knocking him off the tractor. He was killed.

Question: What were the names of some of the guys from this area you served with?

There was Bealer, two Longers, two Crawfords, Bartlet H. Gregory, Raymond Edwards, Pete Dickinson, Skeeter Wolf, and Lyons from Keota. There's also Charlie Plecker, Wilbur Wright, and Dave Brinning. That Wilbur Wright was a character, especially when he got mad. He got really seasick going over. He threw up so hard that his false teeth came out. Bill Longer was killed over there. He was a very nice guy.

(We accompany Bob down to his basement. There was a large photo of the members of the 113th. Behind them were their vehicles lined up in neat rows. Bob starts pointing out people in the photograph. It's like hearing an honor roll read.)

This is Shawn Flynn. That's Charlie Plecker. There's Charlie Snyder, Gilbert Dickinson, Donald Longer, Carson, Rex Dodson, Harold James, Gregory, Marsh Atkinson, and Birdbrain Miller. I can't seem to find Wilbur Wright. Here's Bill Edmondson. Red Lyons was a radioman. There is Sulentic from Montpelier.

Some of it I really enjoyed. I saw places and countries I would have never gotten to see otherwise. My favorite place was the White Cliffs of Dover. There was an English vacation retreat there were all the rich ones went. Oh mother bear, that was nice! The Scots were very nice. I found the English to be catty. We enjoyed the French people. They were altogether different.

I WAS GLAD TO DO IT

Phillip Kneen
Washington, IA

Navy
Pacific

Interview Date:
11 November 2010

Referral:
Dave & Linda Birney

I enlisted in 1941 after Pearl Harbor. I wanted to enlist in the CBs (also called the Seabees) because I was already doing refrigeration. I went down to St. Louis to enlist because they didn't have anything local. They wanted me to go on down to New Orleans but I didn't want to do that. So I enlisted in the Navy there in St. Louis and was sent to Great Lakes. From there I went to a Navy base in California and then to Australia.

We were the back crew for the landing craft and stuff like that. We were stationed on a Navy base in Australia until they had all those islands cleared so we could go in. They put us on an island north of New Guinea. It was named Windy and was uninhabited. There was a number of other nearby islands. Ours was about a mile and a half long and three-quarters of a mile wide. We were there for about two years. All the time we were there, they'd bring back landing craft that had been blown up and we had to repair them. Sometimes the landing craft were brought in because of motor failure and we took care of that. Then they put the landing craft in on another invasion as they slowly worked

towards Japan. The ones we worked on were mainly the 105 feet tank landing craft.

There was also a PT boat repair crew and a CB repair crew on the island. It was interesting from the standpoint that you were a kid away from home. We never had liberty for the two years we were there on the island.

We did some island watching. It didn't involve too much and was pretty safe. We had a little lifeboat we used for recreation. We traded a Liberty ship with something from my machine shop for it. I can't remember what it was. They were always needing something mechanical. So we had a boat that we could use to go all over the islands. It was something different to do.

After the war was over, they shipped us back to the states on a Liberty ship and I was discharged. That's about the extent of my activity so far as the military was concerned. I went in as a 3rd Class Electrician and came out a Chief.

Question: Did you ever have cause to be fearful or aware of a Japanese presence?

I saw one Japanese plane fly over and that's all I saw.

Question: How was the food on the island?

It was pretty good. We had a lot of horse cock. That's what we called bologna. The island was very hot with a lot of mosquitoes and bugs. We lived in tents with a wooden floor raised up off the ground two or three feet. We took pills to prevent malaria and never had a case of it. There were land crabs around but they didn't cause much of a problem.

I, like most of the vets, went into the war to protect the United States. That was really the reason we went in. When I got out of the service, I moved to Mt. Pleasant and went to work for a refrigeration repair crew. When the owner decided to get out, I bought him out and moved the business to Washington. I had $500 dollars mustering out pay and that bought everything he had. That's how I got into the refrigeration business. I had a Model A pickup and away I went. I thought I had the world by the tail. Kneen Refrigeration, our motto was, "We sell the best and service the rest."

I don't think anyone has ever come up to me and asked me what I did in the service until you have. I was willing to forget my service and go on with my life. I did my job, I was glad to do it, and I'm glad it's done. I just wish our boys now don't have to do it.

A Typewriter Commando

C. Rollin "Ed" Edmondson
Washington, IA

Army
N. Africa, Europe

Interview Date:
11 November 2010

Referral:
Barb Edmondson

I enlisted in 1940, eight days after I registered for the draft. I had been in business school and knew how to type. It took me four years to complete the two years of college as I went home to help on the farm during busy times like harvest. I was working at a farm implement store when two WWI veterans suggested I use my education to get a good placement in the army or I would be toting a rifle like they had. The army needed typists so I was a typewriter commando throughout the war.

I worked in Chicago state office the first year getting records of ROTC students updated and then was transferred to Corps Headquarters in the U.S. Postal building. I was assigned to a civil engineer who was a major in the Engineer Corps. This major was a fine person and when he found out I was from Ainsworth, Iowa he asked if I knew his uncle, Ansell Jeffries. I told him, "If it wasn't for the high winds and the railroad tracks, we'd have adjoining land." So I was the perfect example of another case of "not what you know, but who you know."

I had learned that the ratio of women to men in Australia was ten to one because of the war

and everybody was trying to get assigned there. That sounded pretty good so I went to see my boss, who had been promoted by then to colonel and told him I was interested in foreign service. He said, "Oh really. We get those requests all the time." I was informed that we were picked to be in I Corp which was under Patton and scheduled to go in on North Africa. About a week later my colonel promoted me to the rank of master sergeant. I hadn't even sewed my staff sergeant stripes on yet and here I was, a 23-year old master sergeant! When Patton learned that the coast was undefended, he went in three weeks ahead of schedule. So that's how I got my foreign service. We were assigned to the Pay Section and I got into training and personnel work.

One morning we had a Biblical plague of locust while in North Africa. The locusts were migrating and the wind shifted and blew them right over us. The swarm was thick enough it didn't block out the sun but they dimmed it. Of course there was nothing for them to eat in the desert so they went to work on out tents and the ropes. We had to scrape them off and shovel them up. They were great big things, like our grasshoppers only bigger. They had really sharp teeth. They could chew up a tent rope in a hurry. We lived an entire year in those tents before barracks were built for us.

We took over the Shell Oil building in Casablanca. Patton had his headquarters there on the second floor. He refused to use the elevator, preferring to walk up the stone stairs. You can imagine what kind of noise his hob nailed boots made on that stone. Everybody could always hear him coming and they would just scatter! He was liable to tell you anything, including swearing at you. He was not a kind man.

Churchill and Roosevelt met in French Morocco for a summit meeting. I stood in the honor guard through three national anthems, French, British, and American. The British were terrific soldiers. They had lots of experience. We had a few air raids. We had dug pits and put sand bags around them. We'd jump in them when the sirens sounded. I think it only happened five times.

I was in Morocco about twenty months and then transferred to Italy. We landed in Naples in May of '44. I was at Concertina, the original, old capital of Italy. Both the Allied and U.S. headquarters were there. I worked in the U.S. Headquarters, assigned to the Adjutant General's office doing administrative work. We handled all the correspondence, both incoming and outgoing. We had to keep up with all the Army regulations and circulars that governed the war. I went through the war doing that. The last six months I was in Graves Registration. We'd file missing aircraft reports from all over Europe and plot them on map boards. After the fighting was over in an area, we'd send in teams to interview the local people to find out what they knew of the missing planes and airmen. Part of the trouble was that Air Corps switched flight crew members around and that they weren't always sure who was aboard a downed plane. A lot of the time the dead airmen would be buried in the village cemetery.

When WWII started, we had about 150,000 troops scattered all over the world. When it ended, there were 16,300,000 people in uniform. Things really progressed rapidly. By the time we invaded southern France, the Germans had been pushed

back enough that the rest of the war could have been fought in an area the size of Texas.

We had a large POW camp established at Casablanca. We separated the Italian prisoners from the Germans. The Germans were a determined people, I can tell you that. We had to go through them and classify their specialties, like who was a cook, things like that to get them organized. They couldn't believe we would make such an effort to help them. Someone figured out that is was cheaper to ship them back to the United States for internment than ship food and supplies to Africa. The Germans asked where they would land in the U.S. The interpreters told them New York City. They said, "Oh no, that's been bombed off the map." The interpreters replied, "Well that's strange, we just came from there." That was how effective the propaganda was in Germany.

I picked up a Nazi flag and brought it home. The Germans got chased out of southern Italy in a hurry and left a warehouse full of their flags. We of course, passed them out as souvenirs. It measures four by six and is in my office here on a stack by my shelf. It looks like it has never been flown.

I was the first U.S. military person on the ground in Viet Nam. It was still called Indo China in those days. We had to wait three days in Thailand for the weather to clear for the flight. I was on standby diplomatic status. I had learned to speak French in Morocco in WWII but I had to brush up on it in a hurry. I'm pretty sure I was chosen to go because I had some knowledge of the French language. We flew into Tan Son Nhut airport. I was part of a cadre of five that were part of the Military Assistance Advisory Group to the French. We were the first U.S. military sent and I was the first boots on the ground. This was in 1950. We had an office with a compound wall around us and supervised the unloading of military supply ships and kept the records. Our number one houseboy turned out to be a North Vietnamese agent. We lived off the local economy. He'd go to the market every day and buy most of our food and oversaw the other hired help. We didn't learn that he was a spy until returning back to the states.

I shipped out for the states in October of '45.

> *"The Germans asked where they would land in the U.S. The interpreters told them New York City. They said, 'Oh no, that's been bombed off the map'."*

I was an Iowa farm boy and it was just a big adventure. I liked to travel and loved history and geography. Any time I had a day off and could catch a flight somewhere I took advantage of it. That was my education.

Question: Where were some of the places you visited?

I rode camels around the pyramids in Egypt. I visited Athens, Greece. It had been occupied by the Germans during the war. I spent a week in Switzerland. That was like going to heaven. This was during the war. The Swiss government had made arrangements to allow Americans to tour the country. Everything there was electrified, even the railroads. Everything was clean and polished. It was quite a contrast to southern Italy where all the towns had been bombed to rubble.

I was 30-year career Army. I was in Korea in 1957–58 and a number of other foreign countries. I ended up settling in Ames, Iowa, after being an ROTC instructor at Iowa State.

TRIBUTE

Growing up, I was so proud of my dad. He took a lot of pride in being a professional soldier and he enjoyed talking about all the places he had been in the Army. He also took pride in doing things the right way and for the right reason. Those are the lessons he taught me. I am proud of my country and its values, and I am very proud of him.

Barb Edmondson
Washington, IA

Never Really Scared

Ralph Witthoft
Washington, IA

34th Infantry Division
N. Africa, Italy

Interview Date:
11 November 2010

Referral:
Dave & Linda Birney

I knew my draft number was coming up so I enlisted in the 133rd Infantry Regiment in Fairfield in February of '41. That was an army band unit. The 133rd was part of the 34th Infantry Division. We went to Camp Claiborne for training. When the Japanese attacked, we were sent to watch the coast for two weeks. We came back for a while but it wasn't too long. Next we were sent to Ft. Dix, New Jersey. We took the first convoy over to Europe. The ships would change course every 13 minutes to confuse any German subs in the area. The sea was rough. The ship I was on was dirty and the food greasy but I got along alright. Our first port of call was in Northern Ireland. I volunteered to help with the boat going from ship to shore. I remember getting a case of peaches and eating too many of them. We stayed in Northern Ireland for about a year. We usually ate beans for breakfast and lamb soup for supper.

We next went to England for two weeks. It served as a jumping off place for sailing to Oran, Algeria. We followed the troops across North Africa.

Question: So did the band perform for military parades or any time there were big shots around?

Yes, pretty much. I played a clarinet. Our training consisted of two or three hikes and then we'd march back to camp to practice playing our instruments. I think we went to the rifle range a few times.

After Rommel was defeated in North Africa we went into Italy about two weeks after the troops did. The infantry had a hard time taking the monastery (Monte Cassino) on top of a mountain. We were involved in carrying the wounded American soldiers down on stretchers for evacuation. We lost one guy doing that. Just as we reached the base of mountain, wave after wave of British bombers came in and leveled the monastery. It was my understanding that the Americans refused to bomb the monastery. We were all winter trying to take that mountain.

I only saw one bomb dropped near us, landing about 200 yards. It hit and bounced around some. It was a dud. One time a German plane came in low over our bivouac. I would have liked to have shot at it but we had orders not to.

Question: Why was that?

They were afraid we'd shoot somebody else. First we were issued an M-3, then a tommy gun, then pistols, and finally a carbine. I remember that we had guns while stationed in Ireland but no bullets. When we were in a combat zone, the band members also served as CP (Command Post) guards for the headquarters. We were in Italy a long time before saw any American planes flying. It seemed like every plane in the air was German. We did most of our moving at night. Later on in the war, the American planes filled the skies.

We were within 15–20 miles from where Mussolini and his girlfriend were strung up by their feet. I didn't go see the spectacle but some of band members did.

Question: What was your opinion of the Italian people?

We got along good with them. They were glad to see us. The Italians said that the Germans acted aloof, like they were better than the Italian people.

My oldest brother, Art, was in the infantry. He was wounded in the tough fighting in France and Germany. My brother Wayne was drafted and went in after the war. He remained in the United States. Ernest assembled airplanes for Boeing on the west coast. My brother Wilbur saw action serving as a combat engineer in Europe. I'm not sure what he did but I know he rolled out telephone wire. I had cousin from Illinois that was in the OSS. He'd never talk much about what he did.

Question: Ralph, did you ever see General Eisenhower?

Oh, yes, our band played for him.

We got to see Rome and toured the Coliseum and Vatican. We found an old German car that wouldn't run. A couple of the band members were good mechanics and got it running. We had fun with it until the officers found out. They confiscated it for their own use. I wanted to visit Florence but never did make it there.

There's only three of the Fairfield band members left. The other two are Ben Littlejohn and John Jackson from Fairfield. Ben was originally from Ottumwa. He taught school at Ainsworth.

I was never really scared over there.

GLIDE ANGLE OF A BRICK

Glen Seberg
Olds, IA

Navy
Pacific

Interview Date:
26 November 2010

Referral:
Deanna Estes

I was born on a farm down by Swedesburg 87 years ago. I carried a farm deferment and then went to work at my father-in-law's elevator because he needed help and a couple of guys turned me in to the draft board. I thought, "To hell with them, I'm going in on my own," rather than get drawn in. That's the way I felt about it. So I enlisted in the Navy in '42. I was in for three years.

I took my oath at Camp Dodge. Then I went to Farragut, Idaho. They were asking for gunnery mates that could learn Morse code to be a radio gunner on a bomber. I spent six weeks at Farragut learning Morse code. Next I went to Purcell, Oklahoma, for gunnery school. We shot 50s, 30s, and hand guns. We learned how to handle the guns, tear them apart and reassemble them, because knowing that may save our lives someday. Then I went to Lake City, Florida, where we flew out over the Atlantic Ocean on six to eight hour flights. This was being done to train the navigators. That was what we did during the war—train navigators. My job was radio back in when we reached a designated point. Then we'd fly to the next coordinates. We'd go from point A to point B to point C, like that. We always had two navigators onboard. My name came up once to move on to another station. A boy with me wanted to move

> *"I thought, 'To hell with them, I'm going in on my own,' rather than get drawn in."*

on so he took my place. My name never came up again.

One time my radio signal didn't get extended back to base and they sent out the Atlantic patrol to look for us, believing we had gone down. There was a little static over that when we returned to base, but I could show our plane captain from my log that I had sent the signal.

We trained on an old two engine bomber called a PV. There was a pilot, a navigator, and myself. It had a glide angle of a brick. Not good at all. If something went out, you went down. I was a seaman 1st class. I never did make it aboard a ship. I spent all my time in the air.

I stayed in contact with people I served with quite a while after the war. One lived in St. Louis. We stayed in contact with him until he died.

Question: Do you remember hearing about the attack on Pearl Harbor?

I was with a friend out in the country and my dad told me when I returned home. I hardly even knew where Pearl Harbor was. It didn't mean anything to me. Eighteen year olds don't think about those things. I do think about my time flying in Navy whenever I'm on a commercial air flight. It brings back memories. I only got sick once while flying in the Navy and that was after they fed us boiled liver for dinner. I might have gotten sick anyway. I think I flew 1200 to 1500 hours in the Navy.

We had one plane take off and it never climbed above the tree tops. It crashed and burned, killing the six crew members. It just couldn't gain any altitude. That made you think the next time you took off. I don't think they ever figured out why. Back then they didn't worry much about the why, they just pushed the wreck off to side and let it lay.

Some of the guys I know that were in the South Pacific still won't talk about it. I'm sure glad I wasn't in on that. I remember hearing about the atomic bomb being dropped. We were happy because we knew it was over then. I have no regrets about us using it.

We don't go to win a war anymore, we just pussyfoot around. We've lost a lot of good boys over there (in the Middle East) and I don't know if we have gained anything or not. We went in to win WWII. We'd be speaking Japanese or German if we hadn't. It took a lot of money and a lot of lives to win that war. There's no glory in war. I see these nineteen year old soldiers going off to Iraq and they look like kids. Then I think, well, I was only 18 when I went. They want them young so they'll take orders.

My wife and I went on the Honor Flight last Spring. It was wonderful and very interesting. We went out of the New London VFW Post. Some of the vets in my group had emotional difficulty dealing with the WWII Memorial. They'd have to walk out for fresh air. Kids would come up to us in the airports and want their picture taken with us. Parents even had us hold their babies on our laps for photos.

EIGHT DAYS AFTER D-DAY

Arthur Witthoft
Washington, IA

79th Infantry Division
Europe

Interview Date:
3 December 2010

Referral:
Linda Witthoft

I was drafted in 1942 and got married during a furlough home. I grew up on a farm. I've been told that farm boys make the best soldiers and sailors. I had training in Camp Pickett in Virginia. I served in the 79th Infantry Division. I was a 2nd lieutenant. I received a battlefield commission to get that rank. I was wounded in the shoulder by artillery. A German 88 got me. We were going up a hill when I was hit. I don't know where it was at but it must have been close to Paris because that is where the hospital was that they sent me to. Those 88s really make a loud bang. That's why I probably can't hear now. By the time I got out of the hospital, the war was over.

I went in France (at Utah Beach) eight days after D-Day and fought in the hedgerow country. It wasn't good. It was better once we found out what to do. We'd start firing at the Germans and go after them. They'd take off and leave. One day we might be fighting under one army command and the next day under Patton. *(Note: the 79th played a crucial role in the Cotentin Peninsula fighting to free the port city of Cherbourg following D-Day.)*

Question: What did you think of George Patton as a commanding general?
Well, he could swear pretty good.
I remember the first battle I was in. The company commander got fired (relieved) and everyone got separated. I was scared. I carried a BAR or a carbine for a weapon. I remember spending time in a foxhole in the woods somewhere with water standing in the bottom of it. We would pour hot water over our feet to warm them. My wool underwear kept me warm most of the time. I was in the hospital during the Battle of the Bulge.

We didn't have many young kids in our outfit. I was 29 years old. A lot of the older guys would fall out when we hiked because they were too tired to keep up. One time we were almost bombed by our own planes. We could see the bombs dropping right ahead of us. That happened about half way through the war.

I received a bronze star and a purple heart. Growing up, I never thought I'd see any of Europe. I saw France, Holland, Belgium, and part of Germany. A lot of that was riding through towns in 40's and 8's (train boxcars). I was in England a long time before getting over to France. I did not care for England. It was too wet. My favorite country was Germany. The Germans seemed more like people around here.

We were known as the Famous 79th. We saw the trenches where the 79th fought in WWI.

> *"I've been told that farm boys make the best soldiers and sailors."*

Martha Witthoft: I got a letter from Art after he was hit. He wrote that he zigged when he should have zagged. He said that he did a lot of praying over there. We were married and I was pregnant. I was teaching school at the time. I wanted that baby so if anything happened to Art, I would still have part of him. Until the war was over, his son, Bill, only knew his dad as a photo. Art and Bill would take many long walks by themselves to learn to love each other. When Art got home, he was ready to stay home and farm. We've been married 67 years.

Arthur: War is really pretty dumb, when you think about it.

WE HAULED EVERYTHING IMAGINABLE

Cleo McCoy
Crawfordsville, IA

9th Armored Division
Europe

Interview Date:
3 December 2010

Referral:
Dave Birney

I enlisted for one special reason. Don't ask me why, but other than taking a shower, I've been scared of water. I didn't want in the Navy. I enlisted in the Army on February 29th, 1944, and got out in March 29th of '46. I took a bus to Camp Dodge. From there they sent me to Camp Roberts in California for 17 weeks of basic training. I was home for seven days and then went to Baltimore. I got to come home again and then we sailed overseas on August 10th, 1944.

We sailed to Scotland. It took us seven days to cross. Bing Crosby was aboard our ship. He was part of a USO troop. Bing entertained us every night. I can remember him singing "Paper Moon" like it was yesterday. We were on a big French ocean liner. I was told there were 18,000 soldiers aboard. Usually the transport ships had naval escort but we did not. I was scared of water and sick the whole way. I didn't punch my meal ticket once.

Bing was the first one off the ship when we landed in Scotland. From there we went by train to London. We were there a couple of weeks and then crossed the Channel to Cherbourg.

Question: Were you assigned to a regiment yet?
No, but I was in the infantry. My dad was a truck driver in the Army, so I put in for a truck

driver. I had a little experience driving a truck while training in California. We ended up going ashore at Normandy Beach. We could see a lot of destruction once we reached the top of the hill. We were in St. Lo. It was pretty well destroyed. No French were still living in the town. There were still dead bodies of Germans lying beside the roads.

We slept out in two man tents at the repro depot. One evening they read off about thirty names, including mine, and told us to be ready to ship out in the morning. We surmised we were all headed to the front lines but instead we were sent to a small trucking company. There were only 180 men in that company. There was also a colored trucking company with white officers. We were both hooked up with the 9th Armored Division. We traveled in truck convoys much of the time.

Another driver and I shared the same truck. One of us would haul during the day and the other at night. Our company either hauled food or we hauled ammunition. The colored refused to haul the ammo when they got close to the front. So they ended up just hauling the food supplies. We hauled everything imaginable in the way of supplies to the front. We hauled things back from the front, including the bodies of dead Americans and Germans. Our deuce trucks had sideboards

159

that could be folded down for seats. We could haul 20 American soldiers and they could sit. We could haul 80 German prisoners but they had to stand. Those POW's didn't cause any problems. They were tickled to death to be captured. The prisoners rode unguarded. There was no need to send any. They'd seen enough war and were ready to go someplace else. A lot of them came to the United States. I didn't do it, but some of the guys would take knives and watches from the prisoners. I guess I felt too sorry for them.

The Rhine River was Germany's major transportation artery. There were railroad tracks on both sides plus barge traffic. They put the word out that Hitler claimed he would use poison gas if the Americans ever crossed the Rhine. It scared the hell out of me. We were the first trucking company across the Rhine. We crossed at Remagen. The Germans had blown all the other bridges.

I never got into anything too gory. Our worst problem was when we'd be driving at night in a convoy. The trucks only had little bitty tail lights called cat eyes that were hard to see. One night we got strafed and there was a roadblock ahead of us. We crawled under our trucks to wait it out. Our second lieutenant leading the convoy was always getting lost. One time we drove through this small German town and there were American soldiers on the far side of it. They asked, "How's the town? We were just getting ready to take it."

We only lost one man in our whole outfit. He and another fellow were out in the countryside doing something. They weren't messing around. It was night time. They were driving down a road and a couple of soldiers flagged them down. They stopped. The soldiers were Germans dressed in American uniforms. Both driver and passenger were shot but one survived.

One thing that was hard to take was seeing all the disabled American tanks. I remember one that had a helmet sitting on top with a bullet hole through it. We went through the Black Forest. We drove on the Autobahn in 1945. It was every bit of as good as Highway 218. The Germans built things to last. Everything appeared structurally stronger than the way we built today.

> "We could haul 20 American soldiers and they could sit. We could haul 80 German prisoners but they had to stand."

Question: Where were you during the Battle of the Bulge?

We were in France and Luxemburg. Some of the time we were sleeping in tents near Paris in the snow. The roads were icy. We couldn't drive without tire chains. Besides supplies, we hauled replacements from Cherbourg to the Bulge. We lost a bunch of men in the Bulge. Some of the replacements were educated people that didn't know anything about fighting but they were in the Army and had to go. They were scared. They had punched a typewriter but never carried a gun.

We also hauled some Polish people. That was sad. Men, women, and children were getting kicked out of Russia and Germany. They didn't have much of anything including clothing. They were crying. We hauled them back out of danger.

We were based in Cherbourg until Christmas. The Red Ball Express ran from Cherbourg. It was a designated route. After the war ended, they had a pipeline that ran from Cherbourg that delivered gas and oil to Nuremburg. We would fill five gallon jerry cans with gas at the terminal and deliver it to the troops. I was in Wurzburg, Germany when the war ended.

I was glad I went. I learned a lot. The first thing I learned was rank had its privileges. I started out as a private. Then I made corporal. I got in good with the company commander and he made me a staff sergeant.

I was ready to get home as soon as the war ended. I went into the service with a kid from Conesville named Don Abbott. We stayed together the whole way through and became good friends. He was married with a child at home so he had more points and got to come home earlier. My dad wanted me to farm with him and that's what I wanted. I was happy. I still go out to the farm everyday.

THE OVENS WERE STILL HOT

Howard Yoder
Wellman, IA

42nd Infantry Division
Europe

Interview Date:
10 December 2010

Referral:
Becky Palmer, John Howard Yoder

I was drafted in May of '44. I was in Camp Dodge about a week and got sent on a troop train to Camp Roberts in California. I had 17 weeks of basic training there. Following that, I had a week's leave to come home. Then I reported to the 42nd Infantry Division in Ft. Gruber, Oklahoma. The 42nd was called the Rainbow Division. They were getting ready to go overseas. I had infantry training and was selected to go to the field artillery. The division traveled to Camp Kilmer in New Jersey during November. We sailed out of Newark around Christmas. We sailed in a convoy. The convoy could only travel as fast as the slowest ship. We had an oil tanker with us that was always lagging behind. It took us over two weeks to get to France. The water was rough.

I was assigned to kitchen duty. Everybody was growling that had KP duty, thinking it was such bad work. But the good thing was that we got to eat three meals a day and everybody else only got two. Plus, we were in the center of the ship which was a smoother ride than on either end of the ship. There was some seasickness in the center of the ship but not nearly as much as for those on the ends of the

ship. The air conditioning wasn't working when we boarded the ship and didn't for two more days. The sleeping bunks were stacked five high. Everyone was hot and miserable and wearing only their shorts. I woke up one night about frozen. The air conditioner had started working and no one had any blankets.

It was early morning we when we arrived at Gibraltar. They woke everyone up so we could go on deck to see it. Off to the right you could see the lights from Algeria. The Mediterranean Sea was calm compared to the Atlantic. It was like being on a pleasure cruise. We landed and unloaded in Marseille, France. We were loaded on trucks and taken out to the hills on the north side of the city. We slept in pup tents and had hot meals, but it was cold and would get below freezing about every night. It snowed some and it rained some and was miserable. It got muddy when it rained and cold when it snowed. We stayed there 30 days.

In early February we headed for the front. We were issued guns and we loaded in the back of trucks. We had hot meals twice a day and ate K rations for lunch. We slept in buildings at night.

It took us three days to reach northern France. We were to relieve the 45th Division in a small village in Germany. The 45th Division had come up through Italy and hadn't had a break in months. We sat on the line for a while. We got marching orders in the late afternoon one day. I don't remember much from the first night but some of our unit had been in contact with the enemy the next day. Some of the forward observers from our field artillery came back all shaken up. I don't know what they had seen but they were just tight.

I was in the wire section for the telephones. I never had any training for that. I was not even shown how to splice a wire. My rank was corporal. I carried a carbine. It took several days before we started moving forward. We could hear shell fire but couldn't see anything. The area we were in had been fought over for some time. The Americans had pushed the Germans back and then the Germans had pushed the Americans back. Now we were pushing the Germans back again. We were staying by a little house beside a railroad track. The man living there had the job of closing a gate to stop road traffic whenever a train came through. That was his job. My grandmother spoke German and I knew enough of the language to communicate with the help of a lot of hand signals.

We got the Germans retreating and we kept pushing them. I followed along behind, laying wire in road ditches as our infantry advanced. When the front moved faster than we could keep up with laying telephone line, they used radios. Then I got called to pack a radio and accompany a captain and a sergeant. We were far enough back that we could hear the front line but not see it.

One time it took four or five days to get moving forward again. Going forward, I saw this German ambulance sitting on a side hill. Normally, you wouldn't fire on an ambulance. Our people had observed it long enough to realize the Germans were using it as a dummy. The Air Corps was called in to strafe it. We went through that area in the dark of night. There were dead horses, dead people, and their equipment all along the road. We were traveling in a jeep. Everybody drove without

> *"Some of the forward observers from our field artillery came back all shaken up. I don't know what they had seen but they were just tight."*

headlights. We weren't following the guns but there was a danger of running into the barrel of a 105 howitzer because you couldn't see them.

When we got further south, mules were brought up from Italy. We laid telephone with mules across the Harz Mountains rather than following the road. I think we had seven mules. Three of us guys took care of them. We were responsible for feeding and watering them. A half mile roll of wire could be mounted on a saddle like frame atop a mule. The other mules were used as pack animals to carry supplies and water.

By the time we were through the mountains and back on the roads it was April. All the bridges on the Rhine River were out. We crossed the Rhine at Worms, Germany, on a one lane pontoon bridge. We had a scheduled time to cross the bridge as traffic flowed both directions. After crossing the bridge, we traveled a ways through farming country and spent the night in an apple orchard. The apple trees were in bloom. The next morning was Sunday. We had a hot breakfast and attended church. It was one of those outstanding, perfect mornings you remember. There was a Jewish service following ours.

I was out checking lines the next day because we had a phone out. To check a line, you had to pick it up and carrying it in your hand as you walked. There were normally a number of lines on the ground so it was often a challenge to find the one that was broken. We'd tag the lines some of the time which helped or plug into them and see who was answering at the other end. I got into this town around five o'clock and marked the line so I would know where to start the next morning.

After an uneventful night, I walked out to pick up the line where I'd quit the preceding day. I looked up and saw 35 Germans come walking out of an adjacent apple orchard. They were surrendering. A lot of them looked 35 years old. Some looked older. They had a machine gun nest set up in the orchard. They could have got us the evening before if they had wanted to fight. But they didn't. They were ready to quit. I got in front of the Germans and another fellow that was with me got behind them. We walked them up to the village where we were staying. By that time, there were a lot more surrendering Germans up there. Somebody chalked out a circle and that was the POW's perimeter. They had to stay within that line.

Question: Howard, what were your first thoughts when you saw them coming out of the orchard? Did it scare you?

Well, kind of, but they didn't have any guns with them. The first Germans had their hands in the air. That was the only contact I had with the enemy.

We started moving forward really fast after that. We'd come across abandoned German equipment but never see any German soldiers. One afternoon we liberated a barracks full of English soldiers and a few Americans. These were flyers who had been shot down. The Germans had taken pretty good care of them. They didn't really complain about their treatment. They said about once a week the guards would come through the barracks with dogs but otherwise they were treated pretty good.

After that we were at Dachau. It was the stragglers in the division like us that saw Dachau. The 45th Division was also there at the same time. I didn't see any people but the ovens were still hot.

Eleanor Yoder: When my mother was so sick, you told me she looked like those prisoners at Dachau who were just skin and bones.

Howard: Yeah. From then on we pretty much rode in a jeep. The German people were coming out of these little villages and towns with white flags. The burgermeister and a few citizens would walk out to meet us and surrender their town. Sometime in there we had a week or 10 day rest break. We'd been going hard for 90 days. Some of our guys on watch duty discovered a cave where the Germans had hidden their fine art and valuables. Guards were placed on the cave. I was never on the guard duty nor did I ever get to see the cave.

After our rest period was over, we moved on into southern Germany. We met the mayor of Oberaudorf who was an American citizen. He had a farm in Ohio. He spent the war years in Germany. He said he had received three letters from the German government telling him to report for army duty. He wrote on each of them that he was an American citizen before mailing them back.

Southern Germany seemed like the area where my ancestors had probably come from. Each individual area had a different brogue of the language. Some I could understand a lot better than others. We moved into Austria next. We started staying longer in each town between moves.

We had a cease fire order the day before it was announced on the radio that the war was over. After that we were pretty much on our own. In Rosenheim, we stayed a week in a castle owned by the man whose company made all the German ball bearings. We made him live in his garden house. There was nothing organized. Guys stayed in whatever house they chose. In late summer we moved down to Salzburg, Austria, and bunked in barracks. I was put on switchboard duty. We were there several months. We had German POWs living in tents. We'd furnish them the food but they had to cook it. We heated the barracks with wood and the POWs cut it for us. The Germans are good foresters. They used two man chainsaws.

> *"They could have got us the evening before if they had wanted to fight. But they didn't. They were ready to quit."*

They had a drawing for one soldier to go back to the states on a 30 day leave but there was a stipulation that he would have to come back and spend another year in Germany. I put my name in and it was drawn. I figured that with so many men over in Europe, they probably wouldn't send me back. I thought it was worth the chance. I got back to the States the second week in January and got my 30 day leave. When I reported back, I was assigned to Ft. Campbell, Kentucky. From there my unit was sent to Chicago to participate in a big military parade. We rode down Michigan Avenue. We went back to Ft. Campbell and started training again. Then it was time for my discharge which occurred at Ft. Leonard Wood in Missouri. I made it to Iowa City and called my dad to pick me up. And that was it.

Eleanor: The evening before Howard left for the Army, my folks received a telegram saying my brother was missing in action. My brother was in the Army Air Corps stationed in England. He was trained for manning the ball turret gun on a B-17. The regular ball turret gunner was ill so my brother volunteered to fill in for him on that mission. Before he climbed on the plane, he gave his billfold to somebody staying on the ground. Their plane was shot down over Germany. Most of the crew was able to parachute out, but the ball turret is cramped and difficult to get out of. My brother is buried in Belgium. After the war, his pilot came to my parent's home and returned my brother's billfold. So that was not a very good send off for Howard. My brother's name was Carroll Swartzendruber.

Question: Howard, there are people today that claim the Holocaust was all a hoax. After seeing Dachau, what would your response be to them?

They are in complete denial. The people that in that area claimed they didn't know what was going on. You couldn't smell it without knowing what is was. That's probably the one thing I remember most and also the ovens being warm. When I saw how primitive some of the German equipment was, it's a wonder they had the guts to start the war. The Germans had good equipment, but they had the old stuff, too. There was a lot of Hitler Youth in their teens around near the end of the war.

After the war was over, I was in detached service. Our job was to help get people (Displaced Persons) back to where they came from. They'd load up on trains hanging on to anything that wasn't hot. There'd be people even riding on the locomotive's cow catcher.

Question: Howard, is there one message you would give future generations about how war affected you or the world?

I think about all the stuff wasted on war. When you think about Hitler and Mussolini and the type of government those countries had, the people had no way to vote them out.

Dave Brenneman from Joetown was wounded in the hip by a piece of shrapnel. He told me he didn't think it would amount to anything. Then it got infected and he was sent to the hospital. By the time he recovered and got back to his unit, he didn't know anybody but the cooks and bakers. The turnover of infantrymen was that fast.

I still don't care for Spam. Our cook would get creative and fix it different ways but it still tasted like Spam. We'd trade the local people cigarettes and soap for fresh eggs. You could get a lifetime of laundry done with a bar of soap. They didn't waste anything that was hard to get. I was kind of partial to Austria. It was beautiful country.

April 1943—Martha
The troop train pulled from the station
On a warm and cloudless day.
As a woman with a child in arms
Slowly drifts away.

Then back in her quiet farmhouse
Martha sadly bows her head.
And prays for Frankie's safety
Kneeling by her bed.

April 1943—Greta
"Deutschland Über Alles"
Is Helmut's battle cry.
He'll fight for the Führer's glory
But Greta heaves a sigh.

As she hears the cannons booming
She fears for her son's tomorrow.
She begs he God to hear her prayers
For help with coming sorrows.

June 5, 1944—The English Channel
All night eleven thousand planes
Fill the empty sky.
The sound, a lethal chorus
As o'er the coast they fly.

Gliders packed with paratroops
Eerie with blackened faces,
Fly off course in the dark and some
Will land in dangerous places.

Meanwhile throughout the countryside
Brave Frenchmen take a stand.
At risk of life and limb they'll stay
To help reclaim their land.

Now it's time for mothers to run and hide
Their children out of sight.
The land is under siege and skies
Are raining death tonight.

Six thousand ships are massed and stretch
East past the Isle of Wright.
The Allied Forces gather,
Poised and set to fight.

June 6, 1944—Berlin
Wake up Adolph, hurry, hurry—
You'd better look to the sea.
Army, Navy, and Marines
Have their sights on Normandy.

June 6, 1944—Dawn—Frankie
It's D-Day and with his buddies
Frankie's in an LST,
Along with what seems like a million men,
He heads to destiny.

The sea is choppy, he's cold and wet
In the bowels of the boat
His stomach's tight, he jams his hands
In the pockets of his coat.

June 6, 1944—Dawn—Helmut
Fifteen thousand bunkers
Are cemented in the hill.
Artillery has pounded them
But most are holding still.

Helmut waits, atop the wall
Behind his cannon, crouching.
But fear comes creeping as he sees
The Allied fleet approaching.

June 6, 1944—Morning—The Beach
Men and boys are bursting forth
Out from the carrier's maw.
Now they are wading, guns held high
Toward the beach called Omaha.

There's three more beaches on the left
Called Juno, Sword and Gold
Where British and Canadian troops
From their carriers unfold.

More Americans on Utah
Over on the right
Through a hail of German bullets
Rush to join the fight.

June 6, 1944—Mid Morning—Omaha Beach
Now the water is running red
Now the beaches cry
Now bravado turns to dread
As men collapse and die.

And still the ships disgorge more men
Who struggle toward the shore
Who run, who stumble and who fall
And still the pour forth more.

All day the battle rages
No respite for those who
Press forward are bound to keep
Their deadly rendezvous.

June 6, 1944—Evening—the Beach
Night falls, how many cry in pain?
How many men are lost?
How many poss are vacant?
We cannot count the cost.

June 7, 1944—Martha
Martha sits, her child asleep.
Her thoughts are far away.
The radio has brought the news
That rocked the world today.

She's wondering if Frankie
Survived that deadly fray.
She looks at her son and wonders
"What price will this child pay?"

June 7, 1944—Greta
Greta stands by her burned out house
No tears betray her grief.
They've all been shed and now she looks
For shelter and relief.

No lights to guide her, all is dark
The planes will soon return.
The glow from countless embers
Will flare, as more homes burn.
Post D-Day—Martha and Greta
These two who fought on the home front
Lost loved ones on wall and sea.
Martha and Greta, good women, both
Were also the conflict's casualties.

October 1992—Jackie Wells—The Cemetery
Today I came to Normandy
To walk the honored ground.
To view a beach, to touch a cross
And listen to the sound.

Of stalwart men who bled and died
Who now call out to me.
With fervent prayers we may avert
Another such catastrophe.

Here is Arnold Thompson
And Victor Birch is there.
From Iowa they came and stayed,
God Bless this valiant pair.

By this statue did a soldier die,
Thinking of family?
His life blood flowing, knowing that death was a
certainty.

October 1992—Jackie Wells—The Wall
I walk to the right, over terrain
Dotted with Charlois cattle.
Quiet now, but I see Earth's scars
That mark that frightful battle.

The sea is calm and peaceful
With not a ship in sight
The German bunkers empty, yet,
I sense their former might.

I see a man come strolling
With his dog patrolling banks
That once had groaned and trembled
Under German Panzer tanks.

Beneath my feet the one time
Scorched and tortured Earth
With seed and rain and God's good grace
Today has given birth.

To verdant fields, abounding with
A wealth of tiny flowers
Spots of crimson peering up
Snug in grassy bowers.

I look north from this pastoral land
Toward the ever-pulsing sea
That ebbs and flows and gently strokes
The sacred sands of Normandy.

October 1992—Jackie Wells—Cemetery Exit Gate
As I say "farewell" to this hallowed place
In silent reverence
I take with me reminders
Of its bloody violence.

And the men who perished or survived
And I'll say "a job well done"
Your victory that day was more
Than just a battle won.

You fought for rights for everyone
Your courage you displayed
You gave your lives for a way of life
Our thanks will never fade.

March 2002—Jackie Wells—Washington, IA
Strange feelings still return to me
Though its been years, I know
They're triggered by a word, a thought
Or a docu-drama show.

Our a photo in the Journal
Of a decorated vet
Or a vision of Old Glory
Carried by a young cadet.

But I really need no pictures
I can close my eyes and see
Tableaus of D-Day horrors
And I'm back in Normandy.

Remember
Martha and Frankie, Greta and Helmut

Martha sits and muses
Her soul's scars have grown dim
Just a photo on the mantle
Kindles memories of him.

It sits beside a medal
Earned on a foreign shore
By her handsome son, Frank, Jr.
Killed in another war.

No one knows where Greta lies
No her beloved son.
Both are long forgotten
Since the Allied Armies won.
These four who once lived peacefully
Were drawn to war and strife
By greedy, ruthless, brutal men
Who did not value life.

The men who followed different paths
Who led such divers lives
Like other men who served with them
Left parents, children, wives.

Now we must pray for leaders
Who will strive for harmony
So the world will never undergo
Another bloody Normandy.

OMAHA BEACH

Verl Davisson
Wellman, IA

1st Infantry Division
N. Africa, Europe

Interview Date:
30 December 2010

Referral:
Richard Huber

I was drafted Dec 19, 1942, and I was sworn in in Des Moines. They enlisted us and sent us right to Camp Roberts, CA. It was about 4 months from the time I went in until I was on the front line.

I was a casualty replacement in North Africa for the First Infantry Division, the "Big Red One." It's a wonderful outfit. I was in field artillery, with the 105mms. I started out as a cannoneer, then went on as a forward observer, and then I got in as a mechanic. I had a pretty mechanical mind before I went to the service, so they made me a mechanic to work on the trucks.

In North Africa, I got in at the tail end of it, so I really didn't see too much. I was in battle, but it was pretty well over. We hung around there until we made the D-Day landing in Sicily. I landed there on D-Day, H-Hour. I was under Patton, and I liked him. It was dangerous—you knew that. He didn't care what he did or where he did it or what. But you felt safe with him because he was all business. He wasn't a put-on guy; he was all business. If he could do it, you could do it—that was his motto. I think he was a wonderful guy. I

think the war would've went on another 2 years if it wasn't for him.

I couldn't tell you where I landed in Sicily, but I know we lost pretty heavily there. We lost a lot of equipment—we lost our kitchen truck. Then all we had to eat was what we could steal out of gardens and our K-rations. The Germans had mostly artillery. They were prepared. They knew what they were doing. I was in N. Africa, but Sicily—that was big stuff. It was terrifying, especially when you didn't know anything. Another bad thing was that the First Division was mostly old timers. Most of them were volunteers. And they didn't trust us for nothing. They didn't even want to know us, because we didn't know anything. They figured we'd cause them to get killed. And it was kinda rough, because the enemy didn't like us, and our own people didn't like us. I shouldn't say they didn't like us—they didn't trust us. And it was kind of rough to get along with those people. I bet I was in the First Division 6 months before I was accepted, before they knew that you knew what to do. And I think it took that long to be trained to do combat. There was always somebody sticking their head up when they shouldn't be—doing stuff like that—and that doesn't work. I saw a lot more of the war in Sicily—I saw the invasion, I saw the advancing. In North Africa, I really didn't see much of it. In Sicily we got into the Real McCoy.

We had been radioed information that the Germans had dropped a bunch of paratroopers, so everybody started trying to get them. We could see them up there coming down. It was moonlight. We were shooting machine guns, rifles, everything—and we were doing a really good job of it. When it was all over and done we found out it wasn't German paratoopers; it was our own men. We found out when they started hitting the ground that it was our people. We shot down our own paratroopers. They lost a lot of men—and we did it. We were involved in it. They were probably a ½ mile away or so. I never saw one of them personally, though you could see the parachutes coming down.

(In Sicily) I thought I knew everything, but I didn't, because when I got to Omaha Beach…that was something else. That was another war.

After Sicily we went over to England. I was stationed there about 6 months, and then I made the trip to France. I landed during D-Day at Normandy. I landed at Omaha Beach on D-Day. That was a bad place to be. The journey across the Channel that morning was terrible. They served us a wonderful breakfast, but I didn't have it long. I realized we were off the coast of France when we saw all the junk and the boats upside down. Everything mangled up. We couldn't even get to the beach. That was the trouble. Navy, or whoever was on the boats, was just as scared as we were, because they sure didn't want to go in there.

We were in the water off the coast of France from about 6 am until we went in at 11 am. We were supposed to be the first ones in, but we just couldn't get there. The ones ahead of us had all gotten blown up. There was no place to land. There were hundreds and thousands of boats turned over, just upside down. I witnessed the destroyer approach the beach and start firing at pillboxes. Every time it would fire, that ship would just rock way on its other side like it was going to sink, but

> "(In Sicily) I thought I knew everything, but I didn't, because when I got to Omaha Beach… that was something else. That was another war."

then it would come back up again. It was a good sight to see. You couldn't watch too long because there was a lot of stuff being fired out onto us. There were so many bullets hitting the water that it looked like it was raining. It was mostly hand gun fire, machine gun fire from pillboxes up on the bank. There were bulldozers on the beach digging big trenches, and the trenches were just full of people.

Question: What was going through your mind while you watched?

There wasn't much thought to it. It was just "I hope they don't get me." When you get in that position, there's only one way to go, and that's forward. There's water behind you; you can't go back. Finally, there was an opening, and the guy said "I'm not going onto the beach, I'm going to dump you off right here in the water. And you're going to have to make it. I'm not going in there." Normally the boat would go in and hit the beach, but he didn't want to get stranded there.

I had a GMC truck on the landing craft. I was driving a truck carrying the maintenance implements like tires, tools, gas and all that. I had a ½ ton truck on there, and when we landed, they dropped the plank and told us to ramp off. I drove my truck off there and I was in water clear up to my seat. I was sitting in water, but it never missed a beat. That truck never stopped. It went right on in, up onto the beach, on to the dirt. I had spent a lot of time waterproofing it. I was in maintenance and I knew what it took. I did a wonderful job. I had 10 ft pipes on the back for intake and exhaust. They did the trick. A lot of our equipment just got wet. There were a lot of guys that didn't really care—thought it wasn't going to happen anyway. For some reason I was interested in living, I guess. I just enjoyed doing that kind of work. I bet that truck would've run in water clear up to 10 ft.

I drove with the truck in a real low gear. It didn't move too fast. On the beach there was everything; a lot of bodies. I just had to drive. I was getting shot at the whole time, but it seemed like nothing ever hit me. I don't know why. We lost a lot of people. We lost a lot of equipment. We were getting shelled the whole time.

When we hit the beach there was a big hill to go up. We went kind of to the left, up and around to get up to the top. We were in a convoy and we all went together on an old road. It wasn't really a convoy, but more hit and miss. Some had stalled, some had been shot, some had been knocked out. I didn't figure any of us would ever get off Omaha Beach. I thought we were done. It seemed impossible. I think it was around midnight when we got to the top of the hill. It was probably noon that day when we landed at the beach. It took 12 hours to get to the top of that hill, and when we got to the top, we didn't hardly have any equipment. The only time I thought maybe we'd lose the war was on the D-Day landing.

The night of June 6, all of us mechanics went back to the beach to try to salvage trucks that had been lost in the water. By midnight the tide had gone out so there wasn't any water, so the trucks could be recovered. We got a lot of trucks that night and also some guns. The enemy wasn't shelling us much by then. There was a lot of bashing going on, but I don't think it was directed at us. In fact, I don't think they knew that we were down there working.

On D+1 we started advancing, and then we got run back. I was forward observing that day and I know they took over our guns. We just had the four 105s, and they took them over for a short time. Our crew got them back. I was up ahead radioing where to fire to, and they were firing where we told them to shoot. Things weren't going like you thought they should. The enemy went right over our heads—we were in a bridge. We were underneath that bridge and we never made a sound. We didn't shoot at anybody or hurt anybody. We just laid there quiet and they never seen us or heard us.

We didn't have a radio with us. We more or less directed the rest of the crew if they came up behind us. We told them where to go. We were way on ahead of the forward observing, actually. For this they'd take us out in a Jeep load and use us as markers to tell the other people how to get where we were going. We were way ahead of the line company. It's unbelievable.

In the hedgerow country in France, You just never knew where the enemy was, especially at night. You didn't know who was who. When you had guard duty, you had no idea if it was one of your men walking around out there or if it was the enemy. One night trucks and tanks started coming through and it turned out it was all enemy. They were lost. Everybody got lost. They weren't supreme and we weren't supreme. But they'd be down in our territory, and as soon as they found out they were as scared as we were, I think. They all pulled out again. We couldn't stick our heads out because we didn't have anything to ward them off with. There were too many of them and too much artillery. We couldn't match them. But they left again as soon as they found out they were in a hot spot. That happened several times. Germans would break through and take over people behind us. We'd have to turn around and go back to get them out again. The war was going both ways. There were several times we were surrounded, but it didn't matter. It didn't last over four hours. As soon as they found out they were in trouble they'd start going backwards. When the enemy got into our territory, they knew they were too far in. That isn't the way that you fight. You can't fight with it all mixed together. So they would try to get out and then they were lost. It usually happened at night. The same thing happened to us. We'd get into their territory not knowing what we were doing.

Near Saint-Lo, France, another guy and I were loading a gasoline & water 2 ½ ton truck. I was handing cans up to him. A 240mm railroad gun opened up on us and blew a hole in the ground bigger than this room. The shell sounded like a freight train coming, but we no idea where it was going to hit. Evidently, the top of my head was where the shell mushroomed up, and a piece of shrapnel went into my helmet. The other guy got pretty well filled with shrapnel, but he survived. After we got hit we both jumped into nearby foxholes. He was in one and I was in the other. He told me he was hit, and I could feel something running down my neck. I figured it was blood and I just knew I was full of holes, too. Come to find out, it was nothing but sweat. When I got back to camp my master sergeant told me to take my clothes off. He said, "You can't survive that without a hole on you somewhere." But there wasn't a scratch on me!

When the Germans broke through, they had taken us off the front for Christmas break. They drove us way back. They thought we'd be done with the Service. We weren't there 24 hours and the Bulge started. We got back in the truck and went right back. We were there the first day the Bulge started. The good ol' First had to be the first to do everything!

When we got up there, the outfit that was there was shooting (small arms) at us. Our captain got up there some way, and got a hold of the guy with that regiment or whatever, and he chewed him fine for shooting at us! He didn't know what he was doing—fresh from the States—and he thought we were enemy coming up there. And here we were coming up to relieve him. Things weren't going right, and I suppose they told us to go up and help them out. This captain came by us in a Jeep and saluted us, and we didn't salute him! And boy he stopped and told us where we could go and how to get there! Then our captain came over and put him in his place! He told him to get back, and go as far has he could, and never come back. And that's the way it was. We didn't salute nobody on the line. I don't care if it was Patton himself, you did not salute him. And I don't think he'd let ya. Nobody wanted to know who was who. That captain evidently just got over there and thought everyone should salute him. I mean, this was war.

I think I froze my feet in the Ardennes. I remember at first we'd leave our shoes on, thinking that was the way to go. Then we realized that if you take your shoes off and wrap your feet with socks and blankets it was a lot better. It really was, too. Wearing shoes was the worst thing to do. Shoes made your feet get worse. We had overcoats and blankets—not plentiful, but we had 'em. And we dug in. We went so far and had 'em sealed that we could light a candle in there. We usually tried to have 2-3 men together to make more heat. A lot of the holes were there from before. Me and another guy had a hole and we survived alright. A lot of times it was colder than heck, but you expected that. Cold was better than bullets.

The Rhine River was a mess. I don't really know how we ever got across it. We crossed in a pontoon boat. That boat would be here today and tomorrow it would be a ½ mile up the river, and the next day it would be down the river. It kept moving because the German fighter planes would locate it and come in and strafe it. They strafed us when we went across, but we got through. When the planes came over I dove underneath my truck. I had a bunch of chains underneath my seat and they would have saved me. That was the first time we saw a Messerschmidt. We thought he might win the war! We couldn't shoot him down. We had no idea he was going that fast. Dang, they came through and then they were just gone!

One time myself and four or five others were laying on the ground and we heard this noise so we raised up to look. A German plane strafed a row right behind us. If we hadn't raised up it would have gotten all of us, just like a saw blade. You just had to figure that luck was with you. Evidently, I was lucky all the time. It wasn't what you did or who you knew, it was pure luck.

We always protected one another when someone got killed or wounded. We always took care of them, put them on a vehicle and took them to the back. We never left anybody lay. We were also supposed to bury the Germans, which was hard to do. We shot them, why should we bury them? Grave Registration was supposed to take care of it, but there we just too many bodies. So we were supposed to take care of them when we could. A lot of them we just overlooked and pretended we didn't see.

By war's end, Verl earned 6 Battle Stars, 2 Invasion Arrowheads and one Bronze Star, which he was awarded for recovering vehicles & weapons from Omaha Beach the night of 6 June. After returning home from Europe, Verl was a highway patrol man in northern Iowa for several years. In 1948, Verl and his wife Myra returned to the Wellman area to farm. Verl was an active member of the Wellman American Legion for many years.

IT COMPLETELY CHANGES YOU

George Baumbach
Iowa City, IA

102nd Infantry Division
Europe

Interview Date:
3 December 2010

Referral:
Ann Williams

I was born and raised in Wisconsin on a dairy farm. They drafted me. I was 17 and wanted to go into the Navy. Our high school principal had told us that if we passed the first semester of our senior year and then went in the service, we would get our diploma at the end of the year. It sounded good to me. I asked my dad and he said, "No, Siree! No boy of mine is going in the service!"

Dad had it all fixed for my brother and me to buy the farm. My brother was seven years older. He was still at home. So when I got my draft papers, I found out that all I had to do was sign them and send them back. So that's all I did. I picked them up at the Post Office, signed them, and sent them back and never said a word. All at once here I get this 1A card—my Dad didn't quite understand that. He said, "I had this all fixed up for you and Ernie to buy this farm and take it over. You can have my cattle and my machinery." I said, "Dad, you ought to understand now that I'm no farmer. I'm too much like you. I'm a mechanic."

My Dad had been a blacksmith. My brother would have made a good farmer. I told him, "Dad, I'd starve on this farm." I just hated it. Oh, how I hated to milk cows.

Dad finally gave in and I got out of high school at the end of May. In the middle of July I was sworn into the Army. I was 18. I had intended to go to the Navy and I ran into a fellow named Alois J. Collins

that was from a town called Kendall, about 12 or 15 miles from where I lived. We were both being drafted at the same time. He said, "Well, George, why don't you come to the Army with me? Maybe we can stay together."

I thought about it. First of all, I would have liked to join the Marines, but they didn't want anybody then. So, I said, "OK." There was one thing that was a little nicer about it, in the Navy you got to go home seven days and then you had to report for active duty. In the Army, you got 21 days. And that looked good to me. I had a kind of serious girlfriend at the time. It didn't happen to be my wife Peggy; I didn't even know her at that time. I met Peggy while I was in the service.

So, I finally went along with it and joined the Army. And sure enough, my friend and I stayed together. We both went to Camp Haan in California for training in anti-aircraft. Right across the road from us was March Field Air Force Base. Those big old bombers would fly over us. After about a year, we were known as a semi-outfit. We weren't what they call a mobile outfit. A mobile outfit had all trucks and all guns for each gun crew; ours didn't. But we learned to shoot those guns, learned a lot about them. We had to be able to take and pull a machine gun apart and put it back together in the dark. When you were in combat, you never took them apart in the daytime because you never knew what could happen. I was real handy at that stuff. They would pull targets across in front of us when we were out training in the Mojave Desert.

We landed originally in England. We went over on the Queen Mary. We left on a Sunday morning and Friday morning we were there. It zigzagged all the way across. There were 15,000 men onboard. They loaded us on a train that took us to Southampton.

We just stayed in England two weeks to get our new equipment ready. Then they took us across the channel. Our trucks and equipment had to be loaded down in the ship's hold. Then we were on a barge. We were on this ship and there were some barges there and they were going to have to unload us on barges to get us into Normandy. We landed on Utah and Omaha beaches. That was four months after the D-Day Invasion.

We set there on the channel for ten days because of rough seas. That's the only place that I ever got seasick. One afternoon there was a bunch of C Rations all kind of stacked up there. I was supposed to be guarding those and I was sitting up on them so guys wouldn't steal them. I was kind of hungry so I ate one. I should have never done that! Because, see, that boat just swayed and swayed. And boy, all the lumps that came up . . . I was so sick. When we got aboard the barge we were on pulled up next to a Navy barge. It had a bunch of canned foods. It wasn't long before we were all swiping the stuff. We'd turned into a bunch of thieves! Well, they knew that's what we did. They never said much.

There was a Navy crew in there and I still have a feeling to this day that it's the one my brother was in He was a radio man and he studied correspondence on this so he knew the codes and everything real well. I don't know why I didn't venture down there and look him up. I still to this day think that he was there.

Then they took us and put us in big fields there in France (near St. Mere Eglise). It was raining. We put our pup tents up and went to sleep. I finally put my raincoat on the ground. We only had two wool Army blankets for bedding. I was able to sleep that way but I always got wet. It was miserable; it's a miracle that a lot of us didn't get really sick.

I was just coming back from chow one day and our CO says, "Baumbach, get in here!" I just about…well, anyway I thought, "No what'd I do wrong?" Because, well, I could get into a little trouble now and then. He said, "I just transferred you to the 548th as a machine gunner, because they need one more machine gunner." That was an anti-aircraft unit. I said, "That isn't what I wanted, I wanted to stay with my friends. " He said, "Now listen here," and he didn't say it too unpleasant. He says, "You are too dang small to be in the infantry." I only weighed 140 pounds and was 5'6". I had a problem anyway with lifting. So finally I said, "Ah, OK." I finally gave in. My friend Collins from Kendall, Wisconsin, ends up in headquarters. He gets to drive the jeep for the major. Ha! When we were overseas in combat, here he was sitting back in Holland, where the headquarters were, sleeping in a bed every night and all that. We were sleeping on the wet ground.

But then we left there and started going across France. We went through Paris and it was raining at night. We got a little closer to the front line and during the day those little French kids would run up to the side of the truck calling, "Candy! Candy! Chocolate! Chocolate!" We had these hard things that came in a K Ration. The chocolate would just hurt your teeth. So we'd give it to them. Then they would cry, "Cigarette! Cigarette!" Some guys would give them a cigarette and here was the little kid, seven or eight years-old, smoking cigarettes like an old timer.

Well, it was pretty darn miserable at first. We got there the first part of November, 1944. It rained and rained. Oh, God, it was terrible. The first night here comes what we call, "Bed-check Charlie." German planes, every night at 9:00, would drop a bunch of anti-personnel bombs on us; flares and stuff all around us. Of course, you know, here we were kind of greenhorns and we'd think, "What in the world is going on?" But before I got to there they had just had a battle in this place. Our captain

> *"Well, it was pretty darn miserable at first. We got there the first part of November, 1944. It rained and rained. Oh, God, it was terrible."*

got us kind of mixed up and he took us a little too far forward. There were all these dead Germans lying around out there in that field. I think some of them were still bleeding. That really shook me up.

Anyway, the next morning we were out there kind of looking around. I see a silver thing laying there, I reached over and picked it up. There was a group of guys standing over there talking. I said, "What do you suppose this is?" And boy, did they ever scatter! There happened to be a little puddle of water there so I dropped it in. It was an anti-personnel bomb that I had picked up and it could have blown my hand off.

Here's something that happened the very first thing. The guys were laying out telephone wire. They just laid it along the ground because there were trees and stuff like that. The very first day one of the guys walked into a German mine field. He stepped on a land mine and it blew off his one leg and his foot on the other leg. The second leg had to be eventually taken off. Another fellow was with him and that guy was blinded from the explosion and he couldn't see how to get out of there. The guy that lost his legs stuck his stumps down into the ground to stop the bleeding. Finally our sergeant and one of our lieutenants realized they were missing and went looking for them. They knew about where they'd be. My sergeant was a Polack from Chicago named Nowicki. He says, "You can't let them lay out there like that. So he walks out, picks one up, and brings both of them back. An officer named Elliot went with him. Both were awarded the Silver Star for that. I heard later when I went to one of army reunions that the one kid was never right after that. He was always so terribly bitter. You know one thing that war does to you; it completely changes you. You are not the same person that you were when you left as an 18 year-old kid.

First of all…you talk about mud, and rain! Our feet were constantly wet. Our shoes were soaked, our feet were soaked, and a lot of guys ended up with what they called "trench foot." Finally, I was talking to our truck driver and he had just changed the oil in the truck. He said, "Soak you shoes in that oil." So I did and I didn't have any more

trouble with wet feet. The water didn't go through my shoes—the oil caught it. The oil did get on my feet, but it was better than water.

It was so cold. We were sleeping out on the ground and we finally dug out an area. It was big enough for our pup tents to cover. We found some straw and stuff like that to ward off the cold. We had bed rolls in the United States. We had to buy them ourselves but we had to send them home; they wouldn't let us take them overseas.

But we managed to make do. There was a group before us and they had left little platforms. I don't know where they found them; they were made out of some cartons or something. And we found one of those and slid it in the pup tent. Then we could at least be up off the ground. One thing that sticks in my mind is seeing some of our guys eating their dinner. They were sitting on frozen dead German bodies.

> *"One thing that sticks in my mind is seeing some of our guys eating their dinner. They were sitting on frozen dead German bodies."*

Then we got into Holland. There would be kids where we had our garbage dump. They would be out there everyday, picking up stuff and eating out of it. There wasn't much that you could do about it. But we gave them stuff, anything that we weren't eating, we let them have it. That's kind of the way the American soldier was.

From there, all I can remember is that there was a big American cannon. I don't think I ever heard them fire it. It would shoot for miles. We had just entered Germany. Our guns…let me show you a picture. That's a quad .50 caliber. That's what I shot. All these swastikas are planes that our whole unit shot down. But we shot down five of those in one day. I think they were ME 109s and the FW 190.

Question: How did you know how much lead to give those planes to hit them?

You just learned how to shoot the guns to know how far in front of them to shoot. I am in the picture there at one end; that's an Indian sitting in the seat with our sergeant behind him. We called him "Chief."

When you shot the quad .50 it was so loud that you could hardly hear anything else. That's why we are having a little trouble now with my hearing. Those barrels would get red-hot and they would split. So you'd have to take them off and replace them.

One day I had a pair of leather thong gloves. We were supposed to have asbestos mittens. For some dumb reason, I reached up and took a hold of a hot barrel and went, "Oh, oh!" I pulled my hands off it and my gloves just stayed there. Then we finally found those asbestos mittens. All you had to do was unscrew the barrels and back them off two clicks. They had a thing with a spring on the bottom of the barrel that had a clicker that held the gun in place. The rate of fire per gun was around 600 per minute. It fired a lot slower than the German machine guns. You could cut a man in two with them.

It took a lot of training to really get it right. You asked about the lead on the gun…it depended a lot on the direction they were going. If they were going away from you, you shot under them. If they were coming at you, you shot over them. If they were going sideways, you just kind of knew, after you shot at enough targets. I got to the point that I was shooting the targets off all the time.

I was trained for everything. The Chief and I had the same rank. I had just come in but he had been in the outfit from the start. He had seniority on me. We were the best of buddies, even though he was 16 years older than I was. Like I say, you had to know that gun inside and out. You had to know how to load these. You loaded the guns on one side differently than you loaded those guns on the other side.

We loaded our guns on the backend of our 2-1/2 ton truck. We normally had them mounted on heavy trailers but when we got into the mud the trucks just couldn't pull them. The Colonel talked to ordinance to find out what they could do to load the guns on the trucks. Because you had to have the room as that gun went around (traversed). We had so much stuff on that truck. We had gasoline, an ammunition chest, and extra ammunition.

Whenever I got up on there, I would take my cartridge belt off and hang it from a post that the seat was mounted on. I'd stick my bayonet in the top of the post so all I would have to do was just unhook my belt and use the bayonet to hold it. Well, I'm kind ahead of my story . . .

I eventually ended up with only half a bayonet.

To this day, that's the only thing I wish I would have kept from the war.

We were on the truck and getting strafed by German planes. The bullets went straight through us. We stayed there at our post and just kept right on firing. I don't know which planes strafed us at the time. Most generally, they'd come at us with an ME 109 or sometimes a FW 190. That was a little heavier plane. It wasn't quite as maneuverable as that other 109.

Question: Did you ever see the new German jet, the ME 262?

Yes, that was the first jet airplane I ever saw. We couldn't keep up with that speed. I have thought about that a lot of times since. All you could have done was to have started firing way ahead when you first saw that thing coming and just let him fly into it. We would have had to gotten smart to do that.

The first town in Germany we came to was Bach. I remember that because that's the last four letters of my name. The town was nothing but a pile of rubble. But there was one civilian there with wooden shoes. It was winter time. He had no socks on. We went on through there and some other small towns. They were rubble also.

When the Battle of the Bulge started we had enough experience and the ground wasn't as muddy. The Germans started shooting those darn 88s at us. You never knew when they were going to come. Sometimes it just seemed as though they left us alone. It would be as quiet as could be. We'd get brave and crawl out of the dug-outs and then…it would start.

A guy from Texas, our truck driver, had this idea that we build a large dug-out and used a telephone pole for a roof support. It was long g enough for seven or eight of us to lie down in there. We dug the hole down and then we dug a trench along the front so that we could walk in. The part we slept on wasn't quite as deep. He was pretty good at this kind of stuff. He found that telephone pole, and then he found some doors off a building and he laid them over it. They put a bunch of straw on there, and then some dirt. Now it would have never stopped an 88, but it stopped the shrapnel.

One day when we were out there an 88 landed right at the feet of one of one guy. He was the

175

first guy killed in our outfit. You could hear them coming, but of course they told us by time you heard them coming, they are past you already past you. They travelled faster than the speed of sound. But I can still hear the sound they made. It sounded kind of like this "whew, whew, whew" in rapid succession as it went through the air. This (picture) was the second dug-out we made.

One 88 must have landed awfully close to me. We had a foxhole dug; each one of us had to have our own foxhole. But from this dug-out, we had a trench—and that was my idea. We dug the trench out to the foxhole. Because when you stood guard duty at night, you didn't have to expose yourself to get back in the dugout. When the shelling started, I dived into that trench and all at once something gave me the biggest boot. I ended up with a concussion from that shell.

Another thing that we did in this dugout that made it comfortable was that we found what was called a coke stove. There were a lot of people who lived in the valley. That valley was full of coal mines. We found this coke stove that was lined on the inside with fire brick. It wasn't very big. Once you got a fire started in that, it gave off no light and no smoke. The fire burned like a gas burner would—it burned just blue. So we could keep that going all night and we didn't have the fear of Germans seeing us. They had patrols out every night. That kept us pretty warm in there. We did get our feet dry. But we never took our clothes off—never. We didn't take our shoes off—only to dry our feet when we knew we could get them right back on. Our rifles—M1s—were always right next to us. They were loaded all the time. It was a miracle that we didn't have an accident with those.

The night that the Battle of the Bulge started, they shelled the daylights out of us. There was a bunch of what they called prime movers with us. They were like a tank with no top on it. They had a 105mm cannon. There were a bunch of other stuff including tanks. We were getting ready to cross the Roer River. They kept saying the war would be over by Christmas. That's how fast it was moving.

I'll tell you that the shelling started at 3:00 a.m. I had been asleep and woke up and heard what was going on. A couple of guys sitting over there were talking and smoking. The Germans shelled us on all sides. It's a miracle that all five of us on

that truck survived. The odds weren't good. Before the Bulge, they'd send one man from each crew, every day, back into Holland and you would get a shower. Sometimes you would get clean clothes and sometimes you wouldn't. But during the Bulge, there was a whole month that we didn't get clean clothes.

Our truck had to be dug in, too. The next morning after that shelling, the first thing they did was move all those trucks and tanks. Everything left. Here we sat, one lone anti-aircraft outfit. We were all by ourselves. They moved us down to what they called 88 Boulevard and Purple Heart Corridor. This was the road that you traveled back to Holland and then another road crossed it. When we were first going up into Germany, the Germans would shell that road every time they seen a vehicle go down it. That's how it got the name of 88 Boulevard. And boy, when those guys would get on there with a Jeep, every so often you might have to go somewhere, they'd really take off…really fast. The reason they called it Purple Heart Corner, when the trucks were going through there first troops were coming from both directions. MPs were standing up on a stool directing traffic. Every time one got shot off the stool, they would lay him down in a ditch. Then the MP taking his place would get shot. In all there were six of them laying there dead. They were getting shot by ground fire, small arms. The Germans were that close.

After we moved us down here to this spot, then they came along and took our gasoline. They left us our ammunition. They said, "You guys aren't going anywhere." They said we were going to be sacrificed unless we surrendered—and we weren't too apt to surrender without a good fight. That isn't the way we did it. The American soldier at that time was the best. They all hung together. We were all buddies. And there is still that feeling and camaraderie.

When we were left at the cross-roads with our Quad .50, every once in awhile a plane would fly over but then it got too foggy. That is why they had so much trouble at the Bulge, it was foggy and the planes couldn't fly. We just more or less sat there and waited for something to happen.

Like one night, for example, I was on guard duty outside. We had two guys on at once for guard duty because we had telephones and if they wanted to get in touch with you, they just spoke up. They didn't' ring it or anything. Somebody had to be there and every so often we would trade off if so we could get warm because we would be on for four hours at a time. You could have never stood the cold for four hours out there. It was a moonlight night, and all at once, I head this German burp gun. And boy, you could tell right away what it was. The other guy that was on with me was named Woodcock. He says, "What was that?" I said, "That's a German burp gun." We were positioned next to a hedge and there was an opening through there. So we crawled through and we both looked around, but couldn't see anybody. Finally we went back. By the way, just around that corner in the haystack, we had three Germans all winter. But they were only half there. I don't know which half was missing. You got used to being around these dead people.

The next morning we went over to the guys on the .40 mm, they were just across the hedge from us. We were all one gun crew: machine gun crew and .40mm. We could work on either one. I asked, "Did you hear that burp gun last night?" And one guy said, "That's that crazy so and so, he was shooting at rabbits." I said, "You guys don't know how close you got to getting loaded with buckshot! We thought that you were Germans." They never did that again.

In our battery, 548th, we had over 800 people. That included headquarters battery, A, B, C and D batteries. I was in B Battery. In B Battery there was four or eight man crews. We weren't the only Quad .50 in our battery. We had a lot of them. Those other guys shot down more planes than we did.

We had 40 mms that could stop a tank if they hit them just right. We had two of our 40mms all lined up ready for the German tanks. The 40mms could have knocked the tracks off anything. They shot armor-piercing. They'd have six or eight shells, kind of like a magazine, and there were two guys that had to be well-coordinated because one would run the elevation and they both had to work together.

After the Bulge, things got to moving quite rapidly. We had to cross the Roer River and that was tough. Our gun crew was picked to be the first one across. We went up there the night before

and we took an awful shelling. We were in a wine cellar but our guns were parked out front. We had to have a guard out there and oh, that was the creepiest place to pull guard duty. You never knew what was going to be around and you never knew if a bunch of Germans might show up on you.

Anyway, there was an upstream dam on the Roer. The Germans knew that we were there so they broke that dam and flooded the river so there was no going over to cross there. So they finally took us about a mile back to where we had been. We set up right next to the 105mms. There were Piper Cubs used as observation planes flying beyond the front lines. They would radio back to the artillery guys where the targets were. Then the German planes would come right around us and we would have to shoot them. We knew German planes were in the area.

We never had to use our guns to shoot at German ground troops, but we could have. I'd hate to do that, but we did shoot at most anything at times.

Things moved pretty fast once we crossed the river, but when we were sitting there that night, waiting to cross, we were in this small town. The shrapnel was just flying all over the place. You could hear it zinging by your ears. So I thought I'd get under the edge of the truck to at least stop some of it from coming down on me. Well, it was still coming in there pretty bad. So there was a building there behind me and I stepped in the door. The only reason we sat there was because the Germans had blown the bridge out. Our combat engineers put up another one. We got across early the next morning in the dark. I was amazed that our truck driver could stay on the narrow bridge tracks. The truck had no lights on, of course.

That's when I saw that first jet. I don't know how much ammunition I fired. I have no idea. Of course, we couldn't sleep all that night. The next night we didn't sleep either. We went three days without any sleep and didn't find much to eat. As we went in, we'd live off the land. We stopped at this one place that must have been a farm. There was a house there with two geese. Boy, we had a good meal out of the first goose. So we made a crate and took the second one with us. We got a lot of laughs along the way. We cooked the second one but it was so darn tough you couldn't chew it.

There is one other incident that I want to tell you about. This was when the war was almost over. I remember the date so well. It was April 14, 1945. Days later, I turned 20 years old. We were in convoy with the 105s (men of the 380th FA battalion). Our job was to protect the convoy from enemy aircraft. We were going up this road and there were trees about the size of apple trees along both sides. There was no place to get off the road. Germans planes came in to strafe that whole unit. There were four of them. Luckily, we just happened to hit an opening where the farmer must have had just a driveway to get into a field. We happened to hit it just right and pulled into the field. Chief started firing. There were four planes off in this direction and I had one gun that stuck on me so I had to pop it open. Brass would get caught in there once in a while. I had to get that out of there. Then I had .50 going again.

All at once Woodcock on the other side got hold of my arm and started pulling me down. I looked up right into the eyes of a German pilot. His machine guns were firing. If you ever were in front of a gun and they were shooting at you, I mean, each time a bullet fired, the color it was just white. There was a solid white light in that barrel. The plane's machine guns hit the truck and knocked the hood down into the motor, hit the cab, (this was a cloth cab and we never did find it), and there we were, Woody and I, and he pulled me down. I ended up on top of him. I just said to Woody, "This is the end for you and me." I honestly believed it.

The bullets were landing all around us. All I can say is that the Good Lord must have put a protective shield around us. That's when I pulled my bayonet out of the post. I only had half of it left. It had been shot in two. We were so shook up. We wondered how come none of the bullets hit any of our gasoline. A fire would have set our ammunition off and it would have exploded. It would have been all over for us.

We kept right on shooting. Then I saw the guy in the airplane, I could have reached up and touched him. If I had been standing up he would have taken my head off. He came that close. He went down

> "That's when I pulled my bayonet out of the post. I only had half of it left. It had been shot in two."

and just hit the top of the trees. He went down in the field on the other side.

But our truck was all shot up, the tires were going flat. The bullets had even hit the axles and stuff in the rear wheels and the truck was a mess. There was a bag that we kept our stuff for shaving and washing and that was all full of holes. There were bullet holes in the wooden floor, and to this day I could never figure out how that bullet got underneath us in the truck axle. We were right above it. It would have had to have gone through the floor.

So after that, oh man, I was scared. We were all scared. If anybody says they don't get scared in combat, they're crazy or they're lying. Then here come the medics screaming down the road. I think they thought that we would all be dead. It was just the three of us because the rest of the crew didn't need to be up there and they got themselves down in a ditch. The medics drove on up to us; we were standing off by the truck. "Is anybody hurt?" "No." Finally my hand started to hurt. I got hit by something. So the doc took me in to wrap it up and take care of it. He said, "Well now, you can get the Purple Heart for this." Old dumb me says, "It isn't worth the Purple Heart." "Well, yeah, it is," he says.

Well, that was the dumbest thing I did because I would have everything free at the V.A. I can't get it now because the medic didn't have the injury written down.

Three of us were decorated. Two of us got the Bronze Star. Chief, who was doing the shooting, got the Silver Star. He shot down those four planes one right after the other. If they had got into that convoy, well, we saved that whole convoy and kept them from getting killed. He shot all four planes down but the first one he had only damaged. It circled around and came right at us. Of course, he was going to stop us from taking the other ones down, but he didn't get the job done.

The Chief just kept shooting the whole time. They claim the German pilot was dead when he landed but I never found out for sure. Part of that plane's tail was shot off, I remember that. He hit the top of those trees and went right through them.

The sergeant came out real quick and handed us all a bottle of cognac. So, we all got drunk as skunks.

I saw a lot of German surrendering when we came through Germany. We went clear to the Elbe where we met the Russians. We served as a kind of military government in a little town after the Germans surrendered. We saw displaced people all over the place. We also saw American soldiers who had been held in POW camps, only they didn't look like Americans because they were so skinny.

This little Polack tells us that he knows where there is this mass grave. So somebody comes up with the bright idea the bodies have to be dug up. We were ordered to go out and had to stay there. We didn't have to do the digging up part. They just went into town and got a bunch of women to wash the bodies and put them in covers. The thing I remember about the mass grave was how the bodies were stacked like cords of wood. There had to be about 60 of them lying there. One of them had his mouth open. Now was he put in there alive? I don't know. Was he trying to get air? We don't know who they were. There were males and females. Oh, the smell was terrible. That smell was in our mouths for a couple of weeks. Then they had the German men over there digging graves. They had horses and some wagons hauling the bodies that were there. It was decided that one of us would have to ride along with them. I got that job.

I did not help liberate any of the camps, but we were close to them. Part of our outfit—headquarters—ran into a place where the Germans had put a lot of displaced people in a barn with a lot of straw. Then they went in there with gasoline and set it afire. Then some of them would manage to dig out from under the door and the Germans stood out there and shot them in the head. We were very close to that death camp that was so well known but I didn't go up there. I can't remember the name of it. This would have bee close to the Elbe, in that area. These people were Jews, and some of them are still alive. But the American soldiers were told not to feed them because it would kill them. We didn't know that. The soldiers were giving them stuff and then they got terribly sick. Finally the upper echelon got a hold of them and they made a special soup and stuff for them.

I was a private first class, a PFC. They wanted me to stay in. They offered me a 2nd lieutenant commission if I would sign up for three more years and volunteer to go back into Germany with the Army of Occupation. Well, I was already engaged to Peggy. She wrote the nicest letters. I had this feeling that she wouldn't want to go back with me. If you were married or got married your wife could go with you but you would have been there for three years. That rank looked awful nice but I probably would have ended up in Korea.

We got to be such an ornery outfit that they wouldn't leave us in Germany. We were in the town of Krefeld, Germany, just before we crossed the Rhine. You never saw people look at you so hatefully. A German woman was standing there looking at this dead American. She had kind of had a little smile and was laughing. It made Chief so mad he went up behind her and kicked her in the ass. She didn't know what hit her.

Then we stayed in a basement of a railroad depot. The top of the building was all blown away. There was a woman living there. She had some chickens—about a half dozen or so. You know what we did? We ate them. We had found a Dutch oven someplace along the line. We placed the cut up chicken with a little water and a little butter that came with the C Rations. In about half an hour you had the nicest chicken that you'd ever seen.

Interview transcribed by Kathy Tanner.

"STICK HIM, JOHN!"

John L. Fisher
Wellman, IA

1st Cavalry Division
Pacific

Interview Date:
3 December 2010

Referral:
Doris Parks

I spent the first 17 years of my life in Missouri, graduating from high school and then my folks moved back up here in 1952. I was drafted in '42. I should have gone in about a year sooner but my dad got me deferred twice. He was getting up there in years and back then we shucked the corn by hand. He went to the draft board and told them he would need me home until the corn harvesting was done.

I was in the First Cavalry Division, 61st Field Artillery Battalion. I shipped overseas in '43. We sailed to Australia first. It took twenty-one days because we zigzagged so there'd be less chance the Jap submarines could torpedo us. That's why it took so long. We were aboard a German luxury liner cruise ship that had been captured during WWI and converted to a troop transport. They renamed it the *George Washington*. The ship was way overloaded with soldiers. We didn't sail in a convoy or have an escort. We were pretty much on our own.

We spent about six months training in Australia and then went to New Guinea. We weren't there very long and there wasn't much going on, just some skirmishing with the Japs where we were. Our next deployment was to the Admiralty Islands. We were there quite a little bit. Any time we went ashore to take an island, the navy would come in first just shelling the hell out of it, hammering

it with everything they had. You'd swear there couldn't be a living soul still alive but there always was. How in the hell could anyone live through that? There'd be coconut tree plantation of these islands. The coconut trees would be planted in rows and evenly spaced between trees, checked, just like the way we plant corn back then. Any direction you looked at any angle there were rows. There weren't any lower limbs on a coconut tree and we hated those plantations for the lack of cover.

From there we went to the Philippines. The first island we landed on was Leyte. We'd go down the ramp of an LST. I'd drive my jeep in to shore, just like they do in the movies. We later went in on Luzon Island, the same place MacArthur waded ashore, only that we were there three or four days before him. The Signal Corps and the newspapers tried to make it out that MacArthur came ashore the first wave, fulfilling his promise of, "I shall return." The Japs greeted us with small arms fire, machine guns, stuff like that on both landings in the Philippines. It was kind of scary.

The roughest fighting during the war for us was on Luzon. I was with a 105mm howitzer battery and accompanied the Artillery Forward Observer who was an officer. My actual classification was that of a lineman. We strung telephone line and I was the one that climbed the poles. Any time a tank ran over phone line we'd have to go splice it. Sometimes the Japs would sneak in and cut them. Even though I was classified as a lineman, I'd help carry ammunition and go to the front with the Forward Observer and act as a radioman. The radios we used were carried in two pieces, the transmitter and receiver. We'd connect them together once we got to where we were going. The little walkie-talkies weren't much good for what we were doing.

We'd usually be up at the front where the shells were landing. That way the officer who was the forward observer could radio in sighting corrections. The guns would be way back behind the lines. The shells would whistle when they went over. They'd stop whistling a split second before impact. As long as they didn't quit whistling, you knew you were pretty safe. Sometimes the rounds would come in short. It didn't happen very often. Any time it happened we radio back to the guns telling them to cease fire. There was a 15 year old Filipino kid with us one time. He'd carry supplies for us, ammo and plasma, stuff like that. I told the group of us gathered that we'd better spread out as one short round could get us all. Then one came in short, landing ten to fifteen feet from me. This poor kid wasn't very far from me. I looked back at him lying there and he wasn't moving. Someone yelled for a medic but it was too late. I couldn't see no blood on him or nothing. I guess concussion had killed him. I had been standing right next to this kid and would have been killed if I hadn't moved.

We had different forward observation officers directing fire and different teams that accompanied them. The one officer, a new second lieutenant, hadn't been there long and didn't know what the hell he was doing. He went forward with six other guys and gave the guns the wrong coordinates. The first round dropped right on top of them. Only one of the six walked out of there. I would not have wanted to be the officer responsible for directing fire. You'd never forgive yourself for killing your own men. There were only two times that I saw that happen.

When we'd be up with the infantry, sometimes we could see Japanese soldiers ahead of our lines.

"Those little devils were pretty damn good soldiers. We'd let the infantry deal with them unless they got in close to us."

Those little devils were pretty damn good soldiers. We'd let the infantry deal with them unless they got in close to us. Then we'd shoot them. The artillery was usually reserved for strong points like dug in fortifications. We'd shoot the 105s at Japanese tanks. It worked pretty good on them.

There were these hills that the Japanese had fortified and dug in so deep that we couldn't get them out. We called them, "Million dollar hills." Planes would come over and drop gasoline bombs (napalm) and hell, there'd be fire everywhere, not a shred of vegetation left on that damn hill. The side of that hill was just as bare as that road out there. But still those little devils were living, dug in deep down in those caves. We never did get them out. Finally, we set up machine guns and shot in the cave entrances, providing covering fire so guys with satchel charges could blow up the cave's opening, sealing the Japs inside, burying them. This happened not too far from Manila, and we fought there, too.

We pulled into this one place and it was all dry rice paddies, about as level as this table. We were told we didn't need to dig as there were no Japs in this area. Pretty soon all hell broke loose. Our camp was located in a whole chain of big hills and we were in a dead spot where the Japs couldn't hit us with artillery because of the trajectory. Their shells would either go over us or hit the hill in front of us. We were there for two or three weeks and every God blessed night they'd shell hell out us without hurting anybody. Nobody could figure out where the Japanese were hiding so they sent a plane up one moonlit night and the pilot could see the artillery flashes. The guns were being hidden inside caves and they'd roll them out at night to shoot at us. Once we knew where they were, our planes would come every day around noon and just bomb the hell out of those hills. I don't know how any of those little devils survived but they did. They were dug in deep. Finally, we had to seal the caves with explosives like before. We discovered that the Japanese were using American guns and ammunition captured when the Philippines fell in '42 against us.

Every day about one or two o'clock, the Japs

would open up on us with heavy rifle fire. The Japanese had these little mortars, called knee mortars. We didn't mind their rifle fire that much, but they were awfully good with their knee mortars. We were scared of them. They could drop a round right in your foxhole.

One night we were up on this hilltop. The soil was hard and gravelly and we couldn't dig in very deep. The Japanese started shooting tracers at us. I was sharing a foxhole with another guy and pretty soon somebody jumps in on top of us. Of course, we thought it was a Jap. That was about as scared as I got in the war. The guy with me said, "Stick him, John!" I said, "No, you stick him!" Then we noticed the guy we thought was a Jap had a white tee shirt on and we realized it was the sixteen year old Filipino kid that was with us. He hadn't bothered digging his own foxhole, saying he had been too tired. We told him to never jump in somebody's foxhole again as we had about stuck him. The next night he dug his own foxhole.

They used to tell us that, "The only good Jap is a dead Jap." There were a number of Japanese-run concentration camps on the Philippines. God, those poor people held there were real thin. I talked to one guy who was a Methodist missionary who had been held in the camps for four years. He told me that all they'd get was some thin soup every day that didn't amount to nothing. He had two young daughters interned with him. He said you'd about starve yourself trying to keep them alive. One of the daughters died. He also told me to never trust an oriental. You might think he was your friend, he said, but get him a little mad and he was liable to run a knife in your back. That was pretty much the way they were.

I got a Bronze Star out of one place. You know if a lieutenant gives you a direct order and you disobey, he can shoot you right on the spot. On one day we were going up to take a hill. There was no fire, nothing, nobody shooting at us. The troop ahead of us started digging in and all at once the Japs started coming out of the ground like a bunch of gophers and killed a lot of our guys. So we were ordered to retreat, only they didn't call it that. We did a strategic withdrawal back to a gully. This

"He also told me to never trust an oriental. You might think he was your friend, he said, but get him a little mad and he was liable to run a knife in your back."

lieutenant tells this big infantry sergeant to take his men and circle around the hill and charge it from the flank. The sergeant says, "Sir, you can court martial me or shoot me right here, I don't care, but I'm not going back up there nor asking any of my men to. I lost four of my best men in about four seconds up there and I won't go back up there." This lieutenant was at a loss to know what to say at this point.

Our forward observer officer then asked us if we would go with him. I always said that I wouldn't be no damn hero, but I would go anywhere an officer ordered me as long as he went along with me. Anyway, five or six of us crawled on our hands and knees up to this bush near the top of the hillside. I was scared that the Japs were going to kill me that day. The lieutenant unfolded his map with all the coordinates on it. He was a good one and knew what he was doing. He radioed for smoke rounds, saying, "The Japs are shooting at us so much that we can't even get dug in. We'll smoke them out." So all these 105mm smoke rounds started coming in and he'd adjust the fire, saying, "Drop another one." Our guys could get dug in because the Japs couldn't see them. We took the hill the next day.

One day our outfit captured a Japanese officer, equivalent in rank to a major in our army. He was all by himself, lying down next to a mountain stream drinking water. The area was dense jungle and he had no idea anyone was around. We escorted him back down to headquarters at gunpoint for interrogation. Our battery commander was big and hefty and stood six foot four. The Japanese officer was just a little short guy and acting very cooperative. Our battery commander, a captain, said that he could take him the rest of the way. We offered to accompany them but he declined, saying that he thought he could surely handle one little Jap. He put the Jap on top of a weapons carrier for the ride to headquarters. It wasn't long before the Japanese officer jumped the captain and tried to wrestle his gun away. The two of them rolled around in the mud, fighting each other, rolling over and over, our captain screaming, "Shoot him, shoot him!" My buddy was scared he'd hit our captain so he struck the Japanese officer in the head with his rifle butt. That ended the fight. Our captain said, "That Jap held on to me like a leech, I couldn't shake that little son of a bitch."

We went back to a rest camp near Manila. Our whole group that crawled up to the bush was awarded the bronze star. I never gave that much thought but my parents thought I was some great hero when I returned home that November. About that time we heard that an atomic bomb had been developed and the war would soon be over. We were still on Luzon when it was dropped. We thought anything that would end the war was a good deal. I didn't know how terrible it was until afterwards. I spent about a month in Tokyo after the war was over. Women and little kids would give us the "V" for victory sign with their fingers when they would see us. I can't imagine anyone doing that in the United Sates if the Japanese had won the war.

I was a buck sergeant when discharged. I contracted malaria in the Pacific but didn't know it. I had my first bout with it after I came home in '45. I got sick while shucking corn and the doctor told me it was malaria. I resented the Japanese for a number of years but I have mellowed. My daughter even brought a young Japanese college girlfriend home to spend Christmas with us. When the war ended, everything changed.

TRIBUTE

The importance of preserving our veteran's experiences and service must not be understated.

Since the end of WWII, the world has been anxious to put the horror, devastation and atrocities of global war decidedly in the past. Returning veterans came home and tried to get on with their lives. Little was known or acknowledged about the wounded and disabled veterans who quietly fought a private war waged throughout the remainder of their lives. At the same time, veterans that bore no outward scars fought their own wars of guilt, terror, tragedy and what is now known as flashbacks. They also were destined to struggle for the rest of their lives combating the sights, sounds and horror that remained forever locked inside their minds.

I will never forget being startled awake hearing my dad yelling out and struggling with night terrors. He forever lived in a private hell that he could not escape. Flames and aircraft are never a good combination....

Most veterans of combat tell those who ask what it was like,

"Unless you were there you couldn't possibly understand or even imagine what it was like." The depth and breadth of that statement is immeasurable, unfathomable.

As a small boy in a small rural town in west-central Illinois, I grew up amidst WWII and Korean War veterans and their families. My dad was a veteran of WWII. He had been a tailgunner with The Mighty Eighth Army Air Corps. Dad flew with the 384th BG (H), 544th SQD, 41st Bomber Wing. Dad's office was in the tail end of a B-17G named "The Tremblin' Gremlin." It has always been interesting to me how that moniker will at once say very little about dad's involvement in WWII or, for the more informed it can tell nearly everything about his service.

My uncles had served in the European Theater of Operations (ETO) in the Army, Army Air Corps and Merchant Marines, while others fought in the Pacific Theater of Operations (PTO) as Marines and Navy seamen. My Uncle John, after whom I am named, fought in the Korean War as a Marine. Several of my aunts worked in ammunition and armament plants. One aunt served as a Navy Wave as a nurse, ETO.

Some did not come home.

How do you thank a veteran? How do you express the awe and admiration for that kind of selfless sacrifice? How is it possible to grasp the burdens and responsibilities that our veterans have bourn? Each time I meet a veteran of peace time or war, I try always to express my thanks and appreciation. Their response is most often, "Not a problem, Sir. It has been my honor."

Honor.

How blessed we are to have enjoyed the luxury and comfort of living under the liberties and freedoms paid for by our veterans.

Lefty Wilson
Wellman, IA

You Grow Up In A Hurry

Robert "Smokey" Glandon
Washington, IA

740th Tank Battalion
Europe

Interview Date:
3 January 2010

Referral:
Wyatt Glandon

Note: The 740th Tank Battalion was officially credited with knocking out 69 German tanks and 178 other enemy weapons including anti-tank guns, self-propelled guns, flak wagons, and howitzers. In addition, 717 enemy vehicles and 264 planes were destroyed, nine of which were shot down. The 740th Tank Battalion was also credited with inflicting five thousand German casualties and capturing over sixty thousand POWs. Fully equipped, the battalion fielded 68 tanks. During their five months of combat, they had 57 Shermans knocked out.

I was from Sigourney, Iowa. Several of us guys that ran around together knew our number was coming up for the draft. We had a farm and Dad said, "I you don't want to go, I can get you out of it." I said, "No, I'm a-going." Several of us boarded the bus together. My mom hugged me and my dad shook my hand. My brother Marvin was carrying my jacket and handed it to me. Mom told me later that he cried when the bus pulled out. Marvin followed the bus in the pickup truck quite a distance. One of my buddies on the bus with me was also crying. He didn't want to go. I wonder what ever happened to him. I think he was killed.

When we arrived in Des Moines (Camp Dodge) my thought was, "Boy, what did I get myself into?"

We would check the bulletin board after Basic Training ended every day to see where we were to be sent. We had to walk 37 miles the last day of basic training. I didn't want infantry. I wanted to be a tanker. They sent me to Kentucky, Ft. Knox, and later to the Arizona desert for armor training. Most of the guys I served with were from Texas and Oklahoma. I think I was the only Iowan in the entire outfit.

We were stationed as a reserve unit in Belgium when the Bulge hit. The Germans dropped paratroopers behind our lines who supposedly were cutting lines of communication and sniping at artillery batteries. We were sent out to look for them for several days but couldn't locate any. We had absolutely nothing for equipment other than the rifles we carried. A few days later, in the distance, we could see the road we were guarding being shelled. I told the guy with me, "You wait, we won't be here in the morning." Sure enough, they sent us to the front in the morning. We were routed to a depot near Stumont, Belgium, that had a number of junk Sherman training tanks, broken down tanks and other tracked vehicles. That night we had to cobble up parts from one tank to get another one operative. Some were missing radios, things like that. German planes strafed us when were at the depot in Stumont. We shot back at them with everything we had.

In the morning they sent my crew out on a tank destroyer (M 36). It had a big 90mm gun with an open turret. You didn't have anything over the top of you and it started raining on us. This TD didn't have any machine guns so I acted as the loader for the 90mm. We were the second vehicle going down the road. All of a sudden, around a corner, here comes this big German tank. Our lead tank tried to get a shot off but slid sideways into the road ditch. So he couldn't do anything so we took over. That ole ninety knocked him out. We shot him twice. We made sure we got him. The German soldiers inside the tank jumped out. I don't know if anyone got them with machine guns or not. I imagine they did. Later we crawled up and looked inside the Tiger. It was packed full of American cigarettes.

A little later we were pulled back and given our regular tank–an M4 Sherman. This tank had two co-axial .30 caliber machine guns, a .50 caliber at the top of the turret that the tank commander used and a 76mm main gun. I manned one of the .30s. We usually stayed buttoned up during combat. My view was through a movable periscope. Each crew member had a directional side of the tank that he was responsible for watching. There were ear phones inside the tank for the crew to communicate with each other. It was too noisy to hear otherwise. No one fired their weapons without orders from the tank commander. Tanks had radios with long antennas to communicate with each other. The Germans could stand up to the .30s, but when the .50 would open up, they'd turn and run.

I'll guarantee you grow up in a hurry. I'd never been away from home. I was just a kid, 18 years old. You learn a lot real fast. I think the only time I was really scared was the first afternoon in combat. I saw all these dead GI's from the 3rd Infantry lying in a grader ditch and I thought, "Man, this

is the real deal!" It was. You can't be scared all your life. I figured that I would make mistakes if I was scared and get hurt by doing something dumb. One of the closest calls I had was when I walked back down to headquarters one evening to get the mail. It was fine going down but coming back up, bullets started hitting near me. I realized, "Man, they're shooting at me!" I had to crawl back through the deep snow. I guess I was a little scared that day.

The Germans shot a lot of buzz bombs (V-1s) over us while we were in Belgium. We counted over a hundred in one day alone. They were trying to hit Antwerp. They sounded like they were running on a Briggs and Stratton engine. If they ever started missing they were running out of fuel so you'd better look out as they were coming down! One day when had just sat down to eat dinner when this buzz bomb comes chugging over and its engine stops. You should have seen the mess kits go flying as we ran for cover! It exploded in an orchard near us and blew out windows in the chateaux our battalion HQ was occupying.

> "I realized, 'Man, they're shooting at me!' I had to crawl back through the deep snow. I guess I was a little scared that day."

The 740th Tank Battalion spent a lot of time fighting along the side of the 82nd Airborne. The aggressive fighting ability of each outfit was mutually appreciated. This was in the Ardennes. The 82nd had already gotten the heck shot out them by the time we showed up.

One when we were with the airborne, the tank in front of us got hit. I watched this guy bail out. He was standing in the turret and did a back flip to get out. And down the back of the tank he went, just like that! That tank's gunner was killed. The tank in line ahead of that one was hit next and the driver got killed. I've often wondered how they got them (the bodies) out of there. When the German cannon round went through the steel armor it would ricochet around inside the tank. That is what got them. It was a mess. We ran out of ammo that day and they snuck some up to us during the night.

Driving down a road in the Ardennes another day, we stopped to help a wounded paratrooper. He was sitting with his back against a tree. He had a leg blown off. We sprinkled sulfa powder on the wound and tried to help him but he bled to death. In my mind, I can still see him sitting there against that tree.

We would shoot up buildings on both sides of a street when barreling through German held towns. We shot anything that moved. The barrel of my .30 caliber would get red hot. Sometimes the gun would get so hot it would auto fire, meaning it just kept on shooting even with your finger off the trigger. You'd have to twist the ammunition belt to get it to stop feeding. We'd zero our big gun in on buildings off in the distance. *(Note: Shermans typically carried an assortment of 76mm rounds, mostly high explosive with lesser amounts of HEAT and white phosphorous (smoke) rounds totaling approximately sixty in number. In addition, fifty thousand rounds of .30 caliber ammunition was carried, much of it stored in ammo boxes attached to the outside bustle of the tank. Space limitations allowed for only five to six hundred of the bulkier .50 caliber rounds to be carried. In a typical day of combat, the Sherman's crew would exhaust the entire ammo supply before the dark.)*

The 82nd Airborne was the first outfit we helped. When the snow got three to four feet deep the paratroopers would ride on the back of our tanks. One time in the Black Forest (the Ardennes), we saw some paratroopers riding white horses through the deep snow. Weapons and other gear were strapped on their backs.

We'd be sent to whatever regiments needed us the most (including those of the 30th and 63rd Infantry Divisions). The 82nd would call us back from whomever else we were helping whenever they needed a landing zone cleared of Germans for an airborne drop of replacements. For the night jumps they would shoot up flares and then down came the paratroopers. Once we had to travel all night to clear the Germans out of the drop zone. The 82nd was a good outfit. They later sent an official letter thanking us (the 740th Tank Battalion) for our help during the Bulge.

Occasionally, when we had a long distance to travel, our tanks would be loaded on railroad flat cars for transport. These trains were operated by

"He was sitting with his back against a tree. He had a leg blown off. We sprinkled sulfa powder on the wound and tried to help him but he bled to death. In my mind, I can still see him sitting there against that tree."

American soldiers. We'd ride on top with our tank. On one trip, the train men complained about being shot at while going through several of the towns. We gave them a .50 caliber machine gun for defense. I believe that probably took care of their problem.

I remember this one day we were stopped on this road to rest. I was talking to a driver from another tank. We were standing outside on the road stretching our cramped bodies when he said he didn't feel right about today. I replied, "We're going to make it," but he didn't. He got killed by tank fire that same day.

Some of the tanks we faced were the German Tigers. They were huge! You ought to have seen the size (nearly three feet in width) of the track on those Tigers! That is what we would aim for first, trying to knock a track off. Then we would go to work on them. The other Panzer we faced was the Mark V Panther. Both had our Shermans out gunned. The German 88s were a terrific weapon. I don't care what anybody says, they were the best gun in the war.

Our maintenance people welded extra armor plating to the sides of our tanks. Plus, we stacked sand bags as high as possible. We were lucky. Everything big that hit us ricocheted off our armor plating. I think it was mostly artillery rounds. One time we were trapped on a road as there was no place to pull off. The Germans started dropping mortars down on us. Mortars could really hurt the infantry but couldn't do much damage to a Sherman. One mortar round landed on the top of our tank and the sparks entered where we sat through the cracks. I remember getting the back of my neck singed that time.

One place we tried to avoid was the road intersections. Nine times out of ten the Germans had them zeroed in with artillery. If we were driving down a road and could see a cross roads approaching, we'd cut across country to avoid it if possible.

I remember this one night when we didn't take all of a town which we probably should have. Captain Barry told us, "You guys have been cold for three weeks and you are going to sleep warm tonight." Normally we slept inside the tank. It was cramped and so cold in there that the snow on our boots would not melt. So we went into this house and there was an old man in there and all of a sudden he disappeared. We wondered where he went, but did not really pay it any attention. We soon found out, however. The old man went and told the Germans where we were. The house started receiving small arms fire. Me and another guy tried to go out a door at the same time and there wasn't room for the two of us to fit so he crowded first and got hit by gun fire. I looked over at him and saw blood running down his face. I had to run to my tank. I don't know what happened to him but there were medics close by and they probably took care of him.

It was dark outside. I jumped in a tank but it wasn't mine so I had to climb back out. I could hear the Germans talking just behind this row of trees. I thought, "Oh boy, I've got to hurry!" I climbed into my own tank and discovered that because our tank commander, Lt. Loopey, had fired so many .50s that day that the pile of empty shell casing would not allow me to lower the gun enough to fire at the Germans. When the rest of the crew arrived, we pulled out on the road where I could shoot at the Germans with my .30. I fired until I ran out of ammo. Then we backed out and another tank pulled in to take our place. The Germans typically avoided fighting at night so normally we did not have to worry too much about them when darkness fell.

The next morning while we were getting our tank ready, two infantrymen were walking down the street toward a barn. Unbeknownst to them, there were German soldiers hiding inside and they shot and killed our guys. We turned our big gun on them and blew that building to pieces. The Germans did not get out.

One afternoon we knocked out five Panzers in a town. We were fighting with the 82nd that day. Lt. Loopey had us park our tank behind a house where we could remain hidden but still watch the road the German tanks were traveling to enter the village. There was a knocked out Sherman in the middle of the road. We used it as bait. The German tanks thought the disabled Sherman was doing all the firing and they'd be shooting at it.

They would come down off a hill one at a time and we ambushed five that way. The entire tank crew was awarded the bronze star for that action. The infantry had taken refuge in the cellar of a building during this shootout. They didn't want to get killed.

Lt. Loopey was a great tanker and a fine commanding officer. He was awarded a Silver Star and a battlefield commission during the war. All the officers would receive a weekly ration of liquor. Ole Loopey would always try to hide his bottle but we would usually find it and drink it for him. He loved his booze but was a good egg about our thievery. Lt. Loopey was shot in the neck by a sniper while standing in the turret while we were in a German village. He remained with his tank until the loss of blood weakened him to the point he had to be evacuated. He survived the wound and was hospitalized for some time. He was older than the rest of the crew and lived to age 93. Our whole crew was like a family. When you eat and sleep together and share the same hardships you get real close.

We drove through Malmedy, Belgium and saw the bodies of the dead American soldiers shot by the Germans. We stopped to help with the recovery. The bodies were laid out in rows after being located under several feet of snow. Mine detectors were used to locate the bodies. *(Note: Known as the Malmedy Massacre, command elements of Joachim Piper's 1st SS Kampfgruppe machine gunned American POWs, killing 181 soldiers of the 285th Field Artillery Observation Battalion captured during the early phase of the Battle of the Bulge.)*

Every night we would take turns guarding our tank. One night I saw two Germans sneaking out of a house. I was hesitant, trying to decide what do. I opened up on them with the .50 caliber machine gun. They didn't move again. Isn't that awful? I hated to do it but I figured it was either them or me. I felt sorry for our poor infantry, those poor devils, wading through that deep snow. It was horrible for them. You talk about cold, it was terrible cold!

One time we had our tank parked in one place for several days. There was a frozen body of a dead German soldier buried in the snow near our tank. Every time we would walk around, wading through the deep snow, we would stumble over him.

One day we were taking this town in Belgium. We crossed a field to reach the main street of the town. Our tank was in the middle and there was one on each side flanking us. That is how we attacked. In the middle of the street lay this little girl. We were not going to run over her so we stopped and climbed out of our tank. She was dead. We called for an army ambulance and they took her away. I can still see the color of her dress—it was blue. She would have been around 12 years old. Artillery concussion probably got her as there wasn't a mark on her body. It wasn't our artillery that killed her as we had not shelled the town. It was the only time all five of us shed tears together.

Several things about Christmas day stick in my mind. Our field kitchen brought Christmas dinner. Most days we subsisted on those darn K rations and they didn't amount to nothing. We also got bombed on Christmas. We were on one side of a rail yard. The German troops were dug in on the other side and we couldn't get to them. Allied dive bombers were called in to dislodge them. We could watch our dive bombers coming in and releasing the single bomb hanging under the plane. We also got strafed by some of our own P-47 Thunderbolts that flew on the wrong side of the rail yard. Those of us on the ground called them the American *Luftwaffe* when they pulled stunts like that. A sergeant and I hid under a tank for cover. Afterwards, he refused to crawl out. I had to call the medics to haul him away as he had gone crazy, unable to move. There was a house across the street. There had been a German in it cooking something on a stove. A big shell had come through the side of the house making a mess out of his back. He wasn't going anyplace and neither was his supper. I believe we slept that night in this house. We knew a dead German wasn't going to hurt us. Earlier, in a house on the way to this town, we had discovered the bodies of an older couple lying in bed. I think the retreating Germans had shot them.

I did not think much of General Patton. My cousin, Wilmer Dillon, served with Patton. He's gone now. We were supposed to meet up with Patton (the 3rd Army) once near Bastogne but they were late in showing up. They had run out of gasoline.

Aachen was the first large German city the Allies took after three weeks of hard fighting. We stopped as we entered Aachen to check out an American soldier lying in the street that appeared alright. We thought maybe we could help, thinking maybe he had only been knocked unconscious. We couldn't see a mark on him until we turned him over and saw his lungs exposed. He had been hit in the back by something big. The buildings…there were just nothing left of them.

The Siegfried Line stopped us. Engineers brought up TNT and blew off the concrete dragon's teeth but enough jagged edges stuck up to stop our tanks from going over them. So they brought up a tank with a blade mounted on the front. He bulldozed dirt over the stubs to give us a path to cross. The Germans started dropping artillery in on him and dirt was flying everywhere but managed to get the job done.

After crossing the Siegfried Line we noticed something unusual. There was a German woman standing near a wood line watching us. She made no effort to flee. We thought that was pretty odd and wondered if she was a spy. She was right beside this big German pill box that had sleeping quarters in it. Inside the tank we discussed it among ourselves. Someone figured it was likely a German soldier dressed as a woman. Another offered that she was probably acting as an artillery spotter. It was decided we had better shoot her to be safe so that's what we did. We had no choice.

John Butler of Washington was a POW in one of the prison camps we liberated in Germany. He always wanted me to come over and visit with him about it but I never did. There were also Russian prisoners of war at the camp. They were segregated from the English speaking POWs. The guards had already fled. We drove past one of the slave labor camps. I can't remember the name of the nearby town. We noticed the funny smell in the air and could see the chimneys in the distance belching smoke. Someone said it was the dead Jews being

> *"I can still see the color of her dress—it was blue. She would have been around 12 years old … It was the only time all five of us shed tears together."*

burnt. Later we were told that we could go visit the camp to see it for ourselves but I never did.

I was wounded once, but didn't tell anyone. A booby trap went off as I went through a door into a house. Shrapnel hit me in the legs. It burnt more than hurt. That night I felt something in my boot. It was blood. If I had told anyone, I would have been sent back to the medics and they would have made me stay. I would have been separated from my outfit as they would not have waited on me to return. I didn't want that to happen. There were several times during combat when I wondered if I would survive the war. But I told my dad after shaking his hand, "I'll be back." I meant to make good on that promise.

We lost more tanks in the Ruhr Pocket than in the Ardennes. The last morning we were there, we had one half of our remaining tanks knocked out. They pulled us out then and another tank battalion took our place. *(Note: The Ruhr Pocket was the heavy industry area of Germany and was defended by 300,000 German troops. The Allies initially surrounded and bypassed it. Later, the 740th was the tip of the armored spear that split the Ruhr Pocket. Smokey's battalion had been whittled down to only 17 serviceable tanks when they were relieved.)*

> "There were several times during combat when I wondered if I would survive the war. But I told my dad after shaking his hand, 'I'll be back'. I meant to make good on that promise."

Toward the end of the war the Germans knew they were beaten. We were advancing rapidly through Germany. Road blocks were about the only military obstacles we faced. We would scope out a road block before deciding how to approach it. The Germans would set up behind log barricades at pinch points. If there was heavy stuff there like anti-tank guns, we'd open fire on them with everything we had and call artillery in as well. Small stuff could not hurt us so we'd drive right up to any barricade without heavy weapons and the Germans would surrender.

Sometimes we would pass close to a German airfield. We destroyed a good many planes that way. The Germans would scramble and attempt to get planes in the air to escape. We'd wait until they would just get airborne and shoot them down with our 76mm. We thought we might get credit for shooting down an enemy airplane but they never gave it to us.

You would not believe the scene the last day of the war. The roads and streets were packed with armed German soldiers as far as the eye could see. They were marching towards us, throwing their guns off to the side and surrendering. It went on like that all day. There was no way you could drive through them; we would have run over them. During the war, we had one guy get in big trouble for shooting a captured German officer. I think he might have been court-martialed. Nobody said anything if someone shot an enlisted prisoner. It wasn't supposed to happen but it did. The Intelligence people wanted to question the German officers. That was the reason they were off limits.

After the war we had a parade. I have no idea why they wanted one. The officers told us to paint a record of our kills on the cannon barrel of our tanks. Some crews hadn't accomplished much and had trees, outhouses, funny stuff like that painted on their barrels. Our barrel had 21 tanks painted on it. Later we drove all our tanks to a field and parked them in rows and just walked away. Our war was over.

After the war there were thousands of slave laborers *(Displaced Persons, mainly Poles in their area)*, wandering around. These poor people would raid German villages for food and search out camp guards that were in hiding for vengeance. I don't know what they did to the Germans when they found them, but I suspect they were killed. Some of these Germans came to our headquarters, wanted us to protect them.

During occupation I was stationed in Heidelberg, Germany. It's a big, beautiful city. Heidelberg was a university town and declared an open city so it wasn't bombed. I saw many towns where there nothing left. They had been totally leveled.

I was made Sergeant of the Guard numerous times after the war ended. They also gave me a jeep and a driver and a list of towns to visit every day. My job was to have the town's Burgermeister (Mayor) show me the graves of Allied troops buried in German cemeteries. I'd turn in the list of graves I found every evening, usually seven or eight in number and where they were located. I don't know why they wanted to dig them up. *(Note: Graves Registration attempted to recover all the bodies of missing US airmen and soldiers throughout Europe.)* During the winter it got so cold they couldn't keep up with the number of casualties and bury the bodies. The ground was too hard. Corpses were frozen stiff, stacked up like cord wood. They would haul them away in trucks like lumber.

After the war, three of us were issued leave passes to visit Paris. That place is something! Everyone ought to see Paris. Every other building is a tavern. The French people did not want to fight (in the war).

We had a whole pile of German guns we had collected. One day some Air Force guys we played ball with brought some cognac over to trade for souvenirs. They were examining the guns and one discharged as it was being handed back to my buddy. The bullet hit the floor, going down past my leg, but it shot off the end of my buddy's finger. We took him to the medics and later an officer gave us heck but nothing else was ever done about it. Replacement 2nd Lieutenants, called 90-day wonders, avoided us combat veterans as much as possible. The generals who visited our headquarters were very friendly and would make a point to talk to me when I was serving as Sergeant of the Guard. One day I shook hands with four different generals.

I was discharged in New Jersey and caught a flight to Detroit for $37 in an old converted troop transport and then Chicago where we landed in a field.

Note: When we asked Smokey how long it took him to adjust back to civilian life, to get back to normal, Smokey chuckled, replying, "Well, maybe I never did!"

For as long as most local residents can remember, Robert "Smokey" Glandon owned and operated a gasoline service station on the western edge of Washington. He continues to assist his two sons on a part-time basis in maintaining this family tradition of dependable, friendly automotive service.

CHERBOURG

Harvey Holden
Washington, IA

Navy
Europe

Interview Date:
7 January 2010

Referral:
Jim Cuddeback

I enlisted May 10th of '44. I probably would have been drafted later that year. I registered for the draft in 1940. Pearl Harbor was in 1941, but by that time we had selective service drawn numbers and I didn't have a very low number, my brother did, but I did not have an immediate low number. I was married in 1940 so I did have a married deferment of 3A and then my first child was born in '42. So then it was '44 when I enlisted, although I probably would have been drafted that year. My choice was to go to the Navy, not to the Army. You can't go to the Navy through the draft except under very unusual circumstances, and so in order to accomplish that I enlisted. I had one other reason to enlist. I had three brothers in the service at that time and I didn't want anyone to think I was less patriotic than anyone else. I felt I should be in the service. Most my friends were going too. There weren't young people around.

Question: What drew you to the Navy?

I did not want to be a private in the Army in the infantry. It didn't appeal to me at all. The Navy, I thought, would have better living conditions. That sort of thing. I didn't know anything about

shipboard duty. I didn't know anything about that. I thought I would be shipboard a good bit of the time although I never was for any length of time, so that's why I chose the Navy. I didn't want the Marines. Not all months calls allowed any to enlist in the Navy. It just happened that the month of May they were taking some Navy people. Not through the draft but by enlisting.

I did boot camp at Great Lakes in Chicago. And that's a different experience when you come out of civilian life because it's the first time you take orders and you don't discuss whether the orders are right or wrong and most of us weren't in the shape of being able to run great distances or climb ropes or that sort of thing. Basic training develops unity. You are all in it together and some lowly non-commissioned officer is king. We had to be able to swim, not swim far, maybe 30 feet is all. There's always two or three that say "I can't swim. I can't swim." Well, they'd just get thrown in and that's the kind of consideration you got. Whether that does much good if you're out in the ocean 3000 miles from shore is a little bit beside the point but maybe you can stay up for a while. So boot camp is a leveler and it's unit-building and it's teaching you to take orders. We did close order drill and that sort of thing. I didn't realize it at the time it is the Navy's way to select where they're going to send a person.

Boot camp lasted five weeks. On June 20th I started my five day leave and came home. The day after I arrived home Laurine was born so I was here for that and then I didn't see them again until a year and a half later.

I received a rating out of boot camp which was rather unusual. Before enlisting I had a job with the tax commission in Des Moines. I was also a little older than these young guys going in at 18. In 1944 I was 27. They asked one day if anybody could type and three or four of us held up our hands. They asked, "Do you want to take a test on that?" I said "Yes." So the next day I took a test and I had an exceptionally good day typing so they selected me to become a yeoman. A yeoman is really a secretary, a typist. Surprisingly, I got a third class Petty Officer rating right out of boot camp.

I was assigned right out of boot camp. My orders had Far Shore on them but I was so green that I didn't know that Far Shore meant France. At the time I was assigned to this unit, it wasn't even across the English Channel yet. A group of us left for New York after boot camp. Some were assigned to ships and were going to Europe. I boarded the *Queen Elizabeth* troop carrier and sailed across to Glasgow, Scotland. There were 16,000 troops on the ship and I think you could go down a deck or up a deck, but you could not go sideways or lengthwise. The ship was divided and you had to stay in an assigned section.

We didn't have a warship escort because the ship traveled faster than most of the transports. We zigzagged across the northern Atlantic. It was a very smooth ride. It was such a long ship and it didn't plunge in and out. I got terribly seasick coming home, but I didn't going over. We landed in Glasgow and I was transported in the back of Navy trucks driven by 18 year old kids. I never thought I would see the war or live through that ride because they drove like wild people and on the wrong side of the road. We'd be sitting there looking where we were going here it is going around on the outside lane going around on the right. I didn't think I

would get any farther. I took a train down the full length of England to one of the southern ports and I do not remember which one. Portsmouth or someplace would have been the jumping off place.

My first duty station was at Cherbourg, France. I remember that I crossed from England to Cherbourg on August the 6th of 1944. That was D plus 60 you might say. Cherbourg was a 100 year old port that sat on the end of a peninsula. The allied army had secured this peninsula and captured the Germans trapped there. The port facilities had been badly bombed (by the Germans). At first, it could only receive a ship or two but then it was rebuilt as fast as possible.

Our job—and I was still a lowly third yeoman typist—was to schedule more ships to bring in war materials. Cherbourg was the first real port opened on the continent. I was at Cherbourg for maybe four months. Tides are controlled by the moon and high tide is twice a day and low tide is twice a day, but not at the same time each day. I knew nothing about that and I didn't need to know that. I just needed to do what I was told. They would schedule ships to come in at high tide, but some ships could come in most any time. The tide varied as much as 30 feet. That's an awfully lot and not the same at all ports across the world but there are tides every place. A ship could come during high tide and couldn't leave again until some other time, although it would be lighter after unloading and wouldn't have the same draft.

Our unit operated the port of Cherbourg to its capacity and then the port would be gradually expanded by repairing more keys (what they were called) where the ships could dock.

After four months I moved down to another port, Le Havre, which was the same kind of set up. Part of our unit stayed in Cherbourg. We picked up some new people and built a unit. We lived in a school. That was our sleeping quarters and that's another thing about the Navy. They always had clean beds and there's no doubt we lived better than the guys in the trenches. We were unconcerned about sanitation. The bathroom was a hole in the floor and the showers had no doors on them. The cleaning lady came wandering in any old time. She'd come through the door without knocking and everybody would just give her the hardest time and she didn't care. The French don't pay any attention to that kind of thing. By the second week it didn't make any difference anyway.

Le Harve had also been bombed. Our office was in one end of a hotel. It had a fire place in the room. It was the only heat. We would pick up wood window frames and doors, bring them back, break them up and burn them. I don't mean that we had to work in 10 degree rooms or anything like that. We didn't suffer. After about four months our unit commander transferred to Paris. He wanted to be in Paris rather than Le Havre which was just a dumpy little port city. But in his defense the Navy and the Army were starting to use Cherbourg and Le Havre and our unit was going to regulate the traffic flow coming in to the ports in France. Probably the communications would be better out of Paris.

Question: What kind of communication did you have with the ships to schedule them?

Well, they had a communications section but I was in the administrative part of it, but I think it was short wave radio. Communications would come in to us that would be sent on to the ships. That's how they would keep the ports from being clogged up and of course there is so much stuff along the beaches that would be in the channel from the invasion. We wouldn't have anything to do with that.

> *"The French army was a disaster and Gen. De Gaulle was a disaster to the Allies, in my opinion. The French to this day can't protect anything. We knew the French army wasn't contributing very much."*

Antwerp was a major port, but it wasn't usable to the Allies for quite a little while.

Comment: The Germans sabotaged everything when they pulled out. They just wrecked it because logistics was our Achilles heel - getting enough stuff over there was a huge undertaking.

That's right. Everybody knows that the point was to get enough people and material on the ground over there as quickly as possible. The one great advantage we had was that the Germans were fairly well convinced that the invasion was going to be at Calais, the narrow point of the channel.

I was in Paris for eight months. Paris was an open city and did not have bomb damage. Our office building was up on the Arc de Triump. We lived within walking distance. It was an interesting place to be stationed, especially considering that I was in the Navy.

Question: What was your impression of the French people in Paris? Did you interact with them very much?

Don't take this wrong. I said at the time if they turned France over to the women it would be something, as it is with the men running it, it is nothing. The French army was a disaster and Gen. De Gaulle was a disaster to the Allies, in my opinion. The French to this day can't protect anything. We knew the French army wasn't contributing very much. De Gaulle was wanting to be part of the high command and was a complete thumb in the eye every time he got a chance. I did not like De Gaulle or what they thought their cooperation was in the war effort. Most GIs did not think they were doing their part. Montgomery had a lot more ability than any that the French provided. But he was a hard person to work with, too.

Question: Do you think you had a better picture of the war effort from where you were? Did you have maps and all that so you could kind of keep track?

Only what would be in the *Stars and Stripes* and of course I did have a chance to get it all the time where the troops on the ground did not. There would not have been official communications. They didn't care that enlisted men knew what was going on. No, the *Stars and Stripes* gave the Army's version of what was happening. We could tell pretty much where the front was and when they were getting close to taking Paris, that sort of thing. Yes, I would say we knew a little bit about the progress of the war. We had very definite opinions on Patton and turning him loose, but not knowing anything about the problems involved. I'm a big fan of Patton and not a big fan of Montgomery. He was a better military man than the French ever provided, but he was a terrifically hard man to work with, I believe. He must have driven Eisenhower up the wall. Most people loved Bradley and they loved Patton, too. He was a tough cookie. He demanded a lot of the troops.

Cheyenne: Most people have an opinion about Patton, one way or the other.

Harvey: You mean it went either way?

Cheyenne: I think most vets we've talked to are more positive than negative for Patton. Don't you think?

Larry: I'd say it's the other way.

Cheyenne: Really?

Larry: The old saying: old blood and guts George Patton—our blood and his guts. But Patton got the job done, but most people say it came at a really high price. He used up soldiers. He was usually in an attack mode and that's how you fight an armored war.

Cheyenne: On the other hand if they had let him go he would have shaved a year off the war.

Larry: He ran out of fuel. That's what happened. Montgomery wanted the allocation so he could do his thing which was very little. Patton was very demanding, but Eisenhower had a whole army to run and part of that was Montgomery. So Patton could not get enough fuel and other supplies.

Cheyenne: I do think that he spent men, but he also achieved victories. That way do you really lose more men than you would otherwise?

Larry: That's debatable. Eisenhower is criticized for having this broad front. And from what I'm reading it was completely political. He had to keep Montgomery, Patton, and even De Gaulle happy and that's why Patton didn't just spearhead and make a big loop and cut the German troops off.

Cheyenne: I think many of people, not so much in the army, but the public took a dim view of Patton and his hospital scene where he slapped his gloves across the face of a hospitalized soldier.

Larry: Yes, he did it twice.

Cheyenne: That is really unforgivable. Although he was really so proud of the guys that were right there in the front line that he couldn't get it out of his mind that some people were not goldbricking. I think that was the kind of personality that Patton was.

Question: Did you know the Battle of the Bulge was occurring when you were in Paris?

Yes, but it may have been a week late. By that time it may have turned around. My brother Edgar was in the Battle of the Bulge. He was in the quartermaster's part of the army. My brother Chuck was in the Navy. He went to photography school and he flew a little bit, but not in war zones so much. He ended up on Guam. He stayed in the States for two or three years after Pearl Harbor. My other brother, Birchard, was a store keeper and he went to Africa. He was Navy based in Africa for awhile before they went to Sicily and then he was on an aircraft carrier. Ed was probably the only one with bullets whizzing around, I think. It's surprising how many support people it takes for somebody right there on the front. I don't have any idea of the exact number but when you start to think about having the man on the front line supplied with bullets, the water he drinks, with food, and gasoline.

I'm more defensive of enlisted men. But enlisted men they are the lower caste that's for sure. We had officers that were good officers. We had as many as 8 or 10 officers just in my little unit and some of them could impress the enlisted men and some of them didn't care at all about the enlisted men. You kind of got paired up though. If you did good work and they enjoyed working with you without ever crossing that line between officer and enlisted man. I did more work for two of the officers than all the rest of them combined because they would come to me and I would do what they wanted. But you could talk with them and they treated me very well. I went up in rank ending up a first class yeoman in just under two years. I was in a small unit and able to do the work they wanted me to do. My commander offered to make me a chief if I would stay over there another six months after the war. I said "I'm not going to do that." You know I was ready to come home. I had a wife and kids. I said "I'm not going to do that."

I finally got enough points to come home in November of '45. But I came home with not enough points to be discharged. So I had a month's leave in November and then reported back to California on December 1st. I thought I was headed back overseas to replace somebody in the Pacific Theater because they had enough points to come home. I knew I would have points enough soon, but you don't gain as fast in the States. I spent the month of December in Oakland. Nearly froze to death—talk all you want about California! It was cold up there. I finally came back to Chicago in January. I didn't do much of anything until I got out in March. I just put in my time. I almost had some sea duty after the war was all over. Coming home from overseas we came home on a smaller troop ship. It was mostly Army guys were running the ship. I was a passenger only. I was one of fifty Navy guys coming home. I think we got in several storms. The word was you could actually hear the propellers come out of the water. I got so sick and they finally took me down to sick bay.

Question: Did you ever think the ship would capsize?

I thought it might. The word was that we hadn't made any headway that day. That was the rumor that was going around. Whether it was remotely true, I have no idea. That was not very healing either, I'll tell you. So I was on the water 14 days coming home and 5 days going over. That was the only times I was on the water. Coming home I was seasick at least half of those 14 days. I was not much of a sailor. I had good duty.

Times were all together different. We have an all volunteer Army now. The war wasn't all volunteer anything. But, there was a tremendous desire to be part of it whether you were going to be military or a civilian and part of the rationing. There were not divisions within people's minds regarding the support of the troops. The troops were doing their best and needed to have the best and that sort of thing.

Question: If you had a message or a thought you could give the school kids today about WWII based on your experiences what would it be?

I think war is a terrible way to settle an argument. It is the most wasteful, inhumane thing there ever was. Now how we get away from having that kind of a solution between countries, I don't know. But war cannot be defended in any way if you're looking at it from that aspect. Just think of the production that ends up in the bottom of the ocean. You've got to find a better way of solving problems. People's lives are not worth anything (during a war). I have no way of judging if WWII was done well. It came out well. I couldn't begin to think of a better way we could have done this or that. So my general opinion is that war is not a human way of solving problems. I hope youth of today will do better.

Interview transcribed by Jane Cuddeback.

WE COULD HAVE LOST THE WAR

Dick Colby
Washington, IA

Signal Corps
Stateside

Interview Date:
7 January 2011

Referral:
Paula Brinning

I was drafted in March of '46. You were drafted for the duration and six months. A couple of days later, they discharged us and we were allowed to enlist in the regular army for 18 months. This was what I chose to do. I was raised in Pipestone, Minnesota. Our group was taken by Greyhound bus up to Ft. Snelling. Only three of our group had been through high school. A lot of the others were going up for the umpteenth time. They were probably 4F or something.

We were taken next by train to North Camp Polk down in Louisiana. This was a new camp being opened up, replacing Camp Crowder in Missouri. We were put in the Headquarters Company. I was put in with a group that ran an electric mimeograph. We did that all day, mimeographing orders and other Signal Corps document. If we ran out of things to mimeograph, we sat around. For some reason, they didn't bring in the people from Crowder who were supposed to be doing this so we stayed there for a couple of months. Then we were sent to Ft. Dix in New Jersey.

After being in the service for about six months, someone realized that our group hadn't received any basic training nor ever fired a rifle. So we were given two weeks of basic training. When

> *"I remember the shock and let down when France fell…We were scared of Hitler."*

we came back we were considered soldiers. I had an ear infection while in the army at Ft. Dix. I was hospitalized in order to receive an injection of penicillin every four hours. My enlistment ran out when I was there in the hospital so I was given a medical discharge. That put me in a different benefits category which included four rather than two years of college. I spent those four years at Drake and got out of college with no debt.

I entered service as a private and finished as a tech 4 sergeant.

Question: Do you remember hearing about the attack on Pearl Harbor?

It was a Sunday morning and the rest of my family went to church. I was home sick in bed and heard it on the radio and told my family when they came home. I don't think any of us really knew where Pearl Harbor was for sure. It was a year before anyone knew the scope of the devastation inflicted. I remember the shock and let down when France fell. I was in junior high. We were scared of Hitler. I remember Dunkirk. In the beginning, we knew we were in for it.

Betty Colby: I was living in Chicago at the time. There was a kid walking down the street carrying newspapers yelling, "Extra! Extra!" It was the only time in my life I ever heard or saw that happening. We didn't go down and buy a paper. We turned on the radio. It was 1:30 in the afternoon. We got our best information about the war from the newsreels shown at the movie theatres. Even though as news it was delayed somewhat, the newsreels had more impact the printed word in the newspapers. We'd go to the movies just to watch the newsreels of the war.

Question: Did the people stateside have any inkling during the war that Hitler was killing 6,000,000 Jews?

No, not really, not until toward the end of the war. I remember when the American soldiers discovered the concentration camps. The thought at the time was that it was proof of what we had suspected was going on. We had heard about the concentration camps by that time. I think Louie Larsen may have told us about liberating a camp. He farmed for Bob Wiley north of town after the war.

Question: Did either of you know about the Japanese internment camps in the western United States?

It was probably known, but I don't remember knowing.

Betty: I knew about it after the war because I knew a Japanese American that had been in a camp. He had it pretty good because he was a boy at the time. His family had nothing. They had lost everything, their property and everything had been taken away from them. I remember him telling that some of the guards were really nice to him but they just didn't have anything and there they were, perfectly good Americans sitting in concentration camps.

There was a Presbyterian minister at a Grinnell church that had been in an internment camp in the southwest. He was a Nisei (or a native born American whose parents were both born in Japan). He enlisted in the army and went overseas to Europe and came back after the war. He wasn't accepted in the churches in Chicago after the war because he was Japanese. His father had a farm in central California that was just taken away from him when they went to the camp. After the war,

they had no place to go. I guess it just destroyed him.

Question: Do you have a message regarding your perspective on WWII that you would like to pass on to the youth of today?

Looking at it from the home front, the entire country was at war. The wars today don't affect us here at home. We could have lost the war and that would have been devastating. We were scared for a while. I'm glad we didn't know all that happened at Pearl Harbor. We didn't know how bad North Africa was but we knew that we were not doing very well for a while until we got some experience in fighting.

Question: Do you recall a specific event or time when you were no longer worried about the outcome of the war?

I remember Churchill saying it was "not the beginning of the end, but the end of the beginning." I think that was right after the battle of El Alamein in North Africa. I think that's when we started getting a little confidence. We had the Germans on the run. I think after that, no one thought we'd lose the war.

I had a brother that was 5 ½ years older. He enlisted in the Army Air Corps and went to North Africa and then Italy. He was in a ground crew. He would never talk about it. I remember the day he came home from the war. It was a big day for the family.

I managed the United Presbyterian Home for 27 years. I liked dealing with people more than being an administrator.

> *"...and there they were, perfectly good Americans sitting in concentration camps."*

I Don't Regret Going

Robert E. Yoder
Wellman, IA

Civilian Public Service
Stateside

Interview Date:
14 January 2011

Referral:
Personal Contact

I grew up on a farm in the Kalona area and moved to Wellman. I registered with the draft board when I turned 18. That would have been April 15th, 1944. I don't know how everything worked out that got me a 4E classification. I know I went to a minister and filled out a questionnaire and I had to go to an attorney. In August, I was called to go for a physical. Seven of us conscientious objectors left Iowa City with boys going to the military. We rode a bus to Burlington and then boarded an old train put back into service because of the war pulled by a steam locomotive. We traveled to Jefferson Barracks in St. Louis. I was the only one out of the seven conscientious objectors (COs) to pass my physical.

They kind of gave me a rough time and tried to talk me into going into the military. One guy told me he could sympathize with me as he was a Quaker. So I got along fine. I was told to report to Ft. Collins, Colorado, by October 4th, 1944. When I got to the camp, we had three days of orientation and then I went to work. My first job was harvesting sugar beets. They used a tractor

or horse to pull an implement to loosen the sugar beets. Then we'd come along and pull them out of the ground by hand. Later we would cut the tops off and pile them. Then a truck with the side boards folded down would come along and the beets shoveled into them. There was a sugar beet factory in Loveland, Colorado.

Then they had us digging drainage ditches. We'd dig them six feet deep and install six inch bell tile. One time we were digging in a wet place and the sides caved in, burying the two guys ahead of me up to their chins. I was buried up to my knees and the guys behind me were trying frantically to dig us out. Then it was decided to shore up the sides with plywood and a hydraulic jack in the middle to push them apart. I worked on that project quite a while until they announced at the mess hall one evening that they needed people to go up in the mountains to cut trees. I volunteered for that.

We went up in the mountains in January. We were west of Boulder about 21 miles. Our foreman worked for the U.S. Forest Service. We cut beetle infested trees in the Roosevelt National Forest.

The trees were not big. Most were smaller than ten inches in diameter. We cut the trees into ten feet lengths and stacked all the branches so they could be burnt. We used manual, cross cut saws. In the spring when it got too dry to burn, we had to peel away the bark on the stumps and trees up as far as the larvae had worked.

I had my first furlough in May. It lasted for 15 days and I went home to Iowa. I returned to the main camp in Ft. Collins and put to work thinning sugar beets. We used either a hoe or pulled beets by hand to maintain an eight inch spacing. I don't know how long they had us doing that. There were also workers from Jamaica and German war prisoners thinning beets in neighboring fields. We'd see them ride out in trucks every day just like we did.

Question: Robert, who owned the fields you were working in and were they getting free labor from you?

The fields were owned by private farmers. The government charged them a fee for the work we did. I don't know how much, but it was something. We were all volunteers. We never got paid anything by the government. Eventually the Mennonite Central Committee would give us five dollars a month. The first guys didn't even get that. At first, you had to get a pass to go into town to buy something.

After that, I worked on a crew that constructed concrete irrigation ditches along the edges of fields. We had forms and poured a lot of cement. The farmers would use hoses to siphon water from the shallow irrigation ditches to water their fields. There was a large canal close to our camp that carried water from the mountain streams. It'd be full in the summer when water was needed for irrigation. It probably ran 20 miles before reaching the first farm field. I always wondered how much water soaked into the ground before it got to its destination.

Next, I went back up into the mountains and cut trees where a forest fire had gone through. We cut trees six to eight inches in diameter into post's length, peel the bark back, and soak them in a solution to prevent rot. The posts were taken to Buckingham where conscientious objectors would use them as fence post to build fences for farmers.

Question: How many people were at your main camp?

It would vary. A lot of people would come and go. Guys would be sent to work at mental health hospitals and to test dairy herds for the butter content in the milk. Others were sent to Missoula, Montana, to become smoke jumpers. Our camp was an old CCC camp (Civilian Conservation Corps). I'd say there were probably 250 there. There's nothing left of the camp today.

I also worked in Nebraska with the Soil Conservation Service. I did some surveying but mainly worked in a government shop building tool chests like a county agent might use. The surveying involved laying contour lines. I also helped build contours.

Question: Did you have any interaction with the German POWs?

No, we'd met them on the road while they were riding in trucks. There were some Russian Mennonites from Kansas that could speak some German. They'd sometimes yell, "Nice work" in German as we passed their trucks. The Germans would wave back. They'd have a guard with them. I don't know if the POWs had any idea who we were. I had no idea where their camp was located. Chester Miller, the wood cutter from Wellman, was in the military. He was a POW prison guard here in the States. He grew up Mennonite but changed churches later.

Most of work I did was farm related and I enjoyed working in the timber. My last three months at Ft. Collins was spent in the laundry. We washed all the clothes for all the men, doing different dorms on different days. What I really hated was washing the handkerchiefs.

Question: Were there COs besides Mennonite and Quakers?

You wouldn't believe the number of different denominations represented. There were some that didn't even belong to churches that got into CO camps. I would guess there were over 100 Mennonites COs from the Wellman/Kalona area. The Amish boys got drafted just like we did. We had them in our camp.

Question: Did you know of any Mennonites other than Chester Miller that went into the military?

I attended the West Union church. There was another boy in that church that went to the military. He was a fighter pilot. His plane was shot down and he is buried in Belgium. His name was Carroll Swartzendruber. Howard Yoder married his sister, Eleanor. Carroll's name is on his mother's tombstone. It says he is buried in Belgium. There was quite a few more. Harold Stutzman was another one. I had two younger brothers in the CPS that worked in hospitals.

Question: Did you resent that you were required to do some form of government service?

No, not really. Like people say, I wouldn't take a thousand dollars for the experience but I'd hate to go through it again. I don't regret going. I had a lot of experiences.

Back then we (Mennonites) weren't very popular. Things have changed a lot since then. I think the Vietnam War and the peace movement changed things. I also think the kindness and respect the CO's offered to the mental health patients in the hospitals changed the way people thought about us. There were COs that worked in mental health hospital in Mt. Pleasant and also at Ames. Glen Gingerich, the electrician, served in a hospital. During the war, there was a lack of qualified people to do this kind of work and the COs filled the need. There was also a group of COs that built outhouses for the poor in Florida for sanitary health purposes. I know it's hard to imagine people so poor that they couldn't afford an outhouse but it was a different time. Clayton White and Louis Gugel both went in earlier and served in the CPS a lot longer than I did.

Question: Do you remember hearing about Pearl Harbor?

Yes. My folks didn't have a radio. A lot of Mennonites didn't in those days. My aunt called that evening and told my mother that Pearl Harbor had been bombed. I remember that very well. I thought the war would be over before it got to me. I can remember the day Franklin Roosevelt died.

Question: Howard, if you had a message for the youth today regarding WWII what would it be?

I would tell them to do what I did. I don't know what would happen if they had a draft today.

I farmed until 1975 and then worked 20 years at Wellman Lumber.

PEELED THE SHINGLES RIGHT OFF THAT HOUSE

Melvin Jaspering
Washington, IA

5th Armored Division
Europe

Interview Date:
22 January 2011

Referral:
Abe Miller & Stan Meader

I was originally from Warrenton, Missouri. I volunteered for a year of training in 1941. I had been working at Ft. Leonard Wood in Missouri, doing construction work and when I was inducted, they sent me right back there for basic training. On weekends there, I continued to work for my old boss. I ran a steam boiler to heat asphalt for the streets. I had just been issued my uniform and had returned from a week furlough when the war was declared. You can imagine how I felt. I knew I was sunk for the rest of it.

I was sent to a new installation being set up in California called Camp Cooke. A new armored division was being created there. I had been given engineering training at Leonard Wood so they sent four of us to California as cadre. We had to go through basic training again and spent thirteen months training in the desert. I did about everything while at Camp Cooke. I drove the Colonel around. That didn't work at all for me. There was no conversation with him whatsoever. I got tired of that. Then I hauled rations in a 2 ½ ton truck. I didn't like that so I hauled the mail for a while. I didn't like that so they made me a dozer operator.

There was an older fellow with us that ran a dozer. He would not have had to go to war because of his age but he went all the way through with us. He had come out of the logging camps in Olympia, Washington. He trained a bunch of us green horns on the old D-4s. We operated the little D-4s in our engineer companies throughout the war. C Company had the big D-7 diesel and they were more or less one of the fighting units of the engineers. The captain of C Company knew this older fellow before the war and asked him to be in his company. I tracked this guy down in the late '70s and went out west to visit him. He was getting up there in age and said I was the only guy from our outfit that had ever come to see him. He told me that he lost four dozers during the war from artillery. One of his tasks was to blade the approaches for the bridges. He told how the bullets would start whizzing in and ricochet off the blade.

He said he would whistle, "Shall we gather at the river...."

We were scheduled to go to Africa. About the time we were to leave, they ran Rommel out of North Africa. So they sent us instead to Camp Forrest in Tennessee for maneuvers to get us ready to go to Europe.

It seemed like it took us a month of sailing to reach England. We arrived in February of '44. The sea route took us clear up to Iceland. The convoy we were in was the largest of the war. We didn't experience any submarine trouble but the convoy ahead of us had several troop transports sunk. We did some more training in England. It seemed like all we did was train.

Our whole engineering outfit did KP duty for the infantry men scheduled to go in on D-Day. Three times they were loaded up and practiced dry runs in the English Channel for the invasion. For two or three weeks they waited, anxious and disgusted, wondering when they were actually going to go. It was kind of sad when you think about what a messed up deal it turned out to be.

My rank was a T5, same as a sergeant. That's as high as you could go as a truck or D-4 driver. We landed at Utah Beach on July 24th in the middle of the night. We landed as soon as they had enough territory to bring the tanks in. Our outfit was part of Patton's big sweep. It was hedgerow country but I wasn't involved in that. Our truck pulled a trailer that carried my dozer. Then our truck broke down. We waited for ten days for our ordinance people to show up and the war was going on all around us. There were planes flying over all day, dogfights going on and artillery firing, but that was mostly at night. We didn't know who was winning the war. We had our truck camouflaged and a foxhole dug underneath it. We only had two days of rations with us so we had to get food from the French.

Finally I took off with my rifle to where I could hear truck traffic and hitched a ride on a Red Ball Express truck to their company commander. He agreed to tow our truck in and provide a new motor if me and the kid with me would do the work of replacing our old one. After we had

the new engine in and everything worked fine, we still didn't know where the 5th Armored Division was located. We were told to follow the little signs placed along the road intersections with our division's number. On the way a 5th Division soldier flagged us down wanting a ride. He said he had been left behind because he was off fooling around when he shouldn't have been. Our company commander about fell over when we finally pulled in a day later. He didn't know what had happened to us. Another truck had been reported broken down the same time ours was and it was picked up. That had caused the confusion. We'd been gone for close to two weeks. He told us he was going to list us missing in action that very morning.

A large number of Germans in Normandy were trapped by closing the (Argentan-Falaise) gap so they couldn't escape. I think it was the 9th German Army. We captured practically the whole works. Ours wasn't the only division involved but they helped. This happened when our truck was broken down.

"He told how the bullets would start whizzing in and ricochet off the blade. He said he would whistle, 'Shall we gather at the river....'"

I was assigned to the 22nd Armored Engineer Battalion. I was in the Headquarters Company and I think that was one thing that saved me a bunch of times. We acted as a reserve to replace dozers knocked out in the line companies. Anytime we'd go up there would be two squads of combat engineers clearing mines. When they weren't doing that, they fought as infantry. We wore a flak vest. I was issued a burp (or grease) gun. It was good if you fired it single shot but after about the fourth shot on automatic, it'd climb four feet in the air. I got rid of it real quick and carried a Garand.

I lost one dozer from artillery fire. That's when we went in with the combat engineer teams. The artillery opened up pretty close. I jumped off my dozer and got on the other side of a truck. I did a foolish thing. I had dug a big foxhole so others could use it with me if they needed to. I think the German artillery observer was set up close to us and he thought the big hole I dug was for an artillery piece and that's why we were getting shelled. I was lucky. I didn't get a scratch.

Each engineering company had two trucks carrying sections of pontoon bridges. There was a hoist on the back of the trucks to unload the bridges. My job was to help do that and also to use my dozer to smooth up the approach on the shoreline. I did very little of that, however. Usually we used a bigger dozer because we tried to put those bridges up in a hurry before the Germans knew we were there. Sometimes it was done at night.

One night two of us were set up on a canal crossing we'd put in, guarding it with a .30 caliber machine gun. We heard a bunch of people, maybe 10 or 12 walking towards us and they were jabbering but we couldn't tell who they were. They turned out to be a group of liquored up Free French with a German prisoner dressed in civilian clothes. I made enough conversation with them to understand they were taking the prisoner out of town. I asked them how come their prisoner was a civilian? They said this prisoner had been a high ranking German officer in charge of their town and they were taking him out to the country side to get rid of him. I don't know what we would have done with just the two of us sitting there if they had been Germans. Pretty soon they came back laughing and carrying on. They had shot him.

Here's another thing. When we went in at Normandy, what was left of the Free French armored division that had fought in North Africa followed us clear to Paris. I don't think they did any fighting because there wasn't that many of them left. When we reached Paris, our armored division had to stay on the outskirts of Paris and the French demanded to be the ones seen as liberating the city. That was the last we saw of them. Charles de Gaulle thought he'd won the war before we ever got out of there. He took all the credit. That's what I hated about it.

The Germans pulled a lot of their artillery pieces around with a team of horses. Our planes would do a real number of them. By the time we'd come across where a German column had been hit, the Frenchmen had already cut off the hindquarters of the dead horses for food. When we first landed in Normandy, everybody was pretty nervous. One night our sentries shot a couple of cows by mistake that wandered in. They saw something coming

> "He told how the bullets would start whizzing in and ricochet off the blade. He said he would whistle, 'Shall we gather at the river....'"

in the darkness and the sentries hollered at them and they wouldn't stop, so they let them have it. Anybody that tells you they weren't nervous when the artillery was coming in is full of baloney.

We hardly lost any guys out of our company. The companies doing the recon work lost a lot of guys. Our division commander, Major General (Lunsford E.) Oliver, divided up the different elements of the division in to combat teams. Each team had everything it needed, its own tank destroyers, artillery, engineers, and infantrymen. General Oliver pinned a bronze star on me. They didn't really tell you what it was for other than for meritorious service.

Most of the towns we'd advance through had been bombed out. I'd use my dozer to clear the rubble off the streets so our column could keep going. I remember one night pushing a bunch of German trucks that our bombers had caught in this town. A couple of trucks were carrying artillery shells. I was worried about that a little bit. My dozer's exhaust pipe was sticking up in the air quite a ways and I was worried that any German plane flying would be able to see the exhaust and bomb us. But none ever did.

Our column got strafed twice by German ME 109s. There were only one or two planes involved each time. We could see and hear the buzz bombs. A few hit close to us. I've got photos of captured buzz bombs. Then there were the V-2 rockets hitting England. If they could shoot them that far, it wouldn't have been long before they were dropping them on us. I watched anti-aircraft guns shooting at the new German (ME 262s) jets. They always shot way behind them because they were flying so fast. I watched dogfights between those jets and P-28s and P-51s. The anti-aircraft on the ground would open up trying to help our fighters but they stopped that in a hurry because the only planes they were hitting were our own. If the United States had waited another year to enter the war, I doubt we would have won it. The Germans were that far ahead of us technologically.

I had my own experience with a truck mounted .50 caliber machine gun I was manning. The boy that was supposed to be on it wasn't there. I'd never shot a fifty before. It was in January. We could hear the German planes coming and all the shooting. They were coming in low to get our supply lines. I only saw one plane and he came over at tree top level and I started shooting at him. He was down low enough to fly below the roof of this house. I peeled the shingles right off that house as he went by and then he was gone. The house was the officer's quarters and I really caught it for that. That was the only real shooting I did during the war. I think I only shot three rounds through my rifle and that at openings in pillboxes. I was mainly just fooling around, trying to see if I could hit the opening as they were quite a distance away. I earned a sharpshooters badge during basic and trained on the old Springfield rifle.

I worked on the little crossing at Wallendorf. The river wasn't very deep there. You really didn't need a bridge.

Comment: That was where the first Allied troops entered Germany in September. That would make you one of the first Americans on German soil.

The recon squad went in the night before. The next night sergeant picked out some guys and told me to take my bridge truck in along with two or three recon jeeps out of the engineers. They sent a couple of combat teams in and I went with them. Then the Germans started shooting artillery at us and we got out of there. I ran my dozer up on a road behind this town. The German artillery was going bump, bump, bump, but never caught up with us, but we lost a lot of other guys.

Later it was said that here is where the Army made another big mistake. They should have reinforced us and let us go on advancing. It would have ended the war two months earlier. We went in there for only one purpose and that was to pull the German artillery off of Aachen. We lost guys out of our company in that deal. We had one kid who was driving a jeep which got hit. He got out on foot and was saying that he lost all his personal stuff he carried in the jeep. He was a newlywed. The jeep wasn't very far from us. I told him not to try to go back and collect his belongings as it was too dangerous but he slipped out on us and the Germans shot him. He should have stayed with us.

In October we were on an outpost with

Headquarters Company in the Hürtgen Forest. There were six or seven of us in this outpost. We had a .50 caliber machine gun. I don't know how close the Germans were to us but they were probably some distance away. The Germans had a bunch of poles trimmed up for high lines. We had a little chainsaw at that time and cut the poles up in pieces and used them for fortifications on our outpost. We'd take turns manning the fifty during the night, but half the time the guy would fall asleep. We didn't see any action there so it wasn't all bad.

We had two guys from our division up in a little Piper Cub. They were artillery forward observers. They shot down a German spotter plane with their pistols. I was up there cleaning the snow off the runway with my dozer. This was around Christmas. When I finished, the pilot offered to take me up in his plane. I was surprised by how well you could see everything. You could pick out every foxhole in the ground.

The 5th Armored made it to the Elbe River. That was supposed to be my next job, to cut the bank down for the pontoon bridge. Then General Oliver received orders to stay right where he was at, and not cross the Elbe. He was really disappointed and I was really happy. Back in the states he said, "I'm going to take you guys in to Berlin." We just laughed. But we got to within 45 miles of Berlin, which was the closest any outfit got, although there are others making the same claim.

Me and another corporal sat down around a camp fire and drank cognac with a squad of Russian soldiers on the Elbe. That cognac was powerful stuff. There was only one glass. We'd drink out of it and pass it on to the next guy. We never crossed the river so the Russians had to be on our side.

Question: What did you think of Patton?
He was a nutty but a fighting man. He loved to fight. He thought he was reincarnated, did you know that? His jeep driver in France told of Patton recognizing places he had been in battle in a previous life.

We were right beside Camp Dora when they turned all those prisoners loose. We were sitting in a field when saw them coming. The prison guards were walking right along with them but they had surrendered and didn't have any guns. We talked to them. Some of the prisoners had been there for years and others only days. There were Poles, French, Russians and Americans among the prisoners, all captured from different armies. We motioned for them to keep going on back. We heard later on that they were locked in a barn and it was set afire. Anytime somebody poked their head out and tried to escape, they were shot by the Germans. There were a lot of Germans left behind us and they must have recaptured the prisoners we had liberated. We were a recon division. We were called the "Ghost Division" because no one knew where we were half the time. We were 100 miles ahead of where the Battle of the Bulge broke through. *(Note: Camp Dora-Mittelbau was originally a sub camp of Buchenwald where the V-2 rockets were assembled in underground tunnels. In 1944 it was politically separated from Buchenwald and had over 30 sub camps of its own. An estimated 60,000 prisoners served as slave labor.)*

A lot of the German soldiers surrendered when they realized the war was lost. That wasn't true for the SS troops. Around Berlin there were the kids from the Hitler Youth. They'd just as soon shoot you as look at you. Growing up, that's all they knew.

Question: Mel, do you have a message to the youth of today regarding WWII?

I don't think it would hurt anybody to have some military training. I don't know if they should make it compulsory. I think it would be good for some of the younger people to go through basic training.

I had a brother in the 6th Armored Division that was in Korea. He got there late in the war and didn't see combat. I talked to Leonard Zickefoose a time or two while coon hunting. He didn't say too much but he did say he was in the 5th Armored and had a tank shot out from under him. He had to crawl out through the bottom escape hatch. That was about the extent of our conversation. I think he was in the 85th Armored Recon Battalion but I am not certain about that.

George Miller told me he was up there in the Hürtgen Forest and on the edge of the Battle of the Bulge. He never did say a whole lot about it. George Miller did all my dozer repair work.

Ray Musgrove and I got to talking one day at McDonalds. I never had him pictured as a vet nor any idea he had been in the war. I remarked about how cold it was during the Bulge and he said he'd been up there too, and how his overshoes were all shot. He'd been in the infantry and had gotten close to Berlin but I don't know what outfit. *(Note: Mr. Musgrove was in the 83rd Infantry Division.)*

Pete Rich and I started the construction business together. He was in the Pacific.

Major General Lunceford E. Oliver, Commanding General of the 5th Armored Division, Presents Tec 5 Melvin L. Jaspering with the Bronze Star at Bad-Tennstadt, Germany. Photo courtesy of Mel Jaspering.

DOWN HE CAME

Charles Plecker
Ainsworth, IA

113th Cavalry Group
Europe

Interview Date:
28 January 2011

Referral:
Stan McCreedy, Jim Thompson, Joe Wright

I was in the Red Horse Troop. They were all local guys. Casey was the First Sergeant. When I joined, we were sent to Camp Ripley in Minnesota and bivouacked out in a wheat field. The most exciting thing that happened there was when I was on horseback leading a horse packing a machine gun. We hit a nest of bees and strung the pack and machine gun over the countryside. I didn't get stung but the two horses got pretty excited. The mosquitoes up there were about three quarters of an inch long. Our horses had bumps all over their backs from the bites.

We were at Camp Bowie in Texas when the war started. We'd put in a year and were looking forward to coming home. Pearl Harbor ended that. We were in for the duration. It was just one of those things. I started out as a cook but quit when they didn't promote me to head cook. I went to a cook and baking school in San Antonio, Texas, for six months of training. Dale Hyde was the mess sergeant. The head cook was a boozer. When he quit, I felt like I should have gotten the job but the officers brought somebody in from maintenance and gave him the position. I was pretty unhappy and decided to let them run it without me. That's

why my rank stayed as a T-5. I probably shouldn't be telling these stories, but *(chuckling)* most of them are dead. Wilbur Wright came in as a cook after I quit. I didn't spend any time in the kitchen overseas until right before we came home. A lieutenant came by and said they were short of kitchen help and asked if I would help out.

Charles gets out a photograph of the Red Horse Troop taken at Camp Bowie. Pointing to individuals, he starts identifying some of them by name: Max Donaldson, Skeeter Wolf, John Combs, Raymond Glasgow, Ted Williams, Bill Longer, Earl James, Bob Stirling, Francis Reed, Don Beeler, Dave Brinning….

We boarded a ship out of Boston, the *Elizabeth B. Stanton,* for our trip to England. We were part of a huge convoy. The convoy assembled off Newfoundland. Ships everywhere. There were escort carriers loaded down with P-47s and P-51s set on the decks head to tail, with their wings removed. It took 17 days to cross the Atlantic. We slept in bunks stacked six high. We sailed to Greenland and then on to Bristol, England. We got on trains and rode clear down across England to the Lady Smite Estate.

There were bullet holes in those Quonset huts we were staying in. That didn't bother our sleeping at all. The Germans were still bombing England when we arrived but nothing compared to what they'd done earlier. They'd get us out and move us to slit trenches dug at an angle whenever there was an air raid. The German planes would stay pretty high. Those British had an awfully good anti-aircraft outfit. They'd fill that sky full of flak.

The one thing I really remember about boarding ship was that I was on KP duty. The ship had started moving and I did not know it. I put something in a pot and it started to move and that was as close as I ever got to being seasick. I had to go topside to get some air. I didn't get seasick on the LSTs going over to France but a lot of them did. Wilbur Wright was one of them. He got terribly sick. You know Wilbur could swear. When he got off that ship, he looked back at it and said, "If I've got to ride that damn thing back home, I'm not going."

Right before the invasion, they loaded the LSTs and pulled them into inlets all around southern England. There we sat until the night of June 5th. After making the channel crossing, we unloaded our equipment on to a Rhino barge. The Rhinos were constructed of six feet square, hollow metal tanks. If you got bullet holes in one of the tanks, the others would carry it. I drove one of the Weasels, which was made for the snow in Alaska. I was the last guy off the barge. The tide was coming in and I dipped water going down off the ramp, stalling the engine. A big TD-9 caterpillar backed up into the water and towed me on to the beach. All the vehicles had hooks and cables with loops of each end for towing. Our outfit has six of these Weasels. They were tracked vehicles with a Studebaker-Champion engine in it and we'd use a pair of them to pull out halftracks stuck in the mud in Belgium. It's a good thing they had blacktop roads in Europe or we would have been stuck on the beach. You wouldn't believe how muddy it was.

Our Rhino barge was close enough to the landing beach (Omaha) to see what was going on. It didn't look too bad. There were several knocked

"We spent our first night on French soil on the bluffs above Omaha Beach. A P-51 pilot came walking through, lugging his parachute. He said he was the third P-51 shot down by friendly fire over the beach. Everyone was pretty trigger happy."

out tanks sitting here and there that had hit a mine. I never considered that the invasion might fail. Some of others may have. The Rangers had gone up those steep cliffs on rope ladders and loads of guys have come in on those gliders. The rangers went in at 6:00 AM. That's when the main invasion started. We didn't go until 10:00 AM. I'm certain of that as I remember looking at my watch. There wasn't much shooting in our sector by that time. I drove my Weasel right up through a gap in the bluffs by following the track already beat down by DUKWs. Tony Fiala and Glen Fehlhammer were riding with me, sitting up on each corner of the pack, about as far as they could hang out and they were cussing me the whole way, yelling that I was going to get them blowed up. I can still hear those two guys giving me the devil to this day. At the time, I never gave it much thought of being scared.

We lost Bill Longer up above the beach. Him and Glen Murphy were running for the same fox hole and Bill didn't make it. They machine gunned him. Everett Schneider was killed by artillery. Some others didn't come home.

Once on top of the bluff we noticed a medium tank (Sherman) sitting out in this field. It had been knocked out by a landmine. Then here come this Tank Retriever roaring down the highway, going to get the crippled tank and boom, another mine blew off the front corner of him. That was waste of a valuable piece of equipment. Those Tank Retrievers were big, armored semi trucks. Someone should have swept that field for mines first.

We spent our first night on French soil on the bluffs above Omaha Beach. A P-51 pilot came walking through, lugging his parachute. He said he was the third P-51 shot down by friendly fire over the beach. Everyone was pretty trigger happy.

We had a warning of a gas attack while on the bluffs. There's a special sounding loud klaxon warning for gas attacks. We all put on our masks and this fellow from Minnesota named Miller comes running down the hill screaming that he can't find his mask. He's frantic, scurrying around looking for a mask and we're all laughing at him. He shouts, "You son of a bitches are really going to miss me." We never had a gas attack but I held on to my mask until the end of the war, just in case.

We were assigned to First Army Headquarters to provide security for General Hodges. He was with us by the first night and we had guys who drove General Hodges right up to the frontlines in an armored car.

Our headquarters was in Spa, Belgium, when the Bulge hit. We were forced to move back because of the German push. Hodges moved his headquarters back into that same schoolhouse. We were retreating, but the rest of the First Army stayed where they were. We had good winter gear. But the guys at the front without overshoes really suffered with wet, frozen feet.

The Germans sent a lot of buzz bombs (V-1s) over later trying to knock out First Army Headquarters. I've still got a piece of shrapnel in my head from one of them. One day I think we must have been marking targets for the Germans as the buzz bombs just kept coming. We were in an armored car with this long radio antenna and I think they were using it as a marker (triangulating). As soon as we were ordered to go to radio silence, the attack quit. One buzz bomb hit near the schoolhouse General Hodges was using for his headquarters and blew all the windows out. There was a lot of Purple Hearts for glass cuts. Marion Crawford was one of those inside the school house that received a Purple Heart. This was in Belgium and the snow was deep and it was colder than blue blazes. I was wounded by the same buzz bomb that almost got Hodges. I was standing next to a half track and remember hearing the shrapnel pinging off the armor. This all happened on Christmas Eve.

I was standing guard duty Christmas morning when a German plane came in from the south at tree top level. I think they called it a Foche-Wulf 190. He had just finished a strafing run on some six by sixes on the road. That was what he was after. The plane went right over the top of the house we were staying in. Francis Reed opened up on him with one of the guns mounted on a halftrack. I don't suppose we could have hit a barn if it had been out there. Anyway, he veered away to the east,

following a road out of town, climbing rapidly as he went. When the plane was so high it was just a twinkle in the sky, one of our 40mm anti-aircraft guns and a quad fifty opened up on him. A 40mm shell took him dead center, blowing up the plane and down he came. The wreckage plowed a hole about six feet deep in a nearby orchard. Some British soldiers were closest and they were going to leave the German pilot in the plane wreckage, just let him burn. These Brits had a very bad taste for the Germans. Me and my platoon sergeant insisted that they get the body out. He and I pulled off the tail of the plane and there the pilot sat, right behind the engine. The pilot looked young, like he was about seventeen. His head and legs were gone. The British had some big, heavy duty leather gloves and they fished him out. Then they dug a hole by a post and dragged the body over and slung it in like you would a collie dog. Threw a little dirt on him. Then they wrote it all down a little book they carried for that purpose, noting the type of aircraft and where the body was buried, things like that. I imagine that pilot is still probably buried out there in that orchard. The British soldiers were a little rougher than the average American GI.

> *"Then they dug a hole by a post and dragged the body over and slung it in like you would a collie dog...I imagine that pilot is still probably buried out there in that orchard."*

We spent Christmas Day eating turkey with a family in Tsongas, Belgium. An older couple owned the house. Their married daughter, son-in-law, and two grandchildren lived with them. One of those little boys followed me around. He went everywhere I went. There were a lot of people in that little house. The Army provided the turkey and the lady cooked it. We shared it with them. It was sure nice to spend part of a day inside a warm house. About ten years ago I received a letter from that boy. He enclosed a photo of his mother with it. The letter was written in French and I cannot read French. I was always going to take it over the high school to get it translated but I never did.

After they took my Weasel away from me, I drove a jeep. Our job was to scout ahead and find a suitable, safe location to move the command headquarters forward. They'd move up the next day. Then we'd set up all around the headquarters with armored cars to provide security for them.

We went through the Siegfried Line at Aachen. I carried a Thompson during the war. We called them "meat cutters". I had qualified as an expert with the Thompson. I never had to fire it at any Germans.

We freed Buchenwald. When we pulled up, the prisoners were standing outside in old cloth uniforms. They weren't much. There weren't more than fifty left alive in the entire camp. Some of them were German civilians, political prisoners. We were cautioned before we overran the camp not to give the prisoners any K rations or hard chocolate to eat because it would probably kill them. I've got photos of hay racks full of dead bodies, waiting to be put in the furnaces. They had them stacked like cord wood. And not just men, there were women and children, too. *(Note: The sign over the entrance gate to Buchenwald reads, in German, "Each Gets What He Deserves".)*

The German guards had all fled. We found places built under ground where the Germans would run the people into and gas them. Then they would burn the bodies in the furnaces. There was a monument sitting out by the front gate listing the number of prisoners that had been at Buchenwald. It numbered in the thousands. I guess they were proud of it. You know, I don't see how the German soldiers running that camp could tolerate that crap, do you?

Question: Charles, what would be your response to those who claim the Holocaust never happened, it was all a hoax?

There's a woman in Washington that told me it never happened. In fact, I'll even tell you her name. I told her that she was nuttier than a fruitcake and I had the photos to prove it.

The next day we marched the entire town out to the cemetery and made them bury the bodies on the hay racks. Any child old enough to walk was forced to help.

Dave Brinning won over a thousand dollars playing poker on the trip home. He took his winnings to the ship's captain for safe keeping and never gambled again. The trip home only took four days. I farmed until age 65 when my son Marty took over. Then I drove a D-6 dozer for George Miller for 15 years. I haven't been back to Europe and I want no part of it. I've got photos of where

Longer and the others are buried in the cemeteries and that's enough for me.

TRIBUTE

I grew up with a WWII veteran for a dad. His respect for the flag and our country was apparent to me, especially at parades, ball games, etc. This influenced myself and my siblings with that same respect.

I saw the bond he and they had for each other at the annual Red Horse reunion. It had come from a true dependence on each other, working together for an unselfish greater good. They left the bad horrors of war behind them and moved on with a quiet respect for life.

He did not talk of the war very often, but when he did, it came out with an intensity that made you understand the importance.

I once heard my dad and my mom talking late in his life, asking "did we have a good life?" After he passed away, my mom and I went to see the movie " Saving Private Ryan". We heard this same question asked by Private Ryan to his wife.

My great respect for WWII veterans or anyone who has served or is currently serving our country was founded by seeing it from my father's actions, forged from being in WWII.

With great respect and appreciation,

Joe Wright
(Son of Wilbur Wright)
Keota, IA

DISTINGUISHED FLYING CROSS

Lawrence Whisler
Washington, IA

15th Air Force
Italy

Interview Date:
11 February 2011

Referral:
Jim Cuddeback & Dave Birney

I started flying when I was going to school out in Boulder, CO, and that was in 1940. I went out there because I had hay fever really bad and they thought it would be better for me in Colorado. I was born in this house. The government came out with what they called a CPT program, Civilian Pilot Training. And I signed up for it and was accepted, and so that was the summer of 1940 and we flew piper cubs out there and I got my private license.

Well then, the war started, and I signed up for the draft, but I didn't volunteer. I was still going to school out in Boulder when I was drafted in June of 1941. I was inducted in Denver and sent to an armored force training center and took my basic training with the armored force. I didn't like that very well. We were driving tanks, halftracks and jeeps and trucks. After I'd completed my basic training, I was kept over as a company clerk because they found out that I knew how to type.

So anyhow, while I was working in the office, I found out that if you could pass the physical, you could transfer to the Air Corps. So I passed the physical and was accepted. I was sent to the cadet training center in San Antonio, TX, in January of 1942. I graduated from cadets in January of '44. The first six weeks or so there wasn't any flying then, you were taking ground school and all that. I took my primary training at Coleman, TX, flying PT-19s, and I took my basic training at Sherman, TX, flying BT-13s. My advanced training involved flying AT-6s at Eagle Pass, TX.

I was supposed to get some P-40 time in advanced training, but I didn't get any, so after I graduated, I was sent to Dover, Delaware. There was a pool of pilots coming and going there all the time. Some of them were returning from overseas and some of them were like me, waiting for assignment. But anyhow, I went to Eglin Field in Florida and got 10 hours in a P-40, and then I returned to Dover and got about 100 hours in a P-47. Then I went to Hampton Rhodes, VA, and went overseas from there. I was aboard an LST for 28 days and boy those things were rough when you're out on the high sea. There was just seven of us pilots and the rest of them were all Navy boys, and some of them were just being taken overseas for other assignments.

Well anyhow, our orders either got lost or got

mixed up. The ship that we were on was hauling a cargo of diesel fuel oil to Tunisia, North Africa. We sat there on that ship while they unloaded that diesel fuel and they didn't know what they were going do with us air force pilots so they just unloaded us on what would be like on the bank of the canal. And here seven or eight of us were sitting out there and a Navy truck came along and we flagged him down. We told the driver our hard luck story and jumped in that truck He drove us to his base and they put us up there, assigning us cots to sleep on and fed us and all that. The Air Force finally found out that we weren't where we were supposed to be so they sent a ship down there to get us.

We were supposed to have landed in Naples. We finally arrived at our base near there in the afternoon. Sleeping quarters were four man tents. The tent I was assigned to appeared fully occupied by amount of shoes, clothing and everything else. I said "There isn't any room here for me." The guy showing me around replied, "There is today," meaning that at least one of those guys had gotten shot down.

I was assigned to the 325th crew of the 318th Squadron of the 15th Air Force. They had originally been flying P-40s and then they changed to the P-47s. By the time I got there they were flying P-51s. Now there weren't any P-51s used in training anywhere. They were sending them in to combat as quickly as they got them manufactured.

After we got settled there that afternoon, I was told to get my helmet and my flying togs on and one of the veteran pilots would check me out in the P-51, so that's what I did. One of the older pilots showed me what all the gauges and controls were for. He told me to take off and make a few landings to go to altitude with it if I wished. I flew about an hour and the next morning at 6 o'clock I was on my way over to Germany flying my first mission.

That's how much time I had in a P-51. But it was a lot like an AT-6 and it didn't fly any different than any other airplane. So that was my first mission, and like everybody would be, I was as nervous as the devil. I remember that evening

when we got back the guy whose wing I was flying came over to my tent. We visited for a while and he told me that I needed to settle down my nervous flying. He said as a wing man, I was flying either too far ahead or too far behind. He says the thing to do is to set that throttle at the cruising speed. Then he says your distance, if you're getting too close, you need to pull out a little bit, if you're falling behind, you need to pull in a little bit closer. Anyhow, that guy's name was Ben Ambert. Eventually, he got shot down on a mission I was flying with him. We were flying down pretty close to the ground and his plane got shot and was losing oil. He bailed out and he was taken prisoner. I found out from one of the other guys when the war was over that he was released.

In ten days I flew ten missions. I flew every day for 10 days, and I remember on the 11th day, when I woke up it was daylight and everybody else was gone. I thought, well, why didn't they call me? I went to the office to the CQ and he said to get your bags packed up, you're going to a rest camp for a week or so. I flew another ten missions in ten days when I returned. So I had 20 missions under my belt and a lot of the eight guys that I started in with had either gotten lost or shot down.

> "I had 20 missions under my belt and a lot of the eight guys that I started in with had either gotten lost or shot down."

About that time they needed an assistant operations officer. The operations officer was the guy who assigned guys to fly whatever day on whatever mission. He had a lot of other duties too as far as that goes, but mainly he assigned the boys that were flying that day. The officer who held that position had flown probably between 50 and 60 missions. Anyhow he had a girlfriend in Rome that he was living with. The truth of the matter was he needed somebody to do his work for him so he could spend his time down in Rome. So I was made operations officer and I didn't fly near as often and as regularly as I had before because I had other things to do. One of the things that I did every evening was to make a list up of the guys flying the next day and what position they would fly in, providing the weather was good. Our squadron flew 16 planes every day with usually two spares in case a plane developed mechanical or radio problems after taking off. That didn't happen very often. The pilots really appreciated having that schedule because up until then, they never knew whether they were going to fly until someone woke them up in the mornings.

We were stationed at Lake Lesina. That's about 50 miles inland on the Adriatic side of Italy. We found out that we were probably going stay at that location through the winter so we started building a shack out of discarded wooden boxes that auxiliary gas tanks were shipped in. We hauled sand from the beach with a truck and laid bricks on it for the floor. We acquired the bricks from somewhere. Anyhow, we built that shack and I lived in it nearly all the time I was overseas. We didn't have cots in there, we had beds. We acquired them too. We also built a furnace for our shack. We salvaged tubing from B-24s and B-17s and ran it from an outside barrel filled with 100 octane gasoline. We had a valve that controlled the amount of gas dripping in a plate of rocks and that's the way we heated our shack.

Gee whiz, we had an officer's mess hall and Italian fellas that cooked our meals and served them to us and all that. That's one reason why I was gung-ho on getting from the armored force to the Air Force because Jimmy Doolittle knew about taking care of his boys. I really don't have any horror stories to tell and I don't have any missions that really stand out. Most of our missions were high altitude bomber escort. As far as a mission goes, everything was figured back from where ever headquarters decided target time was going to be and from whatever time of day we were going to strike that target.

After I got to be operations officer, I had a telephone right by my bed. I'd usually get a call from headquarters sometime between 11 o'clock and 1 o'clock at night. That's usually when they'd decide the mission. Then you decided from that what time, and also they would tell me when we were supposed to rendezvous with the bombers and about where that would be. Then I would figure the time back from that as to what time the charge of quarters had to call the guys and get them up. They would also tell me what time the briefing was. We would go to group headquarters for briefing if all three squadrons 317th, 318th, and 319th were involved in the mission. We all had the same headquarters and we had the same runway,

same engineering groups. Then after briefing we usually had about one hour before takeoff time. The pilots could go back to the squadron and get something to eat and all that.

Then we would take off in pairs, two at a time. Then after everybody was off and we were circling the field, we would join up into formation and head out. You would climb at about 130 or 140 mph and rendezvous with the bombers. Most of the missions had only one squadron assigned to take the bombers in to target. The Jerrys were real good at hitting the bombers right after they came off of that target because they knew the escorting fighters couldn't stay too close to them until they got a little ways away from the target. Then we'd have another squadron then pick them up and take them home. The first squadron would fly cover until they got home. The bombers were based farther south in Italy than we were. We'd see them fly over in formation about an hour before we'd even take off. When we'd get back to friendly territory, then we could leave them.

After leaving the bombers, a lot of the guys would go off seeing what kind of trouble they could get in to, I was never real strong on that. Another thing, nearly everybody smoked and they'd want to get down below 10,000 feet so they could light up cigarettes and I was never very strong on that either. When I was picking out guys to fly with me, I usually picked guys that I knew didn't smoke or weren't gung-ho on getting down to 10,000 feet so they could smoke.

As the assistant operations officer, nearly every day I would get a list from engineering of planes that needed to be tested. There could be a jillion different things that might go wrong with a plane. Before they could put that back on the line for operations it had to be test op-ed. After the planes had left for the mission in the morning, I'd take my list and fly those planes to check them out. Some of the other guys that didn't go on the mission liked to do that, so I assigned them planes. By the end of the war we had a lot of pilots, but when I first got over there, you were flying just nearly every day.

Question: How many pilots did you have in your squadron at the beginning?
Well, when I first got over there, I don't think we had 20. We'd usually take 18, 16 and two spares up every day. That's one reason why I'd get in 10

missions in 10 days, they were short on pilots. I flew 55 missions during the war. I'd probably had about 20 in when I started working in operations.

I had flown about 40 or so when we got a new squadron commander. I think he was probably on his third tour. He was a peach of a guy. He asked me if I would stay over for awhile and continue working in operations when he took over the squadron. I told him yeah, I would and I did. But on that 55th mission, that was kind of a rough one and we lost some guys. The more I thought about it, the more I thought you know, I can go home if I want to and I'm not trying to prove anything. When I got back that day why I went in, set my helmet down on his desk and asked him if it'd be all right if I go home and he said it was, so that was the last I flew. I haven't flown since I quit flying those missions over there.

Question: I know the bomber crews had a certain number of missions that they complete. Was it the same for the fighter pilots?

I could have quit at 50. I'll be honest about it. I was gung-ho on flying. When I first started over there, I couldn't hardly wait until CQ to come call me in the morning. I was ready to go. Never once, I can truthfully say, never once did I worry about not coming back. It just never entered my head. And boy those German pilots were good, I'll tell you, those Germans, they were flying ME109s and Fulk-Wulfs. If Uncle Sam didn't think that I was good enough to be over there flying combat, he wouldn't have sent me over there. With the training given me and all that, I figured that I was good enough to fly against those Germans.

Question: What was your opinion of the P-51?

It was a joy to fly. I tell you, it had a zip to it. That ME 109 was a darn good plane, but it wasn't any better than that P-51. You could stand up to the best of them with the Mustang. If you needed the speed, boy it had it. The throttle on that thing, it was wired, which you still had some throttle left on the other side of that wire, but you had to break the wire to get it. It was the best prop driven single engine plane ever built.

Question: What was your flight time with all your auxiliary tanks?

Well, the longest flight would be about 6

"I'll be honest about it. I was gung-ho on flying."

hours. That was about our limit as far as gas was concerned. Most of our missions lasted three and a half to four hours. If the German fighters came up to attack you, they were smart enough to do it when you still had your auxiliary tanks attached. They knew that you had to kick off your wing tanks to be very maneuverable.

Question: Would the German fighter planes attack our bombers when they were getting shot at by aircraft fire?

No, it was suicide to go in there.

Question: Did you ever run into anybody during the war from back here that you knew?

Yes, when I was at the pilot school in Richmond for some reason or another I was downtown in the city and I ran into Cloyce Tinnes and his wife Naomi. He was in the Army.

Question: Did you ever see Germany's jet, the ME 262?

No, to the best of my knowledge, the first jet that I ever saw was at the Air Force base in Naples on my way home in February or March of '45. It was one of ours. I watched it land.

Question: What type of special training did you receive in case you had to bail out over enemy territory. What did you have on you and what did they tell you to do if that happened?

Well, I wore lace boots all the time. The reason was, if you did have to bail out and you pulled the rip cord, your shoes wouldn't come off when the parachute opened. I always wore lace boots but a lot of the guys didn't. Another thing about the P-51, you wanted to make certain you bailed out before the tail came off the plane because it went down pretty quickly when that happened. My buddy Ben Ambert I was telling you about broke his arm when he bailed out. After he was taken prisoner, the Germans kept re-breaking his arm. That happened several times.

Comment: Oh my! That makes my arm hurt just thinking about it!

Question: Did they have any survival kit they gave you….a compass or maps or anything?

Well, I'm not sure, I expect they did. One thing I can remember is we had our picture taken with our hair grown longer than we normally kept it.

I've got a picture someplace that shows me dressed up as a civilian. We were supposed to use that picture if we ever did get shot down and taken as a prisoner. I was just gung ho enough that they weren't gonna get me.

Well, one thing I should tell you I suppose. Do you know what the DFC is?

Comment: The Distinguished Flying Cross.

Well, I was awarded the DFC. I don't think there was any one thing in particular, but I fired my guns a few times and I came home different times with a few bullets in my plane. But I never had any real close calls, I really didn't. My engine never got shot up. Boy when that engine goes, well, you've had it. But I was lucky in that way.

Comment: That's a pretty high award, congratulations, I'm sure you earned it.

Well, evidently they thought I did because they're pretty stingy with passing those out.

I was also awarded the Air Medal, but they gave you that at 10 missions, and then every 10 missions after that you got what they called an oak leaf cluster. And so I had the air medal and four oak leafs. My rank was Captain at the end of the war.

One mission I do remember was to the oil fields at Ploesti. That was a long mission. We flew some missions over there and then landed over in Russia and then flew a mission the next day. I was the operations officer then and I don't believe I went on those. I don't remember. We flew a lot of missions over Czechoslovakia, Yugoslavia, Austria, and Northern Italy.

Question: How about the oil refineries at Vienna, Austria?

Yes, yes. The bombers hit them and we provided top coverage. There were records kept of every mission that was flown and those records of my squadron in St. Louis, and they had a fire down there and they were all destroyed. Some place I got a letter from the VA Administration telling me all my records were destroyed. When I came home, I think I had a copy of all those missions that were flown while I was over there, but I don't know where it is.

Question: Did you fly the same plane every time, or try to?

Not really, especially after I got to be operations officer. Some guys had their preference in planes and I'd always assign them to that plane if I knew what it was. But most of the time when I was in operations, I'd fly whatever was left over because really it didn't make a nickel's worth of difference.

Question: How many pilots do you think you lost out of your squadron?

Those guys had been flying a long time before I got there, including down in North Africa. I have no idea how many were lost before I arrived. But there were a lot of guys who were lost after I got over there. I went over with eight guys. At least four of them either got shot down or were missing in action. One guy named Woodson, a big Irishman with a bad temper, got shot down. He made connections with the Yugoslavian underground and made it back. The underground got him to the banks of the Mediterranean and a ship ferried him across to Italy. This was after I was made operations officer and I had to go pick him up. We had a P-51 in the squadron that they'd taken all the armor taken out and a back seat installed. So I flew that P-51 and picked up this Woodson. He was a big guy and I was probably one of the smallest in the outfit. He was so dog gone glad to get back, he just squeezed the pudding out of me. But he didn't fly anymore. He came back to the squadron and was there for a while, but then he went home. Pilots could do that if they wanted to after being shot down. Some of the guys kept on flying but some went home.

I was most fortunate, I'll say that. I don't remember any specific missions that were outstanding as far as trouble that we had, but I do remember one mission on a Sunday. This was before I was in operations and I was flying as a wing man. The target was a telephone communications office in Albania. It was a strafing mission. I remember we went into this little town and I think the telephone building was right at the end of the street. We were shooting the heck out of that building. A P-51 is armed with six .50 caliber machine guns. I can remember flying right down that main street of this little town and we were probably weren't over a hundred, a hundred fifty feet off the ground at about 200-250 mph. The thing is, and this happened to me that day, you get so concentrated on what you're shooting at that you don't realize that you're as close as you are to other stuff like trees. If you don't pull up fast enough, it can kind of be disastrous.

Question: When you would be escorting those bombers, how many German fighter planes would come up on the average?

Usually there might be six or eight of them. There'd be 16 of us above the bombers and we could keep the German fighters off them. Usually the bombers made their run on the target they'd be about maybe 15,000 feet and we'd be at 20 or 25, probably about 5,000 feet above them. We had heaters in our P-51s and I wore long underwear, even in the summer.

Well, as I said, I was gung-ho on flying while I was doing it, but when it was done I got over it. I could've stayed in the Army. I came home here, I was home on leave for a month and then I reported out in California During that time the war had ended in Europe, so I thought for sure I'd be sent to Japan. But they had more pilots than they knew what to do with and if you wanted out you could be discharged. By that time, all I could think about was getting out.

I didn't know what to do once I was out. My brother was farming here at home with my dad and there wasn't enough ground for everybody. I had 37 months schooling coming under the GI bill so I went back to school in Colorado and got a law degree. The one thing that I learned in law school was that I wasn't cut out to be a lawyer. I didn't want to spend the rest of my life looking over those books. I took the bar in Colorado and was admitted to practice out there. I interviewed several places but I never found anything that really looked good to me. In the meantime my brother moved to a rental farm so there was an opening here at home. I came home and started farming in 1949. I am still actively farming. I'm a stubborn old guy. I don't like to give up. Just like that flying. That was my life at the time, that's all I wanted to do and as I said, I never worried about coming home.

Interview transcribed by Jeanne Thomas.

SPLATTERED PRETTY GOOD

Bob McDowell
Keota, IA

80th Infantry Division
Europe

Interview Date:
28 February 2011

Referral:
Daryl Baughman

My memory is not all it should be. After my basic training at Camp Callan, they kept me on as cadre. I trained new recruits on the 40mm and 90mm anti-aircraft artillery. When things broke out and they needed everybody, I was attached unassigned to the 80th Infantry Division under Patton. I was an infantryman. I carried an M-1 Garand. It is quite a gun. I couldn't do it now, but I could put it together in seconds.

We landed at LaHarve in the early fall of '44. We went straight to the front lines. It was the offensive to take the Saar Valley. I remember my very first night. They put me in a foxhole next to a veteran. We were about ten feet from a German gun. A German self-propelled gun came in after we were already set up. It pounded all night. The ground was moving. I was too concerned with the close proximity of that gun to worry about German infantry discovering us. The self-propelled gun moved out at daylight. Then we started advancing again. I got educated in a hurry.

Being under Patton, we were always out so far ahead, that American planes would strafe us. Many times nobody in the higher command knew where we were. We probably shot American planes as much as we did Germans for a while. We threw a lot of words at them.

Question: Did you know they were American planes at the time?

Oh, yeah. We just had to get them out of there. They were just ripping us. It wasn't their fault. Patton didn't stop for anything.

Question: How did the infantry normally advance?

The scouts would be out ahead of us. That was one way. It was the best way. Sometimes Patton's people would push us out ahead of the scouts. That's why we got shot at so much by the American planes. We were the lost souls out there. A lot of times we weren't where we were supposed to be. I don't remember a German plane ever strafing us. Our planes did a good job of keeping them off us.

We were in on the clean up during the Battle of the Bulge. We had winter clothing but it was cold and oh, my Lord, the snow was deep. We didn't really suffer too much except for food sometimes. Then someone would kill a chicken or get some eggs out of a house. We made it into Bastogne (on December 28th). I saw some paratroopers land but that was later. I never talked to them. I only saw a couple come down.

I was worried about crossing the Rhine River because I had never learned how to swim. The Army qualified us by making us jump off the bow of the *Queen Mary* wearing a life jacket. It was a long way down to the water. But I was wounded right before we got to the Rhine. We were advancing across an open field. I got splattered pretty good by artillery. The medic did a wonderful job. I thought it was pretty bad for me until they took me back to the hospital tent. I decided I was lucky. They had seven operating tables set up and arms and legs were coming off. I don't even like to think of it. There were people a lot worse off than me. I was really lucky.

I remember the German houses. They were different than ours. They kept their cows in the house with them. The rural Germans were great people. I got to Paris. It was a fun place. The French people were different. We learned a lot of things we shouldn't have from them. I guess that'd be the best way to put it.

Comment: I'd always read that Patton made everyone wear neckties.

Oh, no, not when you were out in the field. We never wore any. Maybe they had to back in camp or after the war. I was a corporal at the end of the war.

Comment: I see that you were awarded a bronze star.

I helped out. That's all I want to say about it.

Question: Your division took 200,000 German prisoners by the end of the war. Were you involved in any of that?

We were front line troops. We didn't take prisoners.

I saw General Patton in Frankfurt the morning of his jeep wreck that killed him. He was going hunting. There were three or four jeep loads of officers with him.

I attended Iowa Wesleyan and farmed with my father after receiving my BA degree. After he died from a heart attack, I took over the farming operation and ventured out from there. I was involved with Farmland Industries and on the national board of Nation Wide. I sold Pioneer seed corn and was in the café business for five years.

A few of the folks from this area didn't come back.

SHAEF

Robert Martin
Washington, IA

Signal Corps
Europe

Interview Date:
26 February 2011

Referral:
Paula Brinning

When I went to enlist I was told that my name was next on the list to be drafted. I was advised to wait to be called up by the draft board. I went to enlist because I had been worried that I wouldn't be called because I was helping on the family farm. I wanted to serve my country.

I was in the Signal Corps and assigned to SHAEF (Supreme Headquarters Allied Expeditionary Force). General Eisenhower's red light was the top one on the switchboard we operated. I could have listened in on his conservations if I hadn't been so busy connecting other phone calls. Of course, we weren't allowed to do that, but it would have been possible.

We were stationed in London before the invasion of France. The Germans were sending drone, robotic planes over to London, called buzz bombs. You could hear their engine as they approached. The Germans would put just enough fuel in them to get to London and when the engine quit, down they'd come out of the sky, dropping like a rock. One day there was a buzz bomb alert. We were working teletype machines down in a basement of a hotel in London. I wanted to see this buzz bomb but was told to stay down in the basement. Well, I disobeyed orders and went up on

> *"I was in the hotel in Paris with all the big generals were that were running the war in Europe were headquartered."*

the roof of the hotel. And here comes one, heading directly toward me. It was going bop, bop, bop and almost directly over me when the engine noise stopped. It came right down and hit the building across the street, the blast knocking it to pieces. The building I was in had the façade blown off. When I leaned over and looked down, I could see there were people trapped under the front of the hotel which had collapsed onto the sidewalk. I, of course, ran down and helped dig them out. That was quite an experience.

The British tried hanging long chains from blimps to stop the buzz bombs.

I was also in London when the Germans started sending the V-2 rockets over. The people of London feared them the most as there was no warning or noise with them. We'd have to go out and help dig out houses where people were trapped. Residents of London fled the city. It looked like a ghost town.

I was in the hotel in Paris with all the big generals who were running the war in Europe were headquartered. They had a two-position switchboard there that was in very bad condition. A staff sergeant was there who did nothing but try to keep the crazy thing working. They put WAC's on it first but they couldn't handle it because it was too nerve racking. So they put me and another guy on it and we could run it. Every time a red light would come on, we'd have to answer it because it was a general. For eight hours straight we would try to keep ahead of those red lights. One busy day a full colonel came down and boy, was he steaming mad because he was waiting for an important call to come through. He wanted to know what the heck was wrong. He stood there, ready to cuss us out. He watched us for about a minute and turned around and walked out. It was exhausting, fast paced work.

Eisenhower was upstairs in this Paris hotel. I don't remember any of the other general's names. I'd see Eisenhower all the time but I was just a buck private and later promoted to a T5 corporal. I could have done better if I'd had any ambition.

We were working the teletype machine back when the Battle of the Bulge hit. A lieutenant came in and told us to all go up to the street where they lined us up. Every tenth man was issued an M-1 with a grenade launcher. I was the tenth man and I'd never been trained to use a grenade launcher. Because of the losses suffered in the Bulge, we were supposed to get on trucks and head over to Belgium as infantry replacements. Luckily for me, they got it under control before we were shipped out and I returned to my teletype machine.

After we took Frankfurt, we used a German switchboard. The Germans had good equipment. There were one hundred and forty German gals working on this one huge switchboard and they put us GI's in charge of the women. I ended up marrying one of them and brought her back to the states. All the guys in our outfit married German ladies, but ones who were members of the Nazi Party were not allowed in the United States. So those guys who married Nazis had to stay in Europe.

Frankfurt was just a big pile of bricks after all the bombing we did on the city. Everything was in shambles. One of the guys that married a Nazi Party member became a rich man by staying over there. He would trade American cigarettes for damaged building lots in Nuremburg. This guy only had a 7th grade education and he got wealthy. I came back to the states and worked my tail off and never got rich.

A Welsh girl I knew in England took me home one time to meet her parents. Her father worked on old watches, adding jewel inlays to them. I thought that looked pretty interesting. So I went to a watchmaker's school in Denver when I returned to the states. Later I went to a jewelry school in Los Angeles. I became a certified gemologist. I was hired by a jeweler in California in 1950 when he found out I was from Iowa because he had five other Iowans employed and they were his best workers. In 1960 I purchased a different Los Angeles jewelry store with the help of a $45,000 loan from my parents. It was owned by a man from Fairfield, Iowa. When I told him that I was from Washington it pretty much sealed the deal. In 1989, Donald Trump purchased the Ambassador Hotel where my store was located in and my business was forced out. Donald Trump cost me a lot of money. I moved back to Iowa in 1992.

Robert's friend, Virginia Smith, was present during the interview. She said her brother, Harold Luers, was in the infantry and fought in the Battle of the Bulge. He resides in Grapevine, Texas.

ALWAYS WANTED TO BE A PARATROOPER

William Wagamon
Wellman, IA

82nd Airborne Division
Stateside

Interview Date:
26 February 2011

Referral:
Personal Contact

I was going to be drafted and I wanted in the Airborne. I was told I'd needed to enlist to get in the Airborne. I enlisted in May of '46 a week before my high school graduation ceremony. I did my basic training at Ft. McClellan in Alabama and then went to Ft. Bragg, North Carolina for ten weeks of hell. By that time, the 82nd needed new paratroopers but they didn't want anybody that wasn't good. A third of us were wiped out in the first ten weeks of training. From there we went to Ft. Benning, Georgia. Only one third of those that survived Ft. Bragg made it through Benning.

Our days would start at 5:00 AM with an hour of calisthenics. We'd have a three mile run after breakfast every morning. You couldn't stop running for any reason. The only way you could quit running was to pass out. That happened once to me and they carried me back. Field training occupied the remainder of the morning. Whenever we finished a training exercise, we'd do pushups. We were not allowed to walk anywhere.

The Airborne cadre was all WWII veterans. They never said anything about the war but they wanted to make certain we were tough enough to fight one. They'd wake us up in the middle of the night and

> *"The Airborne cadre was all WWII veterans. They never said anything about the war but they wanted to make certain we were tough enough to fight one."*

make us climb trees to retrieve something. They beat the living hell out of us.

I was really scared that I would wash out. They'd wash out anybody with any physical deficiency like having a leg broken as a kid. A steel wheeled John Deere wagon ran over me when I was young and broke my ankle. I had been hit in the eye with a BB gun. I didn't divulge either or I would have been washed out.

I went through glider training and everything else. I got along fine. Then we started training on the 35 feet jump tower. For some reason, I was scared to death at 35 feet and could not properly do my jump technique. During the breaks, I'd climb back up the tower and practice jumping on my own. They told me I was doing it wrong which would cause me wrap up in the chute going out the airplane. They washed me out. I was sick. I went back to the barracks and I hate to admit it, but I balled like a baby. As I was sitting there, three big, mean cadre guys walk in. They asked me "if I was man enough to start over?" They explained that they would intercede on my behalf and talk to the captain and major if I was willing to start from scratch again. The captain later told me this was the first time the Airborne had given a soldier a second chance to qualify as a paratrooper.

Question: Why did they pick you out for special treatment?

Because I was so damn eager, I guess. I did everything three times more than I had to. So I went through all the training again. I was too embarrassed to tell any of the new recruits that I'd washed out. When I went through the training of lashing the equipment down in a glider (for my second time), the new guys were really impressed by how quick they thought I mastered it. They looked up to me as some kind of leader. Later I was made sergeant of the barracks.

Question: Why did you want to be a paratrooper so badly?

I had seen ads about enlisting in the Airborne depicting really sharp looking guys. As a kid I had ruined my grandmother's two really nice umbrellas jumping from high places. I had always wanted to be a paratrooper.

I probably rode ten glider flights. The gliders were made out of plywood and pretty flimsy. The sides would rattle and shake in the turbulence. I was always excited to ride a glider. I just loved it.

I did my five qualifying jumps at Benning. On the first jump, one of the guy's chute didn't open. He was killed. It was not spoken of but there were a number of (I) quit slips handed in after that happened. The Airborne didn't force any one to stay.

I was an operations sergeant in the S3. We were the guys that would plan the field deployments in combat situations. I carried a carbine. I was the world's worst shot with it. Most of the Airborne were good shots. My immediate commanding officer was Lieutenant Richie. He always kidded me in being such a poor shot. He said I would need to carry a machine gun to hit anything. I was part of a headquarters group assigned to the 82nd Airborne Division but we were a step down from the actual division headquarters. Our group did stuff like ordinance.

Before the practice jumps, they'd send out paratroopers to jump first to see what direction the

> *"General Gavin was a living legend and a tremendous guy. Many considered him the best general in the Army."*

wind was blowing. Those guys were called wind dummies. There was a tech 4, a rough son of a gun but a wonderful guy. He would be wind dummy quite a few times. He'd always ask me if I wanted to go with him. This one time General Gavin drove down in his jeep and paid us a visit. He said, "I need another dummy." Lieutenant Richie pointed to me and said, "Here he is." So I got to ride in the plane with Gavin and a bunch of officers who were jumping. What more can a guy ask for? General Gavin was a living legend and a tremendous guy. Many considered him the best general in the Army.

Question: Was Gavin jumping as a wind dummy?

Oh yes! He did that quite often. That's why they called him "Jumpin" Jim Gavin. A lieutenant named Forrest and I were often jump masters. We were supposed to return with the plane following a jump but one time we decided to bail out for fun as the plane was returning to base. What we didn't realize was the plane was flying faster than it normally did for a jump and it was also only 300–400 feet above the ground. When my chute snapped open at that speed, the harness damn near tore me a new heinie. Lt. Forrest almost landed on a one star general's jeep. After rolling up my chute, I looked over there. Lt. Forrest was standing at attention in front of the general. I high tailed it back to my office. When Lt. Forrest arrived, he chewed me out up one side and down the other for abandoning him. The next morning he admitted that the dressing down he gave was all a joke he and Lieutenant Richie had cooked up.

We normally jumped out of either C-46s or C-47s at an elevation of 1100 feet. I made 35 official jumps. The ones Lt. Forrest and I made together didn't count.

The Airborne had a swagger to them. I think it was a natural by-product of the intense training and instilling the attitude that we could take on anyone and come away the victor. Paratroopers and regular infantry "legs" were always getting in bar fights. I boxed while in the service but I wasn't interested in bar fights. I probably boxed in a half dozen matches.

I joined the Army reserves in Washington after leaving the 82nd in 1948. Lt. Richie said he was sorry to see me leave. He and the other officers always volunteered me for anything silly or dangerous like jumping out of airplanes. I joined the reserves because it sounded like the guys were having fun and it paid $25 a month. I was in the reserve six years. After the Korean War broke out, I received a notice calling me up for active duty. My paperwork for joining the reserves had only been sent in the previous week. I went to see Bill Perdock, the commander of our local reserve. I showed him the notice. He put his arm around me, saying, "You don't belong to those bastards, you belong to me." Somehow he got me out of going to Korea.

Lt. Richie was career Army. He telephoned me after coming back from the Korean War. They had jumped at Inchon. He said they lost a lot of the guys I knew while in the Airborne.

My older brother, Arvid, was a MP during the war. He was involved in rounding up the Japanese Americans for the internment camps. It really bothered him to be doing that. He was sick about it. I remember picking him up at the train station in Columbus Junction when he came home on leave. We had no idea what he had been doing in the Army.

I farmed after coming home from the service. I also worked as the manager for the Wellman Telephone Company from 1970 until 1998.

TRIBUTE

In the United States we have the privilege of exercising vast freedoms that no other nation's citizens can enjoy. This privilege did not come without a heavy cost borne by many.

Through this nation's history, past and present members of our armed forces have sacrificed much to preserve our liberties. Their unselfish honorable service has guaranteed that our ideals have continued and remained strong.

World War II was the deadliest military conflict in the world's history. It is calculated that over 400,000 United States soldiers lost their lives. Many communities and families dealt with the loss of loved ones. Our soldiers had to deal with many hardships including the deaths of buddies.

The word "hero" is defined as a "remarkably brave person." Without a doubt, every American soldier who fought in that war is a hero to me. The Midwestern upbringing of the soldiers contained in this book will not permit them to boast as one. However, their modest words about their stories of that time can't conceal the hero that is there.

Our freedoms should never be taken for granted. Our heroes should always be honored, their contributions never forgotten.

Mark Schneider
Mid-Prairie and Keota CSD Superintendent

STANDING STRADDLE OF THE
OPEN BOMB BAY

Tom Mills
Keota, IA

15th Air Force
Europe

Interview Date:
4 March 2011

Referral:
Dean Redlinger

I enlisted in the Army Air Corps in 1942, because I've never been a fan of walking in mud. I heard about an Army Air Corp college cadet training program and enlisted in it in Des Moines. From there, they shipped a bunch of us from the Iowa area down to Jefferson Barracks in Missouri. The area around Jefferson Barracks had a real strong grip in having the best mud in the Midwest. The barracks had not been built yet to we slept on cots under the stars. This was in February. We were issued trench coats and galoshes and slept in them. The tents arrived a few days later. The mess hall was a mile walk away. The food was hot but terrible. I didn't have the most pleasant attitude in the world.

After basic training, I was sent up to Iowa Wesleyan College in Mt. Pleasant along with ninety other guys that had signed up for the college cadet training program. We were put on an old train that should have been dismantled seventy-five years earlier. It even had the old wicker seats. Eighty-eight of the ninety guys from Jefferson Barracks were coughing and hacking so much we were put on sick call when we arrived at the college. But we all survived and got over it. In our six months there, we were given two years' worth of college courses. All I remember is a lot of math and history courses and math was not one of my

favorite subjects. There was some military training as well, close order drill, physical education, that sort of thing.

After college I was sent to Santa Ana, California for more military training. I had signed up for pilot's school. We were given some flight training in Mt. Pleasant where I learned to fly piper cubs. After completing primary flying school at Santa Ana, I was sent to another flying school in Chico, California. One day while playing basketball in physical education, I fell and broke my wrist. Our basketball court was an old rock pile. I spent two months in the hospital with my arm in a cast and not doing a cotton picking thing. The day after being released I was scheduled for a check flight. I hadn't used this arm for two months and had no strength in it. I had to fly with both hands and couldn't pull the stick back with my weak hand. I tried griping the stick with my feet but feet are not made for flying. The flight got a little rough with the checkout pilot hitting his head on the top of the cockpit. He was not at all happy. He screamed at me a little bit and told me to go back and land. The next day I found out that I had washed out, which was probably the safest thing in the world for me to do.

I was reassigned to bombardier school in

Victorville, California. I went through that school with no real problems and received my commission as an officer upon graduation. I was then sent to near Nashville, Tennessee, where I joined my flight crew. People from all over the country that didn't know each other were thrown together to become Air Crew 421. We became like a family. We did our pre-overseas training, practiced flying and bombing, things like that. Then we traveled to the east coast and boarded a ship for Naples, Italy. Upon reaching Naples, they put us on a train for Foggia, Italy, where we spent the next year. After another two or three days of training to get used to the landing strip and stuff like that, we were ready for combat. That would have been in the middle of '44. From then on we were getting shot at.

Question: What was your first mission like? Were you scared?

I was too stupid to be scared. My view was we'd fly a thousand miles, drop some bombs, come home, eat supper and go to bed. I didn't know enough to be scared. As time went on, the more fighters you saw and the more flak you ran into, you realized that the Germans were not playing marbles. They were playing for keeps. We'd lose planes but the missions went on. I was the bombardier on a B-17. On one particular mission we were carrying six five hundred pound bombs. They are lined up three on a side. When the bomb site said it was time, the bombs would launch automatically in sequence so they didn't hit each other. Something happened to the shackles on one side that was holding the bombs and the bottom bomb wouldn't release. As the bombs move down the tract, the little arming wires get pulled out and some little propellers start turning and the bombs are hot. So we had a load of armed bombs on board. If we had hit a dead air bump and the bombs had slid forward, I wouldn't be here today. I left my position forward on the plane and went back to the bomb bay to see what the problem was. One of the enlisted men who knew everything about bombs but what to do in a case like this, said, "Lieutenant, you've got a problem." I said, "What do you mean? You're the expert." He replied, "But you are my superior. You are supposed to tell me what to do." I asked him

"As time went on, the more fighters you saw and the more flak you ran into, you realized that the Germans were not playing marbles. They were playing for keeps."

if he could get the arming wires back in and he said he could not. He did not know what to do. I decided we'd try to chop the bombs out.

Meanwhile, the colonel in command of our formation radioed our pilot wanting to know why our bomb bay doors were still open. Our pilot informed him we still had live bombs jammed up in our bomb bay. His response was, "Get the hell away from here." So we dropped out of formation about a half mile. The bombardier wore his parachute in the front on his chest. I couldn't work with that on so removed it but left the parachute harness on. I hooked an emergency cable on to my harness and grabbed a fire ax. I had to stand straddle of the open bomb bay to swing the ax. I managed to chop them loose and we dropped them in the countryside somewhere.

Question: Did your bomber have a name painted on its nose?

No, flew a lot of different airplanes. The 15th Air Force was hard up for planes. We'd always seem to get old, used ones that the 8th Air Force (flying out of England) didn't want any more. I can't remember ever seeing any new bombers in the 15th. The 8th Air Force was the star of the movie. Clark Gable flew with my brother's crew in England. My brother was a gunner on a seventeen. He flew 25 missions then flew 25 more. We were known as the Forgotten Fifteen.

Question: Did you ever bomb the Ploesti oil fields in Romania?

No, it just so happened as our name wasn't called that day. They'd send out different formations with so many planes each to different places each day the weather was good for flying. It might be 24 bombers to one target and 60 to a different one.

One time the plane coming in behind us was badly shot up and the landing gear wouldn't go down. It cart wheeled when it hit the runway and caught on fire. We were only able to get three of the ten man crew out of the wreckage before it exploded.

A lot of the time we were shorthanded. A B-17 can keep up with the formation on three engines. A lot of times we'd have one engine knocked out at by the end of a bombing run. Sometimes it was from flak but usually it was mechanical failure. These planes were old. We frequently had to abort missions because of mechanical problems. It wasn't like every other time we had trouble, more like one time out of ten. You could fly a B-17 on two engines but it was nominal.

Question: How many bombers could the 15th field at one time?

Gosh, I have no idea. We were in the Fifth Wing and there were five groups in each wing. There be five squadrons in each group and each squadron had twenty planes. That would be 2,500 planes. Of course, they wouldn't all be flying the same day. We'd get days off and some days the weather was too bad to fly. I'd fly eight to ten days a month. The squadron commander would assign each plane its position in the formation. Some of the bombers were B-24s although the Fifteenth had very few of them. We did have some members of the South African Air force flying off the same fields as us. They were flying British Lancasters.

> *"Have you ever heard of the Tuskegee Airman? We had those red tailed P-51s with us. They were amazing."*

We had fighter escort later in the war. Have you ever heard of the Tuskegee Airmen? We had those red tailed P-51s with us. They were amazing. We very seldom saw a German ME-109 or a Focke-Wulf because those Tuskegee boys were there flying cover for us. They cleared the sky. Those guys were good! By the end of the war, we only saw one German fighter plane and he was a mile away. He was acting as a spotter to radio our bearing and altitude to the flak guns.

Flak was our biggest problem. Our gunners never even shot at an enemy fighter. One time we were flying through this mountain pass and there was flak hitting us from above. The Germans had hauled their flak guns up to near the top of the mountain and were shooting down at us. The ground crew would always patch up the holes.

Question: What were some of your missions?

We bombed Vienna, Austria. We bombed troops in northern Italy. We bombed in Yugoslavia, a little bit of France, Germany, Austria, and other places with names I can't seem to remember. Mainly we concentrated on railroad marshaling yards and refineries. If you destroy the railroads, they can't

move anything. If you destroyer the refineries, there's no gas for tanks and trucks.

Towards the end of the war the German Fifth Army massed troops north of Rome with the intentions of eliminating the city, wiping it out. They sent nine bombers including ours. We loaded up with fragmentation bombs with proximity fuses that were set to detonate 50 feet in the air. We flew in at 500 feet. The Germans were camped and only had rifles to fire back at us. We just ripped the daylights out of them. We took out 5,000 German troops camped there. We fragged them.

Question: So you saved Rome? I thought it was declared an open city and the Germans honored that.

Yes. I guess probably so. The German's didn't completely honor Rome's open city status. They did some damage to it before they left.

Question: Tell me about the Norden bomb sight.

It was invented by a Norwegian scientist. It's a mechanical thing that couldn't work but it did. The scientist was put in a mental institution because they thought him crazy. It had increasing and decreasing gears on it. The bombardiers were issued Colt .45s with instructions to put one slug through the face of the bomb sight and one slug through the top of the bomb sight piece if the bomber was shot down. They didn't want it to fall into German hands. We were given instructions to destroy the sight before bailing out if the plane was going down. You had a nice view of everything including the flak coming up. You kept turning knobs until the cross hairs lined up on the target and stayed there. Then you were through. The bomb sight is running the airplane's flight and releases the bombs. They were a delicate piece of machinery. They're obsolete now, of course.

I have a small piece of flak that I saved. It came in through the nose of the plane. I wore a black and white scarf around my neck when operating the bomb sight to keep me warm. I took that scarf off and there was this piece of shrapnel imbedded in the knot. I thought, "Oh, I could have bled to death."

Question: I've read where the planes in the formation would drop their bombs when the lead plane did and so they really didn't rely on the Norden bomb site that much.

Well, it just depended on the circumstances. Sometimes it happened that way. We were supposed to use the bomb sight to acquire the target in case the lead plane missed the target drop for some reason. Usually we bombed on the leader. When his bombs went, you hit a toggle switch and everything goes.

When you're bombing from 30,000 feet, a one degree margin of error is a huge distance on the ground. The Norden bomb sight operated on the assumption that the aircraft was flying level at a constant speed. Hitting an updraft when the bombs were released would throw everything off.

Everything in southern Italy where we were based was black market. The Italian government tried to control everything but couldn't. We went to a black market restaurant for breakfast until it got shut down. There were two classes of people in Italy. The northern Italians were white Europeans and the southern were more African. They looked Sicilian and acted that way.

I ran into Keith Altenhofen from Harper during the war. He was in the same squadron as I was. He ran a furniture store after the war. Howard Greiner was a pilot in the 8th Air Force out of England. He was shot down. We had several planes in our squadron shot down. By the time I had my 50 missions in, the war was over.

I stayed in the service for a year after the war as a training instructor. I considered making a career out of it but got bored with all the inactivity. I got back home in '46. I went to work at the Farmer's Savings Bank in Keota that fall and retired as the CEO in 1985. I still serve on the bank board.

Shirley Mills: We attended our first squadron reunion 32 years after the war. Those guys greeted each other like long lost brothers. We wives heard stories we had never heard before, both funny stories and sad stories. Those guys laughed and cried together the entire time.

NO WAY ANY OF THEM SURVIVED

Bob Ross
Washington, IA

USS *Tucson*
Pacific

Interview Date:
6 March 2011

Referral:
Tom Tanner

I got to go on a four day Honor Flight trip to Washington, D.C. It was a wonderful trip. They told us not to take much cash with us. I only took $40. When I returned home, I laid my two twenty dollar bills on the table. That's what my expenses amounted to. It amazed me how many people at the airports wanted to shake our hands. The trip reminded me of being back in the service. All those old guys back together and just ornerier than heck. Stewart Bell went with me and we shared a room. He'd wake me up at 3:30 every morning wanting to visit.

I enlisted in the Navy in 1944, and I'll tell you why. They drafted 19 boys out of my high school senior class. They didn't even get to graduate. The Navy would let you finish school and graduate if you enlisted with them. My folks really wanted me to graduate. Thirteen days after graduation I was on the bus heading out. They didn't give me much time.

I had 13 weeks of boot camp in Farragut, Idaho. Then I had eight weeks of ship training on Treasure Island in the San Francisco Bay. I shipped out aboard the USS *Tucson*, a light cruiser. They were also called anti-aircraft cruisers. There were 858 men on it and it was 858 feet long. It had six, five inch guns forward and six aft. We had eight quad 40mms and eight twin 20mms. The ship was brand new so we took it out on what's called the shakedown cruise. The last thing you do is run her wide open. The ship vibrated so badly the steel rivets would pop right out of the walls. We got up to a speed of 41 knots which is pretty fast for a ship that big.

We were assigned to Admiral Halsey's Third Fleet. I spent the rest of my time in the service there. We traveled 96,000 miles in the Pacific, stopping at 18 islands. After you passed Pearl Harbor, you got double points. That's why I was only in the service three years.

I only saw the Japanese fleet once and that was off Guam. We did not engage them. We were also in the Marianna's and the Philippines. We had shore leave at the Philippines. We were off shore Okinawa, but this was after all the kamikaze attacks.

We were off Iwo Jima when it was invaded. We got hit pretty hard by Jap planes. When there were that many planes up there, everybody would just point their guns up in the air and fire away. The Jap planes would fly right into the flak. Tracking the planes with the guns was a myth. There was so much stuff up there that they couldn't fly through it. It was like a shield. There were 96 ships in the fleet.

Question: Did that happen off Iwo? I had not ever heard of that.

There were a few things there that didn't get told or publicized. There were a lot of things that happened that weren't supposed to. The Jap planes weren't supposed to get through, but they did. Those Japanese were crazy. You had to be crazy to be a suicide bomber. We were in on that deal.

Our ship was eight to ten miles from Iwo, doing picket duty for the fleet. The island looked like a ball of fire, there was that much shelling. They shelled that island for three days before the invasion. You just knew it wasn't going well. Right before we pulled out of there, Japanese dive bombers hit the destroyer right in front of us, the USS *Boy*. Its superstructure above the deck was blown clear off the ship. There were sailors blown in the water. We sailed right through them. You could hear those sailors hollering at us to stop and pick them up. We couldn't because that would have made us an easy target. That bugged me a lot. It was the worst experience I had during the war, seeing those guys in the water and not being able to do a thing for them. We couldn't even throw them a life preserver.

Question: Do you think any of those guys in the water survived? Did anyone pick them up later?

No, no, there was no way any of them survived. I know they didn't. I've had a couple of nightmares about those guys in the water. I hate to put in bluntly, but they thought the sooner those men drowned and died, the better off they were.

Question; Because of…why?

Because it was going to happen so why prolong it? We young guys on the *Tucson* were cussing the captain for not stopping to help those men. We thought he should have stopped. We didn't realize that he was probably following orders from the admiral.

When we pulled back, we went 40 miles. The idea was that the farther the Jap planes had to fly, the less likely they were to find us. The Japs were on a different program than us. They'd only put in enough fuel to get those dive bombers to us and not enough to get back even if they wanted to. These were kamikaze planes.

Over the three week period we were off Iwo, the Japanese planes probably attacked us ten different days. Roughly half the Jap planes attacking were dive bombers and the other half were fighters. Our carrier planes did an excellent job of shooting a lot of them down before they reached the fleet. When all that was going on, it was so fast you could hardly tell what was happening.

I was a Seaman 1st Class assigned to fire control. That's the aiming and firing of our five inch guns. I was down in what they called the plotting room. There was a big switchboard with three hundred and eight switches on it. There must have been forty miles of electrical wiring in it. It was like a primitive computer and controlled the five inch guns. We had to learn the function of each switch.

There were 32 guys in that division. The chief in charge of it was a fellow from Ottumwa named Morrison. When he found out I was from Washington, he half way took me under his wing, so-to-speak. He was so tanned that he looked like a piece of leather. He had a little drinking problem, however. He'd come back aboard ship drunk after shore liberty and we'd have to hide him from the officers. One time we hid him in a narrow crawl space behind the switchboard. Several officers came down to the plotting room looking for the chief. Of course, we told him that we had no idea where he was. Right after the officers left, he rolled over and the keys he always carried on his belt shorted out some of the electrical wiring. We worked all night to get the switchboard rewired.

We went 65 days without seeing land. After Iwo the fleet backed off, refueled, and moved closer to Japan. There were four aircraft carriers in the fleet. We'd get up every morning at 3:30. All those carrier planes would take off every morning and roar over us. It would take about two hours to launch them all. They'd bomb Japan and come back. We'd back off about 65 miles and get a reload and move back toward Japan. The fleet would sail to within 20 to 30 miles from the Japanese coast before launching planes. We did that for 65 straight days.

After that, when the war was about over, we were given a new assignment. A whole bunch of big

> *"We young guys on the Tucson were cussing the captain for not stopping to help those men. We thought he should have stopped."*

crates were loaded on to our deck from a transport ship. We didn't know what they contained. About 15 guys boarded our ship from the transport to accompany the crates. We couldn't figure out what was going on. We pulled away from the rest of the fleet and headed north towards Japan by ourselves as a diversion. It turned out that the crates contained radios and those 15 guys spent all their time talking on the radios. The idea was to make the Japanese think that the entire fleet was heading to Japan. That was probably the only time I was scared to beat all hell because we were all alone. The sonar on our ships showed submarines getting closer to us. I never like fighting something we couldn't see.

When we were on the Honor Flight in Washington, D.C., the Navy offered to print out the service record of our ships while we toured the Naval Museum. The service record of the *Tucson* came back blank for the time we were on that secret radio mission to Japan. The Naval guys doing the research couldn't believe it. Sixty-five years later and it was still classified.

We were in Tokyo Bay with the Third Fleet when the Japanese surrendered aboard the USS *Missouri*. We were some distance away but watched through binoculars. We only spent four days in Tokyo Bay and on the third day we had shore leave. We toured the big Yokohama Naval Base. It was impressive. They had a map table with perfect models of all 96 ships in our fleet on it.

Then we rode the narrow gauge railroad up to Tokyo. We carried .45 pistols in case there was any trouble but there wasn't any. The first time I saw a guy from Washington, Iowa, was while I was walking down a street in Tokyo. You know, that really kind of surprised the hell out of me. It was Robert Frakes. I knew that he was a pilot on a Third Fleet aircraft carrier. We were never close to the carriers and I couldn't hardly believe running into him. He and I visited for about an hour right there in the street.

We walked through Tokyo and those Japs would just run from you. They were scared to death of us. They had been filled full of propaganda, you could tell that. You almost felt sorry for them. A lot of them were women, of course. They'd just scurry off the streets. We didn't see any Japanese soldiers. I think they were hiding, I really do. We were only in Tokyo for four hours and it was only a couple of days after the Japanese surrender.

Question: Did you see any damage from the fire bombing we did on Tokyo?
Oh, yes, absolutely.

The biggest thing the Navy taught me was that everyone was equal aboard ship. Individually, you weren't worth a damn. You took care of the guy next to you. Rank, skin color or where he was from didn't matter. That's something everyone understood. The Navy taught me a lot of respect for others. I never regretted being in Navy. It taught me a lot things I'll never forgot.

I kept track of many of my buddies after the war and attended one ship reunion. The only guy from back home that I served with during the war was Harry Suter from Crawfordsville. He went through boot camp with me and we served together on the *Tucson*.

You might not appreciate this and my wife doesn't like me to say it, but I will anyway. Ninety percent of the reason the war worked was because we had a bunch of dumb, young people that didn't know what the hell they were getting in to. I mean that. They'd put you in a situation in which you had to do something to save yourself. I didn't have the remotest idea what I'd be doing when I went in. You had no idea of where you'd even be assigned. On those islands in the Pacific and over in Europe, it was pretty tough going. There was a lot of suffering, more than people realize.

I'm certainly no hero and I don't say this for me, but if it hadn't been for the quality of men serving, we would have never won that war. There were a lot of guys in the service that were pretty determined. They weren't going to take defeat even if hell froze over.

Three-fourths of the men you used to meet on the street were WWII veterans. A lot of them are gone now. Serving in the military was something you just knew you had to do. There was never any question about it. When I came home to Washington, I went straight to work for my dad at his auto shop. Later we were known as Ross Auto and Muffler which I ran with my brother.

LIKE DIGGING YOUR OWN GRAVE

Max Hollander
Germanville, IA

843rd Aviation Engineers
Europe

Interview Date:
12 March 2011

Referral:
Steve & Becky Rebling

I bought this house and farm in '46, right after I got out of the service. I was in the 843rd Aviation Engineers, part of the Army Air Corps. We built new airstrips and remodeled some that were torn up. I was drafted in '42. I went in as an electrician and came out a welder. That's the Army's way of doing things. I had a portable welding shop I drove around, always moving ahead. I always had a hot dinner and for the rest of them, that was wishful thinking.

I went to England and went in Normandy at Utah Beach at daybreak. I was 22 years old. There were so many planes overhead it was hard to tell if it was day or night. I had never seen so many aircraft. We had great support. I have a neighbor down the road named Bill Watson that was in the 101st and dropped behind the lines in Normandy. A group of us vets observe Veteran's Day 12 times a year by having dinner together on the 11th of every month. I ate dinner with him yesterday. He'd be a good one for you to talk to.

We rode into the beach on Higgins boats. They dropped the ramp when they got close to shore and

you waded in. Good luck and no return. We were supposed to get a foothold and then move all our equipment in later and get ready to build airfields. We were a long way from being ready to go as we had to establish a foothold first. I went back over there for the 50th anniversary of D-day and had

Max's view looking back on Utah Beach. "This is where we first set foot in France. Notice the column of men coming up the hill. We all came up that same trail carrying everything we possessed on our back. Photo courtesy of Max Hollander.

the opportunity to examine the concrete pillboxes the Germans had overlooking the beach. They had built those to stay. They weren't figuring on leaving. They had living quarters and food pantries so that the Germans could live inside them. The poor infantry had to get behind those pillboxes and come down from above and drop explosives in there to kill all those Germans inside. The infantry went in before us.

Question: When you crossed the English Channel, did you know you were going in the next morning?

Yes, we knew. We had a colonel that forewarned us. He said, "You may not be coming back. This may be your last." It was pretty much as bad as I expected. There wasn't much talking going over. Everybody was scared to death. The water was chest deep where we went down the ramp. We had our bags and everything we owned on our shoulders. We were under fire the whole time. It was difficult getting through the deep water with all the weight we were carrying but we soon hit shallower water. We lost a few guys there. They had weeded us out in our training at Camp McCord out in Washington State and anybody that was a weakling they didn't take. We still lost some of our guys in that deep water that weren't strong enough. They drowned. I drug a couple of them as far as I could take them and I had to let them go. These were guys I had trained with from the beginning. They were my buddies.

I carried a BAR. They were heavy to lug around. At least I had a truck most of the time to put mine in. Those poor infantry men didn't. I have to give Eisenhower a lot of credit for D-day. He was organized. We were supposed to go in a day or two sooner but the weather was bad so Eisenhower called it off. It was plenty bad when we did go.

Question: Did you get seasick crossing the channel?

No, I was used to it by then. I got sick on the boat coming over. I learned to get the top bunk right quick. When we had supper that first night after leaving Camp Kilmer, New Jersey, guys were throwing up like crazy. The floors got so slick we couldn't stand up.

> "They drowned. I drug a couple of them as far as I could take them and I had to let them go. These were guys I had trained with from the beginning. They were my buddies."

We were stuck near the beach for about a week. There wasn't much enemy activity except for snipers. You had to watch out for them. There wasn't much we could do except kill them if we could figure out where they were hiding. We set up our pup tents in a cow pasture and a clothesline to dry our wet clothes. There were 550 guys in our Aviation Engineers outfit. The French people started coming out to help us. Ladies would offer to wash our clothes and bring us food. They were really glad to see us. That was the toughest time we had in actual combat. The rest of the war we were always ten to fifteen miles behind the front lines. We had to sleep in foxholes at night because the Germans were always strafing us. It was quite an experience.

Comment: I'm surprised they sent Aviation Engineers in that early.

Well, they wanted us to get started repairing the airfields. Our equipment was still in England but would come as soon as we got a foothold. (*Note: In General Omar Bradley's book,* A Soldier's Story, *he wrote how critical it was to get airfields operational as quickly as possible to bring in supplies and fly out the wounded. The invasion plan called for having allied aircraft landing above the beach on D-day plus one.*)

I was stationed in the motor pool. The truckers would go back and forth to the beach to get our supplies and ammunition. They'd run day and night, seven days a week. We lived in churches and community buildings if there was any left standing in the villages. Otherwise we lived in our pup tents. After we got a little more established in France, they put up a tent city with eight or ten of us staying together in a larger tent. Sometimes the Army would bring vehicles over that needed repairs and I would weld on them.

We followed Hodges' (U.S. First Army) infantry clear across France. By then, we were building new airstrips for crippled heavy bombers that couldn't make it back to England to land on. We would pour concrete runways for the bomber airfields and use landing mats for the fighters. My job was to weld the ends of the matting together. We couldn't weld at night, of course, the *Luftwaffe* would spot us. It took us around 45 days to complete an airfield, including the time to level the ground with bulldozers and pack it down. Concrete runways took longer than those with mats. All the raw materials for making concrete were shipped over from England and trucks would haul it to us from the beach. During the course of the war, we probably repaired 25 damaged airstrips and built two concrete new ones for the heavy bombers.

We dug foxholes every time we moved. It felt like you were digging your own grave. We'd stay in our tents, sleeping on our cots until the air raid sirens would wake us and we'd have to go to our foxholes. We got pretty good at digging those holes. If it wasn't big enough before, we'd dig it bigger. You get some pretty good buddies when you sleep in a foxhole with them. You'd look out for one another. We had an anti-aircraft battery attached to our outfit but the German planes still strafed us about every night.

I was in Paris when it was liberated. It was a mad house. People lined the streets and there were snipers in the windows. Our guys had to watch out for them. Some of the American soldiers went a little crazy because they hadn't seen a lady for months. Those French women went crazy over the guys, too. Yes, we had quite a parade when we went through Paris. There's a lot of history in Paris. It is a good thing that city wasn't torn up.

We came upon the Dachau prison camp while they were still burning bodies. There were still German guards there when we arrived. They disappeared quickly, running over the hill. We took care of a few of them that didn't run fast enough. We really learned to hate the Germans after seeing Dachau. The way they treated those people was terrible. It wasn't civilized. We saw the showers where the Jews were gassed. We couldn't hardly stand looking at what we were seeing. That and the Battle of the Bulge were the worst things we went through. *(Note: Max showed us some photos of Dachau. They were more graphic and ghastly than any published photos that we have ever viewed.)*

We were in the Ardennes when the Bulge hit.

"I was 22 years old when I stepped off the ramp at Normandy. I can still remember how the water felt as it filled my boots."

The Germans threw their best troops at us. The Germans had everything mined. We pert near had to learn their pattern (of mine placement) so we didn't step on a mine. You could almost see where the mines were after you learned the pattern. Most of the mine fields were rectangular and about the size of this room. You had to stay out of there until the combat engineers came along to clear them. One of my buddies lost a foot stepping on a mine. I didn't see any more of him until I got home. Once you got into a minefield, you had a hard time getting out. The Germans got behind us during the Bulge and we had to retreat through their minefields. It slowed us down some. We were close to Bastogne when we were retreating. We could see the German Panzers in the distance. We wanted no part of them.

We spent as much time at the Red Cross as possible. We took in every USO troop that was available, even got to see Bob Hope. We had the scenic tour of Bavaria when the war ended, saw Hitler's Eagle's Nest. We were repairing an airstrip when they announced the war had ended in Europe. We dropped everything we were doing, never turned another bolt. We even abandoned all of our equipment where it sat. Just walked off and left it. It would have cost too much to ship it home.

The Germans had great highways over there. They are not dumb people, but they were vicious. War ruins you for life. Some of our guys went off the deep end. They never did get back. They were sent home. I never even thought about the war when I came home. I never talked about it or anything. I suspect it was 25 years before I ever said anything about it. I never had any use for the Japs and still don't. They were even more vicious than the Germans. They had no sympathy for life. They might have today, but they didn't when we were headed that direction. We were getting ready to load a boat for Japan when they dropped the atomic bomb. Then we got sent home. So I'd say old Harry Truman saved our lives.

Besides operating a farm in Jefferson County, Max owned the Hollander Insurance Agency in Fairfield. WWII vets from the area volunteered that when they were struggling financially while getting started farming after the war, Max would quietly make their insurance premium payments for them. The insurance company he opened in Fairfield has sold several times but still bears his name.

I was 22 years old when I stepped off the ramp at Normandy. I can still remember how the water felt as it filled my boots. My wife and I were married in New Jersey two months before I shipped out. I told her that she was taking quite a chance. I was too dumb at the time to know how much the war would affect me. It's hard when you have to kill someone to save your own life.

Note: The hands in the photo on the cover of this book belong to 3-year old Carys Miller and 89-year old Max Hollander.

Max (left), in front of his welding truck. Photo courtesy of Max Hollander.

TRIBUTE

(Note: Steve Rebling was present during the interview of his neighbor, Max Hollander.)

As I listened intently to his story, I had the feeling that I had helped him release something that had been bottled up inside of him for way too long. A strange bond overcame us. His tears became my tears as the memories unfolded into an experience I will never forget. It was an experience that must be preserved and repeated over and over again to generations to come. It was not an easy story to tell, but one we must never let die.

His white hair and wrinkled brow oozed with dignity as he spoke of a long time ago. But to him, I'm sure it seemed like only yesterday.

He and his comrades were boys, just boys, yanked from the security of t heir homes and finding themselves half a world away experiencing the horror of war—kill or be killed.

As they jumped into the cold seas at Normandy, I felt the cold water fill my boots. He took me there as the bullets whizzed over our heads. We struggled to drag wounded and dying buddies through the sand and mud to some sort of safety. Together we felt the agony as we saw, one by one, the boys dying. There was an intense fear in a feeling of total chaos. Death seemed almost a welcome relief, and yet somehow, the desire to live triumphed. I was there. I was there a tiny bit, and I'm so glad I was. The more he spoke, the more the memories flooded back to him. They seemed almost endless. He finished and sat there, exhausted from the long journey we had just taken. I shook his hand and thanked him for sharing his story, for being there when his country needed him, and for his part in preserving our freedom. A true American hero! May God bless them all.

*Steve Rebling
Brighton, IA*

PHOTOS OF DACHAU CONCENTRATION CAMP
TAKEN BY MAX HOLLANDER

Photos courtesy of Max Hollander.

THE BEST COUNTRY IN THE WORLD

Ruth Zehr
Keota, IA

German Civilian

Interview Date:
14 March 2011

Referral:
Beverly Zehr & April Cuddeback

I was born in Frankfort, Germany. I can remember getting out of school one day when Hitler was passing through Frankfort on a train. All of us school children were told to smile and wave at him. I could see him sitting at a window in a passenger train car, waving back at us. I'm not certain how old I was at the time, but I was very young.

The war in Europe started in 1939. My dad was a postmaster general in Frankfurt and was moved to Prague, Czechoslovakia. He had been in WWI so he didn't have to join the German army. He spoke eight languages fluently. He ran the German postal service in Prague. I was eleven years when we moved there. I attended a German high school in Prague for four years. In those days, you had to pass an exam to attend high school and pay tuition. After high school, I attended a German university in Prague for two years. We lived in an apartment and had Czech neighbors. I wanted to be able to speak to the people so I learned the Czech language. The Russian, Polish, and Czech languages are similar. German is closer to English. There are a lot of words the same. My maiden name was Fiegler.

Every night at 2:00 AM the air raid sirens would go off and we had to go to the basement. That was when the bombers from England flew over Czechoslovakia on their way to Germany. They never dropped any bombs on Prague, which is a good thing, as it is considered to be the most beautiful city in Europe.

I had an uncle that was in a restaurant having a beer. He made the comment that Hitler was crazy to start a war with England and that it was a war he couldn't win. Someone overheard it and reported him to the police. He was arrested and sent to Dachau concentration camp near Munich. He was my mother's brother. This was in 1939 and we'd been living in Prague about a month. He died in Dachau. We didn't know about the concentration camps until after the war. We thought he was in jail somewhere. The concentration camps were a big secret. Hitler kept it pretty quiet. He had the Jews doing all the manual work in the camps so they didn't have to bring in outside civilian help. If anyone said anything against Hitler someone would show up at your door in the middle of the night and order you to report to the army or navy at five o'clock in the morning. If you failed to show up, you were shot. That's the truth.

Comment: I think the impression most Americans have is that Hitler was adored by the vast majority of the German people.

You know why that is? There was a reason for this. Hitler came to power when Germany was in an economic depression. People didn't have any money to buy food for their children. He started building the autobahn, the German highway. He put people to work and they had money again. That's how he got accepted in Germany. Later on, he wanted to be the head of the whole world.

Comment & Question: Hitler struck a deal with Neville Chamberlain and the French in 1938 to annex the ethnically German dominated Sudetenland region and in six months had basically taken the entire country. Was there resentment by the Czech people to the German presence?

We got along fine with them. My best girlfriend was a Czech. They didn't resent us. I think the Czechs got along better with Germans that came from Germany than the ones already living there. I don't know the reason for that. You know, when Germans met one another on the street in Prague, they didn't give the Nazi salute. They shook hands.

"I can still see the Russians coming down the street in their tanks. We were forced to raise a clenched fist in the air as a salute."

We had food ration tickets issued the first day the war started. Hitler had it all planned out ahead of time. There were different ration tickets for age groups, babies, adults, teenagers and children up to age twelve. The Czechs were given the same ration tickets as the Germans. There were a lot of things you couldn't buy. You couldn't go buy a dozen eggs but you could buy one egg at a time. People didn't have personal cars at that time. They rode streetcars or took a taxi to get around. I rode a streetcar to school every day.

Question: Did you ever see dissidents, Jews or gypsies being rounded up?

No. All I saw was the yellow star they had to wear on their clothes with the word, "Jude" written on it which means Jew in German. One of my best friends was a Jewish girl. She never wore the yellow star but her parents did. She came to visit me in Frankfurt after the war.

Question: How did you get your news of the war? Did everything go through Goebbels' Ministry of Propaganda? Take the fall of Stalingrad for example. Did you hear about that?

Oh, yes. It was in the newspaper and on the radio. I really didn't pay much attention to the war. I was a teenager and more interested in Shirley Temple. I wanted to be a movie star and go to Vienna and take dancing lessons.

While we were in Prague, my dad was transferred to Kiev in Russia. He was sent there not as a worker but as an overseer. A post office was set up in every country that the German army invaded so troops and their families could get mail.

We were hiding in the basement when the war ended. They announced over the radio that any Czechs hiding Germans would be shot. We didn't want to put our neighbor's lives at jeopardy. The partisans had already come to the house and asked if there were any Germans there. They lied, telling them that they had already left. So we went out in the street. That radio announcement forced a number of Germans out of hiding and on to the street. People were shouting names at us. All our jewelry was taken from us. Germans were being killed right out there in the street.

The Russians came later. I can still see the Russians coming down the street in their tanks. We were forced to raise a clenched fist in the air as a salute. I was 17 years old. My mother hid me under a blanket because terrible things were going on.

Everybody feared the Russians. They were made out to be the bad ones. The British and the Americans soldiers were not viewed that way. My mother had a brother living in New York. A lot of Germans had relatives living over here and in England.

Many of the Germans knew the end was coming and they left Czechoslovakia. The postal department had buses and many of the families were leaving on those buses to go back to Germany. My dad wanted us to leave but my mother didn't want to leave her home. My dad left and went back to Frankfurt. We reunited with him after spending eight months in a concentration camp in Lissa.

We were told to walk to this place three or four city blocks away to meet all the other Germans being rounded up. A lot of people were killed on the way there. Sometimes it seemed like whole families had been killed. Their bodies were thrown in the river. Our family walked to the assembly place by ourselves. I did not witness the actual killing. Once we got there, the Czech partisans painted swastikas on our foreheads. Later we walked to the train station where we were put in cattle cars. We did not know where we were being sent. We got off the train at Lissa where there had been a German Army camp. We lived in the army barracks. My family was divided up. My mother was in a camp of older women. They had to do the Russians' laundry. My sister and her two little boys were in with kids. I was in a camp full of teenagers in downtown Lissa. We had to work morning until night hoeing around rows of trees in a nursery. It was hard work and we didn't get much to eat. A lot of the girls would faint while working.

Question: What were conditions like in the camp?

Most of the children starved to death. One of my sister's boys died. Her other son survived the camp but was sickly from it. We'd get some raw vegetables to eat but never any meat. There was a shortage of salt after the war so the vegetable soup didn't have much taste. Even the Czech people didn't have any salt. We were always short of food. My mother told me that if any woman couldn't get up in the morning to wash the laundry, the Russians would beat her. There were around 500 in my camp. There were a number of other camps scattered around.

After being held there for eight months, the Red Cross found out about us and got us released. But only those Germans that could prove they were born in Germany were allowed to go free. The ethnic Germans that had been born in the Sudetenland remained in the concentration camp. To this day, I don't know what happened to them. The Red Cross got us back to Frankfurt. We lived in a bunker until we located my father.

The only thing I saved from our home in Prague was this photo album. I want you to look at this picture of these young children. They are brothers and sisters and that's me in the photo. I was eleven years old. We're sitting on a German tank. Their dad was a general in the German army. Just before

the war was over, he gave his six children poison candy and shot his wife and himself. They were our neighbors. I knew all those kids.

My 18 year old brother served in the German navy. He was killed, but we didn't know what happened. There were a lot of German families that didn't know what happened to their loved ones.

Question: How do you pick up the pieces and rebuild your life after all that?

I still have nightmares. I will as long as I live. The Czechs ran the camps but the Russians would come into the camp at night and do a lot of horrifying things to the women. Some of the young girls were raped. I can still hear their screams. I was lucky nothing ever happened to me. Something like that you just never forget.

Question: Was there much talk about the war in Germany after it ended?

No. People didn't really discuss it. I think everyone was just glad it was over. Everybody would talk about wanting to be in the American or English Zones of Occupation. Nobody wanted to be in East Germany because they were scared to death of the Russians. My sister's husband was in a Russian prison camp for six years after the war ended. It ruined his health. He did not live very long after his release.

> *"I can still hear their screams. I was lucky nothing ever happened to me. Something like that you just never forget."*

You know, that stupid Hitler wasn't even a German. He was from Austria. He was crazy.

Question: Do you remember when Reichsprotector Reinhard Heydrich was ambushed and assassinated in Prague?

Oh, yes. He was a monster.

Comment & Question: He was certainly one of Hitler's favorite henchmen. I've seen German war propaganda film footage showing all these thousands of people in Prague filing by his casket to pay homage. Were you or any members of your family forced to attend?

We would never attend a funeral of a Nazi.

When I go to schools and speak, I tell everybody to thank God that you live in America, the best country in the world.

I met Wayne and his brother, Larry, in 1947. It

was August 17th. It was a hot day and my mother and I went to a restaurant to get something cold to drink. Another lady and her daughter accompanied us. Wayne and his brother and another guy were sitting at a table in the back. Wayne was bashful. The Signal Corps had a night club set up in the rear of the restaurant. The other guy came over to the table and invited us to stay for the band and floor show. Our mothers told us when we had to be home and left. At 10:00 PM, Larry and Wayne walked us home. He was such a gentleman.

We were married on December 1st in 1949. There was a lot of red tape involved for Wayne to marry a German girl. We had to wait for my paperwork to come back from Washington, D.C. I was Lutheran and we were married in Lutheran church in Germany. The ceremony was in the German language. It was a good thing Wayne spoke German so that he knew when to answer, "Yah".

Everybody in Keota made me welcome. It's a very friendly town. People brought cookies and cake to our house when we moved back here. I was the librarian here for eleven years and worked fifteen years in the bank. Wayne worked for the Postal Service for forty years and retired from the West Chester Post Office in 1985.

Wayne's folks were Mennonite. They made me feel welcomed. Five of their six sons served in the military. The parents were not too happy with them. Wayne's folks were Mennonite. Five of their six sons served in the military. The parents were not too happy with them.

Wayne and I returned to visit Germany quite a few times. There are good and bad people in every country. I don't have any hate for anybody. Life is too short for that. Every night I pray that people would get along with everybody else and that there will be no more war.

April 1944. Ruth wearing the coat that was later ripped off her back by a Russian soldier. Photo courtesy of Ruth Zehr.

Circa 1941 or 1942. Ruth (far left) sitting with five of the seven siblings who were later poisoned by their father, a German General. Photo courtesy of Ruth Zehr.

WHAT FEAR TASTES LIKE

Eugene Vogel
Hedrick, IA

101st Airborne Division
Europe

Interview Date:
24 March 2011

Referral:
Mary Vogel

I grew up in the Keota area. Leon Vogel is my brother. Victor was my dad's name. I came out of high school and my very best friend's brother got killed in the war. He wanted to know if I wanted to go in the service with him. So I said, "Yep. Let's go." I had an older brother that farmed with my dad and he was supposed to go. I went down to the draft board and they said that if I went, he wouldn't have to—but he had to go later anyway. So we enlisted.

We went to Camp Fanin, Texas, for training. And then we went right across. It was very short training—I think it was 13 weeks. We went to England, then across the Channel. We went to a place with swine houses on the Rhine River; that's where we went into combat. We were actually on the front line within 100 yards of the damn enemy and never had a shell. We had rifles but we didn't have any shells. We were not issued any ammunition. They were getting us up there too quick. We were sitting in a big old factory up on the Rhine River and Rogers said to me, "You know, we ain't getting this war won sitting here in this room." They put a paper up in the middle of a board and looking for guys to volunteer for the Airborne.

So we both went down and volunteered and they didn't take him (because he had flat feet),

but they took me So then I went on the front line with the 327th Glider Infantry. We covered quite a bit of territory. We went out to Hitler's Hideout—Berchtesgaden—we took that and we had quite a few of those combat days. They kept sticking us in the holes. I learned more in six weeks over there than five years in training camp.

We were on the front line on the Rhine River and I was already qualified for gliders. I had been promoted in the field from PFC to staff sergeant. I volunteered for jump school. They let us come off the line for six or seven days to go to Jump School. We had to pack our own chutes and jump them. And when we got ready to jump they didn't have any Jump Master. So I became the Jump Master and I had never ridden in an airplane before. The first nine times I rode in an airplane, I never landed! I jumped out of it. Then after that we just made pay jump once a month, if possible. My jump training was on Continental Europe in France. Before, when we were in the gliders, we had parachutes strapped on us several times—at least four or five times—to jump behind the lines. Then Patton got there and he rolled right up there the next day and we were supposed to jump behind the lines. They got to where they were supposed to be before we got to do that (jump behind enemy lines). You talk about an army or the military doing something that hadn't ought to—well, it would be like strapping a chute on two civilians and saying, "Come on, you're going to jump behind the lines." You've never had a chute on before, you didn't know what the hell you were doing or nothing and they ain't gonna tell you what to do. But you might rather do that than ride a glider down (that was going to crash).

In a glider you were a sitting duck. For a while I was a jeep driver in the Gliders and you sat in the jeep with the front down and everything. When the glider rides up on its nose, the jeep rolls forward, kind of temporarily tied in there. When it rode forward, it's got a cable hook on the back and it comes back around over the pilot and co-pilot, and that cable is supposed to jerk them up. And you go out underneath. And you're out running around and the glider ain't stopped yet. It doesn't take much training for that, though.

During Operation Market Garden I was in England. I remember we were standing in line and they were going to feed us Thanksgiving turkey. And the turkey boxes said Wellman, Iowa: The Turkey Center of the World. And they put your piece of turkey in your mess kit and your potato and gravy and it was raining and you had to put your rain coat over it to keep your mess kit from running over. I'll never forget that. I never had trouble with being homesick or anything but that was really something. It was raining, and I was eating turkey that came right from home. I was 18 years old.

When I joined the 101st it was just when they started to come out of the Battle of the Bulge. Those were really tough troops that came out of Bastogne. We got in on the tail end of that; and boy they were tough. It was just exactly like they write and talk about it. The reason I got promoted is because they didn't have anyone left.

The enemy troops that we faced were used to getting orders. The Germans had bad commanders. If the Germans weren't held back they would have fought smarter or harder. They did what they were told to do and nothing else. You take a GI and toughen him up like them guys who came out of Bastogne, one of them could whip 50 Germans in a fair fight, because they were tough, boy!

"Those were really tough troops that came out of Bastogne…The reason I got promoted is because they didn't have anyone left."

In Germany, we had a little barn that had two sides and a hay loft on top. And it was about half full of hay. And I was sitting on an anti-tank gun in that shed with the door shut and I heard a railroad gun shot over above and back behind me. The next one landed out in front of me. So I though, "I'd better hunt me a hole." So I climbed down under that anti-tank gun between the trails. And that thing just splintered that barn—that railroad gun. It shot behind me and just took the top off that building and everything and just splintered it. The hay came down on top of me. It didn't start on fire, though.

They didn't look me up because they didn't miss me for a while. It was on a Sunday and pretty soon a guy by the name of Woodbury said, "Hey, my buddy is some place in there." So they came and started digging around and pretty soon they found me. It had stunned me; knocked me out, I suppose. The first thing I heard was Woodbury saying, "I think he is in there, yet." And they dug me out. That one was the closest to meeting my Hallelujah. That shell was pretty hot. The concussion should have killed me; I ain't got no business being here. Those big guns, if you're in a fox hole or can get just below ground level someway or when they go down in a hole, it makes a concussion. It might make you dizzy or think you are dead for awhile but…it all goes up. What's tougher is air bursts because all that comes down.

Those boys that came out of Bastogne—they could hear those shells go over and they could tell if it was going to land in their hip pocket or if it would miss by 50 yards.

It was pretty cold that winter. I got caught back behind the line two or three times, going over on night patrol and getting prisoners, and got caught over there…Germans were all around. I hid out two or three weeks under a brush pile behind German lines. I ate K-rations, what little we had. There were six in my patrol. We were talking to our people (U.S.) with radios. They knew we were there but they didn't have the troops to get us. It was scary. You find out what fear tastes like. We had quite a few rations with us on our patrol because they suspected we might get caught. We put snow in our helmets and drank it. People don't realize what you can stand though, if you have to. We were across the Rhine River and back quite a ways behind the enemy lines. Our troops were back across the Rhine. We were some of the first Americans over the Rhine, probably. We went across in river boats. But they (U.S.) knew where we were the whole time because we were radioing reports to them. They finally drove the Germans back and they came and got us with river boats.

I suppose that I went out on night patrols to get prisoners more than half a dozen times. They kept getting more and more patrols as the war went on because that was the only way they had of finding out how many (enemy troops) were back there. We normally got prisoners every time we went out. The way you did that was to sneak up on them. The way to get them was to get in there and do it. I'll say this; if we took prisoners back at midnight or after, by the next day the men reporting knew everything that they had. They didn't ask them real nice or anything. They interrogated them pretty roughly. After that they were prisoners of war. German soldiers did resist sometimes being taken prisoner. It didn't go well for them, but then again it didn't go well for us either. We had no choice but to get out of there in a hurry if a fire fight broke out. They (U.S.) got a lot of information out of them and it helped us a lot—whether there was a regiment back there or a couple divisions or whatever was back there. It makes a lot of difference.

I will say one thing for old (General) Maxwell Taylor. He would be around some place where you wouldn't think a general would. He was tough. The first one that I met that had a lot of stars on his helmet was Maxwell. That deal that I told you I was in where they shot the barn down? Well before they did that, I was on guard out by the shed. A jeep drove up with just two people in it. He jumped out and he had a thing over his helmet so you didn't know what it was. Maxwell came up there and said, "Soldier, you know how to shoot that (anti-tank) gun?" "No, Sir." "Where's the guy who is supposed to be with you?" And about that time the guy who was supposed to be with me, heard Maxwell. He was down in the basement in

the house and he heard him. And boy, if Maxwell didn't chew his butt out. He said, "You know better than that. Those green troops aren't supposed to be left by themselves." That was Maxwell. And before he got done, he came up and patted me on the shoulder and said, "Don't worry about anything. We're going to do our best to take care of you." If you were jumping a pay jump, he'd just fall right in line and go right with them. He was a good one.

I also ran into (Louis) Mountbatten. He was British. It was in Berchtesgaden. I was a jeep driver and they had about 20 or 30 jeeps hauling these guys up that mountain. Mountbatten came and sat his butt in my jeep. I said, "Good morning, Sir." He said, "Good morning. It's a nice day, isn't it?" And I kind of said, "Well, I don't know. I won't call it a real nice day but it will be alright, I guess." I don't remember saying very much to him but we went up the mountain far enough—the road wound around. He asked me how I was getting along with the war. He also asked me about the British. I told him that most of the time we had trouble with them because while we were off fighting it seemed like they were off drinking tea someplace. So to the top of the mountain and the sun started shining. Mountbatten pulled his raincoat off and I saw his rank and I thought, "Jesus Christ, they are going to court martial me for sure now."

"German soldiers did resist sometimes being taken prisoner. It didn't go well for them, but then again it didn't go well for us either."

That's because I was really putting the stuff to him. After they walked around and looked everything over he did come back and got back into the same jeep with me. I said, "If I said something to offend you, I didn't mean to." He turned out to be a pretty nice guy. We had some real good discussions up there.

I was in Hitler's house several times. I remember the gold elevator. Off to the side of the house they had a place where they kept Göring and Bormann (Nazi leadership) and we pulled guard duty on them. That Göring, I never did like him. If he had made a bad move, he would have been wasted. Each one of them had a big, monstrous car with bullet proof glass. Most of us tried to bring those home but they wouldn't let us. I saw Hitler's staff car there. In fact I drove it. We took it you know… hell it belonged to us! They also had a section of the mountain fenced off for cattle. Boy, we ate some of the best beef! I imagine it was Hitler's beef. He had some nice fat steers.

There was no German resistance when we took Berchtesgaden. When they surrendered they came from everyplace but those Alps (you could hide a hundred soldiers and never miss them). I took a motorcycle away from a German officer. It had a sidecar on it. It was a BMW—a monster of a motorcycle. I could ride a motorcycle a little bit and thought I might as well have that. So I relieved him of that and the sidecar. The strange part of it was that after the war was done I could have sent that thing home. I have often thought of that. Why didn't I send that thing home? Well of course back then I wanted to come home and to hell with the motorcycle!

When the war got towards the end, they sent us up in the Alps to get SS troops. We were supposed to capture them and bring them back. Talk about a SNAFU! To try and catch SS troops in those mountains was a ridiculous thing. We were just wide open, but they never would shoot very much. There was no way in hell that they were going to catch them. We finally just sat trucks down below the mountains and waited them out, knowing they had to eat sometime. We waited and knew they had to get hungry and were going to come down. We wanted to capture them; we didn't necessarily want to shoot them.

Question: Did you run into anyone from back home during the war?

Yes—Floyd Keitel. Floyd ran a grocery store in Keota. He was the first guy I saw over there from back home. We had come back from our shower and I walked into a movie and I saw the back of a guy's head. And I thought, "Boy, I know him." I walked right over the damn chairs and dropped over and I said, "Jeeeezus Cah-rist, Floyd Keitel!" He had been through all the war. Floyd Keitel—I will never forget him as long as I live. I knew him real good in Keota because my folks always bought groceries off him.

Question: Eugene, did your outfit come across any prison or work camps?

We did come across some prison camps. I helped carry people out of one prison camp but I can't remember the name of it. Boy, they looked horrible; they were just skin and bones. It wasn't a real big place but it sure was a no good place. We carried the prisoners out on stretchers. We were helping the Red Cross and the medics. There weren't ovens there but the prisoners were not taken care of very good.

When the war ended they were not going to bring us home. They started getting us tanks and airplanes Because they were going to fly right over to Japan and we were going to jump out with guns and everything. You know that didn't set real good. By that time they had dropped the pill (atomic bomb) and they held us up. So then we stayed over there and then we came back home.

Let me tell you something. They gave me some kind of medicine a while back—like a year or two years ago. It made me have dreams. Man, I'll tell you what…I was fighting the war all over again. I was waking up in bed and hollering and goddamn, what a mess. I called that doctor and I said, "I ain't taking any more of them." He said, "What's the matter?" I said, "I'm having dreams about the war and every other goddamn thing." It was a no good deal.

If I had it to do over again, I would have still signed up with the 101st.

> *"Boy, we ate some of the best beef! I imagine it was Hitler's beef. He had some nice fat steers."*

Didn't Care if you Lived or Died

Bill Watson
Lockridge, IA

101st Airborne Division
Europe

Interview Date:
29 March 2011

Referral:
Max Hollander

I was drafted in 1943. I was in the 907th Field Artillery. While at training Ft. Bragg, my platoon was assigned to the 401st Glider Infantry Regiment of the 101st Airborne Division. Our 75mm howitzers were transported to the battlefield on gliders. When it was time to go overseas, we were shipped to Camp Shanks, New York. After spending two weeks there, we were given a train ride down to the docks. We were put on an old tub. The ship was an old British passenger liner that had sailed the African coast.

The convoy was the biggest of the war. Our ship developed engine trouble in the middle of the Atlantic one night. The rest of the convoy kept going and there we sat. One British corvette stayed behind with us. It was not a good situation to be in. We drifted a day and they finally got the engines running again. We limped back to St. Johns, Newfoundland. We remained in the harbor 30 days until the ship was repaired. We never got off the ship. The ship limped out about ten miles into what was called "Torpedo Junction" on three different occasions and turned back. The fourth time was at low tide and they tore out part of the ship's bottom

haul. An American ship came and picked us up. We returned almost to New York to catch another convoy going over. We were 43 days on the water. I was an airborne sailor!

We landed in Liverpool, England and saw our first evidence of war. The Germans had bombed the docks and bombed the town. We were put on a train. We ended up at a farm which was to be our base. Our barracks were old sheep sheds. They didn't have any shingles so we got wet every time it rained. Finally they moved us all into tents.

Before D-Day, we participated in a practice amphibious landing (Operation Tiger). A beach (Slapton Sands) that looked like Utah Beach was picked out. The Navy had a lot of ships involved in the exercise. A fast German boat, like our PT boat, got in amongst them and sank six of our ships. I don't know how many men were lost but it was a bunch. We went back to doing 20 mile hikes for training.

There weren't enough airplanes available to tow all of us glider riders so the 907th and the 321st Field Artillery rode boats in to Utah Beach on D-Day. Our LST went to Omaha Beach by mistake. Another ship goes by us and this guy with a bullhorn shouts, "You're at the wrong beach!" So we sailed to Utah and went in late morning of June 6th.

Question: Could you see enough of Omaha Beach to tell it wasn't going well?

Oh, yes. There was a lot of smoke and a lot of dead people. We were in the water off Omaha until midmorning.

Question: What were the conditions on Utah when you landed?

It was pretty quiet. There wasn't any German fire hitting the beach. Part of the 907th battery was aboard the *Susan B. Anthony*. She hit a mine and sank. As soon as we unloaded, we started up one of the four causeways that ran inland. We marched quite ways, no one rode. Jeeps pulled the howitzers. We came up to a bridge. The grader ditch was full of gas masks and there is where mine went. We came upon two infantrymen. They told us to be careful. There was a sniper close by they were trying to get.

We got to where we were supposed to be. We set up the battery and started firing. When we laid our gun, we dug a gun pit. Off to the side was an ammunition pit. We had one fire mission where we fired three rounds a minute for 15 minutes. That's what is wrong with my ears. We connected with elements of the 101st that went in by air the first day.

I'd been in France about five days and had a pretty good beard started. From behind me I heard someone say, "Soldier, you will shave." I turned around and said, "Yes, Sir!" It was the two star general in command of the artillery, Tony McAuliffe, giving me that order. We stayed in France for about 30 days before returning to England.

Question: What was it like to suddenly be thrust into enemy territory?

It wasn't nice. There were a lot of dead. I sat down on a dead German to eat the first hot food I had after getting there. He didn't smell too good but I wanted to sit down. We carried food rations for three days and the jeeps carried some, but it was all

"I sat down on a dead German to eat the first hot food I had after getting there. He didn't smell too good but I wanted to sit down."

of a week before we ate our first hot food. The first general killed was from the 101st. His glider hit a ditch and plowed into a hedgerow. I saw that many of the men riding the gliders were just slaughtered. Those gliders carried 15 men and maybe two of them would be alive. That's when I decided to go to jump school.

I went to a jump school in England and did my five qualifying jumps. But I still rode a glider into Holland on Market Garden. We took a 105mm howitzer in on our glider. We had six of those in our company battery. It was a load for the glider. There was bad weather and we didn't get there for six days after the paratroopers went in. They were suffering for artillery and glad to see us.

Question: Can you tell us about "Hell's Highway"?

We had a certain section to hold. The artillery was set up on one of the road. A British truck column was traveling down the road when we arrived. All at once they stopped, dismounted, and got their tea pots out. My sergeant had taken his backpack off and said, "Guard this, Watson." One of the British Guardsman came walking up to help himself to the carton of Camels sitting on top of the backpack. I told him, "You'd better get out of here." I would have shot the son of a bitch. I really would have, because that's what I thought of them. If they hadn't stopped for tea and went on like they have, it wouldn't have been so bad.

The Germans cut the road one night within 100 feet of us. Word was passed down to not do anything but lay quiet. There weren't enough of us to handle that bunch of Germans. There were trucks burning. You could see the Germans in the fire light. We got orders the next morning to turn the guns completely around to shoot the opposite direction. What's that tell you? All we were trying to hold was the road corridor. There were Germans on all sides of us.

Later we were in a low area of Holland called the "Island". The Germans were across the river on high ground. There could be no movement during the daytime. If you moved, you got shot with artillery, a machine gun, or something. We stayed in the basement of an abandoned house. We weren't firing our howitzers at this time in the battle. Our infantry would go back and forth across the river to get prisoners. They had a way of doing it. When they'd come back across the river, our side would fire machine guns and bazookas over the top of them to provide screening cover.

Question: Where you involved in any way when the 101st rescued the British paratroopers from across the river?

No, we didn't know anything about. I think we were backing up another outfit at the time. We were in Holland around 70 days. We went back to France after Holland for R&R and get to replacements.

Within 30 days, we were loaded back in trucks heading towards Bastogne. We didn't have anything for winter gear, no overshoes, no gloves, and half of us without overcoats. It got down to 10 below at times. We didn't have much for weapons either as the rifles and artillery pieces had been turned in to Ordinance. We had about eight hours to get everything back. A lot of those infantry boys had nothing but a stick. When we got up near the front, we took the guns and ammo off the guys coming out. That's how we got resupplied. It was a cold ride up that night in the back of those open trucks. We had no idea what we were getting into. All we knew was there had been a German break through.

Question: How soon did you realize the Germans had you surrounded?

The next night after we got into Bastogne the Germans shot up and captured what was left of the Medical Company. They were set up on the southwestern side of Bastogne. We knew we were surrounded then. It was that quick. We were set up a short ways north near Foy. There was a barn and house. The captian was bunking in the house. I was on the gun from then on. I worked up from a number six position to number one. That meant I got to pull the cord to fire it. The number six man handled the powder and set the fuse.

Question: How did you move up from a number six to a number one position?

When we were Normandy, we had a cease fire order. One guy by mistake set the fuse to zero

rather than turning it to safe. The next time we fired, we had a point blank air burst that about wiped out two gun sections. We fired over 1000 rounds at Bastogne.

Question: Did you ever shoot at a Panzer with your 105?

No. At Bastogne another outfit that had previously been with the 82nd was with us. They got a tank with their 75mm. They fired some type of special round that burnt through the tank and kept on a going. As far as I know, we never shot at anything mechanized, only ground forces. When the siege was broken, we were down to one armor piercing round and one high explosive. Normally we could not see the German troops we were shooting at. We had a forward artillery observer over the hill spotting for us. With those 105s, we could shoot a full circle around Bastogne if needed. They had an effective range of 10 miles.

"When the tree burst came in, you got down in a foxhole and said a prayer."

Question: Did you ever coordinate time on target with other guns?

Yes. You're making me think about a lot of stuff I've forgotten about. I've tried to forget some of this. We had a lot of guys lose fingers and toes from frostbite. All we had to crawl into for protection from the cold was a frozen hole in the ground. The guys that really suffered were those that spent the night lying in the snow along a fence line on outpost duty. I remember drinking water out of a stream with a dead German lying in it.

Foy changed hands a couple of times in the war. We were far enough back that we didn't have to move when that happened. We were hit with a lot of German artillery tree bursts. We were in evergreen forests some of the time, but it was the worst when a shell burst hit the top of a tall oak. There'd be limbs flying everywhere. We'd jump in a foxhole unless we were on a fire mission. Then we would stay right where we were at, manning the gun. A foxhole didn't do you all that much good with tree bursts anyway. You got to the point you didn't care if you lived or died. You got that miserable. When the tree burst came in, you got down in a foxhole and said a prayer. I slept on a pile of ammo one night. I was so damn tired I didn't care.

Question: Was there ever a point when you thought the Germans would win the battle?

No, there was never a moment when we thought Bastogne might fall. I think the mentality was that we're here, and we're going to take it. One plane would bomb Bastogne every night. When we started pushing back the Bulge, we were told that we could rest once we took a certain town. That was our motivation each day.

When we were finally pulled out of Belgium, we were sent back to France. We were assigned to a quieter section of the front in the Alsace region. Later we were sent to the Ruhr River valley. My gun shot 20 shells full of surrender leaflets into Dusseldorf. Near the end of the war the 101st was in the Bavarian region of southern Germany. By then, we were fighting 12 year old German kids. We came across one of Dachau sub camps called Landsberg at the end of April. The town people were ordered to bury the bodies. We knew what we were fighting for after seeing that. I was sent to Liezen, Austria, rather than to Hitler's mountain retreat at Berchtesgaden.

The Russians were across the river when the war ended. I had to stand guard duty. The Russians would come over and try to steal women in the middle of the night. I had a very poor opinion of the Russians.

From the time I left the states until I got back, I was lost. All I ever saw was what was right out in front of me. I usually won't talk about the war.

Emma May Watson: This is the first time anyone has ever sat down and really asked Bill about the war. We went to a reunion of the 101st. I was sitting at a table by myself. All the women I knew were hosting the reunion and were busy working. Bill Guarnere invited me over to his table. His wife gave Bill a funny look but it didn't bother him a bit. I had a lot of respect for Bill and he was really a nice guy.

Question: Bill, did you ever meet Dick Winters?

I saw him some but never really met him. This was when we were in combat. We supported all the line companies in the division with artillery but we helped the 506th Regiment the most. That's who Winters and Guarnere were with. I could have reached out and touched General Eisenhower in England before the invasion. The division was

doing a training jump and Eisenhower walked right by our field artillery.

I carried an M-1 Garand throughout the war. My rank was private first class, although I turned down a promotion to corporal. I received a good conduct medal and a bronze star.

My brother Sherman was a Marine paratrooper until they were disbanded. Then he was transferred to the newly formed 5th Marine Division. As a sergeant, he led the first patrol up to the top of Mt. Surabachi on Iwo Jima.

MISFIT

Sikke Temple
Washington, IA

Army
Pacific

Interview Date:
5 April 2011

Referral:
Dr. Jim Harris

I was drafted in February of '44. I was processed through Des Moines and went to Camp McCain in Mississippi for basic training. It was damp and cold and we all got sick. One of the boys got spinal meningitis. He survived but we were quarantined for quite a while. I couldn't hit the broad side of a barn with the M-1. Once you qualified, you had to go to the target pits. No one liked that job. For some reason, I never could qualify with a Garand.

I was in the 87th Infantry Division, the Golden Acorn division for six months. Wayne Testeroot from West Chester was in the 87th. He and I were inducted at the same time. Harry Whitacre and Easy Jones were in the 87th. I played a coronet in the band. I never expected to be doing that in the Army. Then I went over into a college engineering program. They sent me to Clemson University. Kenneth Cuddeback, was at Clemson, but I didn't know it until afterwards. Then I went up to Boston University, but I wasn't there very long.

Then I got in the Army Air Corps. I had always wanted to be a pilot. I had one foot in the door of Naval ROTC for pilot training while in Ames

before I was drafted. The Air Corps sent me to Greensboro, North Carolina. I had to retake basic training every time I turned around. Next I was sent up to Syracuse University for the Air Corps preflight program. I had one flying lesson in a Piper Cub. They hadn't taught me anything about flying. It was a case of learning by doing. There was bad air turbulence the day I went up and I got air sick. The fight instructor had me land the plane and I about broke the landing gear off. The Air Corps casualties in the European Theater had dwindled by then, so the Syracuse program was cancelled. For a while, they were losing 70-80% of their planes. Charles Lemley was a classmate of mine. He survived his time as a tail gunner over Europe.

This time I was sent to the 78th Infantry at Camp Pickett in Virginia. We were getting ready to go overseas. They had us doing forced marches. At the end of the march, everybody was really dragging, moaning and groaning. It made me appreciate the Air Corps more. The Air Corps always sang when they marched. So do you know what happened? Some darn fool started singing the Air Force song.

They had my name, rank, and serial number so fast you wouldn't have believed it. The next morning I stood before the company commander and he was still boiling mad. I got a lot of guard and KP duty out of that. In fact, he was so upset that when they went overseas he didn't take me. I got quite a break.

I didn't realize it until afterwards, but both of those infantry divisions went into the Battle of the Bulge as replacements. That was about as close to suicide as you could get. I corresponded through the mail with one of the fellows I met in the 87th. I could follow their progress to England, through France and into Belgium. He wrote and told me about the saxophone player getting shot in the head. Then the letters quit coming. I've often wondered what happened to him, other times I am kind of glad I didn't know.

Then I was sent to the combat engineers. At least we had trucks so we didn't have to walk as much. The government was about bankrupt by then so they had a big bond tour. I was in transportation so I was assigned to that for a while. After the bond tour ended, I went home on furlough. When I returned to base, the first sergeant asked me if I would like to go to mechanics or blacksmith school. I chose blacksmith school and was sent to Ft. Kearny, Nebraska. It was good duty but it didn't last very long.

Question: Sometime during all this, didn't you get married?

That was when I was in the combat engineers. Beulah came out but she went back home when I went overseas.

Then I had the chance to go to officer's training school at Ft. Belvedere. My buddy Captain Flynn told me, "Sikke, we're going overseas and I knew you wanted to go so I threw your application in the wastebasket." We loaded all our equipment on a train and went to Camp Stoneman near San Francisco. We boarded a ship for a rough ride to the west side of the Philippines, in the Lingayen Gulf. It was late enough in the war that the ship didn't zigzag much. I got really seasick going over. For a couple of days, I couldn't even move. The war ended while we were in the Philippines.

> *"Then the letters quit coming. I've often wondered what happened to him, other times I am kind of glad I didn't know."*

Supposedly, Bob Hope was there when they announced the war had ended. There was a USO show up in the woods but it started raining so hard that I did not attend. Manila was not a nice place. The city had been destroyed in the war.

Question: There were around 50,000 Japanese troops still fighting in the Philippines when the war ended. Did you see any of them when they surrendered?

I saw one, the general they called the "Tiger of Bataan." They hung that son-of-a-gun on the yardarm. I was at a warehouse with a buddy picking up supplies when he was brought by as a prisoner in an open personnel carrier. The guys standing around cussed the Tiger of Bataan in Japanese and he cussed them back in English.

We constructed some warehouses and did some other engineering projects. I drove a truck most of the time. I was kind of a misfit and didn't get along. They'd usually give me a job where I could be off by myself. I drove a jeep until the officer I was driving got tired of my slow driving. He got all upset one day and told me, "Sike, let's get a-going." So I put the pedal to the floor. I cured him! The next day I wasn't even a jeep driver anymore.

We had good food in the combat engineers. Our guys would steal anything not nailed down and hide it in the trucks. We loaded all our equipment and anything else we could steal on an LSM to go to Japan. An LSM is a smaller vessel than an LST and barely seaworthy. We got caught in the tail end of a typhoon. It was bad. We lacked three degrees of capsizing. When we unloaded in the surf on the coast of Japan, the water was too deep. The first truck and trailer floated off. I was next in line but they stopped me.

I was in Kobe, Japan, for a short time. We had firebombed that city. Everything was destroyed. Buildings had melted down from the intense heat. I was told that the only place the people survived was in the open cemetery. We used bulldozers and a road grader to clean up the roads there. The Japanese people acted pretty subdued.

I had a cousin named Bill Brewer from

Washington who was in the Navy. I believe he was an ensign aboard a destroyer in the North Atlantic. He became a minister.

Cultivating corn is a boring job. I used to think a lot about the war while cultivating. The more I study back on the war, the more depressed I get. My conclusion is that we have not learned a thing. The only way we'll stop wars is when people refuse to fight.

TRIBUTE

To my father (Kenneth Cuddeback), and to all of the other men and women who have put on the uniform and defended our nation's freedom over the years, I say a heartfelt thank you.

Jim Cuddeback
Washington, IA

Almost Hopeless

Donald Dayton
Washington, IA

USS *Lexington*
Pacific

Interview Date:
12 April 2011

Referral:
Nicole (Dayton) McVicker

I grew up in Kalona and enlisted at age 17 right out of high school. We had 24 in our high school class and three or four of the boys were eighteen and got drafted the next day after graduation. So I decided to go ahead and enlist as I would be drafted soon away. That was in 1943. I was in the Navy for two and a half years, got out for a year, then enlisted in the Coast Guard for a couple of years.

I was such a kid that the farthest I'd ever been away from home was to Oskaloosa for a state music contest. So being in the Navy was quite an experience for me. I was in a lot of different places in a shorter time than most. I did boot camp in Farragut, Idaho. From there I went to Memphis, Tennessee, for radio aviation training. Dean Kraft from Wellman was there but he flunked out. I don't know what happened to him after that. Then I was sent to Hollywood, Florida, for aerial gunnery school. I joined my TBF Avenger torpedo bomber crew in Miami. But my pilot decided he wanted to be a night fighter pilot so that left me in the pool of available crew members. From Miami I went to Norfolk, Virginia. Then I was transferred to Quonset Point Naval Station in Rhode Island. From there, it was on to Martha's Vineyard where I worked on equipment. A pilot needed a radioman so I joined his crew in an Avenger. The Avenger

was the largest single prop plane built during the war.

We had our first flight the next day. I don't know what mechanical problem our plane had for certain but the engine just sputtered, caught on fire, and quit. We were flying at only 1700 feet. With the glide angle of an Avenger only 1:1, I knew we were going to be non-airborne very soon. My pilot was a good one and was able to keep the crippled plane level as we descended. He made the mistake of inflating his Mae West (life preserver) while still in his flight harness. That about choked him. The gunner and I were able to get it unbuckled after impact.

Question: Did you sustain any injuries in the crash?

I didn't have any physical injuries but had some emotional ones. A few of months later I went to sickbay with a painful rash around my waist and the flight surgeon asked me if I had suffered any recent emotional trauma. I answered, "Why yes, I have." I was diagnosed with having shingles.

My plane stayed afloat for one minute. Our training kicked in. I'm sure glad I paid attention during training. We got the pilot out and the three of us in a rubber life raft. We were in it for an hour. They told us under the weather conditions we were in that 20 minutes was the maximum that a person could be active and mobile. We went down on December 26, 1944. The air temperature was zero. You know, the eastern United States is a terrible place to live in the winter. The damp cold is worse than what we have here in Iowa.

We were the tail end of the squadron flight. None of the other planes could have seen us go down. Because we went down in mere seconds, there had been no time to use the radio. I knew it was almost hopeless because we weren't getting any closer to land. The tide was taking us out to sea. We were using these plastic paddles and I think that's what kept us alive, the physical movement. We were wearing heavy leather wool lined flight gear and when that gets filled with water it's like lead weight. Getting into a life raft in those conditions…. I don't know how we did it. Hypothermia set in. We were almost completely immobile when the Navy crash boat pulled us in. We did see a PBY float plane and a Coast Guard Widgeon flying around. The waves were 15 to 20 feet. It was a rough sea. Those float planes would have probably crashed trying to land. They were willing to do it but the Navy crash boat got there. They kept us a couple of three days in sick bay for observation.

Question: How long was it before you felt warm again?

You know, I'm never warm. Just ask my wife. Cold bothers me. There was a big write up in the local Martha's Vineyard paper about our rescue. I have a copy of it. The only witnesses to the crash were five kids ranging in age of 11 to 14. The oldest immediately ran to a phone and called the air base, notifying the Operations Officer of the crash. Then he ran and found his father and told him of the crash. His father drove to a sand dune and with the aid of binoculars sighted the craft and noted its approximate location. Then he placed the second call to the air base. Within three minutes of the first call, a search plane was airborne. Other rescue planes and vessels were notified and converged on the area of the crash. That's how were we rescued.

After that I was sent to Groton, Connecticut, then to Bangor, Maine, and back to Groton. I ended up in Alamogordo Air Station in California.

"Hypothermia set in. We were almost completely immobile when the Navy crash boat pulled us in."

From there it was across the Pacific to Ford Island at Pearl Harbor and then to Mali, Hawaii. From there I was sent to Saipan. It was that time that our plane was switched over from a torpedo oriented bomber to a regular bomber. By that time in the war the Japanese fleet had been almost totally annihilated and there was practically nothing left afloat to use a torpedo on. So we trained in what is called glide bombing with rockets and 250 pound bombs. We made attacks on about half a dozen small islands you've never heard of in the Marianna chain. I remember that one of them was named Rota. These were Japanese held islands that had no strategic value and were simply bypassed. There'd be some 20mm anti-aircraft guns on the islands and rifle fire shot at us. Nothing big in the way of anti-aircraft guns. We were bombing them for practice. We did not lose any planes. In two weeks the war was over.

A carrier appeared and we went aboard that and went to Japan. They'd send us ashore on Japan and we would help clean up debris to help them start rebuilding their country. The B-29's had been annihilating Japan long before the atomic bombs were dropped. We went ashore in Kobe and it had been just flattened. There was a big air base on Tinian which was close to Saipan where we were stationed. We'd see wave after wave of B-29's heading for Japan flying day and night twenty-four hours a day. The war couldn't have lasted much longer even if we hadn't dropped the atomic bombs.

Sometimes we'd go ashore by ship and other times by plane. We were stationed on the carrier the USS *Lexington*.

Question: What was it like landing on a carrier?

Frightening. We did it from September to December when I had enough points to go home. Both the landings and the take offs were dangerous things. The planes would cut power to zero when landing on the deck and there were barriers that would stop the plane if the cable hook missed.

I saw a lot of the results from the kamikazes attacks. I saw the carrier, the USS *Franklin*, from the air. It had a hole in its flight deck the size of this house from a kamikaze. I was told that the *Franklin* was about 50 miles off the coast of Japan when it was hit.

Our crew stayed together throughout the war. Our gunner was from Indianapolis and I looked him up while visiting the city in 1964. You can't blame someone today for something that happened seventy years ago. I have never purchased a Japanese vehicle or probably ever will. I suppose the war has something to do with that. It seems to me that every fifteen to twenty years we have another war. We get over with one and everything is fine for a while and then fifteen to twenty years later we have another war. I'm not sure there's any way to avoid it. I don't know if there is an answer.

Ethel and I were married during the war. Ten of the sixteen million men serving were discharged when the war ended. The biggest problem was trying to find a place to live. We lived in cock roach infested dumps. I went to school at the Milwaukee College of Engineering to learn heating and cooling to get a job at Amana Refrigeration. I had a good job but no place to live. We finally found a house in North English where we shared the upstairs with two other families. There was only one bathroom and we cooked on a hotplate.

One day I saw an ad in the *Des Moines Register* by the Coast Guard wanting men for search and rescue. I knew something about that so I enlisted for a couple of the most interesting years of my life. The Coast Guard's mission was to save lives and the Navy had trained us to only destroy. I was stationed in New York City and we covered the coastline from North Carolina up to Greenland. Much of the time I was flying in converted B-17s. We flew international ice patrol. They were wonderful planes. At that time, the Coast Guard was part of the Treasury Department. We would fly over the remote mountain areas of the eastern seaboard in the winter looking for roofs devoid of snow and note their location. The Treasury would then send in their revenuers to look for moonshine stills.

After leaving the Coast Guard we bought a little grocery store in Kinross and ran it for fourteen months. I'd hire out as a day laborer to farmers and worked as a janitor at the school to supplement our income. After selling the store, I worked for a local tea company chain. Ethel had gone to

beauty school when I was in the Coast Guard, and I ended up going to cosmetology school as well. We operated a beauty salon in Washington for 21 years and then opened a cosmetology school in Burlington.

My brother John spent six years in the Navy. He enlisted before the war started. He spent all most all his time at sea in the Pacific. He was on a mine sweeper, a light cruiser, and a carrier escort. He could tell you some stories if he were still alive. He was a water tender in the engine room. He died of lung cancer at age 49 from all the asbestos in the engine rooms. He's buried at West Chester.

TRIBUTE

It has been a pleasure to work with Washington County's Veterans, which I call "my Veterans" as their County Veterans Service Officer. I have never had such a rewarding job and I hope that they all consider me a friend as I do them. Thanks to ALL of them and their families for their sacrifice.

*Sue Rich
Washington, IA*

THE SIZE OF A DOT

Wayne Wasson
Wellman, IA

USS *Hugh W. Hadley*
Pacific

Interview Date:
21 April 2011

Referral:
Jack Seward & Doug Ulin

I spent 12 weeks in boot camp in Farragut, Idaho. That place was a creation sitting next to hell. Oh, it was hot! I was sent to my ship right away, straight out of boot camp. I caught my ship, a newly built destroyer named the USS *Hugh W. Hadley*, in San Pedro, California. We joined Bull Halsey's 5th Fleet in the Pacific.

I was a deck hand and a second gunner's mate. We all had battle stations assigned to us except for the colored guys because they didn't trust them. The coloreds were mainly cooks. My battle station was manning a twin five (inch gun) on the fantail. We were a man short one time so they gave us a colored guy. He took off when the action got a little rough. It was a good thing he didn't go below deck because he would have been killed (by a kamikaze) if he did. Our five inch gun had a shooting radius of eleven mile. I was a loader. I manned a quad 40mm for a while but my eardrums couldn't take the noise. Those 40mm's would rattle your brains. I was in for the duration of the war. I had to sign up for two years active duty with another two years as active reserve subject to being called up.

Our first real action was when bogies were coming in directly for us was at Okinawa. Prior to that, we had sailed past Japanese held islands where the Army and Marines were fighting. Iwo Jima was one of the islands. Two brothers from Wellman, Verne and Junior Goodwin were Marines fighting on Iwo. Neither knew that the other was there. They both survived the battle although Junior got hit in the neck. We went by Iwo at night so we really couldn't see anything. We rarely ever saw land while in the Pacific.

April 1st was D-Day at Okinawa. I was aboard the *Hadley* off Okinawa. We were on the outer ring of the fleet on radar picket duty. The Japanese planes would try to bomb us first. If they missed with the bomb, they'd try to crash into us. The Japanese Betty's would come in low at night, skimming the wave tops and our radar couldn't pick them up. They'd usually attack at night. Our radar could only pick them up when they were a ways off when they came in low. A kamikaze came in low one night trying to get us but he didn't. Another night we shot down our own plane. We didn't know it for six weeks and only then because the co-pilot bailed out and survived. Someone else picked him up. There was another pilot we rescued when his Corsair hit the water. He stayed on board with us for three weeks. He told us that the ocean water appeared black at night except where the ship propellers made it phosphorous in color. He said it shone like a flashlight. It was easy to follow the bright phosphorous trail straight to a ship and that's how the Japanese were finding us. Our ship's captain should have been aware of that. We should have drifted at night. We hated cloudless, moonlighted nights because the Japanese could spot us easier. We'd be at general quarters all night. It'd be like daylight on the ocean. The Japanese sunk one of our fleet's ships every night off Okinawa for 36 days straight. There were some daylight attacks, but not too many.

Question: How'd you see the planes at night to shoot at them?

The five inch guns were radar controlled. About all we had to do was load them. We were knocking down planes we could not see at night. We shot down 23 planes and three hit the ship. After we got attacked, there was enough light you could see the chin straps and the gold teeth of the Jap pilots strafing us.

The *Hadley* was hit on May 11th, 1945, by three kamikaze planes. We had been at general quarters all night. I had just finished breakfast and was taking my shoes off to sleep when they said to man your battle stations. The first kamikaze that hit us came in low with the sun to its back. That's why he wasn't spotted. It struck mid-ship, knocking both engine rooms out. The ship didn't shake when hit. It dropped like a person's knees buckling. Another kamikaze blew off two of the five inch turret guns on a different part of the ship. The open quad 40mm next to us was destroyed. Our sister ship next to us, the USS *Evans*, took five kamikazes to her deck. It didn't sink her either. Destroyers are hard ships to sink unless the tail gets busted out. All the compartments had water tight hatches. Half the compartments could be flooded and the destroyer would still float. We circled around the *Evans* trying to protect her until we were hit. There were over 100 Japanese planes attacking our two

destroyers. That was the record high for the war for just two ships. They looked like a bunch of ducks out there, that's how thick they were. We shot some of them down right beside us with the 40mm, right before they could make contact with the ship. Nearly all the ammunition aboard ship was shot up during the 105 minute attack.

When the abandon ship order went out over the loud speaker, you didn't have to jump off the ship into the water. You could simply step off into it. They didn't have to tell me twice. I was ready to get off that ship, the quicker the better. I stayed with my five inch gun until the abandon ship order was issued. We were already wearing our life jackets, which was the normal operating procedure. We spent 2 ½ hours in the water before being picked up. When you're out there bobbing around in the vast ocean, you felt pretty small, about the size of a dot.

> "The Japanese sunk one of our fleet's ships every night off Okinawa for 36 days straight."

It took the Marine Corsairs almost two hours to get to us to help. They'd get right on top of the Jap planes and run them right into the water. That takes some guts and good flying! I was in the water when I saw that. We were credited with shooting down 25 Jap planes. Our sister destroyer shot down 18. The Corsairs got the rest.

Question: Were you worried about sharks when in the water?

No, you don't have to worry about sharks where bombs are going off. They are a long ways away. The concussion scares them off. Some of the older sailors stayed aboard ship. Our destroyer was heavily damaged but did not sink. We were picked up by a PA, which was the same as a troop transport. Later we were transferred to a small aircraft carrier.

We lost 31 guys. The boilers blew in the engine room. Those men literally got cooked. The doctor said they would have never known what hit them. It was ten days to two weeks before we pulled their bodies out. They'd been in water all that time. When we hooked on to the bodies to pull them out, we pulled them apart. The bodies had to be put in CI cans for burial at sea. Usually they slip a body out from under a flag with two 50 pound projectiles attached for burial at sea. I only saw that done one time, however.

Comment: Experiencing a kamikaze attack had to be pretty scary.

I didn't let myself think about being scared. All you thought about was doing your job, loading those guns as fast as you could. Those five inchers could fire as fast as we could load them. Each bag of powder weighed 28 pounds and the shell weighed 54 pounds. The shells were either set to explode on impact or on timed fuses. We never even took the muzzle coverings off the ends of the gun barrels. We just shot them off.

Our ship would almost always be moving so we wouldn't be a sitting duck. One time, a Jap sub launched a torpedo at the keel of our destroyer. The lookouts on the fantail were slow in spotting its wake. Our captain attempted to evade the torpedo but it takes a long time to turn a ship that big. The torpedo passed underneath the midsection of the ship without exploding. It had been set to run too deep. We figured the Japs had mistaken us for a cruiser which ran much lower in the water.

The second ship I was stationed on was a troop transport. We sailed to China to pick up troops and mostly American civilians and brought them back stateside. It was a slow boat to China. We had 4500 hundred passengers including kids and babies.

The atomic bombs were a bad deal but they saved a lot of lives. They also took a lot of lives.

Question: Wayne, did you ever run into anyone from back home?

Yes I did. I met Porky Milan from West Chester on Treasure Island. That would be James Milan's dad. Treasure Island sits in the San Francisco Bay. I ate Thanksgiving dinner on Treasure Island. The turkeys served were from Wellman, Iowa. I told the guys that bird came from my hometown. I also ran into my cousin, Leonard Wasson in San Francisco.

David Huber was lost on a transport ship going over early in the war. Leonard Wasson was on the carrier *Yorktown*. Leonard's brother, Jasper Wasson, was on another carrier. He lived down in Hungry Hollow near Brighton.

I did not have any trouble readjusting to civilian life. The Navy taught me discipline but I was ready to get out. I became a commercial logger and tree trimmer.

THE HEROES ARE STILL OVER THERE

Mike Orris
Washington, IA

Navy LST
Pacific

Interview Date:
23 April 2011

Referral:
Tina Lewis Montz & Wendell Guy

My twin brother and I were up in the hay mow pitching loose hay one night in July of '44. There was dust and hay chaff down our necks. We looked at each other and decided there must be an easier way to make a living so we threw down our pitch forks and enlisted in the Navy. We were right out of high school and only 17 so we needed our dad's signature but he wouldn't sign because he had been wounded a couple of times in World War One. He didn't want us to go but we went anyway

We had boot camp at Great Lakes. A guy wanted to know if we could swim and we said no, we didn't know how to swim, all we'd done is work on the farm. So he said to jump in the training pool and I went about from me to you and he said I passed (chuckle). That's how we got in. Right afterwards, he said, "I'm an expert swimmer an' I'll live about 20 to 25 minutes longer than you out in the middle of the ocean." I thought that was pretty well put because it was true. We were at Great Lakes about two months I think and then they shipped us to Fort Paris, Florida. It's a little island off of Florida. We had a little bit a training, very little, and they

asked us where we wanted to serve. I wanted to go overseas. I could get $5 more pay a month than the $27 was getting then. That's more than I got working on the farm $.50 a day! That was good pay in those days.

Question: Did you farm with horses back then?
Oh yes, with a team and wagon. We'd get up every morning and milk those 5 cows then go to the field all day. It was hard work, too. We did a lot of thrashing, pitching bundles, and shucking open pollinated corn in the snow. Yes, the good old days.

Well, we rode a tube train from Fort Paris, Florida, to San Diego. It took us six days and we had to be in our dress uniform. We had the windows clear up and it was hotter than Sam Hill and the smoke and soot came in when we went through the tunnels and we had to throw our uniforms away. We couldn't get them clean so they is issued us new ones.

We sailed to Hawaii. We were there just a little while before being shipped on to the Philippines and from there we went to Iwo Jima. We weren't

257

there too long and bunch of us got orders to head for Okinawa before that one war was over. We didn't know what all was going on. There were 320 ships in the convoy.

Question: What kind of ship were you on?

Well I was on four different ones. The first was an LCI, then an APA, and then a cargo ship. While we were unloading the Marines at Okinawa, something happened to the top of our ship and we couldn't bring them in any more so I volunteered to get on an LST. The rest of the time I took Marines in to the shore. Okinawa was different than the rest of the island landings. We shelled the beach for two days and two nights and wasted all those shells because there was no Japanese along the shores. None. They were up in the hills. The Marines and Army infantry went in about two miles before they hit any resistance. I helped take in about five loads of Marines. The LST carried right at 300 troops. Oh, we had them packed in.

Comment: So you'd basically deliver them to the shore, drop the ramp, and off they'd go.

Off they'd go. The invasion started April 1st, 1945, Easter Sunday. Half way through the landings, we went got wounded coming back and we took them to mostly to the hospital ships. That was a mess. They couldn't handle them all so we put some of the wounded on APAs. They were taken mostly to Guam which had a pretty good hospital.

Question: When you were off Iwo Jima was the battle still going on?

Oh yes. We weren't close enough to really see the fighting. The bigger ships were closer than we were. Of course, the Japanese always wanted to hit a battle ship or air carrier or a hospital ship. That's the three they picked on. They wouldn't pick on our little ship.

Question: Kamikazes?

Yes, kamikazes…well, not always, sometimes bombs. My best buddy from Cotter, John (Jack) Duncan, was on the USS *Franklin* at Okinawa and we were right beside it. I got a photo of it. People will tell you it was kamikaze that hit it but it was not. Two bombs hit the ship and killed half the crew. There were 3700 on board and I think it

killed 1500–1600 sailors. The *Franklin* was hit in the middle of the ship, but we saved it. A couple of tug boats got along side it and took it to Guam. It was repaired and back it came.

I didn't even know my buddy was on the *Franklin* at the time. They don't tell you all that. I didn't know that my brother was at Iwo Jima. He was killed there and I didn't even know he was there. Yep, it was kind of sad.

Question: Your brother was a Marine on Iwo?

Yes. A guy from the Marines that was a buddy of his…this fellow that was in the Marines with my brother has a photo, we think it's, he thinks it's my brother but we can't prove it. This fellow sent that photo to me. He worked with me up at the Vets hospital and he brought it up to me. I think this happened when he found out my name was Orris. If the photo isn't of my brother then it's his twin that sure looks like him. See right here, they'd shot him in the back. He'd taken four back before he got shot. But this guy lived through it and he's the one that told me about it.

"I always said that I'd rather take a chance getting killed at sea than in a fox hole."

Question: But this wasn't your twin brother?

No, this was my older brother, Rex. He was 19. His grave is on Iwo Jima. Here's a photo of me at his grave side. That's what I looked like at age 17. After the war was over I got permission to fly from Guam and visit his grave before I came back you home. They put me on a B-29 cargo plane and flew me over to Iwo. I didn't know it was cold up there and gee I 'bout froze to death! I just had on my blue jeans and a short sleeve shirt. The only item in the cargo hold was a bunch of parachutes which I used to cover myself to try to stay warm.

All those graves have been moved to Hawaii now from Iwo Jima. My wife and I've been out three or four times visit his grave. Supposedly all the American bodies have been moved from Iwo Jima but when you're dead, you're dead. It don't make any difference. I always said that I'd rather take a chance getting killed at sea than in a fox hole.

Question: Was Rex in the 5th Marines?

Yes, the 5th Marines Division. That Iwo was a mess. It was bad. Only one half as many got killed there as on Okinawa but still—a death's a death. I know exactly what got killed, I have it written down here, 19,375 were killed at Okinawa and 67,404 wounded. Okinawa was by far the bloodiest battle in the Pacific. It was a bad one. There were 2500 kamikaze planes destroyed in Okinawa, that's quite a few. They damaged 400 Navy ships.

Question: Did you witness at the kamikaze attacks?

Oh, I saw a couple of them coming down. It was early morning, on March 19th, before the invasion. We were in a convoy going from Iwo to Okinawa. We weren't part of the 5th fleet. We were just in the Navy. I saw these five planes approaching. I was on duty so I sent message down to our captain that there were five planes that don't look like American. He said, "Mike, those are just out guys out on maneuver." I replied, "I don't think so." I signaled to another ship ahead of us, a big destroyer, and they wouldn't signal back or anything. Sure enough, that's the attack that got the USS *Franklin* that my best buddy was on. These planes were not kamikazes. They dropped bombs which hit the *Franklin* right in the middle.

It took until June 30th, three solid months before Okinawa was finally secured. But there were tons of Jap soldiers still there, hundreds of them up in the hills. Years afterwards they still were living there. They were something else. You go over to Japan or Hawaii right now and walk down the street. The Japanese people will get five abreast and they won't let you through. They make you go out on the street. That's how ornery they still are. Well, I should get over it but I just haven't.

Donna Orris: I had a Japanese (American) roommate in nurse's training while he was in the Navy. My mother about died when she learned who I was rooming with. Her parents were sent to a concentration (internment) camp because they were Japanese and she went out to be with them. I never saw her after that but I would hear from her a couple of times a year. She could speak pretty good English.

Question: What did she say about the war? She offer any opinions?

Well, no, not really. She was born and raised in America. She was rooting for us.

Mike: I guess you can't hold it against these people now in Japan what their ancestors did but

I wonder if it would happen again what they'd do. I'm just saying.

A person forced to walk around five of them abreast on the sidewalk would be enough to make me mad today. One time over in Hawaii I decided I wasn't putting up with this anymore and shoved my way through them. Of course, they are smaller in stature and I went right through them. They turned around and shook their finger at me. Now the Japanese own 82% of Hawaii. They lost the war but won the island.

I got my initials on Mt. Suribachi on Iwo Jima. I was there visiting my brother's grave and the guy in charge of that island was a Colonel Morris from Ainsworth. He knew who I was of course after we visited and he took me up there to see Suribachi after I visited the grave. I was riding with him and he said, "Why don't you take this rock and scratch your initial down here at the base" and I did. I don't know if it'd still be there or not (chuckle). I'd like to go back and see it just to know.

Question: Did you climb up on top of Mt. Suribachi?

No. Well, we were right up there, on top, but I put my initials at the base of the mountain. There was nothing at the summit but rock when I was there. My brother was where they couldn't wear or have any guns. He was on a hospital ship. He was the medical corps. And they weren't allowed any guns and that's the reason they picked on them. They knew they didn't have any protection. First thing the Japs would do was bomb a hospital ship because they knew it couldn't shoot back. They were ornery.

After Okinawa we sailed back to Philippines for a little while and from there went to Guam. We were there two weeks. That's when I got permission to fly over to Iwo Jima.

Question: What was the atmosphere like when you heard the news that we dropped the first atomic bomb?

Too bad we didn't do it sooner. I knew that's the only way to get them to surrender.

I've been 12 years volunteering up at the VA hospital in Iowa City. I just love working with the WWII and Korean vets. Now it's just changed so much and it is awful. The Vietnam vets have taken over the place. They got an office there now and they want us to subsidize them on every little thing. There's one guy that I work with and he's getting three pension checks. He's 62 years old, he's able and capable as any one of us of work and he brags about it! I just get tired of listening to them complain. The heroes are still over there. Let's put it that way.

Question: When you think back on your whole WWII experience what what's the first thing you think of when you think back on the war?

Well, invasion of Okinawa, I guess. I admire the ones that went in and fought and saved this country. I think I unloaded guys from the 6th Marine Division. There were 1622 killed from that division on Okinawa.

Question: Where there any Marines that refused to get off your LST?

Well, some of them. Some of them got court marshaled. They just didn't want to get off. I had to take a few back to the troop ship. You shouldn't have joined the Marines if you weren't gonna serve.

Question: Did you ever run into anybody that you knew from back home during your time of service?

Nope. All the ones I really knew got killed.

Interview transcribed by Tina Lewis Montz.

My perspective on recording for future generations what World War II veterans contributed to America is, very unselfishly, I will add, almost beyond understanding. Many gave all they could—their lives. Many are buried on foreign soil. We must not forget them.

Often one question comes to mind—what was on their minds when they were called to serve. Some I have visited with say, "I just did my job, nothing special, just what needed to be done, what everybody did." They came home, put the war behind them, picked up their life and family and moved on. Most never even talked about their in the war with anyone.

In my personal case, after serving in the USAF I didn't talk about it. It was several years before I joined the American Legion. I was later elected to serve as Commander and later asked to be the Honor Guard Captain. I started helping our group do Military Funeral Honors.

Families making future end-of-life planning call me with several question regarding what to do. Several times the wives ask what they should do (should they have military rites at the funeral). In speaking with the family, it is usually another act of being unselfish—not wanting to put anyone on the spot or create any extra work. As I am going out the door, the wife will again ask what she should do. I simply explain our country owes her husband his military honors. I tell her I can't tell her what to do, but hope and pray she allows us to do what should be done.

We are about to lose all of our World War II veterans. We must honor them and to tell the younger generations the true history of what they did for America.

Wendel Guy
Washington, IA

I Considered Myself Very Lucky

Carroll Steinbeck
Rubio, IA

66th Infantry Division
Europe

Interview Date:
26 April 2011

Referral:
Jeff Hildebrand

I was on a trip to Burlington the Sunday Pearl Harbor was bombed so I knew I would going into the service. I was a senior at the Richland high school and enrolled in the University of Iowa that next fall. That would have been in 1942. In December, we got the option of enlisting or being subject to the draft. So a lot of us enlisted in what was called the Enlisted Reserve Corps. That guaranteed us we could finish that year of college. Immediately after finishing the college term in May, I went up to Camp Dodge and was inducted in the Army. My brother Kenneth went at the same time. He had been a senior in college and had four years of ROTC. He went immediately into Officers Training School

They sent the whole group of us from Camp Dodge to Camp Roberts in California for basic training. We trained in heavy weapons. While the seventeen week basic training was going on, they came and gave us written examinations. Those who elected to take the exams and passed were

sent to the University of Wyoming at Laramie. I guess they were trying to make engineers out of us by the subjects they gave us. But anyway, I got a year of schooling in. In April they were short of manpower again and sent our group to Camp Robinson near Little Rock, Arkansas. We were there about a week and assigned to the 66th Infantry Division. We took our final months of training at Fort Rucker, Alabama, before going overseas.

We shipped out of New York on November 15th of '44. We took the northern route which was very, very rough. Everyone got seasick. We landed in England on November 27th, on my birthday. I had just turned 21. We were stationed at Dorchester then along came the Battle of the Bulge. This was a couple of days before Christmas. They had everything laid out for the Christmas dinner, turkeys thawing out and everything. We moved out so fast they left the food sitting on the tables. We went to South Hampton and here's where my luck started. My company was one of the last to leave. We were to board the *Leopoldville* but there were already 2,000 paratroopers on board by mistake. So they had to take those people off. It took quite a while to get those men off and our people didn't start boarding until 2:00 AM. They got 2250 men aboard and the rest of us boarded the *Cheshire*.

It was a nine hour trip for the two troop ships to go the 95 miles across the channel to the port Cherbourg, France. We started around eight in the morning and about 2:30 PM we got a submarine alert. The destroyers escorting us dropped some depth charges and 30 minutes later we got another submarine alert. About dusk a torpedo hit the *Leopoldville*. This happened on Christmas Eve. We were only five miles from Cherbourg. It was said that between 300 and 350 men were killed instantly when the torpedo hit. The ship stayed afloat for some time. They tried to communicate with the people on shore at Cherbourg but for some reason did not have the right radio frequency and could not make contact. So they radioed back to Liverpool and reported that we were in trouble. But things got fouled up back there and the message never got passed on. After a while, ships started drifting in to the minefield so they had to drop anchor.

About an hour after the submarine attack, they were able to make radio contact with Cherbourg. We had three British and one French destroyer with us. This British destroyer, the *Brilliant*, tried to pull up along the side of the *Leopoldville* so they could tie the two ships together and start taking people. The waves were high and they were having a terrible time with the ships banging together. Guys were jumping from one ship to the other, some mistiming their jumps and being crushed between the two ships. We were a couple of hundred yards behind and could see this going on. They estimated that 700 got off the *Leopoldville*. There were injured guys tied on to litters and they were sliding off the ships and going overboard.

So anyway, this went on for a long time. The people on shore were celebrating their Christmas rather than manning their post. The officers were having a party and didn't want to be bothered. They really didn't realize what was going on for about two hours and by then it was too late. The ship went down and they estimated there were a thousand guys in the water. The water temperature was 48 degrees. You last for about a half hour.

The big tragedy in all of this was the crew of the *Leopoldville* lowered lifeboats when the torpedo hit and left. It was a messed up deal. The crew was made up of Belgians, Congolese, and British. They failed to alert the passengers on how to lower the lifeboats. They piled their personal possessions in their own life boats and floated away. The GIs had to fend for themselves.

Some small boats finally came out from Cherbourg. They tried to salvage what people they could. The next morning when it became daylight the frozen bodies were laid out on the dock in rows like cord wood. What was left of us set up camp in two man pup tents near there. There was snow on the ground and it was cold. For heat we had a candle in a tin can. They came and hauled the bodies away on flatbed trucks and took them to a cemetery. We had lost so many men, I think the official count was 802, that they didn't want to blame the British or the Belgians. (*Note: None of the crew was lost.*) So they talked to Eisenhower and it was decided to cover it up. So the families were just notified that the men were missing in action. This went on for 50 years before the facts were released to the public. Anyway, it was total foul up. A lot them could have been saved. My roommate from Laramie went down on the *Leopoldville*. I knew a lot of those guys that died.

I was watching the History Channel in 1998 and happened to see a program on the 66th Division. They interviewed survivors from the *Leopoldville*. That was the first time I had seen a public acknowledgement of what happened. The German sub that torpedoed the *Leopoldville* was sunk by a British submarine four months later.

Our division was headed for the Bulge but since we had lost so many men, they moved us in to replace the 94th Division several days after Christmas. They were down in the St. Nazaire/ Lorient region containing a pocket of fifty thousand German soldiers. The Germans were penned up against the coast and our job was to keep them from breaking out and rejoining their forces. They sent us in to relieve the 94th in the dark so the Germans wouldn't know. The snow was almost knee deep. We got in there at eleven o'clock

New Year's Eve and we stayed on line for one hundred and 33 straight days. There were already a half way permanent (defensive) setup but we moved around some. It was a lot better than what some of the rest of them were going through.

I was in a heavy weapons platoon attached to a rifle company. I was the gunner on a 60mm mortar. My job was to sight the mortar. There were five in a mortar team, the squad leader, gunner, and three ammo carriers. One of the ammo carriers was 6'4" and another 6'7". The taller one was named Ed Mills and he played center on the Wisconsin Badger basketball team.

The 60mm had a range of one mile. There was a chart that came with every box of ammo with degrees for range and you'd adjust the level. You'd use an aiming stakes five yards or so out in places you had been a while so you'd know where to aim. A lot of the time you couldn't see the target you were shooting at so you had an observer. We practiced by the hour before going in to actual combat. We had fire missions every day. We could get nine or ten in the air before the first on a hit. We fired a lot of flares at night especially. The flare rounds would burn about thirty seconds, floating down on a parachute. I had trained back in the states on a heavy, water cooled machine gun and the 81mm mortar but was put on the 60mm.

Sometimes we had misfires that you had to carefully dump out of the tube as the shell armed itself when striking the end of the tube. We'd have short rounds as well on occasion. One time an ammo crate of mortar shells had the words, "Do not fire over the heads of friendly troops" written on it. I guess they knew that box was suspect.

The Germans tried to make a major breakout right after we got there. They may have realized they were facing a new outfit. I've read that they were trying to disrupt things in the rear when the Battle of the Bulge was going on. We had a major go around with them then. They were right out in front of us then with machine guns and everything. This happened at night. We fired both high explosives and flares. The Germans had a lot of artillery in the pocket. They were guarding their submarine pens.

One night we moved in to a barn, looking for a good place to sleep in the hay mow. We got in there after dark and got all bedded down and heard a bunch of rustling and movement. Someone turned on a light. The place was full of rats. So we had to turn our face backwards in the sleeping bag so the rats couldn't get to it and let it go at that.

Our front lines were pretty much static. A lot of patrols were sent out, day and night. I went out on day patrols but never night ones. I almost killed my sergeant one night while on guard duty. I was back a little ways from this stone wall so nobody could reach around and get me. I had what was called a grease gun. I could see somebody lean out around the end of that wall and had the trigger about half way squeezed off the guy said, "Hey, Steinbeck." It was my sergeant. He came 15 minutes too early and from the wrong direction. We were both scared when we realized what had almost happened.

Question: How many men went on a typical patrol?
They were squad size, 6–8 men, no more than a dozen. I carried a new type of mortar copied from the Japanese knee mortar. It had a trigger mechanism and you didn't drop a shell down it. One of its big advantages was that you could fire it lying flat and it was a lot lighter to carry. I volunteered to go on patrol and got to use the new mortar.

The country side was mostly open fields and hedge rows. We lost a few men from artillery fire and from going on patrols. We lost one of our best officers on a patrol when it was ambushed. He was machine gunned.

The German lines were about a mile in distance from ours, within the range of their artillery. I never really thought much about the fear factor. I suppose some times were worse than others.

We had one lieutenant who was very, very scared all the time. We loved to torment him. He had someone guard the entrance of his dugout every night. We didn't appreciate having to do this. We'd sneak up some nights and get the guard out of the way and then toss a grenade over behind his dugout just to keep him nervous. He'd never come out and never caught on that we were the ones doing it.

It was one of the coldest winters on record for Europe. We had sleeping bags and winter clothing including overcoats. You usually slept fully clothed, only taking your boots off. I didn't get a decent bath for three months and went four months without sleeping in a bed. You wondered how those people up in the Bulge survived. I considered myself very lucky.

I don't know if you are aware of these figures, but during WWII there were sixteen million in uniform. Of that number, 455,000 died and another 672,000 were wounded. So that means one out of every sixteen were killed or wounded.

We stayed in the Lorient region until VE Day on May 8th, 1945. We waited two or three days for the mines and booby traps to be removed before moving in to this town. There were piles of weapons in the middle of the street, just these huge mounds of German weapons. I picked up a P38 pistol, a Mauser rifle, a bayonet, and German helmet. I sent everything home in the mail except for the P38. I carried it home. I carried a Colt .45 during the war. I would have liked to have taken it home as well but wasn't going to risk getting in trouble by stealing it.

After the war was over, they loaded us up in boxcars and took us to Belgium to be occupation troops. The next morning they sent us back to Marseille, France, to help process boys going home or going to the Pacific. I had too many points to be sent to the Pacific and not enough to come home. We processed one hundred thousand troops. After that, I was loaded in another boxcar and sent to Vienna, Austria and attached to an engineering group. After about a week, they asked if anyone wanted to play football. I signed up and they moved us to a hotel. We practiced during the week and played games on weekends.

After football season was over, they made me an MP. Vienna was divided up into four occupation zones, French, British, American, and Russian. The Russians never stayed in their zone. One day my partner and I were out patrolling and a Russian jeep about ran us over. The Russians always carried their weapons with them. We ran their jeep down and pulled them over. It was an officer and his driver. We planned on taking them back to the Four Powers Headquarters so I got in the Russian jeep and sat next to the driver. The officer was in back where they always rode. They were told to follow our jeep to the headquarters. When it got

time to turn off to the headquarters, the Russian driver kept driving straight back toward the Russian zone. So I grabbed the steering wheel and ran the jeep into the curb. Then we loaded them in our jeep and turned them in. I don't know what happened to them.

You couldn't trust the Russians. I was no lover of the French, either. I liked the Germans better than the French. I didn't have much to do with the British but they were a little different. You couldn't trust the French. Every move we made during the war, the Germans knew about it. The information had to be coming from the French.

I was discharged with the rank of PFC on May 8th, 1946, at Camp McCoy in Wisconsin. It had been three and a half years since I had said good-bye to my brother Kenneth at Camp Dodge. Kenneth was an officer in the Army and never had to go overseas until after the war was over. He ended up a captain in charge of a motor pool. My cousin Kermit was a Navy pilot and flew off of a carrier. I think he was a fighter pilot. My father was on the local draft board. I still have my draft card with his signature on it. He was the one that registered me for the draft.

I went on a four day Honor Flight to Washington, D.C., last September to see the WWII memorial. I've spoken at Pekin School and over in Richland at the Community Center about the war. I weigh the same as I did while in the service so I wear my uniform.

Carroll owned and operated a farm implement dealership and repair shop in Rubio before retiring. He served for many years as the chairman of the Washington County Conservation Board.

It is an honor and privilege for me to have this opportunity to write a brief tribute to the men in this book and to veterans as a whole. The gentlemen interviewed within are truly great Americans. As you read their stories, you will recognize that although these men survived incredible adversity and performed heroic feats, these are ordinary Iowans.

These men are our fathers, brothers, relatives, friends and neighbors. Their greatness came as they were thrown into extraordinary circumstances and how they faithfully and selflessly fulfilled their role. These men were asked to leave their homes and families and reach deep within themselves to fight for family, friends, country and way of life. They experienced all the facets of war that only those who were there can fully realize and appreciate. They fought in jungle, desert, cities, countryside, on islands, from ships and planes in Europe, Africa and Asia and faced the many challenges that these environments provide.

The costs of this war were not slight. There was terror, chaos, pain, loss of friends, hunger, thirst, exposure to the elements, loneliness, fatigue, and the constant awareness that they could die at any moment. When the war ended, these men came home, raised families, began careers, started businesses, assimilated back into America and continued to build the United States into the greatest nation on earth. The end of the war didn't end the effects of the war on those who battled to survive. There were disabilities as a result of injuries received, difficulty in transitioning back into a civilian, mourning of loss of friends, and nightmares of the war that in some cases continue to this day.

I would like to think that every person would like their life to have meaning. That they, and their actions, made positive effects that reached others and was much larger than even themselves. Each veteran in this book and all who fought in World War Two accomplished this. They helped their brothers in arms, prisoners in concentration camps, the allied countries, our United States and the world as a whole. Had the Axis powers not been stopped, our world and way of life would be immensely different from what we have known.

As Americans, I feel we have three enormous responsibilities towards all veterans who fought and continue to fight for our freedom, values, and way of life. First, I feel that we must each strive for greatness in however we are gifted. We must be good stewards of the United States. Rather than being parasitic on America, feeling that our country owes us, I feel we should use our talents to be the best and most successful person we can be. By us, as individuals, striving for greatness, we keep America great and pass it on to the next generation.

Second, I feel we have a solemn responsibility to protect the Constitution of the United States and the freedom it gives us. This document and the liberties it protects was paid for with risks, sweat, blood and lives. Each person, as they are inducted into the military, swears to protect it from foreign and domestic enemies. This high price of freedom is not to be negated with the swipe of a politician's pen from the comfort of his or her office.

Third, I believe we have the responsibility to remember all those who have fought and those who have fallen to give us the way of life we have as Americans today. We must continue to tell their stories and keep them and their families in our prayers.

Finally, I would like to thank Larry Cuddeback and Cheyenne Miller for compiling these interviews. Through them, we keep the memories of these great men alive for eternity.

Jeff Hildebrand
Brighton, IA

WHAT THE HELL HAD I GOTTEN INTO

Marlyn "Hoddy" Allen
West Chester, IA

6th Marine Division
Pacific

Interview Date:
6 May 2011

Referral:
John Capper & Richard Huber

In some ways, the war brought the country into a better period. We had been suffering as a country through the Great Depression for a number of years before the war and it was a terrible time. We were damn poor.

I don't think any of us vets would consider ourselves heroes. We went to war in December in '41. I never had a job, never had a car, never even been on a date. I was almost 18 with no prospects in sight so a couple of us decided to join up. At that time, the Japanese were still taking islands and the Germans taking over one country after another. It was a time in my life when I wanted to do something. It wasn't so much flag waving on my part but rather that I just wanted something to do. I didn't realize what was going to happen.

I hitchhiked from Wellman to Des Moines to sign up for the Marines. I barely made the minimum height or weight requirement. This John Wayne type sergeant in charge there didn't think I belonged in the Marine Corps. After mouthing off to him, he agreed to sign me on. I was called to active duty in May of 1942 and sent to San Diego

for six weeks of training. I remember my first day of boot camp and the bugle blowing so early in the morning I couldn't believe it. Our drill sergeant came out and belittled us worse than anything. He told us he was our mother, our father, our chaplain and we were going to do exactly what he said. And if we tried to get over that fence we'll probably shoot you. He added that, "I've got you for six weeks and then you'll be a Marine." My thought was, "What the hell had I gotten into?" My buddy, Gene Smith, flunked out of the Marines and ended up in the Navy. He struck an officer and was booted out of the Navy.

There were a number of different Indians in boot camp training with us. I learned later that these fellows were later used as code talkers. There were so many different tribes and different languages represented that even if the Japanese had figured out one of the languages they would have been lost on the rest of them.

I completed training on the 19th of July and was trucked that evening to a converted luxury liner docked at one of the ports. We sailed the next morning. We had no idea where we were going. I hadn't hardly been out of the state of Iowa before this. That ship had eight decks and there were five thousand Marines on board. A destroyer escort accompanied us. We sailed for eleven days until we reached a deep water harbor at Pago Pago in the Samoan Islands. Up to this time, we had not received any combat training but had trained with an M-1 Garand. Our job was to defend islands. Later we were transferred to a British held island that they had gotten from the Germans after World War One and set up a defense there. We could not have defended that island if it had been attacked. We were 18 and 19 year old kids. There were a lot of us from Iowa. It was kind of a makeshift deal. At this time in the war, U.S. forces were not conducting any offensive actions against the Japanese.

We trained on that island for several months and were then taken to Pearl Harbor where we joined a convoy. I was assigned to the 22nd Marine Regiment which was an independent regiment, not part of any division. We sailed with the convoy for sixty days and then made several landings in the Marshall Islands. That was our first combat. It brings back memories. There were hundreds of little coral islands in the Marshalls and they made ideal landing strips for our bombers. Our first landing was on one of the bigger islands, Eniwetok. After several days we were pulled off and landed on another island. There were twenty-five hundred Japanese troops on these two islands. I was in a heavy weapons company on a half-track armed with a 75mm howitzer. Our first engagement was to take out a pillbox on Eniwetok. I could see dead Marines lying on the beach where we landed on shore. A lieutenant ran up to us and asked if we could do something about a Jap pillbox. We ran the half-track right up to it and fired two rounds. That took care of it. Later, I peeked inside and saw the two dead Japs were just young kids like us. Young kids have to fight the wars that old men start.

Leaving the Marshalls, we sailed for Guadalcanal in the Solomons where we received more training at a base there. Guadalcanal had been recently captured from the Japanese after hard fighting. There's quite a story about that. They had a heck of a time. There we were joined by another marine regiment to form the First Provisional Brigade. Our next assignment was Guam in the Marianas.

Guam had some small mountains on it and was located closer to Japan. The Japanese had captured Guam early in the war. Our brigade went in on one side of it and a Marine division (the 3rd) went in on the other side. My brother-in-law and several other guys from Wellman were in that division. One thing I felt good about was that there were a lot of natives there that were treated pretty badly by the Japanese. They were very happy to see us.

I was a sergeant and in charge of a half-track. The landing craft ferrying our half-track in to Guam struck a reef off shore and we were told we had go in from that point. But the water was too deep and we sunk our half-track. We ditched our gear and swam about a quarter mile to shore while under fire. There is an advantage to being small. The whole thing (of combat)takes some adjusting. Landing on a beach and seeing a lot of dead bodies was a shock but pretty soon you got to the place where you could block it out. The one thing I will say about the guys we went in with, those in the landing craft, I never saw one that tried to crawl back in and go back to the ship. After you trained that long with the same guys they become closer to you than your own brother. The Marine Corps kind of beat that into your head.

After reaching shore on Guam and getting squared away, we given a second half-track. I had them drive down around the edge of the beach where a stream dumped into the ocean and we buried this one in quick sand. The third one they gave us we kept. We didn't get too involved in the fighting. We did fire into cliffs where there were snipers and stuff like that. We could blow up pill boxes and tanks but the Japs didn't have too many tanks on Guam. But they did have twenty thousand troops there. We never knew what was really going on at the time it was happening. I learned later that the top brass was worried that we would not be able to hold the beaches. There were

> *"Landing on a beach and seeing a lot of dead bodies was a shock but pretty soon you got to the place where you could block it out."*

big battleships out in the ocean firing sixteen inch shells over our heads at night. They told us that one out of every seven marines that landed on Guam were either wounded or killed.

Our half-tracks had armor plating that could stop small arms fire. One of my crew was wounded when they were moving forward but I wasn't in the half-track at the time. We had both HE (high explosive) and armor piercing rounds for the 75mm. The driver and section leader sat up front and the gunner and assistant gunner sat in the back. The gun would recoil 40 inches back. Our half-track also had a .30 caliber machine gun. The American way to fight was to do a lot of shooting, using our overwhelming fire power rather than sight in on an individual target. This was dense jungle and you couldn't see much anyway. The lack of ammunition was never a concern.

After being on Guam about 30 days, the Japanese realized they were defeated. Around four hundred of them got drunk on sake one night and did a banzai charge on the front lines. I was back a ways from the front with our half-track. I couldn't see anything but I could hear the Japs coming and their loud yelling.

Question: What was going through your mind when you heard this?

I was scared shitless. I'll tell you, when you made a landing, there were guys that threw up and others that wet their pants. Just knowing that there was somebody there on that island that wants to kill you is a bad thing to experience. We'd climb down cargo nets hanging on the side of the ship into landing craft. Then the landing craft would circle around until it was our turn to go in. We generally went in on the third wave. Sometimes they land you on the wrong beach. It was usually mass confusion. I made three landings. Guam was the worst because I had to swim ashore.

We were on Guam about 60 days. There were still Japanese soldiers hiding out in the mountains on Guam after it was labeled secured. They used to sneak down at night and booby trap the garbage. Some didn't surrender for twenty or thirty years after the war ended. There was also an American

that hid out on Guam until we took it back from the Japanese.

Next we went back to a base in the Solomons. We crossed the equator quite a few times. I was in the Pacific two and one half years and spent six months of that time on ship. We were on some really bad troop ships. Being that far from Pearl Harbor, we didn't have much in the way of food or supplies. We would scrounge around on the island we took looking for food to eat. The Samoan and Solomons were heavy jungle islands with heat, humidity, and mosquitoes. We had more cases of elephantiasis than malaria.

Another regiment joined us on the Solomons and we formed the 6th Marine Division and they went in on the Okinawa invasion on Easter. I never fought with the 6th Division as I had already rotated back to the states. Just before I got to home I was at the big base on Guadalcanal and we were told there was going to be a general coming to make a big inspection of the troops. We had to have everything all spic & span and we were standing there for hours waiting. To me, seeing a general was like seeing someone like Obama but more important. I was praying that he wouldn't stop to check me out because I was so short. He stopped and talked to two guys in our whole outfit and I was one of them. He asked me how I was getting along and if I was "ready to go in the next operation?" I said, "Yes, Sir!" But I was lying. This two star Marine general was named Shepherd and commanded the land forces on the Okinawa invasion.

My brother Chuck was in the army infantry. He fought in North Africa, Sicily, and Italy. Later he went in the south of France and fought in Germany. He was wounded four times. Some of my Wellman friends on were on Guadalcanal when I was there. I got to see John Capper, Bill Ulin and Vernie Goodwin.

I rotated back to the states in December of '44. After being in the tropics for two and one half years, Iowa felt colder than hell. But I did get to spend Christmas at home. When I took off my shirt, my family remarked on how yellow my skin looked. That was from taking all those adiprene

> *"He asked me how I was getting along and if I was 'ready to go in the next operation?' I said, 'Yes, Sir!' But I was lying."*

tablets we had to take to prevent us from getting malaria. After my leave, I was sent down to Paris Island to coach new recruits on the rifle range. Then I was sent to North Carolina and ready to rotate back to the South Pacific but a lieutenant fixed it so I could remain and continue to help train new Marines. I spent some time at Quantico Base in Virginia and got to travel up to D.C. a lot. There were two Wellman girls working in government offices in the capital that I looked up, Darlene Novy and Ladorra Patterson.

There was a big parade planned to celebrate Navy Day and they wanted six hundred marines that had been overseas to march in it. We trained and trained for that parade. That parade was kind of the highlight of my tour. We marched eight or ten abreast down Pennsylvania Avenue past all the dignitaries. A thousand graduates from the Annapolis Naval Academy marched behind us. The Marines are part of the Navy but Marines don't like to admit it.

The war was over in '45 and my enlistment wasn't up until May of '46 and they wouldn't let me out a day early. They tried to get me to re-enlist. I told them, "You couldn't print enough money!" I think most guys were like me in that they wanted to find a job, settle down with a good woman, and forget about the war.

I am 87 years old and still have a crew I take care of that fixes basements, does tuck work, masonry things like that.

The Wellman Centennial book list 425 servicemen that fought in the Second World War from the Wellman area. Twelve did not come home. Hoddy was one who did.

IF I LOST A LEG,
WOULD IT BE WORTH IT?

John Mielke
Ottumwa, IA

101st Airborne Division
Europe

Interview Date:
14 May 2011

Referral:
Bill & Mae Watson

I enlisted in early 1944. When I was in high school, I was working 52 hours a week and going to school. I was working at a restaurant. During the previous year, the state of Iowa lowered the number of credits you needed to graduate to attend college so I quit in mid-year in 1943. I went up to Ames and didn't realize that you needed to study. I was still working and getting like three hours of sleep at night. They came out with this ASTP program. I signed up for it, took a test somewhere along the line and signed up for the Army as a reserve as I wasn't eighteen yet. So I was in the Army Specialized Reserve Training program and was sent down to the University of Kansas in September. In February of 1944 they ended the program and sent all the reserve people in it to the infantry. I did my basic training in Camp Blanding in Florida. I did my paratrooper training at Fort Benning.

Because of my restaurant experience, I was sent to Cook and Bakery School. Everybody else in that school was 30 to 35 years old. They looked pretty decrepit as far as I was concerned. I figured they'd make me an infantryman as soon as we went overseas and I knew I needed more training for that. I thought that the extra fifty dollars a

month and the fancy boots the paratroopers wore looked pretty good so I joined up. One of the big things about the paratroops was that they were all volunteers. There were good guys in every unit, no question about that. But there were some guys who were there because they had to be. The paratroops joined up because they wanted to. That made a difference. In the paratroopers you knew you could depend on the guy next to you.

I got over to England about the time of the Holland jump (Operation Market Garden). It was September or October. About four or five days out, our ship lost a screw and we couldn't keep up with the convoy. The sea was rough with all the storms and we got completely off schedule. It took us two weeks to cross. Since we had to drop out of the convoy, we made the rest of the voyage without Navy escort. It was a little worrisome. I felt like a duck in a shooting gallery. I could feel the submarines watching us. The water sure looked cold.

Question: Did you get seasick?
No one has ever been more seasick than me. I did a lot of fishing as a kid in lakes and rivers and never even thought about getting seasick. But boy,

I was! I had never seen anything so beautiful or so green as the coast of England.

We were originally supposed to be replacements for the losses suffered by the 101st Airborne in Normandy but didn't arrive in time for the Market Garden jump. We went to Newbury, England, where the 506th was based. There weren't regular barracks. We stayed in huts and it was cold and damp. We were at Newbury a while and then sent to Mourmelon-Le-Grand in France where the 101st was scheduled for garrison duty after finally being pulled off the front lines in Holland. I was assigned to Baker Company, 1st Battalion, 506th Parachute Infantry Regiment.

Question: Did the veterans resent or look down on the new replacements?

No, not in the way that I think you are asking. As a replacement, I didn't have any problems from the veterans like they depicted in *Band of Brothers*. After Market Garden, I think they were happy to see anybody. The barracks or huts we stayed in slept ten or twelve guys. Only one or two of them would be Normandy veterans and some of them had just returned from being released from the hospital. The guys that had seen combat in Normandy were kind of subdued. They'd talk and tell you certain things. They didn't boast or anything like that. We had good conversations. We were eighteen year old kids and we listened.

The guys that were in Market Garden had little use for British General Bernard Montgomery. They offered that if Patton had been running the show, the war would have been over. They spoke of the British armored column stopping for tea breaks all the time, seemingly in no rush to save their British paratroopers fighting for their lives at Arnhem. I heard all kinds of talk like that but I was not there so I don't know.

One of the Normandy veterans had received the DSC and General Eisenhower personally promoted him to the rank of sergeant. He was told that because Ike had promoted him, only Ike could break him. So this guy goes in to town and gets drunk for three days. When he came back he was back to being a private.

We had been at Mourmelon a month to six weeks before the Holland veterans showed up and they were only back a week or two before the Ardennes push. We didn't get assigned to squads or platoons until the Germans broke through. Then it was just zip, bang, boom. The squad sergeants were guys that had been through it and were more concerned that you knew what you were doing.

One of the big problems when the Bulge hit, was that we didn't have much for equipment. Winter clothing had not been issued, either. When we were at Bastogne, we weren't inside a house or anywhere you could get some kind of protection from the elements for two or three weeks. It was so cold and we didn't have any winter clothing. That cold just zips in to you. You'd get so you could hardly even move. Even going to the toilet was a problem. There was no hot food the entire time. You just can't imagine how cold it was. It got to the point that I wondered if I lost a leg, would it be worth it? Could I go home then? I was having those kinds of thoughts.

"We rode to Bastogne in open trucks, like a semi without a lid. It was cold but it got a lot colder."

We rode to Bastogne in open trucks, like a semi without a lid. It was cold but it got a lot colder. We set up outside of Bastogne. Nobody knew where we were. I never did see a map the whole time I was there. A lot of troops were withdrawing past us. When you're going into battle and see troops retreating past you, you don't look at them with great pleasure. We were disdainful of them. We didn't have any ammunition or guns. My sergeant stopped a few of those going past and took their weapons and stuff so each of our squad had something to fight with. I didn't know how much ammunition I needed for combat. I was used to taking ten shells with me pheasant hunting and coming back with three birds. We ended up with a bandolier of M-1 ammo apiece. The guys who had been in combat were upset because they knew that wasn't nearly enough. When we started up this road to Noville, they brought in a truck with ammunition and we all picked up two or three more bandoliers.

Noville was a mess. The 10th Armored was holding Noville. They were one of the few outfits that were following instructions. They had been told not to pull out of Noville and they hadn't.

Noville sat in a valley with high ground all around it and it wasn't a good place to try to defend. The 10th Armored wanted to pull back to Foy. They were notified that they'd be given a battalion of paratroopers. That was us. *(Note: Combat team Desobry, named after its commander, held Noville with 15 Sherman tanks.)*

The first day, our platoon was on a flank guard on high ground. I remember watching all these German tanks coming and attacking Noville. I remember this one tank going fifteen miles per hour over rough ground and firing twice. I looked to see where he had been aiming and saw two big holes in the church steeple. That was the kind of weapons they had. We had it easy that first day, mostly just observing the fighting around us.

That night our platoon moved into town. There was a stone or cement arched gateway that we had to go through to get in to Noville. There wasn't any enemy artillery landing outside of town, it was all landing inside the town, the other side of this gate. My squad was moving to establish a listening post. We had to go through that gate to get over to the other end of town. Going up to the gate, we could see the bodies of our dead in the ditch. The Germans were really shelling Noville. The sky was all lit up with the flashes but every once on a while there'd be a short pause in the shelling. We shot through the gate during one of these pauses and holed up in a little house. We were supposed to watch and let the rear know if we saw anything.

We spent the night and in the morning it was real foggy. We could hear the noise of motors running. We assumed they were tanks. They'd rev the motors up and cut them back, then another would rev up. When the fog started lifting, we could see two German tanks on the other side of the street. They were that close to us. All we had were M-1s and a Thompson, not weapons capable of taking on tanks. One of the guys got word back with something that had wires running from it (probably a field telephone). We didn't have cell phones in those days. Then we got out of there. That was the start of one terrible day.

"Our battalion had 600 men in it when we entered Noville. After roughly two days of fighting, we had suffered 199 casualties."

Our battalion had 600 men in it when we entered Noville. After roughly two days of fighting, we had suffered 199 casualties. Our 40 man platoon was down to 12 people. We lost guys in our squad the first few days. The majority of our casualties came from artillery. I grew up a bunch during the first twenty four hours. I learned a lot. You go through the training and think you are prepared for anything. In combat, you soon find out that there are still a few things you don't know.

We moved several times that day. There were three or four of us left in the squad when we left Noville. We rode out on a 10th Armored Sherman tank. The 10thArmored had mainly tank destroyers left to fight with. I don't know how many foxholes I dug that day. Our platoon was the rear guard for the battalion's withdrawal and our squad was in the rearward position of our platoon so I was one of the last guys leaving ahead of the Germans. There wasn't any snow on the ground at that time. It came later. In two or three days we had retreat to Foy. We remained in the vicinity of Foy. We never got in to Bastogne. We were sent back nearly to Bastogne when the planes started dropping supplies. That's the closest we ever got.

After being resupplied from the air drop, we went back to Foy and found a farm house out in the woods. We had foxholes dug in the woods. It was cold and all we had to eat were C rations. We heard that a kitchen set up in Bastogne was sending out hot food. So we went two at a time down to this house where they had a big tub full of hot oatmeal. I never cared for oatmeal and all I had to put it in was my helmet. But it was the best meal of my life because it was warm. My Christmas meal was a dinner K ration. It consisted of a little can of cheese, saltines, four little pieces of hard candy, and powdered lemonade to mix with melted snow. Anyway, it was not a very good Christmas dinner.

We got shelled with artillery. There was such a thing as TOT—time on target. That's when all the rounds from different guns arrive at the same time. There was a cross roads out in an open field. Every so many minutes the Germans would drop some shells there because there was probably someone going through there. When you were in the woods, you never knew when the shelling would come. I think they would try to catch you out of your foxhole.

Question: Was an artillery barrage the most terrifying thing you faced?

It was probably the most scary thing, but you didn't really get scared by the shelling. Instead, it was here comes those damn things and you thought what you could do to protect yourself. You didn't think about being scared. It was a different mindset. You don't go the nearest foxhole. You went to your foxhole. You'd seek some type of cover if you couldn't get to your own foxhole. It depended on what was going on at the time. It seemed like we never did the same thing twice. Those first couple of days we were in Noville, there wasn't much time we weren't being shelled. You just never knew when the shelling would start.

Question: Did the shelling usually preclude an infantry attack?

We'd always be looking for one when the shelling stopped. Sometimes they attacked and sometimes they didn't. In between the shelling we'd try to stay warm. There were times we'd go on patrols, stuff like that. As a private, I didn't know what we doing, I was just following orders.

Question: Did you ever have Panzers approaching directly toward your foxhole?

No. There were some ten to fifteen yards away but they were going the other way. We were facing SS Panzer Divisions and they were tough. We had a bazooka and one rocket but nobody knew how to use it. A guy shot at a tank but missed it. The tank kept going. Usually the tanks were accompanied by infantry but as I recall, there weren't any that day. Someone would call back for artillery support if there was an infantry assault. We were never overrun by German infantry.

Question: Did you ever experience the German screaming meemies?

Oh yes, they sounded just like they were coming right down your hole. You'd hear them way off coming and you'd swear they were going to get you. My squad leader said that they were a psychological weapon and wouldn't hurt you.

Question: Did you ever light any fires to try to get warm?

Sometimes we would burn the K ration boxes to make coffee. They were coated with wax so the cardboard didn't make much smoke. The Germans knew where we were so it didn't really matter. It never got so cold that my M-1 didn't work. I think the guys that had problems with the M-1s not working weren't taking proper care of them.

Question: Did you learn of General McAuliffe's reply of "Nuts" to the German demand for surrender?

Yes, we heard about it the next day. The Germans had us surrounded and our battalion was surrounded at Noville and cut off from the rest of the 101st.

Question: Did you ever feel that your situation was hopeless?

No, no, no! By God, I'm a paratrooper and there's nobody that can take me on. When we would get drunk and go to town and see an Army Air Corps guy we'd ask for a taxi. When we'd see a Marine in uniform we'd call him a bellboy.

Question: It nice to have you confirm the airborne swagger. How many fights did your trips to town lead to?

There were a few fights, but I tried to steer clear of them.

Question: When Patton's 4th Armored Division arrived in Bastogne on December 26th, how did that make you feel? Did you even know they were there?

I never saw them. Someone told us they had arrived. I thought, "So what?" We were getting along just fine without them. Paratroopers have a different kind of attitude.

I was lucky in that I never got trench foot or frozen toes like so many of the men did. The severe cold affected my legs for ten years after the war. They'd feel like they went to sleep. It didn't happen all the time and finally went away. Sometimes when the snow sticks on the trees or there's fog here in Iowa it will remind of the Ardennes. I still go out in the woods to hunt deer and turkeys. The same thing happens when I see a scene or landscape in the timber, it'll bring back bad memories.

Question: General McAuliffe sent out a Christmas message to the troops that he had printed up. Did you ever see it?

No, I never saw it. I remember hearing about it. We had some snow at Christmas time and it kept getting worse.

That German Tiger tank with that big barreled 88mm was something. It could shoot a shell like a high powered rifle. The Germans would send a small plane, like a piper cub, over every night. You had to make sure you weren't smoking a cigarette or showing any light when he was overhead.

After the Germans had been pushed back from Bastogne, we were sent down to the Alsace Lorraine district. Somebody had screwed up down there and we took over their positions. *(Note: The Germans launched a diversionary offensive in the Alsace to take pressure off their forces retreating from the Bulge, code named operation Nordwind.)* We took over eight positions previously manned by a full contingent of infantry with only the nine guys left in our platoon. That meant eight hours on duty with one hour off. We did that for two or three days before we got some more help.

Question: What did you think of Colonel Sink, the CO of the 506th?

The guys that were the old timers thought he was great. I think they were kind of in awe of him. There's the story about him receiving the DSC for standing up in his jeep and urging his troops forward in Normandy. I always thought he was a little over blown but I shouldn't say that because I didn't have the same experiences with him as the old timers did.

Question: Did you ever talk to Dick Winters from Easy Company?

No, but I knew who he was.

Question: The miniseries, *Band of Brothers*, was based on the 2nd Battalion in the 506th. Do you think they could have made one equally as good about your outfit?

Oh yeah, they could have. We had one or two guys in our company that would have been good.

I'll tell you of one incident. We had made this push through a woods around Bastogne and

"Sometimes when the snow sticks on the trees or there's fog here in Iowa it will remind of the Ardennes."

got separated from our flanking units. Corporal McQuery and I were supposed to go make contact with C Company. The squad leader pointed to some smoke and said, "They should be right over there where the fires are. Get some sleep first." The snow was deep by this time. We left about nine o'clock and went to where we were told to go but it was entirely different than we were lead to believe. There was a little town there. The fires we were looking for had gone out and we were seeing different fires. There was a bunch of disabled vehicles in this town. Some were Germans, some American. We were trying to figure out what to do when we heard some people approaching. So we ducked behind some bushes and here comes about a dozen German soldiers, more or less. They were joking and singing just like they were five miles behind the lines. This guy I was with had watched his twin brother get bayoneted in Normandy while (his parachute was) hung up in a tree so he didn't really like Germans. So he's getting ready to shoot these Germans. There were dozen of them and we don't know how many more were back behind them. It was a bright moonlit night and with all the snow on the ground you could see someone moving a hundred yards. I had an M-1 and he had a Thompson. We could have killed them all without too much of a deal but we would have never gotten out of there because I knew there were more people behind them. I stopped him from shooting, but he really wanted to kill those people.

Question: Did your outfit have the opportunity to take many prisoners while in actual combat?

I don't know that we took very many. There was a story that the 506th got a direct order to take prisoners while in Normandy because they weren't taking them otherwise. I wasn't there so I didn't see it but that was the story.

Towards the end of the war we were making these big pushes. We were riding in trucks and saw these people in pin striped prison garb walking down the road. The people were gaunt and had big eyes that were either dead or were shining because they knew they were free. They were going somewhere but didn't know where they were going. It was heartbreaking to see them. It really made an impression on me. Then when we got in to Landsberg, we found out what was going on. The German people did not know what was going on in the nearby the prison camp so our division commander, General Maxwell Taylor, had the local people go to the camp and bury the dead. *(Note: Landsberg concentration camp was a slave labor work camp operated to produce war material. It was part of the larger Dachau complex.)*

At the end of the war we were in Berchtesgaden, the home of Hitler's Eagle Nest. I saw the Eagle's Nest from the outside but didn't actually go through it. Then we went in to Austria for occupation duty.

Austria is just gorgeous. I liked the Austrian people. They had fought on the other side, of course. Everyone we talked to claimed they had never fought the Americans, it was always the Russians. Whether that was true or false, who knew? The thing I liked about Germany and Austria was that they were clean. I saw fancier bathrooms in German farmhouses than I'd ever seen in the United States. In France, the towns and houses were dirty. I wasn't impressed with England. But that was the war's fault. And the weather was lousy. They had been at war for a long time and didn't have some of things they normally would have had, but they got along. You have to give them credit.

Herman Goering had a castle near the little town of Bruck where our battalion was headquartered. Elements of the 2nd SS Panzer Division guarded his place. They were one of the older German outfits that had fought in Spain, Russia, and every place else in between. They looted liquor and art treasures everywhere they went. We took over all the booze they had hoarded. One of our guys had been a bartender in New York and he estimated there was over twenty thousand dollars' worth of liquor stashed there. The bar would open every night at five. If you were a member of our platoon, you went in there and drank whatever you wanted to drink.

Question: What were your thoughts when you heard that the 101st would likely be sent to invade Japan?
Ah, shit!

I was a private or a PFC during my entire time in the service. I carried a Garand. I wish I had kept one of those rifles. The 101st was kind of dissolved at the end of the war. Guys were sent to other units. I went to the 82nd and came home with them, arriving in the states on New Year's Day, 1946. I marched in the ticker tape parade in New York City. It was an impressive site.

The first thing I did when I got home was sign up for the 52/20 club down at the Post Office. If you were an honorable discharged veteran, you were entitled to twenty dollars of unemployment pay for fifty-two weeks. I was planning on going to the University of Iowa and was up there looking for a place to live when I ran in to a guy I knew and went to work for him. I worked selling shoes for a big franchise based in St. Louis. They moved me from Fairfield to Marshalltown and then to Houston, Texas. My wife got homesick for Ottumwa so we moved back and worked for my father-in-law at his grocery store. Then I went in to sales management for Merrill's for a number of years.

I found my squad leader's name on the internet at a 101st web site. He and I emailed back and forth for several years and then he up and died on me. He lived in California. I went on an Honor Flight to see the World War II Memorial. I thought the whole thing was wonderful. I was upset for a number of years that a memorial had not been built yet.

LIKE A STRONG WIND IN A DRY CORNFIELD

Albert "Fritz" Conrad
Harper, IA

30th Infantry Division
Europe

Interview Date:
20 May 2011

Referral:
Rick Conrad & Ann Tweeton

I grew up In Marion County. I started as a private in the 119th Infantry Regiment, 30th Infantry Division. I was drafted in March, 1942. I was 21 years old. I took a train from Des Moines to Minneapolis and then on to Fort Lewis, Washington, for basic training. After basic we went to San Francisco to help the National Guard do coast patrol and stand guard at one end of the Golden Gate Bridge. There were these big, twin 20 inch guns dug in underground for coastal defense that nobody knew about. The gun emplacement was in solid rock. They were located at the edge of San Francisco north of the bridge. The guns were operated by the Coast Guard. We stayed in the underground living quarters. The guns were electronically controlled and could swing out to cover the Pacific near the Bay. I was told they could hit a ship five miles out.

Question: Fritz, were there any other gun emplacements guarding the harbor other than the ones you were at?

If there were, we didn't get to see them. The worst part about it was we were stationed by a zoo. It was always foggy in San Francisco at night. You'd be standing guard in the dark and when one of those lions would let out a bellow it would send chills down your spine. From there I went to truck driving school in Santa Rosa. We drove trucks up in the mountains at night with no lights on. I was scared to death but passed. All you could see to follow was two little green lights on the rear of the truck ahead of you. You had to keep up or you were in trouble. My brother Adrian was down in southern California and got married. I got a three day pass to go visit him and his new wife.

Early one morning we were loaded on a train

pulled by an old steam engine. We got out in the middle of the desert and the train stopped. We were told that the engine had run out of oil and we would sit for three days. So there we were in the desert with nothing to do. They had chow for us but those weren't sleeper coaches we were riding in. We finally got going again and ended up in Carolina Beach, North Carolina. The train trip took eight days. I rode so many trains during the war that I got sick of them.

You were supposed to get a furlough every six months. After 17 months, I finally got a two week furlough in August to come home. My girlfriend, Jeanette Striegel, was still in school when I left for the service. By then, she was working at the Rock Island Arsenal. I met her in Davenport. We decided to get married on the bus ride home to Harper. It was a stupid, really. We talked to the priest on Wednesday and he talked to the bishop on Thursday. We were married on Saturday. I had to go back in two weeks, of course. Jeanette came out to visit me for her birthday in November. I was confined to camp the night she arrived and couldn't even go get her at the train station. So I gave a photo of Jeanette to the wife of another soldier and she picked her up.

My next move was down to Camp Van Dorn in Mississippi. I had to send a pregnant Jeanette back home then. Camp Van Dorn was the mustering out place to go overseas. We were sent by train to Boston where we caught the boat. It was an old French tub. It wasn't very clean. The rough water had a lot of the guys seasick. Our ship was one in a long line of ships going across the Atlantic. We landed in Glasgow, Scotland and sent down to England. We were put on the waiting list to in on the invasion.

I was with the Old Hickory or 30th Infantry Division. We went in at Omaha Beach about three days after D-Day. It was still hot there.

Question: What was Omaha like three days after the invasion?

It was hell. We landed in a big LCI with a steel ramp on the end of it. The ramp kept the small arms fire from hitting you when you were still on the boat. Then you were in water up to your butt

carrying all your stuff and you had better hustle as it was a quarter mile over to the bluffs.

Question: Were you still getting small arms fire three days after the invasion?

The Germans had pill boxes up on the bluffs. They had machine guns up there shooting at us. The first thing we had to do was get those. If you got underneath them, you could get around them. If you were out in front of them where they could see you through the little holes, you were trouble. We finally made it but there were a lot of bodies floating around. I knew I was in a war. I had had enough of it right then.

Everything I owned was in my duffel bag on another boat and that boat got sunk crossing the English Channel. It was hot out in the Channel as well. There were German subs and planes there attacking the ships. I saw German planes. Normally, the American planes flew in the daylight and the Germans came out at night.

I got hit on July 25th in the battle for St. Lo by two pieces of shrapnel. One was in my shin bone and the other my calf muscle. I could still walk. There wasn't any way to get me out and back to England where the hospital was. The medics treated my wounds with sulfa powder and wrapped my leg up. I stayed on my feet for ten days and then I went down with blood poisoning. My leg started hurting quite a bit then. They finally got a C-47 landed in France. The ambulance they hauled me in to the plane kept getting buzzed by a German fighter plane. But he never shot at us. I was put on a rack with a bunch of other wounded and flown back to England. A doctor in the hospital told me that they might have to amputate my leg. I told him they'd better cut it off above my shoulders if they do. I was kind of cocky back then. I evidently still carry shrapnel in me. With all the metal detectors, they won't hardly let me loose at the airport security these days.

Question: After you were wounded, did they send you back to a rear area?

No, I stayed on my feet giving fire orders to my mortar men. I carried a radio on my back and I use it to give the fire orders. Actually, the only thing that I am really thankful for is that I never

"A doctor in the hospital told me that they might have to amputate my leg. I told him they'd better cut it off above my shoulders if they do."

had to take a rifle and shoot a man. But I know I made a lot of Germans uncomfortable with those 4.2 inch mortars. I had two mortar squads under me. It took three men to carry the mortar. One was on the base plate, one on the bipod, and one carrying the barrel. The rest of the squad carried ammunition. I carried a .45 pistol and a carbine. I couldn't hit anything with the carbine 50 yards away. I might as well have thrown it away. The M-1 Garand was the weapon to carry.

Question: You fought in the hedgerow country. What was that like?

The hedgerows were grown up farm roads. It was a lot like Amish country with just a bunch of poor farmers out there, no nice houses. We'd dig foxholes as close to them as we could. That wasn't always a good thing because a shell coming in would hit the tree tops above you. We'd set up our mortars before dark and pick out the probable approaches the Germans would attack. Then we could lay down a field if fire if any one heard something. We'd fire maybe ten rounds to cover a certain area.

Question: Did the Germans use counter battery on you?

Yes, that was how I got hit, by one of their mortars. If you are going to use mortars, the Germans are going to shoot mortars back at you. That's just how the game was played. It was the same for artillery or small arms.

Question: Do you remember the carpet bombing the Army Air Corps did on the 24th and 25th of July in preparation for the breakout and the 30th Division was bombed by mistake?

Our guys at the front put out red smoke bombs to show the bombers where the friendly lines were located. By the time the bombers arrived, the wind had changed and the smoke had drifted back on us. So the bombs dropped on us. I was right by a hedgerow. It buried me. The bombs rolled that hedgerow over almost right on top of me. I'll tell, when those bombs came down it sounded like a strong wind in a dry cornfield. It was just that kind of sound. My thought was, "Oh Lord, I hope one of them doesn't hit me in the butt!"

Question: Did you know they were our planes?

Oh yes, you could see the markings on them.

They were flying that low. I saw a covey of 13 bombers heading towards me. It was called saturation bombing. Only the first few planes dropped on American positions. They finally got word to the planes and the bombing stopped. The last part of the bombers hit were they were supposed to. Eisenhower was a good man. He was the one that ordered the bombing because we not able to budge the Germans.

I rejoined my unit after being in the hospital almost three and a half months. In fact, my oldest son was born while I was in the hospital. They promoted me two grades to staff sergeant while I was in the hospital. The 30th Division was originally a Texas outfit and promotions for Yankees like me were hard to come by. I didn't want to go back to my unit but I didn't dread it either. I wanted to go home. But somebody had to do it. I rode the train boxcars across France to catch up with my outfit. They were just getting ready to enter Belgium. There was a big stack of letters from my wife awaiting my return. The first letter I opened read, "I just gave Gary a bath." I thought, "Good Lord, I've got a boy!"

> *"My thought was, 'Oh Lord, I hope one of them doesn't hit me in the butt!'"*

Question: Were your two squads still intact when you returned?

No. There were replacements. The turnover rate was three times for every man serving during the war. I'm the luckiest man in the world. I don't know why.

The 30th Division's next big battle was at Liege, Belgium. The Ardennes wasn't too bad except for the German breakthrough (Battle of the Bulge). We were in Kohlsheid, Germany, when the Germans made their big push. My grandmother came over from Germany and I could speak some German. One of my jobs was to tell the German people what we wanted them to do, like having them get out of their house so we could take it over, things like that. We were called out of Germany at midnight on the 17th of December. We did not know where we were going or anything else. The 30th Division had to back up and get around the Germans who were behind us, attacking west through the Ardennes.

In the last big German push during the Bulge,

the first company ahead of us got over run by the Germans. The Germans were running down a hill and got right on top of our boys. We stopped them in the second company. Every company in our battalion had already lost half its strength during the fighting in the Bulge up to that point. That first company was wiped out. There was both German infantry and tanks in the attack. This was up in the mountains. The German tanks also ran out of fuel after that. After we got things straightened out and the prisoners captured, we lined them up and took them back behind the lines. We were outside in the cold most of time unless we could find shelter. Then someone had to stay outside to keep watch. The 25th Division was sent out to replace us for three days. We had to hurry back after two days because they all had frostbite. They must not have been a smart outfit. Our division didn't have a problem with frostbite. We had good winter gear. I don't know what we did differently except use our heads.

> *"I thought that if I could survive this birthday, I'd make a bunch more."*

Question: What did your battalion do to stop German tanks?

We used bazookas. That was the best thing to use against them. Their 88s were superior weapons. Our Sherman tanks were just like decoys. I looked out one night after a big tank battle and counted ten Sherman's on fire. The German tanks shot an armor piercing round that went right through a Sherman. We were up in the northern salient next to the British. We were the first American unit below the British.

Patton was a blow hard. He got us in trouble a lot of times. Patton brought a whole bunch of his tanks up to help us through the Siegfried Line. They got up there and ran out of fuel and there wasn't anything they could do. We had to guard Patton's damn tanks for him so the Germans wouldn't get them. That's what I think of Patton. He might have been a good general, but Rommel had them all beat.

Getting through the Siegfried Line wasn't as bad as we thought it would be. We went up there prepared to knock a hole through it. They had it pretty well fortified. The Germans thought it would stop us but it just slowed us down.

Question: How long did you go without showers or baths when you could actually get clean?

I don't know as I ever got clean, but it was a long time in between baths. We'd sometimes try to wash up in a stream, but of course not during the winter. One time I picked a louse of another guy's collar because only those with lice got a bath, clean clothes and a hot meal.

After the Bulge, we returned to Kohlsheid. A German man we knew greets us, saying, "Oh, we're glad to see you. You were supposed to be here for Christmas." I told him that, "I was sorry I didn't make it." He ran down in his basement and came back carrying a bottle of schnapps. He presented it to me, saying, "This is your Christmas present." His wife told me to look for their two little boys. One was 13 and the other 15 years old. She said the German Army had taken the two away to make soldiers out of them. I said, "Lady, I don't think there's much chance of me finding them but I'll sure try."

We had to wait on the Navy to bring in the LCIs to cross the Rhine River because we didn't have any boats of our own or pontoon bridges. We crossed the Rhine at two o'clock in the morning on my 25th birthday, March the 24th. The Germans were dropping mortars on us the whole way across. I thought that if I could survive this birthday, I'd make a bunch more.

Near the end of the war we had a platoon across the Elbe River. They were ordered back to adhere to a deal worked out by Churchill, Stalin, and Roosevelt. We sat there for two weeks waiting for the Russians to take Berlin. Finally they got it done. We were within 20 miles of Berlin and could have walked right in. The German people wanted the Americans to take Berlin. Some of the Russians soldiers crossed the Elbe over to our side after the war. We got drunk with them.

I had German friends. We weren't fighting the German people. One time I told a group of them that the German people were too quick to agree with anybody standing on a stump. One old boy said, "No, thirty percent have all the guns. What are the others going to do?"

I thought the Belgian people were the most like us, the most Americanized. A lot of them spoke English. A young Belgian girl gave me a little .25 caliber pistol the Germans had given their family. They were told to shoot the American soldiers in the back when they came. I asked her why she was giving it to me. She replied, "We don't shoot people." I laid that pistol under my pillow one night and we pulled out in a hurry the next morning. That pistol got left behind. I did manage to bring a German Luger home. They had a whole truck load of Lugers which they dumped in a court yard. We could help ourselves. We were allowed to bring one thing home and mine was a Luger.

I did not like the French or care for the English either, for that matter. The French really growled at us for being on their territory. They resented us being there. It seems like we have always had to do the fighting for them.

We spent time doing occupation duty in Germany. Then we were sent back to France and waited 30 days for a boat to take us home. The boat they put us on was a Liberty Ship, one of those that bounced like a cork in a tub of water.

Question: So did you get seasick that time?
No. I got smart. I never ate anything. The sleeping bunks were tiered five high. I made sure my bunk was the top one. I was discharged in September of '46. I gave the Army 3 ½ years of my life. My son was 14 months old before I got to see him. I had to convince him that I was part of his family. I was a butcher in three locker plants and then got a job working for the natural gas company here in Harper. I traveled in eight states laying pipeline. I retired in 1983.

I can actually say that I was never really scared during the war. I wasn't smart enough. I am kind of disappointed, though. We really thought that we helped the world and we didn't. We can't control the world. I know there are people that need our help today, but our arms are only so long.

My brother Adrian served but never went overseas. Brother Dick was in Germany. He brought a German war bride home. I had two boys in Vietnam and Rick was in Germany. I've got a grandson in Afghanistan. A friend of mine, Lloyd Hammes, fought in North Africa. He was in some rough stuff and became a POW in Africa.

I wouldn't take a million dollars for what I saw but wouldn't give ten cents to do it again.

THE DIRTY DOZEN

Marion, Bill & Lawrence Swift
Washington, IA

Interview Date:
27 May 2011

Referral:
Sheila Hildebrand & Tracy Swift

Lawrence: When the Army doctors gave me my first physical examination, they told me I had TB. Before that, I had been working on a farm at the time so they gave me a farm deferment. So they sent me home. A doctor in Washington gave me an X-ray and it was determined that I only had a scar on my lung. When I was younger, I had asthma so bad I couldn't hardly go up three flights of stairs. I worked on a farm for four years and the hog dust was making me feel bad enough that I had to quit.

I had military service from April, 1946 to April, 1947, as part of the occupation forces in Japan. We really didn't know what the heck we were supposed to be doing over there. The ordinance outfit I was in didn't do much as far as I was concerned. We repaired trucks but we didn't have any spare parts so the trucks would sit there until the parts arrived. I was stationed close to Yokohama. I didn't really see any bombing damage. I had a chance to go to Tokyo but had no desire in going. We had Japanese girls that did the cleaning for us but other than that, there was no intermingling with the Japanese people. All I was interested in was to stay long enough to get back home.

Bill: I enlisted and was in from 1956 to 1962. I had two years active duty, two years in the active reserve, and two years inactive reserve here in

Washington. From Camp Dodge I spent six weeks at Ft. Chaffee in Arkansas. They couldn't figure out what to do with us. We were sent out for training in the Signal Corps in California. After six months, we were put aboard a ship in Monterey Bay. We sailed through the Panama Canal and on to Europe. I was stationed in Germany and assigned to garrison duty in the 10th Division. Garrison duty involved looking after the Army trucks except for me. I was the duty driver for Company B so I had to drive every day. There was a lot of time spent painting Army trucks. Those trucks had many coats of paint on them.

The barracks we stayed in at Wurzburg had been used by one of Hitler's Panzer divisions. They had been bombed out during the war. The outfit that got there two years before I arrived had to clean and repair them. There were still skeletons in the upstairs rooms of the barracks at the time. They also picked up a lot of souvenirs.

Our real job over there was to watch the border between the American and Soviet occupied zones. We watched the people crossing back and forth. The check points had both radio and telephones for communications. The radio section kept busy manning a radio tower stuck upon a hill. I was in the telephone section and we didn't have anything

281

to do unless we went out on field maneuvers. I was a pole lineman to start with but served as a switchboard operator when we went out on field maneuvers.

Nothing bad happened while I was over there. Every day we had to keep an eye on the Russians. They would drive through our zone in cars watching us. They weren't allowed on our base but could get within a couple of city blocks from us. We'd watch them watch us. If the Russians had ever decided to come across the border, we were the first ones in line to stop them. The border between East and West Germany was already walled. There was barbed wire and a cleared area on either side. The dirt would be raked every day in order to see the fresh footprints of anybody sneaking across. We were worried about the Russians coming across the border. They wanted to expand and the Russians didn't like that we were there.

Wurzburg was a pretty good size town. It was heavily bombed during the war, especially all the German military installations. The city was a church center. All the churches, and there were lots of them, had been destroyed. When you walked downtown, you'd see a lot of buildings that were just rubble.

We did field maneuvers out in an area where a Panzer division had trained. There were massive concrete bunkers with steam heat and slits for firing. There was also a huge railroad gun. The Allies had bombed the train tracks both in front of it and behind it so there it sat.

Question: Did you have much interaction with the German people?
The Army employed some so we didn't have to do KP duty. There was also some doing cleaning work, laundry, tailoring, and barbering. The Germans liked us but didn't like us. Any time you get a bunch of soldiers stationed in a town and going to the taverns at night you're going to have problems. The German people also resented the fact that we didn't obey their laws. For instance, when we drove through town in a truck convoy, we went wherever we wanted to go and there was nothing the Germans could do about it.

Marion: I was drafted and inducted on June 22nd, 1945 at the Jefferson Barracks in Missouri. I did my training in Camp Hood, Texas. I was in the 310th Regiment of the 78th Infantry Division which was part of Patton's Third Army. We shipped out from Camp Shanks in New Jersey aboard the *Leif Erickson* troop ship on the day before Christmas. We sailed to the English Channel and sat there for a day waiting on a pilot to get us through the mine field and into the Rhine River. We sailed up to Rhine to a little town near Frankfort, Germany.

We were supposed to train for guard duty. I pulled guard duty one day. The next day one of the guys in my outfit came down with spinal meningitis. We were quarantined to our barracks for two weeks. Then we were shipped out to Berlin.

In our first orientation session in Berlin we were told about the black market. American Camel and Lucky Strike cigarettes were selling for $150 a carton. We were warned not to sell them for anything less! You'd walk down the street smoking a cigarette and throw the butt away. That caused a lot of smashed fingers from all the German civilians diving after it. They would collect the butts and strip the tobacco out and roll their own cigarettes when they had enough.

We were billeted in a hotel. There was a 30 foot bomb crater beside it and live German ammunition scattered on the ground all over. A large bombed out SS barracks was rebuilt and named the Patton Barracks.

Berlin was a divided city but the Russians acted like they owned it because they had taken it during the war. The Brandenburg Gate was the dividing point between the American and Russian Zone. The Russians held up our convoys and had a policy of harassment. I was in the riot squad. We were allowed in any zone. One of our jobs was to close the taverns up at 10 PM. There usually wasn't any problem except for the occasional Russian getting huffed up. We had several alerts that something bad was going to happen but it never amounted to anything.

One morning at reveille my name along with 20–25 others was called out to train for the medics. I thought that was odd since I was a rifleman, but people were always rotating home and the Army was short of medics. They could only train two or three medics at the hospital so the rest of us trained at the aid station. The medic that trained us had been through the war and was rotating home.

They brought a Russian soldier to me at the hotel that had a bump on his head from getting in a fight with some Germans. As a medic, I had no idea how to treat him so I dropped him off at an English run hospital. The Russian captain in charge of him came around literally in tears. He explained that he was responsible for his soldiers and would be sent to Siberia if he could not account for all of them. He was some shook up. That's how strict they were with their own people. Pretty soon the injured soldier came back because he knew that he had to.

Later I was transferred to a mechanized cavalry unit. The Berlin Wall had not yet been built when I was over there. The German people were courteous to us for the most part. I came home in November of 1946.

Marion gets out his photo collection from Germany. He shows us several photos of himself and his brother George together in Germany. George was in the 10th Armored Division.

Question: Did you ever go see the Reichstag?
I'll tell you a story about that. Off to the left of the Brandenburg Gate was the Reichstag. The roof had been bombed out. Nearby was a doorway at street level that led to Hitler's bunker. Off to the side of it was a dug trench in the ground. It was the length of a body. There were two GI jerry gas cans sitting there. That was supposed to be where Hitler's body was burned.

My brother Bernard was killed in a car wreck near Ankeny in 1944 while home on leave. He was in the Army Air Corps. Bernard never made it overseas.

George enlisted in October in 1943 in the Army Air Corps. George was third in age but he was the first to go to the service. He trained in Texas. Both he and Bernard wanted to be pilots but didn't make the grade. George transferred to the Army and was a mortar squad leader in the 10th Armored Division. He saw lots of combat but didn't talk about it much.

Bill: George told one quite interesting story. They were going in to mop up after they had been shelling this German town. They were going door

to door checking everything out. Right in the center of town was a big white sheet hanging like the Germans were surrendering. So all troops gathered on the main street and started walking toward the white sheet. Hidden behind the sheet was a German tank which opened up on our guys. The ones that weren't killed outright scattered like a covey of quail. George said that really made their company commander mad. He ordered his men to back out and told them that there would not be anything left standing in the town by the next morning. George said they called in the artillery and just absolutely leveled the whole works. The next morning there was only smoke where the town stood. For the next three or four weeks George said that when German people would see their shoulder patch, they were so scared they would leave the area.

Brother Charles "Chick" was in the 87th Infantry Division, part of Patton's Third Army. He was in K Company of the 3rd Battalion of the 346th Infantry Regiment. I think Chick got to Europe around the first of the year in 1945. He saw the Orduff Concentration Camp. Chick was in the Ardennes during the end of the Battle of the Bulge and fought through the Siegfried Line. He always talked about the German 88s and how you could tell it was an 88 by the noise it made. Chick was a runner in the Ardennes. It was bitter cold. One time he loaned his heavy overcoat out to another runner. It never came back.

Lawrence: Chick told me about the time he was a message runner in the Ardennes and he had to cross a four foot high fence. After he climbed the fence, a stream of bullets came in over the top of him. I think that is when he was wounded by the shrapnel.

Marion: He never did get a Purple Heart but he carried shrapnel in him until the day he died.

Question: How did your mother handle having so many sons in the war?
Bill: I was the youngest so I was home during the war. My mother would write to them every Sunday evening. We still have some of the letters she wrote the three oldest boys during the war. We had six sisters. All six of their husbands served in the military. Doris's husband, Raymond Sojka was in the Navy on the South Sea Islands. Jean's

husband, Al Fritz, was in the service. Keith Housel, Esther's husband, was on ship from '42 to '45. Edith's husband, Merritt Wellington, was in Korea. Martha's husband, Dale Hawkins, and Annetta's husband, Doug Chalupa, were both in the National Guard here in Washington.

Marion: I was in the Inactive Reserves for three years after being discharged. I didn't have any work when I came home. I was in the 52/20 club. You received $52 for 20 weeks but you had to show that you were actively hunting a job. The government had a program that trained vets after the war. I worked three years at the John Deere store in Washington. The government bought me $100 worth of tools and helped pay my wage. I got tired of doing that so started farming with my dad and rented ground in later years around the county.

Bill: I worked a year for a farmer right out of high school and then worked for Porter Lee's appliance business for a year. The draft was catching up to me so I decided to go ahead and enlist. After the service, I worked as a welder's assistant for Clark Keating for a while, then went to the Ford Motor Company and then to the *Washington Evening Journal* for 26 years. After that I worked 16 years for the Washington Manufacturing Company and finally got old enough to retire.

Lawrence: I worked as a mechanic for Ross Auto until 1983.

Question: Gentlemen, what would you want future generations to remember about the WWII era?

Bill: They should know that the reason we were in Germany and Japan was because they attacked us. And don't let anyone tell you they didn't have concentration camps because they certainly did have them. War is a bad thing. You see a lot of things you'd just as soon not have seen.

Marion: Berlin had underground air raid shelters on each side of the main street that ran the length of the city. There was an air raid shelter under the Brandenburg Gate that I walked over hundreds of times without knowing it was there. There was an underground manufacturing plant outside of Berlin. There were great big anti-aircraft guns that could be hydraulically raised above ground to shoot at our planes and then lowered back down.

Question: December 7th, 1941, what were your thoughts when you heard about Pearl Harbor?

Marion: Those sneaky son-of-a-guns. I knew Roosevelt wasn't going to put up with that. I had no inkling that war was coming before the Japanese attack.

Lawrence: I wasn't so patriotic that I enlisted. I had only one good eye and was always told that I would not have to go to the service. But they took me after the war was over.

Marion: Here's a photo of the Olympic Stadium in Berlin. Hitler hosted the Olympics in 1936 when Jesse Owens won all those Gold Medals. There's a piece missing out of the lead plaque over there commemorating Jesse Owens. I've got that piece.

The story for our family is that not only all six brothers served, but the husbands of all six sisters served in the military as well. We always referred to ourselves as the dirty dozen.

CASUALTIES BROUGHT IN EVERY DAY

Duane Griggs
Burlington, IA

Medic
Pacific

Interview Date:
29 May 2011

Referral:
Virginia Kaska

I didn't go into the military because I want to, I was asked to. My brother and I were honey producers, which was a good substitute for sugar. About that time the draft board said that one of us had to go to the service. So not being too smart, I volunteered to be the one to go. I grew up in Washington County. Stewart Bell was a classmate of mine.

I went in on November 11th of '42 and spent 38 months in the Army. I spent a week at Camp Dodge up by Des Moines and did my basic training in Kansas City about two blocks from Union Station. It was not a bad place for active military.

I was in Kansas City with a detached military police unit for close to a year. We did military police duty at ritzy clubs and ball fields and helped the GI's find their way through Union Station and keep them out of trouble. We also were sent aboard trains as military police guards to Colorado and Arkansas. Then I was sent to St. Louis and assigned to another detached military police unit and we did the same thing there as we had done in Kansas City. There was a place in Newton, Kansas, where the train would stop and the local ladies would give cookies and cake to all the soldiers. They'd also pass out postcards with a picture of the Kansas Jayhawk on it.

"We could do an appendectomy in 14 minutes and nobody died!"

After being in St. Louis about a year, we were called in and told that there was need for more military police in the Pacific theater. So they took a bunch of us up to Michigan for another three or four months of military police training. Then they decided they needed us worse as medics than MP's in the Pacific. Eight or ten field hospitals were organized in Michigan and I was sent to different hospitals across the country for medical training.

We shipped out of California and it took us a week to get to Hawaii. We laid over there for 30 days and played a lot of ball. It took us another 30 days to reach Okinawa from Hawaii because the ship stopped at every little island on the way there. We landed on Okinawa on April 26th in 1945. I stayed there until December 26th of '45. The war was over by then, of course. I was married with a child at the time that helped me get more points to come earlier.

I wish somebody had told me to go to medical school after my experiences as a medic, but no one did. I worked with surgeons that were top drawer. This was in a field hospital in northern Okinawa. We could do an appendectomy in 14 minutes and nobody died! We often thought that there were so many cases of appendicitis because the soldiers wanted some time off from duty. I worked with one surgeon from New York that did really fine work. He only had one eye but he saved a lot of lives. It was a great experience.

We were attached to the 1st Army. We treated wounded infantrymen. We treated very few if any native people on Okinawa. By the time we landed there, you didn't see many of those people around. I don't know where they were at. Our field hospital was about 25 miles from the front lines. We had guards posted at night.

The first day we landed, about a dozen of us with surgical training were taken to a field hospital five or six miles from the front lines. You could hear a lot of firing that close. Nobody ever got hurt, but you kind of wondered sometimes. When we were at that forward hospital, we treated some wounded Marines as well as the Army soldiers. I think most of the wounds were inflicted by small arms fire. I don't remember doing any amputations. We send anybody that mangled up back to a hospital better facilitated to handle it. I never saw a psychological case commonly referred to as combat fatigue. I was up there about a month.

Question: Did you ever treat any wounded Japanese soldiers?

I don't believe so. I would not have had any problem doing so if there'd been any.

Question: Duane, did you feel like your medical training to be a medic was adequate?

Yes, very adequate. I was a surgeon's assistant. While I was on detached duty to the field hospital up by the front lines, we'd get 50 to 100 casualties brought in every day. I remember seeing 20 to 25 army ambulances lined up waiting to unload. We did not work on assigned shifts. We were there when there was something that needed doing. We were basically on-call all the time. I think the longest stretch I worked was 15 hours. We had enough guys to fill in that you didn't have to work ungodly hours.

Our sleeping quarters were four-man tents. There was a terrible storm while we were there and it was a rough two or three days. The only way for food to be brought in was by plane. B-29s flew in frozen food for us. For the most part, the weather was pretty good while I was on Okinawa.

Question: Was your hospital, except for the comedy, similar to the one depicted on the TV show, MASH?

Yes, I'd say it was similar. There are four of us that were in my outfit still around and we correspond together. The closest one lives in Dewitt, Iowa. My great niece, Cheyenne Griggs, is a medic with the Iowa National Guard and has been deployed to Afghanistan.

I published the West Branch newspaper for three years after the war and then sold it and moved to Scottsdale, Arizona, thinking I could make more money down there. After a year there, I'd lost everything but my wife so I moved back to Iowa and worked for the newspaper at New London. I eventually purchased the paper from the owner and ran it until retirement in 1983. I liked the newspaper business but it's too bad I didn't go to college and get smart.

Question: Do you have a message to convey to future generations about your experiences in WWII?

It is too bad that people all over the world have to fight like they do. What a waste of time and money.

Patriotism More Than Anything

Ivan Ulin
Wellman, IA

USS *Tuscon*
Pacific

Interview Date:
9 June 2011

Referral:
Left Wilson, Jack Seward, Jr.

I enlisted at age seventeen on August 28, 1944. My full purpose was to join the Navy. I don't remember much about hearing of the attack on Pearl Harbor. I'll tell you this, if the Japanese had kept coming, we didn't have anything to stop them. We would have been in a boat load of trouble. I do remember at age 16 being worried the war would be over before I could get in the Navy. It was patriotism more than anything. I wanted a crack at the enemy. But after I got over there, I wished I was back in Iowa.

A bunch of us Iowans were sent from Des Moines to Farragut, Idaho, for 12 weeks of boot camp. Other than going to the State Fair, that was the first time I had been any distance from home. Back then, a trip to Iowa City was a big deal. I had my fill of traveling while in the service.

After boot camp I went to San Francisco to pick up a brand new ship built at Bethlehem Steel, the USS *Tucson*. It was called a CL, which is a cruiser, light, or an anti-aircraft cruiser. There were a lot of Iowa boys aboard ship because the group of us shipped out of Des Moines stayed together during training. Bob Ross from Washington and Harry Suter from Crawfordsville were aboard the *Tucson* with me. Wayne Karr from Wellman and I went through boot camp together but separated after that.

We took the ship out on a shakedown cruise and came back to San Francisco. After getting everything situated, we sailed for Pearl Harbor. We were in a convoy and zigzagged the whole way because of Japanese submarines. The USS *Tucson* was assigned to a task force (TF 38) after arriving at Pearl. The task force had one or two aircraft carriers and battleships in the center surrounded by destroyers in a "V" shape providing picket duty. The Tucson was at the point of the "V" and was the flagship for the destroyers. I think we were part of the 7th Fleet but I was 17 or 18 years old and didn't pay a lot of attention to that stuff.

Leaving Pearl we sailed to a bunch of the islands including Midway, but this was after the fighting on those islands had ended. Then we did shore bombardment for six months. It was all done at night and we never did see land. They never told us what island we were shooting at. I do know we did shore bombardment off the coast of Japan, including Yokohama.

I was glad I wasn't on a destroyer. Our ship was 420 feet long and full of anti-aircraft guns. We had twin six inch turrets and we had six of them, three forward and three aft. We had 16 quad 40mm and 32 twin 20mm guns. I was a gunner's mate on a 20mm. I fed the belt of shells in from the top of the gun.

One time we had a Japanese suicide plane fly between our smoke stacks and hit the water on the other side of the ship. I think this happened when we were off Okinawa doing shore bombardment. This plane was close enough that you could see the outline of the pilot.

Question: And your gun was shooting at him?

Oh, of course! Anything that close is the one you're picking on. Most of them didn't get that close to us. Most of the kamikazes were trying to get past us to sink the flat tops. It was the same for the Jap submarines. We lost some destroyers but we never lost any of the big ships. We never lost any ships from submarines that I was aware of. Most of the ships we lost were from the suicide planes.

Question: Did you have time to get scared when the kamikaze went between the smokestacks?

Oh my God *(laughing)*, yes! They claimed that a lot of those suicide pilots were hopped up on something and I think they were, too. I absolutely don't know how he missed us. Our gun position was up high on a catwalk around one of the smoke stacks. I'm certain he would have killed us if he had hit a smokestack. He was trailing smoke coming in. The pilot might have been passed out or dead.

Every fourth shot on the 20mm was a tracer round. The tracers were so close together it looked like that was all that was coming out of the gun barrel. There were two barrels on our 20mm and it really pumped out the rounds. The gunner wore a shoulder harness and was strapped in so he couldn't go any place. This was because of the recoil and the fact of the gunner standing upright while shooting. We wore ear plugs to protect our hearing. If you were on the weather deck when the six inchers went off, the concussion and noise was pretty bad.

A lot of the equipment during the war was put together too fast. I know that on our ship you couldn't fire the six inch guns too fast or the rivets would pop out of the ventilation system. The six inch guns had to be fired in sequence. If you shot them all off at once, it would capsize the ship.

We went to general quarters almost every

day. It was mostly due to enemy aircraft, but not necessarily the suicide planes. Much of the time it was bombers. If they were flying over us, we were shooting at them. Only the six inch guns could reach the higher altitudes. We were never strafed but we were the target for bombers. No bombs ever landed close but you could hear them whistle as they came down. We had torpedo planes come at us but we were never hit, although I think several destroyers were because we could see the explosions. The torpedo planes came in low enough for us to shoot at them.

One time a mine floated between our ship and an oiler when we were taking on fuel. It looked like a big, horny ball. The wave action from each ship kept it away. It scared us pretty badly. We sunk it with gun fire after it cleared the two ships.

We'd get shore leave on some of the small islands. That usually consisted of two cans of green beer and swimming in the ocean. Sometimes we'd jump off the fan tail of the ship. It was quite a ways to drop. We never worried about sharks. After the war ended, we had liberty in Yokohama.

We were anchored in Tokyo Bay next to the USS *Missouri* when the Japanese signed the surrender treaty. We could see the Japanese officers climbing aboard ship. They were dressed up fit to kill. They looked like they were 50 yards away but it was a lot farther. Everything looks closer than it is over water.

Question: What was going through an 18 year old mind during that?

It wasn't history *(chuckling)*, I'll tell you that. We stood attention on the weather deck, four hours on and four hours off, all that day they were signing the peace treaty.

Unless you were in rough seas, you got use to the wave action rolling the ship. But I got seasick after every time we went back out to sea after being in port. Every time. It took about two hours for me to get over it each time.

I started out as a seaman 2nd class and was promoted to seaman 1st class. I passed the gunners mate 3rd class test, which is a step up, right before being discharged. They offered to make me that

> *"One time we had a Japanese suicide plane fly between our smoke stacks and hit the water on the other side of the ship."*

grade if I would re-up but I wanted to go home. I was just glad the war was over. I haven't wanted to travel since.

My brother Cedric Ulin was a chief petty officer on an oiler in the Navy. He pretty much stayed in U.S. territorial waters. He enlisted right after Pearl Harbor and stayed in for six years. Marlo "Bats" Matthes from Wellman was in the war. Leo Durian came home from the war (ETO) all shot up. He was bedfast. He might have lived another five years. Howard (Hoddy) Durian was in the Navy stationed at Great Lakes. I think Bob Marner from here was killed in war. I believe he was a pilot.

I hauled cream for 11 years for the Wellman Creamery in the Brighton, Crawfordsville, and Keota area after being discharged in April, 1946. I would haul meat and bread to people on my route as a free delivery service. Later I operated the Sinclair (latter the Shell) gas station in Wellman.

It Was Interesting, But I Wouldn't Want to go Through it Again

Bill Brown
Wellman, IA

USS *Yorktown*
Pacific

Interview Date:
16 June 2011

Referral:
John 'Lefty' Wilson

The USS Yorktown *was one of 24 Essex class aircraft carriers built during WWII. She was named in honor of CV5, also named the* Yorktown *which was sunk during the Battle of Midway. The CV10 earned 11 Battle Stars and was awarded the Presidential Unit Citation.*

I enlisted in December of '42, a year after Pearl Harbor. My hometown was Ottumwa. I quit school in my senior year and messed around, spending most of my time shooting pool. My dad told me to get job so I enlisted in the Navy. I went to the Post Office to get an enlistment form and they asked me how old I was. I told them 17 and they replied that I would need to get a parent's signature to enlist at that age. When my dad came home that evening I told him I found a job with no layoffs and it was good for three years. He laughed and asked, "Where did you find a job like that?" I told him, "The Navy!" He looked at Mom and she said, "Well, if that's what he wants to do." So he signed the papers. My two older brothers had gone the previous year.

The Navy let me stay home until after Christmas and then I reported to The Great Lakes Naval Station near Chicago. It was January and 20 below zero. Our commanding officer was fresh from Texas and couldn't stand the cold so we only had to spend about an hour outdoors training each day. Nine weeks of boot camp and I never saw a gun, never hand one in my hands. Too cold to be outside!

After training, we were given a week's leave to go home and then I reported to Norfolk, Virginia, and a brand new carrier, the *Yorktown*. Then we had a shakedown cruise where the pilots practiced both day and night time landings on the carrier. Despite the fact that the almost the entire crew was "green and dumb", the shakedown went well and the pilots performed flawlessly. The ship's captain was a three-quarters Cherokee from Oklahoma who loved his ship and the sailors on it. He did everything possible for his crew's welfare. Three years later he made Admiral and broke into tears when promoted off the *Yorktown*, the ship he had christened.

The *Yorktown* left port in January of '43. On board were the STB torpedo planes, the TBS bombers that could carry a thousand pound bomb, and the new F4F fighters. We took the new fighters over to the Pacific on the hangar deck so no one could see them and kept the curtains closed while going through the Panama Canal. The Zeros had been shooting down the old fighters right and left. For armament, we had 20 and 40mm manned by Marines plus 3 and 5 inch radar controlled guns.

I was on a plane handling crew. There were ten men on a crew and ten crews. We pushed planes around on the flight deck and spotted them. We had little Ford tractors with wide steel wheels to move the planes around. There were also two Jeeps the officers had to use while on shore leave and we used those as well to pull the planes around. We had to remove the chocks from the plane's wheels before takeoff. With all the propellers running, the slipstream was strong enough to blow you off the deck. There were rain gutters cut into the deck and we would have to grasp them with one hand to keep from ending up in the ocean.

> *"They took him down to sickbay and dug 152 pieces of shrapnel out of his body and he went back to flying again."*

I had a friend who was removing the other set of wheel chocks from the same plane that I was working on. There was another plane parked off to the side as it was late getting started and time was being allowed for the engines to warm up. My buddy evidently backed into the tail of the plane, causing it to hit something with its prop which caused pieces of shrapnel to enter his foot, severing toes. I retrieved a stretcher from the catwalk and carried him down the elevator to sickbay. He was gripping my wrist so tightly that it took the medical people some time to pry his hand loose. He was recovering from his wounds when pneumonia set in. He died and was buried in the South China Sea.

The flight commander for the fighters always had two wingmen with him because he was a goldbraid (officer). On one island bombing mission, this flight commander got all shot up, with a shell exploding in his cockpit, knocking out all his instruments and covering him in oil. His two wingmen paralleled him in flight, placing their plane's wing tips under his so he could somewhat fly by feel. This way they brought him all the way back to the carrier. Upon entering the circle to land and without a working radio, the flagman waved the crippled plane in after making only one circle. The cable grabbing tail hook had also been shot out so there was nothing to stop the plane except for the crash barrier. Striking that, the fighter plane tipped up on its nose but settled back down to remain upright. So there he was. They took him down to sickbay and dug 152 pieces of shrapnel out of his body and he went back to flying again.

One of their Task Force numbered 58 ships. The high value targets, usually two or more aircraft carriers, would be center and presumably the safest within the battleships' inner most ring of defense. The next ring or circle would be the cruisers, followed by the anti-aircraft cruisers. The outer picket ring would be the radar equipped destroyers. Kamikaze attacks were the biggest threat at that time. Sometimes they would attack in droves and other times single planes would attempt to sneak in undetected. Fortunately, most Japanese suicide planes were shot down by our carrier based fighters and the gauntlet of anti-aircraft fire delivered by the protective rings of ships.

One day I was standing on the flight deck next to a Lieutenant when I noticed him looking up intently. There was a tiny speck directly overhead in the sky getting bigger. It was a Japanese dive bomber heading straight toward them. This Lieutenant went by me like "Zoom!", like he knew what was coming. Then there was me, acting like a greenhorn, wanting to see the action. Finally the radar controlled anti-aircraft fire drove the Jap off and he veered toward a destroyer which got him, he shot him down.

It was so hot in the bowels of the ship, we always slept on the carrier deck when possible. Most of the crew joined us. One tactic the Kamikaze's used was attack with the sun at their backs. You just could not see them coming. One morning here comes this enemy plane and he is low, skimming the wave tops with the sun to his back and I'm standing out there like a dummy to see what happens. I could see he had a torpedo hanging. He's very close and heading straight for the spot I'm standing on. I thought, "Uh, oh! This is it!" Then there was a loud bang and the plane bounced vertically up and flew level across the flight deck. I could see the Jap pilot sitting in there and I could see his eyes. That's how close he was to me. The plane flew clear of the deck and landed in the ocean and then there was big "Whoomp" of an explosion. I could see that he had already been shot up as he passed by me. The speculation aboard ship was that the Jap pilot must have hit the landing gear button instead of the torpedo release by mistake, with the wheels hitting the water causing the aircraft to skip out of control over the carrier. I think the Man up above was watching over us.

We had one pilot that was hit in the head by a single enemy rifle bullet fired from the ground. He made a perfect landing but passed out when his plane came to a halt. The flight surgeon said that a fraction of an inch difference would have killed him. He recovered and continued flying combat missions. Those pilots just loved to fly. Sometimes our planes would make it back to the ship but run out of fuel while circling to land and the pilots would be forced to ditch in the ocean. They said it was like hitting a cement wall.

One time a plane with a damaged cable hook failed to get stopped and struck a gun turret with a wing and spun into another structure splitting the fuselage in half, right behind the cockpit. The pilot walked away unscathed. Crash landing would often result in the propellers chewing up the wood flight deck. Replacement boards were carried aboard ship for such an eventuality.

At one time, the *Yorktown* had 102 planes on board. Half the flight deck would be covered by planes and the remainder stored down below on the hangar deck. Small planes were sometimes suspended by cable overhead. When general

> *"The speculation aboard ship was that the Jap pilot must have hit the landing gear button instead of the torpedo release by mistake."*

quarters were sounded, I always remained on the flight deck. It was my job to get the planes airborne. We were never close enough to see the islands being bombed or enemy ships attacked. I also did not ever witness an aerial dogfight. Any information regarding pilot success was passed around by the crew as scuttlebutt.

One night a Japanese sub torpedoed and sunk an escort carrier (CVEs) near us. They were nicknamed Kaiser Coffins and were used to ferry replacement planes to the larger carriers like the *Yorktown*. There were four of the escort carrier's planes in the air at the time and they flew to our carrier to land. We got three in but the last one came in wrong and we tried to wave him off but he hit the deck and bounced over the crash barrier and landed atop a plane. We had a crew folding the wings up on that plane and several were killed and their captain was in the cockpit and he was burned up in the fire. We got our fire equipment out and put the hoses together. Some of our parked planes were on fire by then and when the guns started going off, that's when I got out of there. We shoved three or four of our planes that had got burn up over the side. It was around midnight that we got the fire put out and no sooner than that was accomplished the General Quarters siren went off. There were Jap planes right above us. We just got it out in time. We would have been a sitting duck. Things happen.

We were anchored one night off the Marianna's. I received a letter from Mom telling me that my brother, Miller "Fuzz" Brown was on Saipan. So I sought permission to get off the ship and ended up getting dropped off on Saipan and told to follow the one road there and eventually someone would stop and help me find my brother. A truck came along and stopped and gave me a ride to the far side of the seven mile long island where I thought my brother was stationed. I found the hut he was barracked in but he was gone for supper. When he came back, he could not believe seeing me sitting there. I had not seen him in nearly three years. When he saw me sitting there he said, "Where in the world did you come from?" I said, "The same place you did, Ottumwa, Iowa."

We never had a submarine warning but had typhoon warnings. The big typhoons lasted two to three days and were particularly scary with the waves so high as to cover the flight deck. Orders were issued for no one to be topside during a typhoon. We had a new lieutenant that disobeyed the order and was swept off the catwalk, never to be seen again. The smaller destroyers would simply disappear under water at times. *(Note: A typhoon in Dec '44 sunk three destroyers in their Task Force and the* Yorktown *participated in rescue operations for the survivors.)* We tied the carrier planes parked on the flight deck down with ropes. We never lost any planes but the wind and salt water would peel the paint right off of them.

During the war we made a hospital run from Pearl Harbor to San Francisco. Five hundred and fifty cots were set up on the hangar deck. All the wounded were Navy personnel. They ran the ship full bore—35 knots, keeping only a few planes on board in case of enemy submarines. One thousand "fresh boots" boarded at San Francisco for the trip back to the war zone. Man, did they get seasick.

Never did it enter my mind that we would lose the war. It was interesting, but I wouldn't want to go through it again. I spent 37 seven months at sea in the South Pacific and guess where I was discharged—Minnesota! My blood was so thin from the heat and now it was 17 degrees below zero.

There's Nothing Like the Marine Corps

Merrill Frescoln
Fairfield, IA

2nd Marine Division
Pacific

Interview Date:
23 June 2011

Referral:
Julie Hill

I was jerked out of Iowa Wesleyan to go to the service. I had enlisted in the Marines in what was called the VI2 program that would allow us to finish college and become an officer. Due to losses at Guadalcanal of second lieutenants, the Marines decided they needed us sooner. I did boot camp at Paris Island and officer's training in Quantico, Virginia. Upon graduation from Quantico, I was asked what branch of the Marines I wished to serve in and I choose the paratroopers. However, that branch was done away with due to all the paratroopers dropped at Bougainville being blown out to sea and drowning. It was decided that the islands were too small to attempt any more paratrooper jumps. So I was assigned to the infantry and met up with the Fourth Marines in Hawaii.

I was a replacement in the Second Marine Division after Tarawa and fought in Saipan. By golly, that was a pretty rough campaign. Saipan was a turning point in WWII. After Saipan, I

went to Tinian and then to Okinawa. We had five Marine divisions lined up to go into Japan if they hadn't surrendered. There's only myself and one other fellow from Austin, Texas, left alive from my B Company, First Battalion, 6th Infantry Regiment of the Second Marine Division.

I went in on the second wave on Saipan. The first wave never made it ashore. The Japs were zeroed in on them. Not all the second wave made it either. Maybe half of us did. There was a three foot high natural coral wall on the shoreline. I rode in on an amtrack which was bulldozer like and would tilt up and down going over the coral exposing us to artillery and machine gun fire. The driver couldn't see much out of the amtrack because there was only a little hole for him to look through. At that time, I was a second lieutenant. I had my hand on the driver's shoulder guiding him left or right. The driver's name was Keith Mitchell from Packwood, Iowa. The shells were flying all around, going "thump, thump." One artillery shell landed in the water very close to us. Some of the landing craft got hit and some of them didn't. It was darn scary!

The amtrack carried my mortar platoon and we numbered 35 men. We unloaded down a ramp at the rear of the amtrack into the water. I remember laying my carbine down on a five gallon can of drinking water that I was going to carry in to shore. A wave came up and washed over my carbine. I crawled up to a tree that had been blown up. There was a Jap up another tree looking straight down at me but he was shell shocked. He didn't know sic 'em what was going on. I raised my carbine up to shoot him but it wouldn't fire. It had sand in it. I ducked down and put my head behind the blown up tree stump, not that it would have done me much good. That's how I got out of that mess.

We knew we had to get off the beach. At first, we didn't go in very far on the island. After we landed we looked around and didn't see anyone we knew. I took my men up to a railroad track. There were some other guys already there. The battalion was trying to get organized. The Japanese artillery shells started landing closer to us. I thought, "Well, this isn't going to last long!" Pete Lake, the other vet still living in Austin, Texas, was a first lieutenant. He stands up and yells, "Alright Charlie Company, follow me," and he runs across the tracks. I didn't know what to do. This lieutenant had been in combat before so I told my mortar platoon to follow me across the tracks. We came out in an open field and tried to find some cover.

I found a trench the Japs had dug and laid down in it at dark and went to sleep. That night we had a big tank attack. I awoke at 2:00 AM and the guy beside me said, "There's a tank!" We were both kind of huddled together and that doggone tank went right over the top of me. The ground there was solid so the trench didn't cave in or anything. The Jap tank went down the hill a little bit and turned around and faced us. I told the guy with me that I was "going to go down and knock that tank out." He didn't say anything so I walked down towards it and shot it with a grenade launcher and hit its gas tank. I ran back to my trench and then the tank exploded.

> *"The beach landing is the worst part of any campaign. Everything is in a state of confusion."*

Question: Did any Japanese crawl out of the tank?

Two came out of the turret. They acted confused, like they were trying to figure out what happened. I had a sergeant that dropped a hand grenade down a different tank's turret. The Japs came out the side of that tank. That's how he got his. I don't know what happened to the Japs that crawled out of my tank because it was dark. The tanks pulled out of our area around 3:30 AM.

My platoon also had bazooka teams. One team knocked out seven tanks with seven bazooka rockets that first night. The other team went four for four. I found out later that the guy carrying the rockets for the second team threw three of the seven issued away because it was too heavy to carry them all. Those teams were pretty much on their own. They had been through Tarawa and I hadn't. They knew what to do and were pretty sure shots.

My 60mm mortar teams would fire illumination rounds at night so we could see any movement going on out in front of us. Then the riflemen would fire into a movement they could see. The Japs would usually counter attack at night. Some nights they'd try to infiltrate and other nights they wouldn't. I don't think they liked to fight at night any more than we did. They'd do a lot of firing at night, but I don't think they knew what they were shooting at. All we wanted to do at night was get some shut eye. After fighting all day and carrying the weight of all our gear and ammunition, we were beat. As an officer, I always had something that needed looking after. If you stopped during the day and leaned against a tree, you fell asleep. We were that worn out.

The beach landing is the worst part of any campaign. Everything is in a state of confusion. You don't know if you are coming or going. If you make it through the landing you might have a ten percent chance of surviving. The Japanese were in caves back up in the mountains. Some of the caves had big doors and railroad tracks leading out. They had big artillery guns in those caves. They could do some rough stuff. That campaign lasted 23 days and nights. We were the only platoon on Saipan that didn't have anyone killed or wounded by the enemy. A sentry shot one of my guys in the knee by accident. I had an eardrum blown out from a Navy 500 pound bomb that hit too close. An Iowa football player named Al Menino was with me. We both lost our hearing.

Comment: There were a number of Japanese civilians living on Saipan.

Yes there was. I woke up one morning and there was a dead Japanese girl lying next to me. She'd been shot through the forehead. I suppose she had taken up with a Jap soldier and they were trying to slip back to their lines by going through our lines and a sentry shot her. I do know that she was not lying there went I went to sleep.

Question: Did you see any of the Japanese civilians jump off the cliffs at Marpi Point?

Yes, it was at the far end of the island. I saw 30 to 40 commit suicide that way. We didn't care if they jumped off or not. We didn't take prisoners either. They didn't get any Marines as prisoners because we didn't give up. I also witnessed the banzai attacks on Saipan which occurred at the end of the campaign. We were too much for them. We had too much firepower and were better shots.

"I woke up one morning and there was a dead Japanese girl lying next to me. She'd been shot through the forehead."

After three or four days of rest, we landed on the neighboring island of Tinian. It took nine days to take Tinian. It rained all the time we were there making conditions pretty bad for us. Tinian was a lot easier than Saipan.

Okinawa was our second campaign. There's a lot to war. We'd only do about one campaign a year. There was a lot of training involved to get ready and all sorts of supplies to be gathered, even things like drinking water. We trained with the new replacements for six months before the invasion. Our 60mm mortars were replaced by the heavier 81mm mortars. We were used as a decoy force off the southern end of the big island of Okinawa. We feinted three separate landings in our amtracks but would turn back when we'd get in machine gun range of the shore and returned to our LST. It was hoped that the Japs would move their forces to the southern end of the island so when the real invasion went in to the north there would be less opposition. It worked so well that our battalion was not needed and we were sent back to Saipan to

train for the invasion of the Japanese home islands. The kamikazes attacked our Navy ships offshore at Okinawa. I saw ships get hit. I think they never went after us because our LST was such a small ship and the Kamikazes had better targets.

Our 2nd Division was scheduled to spearhead the invasion of Japan. Of course, the dropping of the two atomic bombs cancelled those plans. Two weeks after Japan surrendered, the 2nd Marine Division landed at Nagasaki, the city where the second bomb was dropped. My mortar platoon was the first off the boats and I was the first man of my platoon to step on Japanese soil. There was nothing there that resembled a city, just some smoke and small fires still burning. I did find one brick building but its roof was gone.

Question: What was your opinion of the Japanese soldier?

They were inferior and not well trained. They were up against some stiff competition in the Marines.

I volunteered for the Marines because they had a pretty good reputation. There's nothing like the Marine Corps. It was the most efficient organization I've ever been around. They were a great bunch of men to be around. They had good standing everywhere you looked. They were always proud to be Marines. But I didn't think it was so hot myself for quite a while. It wasn't until I was home from the war that I really started to appreciate the Marine Corps.

I finished college at Wesleyan after the Marines. I ran the grain elevator in Sigourney with my dad for five or six years and then farmed for a living.

HONORED TO BE A PART OF IT

John Koontz
Fairfield, IA

436th Anti-Aircraft Battalion
N. Africa & Europe

Interview Date:
23 June 2011

Referral:
Personal Contact

I was taken in the first draft out of Jefferson County on March 18, 1942. I was gone for 43 months. I took my basic training at Camp Wallace in Texas. I did my training on the 40mm anti-aircraft gun at Camp Irwin in California. I was assigned to Battery B of the 436th Anti-aircraft Battalion. I shipped out of Norfolk, Virginia. We were in an old ship, the USS *Bliss*. It took 18 days to cross in rough seas. I was seasick every day and scared the last day. We docked in Morocco and went to shore. Our ship was torpedoed in the harbor. There were still men on board. Eleven men went missing. Seven were hospitalized with burns and two were killed.

We were part of the initial invasion of North Africa (Operation Torch). The United States thought that the French (Vichy) troops would be friendly but they weren't. We wore an armband showing we were Americans.

Question: Were you ever fired on by the French troops?

No, but we were shot at by Nazi planes. We were right behind the infantry and in front of the artillery. It was that way clear across Africa. Our artillery would fire over our heads and the enemy artillery would fire at us. Our biggest concern was the short rounds from our own guns. We went

through French Morocco, Algiers, and Tunisia.

The first place we set up our guns to guard was the airport at Casablanca. That's where we saw the first German planes. They were the Stukas and the medium bombers. They were going after our planes on the ground. We guarded a number of our artillery groups as well. We had spotters with us. It was their job to identify an incoming plane and determine if it was friend or foe and what kind it was if it was enemy. Actually, by the time we got over there, the German air force was starting to fizzle out in North Africa. Our next deployment was to Oran, Algiers.

We were attached to different infantry divisions. I can't remember what divisions they were. At one time or another, we were part of the 3rd, 5th, and 7th Armies. We served under Patton in Africa and Sicily. We were sent where we were needed. We moved all the time. We had trucks that pulled our guns. We sat on benches in the back of the truck when we traveled. Basically, we'd guard airports, ammunition dumps, and certain road intersections. Our guns were hooked up to a generator and a control box. People were on this box that did the vertical and horizontal tracking. That's what I did. I was a fire control instrument operator. One guy was on the vertical and I was on the horizontal. You'd have to give the plane a little lead. I didn't initially receive training for that. Someone had to leave and I took over that job. I had been trained to operate the generator.

We didn't have a lot to shoot at sometimes but other times we did. Sometimes you could tell when you got a good hit and other times you couldn't. Each battery would be credited when hits were made. Each gun crew would have a quad 40mm and a quad fifty. There were four gun crews in each battery.

Then we went in on the invasion of Sicily (Operation Husky) on July 9th, 1943. We were at the Palermo airport for quite a little spell. This would have been in 1943. We left Palermo for the Messina Straits. We worked our way up the toe of Italy nearly to Florence. We went through Rome. Then we were pulled back to Naples to get ready for the invasion in southern France (Operation Dragoon).

We landed at Marseille on August 15th, 1944. There was some German resistance in southern France but not too much. That's when we had to be careful because the German planes would strafe us. We'd jump in the foxholes the infantry had already left. I can remember that!

Question: I am wondering why you weren't shooting at the German planes?

We weren't set up yet. Every time we moved, we'd have to dig out a big place to set our gun up and sandbag around it. About the time we'd get set up, we'd get orders to move again. Usually we only moved once a day. I think the longest we ever stayed in one pit was two weeks. We were usually close enough to see the front lines. We went through France, Germany, and Austria. I liked Austria the best. An old woman in France came out with a freshly baked apple pie for us to eat as we went on our way. Our battalion was even credited with taking some prisoners.

Question: Were any of your battalion awarded purple hearts?

Oh, yes. Guys would get wounded, usually from shrapnel. Either it was from German artillery or short rounds from our own artillery.

Question: What was your reaction when you heard about Pearl Harbor?

Well, I figured I'd get drafted. It wasn't too long before I was. There were a lot of people that did enlist. I couldn't decide where I wanted to serve so I just waited to be drafted.

It was a different kind of war than they have today. After the war ended, we figured that we had enough points to go home. Instead, we were sent to England to do MP duty. I farmed after coming home. Farmed all my life and we still own it out on the Pleasant Plain road. Later, I even served on the draft board.

Question: John, do you have a message for the young people of today regarding your service during the war?

I was honored to be a part of it. In fact, I went on the one day Honor Flight to Washington, D.C. It was a wonderful day. People honored us every place we went.

A Two Star General

Robert Gamrath
Fairfield, IA

Army Air Corps, 34th Infantry Division
Stateside

Interview Date:
23 June 2011

Referral:
Aaron Kness

To my knowledge, the real story of WWII hasn't been written because it is so damn complicated. The first time I tried to enlist, they wouldn't take me because I was too skinny. I was married and had a son born so I decided to wait until they drafted me which happened five months after the war started. I spent three years, eight and one half months in the Army Air Corps and a total of a little over 29 years in the military. I did serve one little spell in the Navy in 1940. They came out with a 30 day cruise down to Panama that three or four of us thought would be good to go on. We were aboard the USS *Arkansas* and it had a huge wake because they couldn't steer it straight.

The rest of my time was spent with the 34th Infantry Division which was an Iowa National Guard Division. That's not regular army. Both Washington and Fairfield had units in the 34th. I spent close to two years working in the medics before going off to college. As a kid during the Depression, I worked at the Shriner-Johnson drug store 40 hours a week while going to school and 90 hours in the summer. This goes back to tough times. They let me work six months before they paid me anything. Then they gave me twenty dollars before Christmas It figured out to $1.25 per week. A lot of people worked for $50 to $70 a month during the Great Depression.

I joined the Guard when I was 16. Some of my friends went in at age 14. The Reserves were mainly made up of college graduates. My brother was eight years older than me and a graduate of the University of Iowa. He was working for IBM when the war started and went in as a captain.

In 1940 there were only 200,000 servicemen and that included all branches of the military. By 1945 there were 16,000,000. Where'd they all come from? They were civilians and they were all better trained than the National Guard units before the start of the war. You may hear some old guys saying that the Guard units weren't worth much. That's because we didn't have much to begin with. We even had to train with wooden rifles. The people that really won the war were the women in the United States that went to work in the factories. It was old men and women who were building the Liberty ships at a rate of one per day.

I stayed stateside during the war. That wasn't because I tried to duck anything. The first place they sent me was to Ft. Leonard Wood down in Missouri, where we had six to eight weeks of boot training. I was 22 years old when I went to Ft. Leonard Wood. They made me a drill instructor because I'd had previous military experience. Fortunately, I had some knowledge about what was expected of me. After boot camp they sent me to radio school in South Dakota. Then I was sent to the military airport in Atlantic City, New Jersey, for field training. That airport is now a civilian airport and the biggest one in the United States. Then I was sent to another place to prepare for going overseas. Luckily for me, my application for Officers Training School came through. I think being married with a child might have had something to do with it.

When I completed OSC, I was sent to Pawley, New York to cryptographic school. It was for decoding and deciphering messages but there was a lot more to it than that. There was one case where they intentionally coded a message so that the Japanese could read it. This was designed to draw the Japanese Navy out so we could bomb the hell out of them. There were other cases where they'd use American Indians who would put the message in their language and there was no way the Japanese could decipher it. I was the regimental commander of my class and we had parade every evening. They brought in an old World War One veteran to run the class. When I graduated from that school, they moved it to Illinois and took me with them as an instructor. So that's why I didn't have to go overseas.

I didn't have enough points to be discharged until February of '46. I left as a captain in rank. I started a business here and had to rejoin the National Guard Service company to make enough money to stay in Fairfield.

During the war, the 34th Division had 607 days of frontline duty. A Service Company is just what it is called. It has a headquarters company, a band, a medical company, a 4.2 mortar company, and a section called Graves Registration. They're the ones that pick up the dead bodies. I was the Service Company commander. That 4.2 inch mortar company had more short range fire power than a whole company of artillery because they could shoot so much faster. I fired one once and their destructive capability still scares me when I think about it.

We had one boy in my company that was somewhat limited. He couldn't make it through the second year of high school. But our company took him. He did a lot of KP and latrine duty. During the war he was in Graves Registration.

We were up in Michigan doing our two week training one time and scheduled to come home the next day. I checked in at headquarters that evening and there wasn't anyone there. All of a sudden, three or four sergeants showed up saying so and so "is drunker than a skunk and he's got a big knife. He's run everybody out of the mess hall and we can't get it cleaned up so we can leave in the morning." I asked if they had found the 1st sergeant and they said he had gone to the show. I replied, "Well that's great. I haven't been shot at, so now I'll get cut up." So I walk down there and there is 30 to 40 people looking in through the windows and this same limited boy is inside with most of the lights off waving this big knife. I walked in and called him by name, saying, "I'm your commanding officer and I want that knife." He about fell over trying to salute me, he was that drunk. He handed me the knife and I turned around and told the sergeants "to put this soldier to bed and make sure he went to sleep because I wanted to take him home in the morning." This boy had spent two or three years in graves registration picking up dead soldiers during the war and I didn't blame him for wanting to get drunk.

I had to kick a full master sergeant out for being drunk on the job. I also had to send a company commander from Washington home while we were on flood duty for being drunk.

My deputy commander, O.B. Nelson, was the head football coach at Parsons College. The best one they ever had, in my opinion, and a good friend of mine. One time he came out for general inspection wearing tennis shoes. He was ready to take over the company when I planning to retire after putting in three years as company commander but I was promoted up to regiment first. This happened the whole way I was in the service, being promoted about the time I was ready to get out.

The 34th went into Algiers and into Italy. Then they went to England where Eisenhower was in charge. Joe Little was the drum major in the 34th's band company which` was assigned to Eisenhower's headquarters group. Eisenhower would yell, "Hi, Joe" when the band marched by him. He even did this after he became President. I've seen the graves in France and it just breaks your heart.

I became the senior General Officer of 34th Division, Troop Commander. I was four years, three months in grade. I was a two star general. I retired in 1969 as a major general. The National Guard today is entirely different than it was before WWII.

I had dinner with the Lawson brothers last week. They were in town to celebrate their mother's 104th birthday. Bud Lawson was the Adjunct General for the Iowa National Guard. Dick was a four star general that worked as G3 out of the Pentagon and served as an aid to the President. He lives in Virginia.

Evelyn and I just celebrated our 70th wedding anniversary. I'll be 92 next month.

A Lot of them Luftwaffe

Rollie Zihlman
Fairfield, IA

109th Ordinance Company
N. Africa, Europe

Interview Date:
23 June 2011

Referral:
Max Hollander & Steve Rebling

I am 95 years old. My grandparents came from Switzerland. My great grandpa on the other side of the family was named Coppock. He built a church and a dam on the Skunk River in the town that bears his name. I enlisted in the Army and went in on Thanksgiving Day, 1940. I volunteered for one year of service and did almost five. There was a draft then and I took another kid's place. I was the first one from Jefferson County to enlist. People have asked me the name of the kid I replaced but I can't remember. I have since gone to the courthouse to try and look it up but they have no records either.

I first went to Des Moines for a little while and was then sent to Camp Lee in Minnesota in January of '41. It was 30 degrees below up there. It was some cold! We'd go outside and drill for 10 minutes and go back inside to warm up. Then we'd go back out for another 10 minutes. That'd go on for about an hour and a half. One day our captain

said he had good news for us, "We're going back to Iowa." Boy, we were glad!

I was in the 109th Ordinance Company. We serviced artillery and infantry weapons. Next we went to Ft. Riley, Kansas for a little while and then returned to Des Moines. In the summer of '42 we trained in Louisiana. If I remember right, there were 24,000 of us down there training to go overseas. From there we went to Camp Kilmer, New Jersey. We trained there for a while. We arrived in Bristol, England August 18th, 1942. My ordinance company was attached to the 34th Infantry Division. We weren't actually a part of the division. The 34th was the first American division to go to Europe. They arrived in Northern Ireland in March and April.

Our company went in on the invasion of North Africa a day after the infantry and artillery landed at Oran, Algeria. Boy, it was bad. It was bad. There was still a lot of fighting. We were facing German defenders, not the French. We couldn't hardly get landed. There were a lot of dead soldiers floating around with their rifles still slung on their backs. I spent almost a year in Africa, including Tunisia and French Morocco. The Italian soldiers gave up fast. We saw a lot of them *Luftwaffe*.

Question: What was your job in the ordinance company?

We worked on rifles the infantrymen brought in for repair. When one of the big artillery guns went bad, we'd tow them back with a wrecker and work on them. Sometimes the barrels on the .30 caliber machine guns would get too hot and we'd have to replace them. It could be difficult getting them off. The cheaply built grease gun was tough to work on. We didn't have much luck fixing them. Fighting up in the mountains in the mud and wetness was hard on weapons.

We saw thousands of French Arabs. The Sahara Desert is 1200 miles across. We were on the edge of it and it was 130 degrees and no shade. The closest water was 70 miles away and it had to be treated with pills to be safe to drink. We were there about a month and glad to leave.

After running the Germans out of Africa I went in on the invasion of Italy. I spent a year and a half in Naples. Our outfit missed the invasion of Sicily. Italy is about half mountains. I made it to Rome a few times. One Sunday we were taken to Vatican City. That was something to see. There were priests and nuns by the hundreds. We couldn't get within a quarter mile of the pope for all the people. Rome was never bombed.

One time while we were camped at the edge of a mountain back of the lines in Italy, Bob Hope and the movie star Francis Langford gave a show. We were always blacked out after dark so the show was late afternoon. All at once, the German air force came over that mountain strafing and everyone ran for their foxholes. The show was over for that evening! There were other times the *Luftwaffe* bombed and strafed us.

Question: What did Bob Hope and Francis Langford do?

There was a foxhole for them, too. A few times we had to pull back when the Germans made a

push through our lines. It did not take us long to pack up and move out. There were times the German artillery would land pretty close to us. When those 88mms would go off, they'd get your attention. They were powerful guns.

We came across Jews in Italy that had been hiding from the Germans in buildings. They were glad to see us. Hitler was killing them by the thousands. The Italian people were alright. They were friendly. The Germans drank beer and the Italians drank wine. The Russians drank vodka.

I was over in Europe twice. The guys that went in early and had a lot of points got to come home for 30 days. I got home Christmas night in 1944. While I was home, I received a phone call from Camp Kilmer telling me there were no troop trains available so I should stay on leave another month. I returned to Italy on March 1st, 1945.

We were on the Italian/French border the day the war ended. I remember seeing the Air Force planes flying over early one morning heading to bomb Germany. They flew in 'V' formations and looked like geese. An officer said, "It won't be long now." In 24 hours, the war was over.

I was discharged July 5th, 1945 from Ft. Sheridan, in Chicago. I went to work at Burlington Ordinance Plant. I worked there for 31 years. I ran a mower in the summer and a snowplow in the winter. A lot of the buildings were underground. We mowed right over the top of them.

> *"The Germans drank beer and the Italians drank wine. The Russians drank vodka."*

Question: What was it like being already in the service when Pearl Harbor was attacked?

I was stationed in Kansas then. Our captain told us it had happened. Our training intensified and we had new people arriving. The camp I was in the process of converting from horse cavalry to mechanized. I had leave scheduled a week after Pearl Harbor and was worried that it would be cancelled. But my captained let me go.

My hope is that the children being born today don't have to fight a war.

Golden Shellback

Paul Reynolds
Washington, IA

Magic Carpet, *USS Attu*
Pacific

Interview Date:
24 June 2011

Referral:
Personal Contact

I grew up in Des Moines and enlisted in June of 1943 right out of high school. People were more patriotic back then and everybody was going in. I was only 17 so I had to have a parent's signature. Another reason for enlisting was I could choose the branch to military to serve in. I wanted to join the Air Force but my dad wouldn't agree to sign for that but the Navy was okay with him. So that's what I joined. I was 15 when the Japanese attacked Pearl Harbor. The pastor at our small church volunteered to be a chaplain.

Right away they froze the amount of gasoline. You could only buy four gallons a week. The speed limit was lowered to 35mph. My dad worked as a coal distributor. They'd get extra gas coupons to delivery coal. If he had any left over, he'd give them to servicemen to make sure they would have a full tank of gas. I started working at a gasoline service station in Des Moines when I was 14. The government asked people to turn in stuff made out of rubber when the war started because of the

shortage. We had a pile of rubber door mats people left us. I remember a neighborhood lady dropping off a pair of rubber galoshes. She cut them in two so nobody would take them, ensuring they would go towards the war effort.

I got in an accelerated training program called the V-12. We referred to it as 'victory in 12 years or we'd have to put down our slide rulers and fight'. I was sent to Iowa State for several semesters and then the University of Dubuque and later to Illinois State. Then the Navy ended the program and sent me to Great Lakes and then to Mid Shipman's School in the Bronx's in New York City at a place called Frog's Neck. It is still there and right across from the Merchant Marine School. We'd watch them practice drill abandoning ship. We trained on decommissioned private yachts that had been requisitioned at the beginning of the war because the Navy was so short of smaller vessels for sub patrol. We operated put of Long Island Sound and learned navigation and chart reading, piloting, gunnery, and things like that. I remember the time one of the guys wasn't being careful when practicing with the 20mm and almost hit a merchant marine ship.

We were given tours of different naval vessels at the Brooklyn Navy yard including a submarine and a sub chaser. Aboard the sub chaser, the use of the hedge hogs was being explained to us. The hedge hogs were like a shotgun blast of small depth charges that would explode in the water when they hit something. They were used to determine the depth of an enemy submarine by timing their rate of descent. While they were demonstrating how it operated, it accidently went off and dropped a cluster of the hedge hogs through the roof of a barracks next to the shipyard. The detonators were water activated so luckily they did not explode.

The Mid Shipman Officers training program was three months long. Two weeks before graduation I washed out. I could never figure out why. It was probably because they had more officer candidates than the Navy needed at the time. So I applied and was accepted to aviation electronics and was sent to Jacksonville, Florida. I graduated 6th in my class and was given a choice of assignments. I hadn't really seen much salt water yet so I applied for overseas duty. I shipped out of San Francisco on a steamship, the *USS Monterrey*, and was sent to Ford Island which is in the middle of Pearl Harbor, where the Japs attacked. I slept in a hangar about a month and then I answered the call that went out for volunteers to work the ships that were bringing troops home. It was called Magic Carpet.

I was assigned to the electronics division of an escort aircraft carrier, the *USS Attu*, CVE 102. It was named after one of the Aleutian Islands off Alaska. It was good duty. I was a seaman fist class in rank. I was aboard the escort carrier for eight months ferrying Army and Marines home. I don't remember how many rips we made. We stopped at a lot of islands. The natives would paddle out in their dugout canoes wanting to trade for cigarettes. One of the island harbors had Japanese navy caps floating upside down in the water. We took 7000 soldiers off a little island that was so small that I

don't know how they all fit on it. I don't remember the names of the islands but I can recall being in the Philippines, Borneo, New Guinea, and Australia. Australia was our first stop to deliver some paperwork to an admiral aboard a cruiser. It was a 10 day voyage from Hawaii that we made in seven. The funny thing was that the Australian gals knew we were coming. They came out in small boats, water taxis, to meet us. They would call out asking if so and so was on board. Our guys would shout catcalls and throw coins at them. We spent seven days in the Sydney harbor and were granted shore leave. Australia was the craziest place I have ever been. All the women wanted to go to the United States. Part of it was the Australian guys didn't have any money to spend on them and us Yankees did. The first thing they wanted to do was go for tea, which meant to eat a meal. I think we were the main source of food for many of them. You had to be careful what you said to them. Those Australian women were crazy. One gal asked me to get her a uniform so she could go on board with me. There was no way I was going to even consider doing that. Some gals got aboard a cruiser headed for the States as stowaways. The ship was two days out to sea when they were discovered and had to return to Australia to unload them.

"Some gals got aboard a cruiser headed for the States as stowaways. The ship was two days out to sea when they were discovered and had to return to Australia to unload them."

We had 2000 men on our carrier when doing the Magic Carpet. Our ship was designed for 900. Steel bunks were welded to the hangar deck six or seven high. Some of the ships only fed the discharged soldiers they were transporting twice a day but we fed them three meals. We evaporated (distilled) sea water for all our drinking water.

Some of the guys we picked up had been in stiff combat. They had a lot of baggage with them, including alcohol they had picked up from somewhere. After they got drunk one night we had a captain's inspection. All their baggage was inspected. They had everything; typewriters, guns, souvenirs, booze, and a monkey. All the government issue was confiscated and the ship's doctor put the monkey to sleep and threw it overboard. Otherwise, we would have been placed under a six week quarantine if hit port with it on board. The soldier who had the pet monkey took it off a Jap he had killed. It was aboard the barge that ferried the soldiers out to our ship but they wouldn't let him bring it on board. After boarding our carrier, this soldier whistled to the monkey and it raced up the cable securing the barge to our ship.

There were still mines floating in the shipping lanes so we had a mine patrol going on. Our ship had twin 40mm and a five inch gun on the fantail. They use the twin 40mm to sink any mines that were spotted. One time we saw what look liked a small floating island. It took quite a bit of ammo to sink it. I'm not sure what it was, maybe a ship's hull or a dock that had floated loose. The idea was to keep the shipping lanes clear. Another time we picked of an empty LCVP landing craft that was drifting. It had probably broken free of its mooring at Pearl.

Question: What was your typical day like duty-wise on the escort carrier?

We kept busy. I spent four hours a day running the voltage on two generators. The automatic voltage regulators had burnt out so it had to be done manually. I also operated the movie projector aboard ship. I was the electrician on the foredeck for the anchor winches when we went through the Panama Canal. The Canal Zone was 75% off limits to service men. It was mostly a red light district. You could see anything for a dollar. And I mean anything!

We crossed the equator and the International Date Line at the same time. That made you a golden shellback. We underwent the ceremony of kneeling on steel mats to King Neptune and getting poked with copper edged swords. We also had to take a salt water shower. One of the privileges of being a golden shellback was it allowed you permission to spit into the wind.

Question: Did the soldiers and Marines that had seen combat act any different?

A lot of times they would sit quietly together off by themselves.

Stan Wallace from here was a rear turret gunner on a PBM torpedo bomber. I didn't know that until I read it in his obituary. I worked on those electric turrets in the PBMs while in training. 'Mac' McGaffey had the local Pepsi distributorship. He was in the Army stationed in England. I don't

know what he did in the service but he met his wife over there.

I was discharged in 1946 and went back to school at Iowa State studying electrical engineering. This was on the GI Bill. I took some time off from school and got hired by the Burroughs Company. I ended up working 21 years for them, 14 of which were in Ottumwa. They manufactured and service book keeping and adding machines. I worked with all the banks in the area and Rex See told me there'd be an opening in what is now the US Bank in Washington and I started there on 1968.

I hope to go on the Honor Flight this September if my doctor thinks it would be okay.

THE TAIL END OF KNOWING ANYTHING

Kieffer Garton
Washington, IA

13th Armored Division
Europe

Interview Date:
24 June 2011

Referral:
Personal Contact

I grew up on a farm in the Jewell/Humeston area of Wayne County. I didn't know what to do after graduating high school. Everything seemed to be in a turmoil. I looked into joining the Merchant Marines and learned that was one of the most dangerous places to go as far as the number of casualties, but when you're 17, you feel immortal. I ended up enlisting in the Army on September 22nd, 1943 with the understanding that they wouldn't take me until I turned 18. I completed two quarters at Iowa State before being called up.

Over a 1000 guys went through Camp Dodge the day I was inducted. From Camp Dodge I went to Camp Hood in Texas for 17 weeks of infantry basic training. For the first month I was a complete basket case because I was so homesick. Plus, I was sick with bronchial pneumonia and put in the hospital upon my arrival in Texas. I weighed 135 lbs then and 185 lbs after the 17 weeks of training. The Army took good care of us. I had a 28 inch waist and could have licked my weight in wildcats. I stayed in that condition the whole way through service even eating Army chow.

There were approximately 1000 guys in our training battalion at Camp Hood. Thirty-three of us were selected to go to the 13th Armored at

Camp Bowie in Brownwood, Texas. My MOS number indicated I was a volunteer and I think that had something to do with me being selected. By that time in the war, we were fighting on two fronts and losing a lot of men. As far as I know, everyone else went in as a rifle infantryman. That's a real bad deal.

I was assigned to a heavy weapons platoon in Headquarters Company of 16th Armored Infantry Battalion. A lot of the guys were from Texas and Iowa. We trained on water cooled .30 heavy machine guns. There was a four man crew- first and second gunner and two ammo bearers. I was an ammo bearer but we were trained to do everything in case the need arose. Headquarters Company also had a heavy mortar (81mm) and recon platoon and three tanks with 105 howitzers for guns.

In January of '45 we sailed across the North Atlantic in an 85 ship convoy aboard the USS Robin. The waves were 20 feet high and it was rougher than a cob. Everyone got seasick including the Marine gun crew manning the 105 howitzer siting on the stern. We ate three times a day. We had to stand at a counter to eat. You be trying to eat and then here came some vomit sliding by. If you weren't sick before, you were then! Climbing up a ladder when the guy above you got sick was also unpleasant.

We didn't go to England but rather went straight to Le Havre, France. I spent the first night in Europe sleeping under a half-track. Later we were billeted in a large chateau in Normandy. The entire Headquarters Company slept in the attic. There were 22 fireplaces in the attic alone. The Marquis was never there; he stayed in Paris. He owned the village and all the farm ground surrounding it. Time was spent getting our equipment rounded up. I was detailed to unload ammunition off a train. The 13th Armored Division was the last to be sent to Europe. Everybody rode on either tracks or wheels. Nobody walks.

Let me tell you about the first combat we saw. Our armored column was driving down a road in France, we went past a grassy hill with two or three lines of trenches on it with a little house up on the top of the hill. Some dummy German fires on us- the whole 13th Armored Division on that road. So we stopped the half-track, dismounted, and set up our machine gun. Our platoon sergeant was named Sims. He was from Quincy, Illinois. He was so petrified that he froze and wouldn't get out of his half-track. The buck sergeant on the other machine gun in our squad took Sergeant Sims to the company commander at the point of a bayonet. Sims was busted to a private on the spot. He peeled potatoes for the rest of the war.

I received the Combat Infantry Badge and two battle stars. One of those was for the Ruhr Pocket and I can't remember the other one. The Ruhr Pocket had been bombed to rubble. One of the things we found there was hundreds Polish women that had been brought in as slave labor. The Germans had these little foot mines sown everywhere in the rubble. They were wooden so the minesweepers could not detect them. They were designed to blow your foot off which is better (for the Germans) than killing you because it took three guys to take care of the injured. The other thing I remember about the Ruhr Pocket was getting so tired that my entire squad laid down on a sidewalk with all our gear on and slept for eight hours. The Ruhr Pocket was the meanest part of the war I was in. A rumor went around that

American soldiers had executed 22 Germans that had manned an 88mm gun.

We started collecting a lot of German prisoners after the Ruhr Pocket. I remember one time standing guard out in the rain over 30-40 German prisoners. The Germans were in a barn but one end of it was on fire. I wasn't happy about the whole situation. Those POWs started creeping out of the barn. I wasn't going to shoot anyone and those Germans weren't going to cause any problems. Pretty soon we were all standing out in the rain. The barn burnt down.

Question: Did you ever see any German tanks?
I saw knocked out German tanks that were on fire. Tanks would scare you to death. A soldier on foot didn't have a chance. The Germans used horses to transport guns and supplies. They were down to using farm wagons. It makes you wonder what on earth was their incentive to keep fighting. I saw lots of dead horses. It was terrible. I saw a lot more knocked out Sherman tanks. Just about everyone was on fire. I saw a lot of dead Germans draped over stone walls. Most of the walls had broken glass cemented on the tops.

The bravest man in the whole outfit was the doctor, Harold Rosenberg. He wasn't a medic, but a real doctor. He'd run around treating the wounded while the shooting was still going on, standing upright. All he would have had to do was wait five minutes and it would have been safe.

My squad consisted of 12 guys. We all rode in a half track named 'Vera'. All the half-tracks in the company had names that started with the letter V. There was a .50 caliber machine gun in the front turret and two of the water cooled .30 calibers on board. We did not fire them without dismounting and setting up the tripod. Our platoon was unique. Our squad sergeant rode up in the turret. As soon as we stopped someplace, he'd immediately disappear. He'd go someplace every time. When we got ready to go again, he'd show up. Anyway, he was shacking up with the local women.

We were issued .30 carbines as our personal weapons. They were pea shooters. My buddy Bruce Krieger and I carried German Mausers. We zeroed them in on the Maginot Line. Krieger had been a high school math teacher. He was always getting into trouble and getting busted back to private. We carried those Mausers during parade inspection. I figured we'd get court martialed but nobody seemed to care.

Another guy and I were sent to a demolition school. One of our jobs was to probe for buried land mines with our bayonets. We'd flag them and someone else would disarm them later. It was a little unnerving. We also checked buildings for booby traps. I discovered one doorway booby trapped by seeing this little red wire. That was enough for me. I put a warning sign up and got out of there. I spent a lot more time pulling guard duty at headquarters.

We crossed the Rhine at Remagen. They had already quit using the rail road bridge by then. We crossed on a pontoon bridge the engineers built. Then we took off like crazy for Berlin. The German Army was pretty well finished by then. They'd shoot at you once and then immediately surrender, often by throwing a white bed sheet out the window. One time a sniper hiding in a house opened up on us. We had a tank with us. Nobody had enough ambition to go into the house to get the sniper so the tank stuck its gun barrel through the front door and fired a round. That took care of the house.

We only set up our machine guns half a dozen times. We'd set up our machine gun in the daytime by sand bagging the tripod to cover a road intersection about a quarter mile away. We'd zero in or register the gun on that intersection with tracers. At night we would provide intermittent fire on the intersection. It was a hell of a thing for a poor German to be down there on that intersection getting riddled by .30 caliber machine gun bullets.

The guy sitting next to me in the half-track was hit by a mortar fragment but my platoon pretty much went unscathed. The first platoon on A Company always had point and they had all the casualties. The closest I had to be wounded was while standing in the chow line. A guy dropped his grease gun (M3A1 submachine gun) and it discharged, killing him.

In the last days of the war, the executive office of the battalion would have German prisoners brought in one at a time. These POWs all had

"I looked out the same big picture window that Hitler did...."

numbers tattooed on their arms. They were the SS. The executive officer, a jeep driver, and the prisoner would run off and after a while they'd come back and there was no German prisoner. Apparently, they were taking them out and summarily executing them. This probably happened eight to ten times. I was guarding the headquarters so I witnessed this. Finally, they came and picked up the executive officer and took him to the funny farm.

We almost made it to the Elbe River before the whole division turned around and headed south towards Austria. The rumor going around was that somebody needed to be down there in case we had to fight the Russians. We ended up in the little village in southern Germany right next to the Inn River and the war is over. We were just across the river from Braunau in Austria where Adolf Hitler was born. Then all at once, all our equipment disappeared. Tanks, trucks, and our half-tracks vanished. To this day, I have no idea where it went. I think some German junk dealer got it all.

I was on the tail end of knowing anything. I never knew where I was or why I was there. I only knew what they told me and that wasn't much. The individual soldier had no idea what was going on. You were lucky if you knew which way was north. All you knew was what you could see from horizon to horizon.

Our whole company toured the Eagle's Nest at Berchtesgaden. I looked out the same big picture window that Hitler did but the glass was blown out. The Eagle's Nest had been bombed by British Mosquito planes.

The 13th was part of the 7th Army and Patton's 3rd Army. Shortly after the war was over, Patton gave a speech. He never said anything. He just cussed.

The 13th Armored Division was selected to go to the Pacific for the invasion of Japan. The plan was for us to land south of Tokyo on the Pacific side while another armored division landed of the western side and we were to cut the island in two. In July we came back to the states aboard the USS General Grant. It was a bona fide troop ship and a wonderful voyage compared to our trip over to

Europe. We had two good meals a day and we got to sit down to eat them. I'm half way through my 30 day leave, which was routine when you came home, and the war is over—VJ Day!

Since they Army already had plans to send us to Japan, they decided to go ahead and send us but gave us a 45 day furlough. After that was up, I reported to Camp Cook California, which is now called Vandenberg Air Force Base. Down on the beach was all new equipment. All the tanks were the newest models with 90mm guns. I stood guard there a few times. An infantryman is just a glorified guard much of the time. I also spent time copying re-enlistment records by hand. I also spent too much time policing the grounds for cigarette butts. Anyway, they decided MacAuthur had things under control in Japan and the 13th wouldn't be sent. But they did decide to send me individually to Japan and they gave me another 30 leave. So I went home again. I had to report back to Camp Cook just before Christmas.

At that time, my dad had two Ferguson tractors. He purchased a brand new Woods Brothers pull type, one row corn picker. New equipment was so scarce that he had to agree to pick his neighbors corn before they would sell it to him. Dad got his hand his hand buggered up in the corn picker. I went to the Red Cross and told them what had happened and I was needed at home so they interceded for me and I received a 45 day furlough. So there I am, still in the Army and picking corn in Wayne County and it was miserable cold with snow on the ground. While I was home, the outfit shipped back to Camp Hood. Finally, in April of '46, the Army decided I should go home. I was discharged from Jefferson Barracks in St. Louis.

I went back to Iowa State on the GI Bill and got a degree in farm operations. That was the four most wonderful years of my life. I studied part of the time. Des Moines was full of country girls working in the insurance offices. Part of my education was learned at the Green Parrot in Des Moines. After graduation, I went back to farm with my father because I loved to work horses but that didn't last because there wasn't enough land to support us both. In 1947 I started teaching voc ag but didn't really enjoy teaching. I ended up working as an appraiser and farm manager for Doane Ag Services for 39 years out of Tipton and Cedar Rapids.

THE GREATEST OUTFIT

Bill Beenblossom
Washington, IA

Construction Battalion
Pacific

Interview Date:
8 July 2011

Referral:
Mardi Knerr

I got tired of people asking me why I wasn't in the military when I walked down the streets of Washington. So I enlisted in 1945 and volunteered for the Navy CBs. I joined up with the CBs at Great Lakes near Chicago. It was "the greatest outfit I've ever been around." I was appointed Master of the Barracks while at Great Lakes. That meant I was in charge of overseeing the barracks and I was only an apprentice seaman at the time. I went all the way through with my best friend and neighbor, Francis Heck.

We shipped out of San Francisco on October 16th on an APA ship. We stopped at Pearl Harbor. There was still debris everywhere. In 17 days, we were in Guam. I think it stormed 14 of those days. The ship would roll sideways and pitch up 32 feet every three seconds. I didn't get seasick. I made a nest under a gun tub on the bow of the ship and slept in a coil of four inch hauser rope. The high light of the voyage was seeing the flying fish come off the big waves during the storm and land on the ship's deck. Those flying fish were 32 inches long and had really hard heads. They hit the ship's superstructure and drop to the deck. It sounded like somebody dropping rocks. I also saw dolphins at night in phosphorous water. It looked like you could reach out and touch them.

We were part of a heavy equipment outfit on Guam building the new Agana airfield. Coral was run through a rock crusher and mixed with asphalt to make the runway. Coral rock is soft rock similar to limestone. We could dig coral with a dozer as easily as with a backhoe. Every couple of weeks the demolition crew would use a wagon drill to bore holes every 10-12 feet and pack them with dynamite. The blast would loosen the coral rock. We have to get a new pair of shoes every week due to the coral.

When I got over to Guam, they sent me out with a fellow from Oklahoma. He was a D-8 dozer operator and I was his gopher. Two days later, I was operating the dozer and he was sent somewhere else. After running a dozer for a while, I felt comfortable doing whatever they asked me to do. Some of the rocks they had me moving were huge and I got into a few dangerous situations. Once in a while I'd drive a truck when I had nothing else to do.

They made me head of the shop. You didn't have to have any experience. I guess it was a question of who could yell the loudest. We could never get replacement parts to fix equipment. We had a 15 acre field parked full of tandem dump trucks that had little things wrong with them. Nobody had any desire to fix them up. They'd just keep bringing in new ones.

The guy in charge of heavy equipment had a brother in the Merchant Marines. After the war was over, this brother employed mechanics that knew what they were doing repair all the damaged equipment. He loaded the trucks and other equipment on ships and took it all back to the United States. I've often wondered if he is worth any money today.

I saw a couple of guys lose their lives. One was hauling rock, building a breakwater. Some of the rocks were boulders as big as this room. The trucks didn't have a tailgate. The trucks were unloaded by attaching a cable to the front of them and a dozer lifting the front of trucks up. The driver was required to get out of the truck while this was going on. This one time the dozer operator said something to the driver that he couldn't hear. The driver walked closer to where he shouldn't have been a rock crushed him.

There were still Japanese soldiers hiding out in the mountains on Guam. Because of that, some areas were off limits. I did venture once under orders into one of those areas to recover construction equipment. The roads up in the mountains were narrow and snaked around precipices that dropped to the ocean. I drove a lowboy up the mountain and met a school bus full of kids coming down. Luckily, the school bus driver knew what to do and we squeezed past. I widened out a lot of bridges going up. I was supposed to haul back a road maintainer, backhoe, and dozer that had been left up there. When we arrived where the equipment was supposed to be, we found that somebody had run it over the side of the mountain and it was all destroyed. We had been warned that there were thought to be Japanese in the area.

The Japs would sneak down into our camp at night to pilfer supplies. There were guards posted but no one ever saw anything. We lived in 24' x 24' tents down next to the water. It seemed like whenever a tent went unoccupied for over 24 hours, everything inside would be cleaned out. We had trouble with other outfits stealing our jeeps. The CBs didn't get along well with the navy people

but we never had any problems with the Marines. The Marines patrolled the roads. They were the highway patrol on Guam. There was a 25 mph speed limit unless you were hauling asphalt and then it went up to 35 mph. There were also Army personnel on Guam.

Question: Did the idea of Japanese sneaking around your camp at night bother you?
I never lost any sleep over it. I figured that I had as good as chance as anybody of surviving.

One time another guy and I were driving a radio jeep searching for one of our stolen jeeps. We drove past a ravine and heard someone calling for help. We knew better than to stop and continued driving and radioed for another jeep to back us up. Then four of us ventured out on foot. The place was spooky looking. One of us stepped on a stick and there was a loud crack! One guy was so startled he cut loose with his gun. All we ever found was a chicken perched on the porch railing of an empty house cackling away.

Question: Why did you know it was better not to stop?
On Guam, you learned to trust one or two men and let the rest kind of go their own way. I had a buddy from Missouri and one from Massachusetts. They were the two guys I would trust with my life as long as I could see them.

There were small islands around Guam. During low tide, it was possible to walk to some of them. There were American civilians on Guam. Some of the men had their families with them. I spent time building an area for navy families to live. On our trip home, there were 500 women and children aboard ship with us.

I volunteered to go to the Bikini Atoll where they tested an atomic bomb but was not selected. My job would have been to level off the blast crater. Those who went didn't have a good word to say about their time spent there. They did report that the explosion "made a hell of a dent."

There were two civilian outfits working on Guam when I came home. The weather and temperature on Guam were similar to south Florida. I was usually naked from the waist up and never wore a cap. I was so tanned that I looked like a black

> *"They were the two guys I would trust with my life as long as I could see them."*

guy. Now, I'm paying for it. It would rain with no warning. You'd look up and the sun was shining while you were getting drenched. I don't recall ever hearing thunder or seeing lightening. It rained a lot. I was wet more times than I was dry.

My favorite job was pushing crushed coral away from the crusher. I enjoyed it because it was a challenge to keep it level. It was a lot like having a regular job. We'd start at six o'clock in the morning and get off at three in the afternoon.

One thing I did learn over there was that I didn't like Spam.

Julie Beenblossom: I was three years old when the war started. My dad was 40 years old and enlisted after Pearl Harbor. My mother and we four girls went where ever they sent him. He was an administrator at Luke Field in Phoenix, Arizona. He'd been a school superintendent. My dad was named Paul John Jones. The war affected so many people in so many ways. That's how I ended up in Washington. I became very patriotic as a little girl and I am still that way.

Bill: I farmed after coming home and ran a corn sheller with my brother. For three or four years, we averaged shelling 650,000 bushels each year.

TRIBUTE

My sisters and I are very proud of him (Bill Beenblossom) and love to hear his stories. We love him very much.

Mardi Knerr
Washington, IA

THE MOST HATED WOMAN ON BASE

Bess Edwards
Washington, IA

WAVES
Stateside

Interview Date:
16 July 2011

Referral:
Halcyon House

I was in the WAVES (Women Accepted for Volunteer Emergency Service) in the Navy and was based in Ottumwa. I enlisted in 1943 and served through 1945. I had a Specialist S rating and I have no idea what it meant. All I could figure was that it had something to do with the Shore Patrol. I wore an "S" patch on my shoulder. That allowed me to leave the base every Friday evening without needing a pass. Everybody else had to get one. I came back to Washington every weekend. I'd take what was called the "cattle car" from the base to the bus station in Ottumwa and get home that way.

I was in charge of about 500 women. A lot of the girls worked down at the air base on airplanes. That's where they met the "90-day wonders." Those young men were second lieutenants from Iowa City and were being trained as pilots in Ottumwa. My girls thought those pilots were hot stuff and wanted dates with them.

I didn't read the regulations as good as I should have when I first went in. There was a woman lieutenant that was always on me about the girls in my barracks. They weren't wearing their head gear as required and wore red socks when they were supposed to be white only. Things like that. I was 23 or 24 years old at the time and most of the women were younger than me. They'd be gone all day working on the planes. I really didn't have that much to do when they weren't around. They didn't treat me very good. Women can be pretty catty at times. I felt like I was the most hated woman on base. It kind of ruined me for wanting to be around any group of women in the future. They'd have the nerve to ask me to iron their uniforms and borrow my bedroom slippers for their date nights spent in Ottumwa.

I was transferred to Olathe, Kansas. I'm not certain what I was supposed to be doing down there for sure. I remember spending a lot of time swimming and learning how to bowl while there.

My husband Rueben and I were married in 1947. Rueben was quite a bit older than me and died of a heart attack. We had one child together. He was a photographer by trade and we had a photography supply store in Iowa City. My maiden name was Lowe. Bob Lowe was my brother and Dorothy See my sister. I have another unmarried sister at the UP Home. Bob was in the war but I never heard him talk about it. I remarried in 1953 and that lasted 24 years until he passed away.

TRIBUTE

It is a privilege to have an opportunity to write a few remarks about the impact that the service of our World War II veterans continues to have on me. In my work as a judge on the Iowa Court of Appeals, and an Iowa District Court Judge before that, I have often reflected on the significance of the service of our veterans. Access to justice and protection of freedoms would only be dreams if not for those who have sacrificed in order to protect the United State of America from those who hold different ideals.

I moved to Washington County 30 years ago as a young lawyer. Over the course of the years, and through involvement in various community activities, I periodically learned more and more about the sacrifices made and the suffering endured during World War II by many of the men of Washington County. One of the reasons that it took me years to learn even little bits and pieces about their lives during the war is the humility of the whole lot of them. I rarely heard them talk about their experience, but welcomed every opportunity. I remember well a Veterans Day presentation at a local service club meeting where I first heard one of them talk about escaping a

prisoner of war camp; but such talk was rare and underplayed. Every veteran that I have encountered, from the prisoners of war to the state-side supply clerks, conveyed the same ultimate message: they were just doing what was asked of them, and they went on with their lives. They then humbly served our community in nearly every profession and occupation for years and years.

Realizing that they have so much more to share, I am very pleased that the histories of our World War II veterans are being documented in this book; and it is with great expectation that I look forward to reading the accounts of the interviews. To those veterans: Thank you for your past service to and sacrifice for our country during World War II, for your past and present service to the Washington County community, and for your willingness to share your experiences for preservation in this book for the benefit of present and future generations.

Respectfully,

Michael R. Mullins
Judge, Iowa Court of Appeals

VERY APPRECIATIVE

Marie Widmer
Washington, IA

Aid Worker
Europe

Interview Date:
16 July 2011

Referral:
Halcyon House

I volunteered through the Mennonite Church Conference (MCC). I had gone through nurses training in Hutchinson, Kansas. My parents were really poor but I felt like it was something I needed to do. I first went to a CPS (Civilian Public Service) work camp to help the boys there. Next I went to a CPS hospital camp in Michigan. It was there I met a minister with the MCC. He asked me if I wanted to go over to Europe. I told him that I did. Of course, this would be without pay although I did get $15 a month and all our living expenses.

When we got to Europe, we were in a program where we did clothing distribution. The Mennonites had sent many bales of clothing over to Europe. By that time in the war, there was a real need for clothing. In Holland, they wore wooden shoes and they wanted leather ones. I met my husband over there and we were married in Europe.

I was in Holland in 1944. The war was still going on. Things weren't very good in Europe. The American people came and rescued Europe. A lot of Holland had been flooded because the dikes had been broken. Food couldn't be grown in those areas.

After Holland, I was transferred to a different

"The American people came and rescued Europe."

place where we distributed food. The younger people, the pregnant women, and the old people needed the food the worst. Powdered milk, flour, and other food were sent over from the United States. We'd make big kettles of soup to feed the people. I'm not certain the exact number of people we fed every day. It was probably around 200. There just wasn't anything to eat for many of the people. I was over in Europe for two years. I spent six months of that time just cooking food.

Question: Did you ever do any actual nursing on injured people?
Yes, I did some in France. It was for children who had lost their parents. There was a school set up for these orphaned children and I was the nurse there. That was the only real nursing that I did. We made it into Germany. We did both food and clothing distribution there. The destruction was bad. You'd see a bunker or maybe a chimney sticking up. You knew somebody was living there.

The Red Cross was also over there helping. They'd help about half the people in an area and we'd help the other half.

Question: Did you ever see the displaced people used for slave labor?

Oh, yes, the Russian people. There was a group of Russian Mennonites that had been forcibly relocated from the Netherlands to Russia to show the Russians how to farm. The Russians apparently were not good farmers. These Mennonites were traveling someplace to board a ship for Paraguay. The one thing Mennonites are strongly opposed to is killing and they understood that they would not have to serve in that capacity in Paraguay.

We were in one place near Kiel, Germany, were the Jews had been held. There were a number of tiny cells the Jews would be crowded into. I can't remember the name of the camp. I'm 94 years old so my memory isn't as good as it should be.

Question: What was your opinion of the German people?

They were pretty much just like us. We did not have any objection to anybody. We were friends to all. We made connections with the local churches. I had a brother-in-law that ran one of the relief camps. He was invited back to Europe 50 years after the war for a celebration and recognition for all he had done to alleviate the suffering. The people were very appreciative.

When my husband and I returned to the states, we started farming. Jon and Tim Widmer are two of my children you may know. All of my children have done special work for the church.

Two Hundred and Nineteen Days

Peter "Stibe" Flander
Keota, IA

6th Infantry Division
Pacific

Interview Date:
23 July 2011

Referral:
Dean Redlinger & Frank Morris

I graduated from high school in 1943, here in Keota. I turned eighteen in August and by October I was drafted and in the service. The farthest I'd been from home before being drafted was Muscatine. From Des Moines I was sent to Camp Roberts in California where I had 17 weeks of basic training. Then I was sent home on 10 days of furlough. I got to visiting with some other guys home on leave and three of us from Keota were being sent next to Fort Ord in California. The other two were Phil Morris and Fred Wade. We three shipped out of San Francisco on the 27th of April in 1944 on the same ship and were on the ocean for fifteen days without touching port. There were enough food and supplies on that ship for ten thousand people for 15 days. At the time I thought, "That's Washington, Keota, and Sigourney all put together on one ship."

We went to Sidney, Australia. There were 600 blacks on board with us and they stayed in Sidney. Some of us went on to a big replacement depot for the Pacific on the southeastern tip of New Guinea. I was sent to the 1st Infantry Regiment which was part of the 6th Infantry Division. Phil Morris and Fred Wade got sent to different outfits.

After I joined the 6th Division, I discovered there were three other fellows from Keota in my division.

My cousin Omar Flander, was in a field artillery unit attached to the division and Dick Daeley and Matty Hotchkiss were in the 1st Infantry Regiment with me. There were a lot of people with connections to Keota in New Guinea.

In northern Luzon towards the end of the war, our company took a pack train of donkeys or mules loaded up with supplies up in the mountains. There weren't any roads, only paths to follow. We were sent up to relieve the company Matty was in. There sat this guy with a long beard and tired eyes. I looked at him asking, "Matty, is that you?" I couldn't believe it. He replied, "It is, Stibe." He was on his way down the mountain. We didn't realize how close the war was to being over at the time. One of the Japanese units we were facing ended up surrendering to us.

There were rice paddies up in these mountains to an elevation of four thousand feet. They were all built by hand and probably took centuries to construct. There was a waterfall diverted for irrigation. Those rice paddies couldn't be sold. They were handed down from one generation to the next.

There was place the C-47s would drop supplies to us. They'd just push everything out the door then we'd have to go recover it. The ammunition boxes had parachutes attached so they were easy to find. It was all tough hiking up through there.

We heard the news about the dropping of the atomic bomb and all this unbelievable destruction it caused from a Tokyo Rose broadcast. We didn't have any radios but we listened to her when we could because she played our kind of music but it made us homesick. Her story turned out to be true. The next day we hiked the 15 or 20 miles down out of the mountains. There was a camp set up with cots and tents where we could go and rest. The very next day they made us do close quarter drill. Can you imagine that? They wanted to keep us busy. That was the infantry! All we wanted to do was sit and talk or sleep. That ended my two hundred and nineteen days of continuous combat on Luzon. I often wonder how many people today would go back and do the same things we did under the same conditions. We did what we had to because it was patriotic.

Question: Were the Japanese holed up in caves above you in the mountains?

We didn't really know because they had so many caves. They did this in New Guinea too. We thought they were just natural caves but a lot of them were dug caves. They forced prisoners to dig them. They had Asian, Koreans, American, and prisoners from the islands doing the manual labor. There was supposed to be one large cave somewhere in Luzon wide enough for two trucks to pass where gold was buried. It's been reported that six thousand tons of gold looted from Japanese conquered territory is buried in that cave. The slave labor doing the work was sealed inside the cave to keep its location secret. I read about all this later in a book. Of course, we didn't know anything about it at the time.

I carried an M-1 Garand, a good gun. I wished I had purchased one. I took part in military funerals for 65 years but gave it up last year. My legs and back have given out and I can't stand at attention that long any more. I was proud to do it while I could. If I had known I would have been doing it that long I would have had a rifle that could fire,

like an M-1. The old WW1 rifles we carried were worn out.

An infantryman in WWII was paid $50 a month. Being overseas earned an additional $10 dollars a month and combat pay was another $10 dollars. That figures out to an additional thirty cents a day for being shot at. I only received one medal before being discharged and that was the Good Conduct Medal. They didn't give medals during the war in the Pacific because they didn't have any available to issue. Sometime after the war I found out where to write to and be awarded the medals earned so I did that and spread the word to other vets in the area. I also served with the 6th Division in Korea. The war records stored in St. Louis were destroyed in a fire so it was more difficult getting medals for that service. I finally wrote a letter to one of our U.S. Senators and had the medals delivered in 10 days. It goes to show you that things can happen pretty fast in Washington, D.C. if they want them to.

> "We heard the news about the dropping of the atomic bomb and all this unbelievable destruction it caused from a Tokyo Rose broadcast… Her story turned out to be true."

We went to Korea after the war as occupation troops. The Japanese had already left by the time we arrived. It took us ten days of sailing to get there. We landed at Inchon. We had left the tropics and there was snow on the ground. We about froze to death. We were all over southern Korea, driving around making our presence know. There wasn't a lot to do, really. I was a staff sergeant and in charge of an anti-tank gun but it got lost in the move. We had to drive to southern Korea through the mountains to retrieve it. We encountered a number of unmanned road blocks built of brush and trash. We took it to mean someone didn't want us there but we didn't experience any trouble.

New Guinea was jungle or a tropical rain forest. It rained 21 days straight when we were at the replacement depot. If you tried to dig a fox hole a foot deep for protection, you had a well. They fed us salmon 20 of the 21 days we were there. It wouldn't have tasted so bad if we could have eaten it right out of the can, but the cooks always tried to doctor it up. The natives on New Guinea were diseased and unhealthy. The men wore G strings and the women bare breasted. They were taller and blacker than the Filipinos.

Most of the time, we didn't have to go into the interior very far. While I was in New Guinea, I was in on three invasions. They were not real big operations. Our purpose there was to secure enough ground to make landing strips for fighter planes for the upcoming invasion of the Philippines. The fighters were mostly Mustangs and P-38s. We had 87 days of continuous combat there and I was still not 19 years old.

Question: Were you in the Battle of Lone Tree Hill on New Guinea?

There were a lot different stories about Lone Tree Hill because a lot of the time, there was only one tree left on any hill. There was one very similar around Sansapoor.

The Koreans would haul their human waste (night soil) around in tanks to use as fertilizer on the crop fields. Every once in awhile some wise guy would hit one of those with his truck for fun. It's amazing what some people will do when they get a little beer in them. The officers were always asking where their coffee pot was. It was their code word for their liquor. Some of the men drank what was referred to as torpedo juice. It was one hundred ninety proof alcohol. I am not certain where they got it or what exactly it was. It may have been the actual fuel used to propel a torpedo.

My outfit was one of the spearhead divisions that landed on Luzon in the Philippines. We went in so far and secured the land up to the Angat River. We received word to hold there and not to advance any farther and there would be some rangers coming through our lines and they would be advancing on to this prison camp. We had no idea how close we were to it. We thought, "What the heck. We're getting robbed of that." It turned out that liberating that camp was one of the best things we didn't get to do. The rangers were trained especially for this and they knew exactly what they were doing.

The mission was a success. The rangers freed the POWs at the Cabanatuan prison camp. Those guys had been on the Bataan Death March. They made a movie about this raid. We never heard or saw the outcome as we had already moved on by the time they came back through.

> *"The Japs wanted to fight at night and we wanted to fight in the daytime so it was 24/7."*

Question: Did you use passwords at night?

Yes, and it was usually a word like, McGillicuddy, with lots of Ls in it. The Japs couldn't pronounce our "L" sound.

I was a platoon sergeant in Headquarters Company, which consisted of a heavy weapons platoon, an anti-tank platoon, and an ammunitions and pioneer platoon. We were infantry and were put in where ever we were needed. I manned a lot of road blocks with a 37mm anti-tank gun. The Japs didn't have much for heavy equipment like tanks. We had armored piercing for tanks and canister rounds that were like a shotgun shell. They were anti-personnel shells. The Japs wanted to fight at night and we wanted to fight in the daytime so it was 24/7. I had two hundred and nineteen days of that.

We lost our two star division general and our regimental commander. He was a full colonel. They were in our command post. I had just passed through there and heard this, "Brrrrrrp!" A Japanese soldier hidden in a nearby ravine killed them both in one machine gun burst.

One night on the Bataan Peninsula in the Philippines the Japs snuck through our perimeter. The base was set up by a church in a small town. Road guards were sent out. I was road guard west of town. There was the huge explosion and I knew it had to be our ammo dump. We found out later that the Japs were speaking the Filipino language as a disguise in the dark and someone allowed them to pass through the lines. We held tight the next morning as we were surrounded by cane fields and didn't know what was out there. General MacArthur came by to inspect the damage and he got pinned down in the command post by enemy small arms fire. I didn't see it happen but that was the story going around. That was the closest I ever came to seeing him.

I wasn't involved in the fight for Manila but passed through the city one time on the way to guard a big reservoir northeast of there that provided the drinking water for the city. There was a concern that the Japanese would blow up the dam. The Japanese were dug into the mountains waiting for us in what was called the Shimbu Line. We had trouble getting to them on this one hill top.

Their artillery guns were giving us the devil all the time. Our planes would come over and bomb, but couldn't stop them. We learned later that the guns were mounted on tracks in caves dug through the back side of the mountain. They shoot them off and roll them back into caves where the bombs couldn't touch them.

Question: What was your opinion of the Japanese soldier?

If we had to fight with what they had, we would have never won that war. They had very little. They could get by on a handful of rice a day. They were good with what weapons they had. Those little hand held knee mortars were good. By that time in the war, all their supplies coming into the Philippines were pretty well cut off.

There were more men lost from disease and physiological problems than from combat wounds. We took yellow pills every day for malaria. I contracted it once but it was after I was sent back home. The Army gave us a whole series of vaccinations for diseases. The cholera shot was the worst. That one really hurt.

I spoke to a history class over at the high school about my service in the war. One of the kids asked me, "What was the worst thing you saw?" Well, I wasn't going to tell him, or you, or even my wife that. There are things I won't tell anyone. Unless someone had been there, there's no way they could understand it. I remember being around WWI vets and they acted the same way.

Question: Okay, then what was the best thing you ever experienced?

Harry Truman dropping the bomb. I think he had the hardest decision any president ever had to make. Those who opposed it didn't have a son or a father or a husband over in the Pacific

I went to my first division reunion in 1988. There were 30 guys from my company there that I hadn't seen in 43 years. They had all gotten old. I went to another one up in Wisconsin Rapids and that's when you heard the stories.

I worked for the Harper natural gas company for 35 years. I worked inside the compressor building where the engines were. Fritz Conrad worked outside on the pipeline.

There Were Hard Times

Donald Longer
Fort Meyers, FL
(In Washington, IA, attending the annual Red Horse Troop reunion.)

Army Air Corps
Pacific

Interview Date:
31 July 2011

Referral:
Joe Wright

I enlisted in the Iowa National Guard in September 1940, becoming a member of Troop D of the 113th Cavalry. We were known as the Red Horse Troop which was headquartered in Washington, Iowa. The original group numbered 106 local individuals. Troop D was mobilized in January of 1941, and was sent to Camp Bowie in Texas. Our horses didn't make the trip. We were converted to a mechanized reconnaissance unit and equipped with scout cars, jeeps and motorcycles. Our troop then entered a period of demanding training in equipment and field maneuvers in Texas and Louisiana. It was in Louisiana that we encountered signs that read NO DOGS OR SOLDIERS ALLOWED. We were billeted in four man pyramidal tents with wooden floors and a small, inadequate natural gas heater. We had a bugle call for everything. They began with reveille, roll call, mess call, work call, retreat, etc and ended with taps. We were scheduled to complete our training in November of '41 and return to Washington. In late October, we were notified that our National Guard unit had been federalized, which meant we were in for the duration.

After Pearl Harbor, the Red Horse was assigned to border patrol duty at Brownsville, Uvalde, and Del Rio. We manned machine gun positions along the Gulf of Mexico, guarded railroad bridges, and conducted night patrols on highways close to the Mexican border. We were primarily guarding against the perceived threat of infiltration by enemy agents or saboteurs. There was a passenger train that crossed the Devils High Bridge near Long Tree, Texas, and we were tasked with stopping and boarding it for inspection.

Upon relief from our duties as border patrol, I applied for and was accepted to Officers Candidate School (OSC). Although I had wanted to attend the Cavalry OSC, I was assigned to Armored Force School at Ft. Knox, Kentucky. After graduating, I was assigned to the 7th Armored Division at Camp Polk in Louisiana. I was made a Platoon Leader of a Reconnaissance Unit. We received excellent training that included field maneuvers at the Desert Training Center in California. My unit was always assigned to be the point of the entire division, scouting ahead looking for the enemy. I figured my life expectancy in that role was rather brief, so I applied for pilot's training with the Army Air Corps.

My pilot training was in California and New Mexico where I received my wings in March of

1944. My training was in the PT-17, BT-13, AT-17 and the U C-78. Later I trained in the B-25 and A-20. These were the planes I flew in combat. As I recall the A-20 had eight .50 caliber machine guns and could carry six 250 lb bombs.

Our missions in the Pacific Theater were primarily for troop ground support. We conducted air strikes ahead of advancing infantry. We had no direct contact with the ground forces. The infantry would put out colored panels so we could tell where our friendly lines were. We were told not to bomb or strafe behind the panels. Several times the ground troops failed to pick up their panels when they advanced. Once I strafed behind friendly lines. I do not know if I caused casualties.

I do recall one major friendly fire incident. Our squadron commander was leading the group. He selected the wrong village and it was occupied by our troops. I did not drop my bombs, however several pilots including our commander did. Fortunately there were no casualties. When we returned to the air field, the commander told me that I was grounded for not dropping my bombs, however, the order was withdrawn when he learned he had hit the wrong target.

Three months before the war ended we began transition to the B-32 bomber. Not too many people have heard of this airplane. It was built by consolidation and was similar to the B-29, but had greater storage capacity and superior range. I don't think there are any of them remaining.

My last combat mission was on 13 June 1945. I received the news that brother Jack had been killed in action near Batangas, Luzon. I was relieved from combat duty and any further participation in hazardous duty because I had lost two brothers in combat. I had flown 56 combat and 40 combat training missions.

I left my unit in late July for return to the US on a converted cargo ship. Our ship was rammed by a destroyer in Manila Harbor. Our next transport was a Liberty Ship that took 31 days to sail to Seattle. We were bussed to Fort Lawton and then by train to Camp Beale, California. The train rail cars were all wooden seats, no heat and no sleeping accommodations. It was very cold at high altitudes and very uncomfortable for us in our tropical uniforms. The troops in one of the cars broke up the seats and started a fire for warmth.

I elected to remain in the Service. During my military career my duties were Pilot, Squadron Commander, Chief Base Supply, Staff Logistics and Planning Officer, attended Command & Staff College, a Korean and Vietnam veteran. I served at numerous Air Force headquarters and higher commands. After 29 years I retired a Lieutenant Colonel. As I reflect, there were hard times during the wars, but there were many times of personal satisfaction when I knew I had made the most rewarding career choice.

My activities in the civil sector included: owned and operated a Real Estate agency, motel, mobile home park, managed several developments and CEO residential and commercial building company. Community service activities involved fund raising, Kiwanis and military organizations.

By Donald Longer.

TRIBUTE

On October 29, 1943, Private First Class Robert J. Nicola, a graduate of Washington High School Class of 1943, boarded a train bound for Camp Dodge, Iowa, to enter active military service.

On July 26, 1944, Pvt. First Class C. Earl Stoufer, who had left his wife Muriel and his two small children in Fort Dodge, Iowa, sailed out of New York harbor for the European theater of war.

Bob, still a teenager when he reported for duty, recalled his Army days as a grand adventure. He told his family about making friends from other parts of the country for the first time; of eating shrimp for the first time; of his fear of climbing down a rope ladder; of foolishly stealing eggs from a barn and putting them in his pocket while running from gunfire. He didn't talk about the events that earned his combat infantryman's badge and his bronze star.

Earl, who was in his 30s when drafted, found combat unbearable. He participated in four major battles and was wounded with shrapnel which he carried for the rest of his life. He earned four battle stars and a Purple Heart. But he suffered what was then called "battle fatigue" and spent the rest of the war behind a typewriter in France. A letter he wrote detailing his days in the Army is written in third-person, as if he felt separated from what was happening to him.

Both Bob and Earl returned safely home and resumed peacetime lives. Bob played baseball with other returning vets; he dated and married a college girl. He started to work at McCleery-Cumming Co., Washington's calendar factory, where he stayed for the rest of his working life. Earl went to work for Sieg Auto Parts in Fort Dodge and stayed there the rest of his working life. Neither man talked of terror, of seeing carnage and destruction. They took part in saving our world; and then they saved us from sharing their fear. Only as stories like theirs have emerged from books and movies have we gained a glimpse of what they saw and did. How can we ever be grateful enough?

In 1994 Bob offered his son-in-law, Dave Stoufer, the use of a small building on a piece of property he'd bought near his home in Washington, Iowa. Dave thought it would make a fine sound studio for his fledgling audio/video business. Then Dave's friend Tom Marsh dropped by and shared some local history.

"This building has historical significance," he told a skeptical Dave. It turned out that Tom was right. The building at 219 Sitler Drive was the first Iowa National Guard office in Washington. Located next to a large barn that was rented by the Guard for their horses, the block building housed F Troop, (later Troop D), during the 1930s. Bob recalled that as a young boy he watched the mounted Guardsmen ride from the cavalry barn through town to the railroad station where they boarded the train for their annual drill in Texas. When WWII began, the Guardsmen left for Texas with their horses one last time. And when they returned after the war the cavalry rode motorcycles, scout cars and jeeps.

Shadows of those days remained in the Guard office at 219 Sitler Drive. When Dave removed a wall he found the framing of the paymaster's window. As Washington folks dropped by his studio to tell their memories—folks like neighbor John Butler, who shared his story of being a prisoner of war—Dave's imagination was stirred and it wasn't long before he had gathered others who also were excited to create a veterans' appreciation event and a museum. Since that time, F Troop Historical Association has hosted parades with mounted re-enactors; present-day military officers; a restored B-25; a helicopter from the current 113th Iowa National Guard F Troop; and accumulated an ever-growing collection of militaria donated by fellow Iowans.

F Troop Historical Association's motto is, "Our purpose is not to glorify war but to honor its heroes."

As Earl's son and Bob's daughter, we—Dave Stoufer and Rachel Nicola—hope to honor our respective fathers' memories; to provide a place where veterans feel appreciated; where visitors learn more than they knew before about Iowa veterans and their service; and where we all can pause to treasure our freedom and the price with which it was bought.

Dave Stoufer & Rachel Nicola
Washington, IA

Until You Killed Them All

Russell Schafer
Fairfield, IA

1st Cavalry Division
Pacific

Interview Date:
30 July 2011

Referral:
Audra Williams

The 8th Cavalry Regiment was part of the 1st Cavalry Division. The Division fought in the Pacific theatre, seeing action on Negros Island, New Guinea, Manus Island, and later on Leyte and Manila in the Philippines.

I enlisted right after Pearl Harbor. I learned about the attack on Pearl Harbor with two of my buddies listening to a pickup radio after hunting rabbits. My mother said I was too young to go. I looked at my father and told him, "I would rather fight the Japanese than the Germans because them sons of bitches attacked us." My dad said he would sign for me but he did not really want to. I replied, "If you don't, I'll go to Canada and join the army up there."

I had basic training at Ft. Sill, Oklahoma. Basic training was fun. I was in great physical shape from playing football and working and had no problems. Some of the older guys complained a lot.

We first sailed to Australia (1943) where we received training in jungle warfare. They would take us out and drop us off and we had to find our way back. Sometimes that was tough. Australia was full of snakes. They were bad, very poisonous snakes. We'd use clubs to kill them or cut their heads off with our machetes. The biggest snake I saw was in New Guinea. It was twenty-five feet in

length. Someone had shot it.

I was issued a Thompson sub machine gun. I loved that weapon! It was a great gun and I knew how to shoot it! Our battalion was issued a number of the .30 caliber carbines. I didn't think much of them. A buddy and I were in charge of inspecting the allotment and sighting them in. If you could hit the broadside of a wall, they were good enough.

I spent most of my time as a corporal with F Troop of the 8th Cavalry Regiment. Our captain was a full blooded American Indian from western Oklahoma. He was a tough man. He loved to kill Japs. Caucasians were a minority in our regiment. Fifty-two percent of the regiment was made up of Indians and Mexican Americans. They were tough, good fighters. Our Mexicans would rather kill a Jap with a machete than shoot him. When the Japanese would attack us, the Mexicans would purposely let some get in close so they could use their machetes. They'd drop their rifles and swing their machete at a Jap, usually aiming for the head.

We landed on Manus Island (March, 1944). We were trying to take the airfield and the Japs were trying to push us back off the island. The 99th and 82nd Artillery Battalions were there helping us. They had 75mm pack guns that were fired horizontally into the charging Japs. High explosive rounds with one second fuses were used. That tells you how close the Japs were. Later we were told that 3,000 Japanese had been killed that first day.

The Japanese would attack crazy. They'd come and come. The Japanese soldier had no regard for their own life or anyone else's. Hell, all we could do was to just shoot them. They'd just keep attacking until you killed them all. If any of them got through, we would kill them with a knife or bayonet. That happened quite often. I always carried three hundred rounds of ammunition. The clips for the Thompsons held 30 rounds, so I carried 10 of them. It was a lot of weight to carry around.

The Japanese constructed bunkers out of coconut logs, using four on a side and a ton of dirt between them. Those bunkers were tough. They could absorb a 50 lb bomb. We would try to get a flame thrower up close enough to give them a little squirt inside. We begged and begged for tanks to come up and help. Finally, one was sent, a medium Sherman with a 75mm gun. It would pull right up to the bunkers and let go with an HE (high explosive round). No Japs would ever come out. We loved that tank!

We never took any Japanese prisoners. So they came out with an order, offering two weeks leave to Sydney, Australia, to any soldier that brought one in. I remember seeing one of our guys marching two Jap prisoners in at gunpoint and then some smart son of a bitch shot them both before he could turn them in. Boy was he mad! They didn't pay for dead ones.

The Japanese did not try any of the Bonsai attacks after dark. But they did attempt to infiltrate our lines. We did not use passwords at night. Instead, we shot anything that moved. We killed a number of wild pigs that way and they were good eating. But some righteous son of a gun ordered us to stop eating the pork as the pigs had been feeding off the dead American and Japanese bodies.

New Guinea was a big island. It was one of the toughest places you could go. It had everything bad on it. Besides the snakes, there were scorpions and big centipedes and cannibals. "*When the women come out to cut up your remains, just roll to your rifle and blow out your brains. And go to your God like a soldier.*" That is Rudyard Kipling. I was in the hospital in New Guinea and the only thing they

had to read was Kipling. I loved it! I read every page in that damn book and memorized a lot of it.

Salt water was no good to bathe in. I knew where a fresh water stream dumped in to the ocean so I headed down there one day with my soap and rag. So I walked into the creek and I noticed something rolling down into the water from the far bank. It looked like a log. Then another one rolled in. I looked close, and the logs were swimming. I thought, "Russell, you damn fool. You'd better get out of here!" They were crocodiles!

My right leg started going dead on me. Then I had a place on my right side, on my chest that was swollen. The old doctor that treated me inserted a funnel and a syringe two or three times to drain the pus out. That seemed to help. Initially, the doctor was considering taking a rib out and I sure didn't want that.

My leg had something else wrong with it. We had been in a spot on the Admiralty Island in which we were surrounded by the Japanese. They were tossing hand grenades at us and we were throwing hand grenades and everything else back at them. As it turned out, I had been wounded by a small sliver of grenade fragment in my upper leg, causing the femoral nerve to be severed.

I was sent to a little surgical hospital on New Guinea from the Admiralty Islands. The hospital was run by Col. Charles Mayo, from the Mayo Clinic in Rochester, MN. They performed surgeries every day and I had my turn there. He was a tremendous doctor. I spent about a month there. I was sent back to a hospital in the states after that.

I served as a Fairfield police officer for 25 years, spending the last ten years as a plainclothes detective. Later I poured a lot of concrete as a contractor. I caught malaria in the Pacific and had 26 attacks after returning home. I did some crazy things during the war. It wasn't an easy war. I think back now, "How'd that dumb bastard do all that and survive."

Question: Do you still harbor resentment for the Japanese people because of the war?
Yes, I do. I don't have much use for the Chinese either. My outfit fought them in Korea. My advice is to never trust an Oriental.

It's the Real McCoy

George Vorhies
Fairfield, IA

Navy
Pacific

Interview Date:
30 July 2011

Referral:
Bill Watson

I enlisted in the Navy in 1936. I was 17 years old. I hitchhiked to Burlington from Lockridge to enlist. The Henry County Sheriff stopped and gave me a ride part of the way. I'm about half way into Alzheimer's so my memory is bad and I have to think about everything I tell you. I spent some time on what they called North Island in San Diego. I did boot camp in San Diego. My first duty was that of the captain's orderly aboard a vessel. My brothers Harold, Lester and Grant were on the same ship. Some guys from an aviation repair unit came aboard ship. I got to talking to them and thought it was something I would be interested in doing and went to see the captain about transferring. So I was placed in an aviation repair unit back in San Diego. It wasn't long before we were moved to San Pedro, California, and later I was transferred to a carrier.

About that time the guys in the Naval Reserve were being called up because they were getting ready for the war, I guess. Then they had the National Draft Act. A young guy didn't have much choice as to what was going to happen to him. In the Spring of '38, a Hawaii detachment was sent out. I made the trip aboard a troop transport.

I was stationed right in the middle of Pearl Harbor at the Naval Air Station on Ford Island. I was involved in revamping old ships and preparing others for service. We started working on the OS2U bi-planes. Ships had these small float planes that were catapulted off and used for observation. They had some problems with the catapult and we had to fix every one of them. Later we worked any naval aircraft that had mechanical problems.

Question: How close were you on December 7th when the attack came on Pearl Harbor?

I was smack dab in it, on Ford Island. I was on the duty roster that day as an emergency driver. I was on shore until four in the morning attending an American Legion sponsored dance in Honolulu. I didn't get much sleep when I got back before having to answer muster. Before eight o'clock I ran across the street from the barracks to the administration building. If you didn't make muster, the officer of the day might make you come back every hour for the rest of the day.

I heard something and stepped out of the administration building. I looked up and saw this plane over head. Someone remarked, "Who's making all this noise on a Sunday morning?" I could see bombs under the wings of this plane and then he dropped something but I couldn't see for sure what is was. Then he bellied out right over the top of my hangar. Then a second plane is coming in and he is at a lower angle. He cut loose a whole cluster of small bombs. They were incendiaries. A third plane comes in at a steeper angle and drops a great big bomb. That one hit right between our two hangars.

I turned and ran up a flight of steps into the Administration building. There was a sailor I'd never seen before coming in the other door. The officer of the day came out of his night quarters asking, "What's going on out here?" The fellow that came in the other door says, "Sir, a plane just dropped a bomb on that ship out there!" I said," It's the real McCoy, sir, the hangars are burning!" The officer ran over to the foyer and grabbed a brochure, reading aloud what to do in case of an air attack. "Sound the air raid alarm and call out the seamen guard." Then he leaned over and pressed the button for the siren mounted on the roof. It let off one big, long loud wail. This officer then phoned our captain. All the captain said was, "Take cover, take cover!"

The next morning they brought in a Jap plane to the hangar that had crash landed on Ford Island. It turned out to be the first plane that I saw. The intelligence officer examined the cockpit and starts pulling things out. A fellow named Swede Rehnquist from Bloomington, Minnesota, was my sergeant. He was standing on the other side of the plane from me. I'll never forget this. He reached in the cockpit and pulls out a little rag doll that was on the instrument panel and asked the intelligence officer if he could have it. He let him keep it. One of the items discovered in the cockpit was a standard USGS map of Pearl Harbor, just like the ones you could buy for fifty cents. Our hangars were marked in red. That was his target. This plane crash landed on Luke Field. The pilot climbed out shooting with a pistol. One of the Marines shot him dead.

I left the area of the barracks and headed down to the hangars. I could see one of the big battleships starting to turtle or roll over. I'm not sure which one it was. It may have been the USS *California.*

Here's a photo of me at Pearl Harbor that was on the cover of *Look Magazine.* That's me in the foreground with my back to the camera. I'm holding a shovel I was using to clean up debris. We had a bulldozer down there. You can see the wind sock and that's Hagar 38. The hangar across the

street out of the photo had burnt. The big airplane is a PBY. In the distance you can see a flag that is flying from the stern of the *Nevada.* She went down in the channel. Two guys rolled out that work bench and set up a machine gun to shoot at the planes. This big black blob is the destroyer the USS *Shaw* blowing up.

The Japanese attacked in two waves. I watched the planes finish their bombing run at Pearl Harbor and turn toward Hickman Field where they strafed where the Army Air Corps parked airplanes. I don't think any of our Navy planes got up. Some at Hickman did. Most of Navy planes were catapult planes. Every ship had two or three of them.

Our hangar doors had been shattered by shrapnel. There was a concrete wall between two of the hangars. I saw all these guys with their backs to this concrete wall. I yelled at them, "A close hit will bring that whole wall down on top of you." Me and another guy sought cover inside our hangar. We crouched behind a sheet metal locker until we noticed bullet holes clear through it. I told my buddy, "I'm going outside to see one of those son of a bitches come down." By that time, the air was full of anti-aircraft fire. An officer hiding out in another hangar across the way yelled at us to get back under cover, adding, "Don't you know all that anti-aircraft flak will be coming back down?" That's how dumb we were. Shell fire from the ships at Pearl Harbor fell on people in the streets of Honolulu.

Survivors from the attack waded onto shore on Ford Island. They were badly burnt, like they'd been scalded. Their skin hung down off them like wet paper. We brought them in and laid them down on the floor of the mess hall. The captain's and the operation officer's wives were there trying to give them aid. They were the only women I saw there.

There was a worry that the Japanese would land a ground invasion. I was assigned a roof top with my Springfield. I had .30-06 ammunition that I had bummed off the spotters stored in my locker in the hangar. We were saving it for a pig hunt on the big island. Someone carried a heavy machine gun up to my roof top but didn't bring a tripod. So we set it up on a vegetable crate.

Later that night, four planes from the USS *Enterprise* that had dropped off supplies to Wake Island returned to Pearl Harbor. It was dark and when the planes turned on their landing lights, every damn gun at Pearl Harbor opened up on them. It was just a cone of fire. A crow couldn't have gotten through. All four fell over in the cane fields and burned.

I stayed in Hawaii the remainder of the war. I remember preparing planes for the Battle of Midway. We knew it was coming. About that time, they wanted somebody for aerial gunnery training. I heard about it that evening and met the chief in charge of it in the morning and got my bid in early. I asked him what it would involve. He said you'd take the training and then go south. I told him to sign me up. Upon hearing of my plans, one of my buddies said, "Vorhies, you're going get yourself killed." I replied, "Well, if I stay here I'm going die of boredom."

I left Pearl Harbor and went to gunnery school on Barber's Point. Once I got there, I discovered that they really wanted a worker rather than a gunnery student. So I was given a truck to drive back and forth from Pearl Harbor to haul supplies. I built my own shop and was given a metal lathe to operate. My rank was 1st Class Aviation Metal Smith. I made Chief Petty Officer before I came home. All my brothers made it home.

My brother Grant had quite a career. He was a carpenter in the Navy. He was on the beach at Guadalcanal chopping through the bottoms of capsized landing boats to free trapped Marines. He was also on the ship that boarded and captured a German U-boat in the Atlantic. I've got a photo of Grant sitting on the sub's conning tower. The German's had tried to scuttle it. He was one of crew that went inside the submarine. That's the submarine that sits in the museum in Chicago

I had an opportunity to revisit Pearl Harbor after the war with my wife. I wouldn't go. Too many memories, but she really enjoyed it.

THE MOST POPULAR SHIP IN THE BAY

Mike Wheelan
Washington, IA

SS *John Rutledge*
Pacific

Interview Date:
5 August 2011

Referral:
Bill Wagamon

I was drafted in August of 1944 and we left Washington on a bus on a Saturday night. I remember a number of fellows leaning out the windows to kiss their sweethearts goodbye.

We went to St. Louis to be inducted into the service. We were fortunate that they gave us a choice of what branch of the service that we would prefer. This was quite unexpected. All 66 of us signed up for the Navy after listening to a pep talk by a Navy officer.

I was the only one inducted into the Navy. All the rest went to the Army. I am sure it had nothing to do with my skill. The Navy just needed one more to fill their quota. Lucky for me, they started at the back of the alphabet. This was my first experience of how the Navy did things, as I had a mastoid ear and was not to be too associated with water.

I was sent to Great Lakes Naval Center. Boot Camp lasted twelve weeks—long enough to weed out those under age or those who were bed wetters.

It took several weeks to get all of our shots. Another reason that it consumed time was it took several weeks to realize who was really in charge—the officers or the men. We were thoroughly educated, though we had more than our share of mommy-babies.

From Great Lakes they sent us to Norfolk, Virginia, and gunnery school. After gunnery school we boarded a train for New Orleans. I was sick with the flu but I wanted out of Norfolk so bad that I kept quiet.

We boarded a train at Norfolk and headed for New Orleans. On the way through Tennessee, the train stopped for a while. There were several trains on the track. In record time someone found a leaking carload of wine, two tracks over. He came back aboard and shouted, "Halleluiah, there's a car load of wine over there that is leaking." Everyone in the car took off like a flock of ducks. Prior to our departure from Norfolk, I was standing ready to board the train. A Navy officer approached me and asked my name and said, "Seaman Wheelan, here are the orders for all the men in your car. You are in charge of them."

As I sat in the train car looking at all the empty seats, I thought, "Oh, Lord, help." But they all got back on and the train took off headed for New Orleans.

We were assigned for the *John D. Rutledge* transport. I was a gunner's mate 3rd class, part of a Navy crew aboard a civilian merchant marine cargo ship. One of my duties was to man one of the four 20mm anti-aircraft guns. The ship was capped and loaded with tanks, DUKWs, and artillery pieces all on deck. We left there about sundown and proceeded to the mouth of the Mississippi.

I got seasick a little bit the first night on the ocean water. I took off my sweater and shirt and just shivered there for a couple of hours. I had watch. I got a little bit woozy and I put my shirt and sweater back on and I never got sick again, even in rough water.

We passed Cuba on our way to Panama. The trip through the Canal was interesting but uneventful. From there we headed for the Marshall Islands. It took us five weeks.

We stopped at Kwajalein Island for mail. A number of us were up on the captain's deck looking through a big heavy telescope to see land. Much to my surprise, there was nothing left there but a few stumps. All of the trees and vegetation were destroyed when the United States re-took the island.

From there we proceeded through the Caroline Islands and around the north side of the Philippines. Then we went down the west position to Subic Bay where the Marines had landed a couple of weeks before.

We pulled into Subic Bay. Bigger bombs and shells going off gave realization that we were too close to shore. We moved to another location of the bay.

As we were moving, we heard another plane go over head. Everyone opened fire. Thirty or forty ships were unloading at the time. A solid sheet of flame went up where everyone thought the plane was in the night sky.

Skipper told us to cease fire. It turned out that we shot down a PBY Seaplane. On another night at Subic Bay, I suppose it was a Zero came over us and we could tell he was not pulling, he was more gliding, and he dropped two bombs on the ammunition dump. We had to get out of there because there were shells flying all over everywhere.

The Japanese hiding in the mountains would start working on us before dark. The guns were in

caves, they would roll them out and shoot and then take them back in there and we couldn't get them.

There wasn't any Navy ship big enough to do much good. They had moved all the cruisers. Even the destroyer couldn't reach them. They were probably at least five miles away. They had the elevation and could lob them in. Moving after dark was customary. The Japs still controlled the mountain around Subic Bay. They would get a fix on us prior to dark so we had to move when it got dark.

We later got ashore where Pierce, my best friend, got a shave and a haircut. I chickened out. The barber looked too Japanese to be shaving his neck with a straight edge razor.

We later pulled out and went to Manila. There we finished unloading our cargo of 10,000 tons. The cargo consisted of food stuffs, ammunition, and fuel. The top deck was covered with tanks, DUKWs, and artillery pieces.

We then moved on to Leyte Island, where we made a R & R stop so the boys could get a few beers. We moved out of the Philippines into the open seas with about 30 other ships. Whenever we were in enemy waters, we always traveled in groups of ships in a zigzag position. The reason for that is a submarine can plot a straight line course. In maybe half-an-hour, a Jap sub could fall back, plot your course, surface, swing around out of sight, lay in wait to torpedo the ships. If the zigzag course is used by the ships, he cannot plot our course. To watch 30 ships turn a corner a thousand miles from nowhere is an awesome sight.

Our ships left the Philippines and headed south. We crossed the equator without incident and took the customary belt-strap beating for the Old Salts. We saw nothing of Davy Jones' Locker and continued on south to Bougainville in the Solomon Islands.

We loaded the ship with beer. If you have never seen 10,000 tons of beer, it's a lot… and I couldn't drink a drop because Uncle Carl called me into his office before I left for the service. He said, "If you don't drink any alcohol while you are in the service, I will give you $300." And he did.

> *"We later got ashore where Pierce, my best friend, got a shave and a haircut. I chickened out. The barber looked too Japanese to be shaving his neck with a straight edge razor."*

Uncle Carl was an old Spanish American War veteran who knew all the problems of servicemen and alcohol. This was enough incentive for me because I wanted to buy my own farm someday. Uncle was also aware of all the alcohol problems that existed in our family. He, however, never refrained from helping us. I had always respected his advice and felt I was always getting the very best.

From the Solomon Islands, we headed to New Guinea, through the China Sea, which was as yellow as could be. A few days out of Bougainville, we ran into a storm and had to latch down everything. The pitch and roll of the ship seemed impossible to recover from. It seemed impossible to right itself.

We were in convoy again which created more problems of running a zigzag course. It was the first time I was really frightened. We had cold meals for three days and nothing would sit on the table. If we used any Chinaware, it was likely to end up broken on the floor.

We landed in New Guinea. We took on fuel needed to return to the Philippines. Soon we were off the coast about 100 miles from Los Negros. In enemy waters, duty was always four hours on and four hours off.

My station was at the stern of the ship. It happened that Pierce was at his station at the bow. There were always four men acting as lookouts at all times.

About 2:30 in the morning, I could hear Pierce yelling at the top of his voice. We each had microphones but he was so excited that he forgot to turn his on. I said, "Press your button, Bud," which he promptly did. He roared, "Torpedo!!!" The first mate was officer on duty. On that time of night he left the captain's quarters and promptly zeroed in on the white line coming at us and yelled, "Hard left!"

It passed by Pierce. He had the best view as he looked down on it. The torpedo missed us and passed through the convoy harmlessly. We were satisfied with that much excitement for one day.

> "A few days out of Bougainville, we ran into a storm and had to latch down everything. The pitch and roll of the ship seemed impossible to recover from. It seemed impossible to right itself."

However, about 11 a.m., I was back on watch again. I heard somebody say, "I'm dying!" This was before the Blacks were accepted as equals. I heard another voice say, "Go ahead and die you black son of a bitch."

I knew the problem was coming from midship. What had happened was four of the Black galley workers had been peeling potatoes in a tub. One guy made a comment that number two didn't like. So number two drug a peeling knife across number one's wrist. Number two went into the kitchen, picked up a long-blade butcher knife, came back into the potato peeling area and stabbed number one. It went clear through him. Hence the statement, "I'm dying." I heard him say that.

My watch wasn't over, so I didn't get up to that area for about one hour. The deck was covered with blood and the guy was still lying there on deck without any attention as we had no doctor on board. He had died immediately. A death on board ship must be verified by a doctor.

We were still in a zigzag convoy. We signaled for a doctor and a destroyer answered the call. They came along side about 150 feet away. Due to the rough seas, that was probably an appropriate distance. They shot a line (a rope) between the upper areas of the two ships and then pulled a heavier line across with an even heavier line the third time. Because of the problems earlier that morning, we knew there were submarines in the area.

They put a doctor in the boatswain's chair and pulled him across. He probably never forgot that ride because of the extremely rough waters. Because of the roll of the ship he got a real ride. He would be down in the water and then he would be way up in the air. To stop to transfer that doctor would have been unthinkable in enemy waters.

The doctor looked at the man and agreed he was dead. The doctor was ready to go back across. I noticed the captain's door on the destroyer. He roared out of there, grabbed a sailor by the shoulder, pointed to an axe in glass, and gave the sailor a shove. The sailor broke the glass, grabbed the axe and chopped the line between the ships in two. All sorts of things started happening on the destroyer.

The gates across the back of the destroyer were flying open and barrels rolled up to the exits. We couldn't believe that he would drop depth charges that close to our ship because we were not built for that.

The hull of the Liberty Ship was only three-fourths of an inch thick. The destroyer dropped two depth charges. After 150 feet he dropped two more. We were over top of a submarine. The explosions were four big white mounds of sea water. My ankles bothered me for two days. But a large, heavyset fellow, one of the Merchant Marine crew, went down in front of me. The shock bothered him much more than me. I was so frightened that for the first time I wanted a cigarette.

The destroyer seemed satisfied with his work and moved off full throttle to his station in the convoy with us still having the doctor on board.

The ship's carpenter laid out a large square canvas. They laid the Black corpse in the middle, folded it over and sewed it up. We put him over the side. There was no ceremony or chaplain involved. No one had any respect for that man whatsoever.

When we did get to shore, the knife wielder had to go before a military officer. He was granted self-defense. He came back and wanted permission to serve on our ship again. Our Navy officer on board the ship was a radical Southern Negro-hater and said, "You can go to hell."

After that excitement, we headed to the eastern Philippines. We were going back to Leyte again to unload all that beer. There were nearly 10,000 cans of beer in the hold. While in route, during the day, no one was snitching any beer. After dark, it was another matter.

The stack of beer resembled the top of an ant hill. Everyone was pilfering cases of beer. When we got to Leyte, we didn't encounter the inter-service rivalry we were accustomed to, but instead were looked upon as saviors and by far, the most

popular ship in the bay. After all, we had all the beer! After unloading, a crew was sent aboard to retrieve most hidden cases of beer.

From Leyte, we went to San Francisco, then ninety miles up the Sacramento River to Stockton. We went into dry dock. We were losing about fifteen percent of our efficiency because of barnacles on the hull. So they sandblasted us.

We exited dry dock and moved to the loading docks and started loading ammunition. When about half-loaded—this was around August 5th of 1945—every form of communication blasted out that a new type of bomb had been dropped on Japan. A few days later, a second bomb was dropped and the war was over.

The scene in downtown Stockton went from calm to revelry beyond description. Everybody was hugging and kissing, the streets were jammed elbow to elbow. Everyone left their houses, stores, and cars. We had four years of war and it ended with a bang.

In San Francisco it was quite different. There was so much destruction and riots that all military personnel were confined to quarters for 30 days.

We unloaded the ammunition and started loading food stuffs for the Orient. After we were full, we went back down the Sacramento River, then out San Francisco Bay, headed for China.

This was a more relaxed voyage. There were only twelve servicemen aboard this time (compared to the 43 we had before) plus the forty Merchant Marine crew to operate the ship.

We stopped in Japan and unloaded some food stuffs. The next stop was Shanghai, China. We went about fifty miles up the Yangtze River and anchored in Shanghai.

China appeared to be much worse off than Japan. There were hundreds of sampans—little boats in the river—where people lived and where they got their food from. They swam the bottom of the river to retrieve food. You could imagine how little food they could get in a country so poor.

> "We had four years of war and it ended with a bang."

We weren't allowed to go ashore without being searched for food. It could cause a riot, though your intentions were good.

We were transferred off our ship, the *Rutledge,* which had been our home for over a year. We were housed at a race track temporarily. One night someone was shaking our bunk. I was on the top—they were four-high. I figured it was just a drunk so I tried to ignore it. Finally, I turned over and looked down—and there was my Washington school classmate, John Gamble. We had enjoyed a lot of good times together. You can imagine how elated I was to see a familiar face so far from home. When you got to a new locale, they had an area where each state had a big thick book, and you signed that. It was a good thing to have. I don't think it was just a Navy phenomenon. I saw several fellows; I looked them up because their names were in there. To see somebody you knew was special.

There were many sights I saw that were sickening. Here are a couple of examples. There were wooden wheel oxcarts going up and down the streets picking up dead bodies of people who didn't make it through the night. Some were clad only in a newspaper. Another example was the manner in which the Japanese had brutalized the Chinese for years.

After the war was over, the bottom rail was on top. The Chinese would move the Japanese one at a time through the city with their arms outstretched on a pole with leg irons on. Each prisoner would have 30 to 40 people beating on him with anything available. Soldiers moved them through the street. Down the street would be another group doing the same thing. This was repeated more times than we could count. The Chinese surely had their revenge. The Japanese soldiers that were marched through the mobs of the Chinese people were all bloodied. I think some of them didn't survive. I never heard that the Chinese kept a lot of prisoners like Russia did. Russia took millions of prisoners that never got back home at all. A lot of the German prisoners over here did not want to go back home after the war ended.

When I was in China, it wasn't so much the buildings destroyed, as it was their way of life. Their lack of food was a terrible problem. The Japs would wait until the rice was ready to harvest and then they would take it all. It wasn't the Communists at that time; they were in possession of very little of China. I think up into the far north.

We were transferred to a repair ship, the USS *Wharton,* which had been in Shanghai since the end of the war. From Shanghai we went to Panama City through the canal, then to New Orleans and on to Minneapolis by train. En route, the sights I enjoyed most were the cornfields. I was mustered out the 10th of June 1946.

Question: Do you remember hearing about Pearl Harbor?

My brother Don came home on leave and Dad was taking him back that Sunday. Dad came home and we did chores and it was pretty late before we turned the radio on. I'd say it was after dark. That was when we heard the news. I am surprised a ton of our relatives didn't call to tell us.

At the time I don't know that I took it seriously, that it would affect me. But our manual training teacher told us, "You fellows are going to be involved before this is over." And he was right.

Donna Wheelan: I was only a freshman when Pearl Harbor was attacked. I guess it didn't make that big an impression on me at that time. I don't remember the folks talking about it much but they probably didn't talk about it in front of us. They did that a lot. They didn't want us to worry or think about it.

Mike: My brother Don was in the Navy Air Corps. He and another fellow piloted a PBY for quite a while out of Jacksonville, Florida, looking for subs. He had one bad eye. He pulled some shenanigans to get around the test and he got in. He signed something that he knew he had one bad eye. So he was an instructor most of the time and flew a Corsair. He brought one home one time. I was farming. I was plowing along about three miles an hour and I asked him if he would show me what 500 miles an hour was like. So he did—he came pretty close to me. You couldn't follow him. He was over here—and then he was down here. He brought quite a number of planes home. He would bring a mechanic with him and stay overnight.

One night he came in much later than he wanted to. The airport at that time was almost non-existent. It was grass. We lived out by the airport. Dad and I took two cars. Dad was on the northeast corner and I was on the northwest corner of flight to show Don where the fences were. Don thought that I was not in position because he could not imagine the fence where it was. He hit it and went right down a hedgerow. He cut things up pretty bad and he was madder than a hog. But I was where I was supposed to be. This was when the war was going on. He would bring trainers of considerable horsepower home. Don was stationed most of the time in Kansas. Somehow the news got out and he beat it out of here at daylight. Naval personnel based in Ottumwa ended up here about 9:00 in the morning looking for him.

I have seen the write-up that Don had to turn in. He thought that he was getting low on gas so he picked this little Washington, Iowa, airport. He was capable of writing a good report so I don't think he got caught.

Donna Wheelan: I remember them talking about the new bomb. They explained what a terrible thing it was but on the other hand, the Japanese were doing such terrible things you know. They justified it in that way. We were going to lose an awful lot more.

Mike: The atom bomb stopped everything. The Russians were supposed to help conquer the Japanese in China. All they did was go in and take all the machinery out of the factories. They took and kept that one northern Japanese island. The Russians didn't do what they agreed to there. They did very little fighting as I heard; they were just busy stripping the country.

Question: Mike, do you have a message for future generations regarding the war?
I think it is very important that they read up on what the Second World War was about. It was a time that was different than any other time unless it was the First World War. People were one hundred percent against the Axis Powers— not ninety percent. I do not think we could fight WWII today.

TRIBUTE

On behalf of my family, I would like to thank my uncle, Mike (P.R.) Wheelan, for his years of service during WWII and for his willingness to share his story with us. I know that you and Uncle Don and many others sacrificed precious things during those years to serve our country. You were in danger's way for a cause that made the world a better place for me, my brothers, sisters and cousins. We are honored and proud to know you.

With much love and admiration,
Molly Daniel
Charleston, IL

War is Certainly Not Pretty

Russ Bannister
Washington, IA

Army Air Corps
Europe

Interview Date:
11 August 2011

Referral:
Halcyon House

I grew up about a mile from Wrigley Field in Chicago. I saw a lot of ball games including the very first All Star game. It was played in 1934. I saw Babe Ruth, Lou Gehrig, Lefty Grove, and Ted Williams play. I went to all the Bears games. We moved to LaPorte City, Iowa, when I was fourteen.

I'd say that most of the kids that enlisted were looking for something to do and a place where they could get food in their stomachs. There were also some that enlisted out of devotion to country. For my own experience, and I have to be honest, I was a draft dodger until there was no way around being a draft dodger. I waited until it was about time I would be drafted and then enlisted. I had a degree in Business Administration from Northwestern University, graduating in 1941. For some reason they thought me too short to get into the Navy. Can you believe that?

So I went to the Army and stood on the tips of my toes and made it by about half an inch. I joined the Air Cadets. I did fine until they started doing the power stalls and then they'd dive and go back up and quiver and roll and spin. Those acrobatics and I didn't get along. I got air sick and it made me dizzy. My flight instructor said I wasn't long for the Air Corps and he was correct.

I became a weatherman. I did my training at

Chinook Field at the University of Illinois. It lasted about six months. My job was to draw the weather air maps, showing dew points, barometric pressure, and where the fronts were located. This determined if the B-24s could fly the next day. The B-24s flew a different route to Europe than the B-17s, which went the northern route. The B-24s went to Brazil and across to North Africa and then north to air bases. Martha Boshart was a pilot that ferried the B-24s to the edge of Brazil.

We sailed overseas on a small Liberty ship. There were 100 ships in our convoy. Our sleeping bunks were stacked five high. Fresh water was a precious commodity. We tried showering with salt water once. That was the end of that experiment. We stopped in Malta and Algiers. The crossing took 28 days.

I was in Italy with the 12th Air Squadron of the 15th Air Force. I was stationed in La Tagliata at an old British airbase from WWI. I was a staff sergeant. Three of us started making weather maps at 8 o'clock in the morning and finished at 4 o'clock in the afternoon. We'd usually make two maps. As weather observers, we'd continue to work until midnight. I attended a couple of mission briefings and listened to our captain give the weather report. We slept in GI tents.

Question: Did you or your captain ever give out a weather forecast that turned out to be so wrong that it caused a major problem?

You bet we did. One time we had 45 pilots that had completed their required number of missions and were heading for home. They were to fly from our base to Rome but hit thunderstorms en route. We lost 35 of them, all on one plane. Sometimes the officers would disagree on whether or not it was fit to fly. But somebody always had to make the decision and then live with it.

My father died from tuberculosis when I was seven. My mother passed away from a stroke when I'd been in Italy about a month and a half. That probably had the most impact on me of anything that happened during the war. I was 24 and on my own from then on.

I had a chance to fly to Switzerland and spent a week there. I spent time in Venice and Milan. I met an Italian college girl at a dance club in Milan and we had a lot of fun going different places. Either her mother or brother always accompanied us so any thought of romance was out of the question.

Senator Hubert Humphrey flew a B-24 bomber out of a base about a 100 miles north of us. I was given a ride in a B-24 after the war ended. We flew over the Alps. When we got over Munich, they opened the bomb bay doors so I could see the destruction they'd done to the city. War is certainly not pretty.

We spent a week in Rome. It was an interesting place. We even had an audience with the Pope. We got to climb up to the top of St. Peter's Basilica and view all of Rome. They don't let people do that anymore.

We came home in October. There were terrible storms. The ship was out of the water about half the time. When the propellers would come out of the water, the whole ship would shake. We were too scared to get seasick.

Question: Do you remember hearing about the attack on Pearl Harbor?

Yes, I was sitting in my girlfriend's apartment waiting to go to the theater. Franklin Roosevelt came on the radio and gave his historic speech about the attack. It changed me from being a strict isolationist. My thought prior to Pearl Harbor was, "If those people want to kill each other off, why should I give a damn?" It made me feel more interested in trying to do something to save the country. I have to admit that I was willing to take an easy role in the war if it would increase my chance of coming back.

It would be nice if somebody of my age could come back for two weeks and tell everything that happened.

SWING A COMPASS

Max See
Washington, IA

Army Air Corps
Stateside

Interview Date:
19 August 2011

Referral:
Washington Rotary Group

I was in the Army Air Corps. I was drafted. Two of us went up to Des Moines to enlist for pilot training. We bummed a ride with Milo Sorden. That was in October of '42. I was 25 years old. They told me the cut off age was 23 and I was too old. Don Bye was quite a bit younger and they took him. So I thought, the heck with it, I'll wait until I'm drafted. That happened in April of '43.

I did my basic training in Miami Beach. It lasted about three months. We took aptitude and IQ tests. One of the tests was for the Signal Corps. I didn't want any part of it so I didn't try to make a good grade on that. Now on the mechanics test, I tried hard on that one.

Then a bunch of us were sent on a train. We didn't know where we were going and we weren't supposed to know. They kept all the window shades pulled down on the train. We ended up in Amarillo, Texas, at Aircraft Mechanics School. I was in school there from June to December, studying the B-17. We learned how to start, stop, and control a B-17 engine. We learned welding, riveting, sheet metal works, and instruments.

From Amarillo, six of us were sent to Alabama for two weeks and then to Ft. Myers, Florida for gunnery school. Two or three of us didn't qualify because of age for gunnery school and they

couldn't figure out what to do with us.

Next I was sent back down to Florida. I was placed as a permanent part on the line as an instrument specialist on B-17s and B-24s. Both were four engine bombers. I was assigned to Squadron B. I asked the officer in charge if they would send me to instrument school in Eldridge, Illinois, because it was close to home. I ended up being sent for two weeks training in Philadelphia. When I returned to Florida, I found out it was illegal for me to work on instruments. All that work had to be done by civilian contractors. All the instruments were sealed. One of the civilians working on instruments befriended me. He gave me a bottle of shellac so I could reseal the instruments after tinkering with them.

I shared a shop with an electrician. My job was to repair malfunctioning instruments on the training planes. I could start the engines on a B-17 but they wouldn't let me move it. They used a B-26 to tow a target out over the Gulf of Mexico. A bomber would go out with ten students on board for gunnery practice. They'd shoot a .50 caliber out a side window at the target being towed. The pilot would enter into his flight log any problems encountered with the plane. The most common thing I worked on was the cylinder head temperature gauge. When an engine overheated, it was usually from a bad thermocouple caused by all the vibration. The crew chief would report the problem to me. I was a PFC and put in charge of this after three or four months. At one time, I had three sergeants working under me. I made corporal a couple of months before being discharged.

One of my favorite things to do was swing a compass. I'd go out to the runway and stand in front of the bomber with a master compass. The pilot would taxi his plane around to different headings to measure his plane's magnetic compass compared with mine. No magnetic compass was exactly right on every heading. They would be a degree or two off. The farther you flew, the greater the error. That's about the only thing I did for a year.

I spent the rest of my time in Florida, except for three months after the war was over. Then I was assigned to the salvage department. A lot of good stuff got dumped in a hole and buried. I thought it a terrible waste. The only thing they salvaged was boxes of clay pigeons. They were used for gunnery practice. The clay pigeons were sold to a guy in Miami.

Your date of discharge was based on points. I had a wife and child, but I had not been overseas or seen combat. So I was down the list. Being stateside, I was fortunate. I got to come home about every six months on leave. I finally got out in February, 1946.

Question: Which did you think was the better airplane, the B-17 or the 24?

I liked the B-17. It had fewer engine problems and could take more punishment. All we had were B-17's when I started there in Florida. Then they shipped all of them overseas and brought in all B-24's. Then those were sent overseas and they brought in B-17's again. Our line CO was a lieutenant who had flown a B-17 overseas. He spoke highly of them.

Question: Where were you when Pearl Harbor was attacked?

I was up here on East 3rd Street at my folks, having a family reunion. We heard it on the radio that Sunday afternoon. We already knew by the way things were stewing that we'd have to go into the service. But we had no idea when. I'd heard

of Hawaii, but Pearl Harbor and Hickman Field meant nothing to me.

Question: Max, did you run into anyone you knew from back home during the war?

John Perdock, Bill's brother, stopped in to see me once. Don Bye and Daryl Burham stopped by. I saw Cloyd Garret, who worked at Montgomery Wards for years. He was up in Jacksonville and I went up to see him. I ran into another guy from Crawfordsville in downtown Ft. Myers but I can't remember his name.

Garret was in the infantry. Bye and Burham were in the Air Corps. I think Daryl and Everett Burham were first cousins. Everett was a flight instructor in the Air Corps in Enid, Oklahoma. John Yuosling and Gene Tucker were single engine flight instructors in Texas. My brother Clarence or "Mike" saw action in the Battle of the Bulge. He was in the Rainbow Division.

Question: Forty-two people from Washington County were killed during the war. Did you know any of them?

I remember an Edmonson that was one year behind me in school. Bob Shannon was a captain. His B-24 crashed because of weather in Europe and he was killed.

After the war ended, I was stationed in Enid, Oklahoma. I was discharged from Jefferson Barracks in Missouri. My wife and two children were still living in Enid so I had to take the train down to bring them back to Washington. I started working for Milo Sorden at his music store repairing musical instruments in 1939. After the war, I got my old job back. Milo was the guy that drove me to Des Moines when I tried to enlist in the Army Air Corps. I purchased the store from him in 1957. I sold the store to Dean Kurtz in 1981. I'll be 94 in October.

Question: Do you have any message for the youth of today?

I think back how the youth in Germany let one powerful man brainwash them. They need to be careful in not allowing any one man that kind of power or influence.

KEEP THE PLANES FLYING

Max Smith
Washington, IA

Army Air Corps
N. Africa, Europe

Interview Date:
23 August 2011

Referral:
Washington Noon Kiwanis

I grew up in Albia, Iowa. I enlisted April 10th, 1943, in the Army Air Corps. I trained at the University of Oregon and Harvard in the graduate School of Engineering for the Weather Service. I served as a Weather Observer at Goodfellow Field Airbase in Pyote, Texas, Chanute Field in Rantoul, Illinois, and Cazas Air Base in Casablanca, French Morocco. Eleven of us flew across the Atlantic to Africa in a C-54.

My assignment was to the 19th Weather Squadron. I wore a 9th Air Force patch on my uniform. I was primarily in the Weather Service. My job was to keep the planes flying. I donated all my uniforms to the Community Center so they're gone. I was six or seven months in North Africa. When I first got over there, I went from Casablanca clear across North Africa to Egypt in a C-47. We flew into Cairo. Our group of eleven toured the pyramids. I was supposed to go on to India but my orders got changed en route. I carried a gun with me then. Then I was permanently assigned to Cazas Airbase in Casablanca. They wouldn't let anybody except those in charge carry a gun in Casablanca. They were scared of having incidents with the local Arabs.

> *"The weather information I collected could shut a base down. One time my data stopped a general from flying."*

One of my duties was to attach our weather instruments to a balloon and send it aloft. Usually the balloons would go up 20,000 feet in elevation. The instruments would pick up the air pressure, humidity, wind velocity and direction which would be relayed back to us by radio. We'd record this information and transfer it to weather maps before the next mission. Then the meteorologist would analyze the maps.

Sometimes I would have to make my own hydrogen for the balloon in North Africa. Actually, we had someone else make it for us. One time I had to drive to the other side of Casablanca in a 2 ½ ton truck to pick up the hydrogen. The French had one side of the air field. That's where I had my weather station. I had three buildings over there where I worked alone. In one building I had equipment that would pick up the radio signal and run it through instrumentation that would pull out all the weather data. It was kind of complicated. That's why they sent me to Harvard. That's how we obtained the local weather conditions. Information from more distant places came in by wire when we had it. Otherwise, we had to get it any way we could. All this was designed to get the pilots some accurate information so they wouldn't fly into problems. The weather information I collected could shut a base down. One time my data stopped a general from flying.

One night I drove my jeep over to the weather station. I wasn't supposed to go alone but I had to when I didn't have a driver. I pulled up to my two tents about four in the morning. Things didn't feel right. Something felt wrong when I opened the door to the tent but I still had to get the weather information. I must confess that I didn't spend much time looking around to see who was there. I turned every light on I could. They were probably local Arabs looking for food or pilfering equipment. I suspect they were hiding in some of the storage rooms. I would have liked to have had a gun that night. Most of the local Arabs behaved themselves but they were accomplished thieves. Things were actually rather quiet when I was in North Africa. They had things cleaned up by the time I got over there. I'm just thankful I didn't have to carry a gun in combat and kill anyone.

Normally the weather wasn't too bad in North Africa. They weren't flying any bombers out of the Cazas Airbase when I got over there. There were a lot of Italian prisoners of war there. The German POWs had already been sent on.

Question: Did you have much contact with the local Arab population?

Some, but not very much. We called them "wogs." Generally speaking, you had to have an Arab driver when you went through Casablanca. The problem was finding one that could be trusted and spoke English. That was the reason I had to drive myself sometimes. I had to drive through the old part of Casablanca once and that's when I should have had someone with me. We'd venture in to Casablanca when off duty. The USO was there. Parts of the city were off limits. We were to stay away from the old walled city.

Norm Schoonover was an infantryman in North Africa. Norm was in the 34th "Red Bull" Infantry Division. He got shot through the neck and jaw. A sniper got him. He was picked up in time to be saved but he had trouble moving his head back and forth from then on. Norm told a story about being on guard duty when Churchill met with Roosevelt in Casablanca. This was before I got over there. He had to tell Winston Churchill to pull the window

shades down one night in his hotel room because he was violating the blackout order.

My older brother was already in the Coast Guard. He was a pharmacist mate on a hospital ship. He was in the thick of it in the Pacific. They'd treat the wounded from the island campaigns. There were a lot of burials at sea.

I was discharged from active duty April 10th, 1946, but remained in the Active Reserve for 22 years. In 1950 I switched over to the Medical Service Corps and became an optometrist. I was a buck sergeant during the war and a major when I left the Active Reserve. The Iowa Great Lakes were the farthest away from home I'd been before the war. I'd never ridden a train or flown on an airplane. My war experience was interesting to me because I got to see parts of the world I only knew from history class.

Max Smith continued practicing optometry in Washington until his retirement.

ONE OF THE THIRTEEN

Leo "Chub" Hall
Wellman, IA

81st Infantry Division
Pacific

Interview Date:
6 September 2011

Referral:
Jack Seward, Jr.

I was drafted in 1943. Everyone always wants to know how I got in the Army when I couldn't see. When we arrived in Des Moines we were given a physical. The guy ahead of me standing in line for the vision test wore glasses. The examiner told him to remove his glasses and read the smallest line he could. I remember those letters and repeated them when my turn came. When I got out to Camp Cooke in California, I was asked how I had passed the physical with such poor eyesight. When I told the officer, he said that he could get me out of the Army if I didn't want to stay, but I said, "No, I want to stay."

It seemed to me that, at that time in the war, everyone wanted to join the service. My brother was already in the war with the 34th Infantry Division in North Africa, in the medical department. He was in the National Guard before the war started. We grew up ten miles northwest of Wellman. A whole bunch of guys from the North English area were in the National Guard. The Guard was activated when the war started.

All my friends that I grew up with joined the military. I rode the school bus with Carroll

Swartzendruber. He went to the service. The Goodwin boys all went to the Marines. Johnny Capper went. Bob and Red Moothart were also two of my friends that served. After the war Bob told a story about an incident that happened in Germany. A number of GIs were walking down a street and met a woman and a kid. The kid rolled a hand grenade into the Americans, killing one of them. After that, their captain told them, "from now on, if it moved, shoot it."

Roger and Wayne Johnson both served. I ran into Roger while at Camp Roberts. He was in the infantry. My wife, Martha, had a friend named Fladung that did not come home (killed defending Bastogne, 101st Airborne).

There were a large number of conscientious objectors in the Wellman area. I learned later that a number of houses got splashed with yellow paint. This happened after I left in '43. But to tell it like it really was, nobody wanted to go kill anyone, regardless of what church the family attended. Some of wanted to join the military even though their church prohibited it. A few did anyway. I later learned of instances when draft age guys I knew were given an ultimatum by their deeply religious fathers: "If you join to the military, you never set foot in my house again."

I served as a T-4 in the Headquarters Company of the 1138th Combat Engineers. We were part of the 81st Infantry Division. They told us that for every soldier that carried a weapon into combat, there were thirteen others that were needed to support him. I was one of those thirteen. I was initially trained to build bridges. We would individually carry seventy to eighty pound sections of a Bailey bridge and piece them together. When they asked for volunteers to become low speed radio operators, I raised my hand. I thought it would be an improvement over what I was currently doing. My job was to transmit Morse code and voice through a coded message machine. The codes were changed daily. We were supposed to use code most of the time.

Earlier, I was also trained in the use of a device called an odometer. This device was mounted on a jeep and designed primarily for desert warfare where there were wide, open spaces. It operated on compass settings and used a pencil line positioned by two shafts or axis and had four circulating tubes that was supposed to get the operator to within one half mile of a predetermined location from up to three hundred miles away. Since we ended up being sent to islands in the Pacific, the odometer wasn't practical and didn't make the trip with us.

I sailed from Seattle to Hawaii and then stopped briefly in Guadalcanal. Our mail was always addressed to, "somewhere in the Pacific." I spent time on Peleliu and the neighboring island of Anguar. Both islands had already been secured from the Japanese. We were based near an airstrip built by the CB's. We only lost one man from our company during the war and that was from a freak accident. A big typhoon hit our islands. We used DUKWs to travel between Anguar and Peleliu. I was put in charge of keeping track of the DUKWs when the typhoon hit. The high ocean swells made it impossible to even see them most of the time. There weren't any trees left standing on either island after the high winds hit.

We also spent time in New Caledonia and ended the war on Leyte in the Philippines. We were sitting outside on logs watching a movie one evening when they interrupted to announce that the war was over. No one stood up and cheered because we knew we weren't going home yet.

THE LETTERS JUST KEPT COMING

Rex Severt
Washington, IA

Navy Post Office
Stateside

Interview Date:
12 September 2011

Referral:
Personal Contact

I was drafted into the Navy. I had a wife and two awfully nice kids. The farthest I'd been from home was to Washington, Iowa. I did boot camp in Farragut, Idaho. I had a little leave to visit home after boot camp. Then I was sent to Fleet Post Office in San Francisco. There were 4000 working there, all Navy personnel.

There was row after row of boxes that you sorted the mail in. Each box had a name of a different ship or island base. There was a large container for misplaced mail. It included those men reassigned and those killed in action. We very seldom returned a letter to sender for those killed because we wanted to be certain the family was notified by other means. We must have been updated daily on deaths but that was way out of my territory. The Navy was really careful about that. We ran 24 hours a day. I worked the graveyard shift.

Question: Did you ever handle mail that was addressed as "somewhere in the Pacific"?

No, I never saw anything like that. All I handled was 1st class mail. Packages went through a different department. I do know that the Navy went to every effort to find where the recipients were. The Navy would keep forwarding the letter until it was delivered. It wasn't hard work, but it was constant. There was always a stack of letters

waiting to be sorted. The letters just kept coming. I realized how important it was to those sending the letters as well as those receiving them.

I was working as a rural mail carrier for the U.S. Postal Service when I was drafted. I have to assume the Navy had my records and that's why I ended up where I did. I entered service as a seaman and left as a Mailman 2nd class. I served two years. I didn't stay on a base or in barracks. I could live any damn place I wanted and had to eat at restaurants. I received what was called subsistence pay which covered the cost of room and board.

We were required to wear our uniforms at all times. I got brought up on charges by a young shave tail while walking out of a restaurant for having my cap on wrong. I always wore it a little cockeyed like everyone else. It was supposed to sit on your head straight. I was told to be at a Captain's Mast at the Post Office the next morning. I didn't even know what a Captain's Mast was at the time. When I walked into the room, there was the highest ranking naval officer I'd ever seen sitting in a big chair fit for a king or queen. I knew whatever he said was law. I didn't even know how to talk to him but I tried my best to answer his questions in the proper manner. I told him, "Sir, I guess that I was out of proper uniform and I am awful sorry about that." He told me not to let it happen again. He reprimanded me in no uncertain terms, sounding like he would castrate me or something. He added that he never wanted to see me before his court again. I might have been dumb, but I wasn't stupid. I understood what he meant.

I had about as good a duty as one could get in the Navy. It was a job that had to be done. I spent a total of 34 years in the U.S. Postal Service. I spent the last 27 of them as the Postmaster at Wellman.

Being married to a WWII veteran has truly made me understand why they are called the Greatest Generation. They possess a unique inner strength and spirit that can be seen in all aspects of their lives.

Raberta Schafer
(Wife of Russell Schafer)
Fairfield, IA

WE CHEERED EVERY TIME

Doyle Brown
Washington, IA

Army Air Corps
Pacific

Interview Date:
20 September 2011

Referral:
Angela Ellis

I was drafted in 1942. I was 22 years old. Les Dunlap was on the draft board at that time. I asked him for a deferment because my wife was expecting her first child. We lived on a little acreage south of the airport and I worked for a farmer named Marvin Warnick. Then I got a letter in the mail telling me to get ready to go as I was listed as 1-A. I had to have a farm sale that included my six dairy cows. My corn was sold standing in the field and I was off to the war.

I was in Army Air Corp training in Florida when our baby was born. Then I was sent to Will Rogers Field in Oklahoma and placed in a truck company and received training for that in Woodward, Oklahoma. About a year after joining the service, I shipped out of California for Australia. I was aboard the largest ship the U.S. had at that time, the USS *Mt. Vernon*. There were 72,000 troops on board plus the crew. We were packed in like sardines. The ship zigzagged to avoid being torpedoed by Japanese submarines. I didn't think I'd get seasick but I did. I was okay up on deck but you couldn't remain up there all the time.

We went to a number of small islands. I don't remember their names. At New Guinea we got new GMC 6x6 2 ½ ton trucks. They were still in their crates and had to be assembled. We hauled supplies for the Fifth Air Force. A lot of times I would haul gas at night. A big tanker would come in as far as they could in the bay and they'd pipe the gasoline in using a hose. Our job included filling the 55 gallon barrels with gas and capping them. We unloaded the barrels by rolling them off onto tires. We didn't use a ramp. We hauled bombs but they weren't fused so were safe. We hauled supplies up to ten miles inland, to an open field that served as a supply depot. New Guinea had some small mountains and there were still Japanese holdouts but none in the area we were.

There were native inhabitants on New Guinea. They were scurvy looking. They slept in a bunch, side by side like hogs do. Some of the natives were used in work parties. We'd haul them in our trucks. They always wanted to ride in my cab but I would not let them. They were primitive natives that lived off coconuts and bananas. We didn't have any problems with the ones around us.

My wife and Dwight Hayes' wife got to talking and discovered both of their husbands were in New Guinea. When I found out what company he was in, I looked him up. He rode with me at night when I hauled gas so I had someone to visit with.

Dwight was in the photo company and worked in the photo lab.

There was a truck company of blacks that went over to New Guinea before we did. At first, they tried to run us off the road. They acted a little belligerent toward us. They soon learned we could drive the same way they could. They really didn't give us that much trouble.

New Guinea was hot and humid. We took pills for malaria every day. We were told they would likely make us sterile for some time even after we quit taking them. I had my second child born a year after I returned to the states.

We had 55 trucks in our company. Some of the guys would try to drive their trucks up in the mountains and see how far they could get. They burnt out a lot of clutches and ground a lot gears doing that. They were just being 19 year old kids horsing around.

We were in on the invasion on the Philippines. They shipped our trucks ahead of us and we boarded an LST. We could get all our trucks and two or three jeeps and weapons carriers on one LST but they had to really cram them in there. We didn't have any need to carry weapons on New Guinea but they issued them to us for the Philippines.

We stopped in the Dutch East Indies on the way to the Philippines. We flew into Biak on a C-47. We were there only one night. Biak is all coral. They told us to dig in but there was no way you could dig in that stuff. A plane came over strafing that night but none of us got hurt.

We landed on Leyte in the Philippines. The LST we were on couldn't get to the shoreline so we drove the trucks in through water. I drove the tenth truck off the LST. The guy driving the eleventh one said he thought something bad would happen if he drove in so a corporal volunteered to take his place. That truck hit a land mine. The truck cab was blown into splinters. The combat engineers were supposed to have had all the land mines cleared where we drove in but they missed one.

The Navy ships were shooting their big guns over our heads while we were driving in, trying to drive the Japanese back. It was pretty noisy for two or three days. The infantry and combat engineers went in ahead of us.

Question: There was a big naval battle at Leyte Gulf. Were you aware of it at the time?
I knew about it. I don't remember being able to see any of it but I recall seeing our big ships out there. I think I was aware that it was going on.

One night Japanese planes dropped white phosphorus bombs on us. I had a foxhole dug with coconut logs over the top. I had a premonition that I'd better spend the night there and it was a good thing I did. We had 10 guys killed and 10 of our company wounded that night. There were only 100 guys in our company. You could hear the Japanese planes. They sounded like old washing machine motors.

> *"One night Japanese planes dropped white phosphorus bombs on us. I had a foxhole dug with coconut logs over the top. I had a premonition that I'd better spend the night there and it was a good thing I did."*

They kept trying to get an airstrip built next to us for the P-38s. They couldn't haul enough gas flying from their home base to do much combat. The Japs would come over every night and bomb the airstrip while it was under construction. The landing strip was made out of metal mesh crates tied together. When the airstrip was finally done, the P-38s started shooting those darn Jap planes out of the sky. We stood out there and watched. When the P-38s got a hit, the Japanese plane would explode in pieces. We cheered every time!

The Japanese dropped paratroopers on Leyte. We were told to double our guard and to be on the lookout for paratroopers. We heard a story about someone being stabbed through their mosquito netting one night. I wasn't sleeping in my foxhole anymore. I was close enough to the bay that when the tide came in, my blankets in the bottom of the hole would get soaked. We never got very far inland. There were mountains pretty close. We didn't have much to do except sit around. We'd walk up into the hills. There were lots of Japanese bodies lying around. We were far enough back that we didn't see any combat. We got strafed a few times. I don't remember anybody getting hit but a truck tire got blown up. I don't recall any anti-aircraft batteries shooting back. All our company had were carbines.

Filipino civilians would wash our clothes for cigarettes. All that amounted to was them taking the laundry down to the shore and beating it on a rock. Several USO shows came through. We saw Bob Hope a couple of times. They were good shows and we really appreciated them.

We were supposed to go to Luzon next but that was changed. Okinawa was our next island. Things had quieted down quite a bit by the time we landed there. Raymond Kephart was in on the Okinawa invasion. I can't remember what he served in but it seems to me that it was heavy artillery. We were at the north end of Okinawa and had to haul supplies to the south end of the island. There were mountains down toward the south end that ran right up to the edge of the ocean. There was only a one lane road. It took all day to drive to the south end, deliver supplies, and come back. We were on Okinawa when the war ended. We were very, very happy when we were told the war was over.

We went on into Japan as part of the occupation. We drove in a truck convoy from Yokohama to an air base. On the next trip, our truck and another took off by ourselves and got lost in Tokyo. When people saw us, they were so scared that they would run and hide behind their houses. We finally ran into a Fifth Air Force jeep and flagged him down. He led us back to the base but our trucks had trouble keeping up with him.

My brother Kenneth was in the Navy aboard a little LSM. He ferried supplies from ships into shore in the Pacific. My brother Clarence was in the Korean War. Dale, the youngest brother, was in Germany as part of the occupation.

We were shipped home to Seattle and sent to Jefferson Barracks in Missouri where we were discharged. Being away from my wife and little baby girl was the hardest thing for me during the war. I worked at the Cargill plants a while and then hauled bulk fuel for a local Phillips 66 dealer. Then I worked furnaces for Bob Roe for 21 years and my brother's Brown Heating for eight years. My knees were starting to bother me some by then so I took a job managing Autumn Park and stayed there eleven years. After that, I worked a little at True Value and did security work at Modine.

I was privileged to go on an Honor Flight to Washington, D.C. The WWII Memorial made quite an impression on me. It was really special.

SEMPER PARATUS

Wayne Wagner
Washington, IA

Coast Guard

Interview Date:
4 October 2011

Referral:
Paul Reynolds

I was at my uncle and aunt's farm in Lexington for Sunday dinner when we heard about Pearl Harbor. I don't think we realized how significant it was or the number of ships lost until later.

My cousin Everett Davison and I were both born in 1921. He wanted to join the Coast Guard and asked me to join him. We went to Bettendorf to enlist on Labor Day in 1942. Guy Lombardo was racing speedboats on the Mississippi River while we were there. Guys from Iowa, Illinois, and Missouri gathered there and went as a group to Omaha where we were sworn in. Then we were shipped out to Alameda, California for boot camp. We went in as apprentice seamen and made $25 a month. After our 90 days of training, they didn't know what to do with us. They ended up putting us on a train to Seattle. We weren't there very long before we were sent to a CCC camp in Mt. Rainier National Park until they could figure out where to assign us. My cousin and I were placed at Coast Guard stations about 30 miles apart on the Washington coast.

I was assigned to office duty in a Coast Guard station. I ran the radio and did book work. I was a second class seaman by then and received $27 a month. The Coast Guard had its own fleet but I wasn't involved in that aspect of it yet. Most of

the radio traffic was between stations. The chief in charge of our station had me study the blue jacket manual while on duty. It contained all the Coast Guard rules and regulations. Then I was given a test. Passing it made me a seaman first class and I got $30 a month. So we still weren't rich!

I applied for an opening to go to a signalman's school. The school was at a resort hotel up on Mt. Rainier complete with a swimming pool. Lo and behold, I became proficient on Morse Code so they had me teaching a class on it. From there I went back to Seattle for another week or two of training on electrical equipment. Then I was sent down to Cape Blanco, Oregon, to a Coast Guard substation in a lighthouse. Only 20 people worked there. They couldn't use the light on the lighthouse because it might attract Japanese subs. There was an electrical contraption that signaled the ships where the lighthouse was. I ran that, answered the telephone, and operated the radio. The lighthouse was situated up on a high cliff that was the westernmost point in the United States.

Two man beach patrols operated from the lighthouse. They'd be assigned a section of the coastal beach and walk it for eight hours. They'd look for anything unusual. My cousin Everett went out on beach patrol at a different station. He said it was so black some nights you couldn't see enough to find your way around.

I was next sent to Camp Blanco again. After that, I received orders to attend quartermaster's signalman school at Manhattan Beach in New York. I was there three or four months. During that time, Frank Knox, a big shot in the government (Secretary of the Navy) died and there was going to be a big funeral in Washington D.C. and burial in Arlington Cemetery. We had just graduated from school. They offered to give anyone who volunteered to go to D.C. to march in the parade a week's leave when we came back. So that's what I did.

We took a train to Washington D.C. We marched down Pennsylvania Avenue to the cemetery. The casket rode in a caisson drawn by horses. We had drilled during our schooling so we marched pretty good. I can remember hearing the crowds that lined the streets remarking on how good we looked.

I took my week leave to come back to Iowa. It was late April. My dad was sowing oats and there were snow flurries. He farmed with horses all his life. Our farm was five miles south of Washington on the Coppock Road.

When I returned to the west coast, I was assigned to an icebreaker ship named the *West Wind*. It was one of four newly designed icebreakers built in the Kaiser shipyard in Oakland, California. The ship wasn't quite finished so they sent the assembled crew to Catalina Island. There had been a military installation built there during the Spanish American War where we stayed and trained together. My future wife was staying with relatives at San Pedro. I'd go visit her on shore leave. We got married in Los Angeles in 1944.

We took the ship out on its shakedown cruise shortly before Thanksgiving. It was built in the shape of a bathtub and really pitched and rolled. It was 300 feet long and 60 feet wide. It had twin rear propellers and one in the middle of the ship. It had tanks in the bow of the ship that could be filled with water to give it extra weight. Icebreakers work by forcing the bow of the ship on top of the ice. The weight of the ship then breaks the ice. The front propeller also helps weaken the ice by pulling the

> "We marched down Pennsylvania Avenue to the cemetery. The casket rode in a caisson drawn by horses."

water out from under it. Our ship had a five inch gun and a seaplane.

The day before Thanksgiving we had a bad storm. A third class bonsun's mate went on deck to check the lashings on some oil drums and was swept overboard. We went back to search for him but he was lost at sea. The crest of the waves were higher than you could see over. I got seasick during the storm and stayed sick until we reached shore. About everyone got seasick. It stunk so bad below deck from all the vomit that I couldn't remain there. I spent most of the remainder of the time above deck on lookout duty until we reached port. That was the only time I got seasick.

We got issued cold weather gear for a trip to Alaska. We got as far as Seattle and were called back. Russia wanted two of the new icebreakers to keep their northern ports open. I was part of the skeleton crew that remained aboard ship while it was refitted to the Russian's specifications. Then I went on another shakedown cruise with the Russians aboard. After that was over with, I had a week's leave. My wife and I came back to Iowa. That would have been in March, 1945.

When I returned, it was to Treasure Island where there was a Navy base. I was put on shore patrol duty in Oakland. We had to chase young sailors out of bars. The rest of the icebreaker crew was also at Treasure Island. We were assigned to a (Squire class) troop transport, the USS *General D.E. Aultman*. It was 600 feet long and 60 feet wide and had the low profile of an oil tanker. It was built by the Kaiser Company.

After the shakedown cruise, we went through the Panama Canal and sailed to Marseilles, France, to pick up soldiers and nurses to transport them to the Pacific Theater. The war in Europe had ended by then. The Mediterranean Sea was calm but once we past Gibraltar the sea got rough and the soldiers got sick.

When we went back through the Panama Canal we had a guy jump overboard. He did not want to go to the Pacific. Boats were launched to retrieve him. He spent the rest of his time in the brig.

Then we got word that Japan surrendered,

but we still headed to the Pacific. We stopped in Humboldt Bay, New Guinea for supplies. Our next port was Manila. It had been bombed out and was a mess. There was only one path in through all the sunken Japanese ships in the harbor. We unloaded the troops and nurses there. We stayed one night and sailed for Okinawa. We picked up a load of troops there and sailed back to Portland, Oregon, arriving in October.

My three year enlistment was up. I was discharged in St. Louis. I was glad to get out but I kept thinking how lucky I was to have missed all the fighting. I was a green, country kid when the war started. I had not been over a 100 miles from home. I traveled clear across the country a number of times during the war. I had a good learning experience.

The motto of the Coast Guard was *Semper Paratus*. It means always ready. There was a song we sang about it.

Question: Do you remember any classmates that didn't come home?
There was a Jack Wilson, Vernon Beenblossom, Jack Mace and others. Most of the ones killed were in the Army.

I Wanted To Die and Couldn't

Herbert Hammen
Washington, IA

4th Marine Division
Pacific

Interview Date:
11 October 2011

Referral:
Personal Contact

My brother Charles was in Patton's Third Army. He was a medic in the 80th Infantry Division, 319th Infantry Regiment. He was in two bad battles in France. In one, his company was moving up across this bare field. They got shelled so badly and machine guns and stuff firing that they pulled back. There were seven guys left lying out there. Charles went back and took care of them. He received the Silver Star for that. Charles also received a Bronze Star and three Purple Hearts. Charles was badly wounded on December 31st in the Battle of the Bulge. He lived for six days. He was taking care of another soldier when he was hit. Charles was buried in Luxemburg. Since he died in a hospital my mother was sure it was his body in the casket so she had him sent home. The casket came by train and was unloaded on the Freshwaters landing dock.

I was at Camp Lejeune and had leave to spend Christmas at home. I got terribly ill while traveling at the end of my leave back to Lejeune. I took a train to D.C. and a bus from there. That bus made a stop about every five minutes. I thought I'd never

get there. I had no idea where to go when I arrived at night so found an empty hut to spend the night in. The next morning I went to the field hospital and within two hours they had my appendix out. The seventh day I was in the hospital I was told that I was wanted on the phone. It was my mother telling me about Charles. They granted me sick leave to go home for the memorial.

I attended parochial school in Harper. There were only five in my class and I was the only boy. There had never been anyone from Harper in the Marines and I wanted to be one. Some of those kids said that I'd never get in the Marine Corps. I really wanted to prove them wrong. So I enlisted in the Marines in May of '44 and they were supposed to call me up in June. July rolled around and I turned 18 and had to register for the draft. I was given a pre-physical in August. I got called up by the Army in October and had to go to St. Louis for the real physical. After I passed that, I told the guy I wanted to be in the Marine Corps, not the Army. He wrote a big "N" on my paperwork and told me to shove off. The Navy gave me another physical and I told them I wanted to be a Marine, not in the Navy. The Chief Petty Officer said that he "would see what he could do." He went somewhere and came back and said okay. There were only two out of the eight hundred guys in my group that made it to the Marines and I was one of them. Boot camp was down on Paris Island in South Carolina. From Lejeune, I went on a troop train clear across the country to Camp Pendleton in California. We had training up in the mountains and shipped out for overseas in April. I got so seasick that I wanted to die and couldn't. I never ate a thing for eight days. People told me that I'd feel better if I ate something. So I went down to the galley and everything stunk to me. I tried a sip of coffee and didn't make it up the stairs. I sucked on a lemon the eighth day and that seemed to help. We docked at Pearl Harbor but never got off the ship. Then we sailed for Mali. Hell, I got sick again, going from one island to another. I got sick coming home. I'd go out on the deck and watch the horizon. I was too sick to even smoke. I'd get called for guard duty and never leave my bunk. At least they didn't throw me in the brig. I never did get my sea legs. It was good going under the Golden Gate Bridge.

"I still get a lump in my throat when I hear the Marine Hymn."

I was put in the Fourth Marine Division. Their home base was on Mali. They had just got back from Iwo Jima. I was one of the replacements for those killed on Iwo. I was put in a mortar section. My rank was PFC. I shared a tent with four combat veterans. One of the veterans in the next tent over didn't care if he lived or died. He had gone in on Saipan, Tinian, and Iwo. He was even at Pearl Harbor when it got hit. In two or three weeks we were scheduled to land on Japan. We went on maneuvers to train for the invasion. Our division was to lead the assault. The Iwo veterans wouldn't talk about their combat experiences to us replacements. We lost as many Marines the first day on Iwo as we have lost in all of Iraq.

I'm a Catholic and I remember the Father coming out in his jeep on August 15th to say Mass because it is a Holy Day. He had a radio on his jeep. He told us the war was over. We had quite a celebration that night. Someone threw a beer can at the General's car. The next morning, we picked up every scrap of litter on a 25-mile hike.

The veterans with the most points got to go home first. The ship I sailed on had been used to haul Japanese POWs back to the states.

I still get a lump in my throat when I hear the Marine Hymn. When a Marine meets another Marine on the street they always stop and talk. Army guys don't do that. My squad leader was from Virginia. I went to visit him one time well after the war. We had a great time. One of his sons contacted me after he passed away and asked me if I knew about what his dad had done in the war. He had never talked about it.

I lost several Harper friends during the war. I had a neighbor boy, Alvin Redlinger. They never found him. Cletus Berg was killed about the same time as my brother. His brother Ivo also served and married his widow when he came back. There was another guy behind me in school, a Lindencamp, and he was really smart. He was in the Navy and became a commissioned officer and transferred to the Marines. He was killed in Korea. He was riding a Weasel and was killed his first day in Korea. He was the guy in school that told me that I'd never get in the Marine Corps. That's why I wanted to get in worse than ever.

My cousin Everett Hammen was on Wake Island when the Japanese took it early in the war. Somehow he got out, I don't know how. He never talked to me about it. Doc Taylor, the chiropractor, was in the Fourth Marines but worked in the Marine post office. Don Bye that had the shoe store was in the Marines. He moved down to Arizona. He's gone now. Milo Steele was in the Marine Band. They used those guys as litter bearers. Walt Johnson that had the fabric store was in. So were Harold Tucker and Dick Knupp. We had 33 local vets in our Marine league. I had a younger brother in Korea.

I like to travel and have been to every state but Alaska. But one thing is certain, I'm never getting on another ship. It bothers me worse than anything when the young people today show a lack of respect when the National Anthem is played.

BARRACKS NO. 207

Bill Drish
Fairfield, IA

Army Air Corps
Stateside

Interview Date:
15 October 2011

Referral:
Wayne Gould

I was working for Mike Drish on his farm when I heard about Pearl Harbor. I had just driven the tractor in to fill up with gas when he came out and said, "War broke out. The Japanese bombed Pearl Harbor." That was on a Sunday afternoon. I couldn't believe Mike for a while.

I enlisted right out of high school in December of 1943. I went to Camp Dodge in Des Moines and down through Ft. Leavenworth to Wichita Falls. I spent all my time at Wichita Falls, Texas. I was trained as a control operator to help airplanes land and take off. When I got done doing that, they didn't know what to do with me so I was put in charge Barrack No. 207. I had to tell the kids what to do and march them off to chow, things like that. That was about the most fun I ever had in the Army. That's about it on what I had to do, day after day.

Question: What were your duties as a control operator?

I was in a building. My job was to turn the runway landing lights on and off. Wichita Falls was a training base for the B-29s. They were the big

ones. One time a new pilot landed and overshot the runway and flipped the plane over on its back. Nobody was hurt.

Question: What was your typical day like?

I was a corporal in charge of the one barrack. I had to get everyone in my barracks moving in the morning and lined up for roll call. Then I'd head them over for breakfast. At 10:30 every night, I did roll call in the barracks to make sure everyone was present. I'd report anyone not there as AWOL. A lot of guys would go into Wichita Falls and get drunk and not make it back. You'd find them lying out there in the morning.

Question: Did you ever run into anyone you knew from back home?

I ran into Leonard Zickefoose at Wichita Falls. I was taking a bunch of boys into the mess hall and here comes Leonard walking through the door. He was being discharged and was on his way home. Francis Lauderdale was stationed at the same base I was.

Walter Pacha would be a good one for you to talk

to. He spent several years in the Navy. Bob Fritz lives east of Pleasant Plain but I don't know what he did. Ardell Hahn was in four years in the Army and overseas in the (Pacific) islands.

I drove Doc Scheeler to Chicago and he got to telling me stories. He said he and two buddies were lying on a dirt bank one day and a bomb went off close to them. He looked over and his two buddies were dead. He went in on D-Day. He told me stories the whole way to keep me awake.

Albert Everett from Pleasant Plain was on the submarine *Squalus* when it went down. Floyd Johnson was in the Navy. He spent a lot of time up in the crow's nest on a ship. He was up there looking for submarines. He said that during the storms, the ship would pitch to a 45 degree angle. Don Detweiler had photos of a concentration camp. He was involved in the Rhine River crossing.

I can still rattle off my Army serial number. I served with an Indian from Utah. He nicknamed me "Pasquali." I don't know what it meant but that was the name I went by while I was in Texas.

My dad died when I was 11 years old. My family didn't have much money. I started working for area farmers in 1935 and picked up where I left off after the service. My wife worked on Line One at the Burlington Ordinance Plant. She'd come home with powder burnt arms. One of her jobs was putting nuclear substances into bombs. She died of cancer.

I Did It On My Own

Bernard Payne
Washington, IA

USS *Robert I. Paine*
Atlantic

Interview Date:
18 October 2011

Referral:
Randy Payne

I worked as a farm hand for two years after high school. Then I worked for Motorola Radio for two or three years. That was in Chicago. I worked all kinds of radios. I enlisted October 12th, 1942. They gave me my physical in Des Moines and I was sent to Great Lakes Naval Station north of Chicago. I didn't get in on any of the marching or that kind of stuff. All I did was stencil clothes and hand them out to the guys. Next I was in Texas for six months of school. Then I was sent to San Francisco for two or three months. I ended up back in Chicago as an instructor. I did the same thing every day, same as my time spent earlier on an assembly line. I didn't like that kind of work at all.

I was told they needed an electronic technician on the USS *Robert I. Paine* which was a destroyer escort under construction. So I was a Payne on a *Paine*, although they spelled it a little different. I was transferred to this brand new ship and we took it out for the shakedown cruise. They had a high frequency transmitter that was slid in when in use. We got out there and it started raining. Water was streaming in on it. The chief thought something up on the antenna was loose so he sent me climbing the mast to tighten it. I got up 30 to 40 feet and then had to climb out on the yardarm. I had a seat belt on but the ship was tilting so much back and forth that I had to hold on or I would have slid off.

Question: Did you ever get sea sick?
Oh my, I've never been so sea sick. I wished I would die. You'd feel that miserable. Anyway, the captain changed the ship's course so we were going into the waves rather than crossing them at an angle so it wasn't as rough so I could complete my work.

One of my jobs was to set all the frequencies we used on the radios. We had a low frequency land sea channel and an antenna that ran the length of the ship. We could talk to the east coast from clear across the Atlantic. Codes were changed about every day. The IFF (Identification: Friend or Foe) transmitter had a depth charge wired in to self-destruct in case we abandoned ship.

Norfolk, Virginia, was our home port. On our shakedown cruise we went clear to New Orleans. When we pulled up to the dock there, the tide caught the ship and whipped the fantail of our ship around. The twin screws hit one of the sixteen inch wood pilings, chewing it up into cord wood. We made two or three crossings of the Atlantic with bent propellers.

Question: How does a destroyer escort differ from a regular destroyer?

Our ship was 307 feet long and did 24 knots at flank speed. Flank speed is as fast as it will go. A destroyer is 360 feet long and will do 35 knots. We only had three inch guns when we started out. A destroyer had five inch guns and more of them. We had a 360 man crew on the *Paine*. Our job was escorting a block island which was an escort carrier to Casablanca. This ship was a converted flat top and it was carrying a full load of aircraft. It took us three weeks to cross counting the time in the Mediterranean. We had to refuel every five days. We used rolls of coiled rope as fenders when we refueled from the flat top. We made this trip a couple of times.

> *"The last place you want to be is trapped in the bowels of the ship during an attack."*

On one trip towards evening, the aircraft out on submarine patrol were given the word to land on the carrier. This was near the Azores. The carrier had to turn so the planes could land going into the wind. There were four destroyer escorts using their sonar to scan for submarines. The carrier had a new commander and he had his ship make a big, wide circle outside of the water area that had been checked for subs. They got hit by a torpedo in their screws. They knew they were done for and the abandon ship order went out. I was taking a shower when someone yelled that the flat top was hit. I flew out of the shower dripping wet and naked to man my battle station. The last place you want to be is trapped in the bowels of the ship during an attack. All the hatches get sealed and locked to maintain water integrity and you're stuck there. I grabbed a towel and my clothes and took off for the radio shack. I didn't dress until I got up to the radio shack. I could see sailors diving off the fat top. Then they were hit by a second torpedo. It blew the ship's galley up to the flight deck. There were 276 survivors with only seven or eight killed. The flat top sank.

I also witnessed one of the destroyer escorts get hit in the screws by a torpedo. I saw the flash of light from the explosion. That DE lifted up out of the water and then its nose went down and it disappeared under the underwater but it bounced back up. They hooked on and towed it to

Casablanca for repair. Fourteen men were killed on the DE.

I was told there were 15 inches of oil on the ocean surface. Small boats filled with survivors were recovered in the darkness. They'd pull up beside our ship and shine a flashlight. There was a rope ladder hanging down the side but it didn't extend down far enough for the men to climb it. They could only reach it with their hands and they were too exhausted to pull themselves up. Another guy and I climbed down and hauled each one up by their belt. Once they could get a foot in a ladder rung, they could climb to safety. Those poor guys had oil in the eyes, ears, and everyplace you could think of. I gave them nearly all the clothing I had aboard ship.

Question: Were you ordered to climb down the ladder to help or do it on your own volition?

I did it on my own. Those guys not wearing a belt were a real struggle to pull up. All the oil made them slippery. Each one of us was hanging on to the side of the rope ladder.

There were only two men aboard ship that didn't have a specific place to man during general quarters. I was one of them and the other was the chief mechanic. But I was on call 24 hours a day. I'd get called out most every night. They wouldn't turn the radar on until dark.

That was the first and only time I saw the hedgehogs used. Each hedgehog has 35 pounds of TNT and there are 18 of them. They have a little propeller on them which arms the device after it makes three revolutions. They detonate when they hit the ocean bottom or anything in between. They knew how fast the hedgehogs sank and how deep the ocean was. That's how they knew if they hit the submarine. When they launch them all, they set up a pattern over where they think the sub is hiding. The depth charges were shot out by what was called a K gun or rolled off the side. Another DE got the sub that sunk the carrier.

After the flat top was sunk, we were assigned to merchant marine convoy duty. There were 50–60 ships on the convoy. They traveled at 13 knots. There was only our four DE's guarding them. We'd zigzag but the convoy ships would not. The reason we zigzagged was to cover more ocean with our sonar.

Comment: I'd always read that the purpose for zigzagging was for protection from the submarines.

Well, I don't know. That may have been the reason. Every time our convoy got close to southern France the German planes would come out at night and launch torpedoes at the ships. Our radar would pick them up. The German planes would also strafe the ships. Torpedoes are supposed to blow up at the end of their run but these didn't. So we had orders to go back and get rid of one of them. We'd pulled to within 100 feet of the torpedo. The sailors got to use the rifles but being a chief, I had to use a hand gun. It was hard to hit with the ship moving up and down. The torpedo never did explode but we put enough holes in it to sink. Another time a depth charge came loose and was floating through the convoy. We had to go back and sink that. Our captain had the senior rank among the four DEs so we always got the tougher assignments. One time the old man crawled up and laced himself into the 20mm gun turret and tried his luck hitting a depth charge. I don't know if he hit it or not.

I was aboard ship for two years. The first year I was in the crew quarters which were located about in the middle of the ship. When I made chief, they moved me up to about 25 feet from the front of the ship. We were in rough water and near the bow is the worst place to be. I was in my bunk sicker than a dog with straps over me to keep me from falling out of it. All of a sudden the engine stopped and the ship's whistle blasted five times. The chief electrician who'd been in the Navy a long time said, "Boy, something bad has happened! I'm getting out of here." I was so sick all I said was, "Let me know when the water starts coming in." Then the ship made a big lurch that would have thrown you against the wall if you'd been standing. There was a merchant marine ship that had cut in front our ship and knocked eight feet of the bow off. That wasn't very far from my bunk. Luckily, no one was injured.

A bunk mate of mine contracted tuberculosis. I was scared I would get it as my feet would sometimes touch his head while we slept. The sleeping quarters were that cramped. They

transferred him to the flat top which had the only doctor in our convoy. They buried him at sea the next day.

After we ended convoy duty toward the end of the war, we escorted ships in and out from London. I was discharged in February, 1946. My brother Glen served in the Army in the Pacific. I considered making the Navy a career but my mother said she had worried about my brother and I long enough.

I owned and operated Payne's TV north of the square and a radio repair shop out of my house. I am 92 years old. I never ran into one person I knew during the course of the war.

SECOND FIDDLE

Ray Mourer
Rubio, IA

37th Infantry Division
Pacific

Interview Date:
1 November 2011

Referral:
Korwin Hinshaw

I enlisted because I was going to get drafted. That was in the Fall of '42. I spent one semester at Grinnell College before being called up for active duty in February or March of '43. I was inducted at Camp Dodge up by Des Moines and did my Army basic training in Cheyenne, Wyoming. The wind could really blow out there. I shipped out of San Francisco that fall for New Caledonia, which served as a replacement depot. There were submarine nets across the mouth of the harbor at San Francisco that had to be lowered for ships to pass through. We were seventeen days on board the ship, taking a southerly route to New Caledonia.

The Pacific didn't get that much in men and equipment as Europe did. The war effort emphasis was on Europe. We felt that we were kind of playing second fiddle in the Pacific.

I joined the 37th Infantry Division on Guadalcanal. They needed replacements. The fighting was pretty well over with when I got there and it was small scale compared to Europe. But we didn't have much to fight with, either. Guadalcanal had mountains and lots of coconut trees and the Japanese had been there awhile.

From there, we made a landing in Bougainville. Our group went in unopposed. We had artillery on shore by the time we landed and they were firing away at targets. I'd never heard that type of gunfire before and mistook it for dynamite until learning otherwise.

At that time in the war, the Japs had control of New Georgia where they had a big airbase. They flew bombing raids on us daily, especially at night. The only air cover we had was from our carrier based planes. About dark every day, the aircraft carriers would take off to open sea where it was safer. We had some .50 caliber machine guns and some larger anti-aircraft guns, but very seldom did they ever hit anything. There would be at least one Jap plane circling over us all night, sometimes two or three, but never a large fleet of planes. Occasionally they drop a bomb or two, aiming for the airstrip under construction or the ships off shore. The idea was for us to build airstrips on Bougainville so we could have land based fighters and bombers in order to bomb New Georgia.

Bougainville was a jungle island with lots of deep vegetation. It rained practically every day. The Japanese still had control of one end of the island and had us outnumbered, according to what we were being told. When we landed, we only went inland about a mile and (deployed) roughly three miles long. We were also getting reports of a possible landing of Japanese reinforcements, which could have swept us right off that island. We set up a defensive line with pillboxes and cut away the underbrush so we could see clear fields of fire. Then we just more or less sat there while the fighter and bomber airstrips were built.

We'd sleep in foxholes at night. You couldn't smoke, have any light or make any noise. We used passwords at night if we needed to communicate or leave our hole. They were two part passwords and they'd be changed every night. You'd say the first word and second word was the response. Words containing the letter "R" were often used as the Japanese had difficulty pronouncing them. If you forgot the password, you made a point of not leaving your foxhole. It rained a lot at night. The foxholes were muddy, the nights long and cold.

Question: Did the Japanese ever try to infiltrate our lines at night?

Oh, yeah. One night a whole bunch of them attacked. We had good fields of fire established and we were ready for them. Our guns could fire shells (starbursts) that would light up the night like daytime. I don't know exactly how many Japanese attacked, probably three hundred or more. They mainly carried only rifles at night. When they attacked, we started shooting those shells that lit everything up. Our guys were dug in and in the morning the Japs lay so thick you could walk across them. I was up there the next day and they were burying them with a bulldozer.

I had started out carrying an M-1 Garand with an infantry line company. Later, when they found out that I could type, I got a job issuing rations and taken out of the line company and issued a carbine. Ships would bring the food in and we'd unload it. It was mostly canned and powdered food. We'd sort and stockpile the food under trees so the Japanese couldn't spot it.

The few natives living on the island were primitive, appeared almost cannibalistic. They didn't live in anything you'd consider to be a house. They'd just throw up some banana leaves for shelter. The natives were short in stature and suffered from lots of diseases, especially what we called elephantiasis. We had no way to communicate with them.

"We had door-to-door fighting. Room to room. We lost a lot of people needlessly. That was no way to fight."

I looked up a fellow from Brighton that I knew, Lawrence Borkowski, who was a truck driver with the CB's on Bougainville. He had been working on the airstrips, handling the eight feet wire interlocking mats used for the bomber runway surface. Anyway, he told this story about their commanding officer. They were sleeping in their foxholes one night when the Japanese shelled them with their mountain howitzers. One of those five inch rounds hit close to this commander's foxhole and rolled into it, but didn't explode. So the artillery round didn't hurt the officer but it scared him so bad that he had a heart attack.

Our landing on Luzon at Linguyan Gulf was only lightly opposed. There wasn't much more than a few scattered rifle shots fired at us. Our division fought in Manila. We came in from the north, down through Clarke Field. The Japs had used it for an airbase. There were a few shot up Jap planes still there. It was another fifty miles to Manila. There was what they called a Walled City in Manila. I don't know who built it but there was a six foot wall of brick and stone enclosing several square miles of houses. The Japs had taken refuge inside this Walled City. By that time, we controlled both the sea and air and had them surrounded on the ground. They were completely cut off and we could have starved them out. But MacArthur said no, we had to go in and get them. He wouldn't allow our planes to bomb in there either. MacArthur was very unpopular with our division after issuing those orders. We had door-to-door fighting. Room to room. We lost a lot of people needlessly. That was no way to fight.

I saw the American prisoners the rangers rescued from Cabanatuan. These guys had been in captivity since the Bataan Death March. It was terrible. Some of those guys weighed in the eighties. I could count every rib they had. They told about eating mice and crickets. They really went through Hell. The Japs were mean to our prisoners and the Filipinos, too. There was another prison camp down in Manila. We got those prisoners out.

We got orders down from headquarters to take some Japanese prisoners. Until the war was over, we took very few prisoners. A lot of times, they fought to the very last, even the Japanese civilians.

I liked the Filipino people. They were a happy and friendly people. They had tribes similar to our Indian tribes and they all spoke different languages. The Filipinos would come to our camps and trade food for cigarettes. There were a lot of Filipino guerrillas and they fought during the whole war, more or less. They were rough on Japanese soldiers they captured. They'd parade them around the town square and probably eventually killed them. A lot of the Filipinos had ears cut off by the Japanese. It didn't matter if they were male or female. The Filipinos had been treated pretty rough by the Japanese. They had no love for the Japs whatsoever.

Life was cheap. If our leaders (today) had to fight the wars (themselves), we wouldn't have so many wars. The people who have never fought in a war seem to be the ones most anxious to get us in the next one. Wars are worse than you can ever believe. When you are out there fighting, there are no rules. Anything goes. You don't squeal on people. We had some bad eggs. Some of those mean ones, you tried not to make them mad at you. When anybody ever shot (their weapon), it was "always in the line of duty." It wasn't always that way. I think that's how war is.

Over there on those islands, you had no jails. Somebody shoots somebody, what are you going to do with them? The officers that had to deal with those types were half scared of them anyway. Do anything to them and you had to worry about their friends. Put yourself in that position. What would you do? There was no law. Once you got on an island, there was no way to get off. You were stuck there. We had a guy in our company shot one night. Two guys that I knew had been drinking and got into a fight over some gal. Everybody always carried their rifles with them. One guy up and shoots the other one. Nothing was ever done about it that I know of.

We were training for the invasion of Japan when the war ended. We even were shown aerial photos of the beach we were to land on. It would have been a tough, tough go if we had to fight there. A lot of guys believed they would never live to return home. There were a lot of happy people when we dropped the bomb.

I returned to the states in late November in 1945 and finished my education. I taught mostly math and science at Cedar High School, south of Oskaloosa, for a number of years before returning to Clay Township, in Washington County to start farming for a living.

MY BOTTOM DOG TAG

Gilbert Wood
Washington, IA

63rd Infantry Division
Europe

Interview Date:
15 November 2011

Referral:
Dolores Wood

I grew up east of Ainsworth. I graduated high school in 1941. I enlisted in January of '43. There were four boys in my class and the other three were already in the service so I thought I'd better join up. I attempted to enlist in the Army Air Corps, talked to the draft board and sent the paperwork in. When we were loaded up for the ride to Camp Dodge, I discovered that I was in the infantry. I did my basic training in Camps McCain and Van Dorn in Mississippi. It was a rainy and cold. We stayed in tar paper shacks.

I ended up in the 63rd Infantry "Fire and Blood" Division. I was a mortar man in the 4th or weapons platoon of Company G, 2nd battalion, 254th Regiment. That wasn't the same as a heavy weapons platoon. We had three mortar and two machine gun squads in the 4th platoon.

We shipped out of New York City in November, 1944. We had a two week wait there so I got to see a lot of the city. We sailed past the Statue of Liberty. It made me proud to see it. We sailed down the coast to Florida and then across the Atlantic, past Gibraltar into the Mediterranean Sea. We landed in the south of France. After a two mile hike, we

were loaded on World War One vintage forty and eight boxcars. They were called that because they could crowd forty men or eight horses on them. The train took us north to Strasbourg. Then we were taken by truck further north to a little town of Oberhaffen, in the Alsace-Lorraine region of France. The division was split up there. The 254th Regiment was sent south to Colmar to relieve another regiment. We were tasked to taking the Colmar Pocket. The Germans had that area fenced in and fortified. Finally, we marched on foot over the Vosges Mountains. It was January 1945. We'd move and move and it was freezing cold.

I was a corporal and the squad leader of 60mm mortar team. We'd set up in a low area concealed from direct enemy small arms fire. Then I would set a sighting stake in a straight line between the target and the mortar. I had a pair of binoculars and acted as the spotter. The mortar would start zeroing in and I'd give them the range. I had to be up on top to see where the mortar shells were landing.

I wasn't up at the front very long. I got hit too quickly. The last little village I remember going through was Beblenheim. Several miles south of Beblenheim the captain wanted me to spot a couple of German machine gun emplacements and try to knock them out with our mortar. I told him that I would try. I located one of the machine guns and I'm pretty sure I got it knocked out. I fired at the other one but didn't get him. Right after that is when I received the shell burst that took me out. It was probably a German mortar round. I was the only guy in my crew that was injured. Some of the crew was hit pretty bad later, when I was in the hospital. I was wounded in February of '45. I had been in combat three to four weeks.

As I remember it, they threw in a jeep and took me to the battalion aid station. When I came to, there was a doctor poking on me. I asked, "What the hell are you doing?" He answered, "Trying to see if it went clear through." I knew I had also been hit in the hip. They loaded me in an ambulance and took me to a town to be operated on but I cannot remember its name. The ambulance ride was not a smooth one. I think we traveled over the mountains somewhere.

"She said they had to take his left leg off clear up to the hip. I thought then, what am I complaining about?"

When I woke up from the operation, I had a tube stuck in the vein of one arm. The other arm was struck out straight and in a cast. My upper torso was in a body cast. The next day I asked the medic what was wrong with my arm. He told me there was nothing wrong with it. It was placed in a cast to prevent me from rolling over. The doctor wanted me to lay flat on my back for 30 days. They had evidently done some manipulation of the bones and they didn't what me to break them loose again. So I laid there for 30 days.

Next I was sent to a hospital in Aix-en-Provence down by Marseilles. I remained there until they took the cast off. Then I was sent to the First General Hospital in Paris. From there I was loaded on a plane and flown back to the United States. In April I was in a hospital in Topeka, Kansas. I was discharged in Ft. Carson, Colorado.

Comment: You must have been hit pretty badly.
The shrapnel went in my sternum and there is not much remaining of my left rib cage. The right lobe of my liver was torn up. I bled an awful lot.

The doctor said he used four pints of blood and four of plasma on me. The biggest piece of shrapnel was in my thigh. The doctor just pulled it out and sewed my leg up. The shrapnel that hit my sternum also took my bottom dog tag.

I tripped here on the Fourth of July and cracked my hip. The x-rays showed pieces of shrapnel in my hip. The doctor said it blurred the MRI images.

I felt sorry for myself lying there and being wounded until one night around 1:00 AM this feller in the ward starts hollering for more pain medicine. I asked the nurse about him the next morning. She said they had to take his left leg off clear up to the hip. I thought then, what am I complaining about?

It was interesting how some of the French people had their house and barn altogether. They would farm five acres and drink their wine. They were friendly enough to us. I remember this one French fellow came out of house and gave us some applejack to drink at Christmas time. Oh, was it strong! We were glad to get it. Christmas was just like any other day. We spent it outdoors. We were by ourselves. The Germans were good soldiers but they were forced into it by the Gestapo. If they did anything wrong, they were shot by their own people. My brother Glen worked at a German POW camp outside Salina, Kansas. He was originally in the 87th Division as an infantryman and transferred to the Rangers. He developed back trouble while undergoing Ranger training was reassigned to a prison camp. He got to know a lot of the German POW's. A lot of them said they did not to want to fight.

My other brother was named Norman. He was in New Guinea for 39 months with Army Air Corps at an airbase. The Japanese bombed his base a lot. He received a minor wound on his arm during an air raid but declined a Purple Heart. Norman said that if a plane crashed into the jungle that in two days you couldn't find it. The vegetation grew that fast. He came home with malaria.

Eldon Conry, Bob Megchelsen, and Daryl Pearson were classmates of mine that served. Bob was a tail gunner on a B-17. He rode backwards many a mile. Daryl was in the Marines. I farmed and got married when I came home.

Question: Do you remember hearing about Pearl Harbor?

I was riding to Washington with some of my buddies when I heard it on the car radio. We didn't know what to think except we didn't want it to have happened. We were too young to really fathom the magnitude of it.

Dolores Wood: I was at my grandmother's house. I was eight years old. I heard President Roosevelt announce it on the radio as I was going outdoors. President Roosevelt said that the Japanese had bombed Pearl Harbor and we were now at war. I probably didn't understand it at the time but I do recall getting a really scared feeling. I remember my father being called up but was turned down for having first degree flat feet. As I remember, they had a maximum age of 35 to go into the armed services. He was approaching that age. They must have needed men pretty badly as he was called up again. Lo and behold, he no longer had flat feet. He was in the Marines. In the middle of his training in California, his sister in Cedar Rapids got very ill. The Red Cross arranged for my father to come home and visit her. While he was gone, his outfit shipped out and ended up fighting on Iwo Jima. My father missed that, of course, but was in on the occupation of Japan.

Gilbert: I got to go on the Honor Flight on April 26th. Bob Koehler and Bryce Lord were on that flight. That monument was great!

IT KIND OF GETS TO YOU

Walter Pacha
Brighton, IA

USS *Swanson*
Pacific

Interview Date:
29 December 2011

Referral:
Bill Watson, Bill Drish

I enlisted in 1943. I was working on a farm and could have gotten a deferment. But I saw all these other poor devils going and thought I should just as well go, too. I left out of Davenport and went to Great Lakes for boot camp. That was back when they needed people across the pond in a hurry so we didn't get much training.

I shipped out of San Francisco on a troop transport. We had a blackened ship the whole way over. I caught up with my ship, the USS *Swanson 443*, in New Guinea. It was a broken deck destroyer. I was assigned to the fire engine room. There was no chance of advancement there because there were so many guys, so I transferred out and became a machinist. I worked in the steam engine room. I liked that better and it wasn't as hot as the fire engine room. My rank was Seaman 3rd class.

I was also in charge of a small taxi boat that would take the skipper places. I ran the engine and another guy steered it. That was quite an experience. We'd see dead men floating in the water sometimes. They'd have big holes blown through them. We'd report it and someone else would go get them. That happened at Saipan. When we pulled into Saipan, there was nothing there but sugar cane fields and a mill. When we left, it looked like Chicago. They built all kinds

of buildings and paved the roads. There was a big B-29 base built there. There were still Japanese around even though the islands were declared secure. Our B-29s were getting shot at from the neighboring island of Tinian. Our ship and our sister ship patroled around Tinian. We had orders to shoot into every hole we could find. That put a stop to it. I was topside one time. You could see people working on a building. Our guns blew it all to pieces. There were bodies flying everywhere.

One time we dropped depth charges on a Japanese sub. I think we got him. When the depth charges exploded, the rear of the destroyer would raise up. Sometimes we'd come across spent torpedoes or mines floating and we'd have to take care of those.

We were in the Philippines. I had Shore Patrol duty for one day. From what I saw of the beach at Subic Bay, I didn't care to go in there. There was a big naval battle (Leyte Gulf). The Navy was hollering for help. They were just about getting blown apart. Our ship was running wide open to get over there, but it was all over by the time we arrived.

Then we went to Iwo Jima, the island with the big hump at one end. I don't know how many days we went in and blew all day long at that hump and the caves in it. I know we went up there from Saipan all by ourselves three different times. We were the only ship shelling the island until the fleet came in right before they got ready to take it. We had 40mm and five inch guns on our destroyer. When the Marines went in to take it, the Japs were in there somewhere, because they got shot all to heck. I remember seeing the Marines going in to land. The landing craft were getting all shot up. I saw that happening before Iwo. It kind of gets to you. You think, maybe they made it to shore and got shot on the beach.

We operated out of Saipan. We did a little of everything. We had to leave our base on Saipan and sail back to the states for ship repair. We were going to be anchored for a whole month. That's when I decided that I wanted to marry that good looking woman sitting here beside me. So she came out to California and we got married.

Question: Where you involved on the Okinawa campaign?

We were there but kind of on our own. We weren't with the fleet then. We'd shoot at the island. They needed someone to land on Okinawa to act as spotter to guide our shooting. John Lindsay, the former mayor of New York City, was aboard our ship. He volunteered. He never volunteered again. He spent two days in a foxhole. The Army man with him stuck his head up to look out and got shot.

I felt for those Army guys. We had to shoot across them. You didn't know if you had really shot across them. They might have advanced farther than we thought. I think it was that island where they brought the sick ones aboard our ship. We transported them to a hospital ship. After that, we patrolled around the islands and picked up fliers who had ended up in the water. Sometimes it took us a couple of days to find them. The carriers would send out planes to search if the pilots had time to radio back. We'd usually find them by following the calico colored water trail left by the dye if they were in a life raft. One time there were more guys than could fit on the lifeboat. They'd take turns being in the water. The first thing they wanted when they were picked up was cigarettes.

"John Lindsay, the former mayor of New York City, was aboard our ship. He volunteered. He never volunteered again."

Question: Did you see any of the kamikazes?

Oh, hell, they pert near got us once. I don't know how the kamikaze missed the stack. He just shaved the top of it and went in the water. I did not see it. I was pushing powder into the shells. I remember one time when we were under attack and water starting coming in the hole we feed the shells up to the gun. We thought we were sinking. The sea was that rough. There were times we couldn't walk on the deck because of all the water washing over it. It wasn't safe to be topside in a typhoon.

Question: Did you ever get seasick?

Oh, my! When I first got on board, they had my quarters in the bow of the ship where it is the roughest riding. I got so sick they had to move me to the center of the ship. I avoided the sleeping quarters as much as possible because everyone was throwing up. My first duty on the transport ship going over was kitchen detail. Our ketchup was served in gallon buckets. One time the sea was so rough some of the ketchup ended up on the ceiling. We had to use a hose to flush the whole works out.

Our ship could operate about a week on the fuel it carried. Then we would have to refuel from a battleship or carrier. Once we about got it refueling from a carrier. We were pulled alongside of the carrier. A torpedo passed between the two ships. We went to General Quarters but nothing else happened. I saw destroyers back at Pearl Harbor with the whole belly blown out of them. But they were still floating. A destroyer was called a "tin can."

We joined the fleet from our base in Saipan to go to Japan for the invasion. Luckily, the war ended before we got there. That was a blessing. We would have lost a lot of soldiers and Marines. We had to win that war and we had to get in it.

Question: Did you ever run into anyone from back home?

I ran into Bernard Pauley when we stopped at Pearl Harbor for repair. He was aboard a tender we tied up alongside of. We were sure happy when Harry Truman dropped the bomb. Ardell Hahn and Victor Dykes from the Brighton area were in the Army. They made it through all those islands but figured they'd never live through an invasion of Japan.

When the war ended, we came home through the Panama Canal. I was discharged in 1946. I wanted to farm. Everybody told me not to, thinking the country would enter another depression. We rented ground and moved six times. We finally settled south of Brighton.

My brother Gerald was in on the tail end of the war in Germany. He was part of the occupation troops. Delbert Hesseltine was a nose gunner on a bomber that got shot down. He flew out of England. The Germans helped him out of the wrecked plane after it crashed. He very seldom talks about it.

I am glad I went. Before it was all said and done, I would have had to serve anyway.

Highly Classified Radar Work

Stanley Chabal
Washington, IA

Army Air Corps
Stateside

Interview Date:
13 January 2012

Referral:
Dave Birney

I grew up on a farm six or seven miles south of Richmond. I went one semester to junior college right of high school. I figured I'd get drafted soon and didn't have any money anyway, so I quit and went to work for a dollar a day. I was visiting my girlfriend (future wife) in Haskins. Her dad walked out of the house and asked me if I had heard the news. He said, "The Japanese have attacked Pearl Harbor and it's all blown up." I was 21 years old then so I knew I'd be called up soon. Later, I worked as a hired hand on Roy Carter's farm. Roy offered to go to the draft board to get me a farm deferment. I told him not to bother, that it would only be good for three or four months and I would still be gone before harvest. I thanked him, but figured I'd just as well go and get it over with. As it turned out, it worked well for me that I went in when I did.

I was drafted in 1942. Two bus loads carrying 30 people each left from Winga's Café for Ft. Des Moines. That was on May 22nd. We were some of the last men to go through Ft. Des Moines before the WACS took it over. Then everyone went through Camp Dodge. I was sworn in about six o'clock on the Friday night I arrived in Des Moines. On Sunday evening, we were shipped to Camp Crowder, Missouri, south of Kansas City. The first three or four days, they had us out with picks digging up rocks so they could lay sidewalks. There weren't even enough rifles to go around so not everybody was issued one. We were supposed to have basic training there but it wasn't very tough.

Then about 60 of us were sent by train to Camp Murphy near Jacksonville, Florida, to study radio theory. It was a new camp that wasn't even on the map yet. The mosquitoes were bad there. Our low barracks were camouflaged and hidden under the pine trees. Even the roads had been painted green. A security fence had been erected around the camp's perimeter. Our lieutenant told us that if we passed the 16-week college level course on radio theory, we'd be placed into radar. Not one of us 60 men knew what he was talking about. He explained that was the reason we were at a high security installation. He divided us up into three different groups. One group had to fix up the barracks so we could sleep there. The second group was assigned to the mess hall to unpack tableware shipped in crates. The last group had guard duty.

I had guard duty that evening after spending the day in the mess hall. I was given a rifle and told to challenge anybody near the warehouses and to let no one pass by. A drunken lieutenant came walking up. I told him to turn around and go back because I didn't want to have to shoot him. My rifle was an old bolt action Springfield. I'm not certain it would have fired anyway. All the good weapons went overseas.

While I was stationed at Camp Murphy, a German sub dropped off four or five saboteurs on the Florida coast. They were supposed to make their way to New York City to set fire to the hotels but were caught right before they could complete the mission.

We were told we would be noncombatants on the Pacific islands. They added, however, that if the infantry couldn't keep the Japanese back that we were on own. We'd be issued .45 pistols to defend ourselves. Those German subs were sinking ships off the coast of Florida in water so shallow that the ships were still sticking out of the water after they went down. One partially sunken ship sat off in the water adjacent to Camp Murphy as long as we were stationed there. As many as 50 German U-boats were reportedly in operation off the coast sinking several thousands of tonnage every month, mostly at night. Usually all hands went down with the ship. There were three or four big shipyards in Florida and they just kept building new ones. One yard was putting out a new ship every day. The ships built out of cement were the best.

Coast Watchers patrolled the beaches on horseback. Every five miles or so they had a telephone set up to report in. We had blackout conditions at night. You couldn't light a cigarette or nothing.

Martha Chabal: There was a rumor going around up here that there would be a blackout the night I graduated from high school. That was in 1943. And sure enough, there was one. It lasted

about 30 minutes. I don't know why they did it. I think it was just for practice to show people what it would be like.

Stanley: The schooling was tough but I don't think anyone flunked out because they needed us so badly. We had classes from 6:30 AM to 2:30 PM, six days a week. The radar we trained on the 584 gun lane machine converted into portable radar. It had a tower that had to be erected that could be moved in a day's time. We finished training in February, 1943. We were supposed to be cadre to train others. Then we were sent to Georgia to another high security facility where they were working on airborne radar. It took three days to get clearance to go in the base. We spent several weeks there observing and returned to Drew Field in Tampa, Florida.

We were then sent to our disembarkation point to go overseas. Four individuals were selected to remain in the states. I was one of them. Then I waited around for some for the Army to decide where I was to be stationed. My wife and young daughter were staying down in Florida and I was given ten days of leave to take them back home to Iowa. When I returned, the first sergeant told me to report to the medical officer. He asked me if I had asthma. I told him I had it all my life. The medical officer, a lieutenant colonel, said I would not be going with my unit to the South Pacific because of the asthma. He restricted my service to the United States and added two more years to my service time.

"I had to provide five reference names that were not family members for top secret clearance. That's kind of hard when you are only 20 years old."

I was assigned to do highly classified radar work for the Army Air Corps. My old unit was shipped to New Caledonia. I was due to go overseas three different times and lucked out.

Question: What was the nature of your highly classified work?

I had to provide five reference names that were not family members for top secret clearance. That's kind of hard when you are only 20 years old. We were tracking the hit of a 500 pound bomb. The planes dropping the bombs were from the 2nd Air Force flying out of Omaha. We had a ticker-tape like chart that showed when the plane released the bomb. Wind vectors had to be calculated to determine trajectory. An onboard radar scope designed to allow planes to drop bombs through cloud cover was being developed and we were assisting in that. I believe the tests were related to the eventual dropping of the atomic bombs on Japan.

Question: How accurate were they?

They'd usually be five or six miles off. The technology was just in its infancy. A big truck brought in from MIT had a diesel engine in it to supply our equipment with power. The bombing runs were over a golf course. Our next move was to Jacksonville, Florida. There were shipyards, rail yards, and bridges there. A river cut the city in half. The planes flew over Jacksonville and pressed their ground radar button and our instruments would record the accuracy. They didn't drop any sacks of flour or anything so no one got hurt. The new radar could pick terrain features. My job was maintenance and plotter.

We were assigned a guard because the nature of our work. While we were in Jacksonville, the city police kept everyone away from us.

Martha Chabal: Stan could never tell me what he was doing in the letters he wrote me. It bothered me some to think that he was keeping things from me but I also realized it was the right thing for him to do. My father worked for the railroad and could get a train pass to come down and visit me when I was staying down in Florida. I remember one time he carried a crate of six dozen eggs with him. The trains carried a lot of soldiers in those days. He would always give his seat to a soldier that needed one and stand. I think he stood most of that trip.

I was in the Army 13 months before I had my first 10 day leave. That's when I went home and Martha and I got married. I spent seven days as a PFC and was promoted to technical corporal when I started school. Upon graduation, I was made a technical sergeant. They paid me $96 a month. I started out in the Signal Corps. The Army and Signal Corps did a lot of squabbling over who would be in charge of my unit. The Army Air Corps ended up taking it over.

Question: Did you run into anyone from back home while serving?

While I was at West Palm Beach, I ran into George Miller. He used to farm northeast of Washington. He was studying radio Morse code. He was with the Air Corps. My brother Ed went in the Army when I came home in 1945. He guarded American prisoners sent by train from the west coast to prisons as far east as Indiana. There were two guys from my Richmond high school class that didn't come home.

I got out in November of '45. I wanted to stay in the military but had to come home and help my dad farm. I farmed near Richmond until 15 years ago. I went on the four day Honor Flight a year ago in October. We left out of Muscatine. They had a chartered bus to take us around Washington, D.C. The WWII Memorial was my favorite stop. I worked 45 years on the Veteran's Affairs Board in Washington County.

IT WAS FUN AT THE TIME

Dale Johnston
Ainsworth, IA

USS *Salute*
Pacific

Interview Date:
8 February 2012

Referral:
Mike Roberts & Liz Miksch

I enlisted in the Navy right out of Crawfordsville High School. That would have been in the fall of '42. I did my boot camp at Great Lakes. Radar had been recently been developed and I was interested in that. But I soon realized that I did not have enough formal education to complete that. So I was sent to Noroton Heights, Connecticut, which was an old Civil War camp for a course in radio operator procedure. I was able to master the radio code well enough to be assigned to a ship. From there I was sent to Seattle where they were building minesweepers at the Todd Ship Yards.

I ended up on the USS *Salute*, AM 294, a mine sweeper. It was a modern, metal ship. Our crew numbered 115-120 men. We were sent in to destroy Japanese mine fields. Our ship used para vanes with hooks on them out in a V from out behind the rear of the ship to gather up the mines. Once the mines were collected, they'd be lifted up. We would take army rifles, 20 and 40mms and shoot at the mines to explode them. We sailed to San Diego for our shakedown cruise. We were to go out to San Clemente Island for small arms training but a storm came up and we had to turn back. Then we sailed back to Seattle. After that, we headed out into the Pacific.

Our first mission was to rescue a seaplane while we were in route to Hawaii. They radioed us from San Francisco to divert to the plane which was about 250 miles away from where we were at. When we arrived, all the crew was sitting on the wings to avoid getting wet. After getting the crew on board, we hooked a log cable on to the seaplane and towed it to Hilo, Hawaii.

Question: How far away from the mines would the ship be when you shot at the mines?
We hoped to be far enough. We'd usually be about 300 feet away. You know that shrapnel can go a long ways. I was a radio man, so I was always sitting behind steel walls. I heard any messages coming in from the Admiral first and it was my job to inform the captain. I was pretty competent about taking care of myself. That's why I'm here talking to you.

My ship was sunk off Brunei Bay, Borneo. We did quite a lot of mine sweeping work there. One time we were pulling in what we thought was a bunch of seaweed. There was a mine hidden in the seaweed and it blew up, almost blowing our ship in two. Nine sailors were killed.

Question: How were you rescued?

It wasn't hazardous or anything. We were assigned to a working fleet. There were always boats around us working on buoys and things. They effected rescue right away. We were put on barges and then transferred to a larger warship. I think it was the USS *Boise*. We observed a lot of the war while aboard the *Boise* before it brought us back to the states.

I can remember getting on an aircraft carrier. I can also remember the Japanese firing on us while we were mine sweeping Brunei Bay.

Question: So the Japanese were shooting artillery at you while in the bay. Did the warships in the fleet return fire?

Well, the Japanese were sly creatures. They'd usually wait until the rest of the fleet was off someplace different before shooting at us. The Japanese had their guns hidden in caves. They'd roll the guns out and shoot and then roll them back in.

Question: Did you ever see any of the Japanese kamikazes?

Oh, yes. Our ship shot at them. They'd turn tail and run. They wanted to get the heck out of there because our anti-aircraft fire was so accurate. The United States is quite a country. It took the Japanese a while to learn that. The Japanese were crude compared to the Europeans.

I thought seriously about making a career in the Navy. I was a radioman 2nd class and would have been moved up to 1st class if I had stayed in. But I loved Iowa and its soil and wanted to farm so decided not to re-up. I was never drafted into anything. I did it willingly because my country needed me. I've always been an American. I can understand why they take the young people for the service. I would hate to go out there now with my age and wisdom behind me and go through that danger. It was dangerous, but we never thought much about it. It was fun at the time.

My younger brother Kenneth had something to do with radar on a ship in the Pacific during the war. My father was in WWI. He fought in the trenches in France. He went into the service while still a junior in high school. He finished high school after coming home from the war.

Taught Not to Take a Backseat to Anybody

Albion Young
Wellman, IA

11th Airborne Division
Japan

Interview Date:
24 January 2012

Referral:
Barb Edmondson & Jack Seward, Jr.

I enlisted September 16th, 1946. I was attending Coe College and knew I'd probably get drafted eventually. My plan was to finish school on the GI Bill. My induction center was in Minneapolis. I did my basic training at Ft. Knox, Kentucky. I am originally from Donnellson, Iowa. Everyone in my training class of 600–800 at Ft. Knox got shipped out but me. I found out later why. They had been testing people on the ability to hear sound for the Signal Corps and I had tested very high.

I had thought about becoming a professional musician. I was a member of the Cedar Rapids Symphony when I was 17 years old. I played a French horn. As a kid, I grew up poor. I didn't receive any notice in school until I took a music aptitude test. I got favorable treatment from that day on until I graduated.

So they shipped me out to Oakland, California several months after everyone else had left. I never was part of the Signal Corps. I took a Liberty ship over to Japan and got caught in a typhoon. There

were two ships sailing together. The storm broke the screw on the sister ship. There were 90 foot waves. How they kept the ships from rolling over I will never know. You couldn't do anything during the storm. Hardly anybody could eat. The only way you could lay in a bunk was to be strapped in. Yes, I got seasick.

It took us two weeks to get to Japan. We were put in a camp and it wasn't very elaborate. All they had were tents. It rained all the time and we couldn't keep the water out of the tents. I ended up with pneumonia.

I enlisted in the paratroopers within a week of arriving in Japan. I had a cousin in the 11th Airborne up in Sendai. I knew I would be sent up there if I enlisted. Sendai, Japan was where all the trouble was last year (with the earthquake and tsunami). I was placed in the 188th Parachute Infantry Regiment. I received my jump school training in Japan. They tried to make the training pretty rough on you. I remember the mud more than anything. Doing pushups in the mud and then eating in the mud. In jump school they took us over to a 34 feet tower. The drill sergeant gave us a lecture. There were probably 200 of us in the jump school. He told us how dangerous the tower was and how they'd had a guy killed just last week jumping off it. I was certain in my own mind that he was full of bull and just trying to scare us. The more he talked the more I started to chuckle. Then I volunteered to go first. The drill sergeant said, "Well, we will see if you live through it."

So I climbed the tower. I would have had no trouble jumping off by myself, but somebody got behind me and put their foot on my rear end and pushed me off the damn tower. They had a run at the end of jump school that everyone despised. By being the first to jump off the tower, I was rewarded by being dismissed from the run. I wasn't very good at volunteering, but I saw right through that drill sergeant and knew exactly what the hell he was doing. The jump school only lasted a couple of weeks.

I was trained on the 81mm mortar. I also did a lot shooting. I was a pretty good shot with an M-1, a carbine, BAR, and .30 caliber machine gun. I went to Coe College a year before going into the service and was on their rifle team. I wasn't the best shot in the conference, but I was among the best shots. There were better shots. I know I was the best shot at Coe.

I also attended a glider school while in the airborne. We were showed how to tie in equipment on a glider. If you don't get everything tied in correctly, somebody is very likely to get killed. That was pretty sobering.

Question: Did you ever ride a glider?
Oh yes, lots of times. It was a lot of fun. I really wasn't scared. I knew those pilots weren't going to kill themselves. Right before the pilots landed the glider, they'd do a loop over. That was to reduce their speed. That scared the hell out of a lot of guys. I did my five jumps to get my jump wings. I got hurt on one jump when my ankle struck a rock when landing. I got carried out on a stretcher by two crazy Mexican medics that hated each other. In fact, one time I had to put one of them in a head

> *"We were showed how to tie in equipment on a glider. If you don't get everything tied in correctly, somebody is very likely to get killed. That was pretty sobering."*

lock when he had gone after the other Mexican with a samurai sword. All I could think of (while on the stretcher) was that they'd get me up so high and drop me. But they were nice to me.

I had to pull guard duty at an army prison enclosure. They were almost all paratrooper convicts. The Army had a rule: if a prisoner escaped, the guard had to be confined until the prisoner was apprehended. One time a con took off for an open doorway from which he could have escaped. I yelled at him three times to halt. I came within a fraction of a second of killing him. Another time I found a trap door leading to a four feet crawl space between the floors that they were using to escape. A lot of these prisoners were murderers and had no future. I reported my discovery to the officers. They told me I was in grave danger and that they would get me out of it. They said that I would be called out in front of the cons and dressed down in the worst language I'd ever heard and kicked off guard duty. And that's exactly what they did.

After I had been in the paratroopers about six months, the division band came around. My thought was to join them and travel around Japan and lead a better life. So I went to the noncoms and asked for permission to go over and interview with the band. They said, "To hell with that noise. You are staying right here." The band was staying in a tent. So I crawled under the side of the tent and talked to the management, telling them that I'd like to join. They took all the information from me and found out I was a better musician than most of the existing band members. Later, the noncoms called me in and showed me a piece of paper and asked, "What is this, Mr. Young?" It was an order from the division general transferring me to the band to direct it. The noncoms were rather upset with me for disobeying orders. They said I had only one little problem in joining the band as I "was not going to live that long." They acted like they were mad. They gave me the worst drumming for three days that I ever had in my life. I figured the damn fools couldn't kill me and I would live through it. They gave me the worst damn detail they could find for three days and got me up in the middle of the night for a forced march. In the end of three days they called me in again. They were all sitting there laughing. They said their fun was over and I didn't have to do another damn thing until I left for the band two weeks later.

I was a PFC when I joined the band. The band members were all T5s except the sergeants so I got a promotion. There were 32 band members. About half of them were Aztec Indians. They were a pretty crazy bunch that liked to drink. We played for whoever they told us to. They brought in a member of Glenn Miller's band to direct it so I did not have to do the conducting. I had no training in conducting but I think I could have done most of it because I was in an ROTC band in Coe.

Sapporo was the northern most city I was stationed at while in Japan. Everything was in ruins. There wasn't anything taller than the shacks people had built as far as you could see. I was in Tokyo in some of the taller buildings. The Americans did not bomb downtown Tokyo. From the tall buildings, I could look out over the industrial area and see for ten miles. Everything had been bombed, either blown apart or burned up by the incendiary bombs. There was total devastation.

I flew around Japan. You could hitch a ride with the Air Force people and they would fly you around if you were off duty. I flew along the coastline. You could tell those people had it all fixed up so they could kill us if we had tried to go in there. You couldn't conceivably have had anybody from my vantage point who would have had any objection to dropping the atomic bomb. There were caves and concrete fortifications all along the coast. All the people with me were totally convinced it would have been devastating to have tried to invade Japan. There were American airplanes that had been shot down all over the place.

Question: B-29s?
All kinds of airplanes. I don't remember seeing a B-29. I think a lot of them were B-25s. I traveled around mostly by train and you could see the downed planes from the train. I visited the prison

> *"One of the things that made us half mad was the Japanese would come down those narrow streets and try to kick us paratroopers off the streets. That was not going to happen."*

were the Japanese kept people from the Bataan Death March. It was very bad. They had the prisoners underground in a cave some of the time. The steel doors were inch and a half thick. My impression was that it was a hell of a place.

We didn't see a lot of Japanese men. The women and children were in pitiful condition. After two or three days, all the Americans felt sorry for them and gave them everything they could. Guys would steal stuff out of the mess hall to give to the Japs. We never called them anything but "Japs." All the troops developed sort of a friendly attitude toward them. Toward the end of the year I was over there conditions for the Japanese had improved immeasurably.

Question: Did you have any personal interaction with the Japanese?
Not very much. I knew one guy. He was a kamikaze pilot. He could talk enough English that we could sort of converse.

Question: Was this guy disappointed that he didn't get to die for his emperor?
Nope, he sure as hell wasn't. This guy worked for us as an orderly. The kamikaze pilots held the Japanese paratroopers in high regard. The Japanese army didn't have as good of parachutes as we did and ours weren't anything to brag about. Ours usually worked. It was rare when they didn't. I had one malfunction on me. I pulled my reserve chute and the buckle dented the back of my helmet. We jumped at 800 feet. I was in free fall until 300 feet. My reserve chute never opened but my regular one finally did at 300 feet. I was always the last guy on the stick jumping out.

One of the things that made us half mad was the Japanese would come down those narrow streets and try to kick us paratroopers off the streets. That was not going to happen. There would be this mass of humanity coming and they would expect us to step aside for them. I think they did this on purpose. And by God, I never heard of a paratrooper moving out of the way! As paratroopers, we were taught not to take a backseat to anybody.

One thing I wish our governor and legislators had seen was the railroad train that ran 135 mph. This was in 1947. I rode the damn thing. It was an electric train. There'd be people hanging on all over the train. It was not a picture of safety by any means. We also rode ferries between Sapporo and the main island. Three months after I came home a big storm sunk all the ferries.

I had a French language instructor in college that was a member of the French Underground during the war. He died of his wounds at age 45. He never talked about it.

Question: Al, do you remember where you were when you heard about Pearl Harbor?

I learned about it when I got to school Monday morning. I remember going duck hunting that morning before school. I had a cousin at Pearl Harbor. He was a bandsman. I don't know what he was doing.

Question: General McArthur was the military governor of Japan when you were there. Did you have an opinion of him?

The absolute worst. He gave the paratroopers the short shift all the way around. We never had anything, everything from food on down. I don't think he had any use for paratroopers. The 11th Airborne saw God awful action during the war. Some of them were a mess. We didn't know if they'd be better off living or if you would just shoot them right in the center of the head with a .45. They were that psychologically messed up. We had one guy that attacked our sergeant. It was crazy. They drank too much. They just didn't perform that well at all.

After graduating from Coe College, I couldn't find a job so I went on to Law School. I moved to Wellman in 1953 and opened a law office.

"Where Did You Come From?"

Robert Koehler
Washington, IA

USS *San Juan*
Pacific

Interview Date:
24 February 2012

Referral:
Bill Wagamon & Gilbert Wood

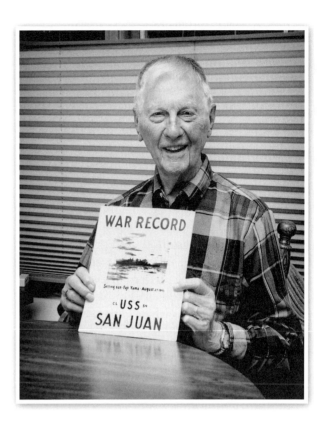

I grew up on a farm three miles from Ainsworth. I entered service 16 May, 1944 and got out on 2 May 1946. I enlisted. A bunch of my high school buddies and I decided we would all enlist together in the Army Air Force. We went to Des Moines but we were told that we needed our parents' permission and were sent home. In the interim, a freeze was put on drafting farm kids. Tom Duncan, Lyle, my brother Marsh and I enlisted in the Navy. We got on a train in Columbus Junction for boot camp at Farragut, Idaho. We had leave to come home after finishing boot camp and got assigned when we returned. Marsh was assigned to an LSV. They took wounded off Iwo Jima and Okinawa. He never would talk too much about it.

I was assigned to an anti-aircraft cruiser, the *San Juan*. Our sister ship was the *Juneau*. That's the ship the five Sullivan brothers went down on. The anti-aircraft cruisers carried a lot of ammunition because of the number of guns they had. That's why the Juneau went down as quick as it did. The first Japanese torpedo hit the keel, crippling the ship. The second hit the ammunition magazine.

The ship was blown in two in a huge explosion. The explosion was so massive they assumed there could be no survivors so the fleet sailed away. Two of the five Sullivan brothers survived the initial explosion and were in life boats but died before any search for survivors was made.

Question: Did you witness that?

No, we weren't over there yet. But we heard about it from guys that were. The *San Juan* was in Everett, Washington for reconditioning when I boarded her in late 1944. We were assigned to Task Force 58.1 in the Pacific. It consisted of four or five aircraft carriers, light cruisers, and lots of destroyers. We were part of Admiral Halsey's 5th Fleet. Our job was to protect the carriers. Some of the carriers we sailed with were the *Saratoga, Lexington, Yorktown, Bennington, Bonhomme Richard* and the *Hornet*. The carriers would come and go so it wouldn't always be the same ones in the task force. We also had British carriers with us some times.

The *San Juan's* main guns were five inch cannons. Three mounts forward and aft, one starboard and one port. They were all twin gun mounts and were radar controlled. The shells had proximity fuses that would cause them to detonate when they got close to a plane. We had one quad 40mm on the fantail and the rest of the 40mms were twins. We had nine 20mms. The 20s and 40s were clip fed. We could put out tremendous firepower. I think we shot down 14 or 15 aircraft. We had a lot of action. We were told that the Japanese were convinced our five inch guns were fully automatic because we could fire them that fast.

We usually weren't directly involved in taking islands. We were out to sea and rarely saw land. We did bombard one small island with our guns. We were never close enough to see the island. Other than that, we were strictly anti-aircraft protection for the carriers. The battles we were in were fought by the aircraft flying off the carriers. They'd take off, fly some place and come back. I think we may have been guarding carriers when Saipan, Iwo Jima, and Okinawa were taken.

The destroyers had the outer ring of defense around the carriers. The next ring was the light cruisers and anti-aircraft cruisers. Closer in were the heavy cruisers and battlewagons (battleships) if there were any in our task force. When we would go to general quarters, all the rings would close ranks and tighten up around the carriers. We'd be close enough to the carriers to pick up pilots from damaged aircraft that went into the ocean. Those pilots would fly right along beside us, waving at us before they went into the water. We had sailors that were good swimmers standing by that would jump in the water and rescue the pilots if it was an emergency. We tried to get them as soon as possible. Otherwise, if we had time, we'd send out a boat to get them.

They put me in sonar first. It was clear down in the bowels of the ship. You sat and listened for the noise of submarines. The odor was of hot metal. I got to the point that I didn't like it so they transferred me to radar. I was on the forward radar mount with one other guy. We watched for torpedoes and listened to the radar. One time when we were on watch, the ship did a violent turn. Over the loud speaker came the order, "All hands on deck. All hands on deck. Torpedo sighted!" That torpedo barely missed the ship. Then our ship quickly turned to where the torpedo had come

from and dropped depth charges where the sonar indicated the sub was. I never saw it, but someone reported an oil slick so we may have got him. Torpedoes leave a bubble trail in the water. That's how you can spot them.

We had another close call. I don't remember what battle it was in. We had bogeys coming in and of course everyone went to their battle station. Mine was in what was called the upper handling room. The gun mount was right above me. Fifty-five pound shells for the five inch guns were loaded in a little elevator below me. The shells were set upright on a little metal pad. When the shell got up to me, I stepped on a little foot pedal that gave me just enough time to grab the shell and hand to another guy who placed it in another little elevator that went up to the gun mount. You didn't dare drop the shell as it could explode. Before I was aboard the *San Juan*, a guy dropped a shell. An entire five inch gun mount was blown up and eight men killed.

I had my accident during action when bogeys were coming in. I was heading to my battle station. Water had come up over the deck in one of the heavy turns our ship made trying to get closer to the carriers. So everything was kind of slick. I was the last guy down the ladder and had my hand over the cowling to close it when my feet slipped. I fell 20 feet through open hatches down through two decks. The guy standing where I landed exclaimed, "My God, where did you come from?" I hit the side of one of the hatches and tore my shoulder blade up. If I hadn't landed on a coil of large rope, my ankles would have probably been broken.

The ship's doctor used something that looked like an ice pick to work on my shoulder. And he cussed the whole time he was probing around. The doctor said the hospital ship was too far away so I'd have to stay on board the San Juan. I had physical therapy for two or three months and went back to handling shells. My busted shoulder blade still bothers me.

I also worked at the Chief's Pantry or CPO mess. That's where the chief petty officers ate their meals. I was a seaman first class. I didn't want to be promoted any higher than I was. I turned down promotions.

We ran up our own Black Panther flag right

below Old Glory when we went on picket duty. It was a red colored panther against a black background. I think we were the only ship to have our own flag.

Question: What the significance or meaning to the flag?

I think basically it was, we are the United States Navy and we are going to kick the hell out of you.

Ulithi was part of the Carolina chain of small coral islands that formed a huge circle. It was said to be the largest natural harbor in the world. There was a little island there named Mog Mog. That's where we went for our R&R. We'd spend a day there and get cigarettes and green beer. The beer wasn't very good. One time when I was there I noticed a guy with the word "Iowa" on the back of his jacket. I thought, "What the heck," I'd go talk to him. So I walked up and tapped him on his shoulder. When he turned around, I was shocked to see Cliff Steele from Washington! We sat together in the shade of a tree, talking and drinking our warm, green beer together.

The Ulithi harbor was considered a secured port. There was a submarine net guarding the entrance. The Japanese held the island of Yap which was also in the Carolina chain. It had an airfield. We had never invaded Yap but the runway was repeatedly bombed so the Japs couldn't launch planes. The Navy would show movies on the fantail of all the ships at night. All the ships would be brightly lit up. They were watching a John Wayne movie one night. I heard an aircraft which didn't sound like one of ours. Then it sounded like it was flying in a steep dive. There was a big explosion and plume of fire from a heavy cruiser that had been hit by a kamikaze. Someone yelled, "Submarine!" I was on watch at the time and radioed the fleet that it was an airplane. You should have seen how fast all those movie projector lights went dark. Then another plane crashed onto the island of Ulithi near the Marine barracks. There was real pandemonium for a while.

We had kamikazes come in during one of our sea/air battles. I can't tell you which one it was.

> *"When he turned around, I was shocked to see Cliff Steele from Washington! We sat together in the shade of a tree, talking and drinking our warm, green beer together."*

The carrier planes had about all left on a mission when the Japanese showed up. One Kamikaze still carrying his torpedo was going to hit our ship. For some reason, he hadn't dropped the torpedo. He was coming in low, not too far above the water. I was in the handling room so I didn't actually see it, but the guys firing the 20's and 40's thought they must have hit the torpedo right on its nose, the explosion was that big. They said that they could see the pilot sitting there in the cockpit. He was that close. All that remained of the kamikaze was a burning tire floating on the water.

Our ship would go out on what was called "Lone Wolf" patrol. We were all by ourselves. No other ships were accompanying us. We were on general quarters pretty much the whole time. This was when our captain would fly the Black Panther flag. Our captain was an aggressive skipper that wanted to cover himself in glory. The first time we did this was before the invasion of the Philippines. We sailed in between some islands in the Philippines. We were ordered to break radio silence to see what we could draw out. Some Japanese bombers came out to monitor us. They stayed out of our gun range. The second Lone Wolf patrol was 30 miles off the Chinese coast. Again, we drew some bombers out but they kept their distance.

We were on general quarters quite a lot. Sometimes it was false alarms. I think they would sound general quarters at night just to shake us out of bed. I don't recall any kamikaze attacks at night but we had to defend ourselves quite often in daylight.

The entire Task Force 58 got caught in the China Sea Typhoon. We were warned about the approaching storm and told to outrun it. For some reason, the entire task force turned and sailed into it. We had just come from Ulithi. Our deck was loaded with new supplies because it all would not fit below deck. Cases of potatoes and other fresh produce were strapped to the deck. When the typhoon hit, it really hit! The instrument that measured wind speed topped out at 240 mph. The wind reached that speed and then the instrument was blown off the tower. The waves were at least 60 feet high. Everything stored on the deck including the life boats was swept away.

Question: Did you lose any ships?

A destroyer escort disappeared. It was just gone. A total of 600 men were reportedly lost in the storm. When the ship was down in the trough of a wave, all you could see was a wall of water. The five inch gun barrels were lowered to an angle that kept the rain water out of them. There was enough roll to the ship that the lower gun mounts had sea water in the gun barrels. The San Juan was not engineered to roll that far. The ship would shutter and groan as it rolled, sounding almost human. A lot of guys got really seasick during the storm. Luckily, I never did.

One of the smaller escort carriers had planes sliding around. They ended up pushing all their planes off their two decks into the ocean. I could see them doing this. This escort carrier was so top heavy that is was in danger of capsizing. The story going around afterwards had the crew running back and forth to the high side on the storage deck to stabilize the ship. I know it sounds like a fairy tale but supposedly that's what they had to do to save the ship. The waves were so bad that the decks on the big carriers got rolled up, just like the old sardine cans when you used a key. Now, when I hear of a tornado warning with 100 mph winds, I don't get too excited.

Question: Bob, where you in the Battle of Leyte Gulf?

Yes we were. That happened soon after we did our first Lone Wolf patrol. We did not go north with Halsey when the Japanese baited him. We stayed with the carriers. The Limey pilots would always come in low and roar over the fleet before landing on their carriers. They always liked to whoop it up after a successful sortie. There were a number of times we almost shot them down because the kamikazes often used the same approach.

When the war ended, the *San Juan* led the entire fleet into Tokyo Bay. I don't know why we got that honor but we did. We stopped long enough to pick up a Japanese naval officer who helped pilot us through the wreckage in the harbor. You could see the Imperial Palace off in the distance. It was raining when we pulled into Tokyo Bay. The next

morning was bright and sunny. You could see the snowcapped Mt. Fuji off in the distance. It was a beautiful sight. We watched the Japanese sign the surrender aboard the USS *Missouri* from about a quarter mile away. When we went ashore to get our POWs released, the Japanese showed us where to dig up weapons they had buried in grease and boxes. I have a Browning .32 caliber pistol and another pistol patterned after the German Luger. Both have Japanese writing on them.

I don't know how many American POWs were got out, but one of them was Pappy Boyington from the fabled Black Sheep Squadron. We went up down the Japanese coast picking up prisoners. I was told that the Japanese guards stood at attention with fully loaded automatic weapons over their shoulders. After the prisoners were released, the Japanese soldiers turned over their weapons. We didn't have any Marines aboard our ship so it was all sailors that went in to get them.

Question: Did you talk to any of the released POWs?

Yes, some of them wanted to talk about the treatment they received and share stories. We didn't bring them back to our ship. There was another ship in the harbor that collected them after we escorted them to the shore. I remember one guy telling about the lack of food in the barracks he lived in. All they ever got was a little fish and a small portion of cold rice, but it was at least good rice and not buggy or wormy like some were fed. The men in his barracks stole enough wire to build a hot plate to heat their rice rations. They had a little heating element they had confiscated someplace and secreted in the floor. They ran a hidden wire from it up to a notch in the light socket. The Japanese never found out about it.

I don't know how many prisoners sailors from our ship freed. It had to be quite a few. Different teams of sailors would go out to different prison camps. All we carried for weapons were pistols and BARs, nothing in between. I got the two pistols after things had quieted down. We were on shore leave at the time. We saw a lot of nice homes in the residential area we walked while on shore leave. There was no evidence of bombing or anything like that. An English speaking Japanese man came out of a nice house and invited us to come inside. We went inside his house. He told us he was glad the war was over. Then he asked, "You like sake?" We told him we had never tasted sake. So we sat down and he clapped his hands. His wife brought out a dusty bottle of sake. He said, "Prewar, good sake, prewar." This Japanese gentleman was a publisher. He said, "I not want this war. I knew we in big trouble." The sake was served in little cups. He stopped us when we went to drink it saying, "Oh no. Me drink first show you it okay." The sake was both good and potent.

Not long after we were in Japan they opened up a place we could dance with geisha girls. Most of them spoke English.

Our ship was part of the Magic Carpet which brought troops home from the Pacific. They stayed on deck because that was the only space we had. We picked the troops up in Pearl Harbor and dropped them off in San Francisco. We made several round trips. I don't know how many guys we could fit on our deck but half of them were on the rail. The ocean between Pearl and San Francisco was always rough.

I also was on the ship's boxing team. I represented the San Juan as a welter weight. I started boxing in boot camp to get out of some of training. I remember one match with a really tough looking character. We sized each other up during the first round. I knocked him down in the second round. He got to his feet and beat the living crap out of me. Later, he sought me out and complimented me on the fight. He said that he was the Golden Glove champion of California and I was the only boxer to ever knock him to the mat.

My brother George fought in Europe and brought home a Walter P38. George fought with Patton's 3rd Army and was in the Battle of the Bulge. He was an infantry man. He told me one story you might be interested in hearing. He and two or three others were out on a patrol behind German lines. They were walking down a road returning to friendly lines when they heard a German patrol approaching. They hid in the tall grass in a grader ditch. The Germans stopped right beside them. George said he could have reached out and touched the feet of one of the Germans. They were taking a cigarette break and talking. George had a good understanding of the language from

> "He said, 'Prewar, good sake, prewar'. This Japanese gentleman was a publisher. He said, 'I not want this war. I knew we in big trouble.'"

hearing our dad speak German with his brothers whenever they got together. The German soldiers were cussing the war and wishing they were home. The German smoking the cigarette threw it down and it landed beside George's face. Then the German patrol turned around and walked off. By that time it was getting dark. George said they realized they wouldn't make it back to the lines in time so they sought out a German farm house to sleep in. A German lady answered the door and let them in. She spoke very good English. She told them they could sleep here but she wanted them out before daybreak. Then she fixed them food to eat. All the guys looked at each other, wondering of this was too good to be true. They were worried that she would turn them in but they were tired and decided to risk it. In the morning she shook them awake, telling them it was time to go.

My oldest brother was named Carl. He was a Lt. Commander in the Naval Air. He was trained to fly off carriers but the Navy decided that he was too old for that so he stayed stateside. He flew admirals around and also ferried damaged planes across the country. Carl spent four years aboard the first *Lexington* right out of high school before he went on to college at Cal Tech. The first *Lexington* was sunk by the Japanese (in the Battle of the Coral Sea) and a second one built and given the same name. During Carl's time spent aboard the *Lexingto*n, they were searching for Amelia Earhart's downed plane.

My cousin, Louie Koehler, was in the army and fought in Europe. About all he would ever talk about was the trip over and the trip back and how seasick everyone got. My good high school friend Daryl Pearson was in the Marines. About all I know is that he saw some pretty rough stuff. He died in a house fire after the war.

I went on the Honor Flight last April. It was a wonderful experience. It was sponsored by Hy Vee and the Corvette Club. More than 80 vets were on the flight at a cost of $72,000. We were given two large envelopes on the return flight. The first contained a dozen letters from elementary school kids thanking us. The second had a beautiful walnut framed plaque provided by the Corvette

Club with my name on it. The inscription read, "Always remembered. America thanks you for your service." What also really impressed me was the reception we received when returning to the Cedar Rapids Airport. Our flight was delayed two hours due to storms and 300 people remained there waiting on us. We were told that nobody left early. People would shake our hand and slap us on the back. They even had a band!

I farmed when I got out of the service. My back bothered me so much from my fall in the Navy that I gave it up when hogs dropped to 10 cents a pound. Then I sold insurance with my father-in-law at Sellers Insurance.

TRIBUTE

I would like to extend a heartfelt "thank you" to all Washington County Veterans. Your sacrifices are deeply appreciated. Washington County has played a key role in protecting the freedoms we all now enjoy. Thank you all.

Ron Steele
Hudson, IA
KWWL News Anchor

I Saw MacArthur Wade Ashore

Ed Bontrager
Wellman, IA

96th Infantry Division
Pacific

Interview Date:
2 March 2012

Referral:
Alvin Miller & Jack Seward, Jr.

I grew up on a farm outside of Kalona. I was drafted in 1943. I went to Camp Dodge for my physical. To begin with, I signed up for a 1W, but (Conservative Amish) Bishop Elmer Swartzendruber wouldn't sign it. I was a bad guy to him because I smoked. The recruiter in Des Moines took me into a room to talk. He was a nice guy. We decided to sign me up for the regular Army. I came back home. My dad said, "Well, if that's the way it is going to be, I guess we'll move to Indiana. I don't want the rest of my boys going into the service." So they moved to Indiana. Four more brothers of mine went to the service. Al served his time in Burma and India. John came in as a replacement in Okinawa. I was in Okinawa when he arrived. From my mother's letters, I discovered that I was stationed not very far from him so I talked to my commanding officer about visiting him. He gave me permission but added that I was "on my own." I started walking down a jeep path and caught a ride almost right up to where John was at on the front lines. They were sleeping in foxholes and tents. John was a BAR man. Another brother was in the medical service stationed in Hawaii.

I was in the 96th Infantry Division and the 381st Infantry Regiment. I did my basic training all along the west coast, from Ft. Lewis in Washington State to Camp Lejeune in California at the Marines base. We trained for amphibious landings there. Once we did that, we knew we were headed for the Pacific islands. We shipped out of San Francisco and sailed to Hawaii. The trip took 21 days. I was only seasick a couple of days.

Leyte Island in the Philippines was the first place I went in. We landed in an LCI, a landing craft infantry. We were on Leyte quite a while. From there we went to Okinawa. I saw MacArthur wade ashore in the Philippines. I was about 100 yards away from the famous photo of him wading ashore.

Question: What did you think of MacArthur?
Oh, I don't know. I never gave it much thought. He was in charge of the Pacific campaign. I was a company cook. We cooked for about 175 men. We didn't drink the local water and relied on water purifiers to treat it. But in war time, you were a little bit of everything. We carried water, ammunition and food to the front lines. We were only about 300 yards behind the front line.

On Okinawa, we were carrying rations up to the front lines. We didn't go together in a group. We went one at a time. Coming back one day, the Japs let loose on a machine gun. The bullets were kicking up right behind my feet and I was running as hard as I could go. I dived into a shell hole and stayed there until it was over with. Then I got out of there and went on.

We'd get shelled by Japanese guns hidden in the caves and by mortars. Most of the rounds would land between us and the front lines. They had one big round we called the buzz bomb because of the different noise it made coming in. It'd leave a hole in the ground big enough to bury a 4x4 truck.

Question: Were you ever involved as a stretcher bearer?

Oh my, yes. We'd have to carry them back from the front lines. When the line moved on, we'd take a truck up to load the dead.

Question: How was Okinawa different than the Philippines?

It was a whole different world. The Philippines was a jungle island. Okinawa was all rock. The Japanese were hiding in caves. We landed on the east shore of Okinawa and went across the island to the western shore, cutting it in two. We were fighting separate of the Marines. We never saw much of them. We ended up pushing the Japs to the ocean. They were on something resembling a flat mountain. The Japanese wouldn't surrender. Some of them did, but most of them went off the cliffs into the ocean. I saw that happen. That was the end of Okinawa.

Question: How'd the infantry get the Japanese out of the caves?

They didn't. Patrols went up with satchel charges and sealed them up. They're still in there. Thousands of Japanese died that way.

Question: Did you ever see the Sugar Loaf where there was so much tough fighting?

Do you mean Sugar Loaf Hill? Oh, yes. I was close enough to see it. In fact, the 96th Infantry was one of the divisions that helped take it.

I think we lost 15,000 men on Okinawa. After Okinawa, we went back to Mindanao Island in the Philippines to rebuild our division to get ready for the big push into Japan. We were still on Mindanao when the war ended. We received word that Japan surrendered in the evening. I'd never seen so much gun fire that night in my life in celebration.

Question: What were your feelings toward the Japanese during and after the war?

We hated them, of course. My feelings have changed somewhat since. The Japanese people are all right now. They know they got beat in WWII.

I returned to the States in December, 1945. I got home the day after Christmas. I was married when I went into the service. My oldest son was born when I was in the Philippines. You had to have 21 points to go home. I had that many because I was married and had a child. After being discharged, I returned to Wellman because my wife was from here. All my brothers made it back okay.

I kept in touch with Lt. Smith from my company. He lived northeast of Cedar Rapids. Members of the company from Iowa and surrounding states used to get together once a year but that ended when so many died off.

I learned about everything you needed to know about life during the war. I'm glad I served but I wouldn't serve in the Army again if I had to do it over. I'd go to the Navy or the Air Force.

THE BLACK FLAG BATTALION

Bill Potratz
Washington, IA

96th Infantry Division
Pacific

Interview Date:
3 April 2012

Referral:
Joyce Letts

I grew up on a farm south of town. My dad was 63 years old and I was the only child so I thought the draft wouldn't take me. I was wrong. I found out after I came home from the service they were going to draft me because I was dating a Mennonite girl and they thought I would join that church and be a conscientious objector. The draft board was going to beat me to it. That was ridiculous. So I decided to enlist in the Air Force (Army Air Corps) if they were going to draft me. That was in 1942.

The Air Force said I didn't weigh enough so they sent me to a training program for glider pilots and flight instructors at Cornell College in Mt. Vernon. Once there I was told to return to Des Moines to sign all my paperwork. They re-weighed me there and discovered that I had gained one pound above the minimum so I had to return to the Air Force. So I left the school at Cornell and was shipped down to San Antonio in February of '43.

I passed all the tests for pilots training but the physical. I was told I had asthma and would have to stay on the ground. They sent me to a navigation

school in Hondo, Texas. Then they came out with the Army's Specialized Training Program (STP). Anybody that tested with an IQ over 125 when they were inducted had to take a test for the STP. There was a lot of mathematics on the test. Don't ask me how I passed it but I did. Next I was sent to Texas A&M in College Station for classification.

After that, we were loaded on a train and rode it for two or three days. We had no idea where we were being sent. We ended up in Chicago studying engineering at the Illinois Institute of Technology. We were there for three terms. Every term 50% of the students were cut. I don't know how I lasted three terms but I did. I went home on furlough after the third term. When I returned everyone was loading up on a train because the STP was cancelled. We were shipped out to Camp White in Oregon to the 96th Infantry Division. We had to go through basic training again.

From there we loaded onto a truck convoy and rode to San Obispo, California, for amphibious landing training with the Marines. Part of the training had us jumping off a 40 feet tower into the water. That was stupid, but we were trained by the Marines and that was the kind of stuff they did. It was rough training but kind of fun, too.

From there we were sent to San Francisco and boarded a ship to Hawaii. In Hawaii, we rode the Pineapple Express to the Schofield Barracks. We were in Hawaii three or four months but spent most of the time aboard ships because we were designated as amphibious troops. We rode around in the Higgins boats and LSTs a lot. The Navy referred to the LSTs as "large slow targets."

Finally we were loaded on a troop ship and headed to the island of Yap which is next to Peleliu. The Marines had just taken Peleliu at a very high price. It wasn't worth what they paid for it and they didn't know what to do with it after they had taken it. So it was decided to skip Yap and land on Leyte Island in the Philippines with the available troops which included the 7th Infantry and 1st Cavalry Divisions besides the 96th.

After arriving off Leyte, they told us to board the Higgins boats but not to take our weapons. We wondered what the heck was going on. All these loaded Higgins boats circled around the ocean off shore and finally headed toward the beach. Then the Japanese artillery opened up on us. We retreated back to our troop ship. That night we had to endure Tokyo Rose mocking us as a bunch of sissies. Another time she told us our wives and girlfriends would by crying after we met the Imperial Japanese troops.

The next day our troop ship deployed the para-veins and swept for mines. Then they told us to take our weapons when we boarded the Higgins boats. I looked out and saw the USS *Alabama*, the USS *New Jersey*, and one other big battleship too far away to read its name. When those battleships let go with their big guns the whole ship moved sideways. We landed unopposed except for a few mortar rounds and went in standing up.

My outfit, the 1st Battalion of the 382nd Regiment, was to advance through the Leyte Valley which was nothing but swamp. It was tough going between the snakes, leeches, and mosquitoes. The Japs didn't like us either. We had some pretty stiff battles in there.

I was an 81mm mortar crew in Company D. I was a PFC by then. I was a corporal when we went into Okinawa. I loved being a corporal. You didn't have enough rank to be in charge of a detail but you had too much rank to be assigned on a detail.

My personal weapon was a .45 automatic. But we weren't always on the mortar. Sometimes we went on patrol. I was lucky enough to carry a BAR then. The Marines taught us to fire the BAR from the hip. You put your right foot back, leaned forward and pulled the trigger as you were starting to fall. The recoil kept you upright.

We were on the mortar most of the time. I was second gunner. I dropped the round down the tube. When we moved I usually carried the tube but sometimes carried the base plate. The ammo bearers were supposed to carry one case of six rounds apiece. Those didn't last long. We'd fire 1000 rounds a lot of days. In the Philippines we used a water buffalo to pack the ammunition. Normally, trucks would bring the ammunition forward. There were supposed to be 10 men on the mortar crew but we never had that many. By the time we got to Okinawa we were down to six men. Two or three were wounded and some were transferred because they thought we didn't need that many. We had a sergeant who acted as an observer (or spotter). We'd usually set up around 150 yards behind the front lines.

Question: Did you have trouble with the Japanese trying to infiltrate at night?
Oh, yes. We got down in our foxholes at night. If you got up and walked around in the dark, you were dead.

MacArthur was told you couldn't conduct a military operation in Leyte valley because it was too swampy. The first couple of days we were making good progress so MacArthur comes walking in to see for himself. The general walked within a few feet of me, standing tall and straight while we were hunkered down. I heard him say, "Keep your heads down boys, or you're liable to get hurt." We liked MacArthur. He was good to us.

One time the Japanese soldiers charged us wearing raincoats. The attack began with a Jap plane strafing us. Then all these Japs came charging down out of the hills yelling *"Banzai!"* We learned later they were wearing raincoats because they had been told that all the American bullets would turn to water.

The Japanese dropped paratroopers on us in Leyte. We thought we had our area all cleaned up. They'd brought in female nurses to the hospital and the 5th Air Corps Headquarters radio section had moved onto a base. We were sitting down watching a movie when I heard low flying planes. I looked up and saw transport planes with the red rising sun on the sides. They dropped the paratroopers beyond my view. A number of outfits thought everything was safe so they didn't bother to post guards at night. The Japanese paratroopers walked down one of the few roads in the area bayoneting people as they slept. Then they drug the bodies out onto the road.

We set up across the road by the 5th Air Corps radio base. We could see Japanese paratroopers over around the radio base. We didn't shoot because we would have damaged our radio equipment. So we waited. That night the paratroopers gathered across the road from us yelling, "Banzai, Banzia! Kill the American pigs." Then they all got to laughing. We didn't think much of it. We were experienced troops by that time. Then a number of them jumped out and stood in the center of the road. Someone yelled, "Let them have it!" Everybody pulled the trigger, even me. Well, that took care of a bunch of them. The rest of the night we threw grenades at them back and forth across the road.

Any time there was a frontal banzai attack you wanted to keep a sharp eye on what was going on behind you as they'd often sneak in troops from your rear. A guy next to me thought he saw movement behind us that night. He pointed at something but I couldn't see anything. That guy watched for an hour and finally opened up with his carbine. That took care of that Jap. He'd been sneaking up inch by inch. At night, the Japanese ruled the roost. The Japanese walked around pretty comfortably at night. Occasionally they'd walk into us by mistake in the dark and everybody would open up on them.

We captured a few of the Japanese the next morning. They were the wounded who couldn't get away.

> "The ward boys, many who were noncombatant Mennonite conscientious objectors, picked up carbines and held the Japanese off for a day."

The paratroopers joined the remaining Japanese soldiers already on the ground and really started causing trouble. They attacked the hospital. The ward boys, many who were noncombatant Mennonite conscientious objectors, picked up carbines and held the Japanese off for a day. Someone asked them later why they didn't read the Bible to the Japanese. I was in the same hospital shortly after that for bloody dysentery and the nurses told me the details. They were sure proud of their ward boys. We were slow getting there to help because the road had all these American dead lying on it. About the time we'd start pulling the bodies off to the side, there be a sniper up in the trees open up on us. That slowed us down. Finally we brought up a flame throwing tank. When the Japs saw a few of their guys getting burned alive up in the tree tops, that changed their attitude. I'd guess the Japanese dropped several hundred paratroopers and from what I saw, they were just kids.

I remember one time in the Philippines they sent us up into the mountains to look for Japs. We fired the one case of mortar shells and one round fell short, wounding one of our guys. We opened the second case and saw that they were all painted yellow. That meant they were practice rounds. Those rounds should have never made it to the front. The officers made me bury the remaining rounds in a sweet potato patch. When we got back, a general court martial was held and they needed the practice rounds for evidence. So they sent me back up the mountain with six other guys to retrieve the case of mortar rounds. We were armed to the teeth. We met some occupation troops up there that advised us to proceed no further as they had lost guys from the Japs in the area. I suggested they go up there and clean the Japs out but they said occupation troops didn't do that sort of thing. Anyway, we continued on and I found the sweet potato patch. We dug up the mortar rounds and returned to camp. It was three days up the mountain and three days back. When we laid out the rounds in the court room, the officers decided to drop the charges.

We were wet 24 hours a day while we were in the swamp on Leyte. Our feet were always wet. You'd take your boot off and it would be full of blood from your skin wrinkling and cracking. River flukes were a problem. Guys would turn yellow when infected. We had a sergeant die from river flukes.

The Japanese were defending the roads going through the swamp. They had coconut log pill boxes set up on the higher ground next to the roads. We'd bring up a tank with a 105mm howitzer on it and that would take care of it. One time a lone Jap officer came charging out of the brush with just a sword to attack the howitzer tank. I guess he thought he was blessed by the Emperor. He didn't make it.

Question: The Japanese rarely surrendered. Did you take many prisoners?

Well, I'll tell what happened our first night on Leyte near Hill 120. We were in the Leyte Valley and the ground was wet. You couldn't dig much in the way of a foxhole. This one kid said he was going to get some dry grass to sleep on rather than the wet ground. We told him no, he had to stay with us and not to leave. But he wandered off anyway and the Japs got him. You could hear them torturing him all night long. This kid was yelling, "Come and help me, come and help me, please. Oh, that hurts." We wouldn't move, no way. The next day we saw their handiwork. I won't go into that. After that, when we came across a Jap, he didn't have a prayer of surrendering. We shot them. We were known as the Black Flag Battalion and that was one of the reasons.

One time we herded the Japs into a big field of dry elephant grass. We put flamethrowers on the edges of the field and dropped incendiary rounds in the middle of the field. That whole field was ablaze at once. We were told not to shoot the Japs to kill them, but to shoot them in the legs so they burned to death.

About 30 of us were sent up in the mountains on Leyte to meet the primitive mountain people. Supposedly these native people fled to the mountains when the Spanish took over the Philippines. We took three or four Filipino freedom fighters with us that could talk the language.

Question: What was your purpose in making the contact?

Who knows? We thought maybe the Japanese were up there hiding out. Those mountain people carried bows and arrows with poisoned darts on the ends.

We went in unopposed on Okinawa. The Japanese chose not to defend the beaches. My outfit was scheduled to go to the front on the third day after the invasion. We got a little careless and didn't properly dig in and exposed ourselves too much. That evening the Japanese shelled the heck out of us. The mortar next to us had their gun destroyed and two guys blown all to pieces. Dirt was flying everywhere. We had just had mail call.

I looked over and Nelson, the first gunner, sitting up and reading a letter. I yelled at him to get down. He said, "My wife was pregnant. I want to see if I have a baby girl or boy before I die!"

We were on the front line on Okinawa for two to three weeks before getting pulled back. Two thousand replacements joined the 96th Division at that time. I had to help train some of them. I don't remember the names of all the hills we took. Tombstone Ridge was a bad one. I lost a lot of my friends there. The Japs had a 320mm heavy mortar. We called them flying boxcars. They flew slowly enough that you could see them coming. You could see the artillery shells in flight right before they hit.

We had a Mexican boy with us. No one could pronounce his name so we called him "Spike." He was a good friend of mine. One time we were crossing this field while being shelled. There were six of us and we went across two at a time so as not to draw sniper fire. The artillery fire was somewhat spaced so we tried to time our run. Spike and I were the last to cross. I heard the gun go off and by that time I had enough experience to know from the sound that we were in serious trouble. We both hit the dirt and the round came in on top of us.

> *"One time a lone Jap officer came charging out of the brush with just a sword to attack the howitzer tank. I guess he thought he was blessed by the Emperor. He didn't make it."*

Shrapnel cut the straps off by backpack and put a whole through my jacket. But neither Spike nor I had a scratch. I never could figure that out. I'll tell you, when the dust settled we were up and moving. Something like that puts the zip in you.

The Japs had 75mm, 105's, and 150mm guns stuck back in caves in the hills. The Navy carrier planes would bomb and bomb trying to get them. Lobo Hill was one placed they bombed a lot. Two planes would come in side by side and drop 500 pound bombs and then climb and the machine gunner in the rear seat would open up. I don't know how many times they tried that and they couldn't do us any good. We lacked 50 feet of reaching the crest of the hill and could advance no farther. We tried for two weeks to take that hill. It rained a lot during that period which didn't help.

Okinawa was the military training ground for the Japanese artillery. They knew every inch of that island. The Japs could drop an artillery shell in your back pocket. An American infantry division that had been in Italy was transferred to Okinawa. We tried to warn them on what to expect at the front lines but they were combat veterans and pretty cocky. They didn't properly dig in. They lasted one night. The Japanese dropped 5000 rounds of artillery on them.

All our drinking water on Okinawa was chemically treated by the Army to make it safe to drink. One time we ran out. Somebody said there was a spring flowing on the other side of the hill. I volunteered to go fill all the canteens I could carry. While there at the spring, a Marine slid in carrying canteens. They were also out of water. As we were busy filling them, a Jap machine opened up on us. All we had were side arms and they weren't much good against a machine gun. Then somebody with a BAR opened up and he took care of the Jap machine gun. The Marine asked where I from. I told him, "The Philippines." He said "I came from Iwo Jima and it was a Sunday afternoon picnic compared to this." I told him the same thing. These weren't the same Japs we fought in the Philippines. They fought harder.

The Japanese had massed troops on Okinawa and planned an amphibious assault through the middle of the island. We were spread thin at that time and would not have been able to hold the line.

Question: So why didn't they do that?

Nelson and I were sitting there with our mortar. I told him "it was too quiet. Something isn't right." So we decided to fire some harassment rounds, dropping a few in one spot and moving on to the next. Roy Nelson and I were in our prime then. We could put nine shells in the air before the first one hit the ground. One of our rounds caused a tremendous explosion that shook the ground. We looked over there and could see pieces of Jap soldiers flying through the air. Then the order was issued for everyone to commence firing. The Japanese started firing their artillery back at us. Generally, they didn't do much of that in the daytime. Evidently they were massing several thousand of their forces and had a lot at stake.

There were five other mortars spread out on the hill we were on. We had set up the preceding night and the Japanese must have had a spotter that knew where we were. Those mortars were soon silenced by the Jap artillery. Our lieutenant had showed us where to set our gun. Roy and I didn't like that spot. It just didn't feel right, like something bad was going to happen. So the next day we moved 100 feet to the other side of the hill where we'd have more protection and dug in. The Jap artillery really worked the spot we had been set up the day before but couldn't locate where we had moved to.

I don't know how many thousands of rounds we fired that day. The range was short, maybe 350 yards. The tube got so hot you could light a cigarette on it. Nelson and I had plugged our ears with toilet paper and we couldn't hear anything. We shot maximum loads with delayed fuses. Those rounds would bury themselves in the dirt before exploding and they destroyed the caves the Japanese were hiding in. It was some hours before we got some help. We fired our mortar for four or five hours straight. Finally it got to the point we were told we could quit firing. That Japanese artillery fire had quit by then and the 4.2 mortars and the Navy would take over.

The next morning here comes this jeep carrying a one or two star general. I thought, oh boy, we're in trouble. He jumps out and says, "They tell me this is the 4th Squad. I came here for one thing. I want to shake the hand of the man that sent that shell over." Nelson pointed to me. I had my photo taken shaking the hand of the general but nothing ever became of it. I felt so tough at the time.

I found out later on that this attack alerted the command that the Japs had an amphibious landing in the making. A search discovered where the Japs had their boats hidden and they were destroyed.

Question: Were you at Sugar Loaf Hill?

I saw the hill, but we didn't take it. The Marines did. I think the 383rd Regiment of the 96th tried to take Sugar Loaf but we weren't involved in that hill but we were in the one right next to it. Sugar Loaf Hill changed the way the Marines fought. They were trained to assault a hill. Sugar Loaf was full of spider holes and caves and the Japs would emerge shooting the backs of the Marines after they charged by. It was terrible the number of men the Marines lost before changing tactics. They finally learned to blow up all the underground and cave entrances with satchel charges before advancing further.

I was also the demolition man in our outfit. I threw the satchel charges. They had 16 second fuses. I remember this one time a Jap came up out of a cave and killed one of our guys. We knew the Jap would throw the satchel charge back out if he had time so we decided to time our run up and drop with two seconds to spare. So me and another guy pulled the cords and ran up to either side of the cave opening and tossed two charges in. It was really a dumb thing to do. If we had tripped or mistimed our run we would have been blown up.

The satchel charges were filled with plastic explosives. They were more powerful than dynamite. I threw more satchel charges into caves than I can remember. Another time I was just getting ready to toss one and somebody told me not to. They had heard a strange noise coming from inside the cave. So this guy crawls in and discovered a woman in labor. So they sent someone back for a stretcher. Then it was discovered we were standing in the middle of a mine field. By the time everything got sorted out and a stretcher was available, the woman had already had the baby. This Okinawan woman refused to be carried in the stretcher and walked out with us accompanying her.

"The worst experience was when had to retreat off Tombstone Ridge. We had to leave our wounded. Some of them were good friends of mine."

Question: Did you ever serve as a stretcher bearer for our wounded?

Oh, yes, lots of times. I volunteered. You'd usually be under fire. I got shot at and missed. You could hear the bullets go zipping by.

Okinawa wasn't even fully taken when they loaded us up and sent as back to the Philippines. Our battalion was down to 92 men. Our battalion went in under strength with only 700 men. We should have had over 1000.

Question: What were your thoughts when you heard about the atomic bomb being dropped?

Praise the Lord! We were set to land somewhere around Yokohama, Japan. We knew what it would be like. It would have been bad. I was supposed to be a squad leader on a recoilless rifle on the invasion. I told my crew we would be lucky to get off three rounds before they got us.

Question: Were you ever wounded?

I had one bullet burn me and make holes in my clothes. I was crawling up a bank trying to get away from a Jap machine gun. They had caught us on one side of a ditch we were trying to cross. The two guys beside me were a little ahead of me. I saw the bullets hit them. The bullets evidently passed on both sides of my neck without hitting me. I picked up a little speed after that. Then a guy opened up with a BAR and took care of the Jap machine gun.

The worst experience was when had to retreat off Tombstone Ridge. We had to leave our wounded. Some of them were good friends of mine. My friend named Kenneth was from Kansas City. He went back for the wounded and never made it back. The Japs got him. I don't know what happened to him. Later we found his dog tags and his rifle. Tombstone Ridge was the first real test we had. We were still learning how to fight on Okinawa. The Japs were well organized and there were a lot of them. Tombstone Ridge was a cemetery. We had just come down a hill onto the ridge. The Japs came running down another higher hill right on top of us. Normally, we could have stopped them with our mortars but we hadn't set up yet. Then those 320mm Jap mortar rounds started dropping on us. We had to get the heck out of there and retreat back up the first hill.

When we were in that area, a Navy destroyer was giving us fire support. One day a wreck of a plane flew over us. It must have come from Japan. It was going after the destroyer and had to clear some trees. When it did, those Navy boys were ready for him. They opened up with everything they had and blew that plane apart.

I didn't really see many kamikazes but I could see the smoke from the ships they had hit. Most of the Navy was farther out to sea.

There were a lot of times we had fun, too. On Okinawa, the natives had public bathing. No one warned us about that.

The Marines had Admiral Nimitz as their commander. I sure didn't like him. Okinawa was the first real Japanese territory we conquered. Nimitz told the Marines, "To the victors, belongs the spoils of war." The Marines could have whatever, including the women. You won't read that in the history books. I did not like it. We rescued one woman from the Marines and this was when they told us about Nimitz's order. There for a while, I thought the Army was going to shoot a bunch of Marines.

The Navy had a lot of people on shore in camps on Okinawa because they had so many ships sunk from the kamikazes. Our outfit was involved in transporting and escorting the civilian population to the north end of the island which had been ravaged by war. One day some of our outfit received orders to saddle up. I was not one of those that went but I heard all about it later. The sailors had gotten drunk and were dragging women out of the line of refugees and raping them. They had a .50 caliber machine gun set up and threatened to shoot our guys. Our people spread out in a line and put a stop to that. They were prepared to shoot the sailors on the machine gun if it looked like they were going to fire.

The Army taught us many things to respect. One of them was women.

Okinawa was a beautiful island. Shuri Castle was like an old time medieval stone castle. The walls were so thick the big naval shells would bounce off. I was never inside the castle, but I was on the outside of it.

A FLYING COFFIN

Robert Stevens
Winfield, IA

13th Airborne Division
Europe

Interview Date:
21 July 2012

Referral:
William Wagamon

I graduated from high school in 1943 and was drafted that August. They were just starting up a new division, the 13th Airborne, when I went in. From Camp Dodge I went to Ft. Bragg for eight weeks of basic training and then received training as a telephone lineman and switchboard operator at Camp Mackall. They gave me the rank of corporal, T5, and then promoted me to corporal in charge of the wire section when the switchboard operator got busted. I was with the wire section the whole time I was in the 13th Airborne.

I was a glider artilleryman. We had to undergo five qualifying flights on the Waco glider. Glider men received 1/3 extra pay. As a corporal, that meant I got an additional $33 every month. Paratroopers received an extra $50 jump pay. I'd tell the paratroopers they were crazy to be jumping out of a perfectly good airplane. They would respond saying is was worse for me to be riding in a flying coffin. I also had four or five practice glider flights over in France.

I was in the 677th Battery. We trained on 75mm guns but my outfit received 105mms when we got to Europe. We had to tear those guns down because of their size and weight and fly them in on two or three gliders. That would have presented a real problem if the gliders didn't land close together. Other than the two pilots, only two soldiers rode on those gliders. Normally the Waco glider carried 13 men.

The Waco glider could carry its own weight but they figured they were probably over loaded most of the time. It had an 84 foot wingspan and was 48 feet long. They had a stall speed of 40 mph. If there was only one pilot available, they'd appoint a soldier to act as the copilot and the pilot would show him how to land the plane if something happened to him.

We scheduled to go in on six different missions but the ground troops got there so fast that they were scrubbed. We were loaded up on the gliders ready to go on three different missions. One of those was Operation Market Garden in Holland. Our last mission was cancelled because the Air Force didn't have enough tow planes. That was the Rhine River crossing. We ended up traveling by truck and crossed the river on a pontoon bridge as part of Patton's 3rd Army. Not all of the 13th crossed the river, but the entire division was awarded a Battle Star.

Question: did you ever have any close calls while training in the gliders?

We had two in France. One time we got into trouble when the glider started roll while being towed. Both the pilots grabbed the release lever while we were flying sideways. Any more of a roll would have crashed us as we were too close to the ground to dive out of it. The other time we were coming into land in what appeared to be a level place but what looked like a road turned out to be a ditch.

We were told that a thousand gliders landed on D-Day and only 13 of them could be used a second time.

It took us 15 days to cross the Atlantic. Our ship was part of a large convoy. We were two days waiting to depart while the Navy destroyers responded to a submarine scare.

We landed at Le Havre in January of '45 after docking overnight at the port of South Hampton, England. We slept in tents and it was cold and muddy.

We were supposed to go fight in the Battle of the Bulge but instead they sent a number of men from the 13th to the 82nd and 101st Airborne as replacements since they had suffered so many casualties. So then we had to train new guys while in France. We had a base camp about 60 miles north east of Paris. We took a train from Le Havre to our base camp, riding in the 40 and eight box cars.

We had one mission cancelled that was supposed to land in Norway. Another mission toward the end of the war had us landing at an airfield close to Berlin so that planes could land to bring in supplies. That mission was also cancelled for some reason or another, probably because the ground troops had already got there.

I was issued a folding stock carbine. I never really saw much actual combat. Our artillery had forward observers and we had to run telephone up to them to communicate. Radios had too much interference and the Germans also monitored

them. I went forward one time with the officer who was the forward observer. We laid the telephone line off a truck. We found an observation point a mile or two behind the front lines. He called in the fire mission. The shells dropped short, with one landing within a hundred yards of us.

We had three artillery batteries with four guns each. My battery had the 105s and the other two had the 75s. We never advanced very far into Germany after crossing the Rhine. Initially, we had fire missions every few minutes. Eventually it worked down to where the batteries could take turns firing. As far as I know, we didn't have too many casualties in our outfit because we were so far behind the front lines. We were close enough, however, to receive counter battery fire from the German artillery. We saw a few of the buzz bombs.

After we crossed the Rhine and things settled down, we received a one day pass to Paris. It just so happened that when the truck carrying my group unloaded us in Paris that they announced President Roosevelt had died. We were devastated by the news.

> "The shells dropped short, with one landing within a hundred yards of us."

They never told us anything more than what it takes to get by. We did what we were told and never asked questions. There are a lot of things I don't remember and some things I wish I didn't remember. I didn't volunteer for the airborne. I was drafted into it. They gave us a choice of being and paratrooper or riding a glider. I choose the glider because they gave those not going to jump school at Ft. Benning a 30 day furlough.

The part of Germany I saw looked a lot like it does around here except the farms are smaller and all the people live in villages. France was the same way. I never had any desire to go back after coming home.

Our division had orders to go to Japan. The dropping of the A bomb saved our necks. I was discharged in January of '46. It was another 20 years before I flew again. It was partly because I didn't have the opportunity but mainly because I did not want to. Flying was a little nerve racking after riding those gliders.

I farmed after the war. You had to apply for a permit from some county board to buy new farm equipment. Veterans received preference. I purchased the first new John Deere A tractor that came to Winfield after the war for $1500. My son David was in the Navy aboard a destroyer escort off the coast of Vietnam. He eventually wanted to farm after coming home so my wife Mary and I moved to town 35 years ago. The 13th Division had 26 reunions and we went to 20 of them. I went on the three day Honor Flight in 2009.

Allen Goff ran the hardware store here. He was a bombardier on one of three B-29s that took off (from Tinian) to drop one of the atomic bombs. They didn't know which plane carried the bomb until after they were in the air. The bomb wasn't on his plane but he took a slug of wonderful photos of what the bomb did.

Leslie (Tim) Bailey was a glider pilot (in the India/China/Burma Theatre). I think he had two missions. He lives in New London. Leonard Schweitzer was in the Army in the South Pacific. He was in the thick of it and wounded several times (and was awarded two Bronze Stars).

Keith Haight was a tail gunner on a bomber shot down over Holland. I think Keith Kongable was a Marine in the Pacific.

Leyte

Baxter Freese
Iowa City, IA

Navy
Pacific

Interview Date:
17 August 2012

Referral:
Ann (Freese) Troyer

My grandfather was chairman of the draft board in Cedar County. I felt like I had to enlist because of how it would look. You can imagine the trouble I would have gotten into if I had received a deferment. I could have gotten a farm deferment. My dad was a farmer. But you know the rumors that would have gone around with my grandfather the president of the local draft board. So I enlisted. I was in an Army program called the ASTP (Army Specialized Training Program) where I had the option of going or staying. I was at the point of getting on the train to go to Kansas City. My uncle, who was an attorney, told my dad that, "if you don't have to go, don't go." Dad took me off the train and we went back home. I enlisted soon after that in the V-5, which was Naval Air Corps and was sent straight to St. Ambrose College in Davenport. I entered active duty 1 March, 1944. I was 17 when I was sworn in at Chicago. I had to have parental signature since I wasn't eighteen yet.

I was at St. Ambrose about six months. I couldn't hack it. My grade school background at Clarence, Iowa, was so devoid of mathematics, chemistry, and the sciences that there was no way I could pass the courses the Air Corps required. So I basically flunked out. But the Navy had a surplus of fliers anyway and washed out 75,000 pilots that year. So the Navy divided us up. Some went on to other

schools in the V-12 program. I chose to go to Great Lakes in the regular Navy. I was there through the fall and winter. Following boot camp, I was put in a company of people that all had previous military experience. So it was basically a company of smart asses because they thought they already knew everything. We had some V-12 movie stars in our companies but I can't remember their names. It was kind of an unruly group but we got along pretty well and never got into trouble. I was there for 12 months.

I then did some SP (shore patrol) for four weeks in Waukegan and Chicago. Mainly it consisted of internal gate security. I tried to get into some trade schools but that was hard to do. The Navy started cracking down because they had too many men. I made myself available for anything that came up and joined a unit called USMD 3749 which was the supply depot. I was sent to San Francisco where I spent a month. The next thing I knew I was aboard a troop ship going under the Golden Gate Bridge and seasick. I was seasick for 33 straight days. I started out weighing 220 pounds and got down to 170–180. I never gained that weight back until after the war.

We were on a fast ship, zigzagging, and not in a convoy. We bypassed Pearl and all the islands and sailed straight for New Guinea. We anchored off the eastern most town in New Guinea, taking on water and supplies for a few days and sailed for Aladia, which is on the extreme opposite side of the island. We were there for two or three weeks while the Navy was making up convoys for the invasion of the Philippines. We had 4000 soldiers and 400 sailors aboard our troop transport. Most of the soldiers were dropped off in New Guinea to be dispersed to go into the battle for the Philippines.

We sailed into Leyte Bay right after the big sea battle took place there. Our ship was full of different soldiers. As we were going through other islands on the way to Leyte, we'd stop and pick up soldiers and Marines that had been through other battles.

Question: Did those veteran troops act different than the green troops you sailed with before?

Oh yes, there were no show offs or anything like that. They had a lot more experience and they let us know that by telling stories. A lot of those guys we picked up had been in the Pacific for the entire war and were heading home after a stop in the Philippines. They were ready to go home, too. The one thing that impressed me on that voyage was the size of the rats on Russell Island. They were huge! All the sailors couldn't get over the size of those rats.

Baxter on the beach at the Navy base. The buildings in the background are part of the Navy Seabee battalion #19. Photo courtesy of Baxter Freese.

Our job in the Philippines was to build supply depots for the 7th Amphibious Fleet. We supplied the LCTs and LCIs and the smaller landing craft. Then we moved up to coast to Samar to build up another base. I spent a year and a half there. We supplied food, ammunition, guns and basically everything the landing crafts needed to operate. We had a separate ordinance base for the weapons and ammunition. My first job was as a night guard on the ammunition depot. I remember it poured rain for the first three nights. They handed me a carbine to carry. That was the first time I had ever had my hands on a carbine. There were still Japanese up in the hills. All I could think about all night was a Japanese firing one bullet in the ammunition and blowing everything up.

Question: How many of those ships do you think you supplied?

Oh gosh, I have no idea. I've never thought of that. Those ships were pretty small and they'd come in hundreds at a time. There were a lot of them. When a ship came in for supplies, I had to sign off for them, give them the final okay. Every ship had a complement that the Navy assigned to them. For example, if you were on an LCI, you got one coffee maker, an ice cream maker, and maybe half a dozen dishes. I could only give out what the Navy said I could. Ships would come in that weren't eligible for an ice cream maker and want one. This one captain came in on a ship with a crew of six. He wanted a coffee maker, an ice cream maker, and an electric fan. I told him that he was ineligible for any of those items because it wasn't in his complement. He asked me what it would take for me to arrange to get him those things for him. I told him that I couldn't because it was not legal. Then he asked me if I wanted a jeep. I was tired of walking that island. The next morning he offered me a brand new jeep painted Navy blue. I didn't hesitate very long. I wrote my conscience off pretty fast. The only problem was that there were only two jeeps on the island. The captain had one and I had one. I was asked a thousand times where I had gotten the jeep. I told them anything that was convenient. I kept that jeep all the way through. We were the only group of enlisted men that had their own jeep.

We didn't have room in the warehouses to store everything indoors. A lot of valuable stuff like Title

10 navigation equipment was stored outside under canvass tarps. We always managed to keep the beer inside under cover because that inhibited the stealing. There was constant pilfering. The shore patrol was in charge of stopping that.

We had a few Japanese planes fly over our base. We could hear distant naval gunfire out in the ocean. There were still some Japanese troops in the hills. We had Japanese POWs interned nearby. It was a small prison camp with maybe a 1000 POWs. They were used in manual labor work details on our base although I was not directly involved with that. The Japanese tortured their prisoners. We did not.

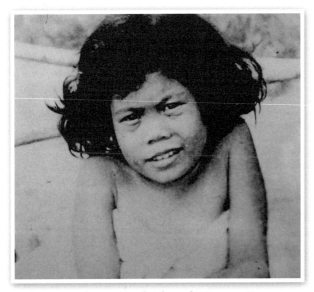

A native Filippino girl. Photo by Baxter Freese.

Question: Did you have any dealings with the Filipino people?

We had no business dealings with them, it was all strictly social until after the war. They were poor, primitive people. They basically lived on rice and fish. They provided laundry services but we never used them. You could buy about anything you wanted from them including their daughters. There was a lot of venereal disease in the Philippines.

We had to take the daily yellow malaria pills. A bunch of us used crushed up pills to dye all our t-shirts and underwear yellow, just to be ornery. We started taking the pills while still on the ship going over. No one in our outfit got malaria that I was aware of.

I was either in the Quonset hut we stayed in or the chief petty officers club on the beach drinking green beer when I heard of the atomic bomb being dropped. We all figured we would be going home pretty soon. Our base was located on a little island four miles long and one half mile wide, and I was kind of tired of it. We were ready to get out of there.

After the Japanese surrendered and the war was winding down, I was offered a commission at the rank of chief petty officer if I would stay on with the Navy and help dispose of equipment. I didn't want it. My rank during the war was store keeper 2nd class. I spent about half my time doing paper work and the other half in the warehouse.

I was up in Banguio, the summer capital of the Philippines in the northern end of Luzon, where the last Japanese were holding out. The last battle of the war was fought there. The city of Banguio was literally shot up. There was a hell of a lot of Japanese prisoners up there. I wasn't aware of any still loose on the ground.

I went through one of the first race war riots after Harry Truman became president. We were basically a black base with a lot of all black stevedores units. The stevedores did all the manual labor, like building the docks and unloading the ships. Most of them couldn't even speak decent English let alone read or write. Everything like mess halls was segregated during the first part of the war. I ate with in stevedores mess because the food was good and I made sure the cooks were well supplied. Then Truman came out with that equality thing to discontinue all forms of discrimination, and the mess halls were combined. The trouble started the first night when the blacks sent people down early to stand in line and save places for their friends. The outnumbered whites got shoved to the back. Then fights broke out. This went on for two or three nights and it kept getting worse. The more the blacks got away with—the more they tried. Finally, they sent in enough SP's to keep order. There were a few redneck whites around, but it wasn't a white problem, it was a black problem.

I could have had a lot of fun at Great Lakes and in San Francisco if I wasn't continually broke. My paperwork never caught up with me so I wasn't getting paid. I was always borrowing money.

Most of the time I could never pay it back because the lender and I would get separated. My fellow sailors took me under their wing and took care of me. I remember borrowing $10 from a real good friend of mine, Leonard Kowalski, from Chicago. After the war when I took cattle to the Chicago stockyards, I tried to locate Kowalski to pay him back. There must be 10,000 Kowalski's in Chicago. I never did find him.

We left the Philippines and sailed to Japan and then through the Aleutians on our way home. The sea was very rough in the Aleutians and the Liberty ship we were riding blew a boiler. I was so seasick I never got out of my bunk when we started out. In the Aleutians, everybody including the crew was seasick except for me. I had it out of my system by then.

One of my old friends I had made acquaintance with from one of the earlier units we had picked up off the islands gave me a real nice .45 caliber pistol. He left for home early and gave me that gun because you never knew whether or not you'd end up in the brig if you were caught with it. I carried that gun with me for months. When I was ready to unload off the boat at Treasure Island (San Francisco) I threw it over the side of the ship. I figured getting caught with it was the only thing that would keep me in the Navy and it wasn't worth the risk. The funny part of the story is about two years ago, I ran down the friend that gave me this gun. He lives in San Francisco about three miles from where that gun rests in the Bay. He asked me about the gun he had given me. I had forgotten all about the pistol until he mentioned it. I told him it wasn't far away.

I was discharged June 20th, 1946. I took advantage of the GI Bill to attend Cornell College. That's where I met my wife, Mary. I worked at a bank in Mechanicsville after graduating. When Mary's dad developed cancer, we moved to the Wellman area to take over his farming operation.

Question: Do you remember where you were when you heard about Pearl Harbor being bombed?
Three of us were in a pool hall in Clarence drinking beer when it came in over the radio. I remember us discussing it. We could not dream it would ever affect us. I was a freshman in high school. Clarence was a German community. If you had a nickel and could curl up on a bar stool and say, "beer," they'd serve you. The other two boys with me eventually got farm deferments.

Mary Freese: December 7th was on a Sunday and my dad decided it was time for me to have another driving lesson. We were driving from the farm to Wellman on gravel and had the radio on. I really didn't get too excited when I heard it. At the time, getting to drive seemed much more important. I think my dad was very concerned but he didn't say much. My dad, Ellery Foster, was a pilot during WWI. He was ready to go overseas when the war ended. He trained at Love Field in Dallas, Texas. He took us down there once to show us the tree he crashed his airplane in.

Baxter: Lou Belcher from Wellman was at Pearl Harbor when it was attacked. He enlisted before the war started. Howard Greiner was B-24 pilot that got shot down in Europe. He's got a lot of stories.

I served on the Iowa Conservation Commission Board, the Iowa Cattleman's Association state board, and other state boards for a number of years. I got back to a lot of the places I was at in the war while being involved in the U.S. Meat Export Federation. That was kind of neat. Those places were bombed out shells during the war and are now modern cities.

Question: Do you have any advice for future generations?
People need to remain aware of what's going on in the country. People complain about the country but won't get involved.

Baxter's infamous jeep. Photo by Baxter Freese.

ANOTHER WAR

Jean Conry
Ainsworth, IA

Army Nurse
Stateside

Referral:
Halcyon House

I have Alzheimer's. It is a terribly debilitating disease. It has erased a lot of my memories.

I was only in (the Service) for a short while. I was a Registered Nurse. I didn't get to Europe. I was an Army nurse. They moved me around a lot. I worked in Muscatine and around Washington D.C. but spent most of my time down in Texas. I can't remember any of the base names. I worked in hospitals while still in training. So I took care of soldiers even before I had graduated with a nursing degree. We cared for both the sick and wounded soldiers.

I can remember being on a hospital floor in Washington D.C. with a bunch of wounded soldiers. We would clean them up and try to help them learn to walk again. A number of them had bad legs.

Question: Did you ever treat or see any soldiers suffering from shell shock?
There was some of that, but I was not around them.

My husband, Eldon, was in the war. *(Note: Eldon Conry was a mechanic in the Army Air Corps. He was stationed in North Africa and Europe.)* I got out near the end of the war. I could have told you a lot more six months ago. Alzheimer's is another war we need to win.

INDEX